Sentencing

Crime and Punishment: Critical Essays in Legal Philosophy
Series Editor: Thom Brooks

Titles in the Series:

Sentencing

Edited by

Thom Brooks
University of Durham, UK

ASHGATE

Published by
Ashgate Publishing Limited
Wey Court East
Union Road
Farnham
Surrey GU9 7PT
England

Ashgate Publishing Company
110 Cherry Street
Suite 3-1
Burlington, VT 05401-3818
USA

www.ashgate.com

British Library Cataloguing in Publication Data.
A catalogue record for this book is available from the British Library.

The Library of Congress has cataloged the printed edition as follows: 2013949705

ISBN 9781409451242

Printed in the United Kingdom by Henry Ling Limited,
at the Dorset Press, Dorchester, DT1 1HD

Contents

PART IV   SENTENCING AS PUNITIVE RESTORATION

PART V   SENTENCING ALTERNATIVES

Acknowledgements

Ashgate would like to thank our researchers and the contributing authors who provided copies, along with the following for their permission to reprint copyright material.

The American Society of Criminology for the essay: Steven N. Durlauf and Daniel S. Nagin (2011), 'Imprisonment and Crime: Can Both Be Reduced?', *Criminology and Public Policy*, **10**, pp. 13–54. Copyright © 2011 American Society of Criminology.

Northwestern University School of Law for the essay: Paul H. Robinson and John M. Darley (1997), 'The Utility of Desert', *Northwestern University Law Review*, **91**, pp. 453–99. Copyright © 1997 by Northwestern University School of Law. Reprinted by special permission of Northwestern University School of Law, *Northwestern University Law Review*.

Oxford University Press for the essays: Andrew Ashworth and Julian Roberts (2012), 'Sentencing: Theory, Principle, and Practice', in Mike Maguire, Rod Morgan and Robert Reiner (eds), *The Oxford Handbook of Criminology*, 5th edition, Oxford: Oxford University Press, pp. 866–94. Copyright © 2012 Oxford University Press. By permission of Oxford University Press; John Gardner (1998), 'Crime: In Proportion and in Perspective', in Andrew Ashworth and Martin Wasik (eds), *Fundamentals of Sentencing Theory: Essays in Honour of Andrew von Hirsch*, Oxford: Clarendon, pp. 31–52. Copyright © 1998 John Gardner, by permission of Oxford University Press; Richard L. Lippke (2007), 'The Case for Retributive Sentencing', in *Rethinking Imprisonment*, Oxford: Oxford University Press, pp. 39–62. Copyright © 2007 Richard L. Lippke, by permission of Oxford University Press; John Braithwaite (2002), 'Setting Standards for Restorative Justice', *British Journal of Criminology*, **42**, pp. 563–77. Copyright © 2002 The Centre for Crime and Justice Studies (ISTD), by permission of Oxford University Press; Andrew Ashworth (2002), 'Responsibilities, Rights and Restorative Justice', *British Journal of Criminology* **4**, pp. 578–95. Copyright © 2002 The Centre for Crime and Justice Studies (ISTD), by permission of Oxford University Press; Clare McGlynn (2011), 'Feminism, Rape and the Search for Justice', *Oxford Journal of Legal Studies*, **31**, pp. 825–42. Copyright © 2011 Clare McGlynn. Published by Oxford University Press. All rights reserved.

Oxford University Press, USA for the essay: Thom Brooks (2014), 'Stakeholder Sentencing', in Julian V. Roberts and Jesper Ryberg (eds), *Popular Punishment: On the Normative Significance of Public Opinion for Penal Theory*, New York: Oxford University Press, forthcoming. By permission of Oxford University Press, USA.

Queen's University Belfast for the essay: Jonathan Doak and Louise Taylor (2014), 'Hearing the Voices of Victims and Offenders: The Role of Emotions in Criminal Sentencing', *Northern Ireland Legal Quarterly*, **64**, forthcoming.

Publisher's Note

The material in this volume has been reproduced using the facsimile method. This means we can retain the original pagination to facilitate easy and correct citation of the original essays. It also explains the variety of typefaces, page layouts and numbering.

Series Preface

Crime and punishment grip the imagination and concerns of both the public and policymakers raising several serious challenges. Can punishment be justified? If so, then what purpose (or purposes) does it have? Which practices best cohere with this purpose(s)? These and many other questions are addressed with rigour and insight in this new book series.

Crime and Punishment: Critical Essays in Legal Philosophy comprises an authoritative and comprehensive set of five volumes reprinting the most influential essays by leading international figures engaged in this field. Each volume is organized thematically with a general introduction to provide an accessible launching pad to the latest research.

The first volume is on *Retribution*. This approach to punishment is widely held to be the oldest such view. Retributivists traditionally claim that punishment must be deserved and proportionate to what is deserved. This volume of essays covers several topics, including desert, proportionality, retributivist emotions, capital punishment and mercy. The second volume is a collection of essays about what is often regarded as the second oldest theory of punishment: *Deterrence*. This is the idea that punishment is justified by its effectiveness at deterring potential future offenders from committing crime. Topics covered include deterrence and crime reduction, incapacitation and the death penalty.

The next two volumes focus on particular issues. The third volume examines the latest research into *Shame Punishment*. Shame punishments are understood in multiple ways, such as an attempt to improve crime reduction through deterrence or as an effort at moral education. This volume covers topics, such as shame and desert, shaming and dignity, shame and deterrence, and shame and restorative justice. The fourth volume is *Juvenile Offending* and it considers whether we should punish offenders differently because of their age as well as how this might be best achieved. Topics included are risk factors, the justification of punishing youth differently from adults and restorative justice for juvenile offenders.

The final fifth volume is about punishment as imprisonment: *Sentencing*. This volume examines sentencing in theory and practice, the Model Penal Code and use of sentencing guidelines, punitive restoration and the unified theory of punishment and alternatives to sentencing.

This *Crime and Punishment: Critical Essays in Legal Philosophy* book series covers exciting and innovative contemporary work by the leading international figures in the field today writing on retribution, deterrence, shame punishment, youth offending and sentencing. Each essay has been carefully selected for inclusion to ensure the seminal work available in English is brought together in one series for easy reference by students, practitioners, scholars and the general public.

THOM BROOKS
Series Editor
Reader in Law, Durham Law School, Durham University

Introduction

Sentencing is a practice that is both widespread and controversial. Every modern state sentences convicted offenders for their crimes. But what justifies the imprisonment of democratic citizens? If they can be justified, how do we determine the severity of sentences? Does the theory of punishment connect closely with its practice? Should we support one purpose for sentencing or multiple purposes? Or should we reject sentencing in favour of alternatives to imprisonment? This book brings together the leading work on sentencing from the dominant international figures in the field. Sentencing is examined from various critical perspectives, including the relation of theory and practice, the Model Penal Code and development of sentencing guidelines, the link between sentencing and emotions, punitive restoration and sentencing alternatives such as restorative justice.

This introduction will consider each of these topics with primary reference to the important contributions to our thinking about sentencing carefully selected for inclusion in this collection. This survey of leading work will highlight the key debates and issues pertaining to contemporary research about sentencing.

Sentencing: Theory and Practice

The first part examines the relation between the theory of sentencing and its practice. Andrew Ashworth and Julian Roberts (Chapter 1) launch the book with a critical survey of sentencing aims and guidelines introducing readers to many of the key ideas and considerations shaping sentencing policy. They consider the three general purposes for sentencing: retributivist desert, deterrence and rehabilitation which I will discuss in turn.

Retribution and its desert theory is perhaps the oldest theory of punishment. It is a broad tent that can be defined different ways (Brooks, 2014a). The standard view is that retribution claims that punishment is justified when it is deserved and no more than deserved. Retributivism has enjoyed lengthy popularity, in part, because it captures certain elements that many find essential for punishment to be justified. The first is that a person must deserve punishment to be punished: innocent people cannot be sentenced because it would be undeserved. The second element retribution captures is that there is a strong link between the crime and its punishment: the worse the crime, the more severe its sentencing.

Problems may arise when we examine 'desert' more closely. For retributivists, an offender *deserves* punishment where he is *morally responsibility* for *wrongdoing*. Punishment is not deserved where someone lacks moral responsibility for some act – and, unsurprisingly, most retributivists reject the use of strict liability because it takes no account of moral responsibility. Furthermore, what counts is our moral responsibility for wrongdoing which is often understood as performing some bad act. For example, a retributivist would argue that thieves and murderers should both be punished where each is responsible for their crime, but murderers should be punished more than thieves because murder is more evil than theft.

The problems that may arise here are that not all offences require moral responsibility: retributivists must either substantially rewrite the criminal law to avoid supporting a theory that can address some, but not all offences. A second problem is that not all offences are 'bad' or 'immoral' in any obvious way, such as the failure to register a new birth or illegal parking. Retribution captures some important elements of desert and proportionality, but theory and practice appear to diverge widely (Brooks, 2012, pp. 15–34).

Deterrence has been defended as a second, alternative purpose for sentencing (Brooks, 2014b). This is the view that punishment is justified where it deters potential offenders from committing crimes through the penal threats. The idea is that criminal justice should secure crime reduction and this is an element about punishment that is surely attractive: it would be difficult, if not impossible, to accept a criminal justice system that made crimes more likely. But the problems quickly mount up. One issue is whether the state should be in the business of threatening its citizens with punishment to act lawfully. A second is the classic worry about deterrence: if punishment is justified by its deterrent effects, would this view of punishment justify sentencing an innocent person if this had positive consequences? A third problem is that it is difficult to know how much deterrence is a factor. We can measure crime trends over time and see how many known crimes have increased or decreased, but we have no convincing gauge on how many *potential* crimes were *almost* committed if not for the penal threat attached to the crimes in question (Brooks, 2012, pp. 35–50).

Rehabilitation is the final penal aim considered (Brooks, 2012: 51–63). This is broadly the view that the purpose of sentencing is to reform offenders so that they avoid future criminality. This view also captures something important: most offenders will eventually become released and so there could be positive consequences in tackling future reoffending by therapeutic interventions. There are also several challenges: if the aim is to rehabilitate, should we punish a thief more than a murderer if the former is more difficult to reform?

Each of these three views about punishment has been defended as *the* main aim of sentencing. Interestingly, all three typically figure in sentencing guidelines used to determine how to punish convicted offenders. While more will be said about sentencing guidelines below, Ashworth and Roberts offer an engaging and well-crafted survey of many of the issues and penal aims that will appear again and again throughout this collection.

But what about the role of victims? John Gardner (Chapter 2) argues that the justifiability of punishment is closely connected to the injustice of victims seeking justice independently of the state through retaliation. The criminal law has long endorsed a displacement function: the victim is displaced as the main actor in criminal proceedings and replaced by the state. While the criminal harm may have been met on the victim, it is the state alone that can take action against the offender. This has historical roots: the displacement function had the purpose of ending feuds, duels and vendettas.

There has been a steady call for victims to have greater involvement in the trial and sentencing process. Recent proposals include the use of victim impact statements that might help influence the judge's decision on determining sentences. Gardner argues that victims ought not to become parties to the criminal trial or administrators of sentencing in order to permit them some measure of retaliation or vengeance. This is because doing so would not further the cause of justice. Instead, it would undermine the main objects of why there is a displacement function in the first place.

Steven N. Durlauf and Daniel S. Nagin (Chapter 3) consider sentencing from a different perspective. What should be the relationship between crime and imprisonment? Some might argue that there is an inverse relation so that you get less crime when more are sentenced. Durlauf and Nagin argue that we should aim for less crime with less imprisonment. They base this view on empirical findings, such as the relatively modest deterrent effects of increasing already lengthy prison sentences and substantial marginal deterrent effects can be achieved through improved visibility of the police.

Durlauf and Nagin also find that imprisonment may have a possible *criminogenic* effect (p. 56). This is the problem that greater exposure to imprisonment may contribute to higher risks of future reoffending. Prisons do not work, but rather may create work for themselves in a self-defeating situation. If we want to achieve better crime reduction, there are alternatives to sentencing that might make this possible. Their attractiveness as policies is that a sound stance on sentencing should be less crime and less use of prisons. So a good policy on sentencing is to use less of it.

Sentencing is about imprisonment. Richard L. Lippke (Chapter 4) focuses on a strange absence in most of the sentencing literature. Different scholars consider various purposes for punishment or debate satisfactory lengths of sentencing for competing types of offenders. But does a theory of punishment help us understand not only the justification of punishment and its severity, but also address the conditions under which punishment is endured? For example, many find it satisfactory to provide answers to queries about why thieves should be punished and how much they should be punished. But *how* should they be punished during their imprisonment?

Lippke offers an engaging analysis that defends a retributivist theory of punishment: punishment must be deserved and proportionate to what is deserved. This view is built on the idea that offenders deserve punishment because of their moral responsibility for some wrongdoing. For Lippke, a retributivist theory about imprisonment must guarantee that offenders are protected from any criminogenic effects from their sentencing. If punishment contributes to offenders becoming more likely to reoffend, then punishment might be undermining the moral responsibility of offenders. If punishment is about just deserts, then such a scenario presents a clear injustice and not what any offender would deserve for his crimes. One implication is that the use of 'supermax' prisons (whereby offenders are imprisoned in relative isolation with little, if any, direct contact with other persons) fails to meet the retributivist test. Lippke defends a compelling argument about how theories of punishment must speak to issues such as prison conditions with rich reflections on how theory and practice interrelate.

The last essay in this first part is on the place of public opinion in sentencing. Stephen Shute (Chapter 5) examines the extent to which sentencing permits or requires taking public opinion into account. Shute finds that the official view in England and Wales is of 'mandatory exclusion' whereby public opinion ought not to be considered when determining sentencing (p. 123). Moreover, the potential relevance of public opinion for determining sentences is broadly lacking in much of the academic literature of this time. That said, Shute identifies shifting currents in the Court of Appeal (Criminal Division) towards a greater recognition that public opinion should be understood as a relevant factor. This is an important development which continues today. Shute's insightful commentary helps chart the problems and prospects of how this development might continue to take shape.

Sentencing Guidelines and the Model Penal Code

Sentencing decisions are often determined through the use of sentencing guidelines. Contemporary guidelines have an origin in the so-called Model Penal Code (MPC). The MPC was designed to address a specific problem. Since America's founding, each of the 50 states developed individual criminal laws governing the definition of offences and frameworks for deciding sentences. The problem was that there were wide differences in how crimes and punishment functioned from state to state. The MPC was an attempt to create a model that could be used by each state to revise their criminal law and bring greater regularity across states. People drawn from a number of different relevant backgrounds came together to design the MPC and it was published in 1962. It has since become highly influential and it helped shape federal sentencing guidelines and the guidelines for many US states. The MPC has also been influential for the sentencing guidelines used in England and Wales, Scotland and other jurisdictions.

The essays in this part consider sentencing guidelines from multiple perspectives. Paul H. Robinson and John M. Darley (Chapter 6) consider 'the utility of desert'. The two leading rationales for punishment are retributivism (or desert) and consequentialism (such as deterrence or rehabilitation). These rationales are often thought to be irreconcilable: the amount of punishment that an offender might be said to *deserve* may depart widely from what sentence might be expected to bring about beneficial future *consequences*. Robinson and Darley argue that although retribution and consequentialism might, in fact, be irreconcilable, the design of sentencing policy in terms of desert can be justified in consequentialist-friendly utilitarian terms. Punishing just deserts promotes beneficial consequences, such as facilitating the creation of shared norms and the moral credibility of the criminal law. Together, these benefit law-abidingness by the public. Robinson and Darley proceed to then put some flesh on these bones and show how sentencing guidelines might be designed to satisfy this goal.

The second essay in this part by Paul H. Robinson, Geoffrey P. Goodwin and Michael D. Reisig (Chapter 7) pursues this project further. They begin with the recent development that the Model Penal Code – which endorses multiple penal purposes (which we might call *penal pluralism*, an idea I will return to later) – had been revised to accept desert as the primary distributive principle for criminal sentencing. This revision brought worries that sentencing would become too punitive if desert were a primary focus and that the ability of the criminal justice to provide effective crime control would be undermined.

Robinson and colleagues argue that this revision of the Model Penal Code should be broadly welcomed. This is because desert is much closer to the public's views about justice than crime control. Furthermore, the evidence is that the assumption that the public possesses punitive intuitions about justice is rejected. Additionally, those who worry about improving crime reduction should support the primacy of desert: doing injustice by departing from public views about desert has not insignificant crime-control costs too often overlooked. Good sentencing policy should have desert at its heart and doing so could promote beneficial consequences.

Rachel E. Barkow (Chapter 8) critically examines the development of sentencing commissions since their launch in 1978 in the USA and the sentencing guidelines produced from 1980. She argues that the diversity of guidelines produced during this time is a product of a core tension between experts and politicians. Or, in other words, sentencing guidelines arise from a kind of tug of war between expert knowledge and political realities. The problem with finding any such balance is the politics of crime and sentencing is believed to be overly punitive which may undermine the constructive space offered to experts. If guidelines should be evidence-based and effective, sentencing commissions must take extra care to avoid domination by their political masters. Otherwise, good policy-making is likely to be undermined by the false impressions held by non-expert politicians. In addition, guidelines should go further and address prosecutorial discretion as well as the role of the jury.

Sentencing guidelines in England and Wales help magistrates and judges determine sentences in normal cases. There may be situations whereby they might depart from their use. But when and how can this be justified? Andrew Ashworth (Chapter 9) probes this matter with great erudition and critical insight. He examines departures from the guidelines for sentencing both above and below (including considerations of mercy) with recommendations on how the current law is best understood and how judicial opinion should be improved. Ashworth argues that departures from sentencing guidelines can be warranted, but there is a real need to develop certain points of good practice to enhance the effectiveness of sentencing guidelines.

This part concludes with an important essay by Ian Edwards (Chapter 10) on the relation of victims to sentencing guidelines. The Coroners and Justice Act 2009 obligates the Sentencing Council to have regard to 'the impact of sentencing decisions on victims of offences' when determining sentencing guidelines. Edwards expands his discussion to include the use of guidelines in Australia and the United States in a comparative critique. He argues that incorporating victims into sentencing commissions could promote beneficial effects, such as improving public confidence, that should be broadly supported.

Sentencing and Emotions

Sentencing might be thought to be rational, not emotional. Justice flourishes after calm reflection rather than through judgments based on sentiment or intuitions. Sentencing is about objectivity rather than subjectivity. Jonathan Doak and Louise Taylor (Chapter 11) believe this view is based upon a mistake. They argue our emotions can help enrich our criminal justice system through what they call a therapeutic jurisprudence that may lead to a positive transformation in the relation between victims and offenders. This 'emotionally intelligent' approach to sentencing advocates the use of narratives because of their emotional importance. Improving the use of emotions in sentencing can strengthen therapeutic healing, strengthen procedure justice, improve the quality of decision-making and transform relationships. This is because emotionally imbibed narratives help us connect with the experiences of loss faced by victims and remorse expressed by offenders. These may help transform relations between victims, offenders and others in constructive ways that promote healing.

Sentencing as Punitive Restoration

This part examines a new development in criminal justice and sentencing policy. There is a hot debate between those who argue for the use of prisons and reformers that call for their general abolition and replacement by alternatives, such as restorative justice. The first group argue that imprisonment can be justified and that it is worth justifying. The second group claims prisons are most often unwarranted coercive state action that is routinely counterproductive:

instead, we require less formal, less punitive and more flexible models. The first pro-prison group highlights that public confidence in the criminal justice system is low. The use of prison is a vivid reminder of the state's commitment to justice being done and being seen to be done. The second anti-prison group highlights that penal alternatives have been demonstrated to achieve higher participant satisfaction rates (including for victims), improved crime reduction rates and greater savings where used. The problem for the first pro-prison group is that the prison is highly expensive for modest benefits in terms of tackling reoffending. The problem for the second anti-prison group is that alternatives lack much public support and their use is often limited to minor crimes by minors.

Punitive restoration is a bridge between these two extremes.[1] It seeks to promote a restorative justice-friendly model with a greater punitive element to expand the beneficial effects of penal alternatives while securing public confidence. One key part of punitive restoration is the reinvention of prison to improve its potential effectiveness. Prisons as we find them may underperform, but, if they are to be continued for use, we can and should reimagine them in new ways to improve penal outcomes.

The first essay in this part examines the use of 'creative rehabilitation' in prisons through the promotion of art. Briege Nugent and Nancy Loucks (Chapter 12) looks at the charity Artlink Central's work over two years at Scotland's main prison for women. They find positive impacts on offenders, such as helping inmates with mental health issues and the development of self-confidence. Nugent and Loucks argue innovative arts programmes can be a useful way of helping rehabilitate offenders, including the most vulnerable inmates and persons who may have become alienated from the formal education system. Inmates can meet others and establish crucial pro-social interests promoting mutual support and benefit (p. 384). While these programmes secure positive outcomes and high satisfaction from inmates, creative rehabilitation is too often an 'add-on' rather than a fundamental element in sentencing policy. Nugent and Loucks argue it is time to re-evaluate this situation.

Punitive restoration can also be secured through the use of brief, but intensive rehabilitation. This is because prison can have a restorative role through targeting the reformative needs of offenders in ways best achievable through secure confinement. Many offenders have the problem that they possess several risk factors for offending, including financial insecurity, unemployment, housing insecurity, mental health problems and drug and alcohol abuse. These factors can be difficult to tackle where offenders remain situated in and influenced by negative support networks. The prison can be a place that could offer a 'cooling off' period and place of brief refuge from these and other problems for offenders for their short-term and long-term benefit (see Brooks, Chapter 14, pp. 436–37). So while alternatives may bring many benefits that can and should be exploited better, prison can also play a far more effective role in offender rehabilitation and crime reduction if redesigned in relatively straightforward ways like this.

One excellent example is research by Devon L. Polaschek (Chapter 13) in the use of intensive rehabilitation of violent offenders in New Zealand. He demonstrates improved crime reduction rates of 10 to 12 per cent reconvictions for inmates completing violence prevention programmes from over three and a half years of both high- and medium-risk offenders for

---

[1]   Punitive restoration is a view first promoted only recently by Thom Brooks which builds off existing research into sentencing and its alternatives (see Brooks, 2012).

all offences. Interestingly, Polaschek finds non-completion of treatment also secures similar improvements in crime reduction. He finds that carefully designed and delivered rehabilitation can reduce risks to the public and offenders of future reoffending.

The first formal exposition and defence of the theory of punitive restoration is found in Thom Brooks (Chapter 14). The theory is developed in a specific context. Sentencing has developed through the use of guidelines influenced by the Model Penal Code. This Code endorses several purposes for punishment (or *penal pluralism*), such as desert, deterrence and rehabilitation. The problem is that there is no clear normative framework to justify either (1) the selection of the particular purposes identified and included in the Code or (2) how penal pluralism can be theoretically coherent. So while penal pluralism is a feature of our everyday practices (whereby judges determine sentences with regard to multiple and different principles), it is under-theorized and potentially incoherent. This charge of incoherence is the view of virtually all philosophers of punishment. They make the point that different purposes can be contradictory: what sentence an offender deserves can be very different from what sentence best promotes future consequences. Therefore, philosophers have argued the Code should be radically redesigned to abandon penal pluralism and endorse one, not many, principles – although it is hotly contested which principle is best.

Brooks defends a 'unified theory' in an attempt to argue for a theory of punishment that can provide a compelling account of coherent penal pluralism. He accepts that retribution may be at odds with deterrence so combining *theories* may be impossible. But we might instead seek to combine *principles* instead of theories. So the goal is to marry retribution with deterrence and other theories, but instead penal purposes like desert, crime reduction and reform. Brooks argues that we require a new framework to justify punishment and the different principles that can play a role. He defends a rights-based framework whereby the criminal law is understood as an attempt to protect our rights: in effect, crimes are rights violations as attempts to undermine our rights. Punishment is a response to crime that is justified where it can serve as a means to restore, protect and maintain the rights we endorse through our criminal law. Punishment gives effect to a 'restoration of rights' through different or multiple penal purposes where relevant. Sentencing can be determined in relation to one or more purposes when relevant where the purposes pursued support the wider end of protection and maintaining our rights. This is the unified theory of punishment: it is possible to justify a compelling penal theory that endorses penal pluralism in a coherent framework. This theory has the attraction of bringing together multiple purposes (desert, crime reduction, rehabilitation and others) shedding light on a kind of 'grand unifying theory' of punishment.

But what might this look like in practice? Brooks uses the example of punitive restoration as an illustration of a unified theory of punishment. Punitive restoration is a response to crimes as rights violations that seeks the restoration of rights in a particular way. The restorative justice framework achieves desert by punishing only the guilty, crime reduction and offender rehabilitation by the evidence it achieves improvements in reducing reoffending and at significant savings. Punitive restoration is different from the standard view of restorative justice because punitive restoration rejects the position that restoration cannot include imprisonment or its threat. Instead, punitive restoration accepts prisons may underperform in terms of rehabilitation and its effects, but redesigning the prison so that we see more high intensive treatment (supported through reductions in both overall time served and, if successful, savings from future crime reduction) to enable restoration. Plus, the failure of offenders to honour restorative contracts typically leads to the start of a new trial. Punitive restoration, which would incorporate possible minor sentences in restorative contracts, could include from the outset a possible suspended sentence if a restorative contract is broken. This could secure penal pluralism in a concrete policy that might lead to significant improvements in criminal justice effectiveness and public confidence.

Thom Brooks (Chapter 15) examines punitive restoration in greater detail. Punitive restoration is not only a way to achieve a unified theory that expands the benefits of restorative justice to more offences without sacrificing public confidence. Punitive restoration is also a way to better include the public in sentencing matters for reasons of justice. Restorative conferences are settings where victims and offenders meet together with support networks, community members and a trained facilitator to engage in a constructive dialogue about the effects crimes have had on those involved. The idea is that mutual understanding can be achieved and the results are strongly encouraging. Both victims and offenders claim much higher satisfaction rates with restorative justice than the trial.

A problem is that public opinion is often believed too unreliable and punitive to be taken seriously in sentencing matters. Brooks argues that expanding the possible range of penal outcomes for restorative contracts can be a welcome development. One reason is that the public involved in these conferences will not be uninformed, but actively participant. This will help ensure their views about outcomes may be more likely to meet the appropriate standards of justice served and the needs of offenders. Indeed, the evidence is this is correct given the improvements in outcomes. A second reason is that with greater understanding the public has been shown to be even more lenient than judges in some cases. Greater inclusion of the public can be acceptable within the set parameters of the restorative conference.

Punitive restoration through the use of the restorative conference is also a view built upon a view of justice. This is the idea of stake-holding whereby those who have a stake should have a say. The restorative conference allows all stake-holders – including victims, offenders and the public – to have their say and for this reason it is to be especially welcome. If those who have a stake should have a say, punitive restoration is the only model that can provide us a compelling view about how this could be achieved. And it is based upon a unified theory of punishment.

Punitive restoration remains an idea in its infancy. However, there appears much future promise for further growth. Predictions about sentencing policy are usually hazardous, but it seems clear that punitive restoration is likely to increase in popularity and use in sentencing policy in future. It occupies a space to be watched closely with interest.

Sentencing Alternatives

The final part of this book considers a debate around particular sentencing alternatives: restorative justice. The first essay is by John Braithwaite, widely regarded as the most prominent contemporary champion of restorative justice. Braithwaite (Chapter 16) considers the standards that might govern the use of restorative justice which he identifies as limiting, maximizing and enabling. Together, these three standards form multidimensional criteria for evaluating restorative justice programmes. (This has unexplored potential analogies with multidimensional criteria found in the penal pluralism of most non-restorative sentencing guidelines.)

Restorative justice is defended as an attractive alternative to the use of prisons for many of the reasons stated above: restorative justice achieves crime reduction with higher participant satisfaction at significant savings. Braithwaite adds a further claim about justice: restorative justice is about a *restoration*. While punitive restoration is about the restoration *of rights*, Braithwaite claims restorative justice is about the restoration of a moral equality between offenders and the community. This requires, in this view, that restorative justice is based upon the foundations of a republican theory of freedom whereby freedom is understood as non-domination. Restoration can only be securely guaranteed where different parties can 'restore' their unequal moral standing. Non-domination is essential to ensure the overcoming of such inequalities and the fostering of constructive, positive future relationships.

The following essay is a powerful critique of restorative justice by Andrew Ashworth (Chapter 17). He argues that restorative justice has been widely held as a highly promising alternative to traditional sentencing. Ashworth notes it is practice-led with the consequence that there is no one conception of 'restorative justice', but instead many. He raises several significant challenges to the use of restorative justice in terms of its project, role and justification. For example, perhaps we should restore unequal relationships between citizens and so restorative justice may appear attractive. However, why think that all such inequalities are only the rest of crimes? Or why believe only those inequalities formed by crime deserve restoration? And what is it that is being restored? Ashworth's challenges force us to reconsider whether informal procedures like restorative justice can guarantee the necessary safeguards we demand from the criminal justice system. While many claim restorative justice is the future, Ashworth's critique raises serious concerns that any future restorative model must address.

This book concludes with a revelatory essay by Clare McGlynn (Chapter 18). She examines the punishment of rape. McGlynn argues that debates over how to best prosecute rape and punish rapists can be improved. Many focus on the need to secure more convictions and greater severity of punishment as scholars, including many feminists, endorse the strategy of reforming traditional approaches to crime and punishment. McGlynn claims this can lead to problematic situations where victims feel marginalized and find justice elusive.

She argues that we should consider the use of restorative justice to secure justice for rape victims. McGlynn focuses on recent proposals by Susan Miller for how restorative justice could become more central in these cases. McGlynn argues that while Miller offers a strong case, it is hampered by its being limited to post-conviction use only. Instead, McGlynn claims that we should endorse a more expansive understanding of restorative justice – not dissimilar to the perspective of punitive restoration noted in the previous part – and criminal justice.

Conclusion

Sentencing is at the coalface of criminal justice for the public and policy-makers. This is because the decision to criminalize is also a decision about punishment. This often, but not only, includes the use of prisons. How might imprisonment be justified? What role(s) should sentencing play in criminal justice? How should sentencing guidelines be developed and improved? Should we endorse a unified theory of punishment of penal pluralism? Or should we support one rationale and not others? What, if any, alternatives to sentencing have promise? Is punitive restoration a viable compromise? These and many other questions are addressed across a wide range of topics drawing together different theoretical resources and rich empirical, comparative studies. This collection brings together the leading critical work on sentencing. These essays seek to deepen our collective understanding of this important view of punishment to shed greater light on future possibilities for current practices.

References

Brooks, Thom (ed.) (2014a), *Retribution*, Farnham: Ashgate.
Brooks, Thom (ed.) (2014b), *Deterrence*, Farnham: Ashgate.
Lippke, Richard L. (2007), 'Minimum and Extreme Conditions of Confinement', in *Rethinking Imprisonment*, Oxford: Oxford University Press, pp. 104–28.

Part I
Sentencing: Theory and Practice

[1]

SENTENCING: THEORY, PRINCIPLE, AND PRACTICE

Andrew Ashworth and Julian Roberts

The passing of a sentence on an offender is the most public stage of the criminal justice process. Sentencing attracts widespread media coverage, intense public interest—and much public criticism. Selective news coverage, populist journalism, and the complexities of sentencing help to explain why polls conducted in all western nations routinely demonstrate that most people believe their courts to be too lenient[1] (see Hough and Roberts, this volume). When researchers provide sufficient information about sentencing decisions, the 'punitiveness gap' between the public and the courts diminishes greatly—but it is the polls that attract headlines.

This chapter begins by examining the various rationales for sentencing and then explores sentencing procedures and practices, including both custodial and non-custodial sentencing. We also discuss the sentencing guidelines that have been issued over the past decade in England and Wales. Throughout the chapter our focus is upon sentencing in England and Wales. However, since many of the problems confronting sentencing and indeed the solutions to those problems are shared by many countries, we also periodically provide illustrations from other common law jurisdictions.

RATIONALES FOR SENTENCING

When a court passes sentence, it authorizes the use of state coercion against a person for committing an offence. The sanction may take the form of some deprivation, restriction, or positive obligation. Deprivations and obligations are fairly widespread in social contexts—e.g. duties to pay taxes, to complete various official forms, etc. But when imposed as a sentence, there is the added element of condemnation, labelling, and censure of the offender for the offence. In view of the direct personal and indirect

---

[1] Thus in 2011, three-quarters of the polled public in England and Wales expressed the view that sentencing was too lenient (see Ashcroft 2011 and Hough and Roberts, this volume).

social effects this can have, punishment requires justification. In order to understand punishment as a social institution and to understand the tensions inherent in any given 'system', there is benefit in identifying the principal approaches to sentencing. Among the issues to be considered are the behavioural and the political premises of each approach, its empirical claims, and its practical influence.

DESERT THEORIES

Retributive theories of punishment have a long history, going back to the writings of Kant and Hegel. In their modern guise as the 'just deserts' perspective, they came to prominence in the 1970s, propelled by the alleged excesses and failures of rehabilitative ideals (von Hirsch 1976). Desert theorists argue that punishment is justified as the morally appropriate response to crime: those who culpably commit offences deserve censure; this censure should be conveyed through some 'hard treatment' that prompts the offender to take the censure seriously, but the amount of hard treatment should remain proportionate to the degree of wrongdoing, respecting the offender as a moral agent (see von Hirsch and Ashworth 2005).

The justification for the institution of state punishment also incorporates the consequentialist element of underlying general deterrence: without the restraining effect of a system of state punishment, anarchy might well ensue. Some, notably Duff (2000), tie further consequentialist aims into a fundamentally retributivist justification, arguing that punishment ought not only to communicate justified censure but also to persuade offenders to repentance, self-reform, and reconciliation. The behavioural premise of desert is that individuals are and should be treated as responsible (though occasionally fallible) moral agents. The political premise is that all individuals should be respected as moral agents: an offender deserves punishment, but does not forfeit all rights on conviction, and has a right not to be punished disproportionately to the crime committed.

Proportionality is the key concept in desert theory. There are two forms of proportionality. *Cardinal proportionality* concerns the magnitude of the penalty, requiring that it not be out of proportion to the gravity of the conduct: five years' imprisonment for theft from a shop would clearly breach that, as would the imposition of a trivial penalty for a very serious offence. *Ordinal proportionality* concerns the ranking of the relative seriousness of different offences: to what degree is rape more serious than robbery, for example? In practice, much depends on the evaluation of conduct, especially by sentencers, and on social assumptions about traditional (e.g. street crime) compared with new types of offence (e.g. commercial fraud, pollution). In theory, ordinal proportionality requires the creation of a scale of values which can be used to assess the gravity of each type of offence: culpability, together with aggravating and mitigating factors, must then be assimilated into the scale. This task, which is vital to any approach in which proportionality plays a part, makes considerable demands on theory (see von Hirsch and Ashworth 2005: Appendix 3; Ashworth 2010: ch. 4); some would say that decisions on relative offence-seriousness can never be more than contingent judgements which bear the marks of the prevailing power structure.

DETERRENCE THEORIES

Deterrence theories regard the prevention of further offences through the threat of legal sanctions as the rationale for punishing. There is little modern literature on individual deterrence, which sees the deterrence of further offences by the particular offender as the measure of punishment. A first offender may require little or no punishment, while a recidivist might be thought to require an escalation of penalties. The seriousness of the offence becomes less important than the prevention of repetition. Traces of this approach can certainly be detected in the treatment of persistent offenders and so-called 'dangerous offenders' in contemporary sentencing, as noted below.

More attention has been devoted to general deterrence, which involves calculating the penalty on the basis of what will deter others from committing a similar offence. Leading utilitarian writers such as Bentham (1789; cf. Walker 1991) and economic theorists such as Posner (1985) develop the notion of setting penalties at levels sufficiently severe to outweigh the likely benefits of offending. The behavioural premise is that offenders are predominantly rational, calculating individuals—a premise that criminologists may call into question. The political premise is that the greatest good for the greatest number represents the supreme value, and that the individual counts only for one: it may therefore be justifiable to punish one person severely in order to deter others effectively, thereby overriding the claims of proportionality. This reasoning depends on convincing empirical evidence of the effect of deterrent sentencing on individual behaviour. This requires, among other things, demonstration that people are aware of the level of likely sentences; and that they desist from offending largely because of that sentence level and not for other reasons. A careful analysis of the general deterrence research by von Hirsch *et al.* (1999) found that there is evidence of a link between the *certainty* of punishment and crime rates, but considerably weaker evidence of a link between the *severity* of sentences and crime rates (see also Doob and Webster 2003; Bottoms and von Hirsch 2011).

REHABILITATION

The rationale here is to prevent further offending by the individual through rehabilitation, which may involve therapy, counselling, cognitive-behavioural programmes, skills training, etc. Still a leading rationale in many European countries, it reached its zenith in the United States in the 1960s, declined in the 1970s, and then began to regain ground in the 1990s (see von Hirsch, Ashworth, and Roberts 2009: ch. 1). A humanitarian desire to help those with obvious behavioural problems has ensured that various treatment programmes continue to be developed. The key issue is the effectiveness of various interventions, and there is a long-running debate about the concept and the measurement of effectiveness (e.g. Lloyd *et al.* 1994). The reality is that certain rehabilitative programmes are likely to work for some types of offender in some circumstances. The 'What Works?' movement rekindled interest in various programmes for behaviour modification, with the development of 'accredited' programmes in prisons and as part of community sentences (see McGuire 2002; Harper and Chitty 2005), but a sober assessment of the available results demonstrated that the claims made by the Home Office and other protagonists have not been translated into practice (Bottoms 2004).

The behavioural premise of rehabilitative theory is that criminal offences are to a large extent determined by social pressures, psychological difficulties, or situational problems of various kinds. The political premise is that offenders are seen as unable to cope in certain situations and in need of help from experts, and therefore (perhaps) as less than fully responsible individuals. The rehabilitative approach advocates that sentences should be tailored to the needs of the particular offenders: in so far as this needs-based approach places no limits on the extent of the intervention, it conflicts with the idea of a right not to be punished disproportionately. Its focus instead is upon the diagnosis, treatment, and completion of accredited programmes. 'Diagnostic' tools such as the pre-sentence report are seen as essential to this approach to sentencing (see Raynor, this volume).

INCAPACITATION

The incapacitative approach is to identify offenders or groups of offenders who are likely to do such harm in the future that special protective measures (usually in the form of lengthy incarceration) are warranted. The primary example of this in England and Wales, originally introduced by the *Criminal Justice Act 2003*, is the IPP sentence (Imprisonment for Public Protection), prescribed for certain offenders classified as dangerous. The nature of this sentence is discussed later in this chapter. Incapacitation has no behavioural premise. It is neither linked with any particular causes of offending nor dependent on changing the behaviour of offenders: it looks chiefly to predicted risk and to the protection of potential victims. The political premise is often presented as utilitarian, justifying incapacitation by reference to the greater aggregate social benefit and therefore sacrificing the individual's right not to be punished disproportionately to the wrongdoing. The repeatedly confirmed fallibility of predictive judgements (e.g. Monahan 2004) calls into question the justification for any lengthening of sentences on grounds of public protection, and yet the political pressure to have some form(s) of incapacitative sentence available to the courts has been felt in most countries. If this is the reality of penal politics then there is surely a strong case for procedural safeguards to ensure that the predictive judgements are soundly based and open to thorough challenge.

RESTORATIVE AND REPARATIVE THEORIES

These are not regarded as theories of punishment. Rather, their argument is that sentences should move away from punishment towards restitution and reparation, aimed at restoring the harm done to the victim and to the community (see Hoyle, this volume). Restorative theories emphasize the significance of stakeholders in the offence (not just the state and the offender, but also the victim and the community), the importance of process (bringing the stakeholders together in order to decide on the response to the offence), and restorative goals (usually some form of reparation to the victim and 'restoration' of the community). There are many variations of restorative justice in different countries, some established in law and others at an experimental stage, and an assessment cannot be given here (see Dignan 2005). They are often based on a behavioural premise similar to rehabilitation for the offender, and

870   ANDREW ASHWORTH AND JULIAN ROBERTS

also on the premise that the processes help to restore the victim; their political premise is that the response to an offence should not be dictated by the state but determined by all the interested parties, placing compensation and restoration ahead of mere punishment of the offender, and encouraging maximum participation in the processes so as to bring about social reintegration.

Victim personal (impact) statements

There are other victim-oriented initiatives at sentencing. One that is widespread in both European and common law countries is to allow victims to submit a 'victim impact statement' (VIS) to the court, detailing the effects of the crime from their point of view. In England and Wales this is known as a 'victim personal statement' and may be submitted to any sentencing court. The VPS has been a feature of sentencing in this jurisdiction since 2001 but has been used in US jurisdictions, Canada, Australia, and New Zealand for many years now (Roberts 2009). The VIS has generated considerable research, and has spawned much heated debate as to whether it is either appropriate in principle or desirable in practice, and whether there are benefits associated with victim impact statements (see Erez 1999; Sanders *et al.* 2001; Chalmers et al. 2007; Edwards 2004). It is worth distinguishing between jurisdictions which allow a victim to provide only a description of the harm and others where the statement may also include the victim's opinion on the appropriate sentence. Criticism of the victim impact statement has focused on the latter form of victim participation. Allowing victims to make specific recommendations for sentence raises deep questions about crimes as public and/ or private wrongs (see Ashworth 2010: 382–7).

SOCIAL THEORIES

There has been a resurgence of writings which emphasize the social and political context of sentencing (see Duff and Garland 1994: ch. 1). Important in this respect are Garland's (1990) analysis of the theoretical underpinnings of historical trends in punishment, and Hudson's arguments (1993) in favour of a shift towards a more supportive social policy as the principal response to the problem of crime. Those who have been influenced by Hart's distinction (1968) between the general justifying aim of punishment (in his view, utilitarian or deterrent) and the principles for distribution of punishment (in his view, retribution or desert) should consider the challenge to this dichotomy in Lacey (1988). She argues that both these issues raise questions of individual autonomy and of collective welfare and we should address this conflict and strive to ensure that neither value is sacrificed entirely at either stage. In developing this view she explores the political values involved in state punishment and argues for a clearer view of the social function of punishing.

Sentencing rationales in practice

It will be evident from the foregoing discussion that the various objectives for sentencing point in different directions. Despite this obvious conclusion, in 2003 the then government proclaimed that it was taking a significant step towards consistency in English sentencing by enacting section 142 of the Criminal Justice Act 2003, which provides:

(1) Any court dealing with an offender in respect of his offence must have regard to the following purposes of sentencing—

    (a) the punishment of offenders,
    (b) the reduction of crime (including its reduction by deterrence),
    (c) the reform and rehabilitation of offenders,
    (d) the protection of the public, and
    (e) the making of reparation by offenders to persons affected by their offences.

Three difficulties arise with lists of purposes such as that found in section 142. First, the objectives are potentially conflicting (except for reparation which can sometimes be achieved alongside another purpose). Second, no direction is provided as to whether one objective is particularly appropriate for certain cases—whether, for example, deterrence should be uppermost in a court's mind when sentencing corporate offending. Third, as the Home Office Sentencing Review (2001) pointed out, the evidence for (b), (c), and (d) is weak. It is therefore unclear on what evidence an individual sentencer could make a rational choice among the various purposes. For these reasons, lists of this kind have been criticized in the academic literature. England and Wales is not alone in taking this approach to providing guidance regarding sentencing objectives. Similar lists of objectives have been placed on a statutory footing in New Zealand and Canada, and the US guidelines manuals provide a similar range of options for sentencers in the US jurisdictions (e.g. Minnesota Sentencing Guidelines Commission 2010).

However, the Criminal Justice Act 2003 contains other provisions that may be used to clarify matters. Section 143(1) states that:

In considering the seriousness of any offence, the court must consider the offender's culpability in committing the offence and any harm which the offence caused or was intended to cause or might foreseeably have caused.

Further, when the Act sets the threshold for community sentences and for custody, and the standard for the length of custodial sentences, it uses 'the seriousness of the offence' as the key indicator. On this basis the Sentencing Guidelines Council (now the Sentencing Council) issued a guideline entitled *Overarching Principles—Seriousness*[2] to the effect that the proportionality principle enshrined in section 143(1) should be used by sentencers as the touchstone. That is fully consistent with the thresholds set by the 2003 Act, but leaves the 'pick and mix' approach of section 142 somewhat in limbo.

It is hard to know how the various rationales for sentencing affect sentencing practice. Judges often refer to general deterrence, most notoriously in the judgment in *Blackshaw* [2011] EWCA Crim 2312, where sentences significantly above the guidelines were approved for offenders involved in the riots of August 2011, on grounds of general deterrence. There was no recognition of the weakness of the evidence for general deterrence, or other objections. Parliament too has legislated for mandatory sentences— for example the mandatory minimum of five years for possession of certain firearms, in section 287 of the Criminal Justice Act 2003—based on a deterrent rationale.

---

[2] All guidelines referred to in this chapter are available at: www.sentencingcouncil.org.uk.

Protection of the public (incapacitation) remains as an exception to the proportionality principle when dealing with so-called dangerous offenders, and those provisions of the 2003 Act are discussed below.

The reform and rehabilitation of offenders is a relevant purpose once the court has decided that a community sentence of a particular level is justified by the seriousness of the offence: in those cases, therefore, the proportionality principle must be applied first, and once the threshold is passed, the possibility of achieving a rehabilitative purpose enters the equation. All these points will be taken further below. What they suggest, and as the seriousness guideline states, is that proportionality should be the sentencer's guide, except in dangerousness cases, but that within the framework of a proportionate sentence it may be desirable to aim for rehabilitation. A reparative measure may also be possible.

In so far as the proportionality principle holds sway, it places some limits on the use of state power over those who offend. Even approaches that are critical of desert theory, such as the republicanism of Braithwaite and Pettit (1990) and the communitarianism of Lacey (1988), recognize some limits to state power at the sentencing stage. The argument that desert theory leads to harsh penalties is not sustainable by reference to international comparisons (von Hirsch and Ashworth 2005: ch. 6), although it does need to be combined with the principle of penal parsimony to ensure that a movement towards punitiveness is avoided.

THE MECHANICS OF SENTENCING IN ENGLAND AND WALES

In this part of the chapter some basic elements of the law and practice of sentencing are set out. The various stages of a criminal case are discussed, together with the procedures which surround the sentencing stage itself.

THE SELECTION OF CASES FOR SENTENCE

Courts pass sentence in only a small proportion of the crimes committed in any one year. The explanation for this is to be found in the concept of 'case attrition' in the process from the commission of the offence through to the imposition of a sanction in cases which proceed that far. As Maguire demonstrates in Chapter 8 of this volume, the attrition rate in England and Wales comes about because only a small minority of all crimes committed are reported, recorded, detected, and prosecuted to conviction.

The most recent statistics illustrate the phenomenon. In 2009 approximately 9.5 million crimes were reported to the British Crime Survey (Ministry of Justice 2010b: Table 1A). A total of 4,338,604 crimes were recorded by the police and a sentence was imposed in 13 per cent of these cases (Home Office 2010a: Figure 1.1). However, since a large proportion of crimes are not reported to the BCS, it is likely that only approximately 3 per cent of all offences in any given year result in court sentences. This is not to suggest that sentencing is unimportant, for it may have a social or symbolic importance considerably in excess of the small proportion of crimes resulting in a sentence. But these statistics do suggest the need for caution in assessing the crime-preventive effects of sentencing. Theoretical rationales which look to the consequences of sentencing may over-estimate its potential for reducing overall rates of criminal behaviour.

The selection of cases for sentence is not merely a quantitative filtering process. There are also various filters of a qualitative kind, some formal, some informal. The role of the regulatory agencies is significant: the Health and Safety Executive, the Environment Agency, and various other regulatory bodies tend to regard prosecution as a last resort (see, e.g., Hawkins 2003). These and other agencies, such as HM Revenue and Customs, also have various means of enforcing compliance without resort to prosecution, such as warning notices or the 'compounding' of evaded tax and duty. Even though the orientation of the police and the Crown Prosecution Service is more towards prosecutions in court, they have various out-of-court disposals which are being used increasingly. When an offence is reported to the police, the choice among alternative courses (e.g. no further action; informal warning; Penalty Notice for Disorder; cannabis warning; fixed penalty notice; or passing the case to the Crown Prosecution Service with a view to prosecution) has relatively low visibility (see further on these issues Padfield, Morgan, and Maguire, this volume). If the CPS take over the case, they too have the alternatives of offering a conditional caution (specifying certain conditions, compliance with which will lead to the dropping of the charge) or of returning the case to the police with a view to a simple caution.

The Code for Crown Prosecutors (2010) states that a prosecution should not be brought unless there is a realistic prospect of conviction on the charge, but allows the CPS not to prosecute if to do so would not be in the public interest. At the stage of plea the system contains strong incentives to plead guilty, and there is no shortage of empirical evidence that negotiation is a familiar part of justice in magistrates' courts and in the Crown Court (see Ashworth and Redmayne 2010: ch. 10). In summary, therefore, the offences for which the courts have to pass sentence are both quantitatively and qualitatively different from what might be described as the social reality of crime. The courts see only a small percentage of cases. Even if it may be assumed that these are generally the more serious offences, how they are presented in court may be shaped as much by the systemic drivers towards guilty pleas, and by the working practices and priorities of the police, prosecutors, and defence lawyers as by any objective conception of 'the facts of the case' (see further Sanders and Young, this volume).

CROWN COURT AND MAGISTRATES' COURT

In most jurisdictions there are two or three levels of criminal courts. In England and Wales there are two levels: the Crown Court deals with the more serious cases and the magistrates' courts with the less serious. The Crown Court sits as a trial court with judge and jury. Some two-thirds of Crown Court cases involve a guilty plea, and these are dealt with by judge alone—juries play no part in sentencing in this jurisdiction.

In almost all other common law jurisdictions sentencing is conducted by professional judges; England and Wales is almost unique in using lay adjudicators (members of the public who have been appointed magistrates). The lay magistracy has existed for over six centuries in this jurisdiction. There are approximately 28,000 lay magistrates in England and Wales, and they usually sit in benches of three, assisted by a legally-trained adviser. Alternatively some magistrates' courts, particularly in large cities, have a professional District Judge. The maximum sentence in a magistrates' court is six months' imprisonment or a total of 12 months' imprisonment if there are two or more convictions. In 2009, fully 93 per cent of all offenders sentenced were disposed of in the magistrates' courts (Ministry of Justice 2010a).

For many offences a magistrates' court has the power to commit an offender to the Crown Court for sentence if it believes that its own sentencing powers are inadequate. Finally, it should be mentioned that the number of offenders dealt with in the magistrates' courts has declined in recent years, as a result of the greater use of out-of-court penalties: this raises serious questions of principle about the quasi-sentencing powers given to the police and prosecutors (out-of-court penalties, conditional cautions), and about the proper functions of a criminal court (see Padfield, Morgan, and Maguire, this volume).

COURT OF APPEAL OF ENGLAND AND WALES

There is the possibility of appeal against sentence, from magistrates' court to Crown Court, or from Crown Court to the Court of Appeal. The Court of Appeal, Criminal Division, presided over by the Lord Chief Justice and the Vice President of the Criminal Division, hears all appeals in criminal matters from the Crown Court. The sentencing caseload of the criminal division has increased in recent years. In 2009, there were 7,195 applications for leave to appeal, and of these fully three-quarters were sentence appeals (Ministry of Justice 2010d: 156). Of the 2,136 appeals involving sentence heard in that year 1,484 or 73 per cent were allowed (Ministry of Justice 2010d: Table 7.7).

MAXIMUM PENALTIES

In most countries the legislature sets the maximum sentence for each offence. This is the position in England and Wales, except that there remain a few common law offences which have no fixed maximum (e.g. manslaughter, conspiracy to outrage public decency). Parliament has set the maxima at different times, in different social circumstances, and without any overall plan, often based on the number of years for which offenders were transported to Australia in earlier centuries (Radzinowicz and Hood 1990: ch. 15). The legislature in this country (and most other common law countries) continues to assign and revise maximum penalties on a piecemeal basis. For example, in England the Criminal Justice Act 2003 raised the maxima for many summary offences, and the maximum for causing death by dangerous driving was increased from 10 to 14 years. As we shall see below, a small number of offences have a mandatory sentence or a mandatory minimum sentence.

THE RANGE OF AVAILABLE SENTENCES

In this section we will begin by summarizing the principal disposals available to a sentencing court in England and Wales, after which we shall discuss the relative use of these disposals over the past decade.

Beneath the maximum penalty for the offence, the court usually has discretion to choose among alternative disposals. In England and Wales the available sentences may be represented in terms of three tiers. At the lowest level are the so-called 'first tier' sentences. These include the *absolute discharge*, usually reserved for a small number of cases of very low culpability; the *conditional discharge*, where the condition is that the offender does not re-offend within a specified time (one, two, or three years), and breach of which condition means that the offender will be sentenced for the original offence as well as the new offence; and the *fine*, still much used for summary offences (the least serious) but declining in use for other offences.

Courts are required to take account of the means of the offender when calculating a fine, but there has been resistance to the adoption of the kind of 'day fine' system operating in many other European countries. The day fine permits courts to ensure that the magnitude of the imposed fine reflects the offender's ability to pay (Ashworth 2010: 327–38). The Carter Review (2003: 27) argued that 'fines should replace community sentences for low-risk offenders', suggesting that some 30 per cent of community sentences ought to be replaced by fines, but no formal steps have been taken to bring that about.

The second tier of sentencing is occupied by *community sentences*. For the last 30 years it has been official policy that the courts should use community sentences instead of some shorter custodial sentences; in practice the use of community sentences has increased, but the numbers of short custodial sentences have also increased, albeit at a slower rate than other prison sentences. The 2003 Act retained the requirement that a court should not impose any community sentence unless satisfied that the offence is serious enough to warrant it; and also the requirement that, if the court decides that the case is serious enough, it should ensure that the community order (a) is the most suitable for the offender, and (b) imposes restrictions on liberty which are commensurate with the seriousness of the offence (Criminal Justice Act 2003, section 148(2)). In many such cases a 'pre-sentence report' will have been prepared by the Probation Service to 'assist' the court. The theory and practice of community sentences are discussed by Raynor in this volume, and the 12 possible requirements (including supervision, unpaid work, drug rehabilitation, and so on) are set out there. The legislation provides for the possibility of imprisonment on breach. However, the relevant guideline states that 'custody should be the last resort, reserved for those cases of deliberate and repeated breach where all reasonable efforts to ensure that the offender complies have failed' (Sentencing Guidelines Council 2004: para. 1.1.47[3]).

Finally, there are the third tier sentences. A *suspended sentence order* should only be imposed when the court is satisfied that a custodial sentence is unavoidable, and that the court would have imposed imprisonment if the power to suspend had not been available. A court is empowered to suspend a sentence of imprisonment of up to 12 months for a period of up to two years, and the court may add to the order one or more of the same 12 requirements that apply to community sentences (see above). On breach of a suspended sentence order the court must activate the prison sentence unless it is unjust to do so. The other third tier sentence is *immediate imprisonment*,

---

[3] Available at: www.sentencingcouncil.org.uk.

and this will be discussed in detail in the paragraphs below. At all three tiers there are separate orders for young offenders (see Morgan and Newburn, this volume), and also some separate orders for mentally disordered offenders (see Peay, this volume).

In all cases involving death or injury, loss or damage, the court must consider making a *compensation order*, requiring the offender to make compensatory payments to the victim according to the offender's ability to pay. The court may also, where appropriate, impose one of several preventive orders—for example, an anti-social behaviour order, a sexual offences prevention order, a serious crime prevention order, and so on. In drug trafficking cases there are mandatory provisions requiring the judge to consider making a *confiscation order*, requiring the offender to yield certain assets to the court, and the Proceeds of Crime Act 2002 (UK) makes confiscation orders available in other serious cases too.

SENTENCING PATTERNS IN ENGLAND AND WALES

Figures 29.1 and 29.2 reveal sentencing patterns for indictable offences in the magistrates' and Crown Courts in 2009. As can be seen, community orders are the most frequent disposal for indictable offences in the magistrates' courts (accounting for 39 per cent of all cases), followed by fines (23 per cent), suspended sentences (20 per cent and custody (13 per cent; see Figure 29.1). Reflecting their more serious caseload, in the Crown Court immediate custody was imposed in over half the cases (57 per cent), followed in frequency by suspended sentences (21 per cent) and community orders (16 per cent). Fines accounted for only 2 per cent of cases (see Figure 29.2).

Table 29.1 summarizes trends for the principal sentences imposed for indictable offences over the last decade (2000–9). Several important trends are worth noting. First, the volume of cases sentenced changed little during this time, increasing by only

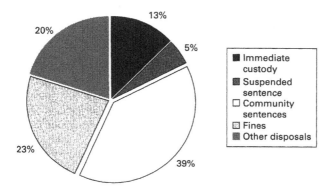

Figure 29.1 Sentences imposed, indictable offences, magistrates'courts, 2009
Source: Ministry of Justice (2010b).

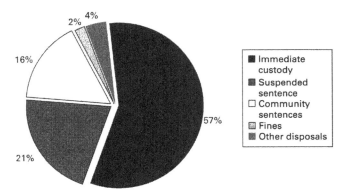

Figure 29.2 Sentences imposed, indictable offences, Crown Courts, 2009
Source: Ministry of Justice (2010b).

1 per cent. Second, the proportionate use of immediate custody remained stable at one quarter of all cases; this explains the fact that the number of prison sentences, which had increased from 1993–2000,[4] levelled out over the most recent decade. Third, following the re-introduction of the suspended sentence in 2005, the use of immediate custody fell only slightly (see Table 29.1). This suggests that courts sometimes use suspended sentences where they would otherwise impose a community sentence, not an immediate custodial sentence.

Fourth, the proportionate use of fines declined—from 25 per cent to 17 per cent of all cases from the beginning to the end of the decade. A fine was the most severe sanction in 82,110 cases in 2000, declining to 56,029 in 2009. Where did these cases which previously resulted in a fine go? As can be seen in Table 29.1, the decline in fines was accompanied by a dramatic increase in the use of suspended sentences of imprisonment due to their revival in 2005 (see above). This may be described as 'up-tariffing' —by which we mean the increasing tendency to impose a more severe sanction. Suspended sentences accounted for less than 1 per cent of cases in 2000, but 10 per cent in 2009, while community orders rose to account for 33 per cent of cases in 2009 from 30 per cent in 2000 (see Table 29.1).

VARIATION IN SENTENCING OUTCOMES

Alleged inconsistencies in sentencing have been a cause for concern the world over—ever since the first scientific analysis was published in 1932 (Gaudet, Harris, and St. John 1932). Since then, empirical research in the United States, Canada, and other countries has repeatedly demonstrated variability in sentencing, across a range of different methodologies (e.g. Austin and Williams 1977; Palys and Divorski 1987).[5]

---

[4] Over the period 1995–2002, the custody rate for indictable offences increased from 22% to 28% (Ministry of Justice 2009: 6).

[5] Where there are fairly high maximum penalties and a wide range of available sentences, inconsistency might appear to be an obvious consequence. Yet even before there were many statutory restrictions and

878   ANDREW ASHWORTH AND JULIAN ROBERTS

Table 29.1 Sentences imposed, all indictable offences, 2000–2009, number of cases and percentage of all cases

	Immediate Custody	Suspended Sentence	Community Order	Fine	Other Disposals	Total cases sentenced
2000	80,784	2,453	97,948	82,110	65,368	326,210
	25%	<1%	30%	25%	20%	(100%)
2001	80,273	2,139	102,063	77,466	63,401	323,203
2002	85,151	1,963	110,768	78,470	62,355	336,744
2003	80,794	2,055	109,648	78,250	65,238	333,930
2004	79,938	2,143	111,784	65,095	60,120	316,937
2005	76,291	5,610	111,724	58,433	60,150	306,598
2006	73,532	20,799	102,971	51,628	53,607	302,537
2007	74,037	27,254	105,142	49,463	56,362	312,258
2008	79,058	28,455	102,782	49,646	55,959	315,900
2009	80,239	31,119	107,852	56,029	51,907	327,146
	25%	10%	33%	17%	16%	(100%)
change 2000–09	<1%	+1,200%	+10%	-32%	-21%	<1%

Notes: row percentages rounded.
Source: Ministry of Justice (2010b).

In magistrates' courts, where most sentencing takes place, local variation is a long-standing phenomenon. Hood (1962) showed that some courts in England are 'probation-minded' and others are not, while Tarling demonstrated that much variation in outcomes remained even after accounting for the different 'mix' of offences coming before the courts (Tarling *et al.* 1985). The latest statistics show that the immediate custody rate for indictable offences in the magistrates' courts varied from a low of 5 per cent in Wiltshire to 18 per cent in the West Midlands (Ministry of Justice 2010a: Table 5(ii)).

Variations are also to be found in the Crown Court. In 2009 the custody rate for indictable offences in the Crown Court varied from 44 per cent in Durham to 64 per cent in Kent (Ministry of Justice 2010a: Table 5(ii)). The average custodial sentence imposed also varied significantly—from a low of 20 months in Norfolk to a high of 31 months in Sussex (Ministry of Justice 2010a: Table 5.2). In their survey of sentencing in both levels of courts in the mid-1990s, Flood-Page and Mackie (1998) found that 'attempts to predict sentences on the basis of case factors were not particularly successful', indicating wide differences in the way that community sentences, in particular, were used. More recently, Mason *et al.* attempted to explain variation in sentencing practices by differences in the seriousness of cases and characteristics of offenders appearing for sentence but concluded that these factors were insufficient. They note that 'some kind of local "court culture" is at work which perpetuates differences in sentencing outcomes for comparable cases' (2007: 26).

guidelines, judges expressed themselves as having little choice in the sentences they passed: 'the least possible sentence I can pass…' 'I have no alternative but to …' (Ashworth *et al.* 1984: 53–4); 20 years later the sentencers interviewed by Hough *et al.* (2003: 38) expressed themselves similarly.

While discretion is important to enable sentencers to take account of the wide range of factors that might be relevant, it does leave decision-making open to factors irrelevant to sentencing. For example, Hood's (1992) study showed that at some courts black offenders were significantly more likely to receive custody than similarly situated white offenders. Hedderman and Gelsthorpe (1997) found variations in the sentencing of men and women that cannot be explained by case factors, and showed that sentencers' attitudes may explain why women are fined less frequently and given certain community sentences more frequently than men. Judges tend to argue strongly against any curtailment of 'their' discretion, but rarely acknowledge the risks of discrimination, individual idiosyncrasy, and other irrelevant influences which accompany discretion that is not well structured or well monitored (see Hudson 1998).

INFORMATION ABOUT THE OFFENCE AND THE OFFENDER

Courts depend for their information on what they hear or what they are told. Since over 90 per cent of cases in magistrates' courts and almost three-quarters of cases in the Crown Court (see below) involve guilty pleas, the main source of information about the offence is likely to be the statement of facts which the prosecutor reads out. It will usually have been compiled by the police, and the way in which it describes or omits certain factors may reflect a particular view of the offence, or perhaps a 'charge-bargain' struck with the police (see Sanders and Young, this volume).

In addition to the prosecution statement of facts, the court may acquire further perspectives on the crime from the defence plea in mitigation, and from a pre-sentence report (if available). Any account of 'the facts' is likely to be selective, determined to some extent by the compiler's preconceptions. It is likely that judges and magistrates will be influenced by the selections made by those who inform them, as well as by their own perspectives. The prosecution's account of the facts may be disputed by the defence. In a trial there is usually an opportunity to resolve these matters, but this is not always so: some facts relevant to sentencing are irrelevant to criminal guilt. The greatest difficulty arises where the defendant pleads guilty but only on a 'basis of plea' more favourable than the version presented by the prosecution. The courts have developed a procedure for resolving most such issues by means of a pre-sentence hearing, known as a '*Newton* hearing' at which evidence is presented and witnesses may be heard.[6] Since the outcome can have a considerable effect on the length of a custodial sentence, procedural fairness at this stage is important.

In England and Wales a court may obtain information about the offender from at least five sources: the police antecedents statement; the defence plea in mitigation; a pre-sentence report; a medical report; and the offender's own statements in court.

The contents of the *antecedents statement* are regulated by the Consolidated Practice Direction (Ministry of Justice 2010e: III.27). They are compiled by the police from the Police National Computer, and should always contain personal details and information about previous convictions and previous cautions. The purpose of a *defence plea in mitigation* is to show the offender and offence in the best light. The purpose of a *pre-sentence report* is to assist the sentencer by providing information regarding

---

[6] After the leading case of *Newton* (1982) 4 Cr App R (S) 388.

the offence, the offender, and related matters. The form of the report is regulated by National Standards for the Management of Offenders (2007): the report should focus on 'the risk of serious harm posed by the offender, the likelihood of reoffending, and factors that need to be addressed to support desistance from further offending'. A *psychiatric report* is relatively rare, but a court may decide to call for one, and is obliged to obtain one before passing a custodial sentence if the defendant is or appears to be mentally disordered (see further Peay, this volume). The impact of the offender's demeanour and conduct in court is difficult to gauge, but judges recognize that they take account of it and tend to feel that sentencing would be even more difficult if they did not see the offender in person (Cooke 1987: 58; Ashworth *et al.* 1984: ch. 3). This fifth source of influence serves to demonstrate that the impact of information received by a court may be mediated by the attitudes of the sentencer (Shapland 1987).

REPRESENTATION AT SENTENCING: ROLE OF ADVOCATES

In most common law jurisdictions prosecutors take an active role at the sentencing hearing, usually placing a specific sentence recommendation before the court. Sometimes the prosecutor and defence advocate submit a 'joint submission' at sentencing, usually following plea discussions. Traditionally, English prosecutors make no such sentence recommendation. This practice is changing; prosecutors are now encouraged to be more active at the sentencing stage. The Code for Crown Prosecutors (Crown Prosecution Service 2010: 11.1) states that the prosecutor should draw the court's attention to aggravating and mitigating factors disclosed by the prosecution case, to any statutory provisions or relevant guidelines, to any victim personal statement, and (where appropriate) to the 'impact of the offending on the community'. Some of what is said by an advocate making a defence plea in mitigation will bear directly on the sentence, and the advocate may propose a particular course to the sentencer. However, both prosecution and defence advocates have a duty to prevent the judge from passing an unlawful sentence, and to remind the judge of any relevant sentencing guidelines.

THE EVOLUTION OF A CUSTODIAL 'TARIFF'

Apart from the few mandatory and minimum sentences, discussed below, the general English approach is to set a fairly high maximum sentence for each offence. One consequence is that most day-to-day sentencing practices are little affected by legislative constraints. For Crown Court sentencing, some normal ranges or starting points have developed over the years, often termed 'the going rate' by judges and 'the tariff' by others. Historically the idea of 'normal' sentences can be traced back at least as far as the 'Memorandum of Normal Punishments' drawn up by Lord Alverstone, the Lord Chief Justice, in 1901 (Radzinowicz and Hood 1990: 755–8). Since 1907 the Court of Criminal Appeal, and since 1966 its successor the Court of Appeal (Criminal Division), has shaped aspects of the tariff. Increased reporting of Court of Appeal judgments on sentencing assisted the concretization of sentencing principles, and the publication of the first edition of Thomas's *Principles of Sentencing* (1970) was a landmark in the development of a common law of sentencing.

The evolution of the custodial tariff was largely driven by the judges, and in the 1980s the Court of Appeal began to issue a few 'guideline judgments' which formalized the 'going rate' for certain offences. Lord Lane, the then Lord Chief Justice, would occasionally take a particular case and, rather than giving a judgment on the facts alone, would construct a judgment dealing with sentencing for all the main varieties of that particular crime. The first of these was in the case of *Aramah*,[7] where guidance was given on sentencing levels for the whole range of drugs offences.[8]

SENTENCING GUIDELINES

Sentencing guidelines now exist in many jurisdictions. The oldest—and the most researched—are found in the United States, where guidelines originated in the 1970s. Many US states use two dimensional sentencing grids. One dimension is the seriousness of the crime and the other the offender's criminal history. For any given offence, the guidelines will specify a sentence length range for each of a number of categories of criminal history. A sentencing court in a state like Minnesota must impose a sentence within a relatively narrow range. If it wishes to impose a less or more severe sentence the court must find 'substantial and compelling' reasons why the guideline sentence is not appropriate (see Frase 2005 for discussion).

The US-style systems have been rejected by many other jurisdictions. The guideline system in England and Wales, and proposals made in New Zealand, for example, aim to structure sentencers' discretion yet allow more flexibility than the US grid-based schemes (see Young and Browning 2008 and, generally, von Hirsch *et al.* 2009: ch. 6). Other countries such as Sweden have developed what may be described as 'guidance by words'—instead of numerical guidelines the Swedish system articulates principles with which to guide sentencers (see Jareborg 1995). Finally, a number of other countries such as South Africa and Canada have resisted calls to develop sentencing guidelines, and judges in these jurisdictions continue to sentence as they have for decades, enjoying wide discretion and guided only by appellate review (see von Hirsch *et al.* 2009: ch. 6).

EVOLUTION OF STRUCTURED SENTENCING IN ENGLAND AND WALES

The process of formalizing the tariff through occasional guideline judgments (see above) may be seen as the first phase of the 'guideline movement' in England and Wales. The second phrase was initiated by the Crime and Disorder Act 1998, which created the Sentencing Advisory Panel. The Panel drafted possible guidelines for

---

[7] (1982) 4 Cr App R (S) 407.

[8] This judgment was subsequently revised (in *Aroyewumi* (1995) 16 Cr App R (S) 211) so that its guidance is calibrated according to weight and purity level rather than estimates of 'street value', and parallel guidance for newer drugs was added in other judgments (e.g. for 'Ecstasy' in *Warren and Beeley* [1996] 1 Cr App R (S) 233).

sentencing particular offences, conducted public and professional consultations, and then sent its 'advice' to the Court of Appeal. The court was then free to adopt the proposals, or to amend or reject them.[9]

A new phase in the development of guidelines was ushered in by the Criminal Justice Act 2003. The Panel still operated in a similar fashion, but its function was to formulate advice for a body called the Sentencing Guidelines Council. The Council received the Panel's advice (draft guideline), discussed it, issued its own draft guideline for consideration by the Minister for Justice and the Justice Committee of the House of Commons, received their comments, and then formulated what is termed a 'definitive guideline'. Courts were required to have regard to such guidelines and to give reasons if they wished to depart from an applicable guideline. During this period the guideline movement surged forwards, with the result that most cases in the lower courts were covered by the Magistrates' Court Sentencing Guidelines (2008), and in the Crown Court the bulk of cases now fall within guidelines.

In 2010, sentencing in this jurisdiction entered a new era (for a history of the guidelines to that point see Ashworth and Wasik 2010). The Coroners and Justice Act 2009 introduced a number of important changes to the sentencing environment. The reforms introduced by the Coroners Act may be traced to two significant developments. The first was a review of the use of imprisonment conducted by Lord Carter in response to the high and rising prison population in this jurisdiction. In his report Lord Carter proposed a Working Group to consider the utility of a sentencing commission for England and Wales (Carter 2007) and one was duly created by the government in the spring of 2008. The Sentencing Commission Working Group conducted a limited review of sentencing guidelines in other jurisdictions and issued a public consultation document which attracted considerable response from the judiciary and other stakeholders in the sentencing process. A consensus emerged from respondents that a grid-based guidelines system such as that found in Minnesota and other US jurisdictions was not an appropriate model for England and Wales. The Working Group recommended a revamp of the current arrangements rather than adoption of a completely new system of guidelines (Sentencing Commission Working Group 2008).

These developments resulted in the Coroners and Justice Act 2009. This legislation introduced a number of changes to the sentencing guidelines in England and Wales (see Roberts 2011a). First, it amended the duty of a court to comply with the guidelines. Under the previous regime the statute stated that courts 'must have regard' to any relevant guidelines. Section 125 of the new Act states that:

(1) Every court—
   (a) must, in sentencing an offender, follow any sentencing guidelines which are relevant to the offender's case, and
   (b) must, in exercising any other function relating to the sentencing of offenders, follow any sentencing guidelines which are relevant to the exercise of that function,

unless the court is satisfied that it would be contrary to the interests of justice to do so.

---

[9] Usually the Panel's proposals were accepted in most respects, and found their way into a guideline judgment delivered by the Court of Appeal (on, e.g., racially aggravated offences, child pornography, handling stolen goods, and burglary).

Second, the previous statutory bodies have been replaced by a single authority, the *Sentencing Council of England and Wales*. The new Council retains a judicial majority among its 14 members. Before being replaced by the Sentencing Council in 2010, the Sentencing Guidelines Council had issued definitive guidelines for a range of offences. These guidelines remain in force until such time as the Sentencing Council revises and re-issues them—a task which will take several years to complete. In the meantime, the new Council has started issuing its own guidelines. These assume a rather different structure than the SGC Guidelines. The first new guideline—which came into effect in June 2011—relates to the assault offences (see sentencingcouncil.org.uk).

EXAMPLE OF ENGLISH GUIDELINES

The new format of guideline requires a sentencing court to follow a clear methodology in determining sentence (see Roberts and Rafferty 2011 for further discussion). Let us consider a specific offence to illustrate how the guidelines function. The definitive guideline for causing grievous bodily harm (Offences Against the Person Act 1861, section 18) identifies three overlapping ranges of sentence length, each range relating to a separate category of seriousness. The ranges are: 9–16 years' custody for the most serious assaults; 5–9 years' custody for cases of intermediate seriousness, and a 3–5 years' custody the least serious forms of causing grievous bodily harm.

As a court moves towards determining the sentence to be imposed it will follow the guideline which identifies a series of nine steps. The first task is to determine which of the three levels of seriousness is appropriate for the case appearing for sentencing. The court takes into account the principal elements of the case to be sentenced—for example the degree of premeditation and whether a vulnerable victim was deliberately targeted—to determine which of the three ranges is most appropriate. Thus the most serious cases which involve a high level of harm and a high level of culpability on the part of the offender will fall into the category with the longest sentence length range (9–16 years). Once a court has determined which category range is appropriate it will use the starting point sentence within the range as a point of departure. For the most serious category the starting point—from which a court will calculate a provisional sentence—is 12 years' custody.

The second step is to 'fine tune' the sentence within the chosen range by considering other, less important factors which relate to the seriousness of the crime as well as personal mitigation. These factors include circumstances such as an abuse of power by the offender, any attempt to conceal evidence, or the fact that the crime was committed while the offender was on licence. Personal mitigation includes factors such as an absence of prior convictions, remorse, and any attempts by the offender to address addictions or other problems associated with offending. Having completed this, the court then follows a series of seven other steps to determine the final sentence. For example, step 4 requires a court to take into account whether (and when) the offender entered a guilty plea (see below for further discussion). Figure 29.3 provides a summary of the steps contained in the sentencing guideline for the offence of causing grievous bodily harm with intent.

884   ANDREW ASHWORTH AND JULIAN ROBERTS

Figure 29.3 Summary of Sentencing Guideline Structure in England and Wales[1]

Offence: Causing Grievous Bodily Harm with intent[2]

Total Offence Range: 3–16 years' custody

Step 1: Use the factors provided in the guideline which comprise the principal elements of the offence[3] to determine the offence category which is appropriate:

Category 1: Greater harm[4] *and* high culpability

Category 2: Greater harm and lower culpability *or* lesser harm *and* higher culpability

Category 3: Lesser harm *and* lower culpability

Step 2: Use the *starting point* from the appropriate *offence category* to generate a provisional sentence within the *category range*. The *starting point* applies to all offenders irrespective of plea and previous convictions. The guideline contains a list of additional aggravating and mitigating factors. These factors affect crime seriousness[5] or relate to personal mitigation[6] and should result in upward or downward adjustment from the *starting point*.

Offence category	Starting point	Category sentence range
1	12 years	9–16 years
2	6	5–9
3	4	3–5

Step 3: Consider if any reduction in the provisional sentence should be made to reflect assistance offered or provided to the prosecution.

Step 4: Consider the level of reduction appropriate to reflect a guilty plea.[7]

Step 5: Consider whether the offender meets dangerousness criteria necessary for imposition of an indeterminate or extended sentence.[8]

Step 6: If sentencing for more than one offence apply the totality principle to ensure that the total sentence is just and proportionate to the total offending behaviour.

Step 7: Consider whether to make a compensation order and/or other orders.

Step 8: Give reasons for and explain the effect of the sentence on the offender.

Step 9: Consider whether to give credit for time on remand or bail.

---

[1] Note: complete guideline available at: www.sentencingcouncil.gov.uk

[2] Section 18 Offences against the Person Act 1861; maximum penalty: life imprisonment.

[3] E.g., victim was particularly vulnerable; offender played a leading role in a gang; premeditation.

[4] Greater harm means that serious injury must normally be present.

[5] E.g., victim forced to leave her home; offence committed while offender on bail.

[6] E.g., remorse; no previous convictions; offender is sole provider for dependent relatives.

[7] To a maximum of one third if plea entered at first possible opportunity.

[8] E.g., a life sentence; imprisonment for public protection (IPP) or an extended sentence.

The English sentencing guidelines allow courts considerable variation when determining sentence and are more flexible than the two-dimensional sentencing grids found in states such as Minnesota. What remains unclear for the present at least is the extent to which the guidelines have promoted consistency in sentencing—one of the primary objectives of any sentencing guidelines system. Although the US sentencing commissions routinely collect data showing the proportion of sentences imposed outside the guidelines, this has not been the case in England. However, one of the statutory duties of the Sentencing Council is to monitor the impact of its guidelines, so more comprehensive information will become available as the Council fulfils this duty (see Sentencing Council 2011).

LEGISLATIVE REQUIREMENTS FOR CUSTODIAL SENTENCES

Legislatures generally set the maximum sentence for each offence, but in some systems they go further. In England and Wales three further forms of legislative intervention may be identified.

MANDATORY SENTENCES

There has long been a minimum sentence of disqualification from driving for 12 months on conviction for drunk driving. Mandatory minimum prison sentences were introduced in 1997 following a fierce battle between the Home Secretary and the senior judiciary (see Dunbar and Langdon 1998: ch. 10; Ashworth 2001).

One provision requires a court to impose a minimum sentence of seven years for the third Class A drug-trafficking offence, unless it would be 'unjust to do so in all the circumstances'. In fact most such offenders would receive at least seven years anyway, and therefore this minimum sentence has impinged little on sentencing practice. A second provision requires a court to impose a minimum sentence of three years for the third domestic burglary conviction, so long as the offender is aged at least 18 and each burglary was committed after the previous conviction for burglary. A court is not bound to impose the minimum if it would be 'unjust to do so in all the circumstances'. It is not clear to which extent this minimum sentence has deflected courts from their normal approach.

The Criminal Justice Act 2003 introduced a further mandatory minimum sentence: for possession of prohibited firearms a court is required to impose at least five years' imprisonment (three years' if the offender is under 18). This is a much stronger provision than the others just discussed, since it applies to a first offence and courts may impose a lesser sentence only in 'exceptional circumstances.'

SENTENCING FOR MURDER

The 2003 Act also altered the sentencing approach for murder. Since 1965 a court sentencing an offender for murder has been bound to impose life imprisonment. The trial judge would propose a minimum term, reviewed by the Lord Chief Justice, but the final decision would be that of the Home Secretary. On expiry of the minimum term, the murderer would remain in prison until deemed not to present a risk to the public, and would then be released on licence (and subject to recall) for the rest of his life. Following judgments of the European Court of Human Rights and the House of Lords in 2002 that fixing the minimum term for a life sentence is a sentencing decision and must be carried out by a court, the Home Secretary relinquished his jurisdiction but Parliament introduced statutory restrictions on the court's powers. Section 269 of the Criminal Justice Act 2003 requires a court, when setting the minimum term to be served by a person convicted of murder, to have regard to the principles set out in Schedule 21 to the Act. The Schedule indicates three starting points:

- a whole life minimum term for exceptionally serious cases, such as premeditated killings of two people, sexual or sadistic child murders, or political murders;
- 30 years for the most serious cases such as murders of police or prison officers, murders involving firearms, sexual or sadistic killings, or murders aggravated by racial or sexual orientation; and
- 15 years for other murders not falling within either of the higher categories.

In 2009 the Minister of Justice added a further starting point, one of 25 years for murder with a knife carried to the scene. However, the language in Schedule 21 is not constraining, and judges may take account of aggravating and mitigating factors when calculating the minimum term.[10] It remains controversial whether it is right to have a mandatory sentence for murder,[11] in view of the considerable variations in the gravity of the offence; and, if so, whether the minimum terms are too high. The current Coalition Government has described Schedule 21 as 'ill thought-out and overly prescriptive' (Ministry of Justice 2010c: para. 170), and so some loosening of Schedule 21 in favour of guidelines seems likely.

STATUTORY RESTRICTIONS ON CUSTODIAL SENTENCES

Most jurisdictions attempt to regulate the use of custody by the courts, often by means of statutory restrictions on the imposition of custody. In states with sentencing guidelines the location of an offence within the sentencing grid determines whether custody is an option for the court. In jurisdictions without guidelines there is often a statutory restriction, or direction to courts to use custody only as a last resort, or only when no other sanction is sufficient to achieve the objectives of sentencing.

The Criminal Justice Act 2003 established two significant principles: by section 152(2) a custodial sentence should not be imposed unless the offence is too serious for a community sentence or fine, and by section 153(2) any custodial sentence must be 'for the shortest term . . . commensurate with the seriousness of the offence'.

---

[10] *Sullivan* [2005] 1 Cr App R (S) 308.

[11] Advocates of the mandatory life sentence for murder frequently cite public opinion as a justification for this sanction. However, in the only empirical test of public attitudes, researchers found that the public were not strongly attached to the mandatory life sentence. When asked to sentence cases of murder members of the public often favoured definite terms of imprisonment (see Mitchell and Roberts 2011).

These judgments depend on proportionality, as mentioned earlier. The Sentencing Guidelines Council established guidelines on the application of the custody threshold, stating that its clear intention 'is to reserve prison as a punishment for the most serious offences' and that 'passing the custody threshold does not mean that a custodial sentence should be deemed inevitable', since there may be personal mitigation or 'a suitable intervention in the community which provides sufficient restriction (by way of punishment) while addressing the rehabilitation of the offender to prevent future crime' (SGC, *Overarching Principles—Seriousness* 2004).

AGGRAVATION AND MITIGATION AT SENTENCING

When courts are determining the seriousness of an offence—the harm caused or threatened and the offender's culpability—they should have regard to its aggravating and mitigating features. Among the mitigating factors listed by the SGC (*Overarching Principles - Seriousness*) are various forms of reduced culpability (e.g. mental disorder, financial pressures) and a good previous record. Courts also recognize mitigating factors that have no bearing on the offence or the offender's culpability—the impact of the sentence on others, an act of heroism by the offender, the payment of compensation to the victim, or assisting the state in prosecuting other offenders (Ashworth 2010: ch. 5.4). The interplay of these factors is critical where a case is 'on the cusp' of custody: in such cases Hough *et al.* (2003: 36–8) found that in custody cases sentencers placed more emphasis on the nature of the offence or the criminal record, whereas in the non-custodial cases the emphasis was on factors personal to the offender. Subsequent research by Jacobson and Hough (2007) involving court observations and interviews with sentencers has demonstrated the importance of personal mitigation; in approximately a third of cases personal mitigation was the major factor reducing the sentence from immediate custody to a community penalty (see Roberts 2011b for further discussion of sentencing factors).

PREVIOUS CONVICTIONS

How significant should a bad criminal record be in sentencing? The common law principle was the 'progressive loss of mitigation': a first offender received substantial mitigation, which would be lost after the second or third conviction, but it would not be right to 'sentence on the record' and to impose a penalty disproportionate to the seriousness of the offence committed (Ashworth 2010: ch. 6). This principle succumbed to a silent eclipse during the 1990s, and section 143(2) of the Criminal Justice Act 2003 now proclaims an entirely different approach—that a court must treat each previous conviction as an aggravating factor if its relevance to the current offence, and the time that has elapsed since that conviction, make it reasonable to do so. This section suggests a recidivist premium and is reminiscent of the US guidelines where sentence lengths are progressively increased to reflect higher numbers of prior convictions (see Roberts 2008 and von Hirsch *et al.* 2009: 148–62).

888   ANDREW ASHWORTH AND JULIAN ROBERTS

GUILTY PLEA DISCOUNT

Perhaps the most significant mitigating factor is the guilty plea. Well established at common law, the 'discount' is set out in section 144 of the Criminal Justice Act 2003. The guilty plea rate has steadily increased from 63 per cent in 2005 to 71 per cent in 2009 (Ministry of Justice 2010d: 98). The Sentencing Guidelines Council issued a definitive guideline on *Reduction of Sentence for a Guilty Plea* (2007), which recognizes various pragmatic reasons for the discount—saving cost, avoiding trials, reducing anxiety among victims and witnesses. Despite the existence of a definitive guideline regarding the guilty plea discount, the Coroners and Justice Act 2009 explicitly directed the Sentencing Council to produce a guideline on this matter, and one is scheduled to be issued at some future date.

The current guideline establishes a sliding scale, with a maximum reduction of one-third for a guilty plea indicated at the earliest opportunity, reducing to one-tenth if the guilty plea is tendered 'at the door of the court'. The guideline also states that 'the reduction principle may properly form the basis for imposing...an alternative to an immediate custodial sentence'. Thus the guilty plea discount may well make the difference between prison or not, and the statistics bear this out —for example, the custody rate was significantly higher for offenders who pleaded not guilty (69 per cent vs. 55 per cent; Ministry of Justice 2010a: Table 2p). In addition, the average sentence length for offenders convicted on a not guilty plea in 2009 was more than double the length for those who pleaded guilty (47 months vs 22 months; Ministry of Justice 2010a: Table 2p).

Such substantial discounts create considerable pressure on defendants to forgo the right to trial which goes with the presumption of innocence. Where defendants are advised that the discount may make the difference between a custodial and a non-custodial sentence, the risk of innocent people pleading guilty is particularly high.[12] Finally, a very substantial discount for a guilty plea may also have adverse effects on principled sentencing. If the primary determinants of sentence are crime seriousness and culpability, allowing a large discount for a guilty plea will undermine these considerations. After all, even though a guilty plea saves the state's resources and spares victims and witnesses from having to testify, the plea is unrelated to the seriousness of the offence or the offender's level of culpability.

'DANGEROUSNESS' SENTENCES

Despite the poor prospects of accurate prediction, governments in many countries regard it as politically necessary to have some kind of 'dangerousness' statute,

---

[12] A further development heightens this risk. The Court of Appeal has altered its position on judges giving indications of sentence, and it is now possible for a defendant who has pleaded not guilty to ask the judge what would be the maximum sentence imposed if the defendant were to change the plea to guilty at this stage (*Goodyear* [2005] Crim LR 659). If the judge indicates a community sentence, and counsel suggests that it would be custody if the defendant persisted in pleading not guilty and were convicted, then the pressure on the defendant would be enormous. (A similar procedure of advance indication of sentence is available in magistrates' courts.)

proclaiming greater public protection from sexual and violent predators. In England and Wales the Criminal Justice Act 2003 adopted this approach and introduced a three-pronged strategy against 'dangerous' offenders. Thus, where the offence had a maximum of life imprisonment, the court was required to impose life imprisonment if the court found that the current offence was serious enough to justify a life sentence, and if the offender was 'dangerous'. If the offence was 'serious' but either did not carry life imprisonment or was not sufficiently serious, the court was required to impose a sentence of imprisonment for public protection. The Imprisonment for Public Protection (IPP) sentence is hardly less constraining than life imprisonment, in the sense that the court sets a minimum term, after which release is only when the Parole Board thinks the risk to the public no longer justifies imprisonment, and release is on licence indefinitely. Then there is the third form of sentence, the extended sentence, composed of the proportionate sentence for the offence, plus an extension period (on licence with conditions) for a violent offence or a sexual offence.

The condition that must be fulfilled before a court imposes any of these sentences is a finding that 'there is a significant risk to members of the public of serious harm occasioned by the commission by him of further specified offences'. The Court of Appeal delivered a 'guidance' judgment on the 'dangerousness' provisions which identified three separate issues.[13] First, the 2003 Act leaves the key term 'significant risk' undefined: the choice of 'significant' rather than 'substantial' may suggest a widening of the net, but the Court of Appeal requires a risk that is 'of considerable amount or importance'. Secondly, there must be a significant risk of this offender committing further 'specified' offences. And thirdly, those offences must be such as to put members of the public at significant risk of serious harm. 'Serious harm' means 'death or serious personal injury, whether physical or psychological'. However, a court was required to have regard to section 229, which created the presumption of significant risk of serious harm where an offender over 18 has been convicted of another such offence; a court should assume this unless, having considered the nature of the offences and any reports about the offender, it considers that it would be unreasonable to regard the risk as significant.

The 'dangerousness' provisions in the 2003 Act were a penological disaster. They were mandatory, and they spread the net so widely as to perpetrate real injustice by subjecting relatively low-level offenders to indefinite imprisonment. Moreover, the planning was so poor that the prisons were unable to provide sufficient courses for IPP prisoners to complete in order to secure their release (see, e.g., House of Commons 2008: paras 39–85). The Government recognized some of these criticisms, and in 2008 the mandatory element of the 'dangerousness' sentences described above was removed, and the threshold for imposing such a sentence was increased to crimes 'worth' four years' imprisonment. However, a recent government document refers openly to 'the limitations in our ability to predict future serious offending [that] call into question the whole basis on which many offenders are sentenced to IPP' (Ministry of Justice 2010c: para. 186). The current proposal is to abolish IPP sentences in favour of automatic life

---

[13] *Lang* [2006] Crim LR 174.

890 ANDREW ASHWORTH AND JULIAN ROBERTS

imprisonment for the second serious offence, provided that the offences reach a high threshold of seriousness. There remains an urgent need to reconsider the cases of the many people subjected to IPP sentences between 2003 and 2008 and still imprisoned.

CUSTODIAL SENTENCES AND EXECUTIVE RELEASE

The practical meaning of a prison sentence varies from country to country depending upon the nature of early release provisions. The current situation in England and Wales is that all prisoners serving determinate sentences are released after serving one-half, and are then on licence under supervision (with requirements) until the end of their sentence. Release at an earlier point is possible through the operation of Home Detention Curfew (see Padfield, Morgan, and Maguire, this volume). Decisions on release from sentences of imprisonment for life or imprisonment for public protection, imposed under the 'dangerousness' provisions of the 2003 Act, continue to be made by the Parole Board. Research has shown the risk assessments made by the Parole Board to be unduly conservative in many cases (Hood and Shute 2000).

Release policies are one of the factors that impact on the size of the prison popula-tion. Between 1995 and 2009 the English prison population grew by 32,500 inmates or 66 per cent (Ministry of Justice 2010a: 2; see further Liebling and Crewe, this volume). The judiciary and the magistracy tend to explain this as a response to what they regard as the climate of opinion in society, fuelled largely by political and media rhetoric. Despite strong evidence of widespread public misunderstanding about sentencing lev-els (see Roberts and Hough 2005: 69–71), politicians and the media continue to press for severity. An escalating response to previous convictions and to breaches of court orders has also played a major part in the trend to severity.

Some mandatory or minimum sentences exist, opposed by the judges who point to the need for discretion in sentencing. However, to follow up the earlier discus-sion, discretion has its disadvantages as well as its advantages. It is a good thing to avoid mechanical sentencing and rigid controls which prevent courts from taking account of particular factors in individual cases. But it is undesirable to allow different approaches that may result in discrimination on grounds of race (Hood 1992) or gen-der (Hedderman and Gelsthorpe 1997), or allow individual judges to pursue their own policies, or local courts to follow local traditions. There is an urgent need for research to assess the effectiveness of guidelines in terms of shaping the decisions of the courts.

Vital to the success of the 2003 Act in moderating levels of custodial sentenc-ing are decisions around the custody threshold. Where sentences have tended to be ratcheted up, they need to be brought down again. The previous Government consid-ered bringing forward legislation on unit fines, as part of a strategy to revive the use of financial penalties, but nothing happened. Both the 2003 Act and the Council's guideline makes it clear that substantial fines may be used for fairly serious offences, as an alternative to a community sentence, but the real issues are at the other end of the scale. Courts, politicians, and newspaper editors must be persuaded that what appears to them to be a low or 'derisory' fine may make considerable demands on the financial resources of an offender on state benefits. Unless this bridge is crossed, there is little prospect of reducing the number of less serious offenders receiving community sentences.

Where cases are serious enough to justify the imposition of a community sentence, courts must follow the guidelines in distinguishing between the three levels of community sentence (low, medium, and high) and in ensuring that the resulting order is proportionate to the seriousness of the offence. In effect, courts must be prepared to give another community sentence after one has failed: the penal ladder should not be shortened because there is only one form of community sentence, but rather courts must try different programmes and requirements if the offence(s) fall(s) short of justifying imprisonment.

Likewise, the malfunctioning of the suspended sentence must be avoided: exactly how the courts locate it in their sentencing practice will determine whether it is applied to offenders who would otherwise have received an immediate prison sentence (as it should be) or to offenders who might hitherto have been given a community sentence. In the training of magistrates and of judges, this will be a key issue. There is much that is positive in community sentences, with evidence of a determination to reduce re-offending through some imaginative programmes, but the underlying framework remains strongly punitive and the various malfunctions described above might operate so as to increase rather than to decrease the punitiveness of the whole system.

Finally, the role of previous convictions and sentencing for breach must be highlighted. The 2003 Act's provision on previous convictions appears to endorse the 'cumulative' sentencing of repeat offenders,[14] but also there is a growing number of preventive orders imposed on offenders, which may then lead to breach. The rise of the preventive order is evident from provisions in the Sexual Offences Act 2003 for sexual offences prevention orders and risk of sexual harm orders, which join other preventive orders such as travel restriction orders, football spectator banning orders, and exclusion from licensed premises orders. Breach of any such order is an offence carrying imprisonment.

CONCLUSIONS

Over the past decade, sentencing has evolved more rapidly in England and Wales than any other common law jurisdiction. In addition to the proliferation of definitive guidelines, Parliament has introduced a series of legislative amendments affecting sentencing and early release from prison. In 2010 the current Coalition Government issued a Green Paper entitled *Breaking the Cycle: Effective Punishment, Rehabilitation and Sentencing of Offenders*. Consistent with the general intent of the Government to reduce the costs of public services, the Green Paper proposed to increase the extent to which offenders make financial reparation to 'victims and the taxpayer' (Ministry

---

[14] Section 142 of the Act states that courts should consider each prior conviction to aggravate the seriousness of the offence (and thus the severity of the sentence) in the event that it is reasonable to do so.

892   ANDREW ASHWORTH AND JULIAN ROBERTS

of Justice 2010c: 20). At the time of writing (July 2011), the Government has just published its response to the Green Paper. In that response the Government has expressed an intention to work with the Sentencing Council to promote the greater use of financial penalties; to review current arrangements regarding the sentencing for serious sexual and violent offenders; and to simplify a number of elements of sentencing law. It is anticipated that Parliament will put forward a reform Bill late in 2011 (Ministry of Justice 2011).

Sentencing has changed significantly in England and Wales over the last decade. Of all developments, the most promising would appear to be the evolution of sentencing guidelines. The Sentencing Council of England and Wales has, as noted, issued a new format of sentencing guidelines and will continue to issue additional guidelines over the next few years. Sentencers in this jurisdiction now have more structure and guidance than at any previous time, and the benefits in terms of fairer and more principled sentencing cannot be under-estimated.

■ SELECTED FURTHER READING

Readings on rationales for sentencing and related issues may be found in: A. von Hirsch, A. Ashworth, and J. V. Roberts (eds) (2009), *Principled Sentencing: Readings in Theory and Policy*, 3rd edn, Oxford: Hart Publishing; M. Tonry (ed.) (2011), *Why Punish, How Much? A Reader on Punishment*, Oxford: Oxford University Press; R. A. Duff and D. Garland (eds) (1994), *A Reader on Punishment*, Oxford: Oxford University Press. See also A. Ashworth and M. Wasik (eds) (1988), *Fundamentals of Sentencing Theory*, Oxford: Oxford University Press. Monographs on sentencing theory include: N. Lacey (1988), *State Punishment*, London: Routledge; R. Duff (2000), *Punishment, Communication and Community*, New York: Oxford University Press; and A. von Hirsch and A. Ashworth (2005), *Proportionate Sentencing*, Oxford: Oxford University Press.

Sentencing texts include: A. Ashworth (2010), *Sentencing and Criminal Justice*, 5th edn, Cambridge: Cambridge University Press; and S. Easton and C. Piper (2008), *Sentencing and Punishment: The Quest for Justice*, 2nd edn, Oxford: Oxford University Press. The website of the Sentencing Council of England and Wales also provides a wealth of material about sentencing and sentencing guidelines in this country: www.sentencingcouncil.co.uk.

For international sentencing see the special issue of the *Federal Sentencing Reporter* published in April 2010; A. Freiberg and K. Gelb (eds) (2008), *Penal Populism, Sentencing Councils and Sentencing Policy*, Cullompton: Willan; C. Tata and N. Hutton (eds) (2002), *Sentencing and Society: International Perspectives*, Aldershot: Ashgate Publishing; M. Tonry and R. Frase (eds) (2001), *Sentencing and Sanctions in Western Countries*, New York: Oxford University Press.

■ REFERENCES

ASHCROFT, LORD (2011), *Crime, Punishment and the People*, London: House of Lords.

ASHWORTH, A. (2001), 'The Decline of English Sentencing', in M. Tonry and R. Frase (eds), *Sentencing and Sanctions in Western Countries*, New York: Oxford University Press.

—— (2010), *Sentencing and Criminal Justice*, 5th edn, Cambridge: Cambridge University Press.

—— *et al.* (1984), *Sentencing in the Crown Court*, Oxford: Centre for Criminology, University of Oxford.

—— and REDMAYNE, M. (2010), *The Criminal Process*, 4th edn, Oxford: Oxford University Press.

——and WASIK, M. (2010), 'Ten years of the Sentencing Advisory Panel', in: Sentencing Guidelines Council and Sentencing Advisory Panel. *Annual Report.* Available at: www.sentencing.council.org.

AUSTIN, W. and WILLIAMS, T. (1977), 'A Survey of Responses to Simulated Legal Cases: Research Note on Sentencing Disparity', *Journal of Criminal Law and Criminology*, 68: 305–10.

BENTHAM, J. (1789), *Principles of Morals and Legislation*, London: W. Pickering.

BOTTOMS, A. (2004), 'Empirical Research relevant to Sentencing Frameworks', in A. Bottoms, S. Rex, and G. Robinson (eds), *Alternatives to Prison: Options for an Insecure Society*, Cullompton, Devon: Willan.

——, GELSTHORPE, L. and REX, S. (eds) (2001), *Community Penalties: change and challenges*, Cullompton, Devon: Willan.

——and VON HIRSCH, A. (2011), 'The Crime Preventive Impact of Penal Sanctions', in P. Cane and H. Kritzer (eds), *The Oxford Handbook of Empirical Legal Research*, Oxford: Oxford University Press.

BRAITHWAITE, J. and PETTIT, P. (1990), *Not Just Deserts*, Oxford: Oxford University Press.

CARTER, LORD (2007), *Securing the Future*, London: Ministry of Justice.

CARTER REVIEW (2003), *Managing Offenders, Reducing Crime*, London: The Strategy Unit.

CHALMERS, J., DUFF, P., and LEVERICK, F. (2007), 'Victim Impact Statements: Can work, Do work (for those who bother to make them)', *Criminal Law Review*, (May) 360–79.

COOKE, R. (1987), 'The Practical Problems of the Sentencer', in D. Pennington and S. Lloyd-Bostock (eds), *The Psychology of Sentencing*, Oxford: Centre for Socio-Legal Studies, University of Oxford.

CROWN PROSECUTION SERVICE (2010), *Code for Crown Prosecutors*, 2010. Available at: www.cps.gov. uk/.

DIGNAN, J. (2005), *Understanding Victims and Restorative Justice*, Maidenhead: Open University Press.

DOOB, A. and WEBSTER, C. (2003), 'Sentence Severity and Crime: Accepting the Null Hypothesis', *Crime and Justice: a Review of Research*, 30: 143.

DUFF, R. A. (2000), *Punishment, Communication and Community*, New York: Oxford University Press.

——and GARLAND, D. (eds) (1994), *A Reader on Punishment*, Oxford: Oxford University Press.

DUNBAR, T. and LANGDON, A. (1998), *Tough Justice: Sentencing and Penal Policies in the 1990s*, London: Blackstone Press.

EDWARDS, I. (2004), 'An Ambiguous Participant: The Crime Victim and Criminal Justice Decision-Making', *British Journal of Criminology*, 44: 967–82.

EREZ, E. (1999), 'Who's Afraid of the Big, Bad Victim', *Criminal Law Review*, 545–56.

FLOOD-PAGE, C. and MACKIE, A. (1998), *Sentencing Practice: an examination of decisions in magistrates' courts and the Crown Court in the mid-1990s*, Home Office Research Study No. 180, London: Home Office.

FRASE, R. (2005), 'Sentencing Guidelines in Minnesota, 1978–2003', in M. Tonry (ed.), *Crime and Justice*, Chicago: University of Chicago Press.

GARLAND, D. (1990), *Punishment and Modern Society*, Oxford: Oxford University Press.

GAUDET, F., HARRIS, G., and ST. JOHN, C. (1932), 'Individual Differences in the Sentencing Tendencies of Judges', *International Journal of Criminal Law, Criminology and Political Science*, 23: 811–18.

HARPER, G. and CHITTY, C. (eds) (2005), *The Impact of Corrections on Re-offending: a review of 'what works'*, Home Office Research Study 291, London: Home Office.

HART, H. L. A. (1968), *Punishment and Responsibility*, Oxford: Oxford University Press.

HAWKINS, K. (ed.) (1992), *Discretion*, Oxford: Oxford University Press.

——(2003), *Law as Last Resort*, Oxford: Oxford University Press.

HEDDERMAN, C. and GELSTHORPE, L. (1997), *Understanding the Sentencing of Women*, Home Office Research Study No. 170, London: Home Office.

HOME OFFICE 2000), *National Standards for the Supervision of Offenders in the Community*, 3rd edn, London: Home Office.

——(2001), *Making Punishments Work*, London: Home Office.

HOOD, R. (1962), *Sentencing in Magistrates' Courts*, London: Tavistock.

——(1992), *Race and Sentencing*, Oxford: Oxford University Press.

——and SHUTE, S. (2000), *The Parole System at Work*, Home Office Research Study No. 202, London: Home Office.

HOUGH, M., JACOBSON, J., and MILLIE, A. (2003), *The Decision to Imprison*, London: Prison Reform Trust.

HUDSON, B. (1993), *Penal Policy and Social Justice*, London: Macmillan.

——(1998), 'Doing Justice to Difference', in A. Ashworth and M. Wasik (eds), *Fundamentals of Sentencing Theory*, Oxford: Oxford University Press.

JACOBSON, J. and HOUGH, M. (2007), *Mitigation: The role of personal factors in sentencing*, London: Prison Reform Trust.

LACEY, N. (1988), *State Punishment*, London: Routledge.

LLOYD, C., MAIR, G., and HOUGH, M. (1994), *Explaining Reconviction Rates: a critical analysis*, Home Office Research Study No. 135, London: HMSO.

MCGUIRE, J. (ed.) (2002), *Offender Rehabilitation and Treatment: Effective Programmes and Policies to Reduce Re-Offending*, New York: John Wiley.

MASON, T. et al. (2007), *Local Variation in Sentencing in England and Wales*, London: Ministry of Justice.

MINISTRY OF JUSTICE (2009), *Story of the prison population 1995–2009. England and Wales.* Available at: www.justice.gov.uk.

894 ANDREW ASHWORTH AND JULIAN ROBERTS

—— (2010a), *Sentencing Statistics: England and Wales 2009*. Available at: www.justice.gov.uk.

—— (2010b), *Criminal Statistics: England and Wales 2009*. Available at: www.justice.gov.uk.

—— (2010c), *Breaking the Cycle: Effective Punishment, Rehabilitation and Sentencing of Offenders*. Available at: www.justice.gov.uk.

—— (2010d), *Judicial and Court Statistics 2009* Available at: www.justice.gov.uk.

—— (2011), *Breaking the Cycle: Government Response*. Available at: www.justice.gov.uk.

MINNESOTA SENTENCING GUIDELINES COMMISSION (2010), *Sentencing Guidelines and Commentary*. Available at: www.msgc.state.mn.us/.

MITCHELL, B. and ROBERTS, J. V. (2011), 'Public Attitudes Towards the Mandatory Life Sentence for Murder: Putting Received Wisdom to the Empirical Test', *Criminal Law Review*, 6: 456–65.

MONAHAN, J. (2004), 'The Future of Violence Risk Management', in M. Tonry (ed.), *The Future of Imprisonment*, New York: Oxford University Press.

PALYS, T. and DIVORSKI, S. (1987), 'Explaining Sentence Disparity', *Canadian Journal of Criminology*, 28: 347–62.

POSNER, R. (1985), 'An Economic Theory of the Criminal Law', *Columbia Law Review*, 85: 1193–231.

RADZINOWICZ, L. and HOOD, R. (1990), *The Emergence of Penal Policy in Victorian and Edwardian England*, Oxford: Oxford University Press.

ROBERTS, J. V. (2008), *Punishing Persistent Offenders*, Oxford: Oxford University Press.

—— (2009), 'Listening to the Crime Victim: Evaluating Victim Input at Sentencing and Parole', in M. Tonry (ed.), *Crime and Justice*, Vol. 38, Chicago: University of Chicago Press.

—— (2011a), 'Sentencing Guidelines and Judicial Discretion: Evolution of the Duty of Courts to Comply in England and Wales', *British Journal of Criminology*, 51: 997—1013.

—— (ed.) (2011b), *Aggravation and Mitigation at Sentencing*, Cambridge: Cambridge University Press.

—— and HOUGH, M. (2005), *Public Attitudes to Criminal Justice*, Maidenhead: Open University Press.

—— and RAFFERTY, A. (2011), 'Structured Sentencing in England and Wales: Exploring the new Guideline Format', *Criminal Law Review*, in press.

SANDERS, A., HOYLE, C., MORGAN, R., and CAPE, E. (2001), 'Victim Impact Statements: Don't Work, Can't Work', *Criminal Law Review*, 447–58.

SENTENCING COMMISSION WORKING GROUP (2008), *Sentencing Guidelines in England and Wales: An Evolutionary Approach*, London: SCWG.

SENTENCING COUNCIL (2011), Crown Court Sentencing Survey: Experimental Statistics, London: Sentencing Council.

SHAPLAND, J. (1987), 'Who Controls Sentencing? Influences on the Sentencer', in D. Pennington and S. Lloyd-Bostock (eds), *The Psychology of Sentencing*, Oxford: Centre for Socio-Legal Studies, University of Oxford.

SHUTE, S. (1999), 'Who Passes Unduly Lenient Sentences?', *Criminal Law Review*: 603

TARLING, R., MOXON, D., and JONES, P. (1985), 'Sentencing of Adults and Juveniles in Magistrates' Courts', in D. Moxon (ed.), *Managing Criminal Justice*, London: HMSO.

THOMAS, D. (1970), *Principles of Sentencing*, London: Heinemann.

VON HIRSCH, A. (1976), *Doing Justice*, New York: Hill and Wang.

—— and ASHWORTH, A. (2005), *Proportionate Sentencing*, Oxford: Oxford University Press.

——, ASHWORTH, A., and ROBERTS, J. V. (eds) (2009), *Principled Sentencing: Readings in Theory and Policy*, 3rd edn, Oxford: Hart.

——, BOTTOMS, A., BURNEY, E., and WIKSTRÖM, P-O. (1999), *Criminal Deterrence: an Analysis of Recent Research*, Oxford: Hart.

WALKER, N. (1991), *Why Punish?*, Oxford: Oxford University Press.

WASIK, M. (1985), 'The Grant of an Absolute Discharge', *Oxford Journal of Legal Studies*, 5: 211.

YOUNG, W. and BROWNING, C. (2008), 'New Zealand's Sentencing Council', *Criminal Law Review*, April, 287–98.

[2]

Crime: in Proportion and in Perspective

JOHN GARDNER*

1. THE DISPLACEMENT FUNCTION

What is the criminal law for? Most explanations nowadays focus exclusively on the activities of criminal offenders. The criminal law exists to deter or incapacitate potential criminal offenders, say, or to give actual criminal offenders their just deserts. In all this we seem to have lost sight of the origins of the criminal law as a response to the activities of *victims*, together with their families, associates and supporters. The blood feud, the vendetta, the duel, the revenge, the lynching: for the elimination of these modes of retaliation, more than anything else, the criminal law as we know it today came into existence.[1] It is important to bring this point back into focus, not least because one common assumption of contemporary writing about punishment, including criminal punishment, is that its justifiability is closely connected with the justifiability of our retaliating (tit-for-tat, or otherwise) against those who wrong us.[2] The spirit of the criminal law is, on this assumption, fundamentally in continuity with the spirit of the vendetta. To my mind, however, the opposite relation holds with much greater force. The justifiability of criminal punishment, and criminal law in general, is closely connected to the *un*justifiability of our retaliating against those who wrong us. That people are inclined to retaliate against those who wrong them, often with good excuse but rarely with adequate justification, creates a rational pressure for social practices which tend to take the heat out of the situation and remove some of the temptation to retaliate, eliminating in the process some of the basis for

* School of Law, King's College London. I am grateful to participants in a staff seminar at the University of Nottingham, and particularly to Paul Roberts, for putting this chapter through its initial paces. Later drafts benefited from Stephen Shute's generous help and advice.

[1] For those who accept that ancient criminal law had this *raison d'être* but who doubt whether it has done much to shape criminal law 'as we know it today', I commend J. Horder, 'The Duel and the English Law of Homicide', (1992) 12 *Oxford Journal of Legal Studies*, 419.

[2] For instance: P. F. Strawson, 'Freedom and Resentment', (1962) 48 *Proceedings of the British Academy*, 187; J. M. Finnis, 'Punishment and Pedagogy', (1967) 5 *The Oxford Review*, 83; J. G. Murphy and J. Hampton, *Forgiveness and Mercy* (Cambridge, 1988); M. S. Moore, 'The Moral Worth of Retribution' in F. Schoeman (ed.), *Responsibility, Character, and the Emotions* (Cambridge, 1987).

excusing those who do so. In the modern world, the criminal law has become the most ubiquitous, sophisticated, and influential repository of such practices. Indeed, it seems to me, this displacement function of the criminal law always was and remains today one of the central pillars of its justification.

This is not to deny the justificatory importance of the criminal law's many other functions, several of which obviously do focus on the activities of offenders. As students of criminal law we have all been brought up on the idea that the various arguments for having such an institution are rivals, each of which takes the wind out of the others' sails. We must, therefore, decide whether we are retributivists, or rehabilitationists, or preventionists, or reintegrationists, or whatever else may be the penological flavour of the month. If we insist on an intellectual 'pick and mix', we are told, we can maybe get away with allocating different arguments strictly to different stages of the justification, e.g. deterrence to the purpose of criminal law in general and retribution to the justification of its punitive responses in individual cases.[3] Still, we must make sure the rival arguments are kept strictly in their separate logical spaces, or else, according to received wisdom, they tend to use up their force in clashes with each other.[4] To my way of thinking, however, this supposed rivalry among justifications for criminal law and its punitive responses is illusory. The criminal law (even when its responses are non-punitive) habitually wreaks such havoc in people's lives, and its punitive side is such an extraordinary abomination, that it patently needs all the justificatory help it can get. If we believe it should remain a fixture in our legal and political system, we cannot afford to dispense with or disdain any of the various things, however modest and localized, which can be said in its favour.[5] Each must be called upon to make whatever justificatory contribution it is capable of making. If and to the extent that the criminal law deters wrongdoing, that is one thing to be said in its favour. If and to the extent that it leads wrong-doers to confront and repent their wrongs, then that counts in its favour too; likewise the power of the criminal law, such as it is, to bring people with mental health problems into contact with those who can treat their conditions, to settle and maintain the internal standards of success for social practices such as marriage and share-dealing, and to stand up for those who cannot stand up for themselves. Even apparently

---

[3] The classic version of such a structured hybrid justification is H. L. A. Hart, 'Prolegomenon to the Principles of Punishment' reprinted in his *Punishment and Responsibility* (1968). A different variation is to be found in A. von Hirsch, *Censure and Sanctions* (1993).

[4] For more or less frank expressions of this anxiety, see N. Lacey, *State Punishment: Political Principles and Community Values* (1988), p. 46 *et seq.*, esp. at 52; P. H. Robinson, 'Hybrid Principles for the Distribution of Criminal Sanctions', (1987) 82 *Northwestern University Law Review*, 19, esp. at 31–4; N. D. Walker, *Why Punish?* (1991), 135–6; R. A. Duff, 'Penal Communications: Recent Work in the Philosophy of Punishment', (1996) 20 *Crime and Justice*, 1 at 8. More theoretically, puritanical critics go further, and argue that mixing different arguments for the justification of punishment is doomed irrespective of attempts to keep them in separate logical spaces: e.g. J. Morison, 'Hart's Excuses: Problems with a Compromise Theory of Punishment' in P. Leith and P. Ingram (eds.), *The Jurisprudence of Orthodoxy* (1988); A. Norrie, *Law, Ideology and Punishment* (1991), pp. 125–35.

[5] Contrast the position recommended by A. G. N. Flew in 'The Justification of Punishment' in H. B. Acton (ed.), *The Philosophy of Punishment* (1969), where the justification of punishment is held to be 'overdetermined' by the many reasons which count in favour of punishment.

trivial factors such as the role of the criminal law in validating and invalidating people's household insurance claims must be given their due weight. All of these considerations, and many others besides, add up to give the institution whatever justification it may have, and to the extent that any of them lapse or fail, the case for abolition of the criminal law comes a step closer to victory.

It is true, of course, that sometimes the considerations conflict, i.e. in some cases some of the considerations which support the criminal law's existence point to its reacting in one way while others point to its reacting in a dramatically different way, or not reacting at all. Sometimes it is even the case that considerations which partly support the criminal law's existence turn against it, and partly support its eradication. The only general thing that can be said of such conflict cases is that they reinforce still further the need for the criminal law to muster whatever considerations it can in its own defence, since by their nature these cases pit additional arguments against whatever course the law adopts for itself. So the existence of such cases strengthens, rather than weakens, my main point. It is also true that different arguments contribute to justifying different aspects or parts of the criminal law to greater or lesser extents. Considerations of deterrence do not support the criminalization of activities which cannot effectively be deterred by criminalization, and considerations of rehabilitation do not support the criminal conviction of people who cannot effectively be rehabilitated. In similar vein, the criminal law's function of displacing retaliation by or on behalf of victims does not support the criminalization of victimless wrongs, or of wrongs whose victims do not offer or inspire retaliatory responses. Criminalizing these wrongs will fall to be justified on an accumulation of other grounds, or else not at all. That still leaves the displacement function, however, as a central pillar of the criminal law's justification. By describing it as a central pillar I mean only that some core parts of the edifice of the modern criminal law cannot properly remain standing, in spite of the existence of other valid supporting arguments, in the absence of the law's continuing ability to pre-empt reprisals against wrong-doers. In this chapter, accordingly, I want to sketch some of the major and (I believe) escalating difficulties of principle and practice faced by the modern criminal law in attempting to fulfil this displacement function and keep the heart of its edifice intact.

2. HUMANITY AND JUSTICE

To continue fulfilling its displacement function satisfactorily has always been a grave challenge for the criminal law, because by the nature of the endeavour there is very little margin for error. On the one hand, the criminal law's medicine must be strong enough to control the toxins of bitterness and resentment which course through the veins of those who are wronged, or else the urge to retaliate in kind will persist unchecked. On pain of losing a central pillar of its justification, therefore, the criminal law cannot afford to downplay too much its punitive ingredient, the suffering or deprivation which it can deliberately inflict on the offender

in response to the wrong. In the end, particularly in the absence of genuine contrition from the offender, that deliberate infliction of suffering or deprivation
may be all the law can deliver to bring the victim towards what the psychother-
apists now call 'closure', the time when she can put the wrong behind her, finally
laying to rest her retaliatory urge. On the other hand, the law's medicine against
that same retaliatory urge cannot be allowed to become worse than the affliction
it exists to control. It must stop short of institutionalizing the various forms of
hastiness, cruelty, intemperance, impatience, vindictiveness, self-righteousness,
fanaticism, fickleness, intolerance, prejudice, and gullibility that the unchecked
desire to retaliate tends to bring with it. On pain of sacrificing a central pillar of
its justification, therefore, the criminal law cannot simply act as the proxy retaliator any more than it can simply dilute its punitive side to the point where it is
incapable of pacifying would-be retaliators.

As if this perennial predicament were not difficult enough for the criminal law,
two further rational constraints upon the modern State have only served to compound the problem as we face it today. The first is the modern State's powerful
duty of humanity towards each of its subjects. To avoid surrendering the whole
basis of its authority—as the servant of its people—the modern State in all of
its manifestations is bound to treat each of those over whom it exercises that
authority as a thinking, feeling human being rather than, for instance, an entry
on a computer, a commodity to be traded, a beast to be tamed, a social problem,
an evil spirit, a pariah, or an untouchable. The anonymous bureaucratic machin-
ery of the modern State which came into existence to honour this duty is also,
notoriously, the main contemporary cause of its violation. It is a depressingly
short step from stopping thinking of someone as a serf to starting thinking of
them as a statistic. But even if the pitfalls of bureaucratization are avoided, the
practice of punishing criminal offenders inevitably calls the State's humane
record into question, because of the element of deliberately inflicted suffering or
deprivation which punishment by definition imports. Such an infliction of suffering or deprivation by the State cannot be justified solely on the ground that worse
suffering or deprivation will be avoided as a result, even if the suffering which will
be avoided as a result is suffering that would otherwise be deliberately inflicted on
that very same person by other people's reprisals against her. The State's duty of
humanity to each person has an agent-relative aspect, i.e. it emphasizes the State's
own inhumanity towards a person and not just the sum total of inhumanity
towards her which occurs within the State's jurisdiction or under its gaze.[6]

---

[6] I cannot offer a proper defence of this claim here. For those who are interested, the basis of such
a defence lies in the fact that the moral duties under discussion in this section occupy the lower level of
a two-level approach to moral reasoning. They summarize and organize certain ultimate moral
considerations, but are not ultimate moral considerations themselves. Therefore they tend already to
display some sensitivity to the limits of our possible compliance with ultimate moral considerations.
One familiar indication of this is to be found in the philosophical myth that 'ought implies can'. It is a
somewhat perplexing myth. Nobody denies, I think, that one can have *reason* to do what one cannot
do. Otherwise where is the rationality in frustration? But many say that one cannot have a duty to do
the very same thing, i.e. that there cannot be a *mandatory* reason to do the impossible. That seems to
me to be a mistaken view, but it is an understandable extrapolation from a wide range of cases in which

Crime: in Proportion and in Perspective 35

This means that, other things being equal, the State's proper response to the fact that a wrong-doer is faced with the threat of retaliation is to protect the wrong-doer rather than to punish her, even if, thanks to the ruthlessness and cunning of the would-be retaliators, punishing her promises to be more effective in reducing her overall suffering.[7]

For punishment to be a morally acceptable alternative to protection, the State has to assure itself not only that the measure of punishment controls retaliation while stopping short of becoming a mere institutionalization of the retaliator's excesses, but also that the act of punishment affirms, rather than denies, the punished person's status as a thinking, feeling human being. That is not impossible. Many familiar features of modern criminal law, including some important substantive doctrines of the general part as well as many procedural, evidential, and sentencing standards, reflect the State's successive efforts to meet this condition. Together these features are supposed to ensure that trial and punishment for a criminal offence affirms the moral agency and moral responsibility of the offender, and in the process (since moral agency and moral responsibility represent a significant part of what it is to be a human being) affirms the offender's humanity.[8] For the reasons just outlined, I regard the constancy of this affirmation as a *sine qua non* of the criminal law's legitimacy. In saying this I am not retreating from my earlier claim that the function of displacing reprisals against wrong-doers is a central pillar of the criminal law's justification. I am only adding the complication that, for better or worse, this function cannot always be legitimately performed by the criminal law.

That point is reinforced when we move from the State's duty of humanity to its parallel, and no less important, duty of justice. Questions of justice, unlike questions of humanity, are questions about how people are to be treated *relative to one another*. Some contemporary political philosophers imagine that all questions dealt with by the institutions of the modern State should be dealt with, first and foremost, as questions of justice. 'Justice' as John Rawls put it, 'is the first virtue of social institutions'.[9] The basic thought behind this view is the sound

what people cannot do is already taken into account in shaping their moral duties, because of the sheer pointlessness of their having a moral duty to do what they cannot do. This means that the level of moral duty can be sensitive, as the level of ultimate moral concern is not, to the limits of our ability to comply. And since I cannot lead your life for you, my possible compliance with agent-neutral considerations based on the value of your goals and projects is limited. This lends an agent-relative dimension to my duties when your goals and projects are implicated in them. That holds for the State's duties as well. It means that the State, like other agents, is morally bound to have a low-level focus on its own moral compliance, systematically but not corruptly concealing morality's higher-level agent-neutrality.

[7] That might include e.g. providing a safe house, or taking criminal libel proceedings against those who make public accusations in a way which will incite reprisal. The demand for protection applies *a fortiori* to those who did wrong but who were acquitted at law, where reprisals not only threaten the wrong-doer but also challenge the law's own authority to deal with the wrong.

[8] I have discussed some aspects of the substantive criminal law which contribute to this aim in 'On the General Part of the Criminal Law', in R. A. Duff (ed.), *Philosophy and the Criminal Law* (1998).

[9] J. Rawls, *A Theory of Justice* (1971), p. 3. Rawls' slogan can bear various interpretations apart from the rather literal one I have adopted in the text. On one very different interpretation, Rawls was only saying that justice is the *last resort* of social institutions, i.e. when all else fails social institutions

liberal one that under modern conditions the State should keep its distance from its people, leaving them free to make their own mistakes. Casting all questions for the State in terms of justice is one possible way to ensure this distance because, as the old adage goes, justice is blind. To do its relativizing work, justice must isolate criteria (although not necessarily the same criteria in every context) for differentiating among those who come before it. And to give these criteria of differentiation some rational purchase, they must be implemented against a background of assumed, but often entirely fictitious, uniformity. The just person, if you like, refuses to take sides in order to take sides; she artificially blinds herself to some qualities of people and aspects of their lives in order to be able to make something of the other differences between them. Rawls memorably conveyed the idea when he spoke of 'the veil of ignorance' behind which just policies are conceived.[10] Now, as many of Rawls' critics have demonstrated, it is very doubtful whether cultivating this kind of artificial blindness to some of our qualities and some aspects of our lives is the proper way for the modern State as a whole to keep its distance from us. It leads to the wrong kind of distance, a remote and sometimes callous disinterest in people's well-being, which the State cannot legitimately, or even (some say) intelligibly, maintain across the board.[11] On the other hand, there is very good reason to think that at least one set of institutions belonging to the modern State, viz. the courts of law, should normally keep their distance from us in precisely this way. Courts are law-applying institutions, and it is in the nature of modern law, with its 'Rule of Law' aspiration to apply more or less uniformly to all of those who are subject to it, that questions of how people are to be treated relative to one another always come to the fore at the point of its application. If we pursue this line of thinking, which of course calls for much more detailed elaboration, justice does turn out to be the first virtue of the courts even though not of other official bodies. The courts' primary business becomes, as the law itself puts it, 'the administration of justice'.

In the criminal law context, where (if the Rule of Law is being followed) the substantive law is relatively clear and certain, the most obvious everyday impact of the court's role as administrator of justice is in the procedural and evidential conduct of the trial—in determining, for example, the probative relevance and prejudicial effect of certain background information about offenders and witnesses, or the acceptability of certain modes of examination-in-chief and cross-examination. In these matters the court's first priority is to specify the density of its own veil of ignorance, the scope of its own blindness, the limits of forensic cognizance.[12] And it must do the very same thing once again at the sentencing stage

---

should at the very least be just. See J. Waldron, 'When Justice Replaces Affection', (1988) 11 *Harvard Journal of Law and Public Policy*, 625.

[10] *A Theory of Justice* (1971), 136 *et seq.*

[11] Both the conceptual and the moral objections are represented in M. Sandel, *Liberalism and the Limits of Justice* (1982), 24–8 and 135–47. Likewise, with a strikingly different twist, in J. Raz, *The Morality of Freedom* (1986), 110–33 and 369 *et seq.*

[12] Isn't there a basic problem with letting an institution decide what it shall take notice of? Doesn't it have to know what it should not know in order to know whether it should know it? True enough.

of the trial where the law, rightly attempting to adjust for the inevitable rigidity and coarseness of its own relatively clear offence-definitions, typically leaves the court's options more open. Of course, in approaching these sentencing options, the court cannot ignore the State's duty of humanity, in the fulfilment of which the State's law-applying institutions must also do their bit. This is a duty which also has implications for sentencing. In the name of humanity, there must always be space for something like a plea in mitigation to bring out the offender's fuller range of qualities, the wider story of his life, some of which was necessarily hidden behind the 'veil of ignorance' during the earlier parts of the trial. But we may well ask: what is it, exactly, that falls to be mitigated when a plea in mitigation is presented to the court? If I am right so far, what falls to be mitigated is none other than the sentence which is, in the court's opinion, required by justice. Identifying a just sentence is thus the proper starting-point. A court which begins from some other starting-point, some other *prima facie* position, is a court which fails to observe its primary, and indeed one may be tempted to say definitive, duty.

Again, nothing in this proposal detracts from my original claim that the control of reprisal is a central pillar of the criminal law's justification. The proposal merely introduces a further troublesome complication. The complication is that, while the control of reprisal forms a key part of the argument for having criminal law and its punitive responses in the first place, those who must implement the criminal law and its punitive responses cannot legitimately make the control of reprisal part of *their* argument for doing so.[13] Displacement of retaliation is a reason for punishment which cannot be one of the judge's reasons for punishing. Judges cannot begin their reasoning at the sentencing stage by asking: What sentence would mollify the victim and his sympathizers? Instead they should always begin by asking: What sentence would be just? I should stress that I am not assuming at the outset that these two questions are unconnected. At this stage I mean to leave open the possibility that, for example, victims and their supporters might want nothing more than the very justice which it is the court's role to dispense, so that doing justice will reliably serve that ulterior purpose. My only point is that the courts should not share in this ulterior purpose themselves; they should insist on thinking in terms of justice irrespective of whether doing so serves the further purpose of pacifying retaliators. For the criminal court, justice is an end, and that remains true even if, for the criminal justice system as a whole, justice is at best a means. In this respect, the criminal court in a modern State is a

---

That is why, in trial by indictment, the *voir dire* exists to separate the function of determining what will be hidden by the veil of ignorance from the function of deliberating about guilt and innocence behind the veil of ignorance. This double-insulation against unwitting prejudice provides a major part of the case for retaining a right to jury trial whenever serious criminal charges are laid. On the question of a criminal charge's seriousness, see sections 3 and 4 below.

[13] This helps us to see why as theorists we should not fear the multiplicity of considerations which add up to justify the practice of criminal punishment. As administrators of justice judges are heavily restricted in their access to many of these considerations, and thus do not have to face all the conflicts among them in their raw form. I have discussed this in greater depth in 'The Purity and Priority of Private Law', (1996) 46 *University of Toronto Law Journal*, 459.

classic bureaucratic institution. It has certain *functions* which cannot figure in its *mission*, and which therefore cannot directly animate its actions.

It is not surprising that this distinctively bureaucratic aspect of courts, and especially criminal courts, has been a cause for much complaint, particularly among victims of crime and their sympathizers, who accuse the courts of leaving them out in the cold, being out of touch with their concerns, stealing their cases away from them, etc. I already mentioned the challenge of maintaining a humane bureaucracy, and maintaining humanity towards victims is an aspect of that challenge to which I will return at the very end of this chapter. But in the context of the criminal law, the pre-eminence of the court's duty of justice creates a prior difficulty, which this discussion was designed to highlight, and aspects of which will occupy our attention over the next few pages. As I explained before, in fulfilling its displacement function the criminal law must always walk a fine line between failing to pacify would-be retaliators and simply institutionalizing their excesses. What we have just added is that under modern conditions an extended section of this fine line, the section which passes through the domain of the courts, must be walked wearing justice's blindfold. What hope can we have for the criminal law's fulfilment of its displacement function under these conditions?

3. THE PROPORTIONALITY PRINCIPLE

In exploring this question, I want to focus attention on one particular principle of justice which is of profound moral importance for the criminal courts in their sentencing decisions, namely the principle that the punishment, if any, should be in proportion to the crime. I choose this principle not only because of its moral importance (to the explanation of which I will return presently) but also because so many people apparently read it as a principle which focuses on how the offender is to be treated relative to her victim or victims, and thus see it as a straightforward way of having the retaliatory impulses of victims systematically reflected in the administration of justice. To my mind, this victim-oriented reading is a serious misreading of the proportionality principle. The State's duty of justice, like the State's duty of humanity, has an important agent-relative aspect. The relativities with which the modern courts must principally contend under the rubric of justice are relativities between the State's treatment of different people, not relativities between how the State treats someone and how that someone treated someone else.[14] Therefore the question of proportionality in sentencing which concerns a modern criminal court is primarily the question of whether this offender's sentence stands to his crime as other offenders' sentences stood to their crimes. This means that the proportionality principle does not in itself specify or even calibrate the scale of punishments which the State may implement, but simply indicates how different people's punishments (or to be exact their *prima facie*

---

[14] See n. 6 above.

punishments before any mitigating factors are brought to bear) should stand *vis-à-vis* one another on that scale.[15]

It does not automatically follow from this, however, that the victim's predicament or perspective cannot properly be introduced into the court's deliberations under the heading of proportionality. According to the proportionality principle, the sentence in a criminal case should be proportionate to *the crime*. If the court can point to features of the crime committed in the case at hand which make it more or less grave than other comparable crimes that have been dealt with by the courts, then the proportionality principle plainly points to a corresponding adjustment of the *prima facie* sentence. It means that everything turns on the applicable conception of 'the crime' and the specification of its axes of gravity. Now it may be thought that the law itself sets these parameters, so that the matter is simply a technical legal one. Crime, some will say, is a purely legal category, and a crime is none other than an action or activity which meets the conditions set by law for criminal conviction.[16] Thus 'the crime' referred to in the principle of proportionality can be none other than the crime as legally defined. It would follow that whether the victim's predicament or perspective is relevant under the heading of proportionality would depend only on whether the legal definition of the crime made specific mention of it. A crime defined in terms of the suffering or loss inflicted upon its victim would leave space for, even perhaps require, the degree of that suffering or loss to be brought to bear on the sentence under the proportionality principle, thus giving some aspects of the victim's predicament or perspective a role in the court's deliberations under the heading of justice. But a crime without such a definitional feature would naturally leave no such space and offer no such role to victim-centred considerations.

In fact, the problem is much more complicated than this. It is true that crimes are, in one ('institutional') sense, just activities which meet the conditions for criminal conviction. But criminal conviction is an all-or-nothing business. Questions of gravity can certainly be a relevant factor, on occasions, in determining which of a number of related crimes the accused should be convicted of, e.g. whether he is a murderer or a manslaughterer, a robber or a thief, etc. But for any *single* criminal offence considered by the jury or magistrate the ultimate answer can only be guilty or not guilty; gravity is neither here nor there.[17] What is more, where the rule of law is properly observed, criminal offences are defined so as to

---

[15] Thus I am going to be writing about what von Hirsch calls 'ordinal proportionality' rather than 'cardinal proportionality': von Hirsch, *Censure and Sanctions* (1993), 18–19. As it happens I also believe in a principle of cardinal proportionality, but it has a very different foundation and applies to the legislative business of setting sentencing maxima rather than to the sentencing stage of criminal trials. It is also worth mentioning that both cardinal and ordinal principles of proportionality need to be applied with the State's duty of humanity in mind, since this forbids cruel or brutalizing punishments even when these would be proportionate. None of this affects the substance of my argument.

[16] G. Williams, 'The Definition of Crime', [1955] *Current Legal Problems* 107.

[17] It is true that the Scots allow for 'not proven' as a *tertium quid*, but of course it still has nought to do with the gravity of the crime. The American solution of 'first degree' and 'second degree' crimes may look at first like another counter-example, but all it does in reality is multiply the number of separate crimes to which the 'all or nothing' guilty/not guilty decision must be applied.

facilitate exactly this kind of 'all or nothing' decision-making. Rape, in England, is sexual intercourse without consent undertaken in the knowledge of, or reckless as to, the lack of consent. Grey areas and borderline cases of consent, sexual intercourse, knowledge, and recklessness have all been, so far as possible, defined out.[18] There is nothing in the definition of rape, apart perhaps from the difference between the knowing rapist and the reckless one,[19] that could conceivably afford a sentencing judge any significant axis of gravity. So does the proportionality principle, by itself, prescribe the same sentence for all knowing rapists, irrespective of their brutality, treachery, bigotry, cowardliness, arrogance, and malice? This challenge cannot be avoided by observing that most crimes do harbour some residual questions of degree in their definitions—that grievous bodily harm is more grievous in some cases than in others, that some acts of dishonesty are more dishonest than others, etc. That is not the point. The point is that, where the rule of law is observed, individual criminal offences are not defined in law so as to retain a topography of gravity for the sentencing stage, but rather so as to flatten that topography, so far as possible, for the all-or-nothing purposes of conviction and acquittal. There is no reason to think that a definition crafted primarily for one purpose, viz. that of flattening the rational variation between different cases of the same wrong, should be regarded as authoritatively determining the scope of the court's veil of ignorance when its job turns, at the sentencing stage, from eliminating such rational variation to highlighting it. There is no reason to assume that the court will find all, or any, of the relevant variables still inscribed on the face of the crime's definition.

It follows that, for the purpose of the principle that the sentence should be in proportion to the crime, we need to go beyond a purely institutional conception of the crime. I do not mean to write off all institutional circumscriptions. It seems to me to be a sound rule of thumb, for example, that evidence which was inadmissible in the trial on grounds of its irrelevance to the charge before the court should not be taken into account when the gravity of the crime is being assessed for the purposes of proportionate sentencing. That an act of dangerous driving caused death should be treated as irrelevant to the gravity of the crime if the crime charged is dangerous driving rather than causing death by dangerous driving. No doubt this is bound to frustrate victims of crime and their sympathizers who may have little patience with the due process principle that people should only be tried for the crimes with which they are charged and sentenced for the crimes which were proved against them at trial—recall that the predictability of such impatience was among the factors which justified the State in monopolizing retaliatory force to begin with. But be that as it may, the due process principle *itself*

---

[18] *Olugboja* (1981) 73 Cr App Rep 344 and *Linekar* [1995] 2 Cr App Rep 49 illustrate the law's attempts to turn certain grey areas between consent and non-consent into brighter lines. *Kaitamaki* [1985] AC 147 does the same with respect to 'sexual intercourse'. The *mens rea* elements were hotly debated in the early 1980s, but the debate was simply between two different ways of artificially stripping grey areas from the concept of recklessness, the broader contrived definition in *Pigg* [1982] 2 All ER 591 giving way to the narrower one in *Satnam S* (1983) 78 Crim App Rep 149.

[19] cf. *Bashir* (1982) 77 Cr App Rep 327.

requires that we go beyond a merely institutional conception of the crime. To implement the principle of due process, just as to implement the principle of proportionality in sentencing, we need some grasp not only of the crime's legal definition but equally of what counts as the *substance* or the *gist* or the *point* of the crime as legally defined—and that is an unavoidably evaluative, non-positivistic issue.[20]

Here, for example, are a couple of classic due process questions. Apart from the charge spelt out in the indictment or summons, were there other lesser offences with which the accused was also implicitly being charged, which did not need to be spelt out? And when does the defendant's previous wrong-doing pass the 'similar fact' test, so that evidence of it is relevant for the purposes of proving the offence charged on the present indictment? Lawyers have often struggled to answer these questions in institutional terms, by pointing to features of crimes which figure in the positive legal definitions.[21] But that, as we should all have realized by now, was always a false hope. One cannot apply or even adequately understand these questions without developing what we may like to call the moral map of the crime, highlighting evaluative significances which may be missing from the law's pared down definition. Thus even if, as I suggested, the principle of proportionality in sentencing does usefully borrow some institutional circumscriptions from the due process principle, that ultimately just reiterates rather than eliminates the fundamentally evaluative, non-positivistic question of what counts as 'the crime' for the purposes of assessing the proportionate *prima facie* sentence. One still needs a moral map of the crime, and the question remains, after all this, of whether the predicament or perspective of the victim can figure anywhere on that map.

4. PERSPECTIVES ON CRIME

One significant strand of the literature on criminal law and criminal justice proceeds from the thought that many, if not all, crimes are covered by one and the same moral map. This is the map of the offender's *blameworthiness* or *culpability*. Following this map leads to a specific interpretation of the principle of proportionality, according to which making the sentence proportionate to the crime means making the sentence proportionate to the offender's blameworthiness or culpability in committing the crime.[22] Let's call this the 'blameworthiness

---

[20] This is not a criticism of legal positivism. Legal positivists hold that validity of a law turns on its sources rather than its merits. That does not prevent them from holding that legal reasoning reflects on the merits as well as the sources of laws, since there is no reason to suppose that legal reasoning is only reasoning about legal validity. See J. Raz, 'On the Autonomy of Legal Reasoning', (1993) 6 *Ratio Juris*, 1.

[21] See *Novac* (1977) 65 Cr App Rep 107 and *Barrington* [1981] 1 All ER 1132 to see how the issue arises in relation to the similar fact doctrine; concerning counts in an indictment, the issue is well-illustrated in the leading case of *Wilson* [1984] 1 AC 242.

[22] A random selection: H. Gross, 'Culpability and Desert', in R. A. Duff and N. Simmonds (eds.), *Philosophy and the Criminal Law* (ARSP Beiheft 19, 1984), p. 59; C. L. Ten, *Crime, Guilt, and*

interpretation' of the proportionality principle. In the minds of many adherents as well as many critics, the proportionality principle in its blameworthiness interpretation systematically excludes victim-centred considerations from the proper scope of the court's *prima facie* sentencing deliberations. The pivotal thought behind this is that a person's blameworthiness in acting as she did is a function of how things seemed to her at the time of her action.[23] It may of course be a more or less complex function. On some accounts of the function, blameworthiness increases or decreases according to how much of the evil of her action the agent appreciated. For others, it is a question of how much the agent should have appreciated, given the various other things she knew at the time. Either way, the crucial manoeuvre so far as blameworthiness is concerned is supposedly to look at the situation *ex ante*, from the perspective of the perpetrator. But that perspective, it is often claimed or assumed, is fundamentally at odds with the perspective of the victim, who looks at the wrong *ex post* and is interested not so much in how things may have seemed to the perpetrator, but rather in how things actually occurred or turned out.[24] On this view the victim and those who sympathize with him are aggrieved first and foremost because of what he suffered or lost at the perpetrator's hands, whether or not the perpetrator appreciated or could have appreciated the full extent of this loss or suffering at the time of acting. If that is so, then the conception of the crime which lies at the heart of the proportionality principle on its blameworthiness interpretation is not the victim's conception. In fact it is diametrically opposed to the victim's conception. If anything, the proportionality principle in this interpretation seems to oblige courts systematically to *compound* the frustration of victims and their sympathizers, and hence to *aggravate* their retaliatory instinct, by insisting on seeing things the offender's way and hence (through the already aggrieved eyes of victims and their sympathizers) doggedly taking the offender's side in the whole conflict. Thus, on this

Punishment (1987), p. 155 *et seq*; A. Ashworth, 'Taking the Consequences' in S. Shute, J. Gardner, and J. Horder (eds.), *Action and Value in Criminal Law* (1994), p. 107 at pp. 116–20. Von Hirsch also makes culpability the only axis of crime-seriousness when he introduces the proportionality principle on p. 15 of *Censure and Sanctions*. But contrast the more complex 'harm-plus-culpability' standard used for proportionality on p. 29 of the same volume, and elsewhere in von Hirsch's work, e.g. in his *Past or Future Crimes* (1985), p. 64 *et seq*. See further n. 30 below.

[23] Among diverse writers who allocate blameworthiness on these terms we find D. Parfit, *Reasons and Persons* (1986), pp. 24–5; S. Sverdlik, 'Crime and Moral Luck', (1988) 25 *American Philosophical Quarterly*, 79; R. Swinburne, *Responsibility and Atonement* (1989), pp. 34–5. D. Husak and A. von Hirsch, 'Culpability and Mistake of Law' in *Action and Value in Criminal Law* (1994); Ashworth, 'Belief, Intent and Criminal Liability' in J. Eekelaar and J. Bell (eds.), *Oxford Essays in Jurisprudence: Third Series* (1987), p. 1 at p. 7.

[24] Talk of the 'victim perspective' and the 'perpetrator perspective' on wrong-doing will be familiar to those conversant with the literature on anti-discrimination law. See A. D. Freeman, 'Legitimizing Racial Discrimination Through Antidiscrimination Law: A Critical Review of Supreme Court Doctrine', (1978) 62 *Minnesota Law Review*, 1049. The version of the distinction relied upon here is slightly less ambitious than Freeman's, although the two are closely related. The distinction I am speaking of figures prominently in Sverdlik, 'Crime and Moral Luck' (n. 23 above) and in A. Ashworth, 'Punishment and Compensation: Victims, Offenders and the State', (1986) 6 *Oxford Journal of Legal Studies*, 86 at e.g. 96. cf. also J. Coleman, 'Crimes, Kickers and Transaction Structures' in J. R. Pennock and J. W. Chapman (eds.), *Criminal Justice* (Nomos XXVII, 1985), p. 313 on the contrasting 'economic' and 'moral' perspectives of tort law and criminal law.

view of the matter, fidelity to the proportionality principle scarcely militates in favour of the sentencing process making a systematic positive contribution to the fulfilment of the criminal law's displacement function.

There is, however, a great deal of confusion in this line of thinking. I can only scratch the surface of a few of the problems here. The problems start with a failure to spell out what blameworthiness or culpability *is*, which leads to an oversimplification of the principles on which it is incurred. Blameworthiness has a four-part formula. To be blameworthy, one must (a) have done something wrong and (b) have been responsible for doing it, while lacking (c) justification and (d) excuse for having done it. Each of elements (a), (b), (c) and (d) can undoubtedly be sensitive, to some extent and in some respects and on some occasions, to how things seemed to the blameworthy person at the time of her action. Elements (c) and (d) in fact incorporate an across-the-board partial sensitivity to the *ex ante* perspective of the perpetrator. Take element (c) first. An action is *justifiable* if the reasons in favour of it are not defeated by the reasons against; but it is *justified* only if the agent acts for one or more of those undefeated reasons.[25] It follows that a purported justification based on considerations unknown to and unsuspected by the agent at the time of the action is no justification at all. Thus justification always does depend, in part, on how things seemed to the agent at the time of the action. Conversely, justification also depends, in part, on how things actually were. No matter how things seemed to the agent, if the reason for which she acted was not in fact an undefeated one then she can have no justification. If she fails the test of justification on this score, the agent must retreat to element (d), the excuse element, to resist the allegation of blameworthiness. Here we find an additional sensitivity to the *ex ante* perspective of the perpetrator: here the agent can rely on what she mistakenly *took* to be undefeated reasons for her action, provided only that she was justified in her mistake. But again this last proviso shows that even excuses are not entirely insensitive to how things actually were; for whether the agent was excused by her mistakes depends on whether her mistakes were justified, and that in turn depends, like any justification, on whether there really were undefeated reasons for her to see the world as she did.[26] So in both elements (c) and (d) we have questions which focus on how things seemed to the agent *as well as* questions which focus on how things really were. Justification and excuse have some across-the-board agent-perspectival dimensions, but are neither of them a pure function of how things seemed to the agent at the time of the action.

Things get more complicated still when we add elements (a) and (b) to the stew. It is tempting to think that wrong action is the mirror image of right or justified action, so that, adapting from the account of right or justified action just outlined, whether one's action is wrong depends on whether the reasons in favour of performing it were defeated by the reasons against and whether one

---

[25] I have defended this account of justification in 'Justifications and Reasons' in A. P. Simester and A. T. H. Smith (eds.), *Harm and Culpability* (1996), p. 103.

[26] Ibid, at pp. 118–22.

acted for one of the latter reasons. Thus obviously no action could be wrong if the agent had no inkling of anything that made it wrong. But right and wrong are in fact dramatically asymmetrical. There are many more ways of doing the wrong thing than there are of doing the right thing. In particular, there is no general sensitivity of wrong-doing to the reasons for which one acted. It is perfectly true that some wrongs, e.g. deceit and betrayal, cannot be committed without certain knowledge or belief on the part of the person who commits them, and others, such as torture and extortion, require a certain intention. But this is not true of all wrongs. One may do wrong by breaking a promise or neglecting one's children quite irrespective of what one knew or had reason to know, and *a fortiori* quite irrespective of why one did it. The same holds true, I believe, of killing people or wounding them, damaging their property, poisoning them, and countless other wrongs which are of enduring importance for the criminal law. It is wrong to kill people or wound them, and one may kill someone or wound them by playing with intriguing buttons or switches which were none of one's proper concern, quite irrespective of whether one knew or had grounds to know the true awfulness of what one was doing. If one's *ex ante* perspective is to be relevant to one's blameworthiness in respect of such killings or woundings, on this view, it must be relevant by virtue of some other element of blameworthiness, such as the justification or excuse element. To be sure, it may also be relevant to one's responsibility, element (b) of the blameworthiness equation. But again its relevance here can only be occasional and limited. To deny that one was a responsible agent one must not only deny that one knew what one was doing, but also point to some underlying explanation such as psychotic delusion, infancy, or (on some views of the phenomenon) hypnosis which puts one temporarily or permanently out of reach of reason so that normal rational standards of justification and excuse do not apply to one. This is a very limited (and decidedly 'bottom of the barrel') opening for one's ignorance to affect one's blameworthiness. So again there is nothing here to make blameworthiness, in general, into a function of how things seemed to the agent at the time of his or her action. In fact, the influence of elements (a) and (b) in the blameworthiness equation fragments and complicates the conditions of blameworthiness even further, so that very few things can be said, in general, about the balance of agent-perspectival and non-agent-perspectival factors which will bear on the net blameworthiness of the agent.

Whatever one may think about the details of this elaboration of the conditions of blameworthiness, it draws attention to one crucial point which is far too easily overlooked. The crucial point is that there is no such thing as blameworthiness at large, or blameworthiness *tout court*. Our blameworthiness is necessarily our blameworthiness in respect of some specific action or activity we engaged in, such as killing, wounding, deceiving, betraying, torturing, or breaking a promise.[27]

---

[27] While we are blameworthy only in respect of actions, we are *to blame* in respect of consequences. To be to blame for a given consequence, we must be *responsible for* that consequence. Doesn't this complicate element (b) of my blameworthiness equation, which spoke only of responsibility for *actions* and therefore (you may say) swept under the carpet the further agent-perspectival

Crime: in Proportion and in Perspective 45

And whether and to what extent our blameworthiness is a function of how things seemed to us at the time of our action depends in very large measure on *which* action or activity we are supposed to be blameworthy in respect of, since different agent-perspectival conditions for blameworthiness evidently come into play for different actions and activities. Now there are those who try to make the determination of which action or activity we engaged in *itself* a function of the way things seemed to us at the time when we acted. Their response to my example of the person who kills unwittingly by playing with intriguing buttons and switches is to deny that it involves a killing, not just because killing in particular is held to be, like deceit, an action with some definitive knowledge requirement, but rather because the scope of agency is always, so to speak, in the eyes of the agent. Fundamentally, we do only whatever we take ourselves to be doing.[28] Personally, I find this a deeply counter-intuitive account of human agency.[29] But more importantly for present purposes, if this account of human agency is accepted, it makes a mockery of the process of determining blameworthiness which I outlined in the previous paragraph. We cannot ask, as I asked in the last paragraph, whether the killer was a responsible agent when he killed, or whether he had any justifications or excuses for doing it. For on this account of human agency *there was no killing*. The most the agent did was press buttons, or fiddle with things that didn't concern him. Having no possible inkling of the death-dealing aspect of what he was doing, he didn't kill anyone. All the hard work which the piecemeal doses of subjectivity in the separate elements of blameworthiness were supposed to do is thus pre-empted by a massive and all-consuming injection of subjectivity in the doctrine of human agency to which it is applied. We are not deprived of our (admittedly controversial and seriously under-specified) answer to the question of whether the button-presser was a blameworthy killer. We *are summarily deprived of the question itself*.

If we rescue the question, as I am sure we should, by jettisoning the extremely restrictive account of human agency which put it out of bounds, we can instantly see that the juxtaposition with which this section began was grievously exaggerated. There is no automatic and comprehensive opposition between assessing the

conditions of responsibility for consequences? The answer is no. Whether we are responsible for consequences is already taken into account in element (a) of the blameworthiness equation. In the relevant sense, we are responsible for those consequences which contribute constitutively to the wrongness of our doing as we do. We are *to blame* for those consequences, accordingly, when that condition is met and elements (b), (c) and (d) of blameworthiness are also present. There is thus no further question, on top of those already anticipated in my blameworthiness equation, of whether our responsibility or blame extends to a particular unforeseen or unforeseeable consequence of our actions. Much effort in moral and legal philosophy has been wasted thanks to the mistaken assumption that one has two bites at the cherry: first one can deny that one was blameworthy in respect of the action and then one can deny, separately, that the blameworthiness extended to a given consequence of the action. In fact the correct answer to the first question necessarily settles the second.

[28] cf. Elizabeth Anscombe's misleading remark in *Intention*, 2nd edn. (1963), p. 53: 'What happens must be given by observation; but . . . my knowledge of what I do is not by observation'. Ashworth's 'Taking the Consequences' is an example of a work which rigorously implements the highly subjectivized account of agency which this remark may be taken to support.

[29] I also believe it is incoherent: see 'On the General Part of the Criminal Law', n. 8 above.

gravity of a crime in terms of the offender's blameworthiness and assessing the
gravity of a crime according to the way it impacts upon its victim. That is
because, to assess the offender's blameworthiness we must begin by asking
'blameworthiness in respect of which action?' and this requires us to interrogate
our account of human agency. Since on any plausible account of human agency
there can be actions which are, like killing and wounding, defined at least partly
in terms of their actual impact upon other people independently of the way things
seemed *ex ante* to the perpetrator, it follows that an inquiry into the perpetrator's
blameworthiness cannot be made independent of this impact. In fact, if we were
to examine more thoroughly the so-called 'victim perspective' with which we
started, I think we would find that the link between the blameworthiness of an
offender and what irks the victim or her sympathizers is even more intimate than
this last remark suggests. I believe it is the action of killing or wounding, complete
with (but not limited to) the death or wound it involves, that normally aggrieves
victims and their sympathizers and sparks their retaliation. Thus the starting-
point of the blameworthiness inquiry—the action which was wrongful—is also
the normal trigger for retaliatory responses on behalf of the victim. Of course
there may be differences of perception and emphasis. It is true, for example, that
excuses tend to be looked upon less generously by victims and their supporters
than their importance for blameworthiness would indicate. Victims and their
supporters may also have trouble with some justifications where their interests
were not among the main reasons in favour of the justified action, and they may
be more doubtful than the court might be, especially under the influence of psychiatric testimony, about a wrong-doer's supposed lack of responsibility. This
means that the blameworthiness inquiry could certainly drive some wedges
between the court's proportionality-driven thinking on matters of *prima facie*
sentencing and the demands of victims and their supporters. But one only drives
wedges between surfaces which are in their original tendency attached to one
another. On my account that is exactly the situation with the offender's blameworthiness and the victim's grievance. It follows that there is no fundamental
opposition of perspectives, no chasm of understanding, dividing the blameworthiness interpretation of the proportionality principle from the demands of
those whose retaliation must be displaced if the criminal law is to fulfil its
displacement function.

Here I am talking as if the blameworthiness interpretation of the proportionality principle came out basically unscathed from the process of correcting the
analysis of blameworthiness which went into it. But of course it did not. What we
have discovered in the process of explaining the concept and conditions of
blameworthiness is that it makes no sense to prescribe, simply, that the sentence
in a criminal trial should be in proportion to the offender's blameworthiness in
committing the crime. For that prescription falls into the trap of presenting
blameworthiness as an independent quantity, something that one can have more
or less of *tout court*. Now that we have brought to mind the important point that
blameworthiness is always blameworthiness in respect of some action, the

Crime: in Proportion and in Perspective   47

blameworthiness interpretation in its original form should be replaced by a sharper ('modified blameworthiness') interpretation of the proportionality principle according to which the sentence should be in proportion to the offender's wrongful action, adjusted for his blameworthiness in respect of it.[30] This reinterpretation, with the slightly more complex moral map of a crime it implies, makes several important advances over the simpler blameworthiness interpretation it replaces. Let me mention just two of them here.

First, the modified blameworthiness interpretation helps to bring out what *justifies* the proportionality principle, and lends it the moral importance in the courtroom that I so confidently spoke of earlier. Although a principle of justice, the proportionality principle also contributes directly and powerfully to the court's compliance with the State's duty of humanity, and it takes much of its moral force from that contribution. As already mentioned, the State's duty of humanity requires it to affirm the moral agency and moral responsibility of those whom it punishes. The proportionality principle in its modified blameworthiness interpretation puts both the offender's agency and her responsibility centre stage. To ask about the offender's blameworthiness is to emphasize her responsibility. That is not only because element (b) of the blameworthiness equation is the element of responsibility. It is also because questions of justification and excuse— elements (c) and (d)—are applicable only to responsible agents, so that applying standards of justification and excuse to people is an assertion of their responsibility. But on top of that the modified blameworthiness interpretation brings out the importance of questions about the offender's agency which are not highlighted in the simple blameworthiness interpretation. It reminds us that treating someone as an agent is of importance quite apart from treating them as responsible. Even someone who is not responsible for their actions is an agent, and should still be treated as one. True, the duty of humanity as I expressed it goes further, and demands that offenders be treated as *moral* agents and as *morally* responsible. This arguably introduces further complications which point to a need for some further modification of the modified blameworthiness interpretation. Nevertheless the complications do not alter the main point, which is that by punishing people in proportion to their crimes, where those crimes are mapped according to the actions which made them wrongful adjusted for the offender's blameworthiness in respect of them, the court contributes decisively to the affirmation of the offender's humanity which is a *sine qua non* of the legitimacy of any modern State punishment. But remember that this is a function of the modern State's special duty of humanity towards its people, which comes of its claim to

---

[30] Compare this with von Hirsch's more complex version of the proportionality principle, mentioned in n. 22 above, which requires the crime to be in proportion to blameworthiness-plus-harm. Von Hirsch's principle comes close to mine in several ways, but still seems to leave blameworthiness as a free floating quantity. It may be said that it does not float free because it is now attached to a harm. But harms cannot be blameworthy. Only *doing* harm can be blameworthy. If von Hirsch's principle is that the sentence should be in proportion to the harm-doing adjusted for the harm-doer's blameworthiness in respect of it, then the only thing which divides us is that I refuse to reduce all wrongdoing to harm-doing. This has consequences: see n. 32 below.

authority and its associated role as servant of its people. Those of us who stake no similar claim to authority and have no similar role in other people's lives are not covered by the same strict humanitarian duty towards them.[31] Thus the strictness of the court's attention to questions of moral agency and moral responsibility need not, rationally, be mirrored in all interpersonal transactions between wrong-doers and people they wronged, or supporters, or even onlookers. That is one important reason why the victim of a crime and his or her sympathizers may sometimes *quite properly* (i.e. independently of their various impatiences, hastinesses, prejudices, etc.) have less time for the niceties of blameworthiness than the court is morally required to have.

Secondly, the modified blameworthiness interpretation has the advantage that it alerts us to the *limitations* of the proportionality principle as a principle of justice for scaling criminal sentences. The principle's usefulness depends first on the court's ability to discern what is supposed to be the wrongful action in the crime, and then the court's ability to compare this action with other actions, before it can even start to settle degrees of blameworthiness as between them. This may not always be possible. Some pairs of wrongful actions are incommensurable. It means that the proportionality scale will not always be perfectly transitive.[32] The adjustments for differential blameworthiness required by the modified blameworthiness interpretation of the proportionality principle can only take effect within the transitive parts of the scale. It may be possible to compare a less blameworthy robbery with a more blameworthy theft. But it will not necessarily be possible, even in principle, to assess a more blameworthy theft alongside, say, a more blameworthy assault. Here sentencing practice may have to move in relatively independent grooves, with guidelines that do not add up to a comprehensive code. The axes of gravity that operate at the sentencing stage will not necessarily, or even typically, allow the gravity of each crime to be plotted relative to that of every other crime. That, in my view, is no violation of the proportionality principle, nor on the other hand an indictment of it, but rather one of its welcome implications. The idea that all crimes are covered by a single moral map has, on closer inspection, very little to recommend it.[33]

---

[31] Although, as I have assumed throughout this chapter, we all have various more limited duties of humanity towards each other. Extra-judicial punishers such as teachers and parents are covered by the State's stricter duty to the extent that they echo the State's claim to authority and its basis.

[32] In their classic article 'Gauging Criminal Harm: A Living-Standard Analysis', (1991) 11 *Oxford Journal of Legal Studies*, 1, A. von Hirsch and N. Jareborg argued that all harms with which the criminal law should be concerned are commensurable, allowing a transitive sentencing scale under the proportionality principle. I think they are wrong about the commensurability of harms, and about the commensurability of living standards on which their argument was based. But even if they are right, it is a long way from the doctrine that all harms are commensurable to the doctrine that all *wrongs* are commensurable, since a wrong is an action, and even when it is an action defined in terms of the harm done, the harm done is only one constituent of the wrong. This means that von Hirsch and Jareborg still have some way to go to show that the proportionality scale is transitive. And here I am granting the generous assumption that elements (b), (c), and (d) of the blameworthiness equation do not introduce yet further incommensurabilities. On the proliferation of incommensurability in an action-centred view of morality, see Raz, *The Morality of Freedom*, (n. 11 above) p. 321 *et seq*.

[33] See my 'On the General Part of the Criminal Law' (n. 8 above) for a much closer inspection.

5. Filling the Displacement Gap

The foregoing does something to explain how the courts, as blindfolded administrators of justice, can in spite of their blindfolds systematically help to fulfil the criminal law's displacement function. Even though the justice that victims and their sympathizers want (which is primarily justice between offender and victim) is not the justice that courts are licensed and required to provide by the proportionality principle (which is primarily justice between offender and offender), the proportionality principle, correctly interpreted, nevertheless shares some of its basic moral geography with the retaliatory logic of victims and their sympathizers. For some distance, courts and retaliators travel on the same path even though the former cannot, consistent with their mission, deliberately track the latter. But as I have also attempted to show, the two paths do diverge at certain obvious points. First, as I started section 2 by explaining, to preserve the legitimacy of the criminal law's monopolization of retaliation the courts must stop short of institutionalizing the excusable but unjustifiable retaliatory excesses of victims and their sympathizers. Second, as I explained in section 3, the principle of due process means that the wrongful action at the heart of the offender's crime cannot always, in the eyes of the law, and notably for the purposes of sentencing, be the same wrongful action which inspires retaliation by or on behalf of victims. The need to restrict the trial to the substance of the charges with which it began may lead to some differences between the victim's perception and the law's rendition of what the offender has done, even when the victim is not driven to retaliatory excess. Finally, the requirement to adjust the sentence for the offender's blameworthiness may, as I just explained in section 4, drive some extra wedges between the court's sense of proportionality and the victim's retaliatory inclinations, even where those inclinations are not excessive and there are no due process impediments to their reflection in law. The court, as an agent of the State, owes a duty of humanity to all which may often exceed the duty each of us owes to other people, and which therefore requires the court to affirm each offender's moral agency and moral responsibility more conscientiously than need be the case in many of our ordinary interpersonal transactions, including transactions with those who wrong us. These three factors add up to constitute what I will call the 'displacement gap' in criminal sentencing: the gap between what retaliators want and what the courts can, in good conscience, deliver.

Traditionally, this displacement gap has been filled by the law's own wealth of symbolic significances. What was confiscated from victims and their sympathizers in point of retaliatory force has traditionally been compensated by the ritual and majesty of the law, and by the message of public vindication which this ritual and majesty served to convey. At one time it was the ritual of the punishment itself which made the greatest contribution. The pillory, the stocks, the carting, the public execution, and various other modes of punishment involving public display allowed the State to close the displacement gap by exhibiting the offender in all his shame and humiliation, in all his remorse and regret, while the proceedings remained under some measure of official control to limit retaliatory excess.[34] But of course a new penal age dawned in the nineteenth century which put the offender out of reach and out of sight in the prison, where measured punishment and control of retaliation could be more successfully combined, both with each other and with the new disciplinary ambitions of supervision and rehabilitation.[35] From then on, the burden of providing ritual and majesty to fill the displacement gap was to a large extent shifted off the shoulders of the punishment system (which was now practically invisible to the general public except in the gloomy expanse of the prison walls) and onto the shoulders of the trial system instead. The courts themselves now had to offer the would-be retaliator the kind of public vindication which would once have been provided by the act of punishment, and the ritual and majesty of the courtroom had to substitute for the ritual and majesty of the recantation at the gallows. Of course the pressure to get this substitution exactly right was eased by the fact that the prison would to some extent protect the offender against the retaliator even if the displacement gap had not been successfully filled by the court. But it was still crucial that the trial itself should offer the victim and his sympathizers some symbolic significances which would divert them from taking the matter into their own hands e.g. if the offender was acquitted, or if a custodial sentence was not used, or once the custodial sentence had expired. For this purpose the court could only rely on continuing respect, indeed deference, for its own heavily ceremonial processes and practices. If the court's processes and practices were to fall into disrepute, if they came to be seen as just distracting frippery, then the vindicatory symbolism of the trial would be lost and the displacement gap would open wide for all to see. We would then face a major legitimation crisis in the system of criminal justice.

My view is that we now face this crisis in Britain, and for the very reason I have just given. During the 1980s and 1990s the steady creep of the ideology of consumerism has led people to regard the courts, along with many other key public institutions, as mere 'service providers' to be judged by their instrumental achievements. League tables, customer charters, satisfaction surveys, outcome audits, and efficiency scrutiny became the depressing norm. Respect for valuable public institutions declined at the same time as expectations of them increased. Even among those who took themselves to be anti-individualistic, the demand that institutions should become more 'transparent' and 'accountable' came to be regarded as orthodoxy, and euphemistic talk of 'cost-effectiveness' became

---

[34] How could the death penalty ever have been consistent with limiting retaliatory excess? Surely nothing could ever have exceeded death? Wrong. That one died with one's soul cleansed by confession or recantation was one mercy. That one died after judicial proceedings in which one was able to put one's defence, and therefore treated as a responsible agent, was another. On the mistaken assumption that the widespread availability and use of the death penalty in early-modern England was a sign of sheer brutality in criminal justice policy, see J. A. Sharpe, *Judicial Punishment in England* (1990), p. 27 *et seq.*

[35] The line of thinking in this paragraph obviously owes something to M. Foucault's *Discipline and Punish: The Birth of the Prison* (1977). I hesitate to specify exactly what.

acceptable. All this was, essentially, a corruption of a sound idea, which I mentioned at the outset—the idea that modern government is the servant of its people. It was mistakenly assumed that since public bureaucracies existed to serve social functions, ultimately serving people, they ought to be judged by the purely instrumental contribution they could make to those social functions, and hence their instrumental value for people. But it was forgotten that many social functions were not purely instrumental functions, i.e. many institutions made an intrinsic or constitutive contribution to their own social functions. The mission of such institutions, to return to my earlier expression, was partly integral to their function. The National Health Service and other organs of Beveridge's welfare State are the most familiar examples in Britain; people who regard themselves as collectivists should rue the day they ever tried to defend these in purely instrumental terms, which was the day they surrendered to the creeping individualism of the consumer society. But the criminal courts exemplify the point even more perfectly. Historically they filled the displacement gap in criminal justice by their own (to the public eye) bizarre and almost incomprehensible processes, their own special black magic if you like, which lent profound symbolic importance to their work. But armed with new consumerist ideas people came to see all these processes as mere frippery. They came to ask what the courts were *achieving* by their black magic, and whether it was giving them the *product* they wanted, whether this was the *service* they were looking for, and of course those questions quickly broke the spell. The courts could no longer fill the displacement gap from their own symbolic resources, since their own symbolic resources had been confiscated by the popular expectation of raw retaliatory results.

The consequence of this rapid social change is that the displacement gap is now an open and suppurating social wound, and the threat of retaliation by or on behalf of aggrieved victims of crime looms ever larger. The courts themselves sometimes feel the pressure and feel constrained to penetrate their own veil of ignorance, abandoning their mission to do justice where, as increasingly often, it parts company with their function to displace retaliation. That seriously violates their duty as courts, which is above all the duty of justice, and which positively requires them to stay 'out of touch with public opinion' on matters of sentencing policy. Meanwhile populist politicians pander to retaliatory instincts by threatening to publish names and addresses of ex-offenders, to force ex-offenders to reveal old criminal records, even to license vigilantes in the form of private security guards—all in order 'to hand justice back to the people'. What they do not appear to appreciate is that all of this makes the justification for the criminal law less stable, not more so. For if the criminal law cannot successfully displace retaliation against wrong-doers, but instead collaborates with it, then a central pillar of its justification has collapsed.

I do not mean to suggest that the courts' recent well-documented waking-up to the existence of victims is in every way a bad thing. There has been, for as long as anyone can remember, a tendency for criminal courts, with typical bureaucratic abandon, to pretend that nobody was concerned in their processes but themselves. Victims of crime, in particular, were kept badly informed and given no quarter at all in the operation of the system. Except insofar as they were witnesses, they were expected to find out for themselves where and when the trial would take place, to queue for the public gallery, to sit with the accused in the cafeteria, etc. In their capacity as witnesses, meanwhile, no concessions were made for the special difficulty of confronting those who had wronged them. Much of this amounted to a violation of the State's duty of humanity towards the victims of crime, and to the extent that it still goes on, it still does.[36] The courts should remember that victims, as well as offenders, are thinking, feeling human beings. But this has absolutely no connection with the far more sinister contemporary campaigns to turn victims into parties to the criminal trial or administrators of criminal punishments, or in some other way to hand their grievances back to them.[37] That victims do not try, convict, sentence, or punish criminal offenders, and have no official part in the trial, conviction, sentencing, and punishment of criminal offenders, is not an accident of procedural history. It is, on the contrary, one of the main objects of the whole exercise.

[36] On which see Helen Fenwick, 'Rights of Victims in the Criminal Justice System: Rhetoric or Reality?' [1995] *Criminal Law Review* 843.

[37] A prescient manifesto for criminological consumerism was N. Christie, 'Conflicts as Property', (1977) 17 *British Journal of Criminology*, 1, which spoke of conflicts being 'stolen' by criminal law and needing to be 'returned' to the parties through procedures which were 'victim-oriented' as well as 'lay-person-oriented'.

[3]

Imprisonment and crime

Can both be reduced?

Steven N. Durlauf
University of Wisconsin

Daniel S. Nagin
Carnegie Mellon University

S ince 1972, the rate of incarceration in U.S. state and federal prisons has increased every year without exception from a rate of 96 prisoners per 100,000 population in 1972 to 504 prisoners per 100,000 in 2008 (BJS, 2008).[1] Counting those housed in jails, the nation's total incarceration rate has surpassed 750 per 100,000 (Liptak, 2008). Accompanying the 40-year increase in imprisonment has been a companion growth in corrections budgets from $9 billion in 1982 to $69 billion in 2006, which is a 660% increase (BJS, 2008).

Much research has been done on the effect of this increase in incarceration on crime rates as well as on the social and economic costs of the ensuing fivefold increase in the nation's imprisonment rate. The point of departure for this article is the recognition that sanction policies that reduce both crime and punishment have the desirable feature of avoiding not only the costs of crime but also the costs of administering punishment. As a theoretical matter, this observation is certainly not new and was recognized at least as long ago as Becker (1968). Of course, the policy question is whether, relative to the status quo, alternative policies exist that can achieve these simultaneous effects. In this article, we argue that it is a realistic possibility that crime, prison costs, and imprisonment numbers can be

We thank Amanda Agan and Xiangrong Yu for outstanding research assistance. Four anonymous reviewers as well as Senior Editors Richard Rosenfeld and Lawrence Sherman have provided very helpful suggestions on a previous draft. Direct correspondence to Steven N. Durlauf, Department of Economics, University of Wisconsin—Madison, 1180 Observatory Drive, Madison, WI 53706 (e-mail: sdurlauf@ssc.wisc.edu); Daniel S. Nagin, Heinz College, Carnegie Mellon University, Pittsburgh, PA 15206 (e-mail: dno3@andrew.cmu.edu).

1. Incarceration rates in state prisons declined slightly in 2009, but increased incarceration in federal prisons resulted in a small increase in the combined state and federal incarceration rates (Pew Center for the States, 2010).

reduced simultaneously if policy makers shift their focus from a primary reliance on severity-based policies, mandating lengthy prison terms, to a focus on a more effective use of police to make the risks of crime clearer and the consequences of crime faster and more certain.

We make no claim about the novelty of our overall policy contention that, given the set of sanctions in place in the current criminal justice system, a simultaneous improvement is possible. In many ways, our position echoes claims advanced in two recent books, Mark Kleiman's (2009) *When Brute Force Fails: How to Have Less Crime and Less Punishment* and David Kennedy's (2009) *Deterrence and Crime Prevention: Reconsidering the Prospect of Sanction.* Aspects of our position also might be found in the commentaries of authors such as Clear (2007), Doob and Webster (2003), Garland (2001), Irwin (2005), Tonry (2004), Useem and Phiel (2008), and Western (2007). Our hope is that the particular framing of the arguments we provide will provide an impetus for a reorientation away from the severity-oriented, crime-prevention strategies that have prevailed for the last 40 years toward more certainty-oriented, crime-prevention strategies.

The evidentiary bases for our conclusion are taken from recent reviews of the empirical studies on deterrence conducted by the authors and colleagues.[2] These reviews led us to the following broad empirical conclusions that inform our policy views:

1. The marginal deterrent effect of increasing already lengthy prison sentences is modest at best.
2. Increasing the visibility of the police by hiring more officers and by allocating existing officers in ways that heighten the perceived risk of apprehension consistently seem to have substantial marginal deterrent effects.
3. The experience of imprisonment compared with non-custodial sanctions such as probation, sometimes called specific deterrence, does not seem to prevent reoffending. Instead, the evidence suggests the possibility of a criminogenic effect from imprisonment.

Together, these conclusions have a range of policy implications; most important, they call into general question the efficiency of current sanction policies and point in directions along which these policies should be changed.

This article is organized as follows: In the next section, we discuss the conceptual framework for the determination of criminal behavior that explains why, theoretically, crime can be reduced without an increase in the resource commitment to the criminal justice system. The theoretical possibility of a cost-free reduction derives from a shift toward certainty-based as opposed to severity-based sanction policies. We also argue that for a sanction policy to reduce both imprisonment and crime simultaneously, it must deter in addition to incapacitate would-be criminals. Thus, the possibility of deterrence is crucial to the goal of reducing prison populations without incurring higher crime rates. The next

---

2.   Our conclusions derive from Durlauf and Nagin (in press), Apel and Nagin (2009), as well as Nagin, Cullen, and Jonson (in press); this article will rely especially heavily on Durlauf and Nagin.

section reviews and critiques the empirical evidence on the deterrent effect of severity-based and certainty-based sanction policies. Policy and research recommendations are discussed in the last section.

At the outset, we note two important restrictions to the scope of this article. First, we restrict our attention to changes in sanction policy that have the potential to reduce both imprisonment and crime. Imprisonment and crime might be reduced by making greater investments in non-sanction-related policies. For example, evidence is mounting regarding the effectiveness of early childhood development programs in reducing criminality (Heckman, Malofeeva, Pinto, and Savalyev, 2010; Piquero, Farrington, Welsh, Tremblay, and Jennings, 2009).[3] We restrict our attention to sanction policies, in part, because non-sanction-related policy alternatives have received considerable attention elsewhere. Even more important, we think it valuable to consider the restricted question of whether the current level of investment in the criminal justice system is allocated most effectively among its various components. As we observe in the Policy Implications and Future Research section of this article, the mechanics of shifting resources from imprisonment to policing is institutionally difficult because the former is primarily a state and federal function and the latter is primarily a local government function. Notwithstanding, both functions are understood by policy makers, mostly elected officials, to be components of an integrated system to control crime and punish criminal wrongdoing. Shifting resources from the criminal justice system to other activities such as education or early childhood development in our judgment would pose far more daunting institutional and political challenges to justify to policy makers. We, thus, restrict our attention to the issue of reallocation of resources within the criminal justice system.

Second, we note that our analysis does not address incapacitation effects, which constitute a logically independent way of reducing crime from deterrence. We recognize that the possibility that incapacitation effects are large represents a potential challenge to our objective of reducing crime and imprisonment, and we will return to this point in the Policy Implications and Future Research section.

Key Concepts

Discourse about deterrence often takes the form of one side, with one side, mostly, but not always, economists arguing that sanction threats always deter and the other side, mostly, but not always, criminologists arguing that sanction threats never deter. Based on our assessment of the existing evidence, it would be unwise for criminologists to ignore that deterrence should be part of any coherent crime-control policy. However, when deterrence effects are

---

3. Borghans, Duckworth, Heckman, and ter Weel (2008) provided a recent survey of the state of knowledge of the development of cognitive and non-cognitive skills. An important theme of recent research is the relative manipulability of non-cognitive skills such as self-control, which has obvious implications for criminal behavior.

unpacked, it is clear that sanction threats are not universally efficacious as magnitudes of the deterrent effects range from none to seemingly very large.

In this section, we discuss possible reasons why substantial heterogeneity persists in the size of deterrent effects and the implications of such heterogeneity for sanction policy. In particular, we discuss the conceptual basis for our claim that it is possible for changes in current sanction policy to reduce both crime and imprisonment. To this end, we make three related points.

First, levels of deterrence always depend on the interplay of the certainty and severity of punishment. Thus, it is meaningless to say that one is more important than the other in determining the strength of deterrence or the level of the crime rate. However, it is meaningful to consider the relative magnitude of the deterrent effects of certainty and severity resulting from changes in their status quo levels and, therefore, to make claims about their relative importance at the margin.

Second, a sanction policy that reduces crime solely by incapacitation necessarily will increase the rate of imprisonment. In contrast, if the policy also prevents crime by deterrence, then it is possible that it will be successful in reducing both imprisonment and crime. Hence, the rejection of deterrence as a crime-reduction mechanism implicitly can constitute a reason for mass incarceration.

Third, if the experience of imprisonment is criminogenic, then an added benefit of sanction policies that reduce both crime and imprisonment is that it likely averts reoffending attributable to the possible criminogenic effects of the prison experience. Although these criminogenic effects have yet to be documented with much precision, their possible existence reinforces our general policy recommendation.

The Interplay of Certainty and Severity in Producing Deterrence

The theory of deterrence is predicated on the idea that a sanction regime, by affecting the relative anticipated costs and benefits of a crime, can lead at least some members of a population to choose not to commit crime. Sanction regimes, from this perspective, simply raise the anticipated costs of criminal activity. As such, one of the key concepts of deterrence is the severity of punishment. In the context of this article, severity refers to sentence length, which we denote by L. Severity alone does not deter; the likelihood of a punishment's imposition also matters to the criminal choice. The offender first must be apprehended, presumably by the police. He next must be charged, prosecuted successfully, and finally sentenced by the judiciary. None of these successive stages in processing through the criminal justice system is certain. Thus, another key concept in deterrence theory is the certainty of punishment, which we denote by p. In this regard, the most important set of actors are the police; absent detection and apprehension, conviction or punishment is not possible. For this reason, we discuss separately what is known about the deterrent effect of police.

Durlauf and Nagin

In its simplest form, the economic model of deterrence theorizes that would-be offenders compare the expected utility under the choice of committing a crime with the expected utility of not committing a crime. These types of calculations cannot be reduced to the sum of a function of p and a function of L; the two terms interact in determining the expected costs and benefits of a crime. Durlauf and Nagin (in press) provided formal algebraic descriptions of this interaction,[4] but the basic intuition is evident when one considers that no level of severity will deter when no prospect of actual punishment is present (i.e., $p = 0$) just as certain punishment (i.e., $p = 1$) will not deter without severity (i.e., $L = 0$).

Moving beyond these extreme, and admittedly fanciful, cases, the interaction of certainty and severity in producing deterrence has a basic implication for the arguments that we will advance here; the deterrent effect of a change in p will depend on the level of L, and conversely, the deterrent effect of a change in L will depend on the level of p. Thus, even though we make reference throughout this article to the deterrent effects of certainty and severity, it is important to understand that these references concern incremental changes from the status quo levels in p and L, namely incremental changes in p at prevailing levels of L or, alternatively, incremental changes in L at prevailing levels of p. Because certainty and severity interact, it does not follow that incremental changes in p (at prevailing levels of L) and incremental changes in L (at prevailing levels of p) always will be equally effective in generating deterrence. In Durlauf and Nagin (in press), we discussed in detail the reasons why the magnitude of deterrent effects depend upon the interaction of certainty and severity and why certainty and severity effects themselves might be heterogeneous because of heterogeneity in individual characteristics and in criminal opportunities.

As will be described in the next section, the empirical support for the deterrent effect of certainty is far stronger than for severity. Several theoretical explanations suggest why this finding should not be regarded as surprising. Prison sentences necessarily are experienced over time and with delay from the time of the criminal act. Both might contribute to the dearth of strong evidence of a severity effect. In economics, the concept of discounting is used to explain why future consequences might be given less weight than present consequences.[5] Criminals might have higher discount rates than the typical member of the population. Indeed, much psychological and criminological research documenting the present orientation of criminal offenders (Jolliffe and Farrington, 2009; Moffitt,

---

4.   One easy way to see the interaction is to consider the expected utility of committing a crime. Assume that the utility of committing a crime and not being apprehended is the same as being apprehended and given a sentence of length 0. Assume that apprehension means that a sentence of length L is received with certainty. The expected utility of a criminal can be written as $pU_C(L) + (1 - p)U_C(0)$, where $U_C(\cdot)$ denotes the utility of a crime as a function of sentence length. It is immediate that certainty and severity interact as is shown the fact that p is multiplied by $U_C(L)$ in the expected utility calculation.

5.   See Polinsky and Shavell (1999) for a formal analysis of the importance of discounting in determining the effects of changes in sanction severity.

1993; White et al. 1994; Wilson and Herrnstein, 1985) strongly supports this possibility. Furthermore, present orientation might cause would-be offenders to be far more attentive to cues related to the likelihood of apprehension than to the future punishment they will receive in the event of apprehension. For example, would-be offenders might be affected little by the prospect of a 50% increase in sentence length from, for example, 10 to 15 years but might be affected greatly by a 50% increase in apprehension probability from, for example, .2 to .3 even though each policy means that a given crime is associated with the same expected number of years of time served. Also, as discussed in Durlauf and Nagin (in press), other factors that might result in differential deterrent effects of certainty and severity are cognitive biases resulting in the overweighting of small (and large) probabilities; perhaps paradoxically, these biases operate in a way that might render subjective beliefs about the probability of apprehension sensitive to the actual probabilities.

The Interrelationship of the Crime and Imprisonment Rates

Our emphasis on deterrence stems from our interest in identifying policies that can reduce imprisonment and crime rates simultaneously. An essential feature of this perspective is that the imprisonment rate and crime rates are treated as joint outcomes of sanction policies determining certainty and severity of punishment. One implication of this perspective is that the imprisonment rate should not be regarded as a policy variable per se but should be treated appropriately as an outcome of sanction policies determining who goes to prison and for how long.

 Blumstein and Nagin (1978) examined the relationship of imprisonment and crime rates in the context of a model that allowed for both incapacitation and deterrent effects. Two critical findings of their analysis were that, in the absence of deterrent effects, a logically necessary trade-off takes place between imprisonment and crime rates and that the presence of a deterrent effect is a necessary condition for the possibility that a change in sanction policy could reduce crime and imprisonment rates simultaneously. The intuition for this conclusion is straightforward; crimes averted by incapacitation necessarily require the incarceration of the individuals who otherwise would be committing crimes outside the prison walls. However, if deterrent effects are present, then heightened sanction risks, when perceived as credible, can result in both lower crime rates and lower imprisonment rates. Again the intuition is straightforward; deterred crimes mean that no one can be punished for them.

 That said, the presence of deterrence effects does not guarantee the existence of such policies. What are the technical requirements for a change in sanction policy to reduce both imprisonment and crime? The concept of an elasticity from economics can be used to characterize what is needed. An elasticity measures the absolute value of the percentage change in some outcome variables with respect to a 1% change in another variable, holding other variables constant. Formally, suppose that the crime rate C is functionally dependent on certainty and severity (i.e., $C(p, L)$). Let e_p and e_L denote the elasticities of the crime rate with respect to p and L, respectively. The Blumstein and Nagin (1978) analysis demonstrated that a 1% increase in either p or L will induce a sufficiently large reduction in the crime rate to reduce the imprisonment rate also if the respective elasticity of the crime rate with respect to the policy variable is greater than 1. Conversely, if the magnitude of either elasticity is less than 1, then the decline in the crime rate associated with an increase in that sanction policy variable will not be sufficiently large to avert an increase in the imprisonment rate. In turn, Blumstein and Nagin showed that, for either e_p or e_L to exceed 1, a deterrent effect must be present. The intuition for this result has been stated already; crime prevention by incapacitation necessarily requires the incarceration of an individual who otherwise would be criminally active. Technically, this concept ensures that e_p and e_L must be less than 1. However, if deterrent effects are present, then crime reduction does not necessarily require the actual incarceration of individuals who otherwise would be committing crimes. This outcome makes for the possibility of simultaneously having both less crime and less imprisonment. We will illustrate this possibility in a later section with a numerical example.

Although we have treated p as a policy variable, it is important to recognize that its role with respect to the criminal decision process can be complicated. For criminal decisions, what matters is the subjective probability a potential criminal assigns to apprehension (i.e., p^e). This subjective probability can be affected by the police in various ways. Most obvious, presumably a relationship exists between the subjective belief p^e and the objective probability p. Conventional notions of rationality, at least in economics, impose the restriction that $p^e = p$, but increased objective certainty of punishment will induce deterrence so long as p^e is an increasing function of p. This can happen through several channels. The experience of capture might cause the apprehended offender to revise upward his estimate of apprehension risk and thereby deter him from future crime. Indeed, Anwar and Loughran (2009), Hjalmarsson (2009), Horney and Marshall (1992), and Lochner (2007) found evidence that such risk updating seems to occur. Furthermore, other criminals might gain new information about the risk of apprehension from the apprehension experience of criminal compatriots, but the limited research on such indirect experiential effects suggests that they are small (Lochner, 2007).[6] Announcements of changes in police expenditures and the like can lead directly to upward adjustments of the probability of punishment. So, even if one rejects the economist's notion of rationality when modeling how crime choices are made, the policy variable p still matters.

Our emphasis on crime and imprisonment rates as joint outcomes of the sanction regime also has the implication that the clearance rate for crimes (i.e., the percentage of actual perpetrators of crimes who are apprehended) is an incomplete signal of the certainty

---

6.   The presence of indirect experiential effects from enforcement might be context specific. Many European countries require television owners to pay a licensing fee. Electronic means are used to detect non-compliers. Rincke and Traxler (in press) found substantial evidence of enforcement spillover effects whereby enforcement action against an identified non-complier seems to increase compliance rates in nearby households.

of punishment posed by the police because it does not incorporate the probability of apprehension and, hence, the punishment that existed for criminal opportunities that were not acted on because the perceived risk of apprehension was deemed too high (Cook, 1979). For example, a would-be robber of a liquor store is unlikely to carry out the robbery if an occupied police car is parked outside. More generally, would-be offenders might be deterred from committing a crime even if the apprehension risk is less than certain but is still judged to be too high because of the overall presence of police or other threats of apprehension. We emphasize the distinction between the probability of punishment for targets that were acted on and the probability of punishment attending targets that were not acted on because the latter are an example of the way a deterrence-based mechanism can prevent crime without actually having to apprehend a perpetrator of a crime to demonstrate the "price of crime."

This observation serves as a point of departure for illustrating with a concrete, albeit stylized, example of how a deterrence-based policy with an elasticity greater than 1 might reduce both crime and imprisonment. Assume that each individual has a probability of 50% of facing a criminal opportunity. Suppose that in this stylized world would-be criminals will take advantage of all criminal opportunities with a risk of apprehension less than 35% and that two types of criminal opportunities exist—good opportunities from the criminal's perspective that have a risk of apprehension of 10% and marginal opportunities with a risk of apprehension of 30%. The latter are described as marginal because their attendant risk of apprehension is only just less than the 35% threshold of acceptability. Suppose also that 75% of criminal opportunities are marginal and that 25% are good. In this world, all criminal opportunities are exercised, so the crime rate is 50%. The clearance rate, which is the apprehension rate for crimes actually perpetrated, is 25% (25% = 25% × 10% + 75% × 30%). The imprisonment rate is 12.5% (12.5% = 50% × 25%).

Suppose now that a new police chief introduces innovations in policing (e.g., problem-oriented policing [POP]) that increase the risk of apprehension at both good and marginal opportunities by 50%—from 10% to 15% for the good opportunities and from 30% to 45% at what previously had been marginal opportunities. We use the past tense to describe the marginal opportunities because they would no longer be taken advantage of because their risk of apprehension now exceeds the 35% apprehension risk maximum that criminals will tolerate.

This policing innovation will have the following distinct effects: First, by deterring criminals from taking advantage of what previously had been marginally favorable targets, the crime rate will be reduced from 50% to 12.5%. Second, by limiting criminal activity to the good opportunities, the clearance rate declines from 25% to 15% even though the police, in fact, have become 50% more effective in producing a threat of apprehension. Third, and most important for our purposes here, fewer actual apprehensions will occur not only because of the decline in the rate of apprehension at the criminal targets that actually are acted on (i.e., the good targets) but also because of the 50% decline in the crime rate; together, these two reductions combine to reduce the imprisonment rate under the new regime to 1.875%. We emphasize that the reduction in prison population is not attributable to the ineffectiveness of the police. To the contrary, their increased effectiveness in deterring crime in the first place decreased the flow of captured criminals into the criminal justice system. This hypothetical case thus illustrates how a policy change, in theory, can reduce crime and imprisonment rates simultaneously.

Do policies with elasticities greater than 1 exist? The following section will assess the empirical evidence on severity and certainty, whereas the last section derives policy conclusions from the empirical literature. Our final section will advance the claim that although evidentiary support does not exist that any particular policy is associated with an elasticity greater than 1, one can identify high and low elasticity policies with confidence. The most likely candidates for policies with high elasticity policies involve the use of police to increase the risk of apprehension, which in turn increases p, whereas it seems that the elasticities with respect to severity are low. However, this result is not the end of the story. These two findings suggest that a change in the current sanction regime toward one with higher certainty and lower severity when combined can reduce both crime and imprisonment even if the certainty policy has an elasticity less than 1; all that is required is that the certainty policy have a larger elasticity than the severity policy.[7] It is for this reason that we believe the answer to our title question is a tentative "yes."

Potentially Criminogenic Effect of the Experience of Imprisonment

Our discussion so far has accepted the conventional wisdom that increases in either p or L will decrease the crime rate. The third argument that we make is that good reasons exist to believe that this is not always the case.

In criminology, the term *general deterrence* is used to describe the behavioral response to the threat of punishment, whereas the term *specific deterrence* is used to describe the behavioral response to the experience of punishment. Because the mechanisms underlying general and specific deterrence are conceptually distinct, no inherent contradiction persists in one being operative and the other not. Indeed, as an empirical matter, this might be the case. Evidence of general deterrent effects is strong, whereas little evidence is found of specific deterrent effects. In fact, if anything, the evidence suggests that the experience of imprisonment might have a criminogenic rather than a specific deterrent effect.

The logic of specific deterrence is grounded in the idea that if the experience of imprisonment is sufficiently distasteful, then some of the punished might conclude that it is an experience not to be repeated. The structure of the law itself also might cause previously convicted individuals to revise upward their estimates of the likelihood and severity of punishment for future law breaking. The criminal law commonly prescribes more severe penalties for recidivists. For example, sentencing guidelines routinely dictate longer prison

---

7.   Note that we are not arguing that the change meets a cost–benefit test because we do not address the
      relative costs of severity and certainty policies.

sentences for individuals with prior convictions. Prosecutors also might be more likely to prosecute individuals with criminal histories. Additionally, the experience of punishment might affect the likelihood of future crime by decreasing the attractiveness of crime itself or by expanding alternatives to crime. While imprisoned, the individual might benefit from educational or vocational training that increases postrelease non-criminal income-earning opportunities (MacKenzie, 2002). Other types of rehabilitation are designed to increase the capacity for self-restraint when confronted with situations, like a confrontation, that might provoke a criminal act such as violence (Cullen, 2002).

However, several reasons exist for theorizing that the experience of punishment might increase an individual's future proclivity for crime. One argument relates to the effect of the experience of crime on expectations about the prison experience. Although some individuals might conclude that imprisonment is not an experience to be repeated, others might conclude that the experience was not as adverse as anticipated. Other reasons have to do with the social interactions induced by imprisonment. Prisons might be "schools for crime" where inmates learn new crime skills even as their non-crime human capital depreciates. Associating with other more experienced inmates could lead new inmates to adopt the older inmate's deviant value systems or enable them to learn "the tricks of the trade" (Hawkins, 1976; Steffensmeier and Ulmer, 2005). Being punished also might elevate an offender's feelings of resentment against society (Sherman, 1993) or might strengthen the offender's deviant identity (Matsueda, 1992).

The experience of imprisonment also might increase future criminality by stigmatizing the individual socially and economically. Much of the evidence shows that an important part of the deterrent effect of legal sanctions stems from the expected societal reactions set off by the imposition of legal sanctions (Nagin and Paternoster, 1994; Nagin and Pogarsky, 2003; Williams and Hawkins, 1986). Prior research has found that individuals who have higher stakes in conformity are more reluctant to offend when they risk being exposed publicly (Klepper and Nagin, 1989a). Although the fear of arrest and stigmatization might deter potential offenders from breaking the law, those that have suffered legal sanctions might find that conventional developmental routes are blocked. In their work on the 500 Boston delinquents initially studied by Glueck and Glueck (1950), Sampson and Laub (1993) called attention to the role of legal sanctions in what they called the process of cumulative disadvantage. Official labeling through legal sanctions might cause an offender to become marginalized from conventionally structured opportunities, which in turn increases the likelihood of subsequent offending (Bernburg and Krohn, 2003). Sampson and Laub (1993) proposed that legal sanctions might amplify a "snowball" effect that increasingly "mortgages" the offender's future by reducing conventional opportunities. Several empirical studies support the theory that legal sanctions downgrade conventional attainment (Freeman, 1996; Nagin and Waldfogel, 1995, 1998; Sampson and Laub, 1993; Waldfogel, 1994; Western, 2002; Western, Kling, and Weiman, 2001) and increase future offending (Bernburg and Krohn, 2003; Hagan and Palloni, 1990).

A recent review of the literature on imprisonment and reoffending by Nagin et al. (in press) concluded that on balance the research findings pointed more to a criminogenic effect than to a preventive effect. Specifically, most studies find higher recidivism rates among individuals receiving custodial sentences regardless of sentence length than among individuals receiving non-custodial sentences even with extensive statistical controls for potentially confounding factors. They also report that evidence on the relationship between sentence length and recidivism is mixed. If the fact of imprisonment as opposed to the length of imprisonment is the relevant source of higher recidivism, then this fact would suggest an even more radical policy change than we propose, namely that criminal sanctions other than imprisonment should be used. We do not pursue this line of argument here.

From a theoretical perspective, the potentially criminogenic effect of the experience of imprisonment might serve as an additional deterrent to sufficiently farsighted would-be criminals. Although the large body of evidence on the present orientation of offenders leaves us skeptical that on the margin this additional source of deterrence is large, the point still stands that if the prison experience is criminogenic when deterrence fails, then ex-prisoners will be more, not less, crime prone because of their prison experience. Thus, sanction policies that reduce both crime and imprisonment might have the added benefit of averting the potentially criminogenic influence of the experience of imprisonment.

It is important to emphasize that the existing literature suggesting a criminogenic effect to prison is far from decisive. The literature has yet to be subjected to the sort of careful identification analysis that one observes, for example, in the study of social interaction effects. Blume, Brock, Durlauf, and Ioannides (2010) provided an extensive discussion of identification problems in social interactions; we believe it is fair to say that the literature on peer effects in prisons, for example, generally has not been subjected to a rigorous evaluation of the conditions studied by Blume et al., which can produce spurious evidence of social influences. Hence, our claim is that criminogenic effects are theoretically plausible and are consistent with several empirical studies.

Empirics

In this section, we discuss the evidentiary support for our claims, focusing on the more recent literature that largely began emerging in the 1990s.[8] We consider this literature in two stages. First, we consider aggregate regressions studies. These studies come in two forms. One form examines the relationship between aggregate imprisonment rates and aggregate crime rates, and the other form examines the relationship between crime rates and aggregate

---

8. The first wave of deterrence research that involved a substantial number of studies was conducted in the 1960s and 1970s. These studies suffered from numerous statistical flaws that are detailed in Blumstein, Cohen, and Nagin (1978). In our judgment, these flaws are so serious that this wave of research does not contain any empirical findings that might be used for formulating policy.

measures of police level, measured, for example, by per capita public expenditures on police. The level of aggregation for the imprisonment and crime studies is typically states, whereas the level of aggregation for police and crime studies is usually cities. We conclude that studies of the relationship of imprisonment rates to crime rates are deeply flawed for both statistical and theoretical reasons. Our conclusion about the usefulness of the aggregate regression literature on policing is less negative but still circumspect. We then consider studies that examine the deterrent effect of specific policies or interventions. It is this literature that most influenced our policy claims. Readers who are not interested in the technical reasons for our reservations about the aggregate regression studies might wish to move directly to the section titled Severity-Enhancing Policies.

Aggregate Imprisonment and Crime Studies

A large literature exists that studies the relationship between aggregate imprisonment and crime rates. To provide a general assessment, we follow a recent important review by Donohue (2009: Table 9.1) that identifies six major published journal articles that examine the relationship between aggregate crime rates and imprisonment rates. Each of these studies finds a statistically significant negative association between imprisonment rates and crime rates, and each has been interpreted as implying that higher imprisonment rates result in lower crime rates. These studies would seem to represent a prima facie case against our view that it is possible to reduce imprisonment and crime simultaneously.

In fact, these studies should not be interpreted this way. A detailed critique of these studies appears in Durlauf and Nagin (in press); here, we highlight the main problems.

The first and perhaps most important problem with aggregate incarceration/ imprisonment studies is that they fail to evaluate how alternative policies jointly affect crime and imprisonment. As such, the studies are not policy relevant. These studies generally ignore three points emphasized in the previous section. The first is that the prison population is an outcome of the overall sanction policy; the population is not a policy variable per se. Changes in the size of prison populations only can be achieved by changing policies that we have summarized through the certainty of punishment p and the severity of punishment L. Second, in choice-based theories of criminal behavior, the deterrence response to policy changes affecting either p or L generally will not be uniform and, instead, will depend on, among a range of factors, the current values of these variables. This heterogeneity in deterrent effects forms the basis for a third point emphasized in the previous section: A logically necessary inverse relationship does not exist between the imprisonment rate and the crime rate. Depending on the magnitude of the deterrence response evoked by a sanction policy, a declining crime rate might be associated with either a declining or an increasing imprisonment rate. Together, these three points illustrate the general idea that aggregate crime rate and aggregate imprisonment rates are equilibrium outcomes, so their relationship will depend on the way that the individual and the institutional factors that determine outcomes on an individual level aggregate across a population.

The exception to our broad claim that imprisonment/crime regressions are not policy relevant is Levitt (1996), which is the one aggregate crime/imprisonment study in Donohue's (2009) survey with a methodological approach that we endorse. This study is based on studying the effects of court orders requiring reductions in prison populations as an instrument, reasoning that such orders will cause a reduction in the imprisonment rate that is unrelated to the endogeneity of the imprisonment rate. He found that a prisoner reduction precipitated by a court order can lead to a short-term increase in the crime rate. Levitt's analysis, however, speaks to a different policy question than ours, namely the effect of court orders. In Durlauf and Nagin (in press), we discussed why his findings are not informative about the effect on the crime and imprisonment rates of a change in the certainty and severity of sanctions.

A second general problem with the imprisonment and crime literature follows from our argument that each is an equilibrium outcome, namely that the existing literature does not admit a causal interpretation between the variables under study. As discussed in the section titled The Interrelationship of the Crime and Imprisonment Rates, crime rates affect imprisonment rates even as imprisonment rates might be affecting crime rates. Statistically disentangling cause-and-effect relationships in this setting is challenging, and these studies suffer from basic limitations in establishing causal claims. One problem in many of these studies is the confusion of the word *causality* as is understood in an econometric sense (and involves the marginal predictive value of one variable with respect to another) with the "causality" in a substantive social-science sense, which involves manipulations of one variable in the context of a model of behavior. Four of the six analyses studied by Donohue (2009)[9] are based on the application of time-series analyses that in essence look for dynamic correlations between the levels of crime rates and imprisonment rates (or for changes in the two series). Any claim that these correlations imply a counterfactual-based causal relationship between imprisonment rates and crime rates has been recognized for a long time to be invalid. The fact that levels or changes in one variable help to predict additional levels or changes in another variable does not imply causality as the term is understood in social science. One obvious reason is that a third factor might be influencing each. A less obvious issue, known as the Lucas critique in economics (see Ljungvist, 2008 for an introduction), is that the dynamic equilibrium statistical relationships between variables such as incarceration rates and crime rates are a function of the "structural" determinants of the sanction regime, such as the menu of potential penalties for a given crime, the rules by which police resources are employed, and so on.

The problem of spurious claims of causality from correlation also apply to Levitt (1996) and Spelman (2005), which are the two studies in Donohue's (2009) survey that

---

9.   The studies are Marvell and Moody (1994), Becsi (1999), Spelman (2000), and Liedka et al. (2006). Spelman (2008) is the state of the art in time-series analyses of imprisonment and crime. Although the study explores important issues of model specification, it also suffers from the criticisms we have made.

use instrumental variable analysis to address simultaneity bias. With respect to Levitt (1996), Liedka et al. (2006) argued that prison-overcrowding litigation is a function of the incarceration rate; hence, both could move positively as a result of a common factor. In Durlauf and Nagin (in press), we questioned whether this critique is particularly compelling in the absence of information on the political economy of overcrowding litigation. Spelman (2005), focusing on counties in Texas, regressed changes in county-specific crime rates against changes in public order, arrest and incarceration rates, and some set of controls. The arrest and incarceration rates then are instrumented using lagged values of variables such as police resources, republican voting, and jail capacity. No explanation is given as to why these instruments are valid (i.e., why they should not appear in the original crime regression). This issue is not an idle quibble. The error in a crime rate/incarceration rate regression is made up of every crime determinant that is omitted from the regression, which includes unmodeled dependence in the crime rate process. Republican voting, for example, is informative about values, which presumably directly affect individual crime choices. Instrumental variables are difficult to justify in a crime regression in which the determinants of crime are undertheorized. We consider the problem of reverse causality more serious for Spelman than for Levitt because Levitt uses such a narrowly defined instrument so that it is easier to think about its determinants (and so make a case for validity) as opposed to the ad hoc collection of instruments found in Spelman.

Third, basic statistical problems are found in these studies. Each study employs linear functional forms that do not represent aggregations of individual decisions except under special cases (see Durlauf, Navarro, and Rivers, 2008, in press, for discussion). These studies also fail to evaluate systematically the effects of assumptions about model specification on their findings. As delineated in Durlauf and Nagin (in press), these assumptions include the choice of which control variables to include in the crime model and the choice of the degree of parameter heterogeneity that is allowed across geographic units. These choices are known to matter in other contexts. These issues are examples of the problem of model uncertainty; the qualitative questions that one wishes to study, such as the imprisonment/crime relationship, do not provide guidance on the statistical model to employ. This reason is well known as to why different articles come to opposing conclusions using the same data set.

Aggregate Studies of Crime Rates and Police Levels

The companion literature to the imprisonment and crime literature examines the relationship between resources committed to policing and crime rates. Studies include Corman and Mocan (2000), Evans and Owens (2007), Levitt (1997, 2002), Marvell and Moody (1994), as well as McCrary (2002). With the exception of McCrary (2002), these studies consistently found evidence that larger resource commitments to policing are associated with lower crime rates. Even for this exception, Levitt (2002) effectively argued that McCrary's findings did not overturn Levitt's general claim of police effectiveness.

The aggregate policing and imprisonment literatures share common features. Both rely on panel data sets tracking crime rates in heterogeneous locations over time—states for the imprisonment literature and cities for the police literature. Both also use similar econometric methods. As such, these studies are subject to many of the same criticisms that we have raised for incarceration and crime regressions. At the same time, the import of our criticisms is less severe in some respects. Unlike the imprisonment regressions, all studies reviewed in Durlauf and Nagin (in press) that employ aggregate police regressions address the following meaningful policy question: Does the level of resource commitment to policing affect crime rates?[10] Changes in the number of police or expenditures on police is subject to policy choice in a way that the imprisonment rate is not. Furthermore, Granger causality receives less emphasis in the police regressions literature than in the imprisonment literature, so although Marvell and Moody (1994) explicitly used Granger causality notions, whereas Corman and Mocan (2000) did so implicitly, neither Levitt (1997, 2002) nor Evans and Owens (2007) fell into the misinterpretation of marginal time-series predictive power as evidence of causality in a counterfactual sense. Read in isolation, our conclusion is that the evidentiary strength of aggregate police/crime studies is limited by inadequate attention to model uncertainty and to aggregation but not by asking an ill-posed question.

This criticism is far less damning than the absence of a well-posed policy question, which in our view places the imprisonment/crime literature in a different class than the police/crime literature. Given the statistical problems and the absence of a well-posed policy question that plague aggregate imprisonment/crime regressions, the statistical limitations of aggregate police/crime studies, and the nonexistence of any aggregate severity/crime studies, the evidentiary support for our general policy claims necessarily is limited if one is restricted to these studies. Simply put, the most favorable interpretation of the aggregate regression evidence is that some reason exists to believe that increased policing reduces crime. But this, by itself, does not imply that a shift from severity to certainty will be efficient. Fortunately, direct and strong evidence with respect to severity and certainty effects can be found in targeted studies of particular policy changes, which we describe in the next section.

Severity-Enhancing Policies

Surprisingly few studies use specific policy changes to evaluate the deterrent effect of changes in severity. The earliest post-1970s attempts to measure severity effects analyzed the deterrent impact of sentence enhancement for gun crimes. A series of studies (Loftin, Heumann, and McDowell, 1983; Loftin and McDowell, 1981, 1984) examined whether sentence enhancements for gun use in committing another type of crime such as robbery

---

10. To be fair, the way in which police resources are employed (e.g., more police vs. higher salaries) might be determined by the crime rate, political economy, and so on so that the comparison of particular measures of police activity are not necessarily strictly exogenous policy interventions; hence, the difference between aggregate police/crime regressions and aggregate imprisonment/crime regressions is not as black and white as we have described. We thank Richard Rosenfeld for raising this point.

deter gun use in the commission of crime. Although the findings are mixed, this body of research generally has failed to uncover evidence of a deterrent effect (but see McDowall, Loftin, and Wiersema, 1992).[11] One important caveat is found with respect to extrapolating these studies to understanding the link between deterrence and severity. The same literature that found that gun penalty enhancements were ineffective also found that these laws generally failed to increase the sentences actually received in gun-related crime prosecutions. Thus, gun-using criminals might not have responded because the real incentives were not changed.

Numerous studies have examined the deterrent effect of California's "Three Strikes and You're Out" law, which mandated a minimum sentence of 25 years after conviction for a third strike-eligible offense. Zimring, Hawkings, and Kamin (2001) concluded that the law reduced the felony crime rate by at most 2%, finding that only those individuals with two strike-eligible offenses showed any indication of reduced offending. Other studies by Stolzenberg and D'Alessio (1997) and by Greenwood and Hawken (2002) also examined before-and-after trends and found similarly little evidence of crime-prevention effects. These studies did not conduct a cost–benefit analysis of the trade-off between the benefits of this crime reduction and the attendant increases, which limits the policy relevance of their findings because the notion of a small effect is not compared with the cost of the policy.

In our judgment, the most persuasive study of the three strikes law is by Helland and Tabarrok (2007), who studied both the effects of the law on crime as well as assessed its cost effectiveness. This analysis focuses exclusively on whether the law deterred offending among individuals previously convicted of strike-eligible offenses. Helland and Tabarrok compared the future offending of individuals convicted of two previous strike-eligible offenses with that of individuals who had been convicted of only one strike-eligible offense but who, in addition, had been tried for a second strike-eligible offense and ultimately were convicted of a non-strike-eligible offense. The study demonstrated that these two groups of individuals were comparable on many characteristics such as age, race, and time in prison. Even so, it found that arrest rates were approximately 20% lower for the group with convictions for two strike-eligible offenses. The authors attributed this reduction to the greatly enhanced sentence that would have accompanied conviction for a third strike-eligible offense.

As is standard in studies of this type, the interpretation of the findings in terms of the marginal deterrence effects of the three strikes law is contingent on the comparability of two

---

11. McDowall et al. (1992) combined data from the different locations they had studied previously for evidence of a deterrent effect of sentence enhancements. Although none of the individual site analyses produced evidence of a deterrent effect, the combined analysis did. For several reasons, we are skeptical of the combined analysis. First, it is vulnerable to many criticisms we have leveled at aggregate regression analyses. Second, their finding that at the individual sites the laws were ineffective in increasing sentence length suggests that the null findings at the individual sites were not a result of a lack of statistical power that might be remedied by combining data across sites. Third, the approaches taken to combining the studies contain numerous ad hoc assumptions that raise separate concerns about whether their findings are robust.

groups who are under study. Some reasons are available as to why unobserved individual differences might be present; for example, those individuals who were convicted of a second non-strike-eligible offense might have had better legal representation than those that were convicted of a second strike-eligible offense. In such a case, the incentives for additional crime commission might differ for reasons outside the penalty differential. Another reason for non-comparability might be that those convicted of a non-strike-eligible offense are simply better criminals than those convicted of a strike-eligible offense in the sense that they are better able to generate alibis, avoid leaving evidence, and so on. Our own view is that the concerns raised by these potential sources of unobserved heterogeneity are sufficiently speculative that we find the Helland and Tabarrok (2007) results persuasive. Helland and Tabarrok also conducted a cost–benefit analysis and concluded that the crime-reduction benefits likely fall far short of the aggregate cost of the increase in imprisonment induced by the law. They go on to argue that a financially comparable investment in policing that primarily affects the certainty of punishment are likely to yield far larger crime-reduction benefits. We return to this observation in the following discussion.[12]

Other sentence enhancement policies also have been examined to uncover possible deterrence effects. Kessler and Levitt (1999) examined the deterrent impact of another California sentence enhancement law—Proposition 8 passed in 1982. Proposition 8 anticipates the "three strikes" laws passed by many states in the 1990s. Their aim was to distinguish the deterrent effects from the incapacitation effects. Most state criminal statutes provide for a sentence enhancement for repeat offenders. Proposition 8 increased the severity and scope of those enhancements and mandated their application. For example, before Proposition 8, sentence enhancements pertained to persons with prior imprisonments, whereas after Proposition 8, enhancements were widened to pertain to prior convictions and were lengthened. Kessler and Levitt (1999) argued that before the enactment of Proposition 8, repeat offenders covered by the Proposition still were sentenced to prison, just not for as long. Thus, any short-term drop in crime rate should be attributed to deterrence rather than to incapacitation. They estimated a 4% decline in crime attributable to deterrence in the first year after enactment. Within 5 to 7 years, the effect grew to a 20% reduction. The longer term estimate includes incapacitation effects. Indeed, Kessler and Levitt acknowledged that the incapacitation effect might dominate the deterrent effect.

Webster, Doob, and Zimring (2006) challenged the basic finding of any preventive effects. Kessler and Levitt (1999) examined data from every other year. When all annual data are used, Webster et al. (2006) found that the decline in crime rates in the affected categories began before Proposition 8's enactment, and the slope of this trend remained

---

12. Shepherd (2002) also found crime-prevention effects for California's three strikes law, mostly from a reduction in burglaries. The aim of the analysis was to estimate the total deterrent effect of the law as reflected in the article's title: "Fear of the First Strike. . ." The validity of the findings are difficult to judge because the statistical analysis rests on many questionable assumptions (e.g., that police and court expenditures are independent of the crime rate).

constant through implementation. But see Levitt (2006) for a response and commentary supportive of Webster et al. by Raphael (2006). Our assessment of the debate is that the evidence in Kessler and Levitt on deterrence is relatively weak as a result of issues concerning the comparability of the crime series used by Kessler and Levitt to uncover the effect of Proposition 8 via contrasts with the crime series for the Proposition 8 crimes but not for other reasons that have been alleged.[13]

A different class of studies tries to uncover deterrent effects by studying the effects of differences in punishment severity for minors versus adults. For most crimes, the certainty and severity of punishment increase discontinuously after reaching the age of majority when the jurisdictional authority for criminal wrongdoing shifts from the juvenile to the adult court. In an extraordinarily careful analysis of individual-level crime histories from Florida, Lee and McCrary (2009) attempted to identify a discontinuous decline in the hazard of offending at age 18—the age of majority in Florida. Their point estimate of the discontinuous change is negative as predicted but is minute in magnitude and not even remotely close to achieving statistical significance. Similarly, Hjalmarsson (2009) found no evidence of reduced offending when juveniles reach the age of majority, but interestingly, the study did find evidence that perceptions of the risk of imprisonment increase.

The finding that the young fail to respond to changes in penalties associated with the age of majority is not uniform across studies. An earlier analysis by Levitt (1998) found a large drop in the offending of young adults after they reached the age of jurisdiction for the adult courts. For several reasons, we judge the null effect finding of Lee and McCrary (2009) more persuasive in terms of understanding deterrence. First, Levitt (1998) focused on differences in age measured at annual frequencies, whereas Lee and McCrary measured age in days or weeks. At annual frequencies, the estimated effect is more likely to reflect both deterrence and incapacitation; hence, Levitt's results might be driven by incapacitation effects rather than by deterrence per se. Second, the Lee and McCrary analysis is based on individual-level data and avoids problems that can result because of aggregation (Durlauf et al., 2008, in press). On its own terms, the individual-level data studied by Lee and McCrary are unusually informative because they also contain information on the exact age

---

13. Levitt (2006) responded to Webster et al. (2006) by arguing that they failed to estimate the same model that he analyzed with Kessler. Specifically, Kessler and Levitt (1999) compared changes in crime rates before and after Proposition 8 for crimes affected by the proposition with changes before and after the Proposition in other crime rates in California and compared the Proposition 8-affected crime rates for the same crime rates outside of California. As such, Levitt, in our view, correctly faulted Webster et al. (2006), who focused on changes in the crime rates for the Proposition 8 crimes but not as compared with changes in others, which is the appropriate strategy. However, Raphael (2006) called into question the validity of the comparison groups used by Kessler and Levitt. Webster et al. also raised this issue. In his response, Levitt fairly noted that it is a matter of judgment and questioned whether Webster et al. have shown that it matters in the examples they raise. In our view, Raphael's criticism of comparability, when combined with the Webster et al. versus Levitt exchange, is persuasive in calling into question the Kessler and Levitt conclusions on the effects of Proposition 8.

Durlauf and Nagin

of arrestees, which allows for the calculation of short-term effects of the discontinuity in sentence severity (e.g., effects within 30 days of turning 18).

In summary, the literature on whether increases in prison sentence length serves as a deterrent is not large, but several persuasive studies do exist. These studies suggest that increases in the severity of punishment have at best only a modest deterrent effect. We reiterate, however, the point emphasized in the section titled The Interplay of Certainty and Severity in Producing Deterrence that this conclusion concerns changes in the severity at margin. In this regard, it is important to note that most research on sentence length involve increases in already long sentences. Some evidence suggests that Massachusetts's Bartley–Fox gun law mandating a 1-year prison sentence for unlawful carrying of gun might have been a deterrent (Wellford, Pepper, and Petrie, 2005). Furthermore, we subsequently discuss experiments showing short but certain incarceration deters. We thus see a need for research on the likely non-linear relationship between deterrence and severity. But for our purposes, it seems that the marginal deterrent value of increased sentence length at current levels is small for contexts in which sentences are currently long.

Certainty-Based Policies

Studies of certainty-enhancing policies typically focus on the deterrent effect of the police. Relatively little research is available on the deterrent effect stemming from the certainty of prosecution or sentencing to prison conditional on apprehension. So although much is known about how one of the primary determinants of certainty affects crime via specific policies, the effects of changes in policy with respect to the other primary actors, prosecutors, and judges have yet to be examined.[14]

The police might prevent crime through many possible mechanisms. Apprehension of active offenders is a necessary first step for their conviction and punishment. If the sanction involves imprisonment, then crime might be prevented by the incapacitation of the apprehended offender. The apprehension of active offenders also might deter would-be criminals by increasing their perception of the risk of apprehension and thereby the certainty of punishment. Many police tactics such as rapid response to calls for service at crime scenes or after crime investigation are intended not only to capture the offender but also to deter others by projecting a tangible threat of apprehension. However, as emphasized in the section titled The Interrelationship of the Crime and Imprisonment Rates, police might deter without actually apprehending criminals because their presence projects a threat of apprehension if a crime were to be committed.

---

14.   Several studies conducted in the 1970s examined the deterrent effect of conviction risk, usually measured by the ratio of convictions to charges (Avio and Clark, 1974; Carr-Hill and Stern, 1973; Sjoquist, 1973). These studies suffered several important methodological limitations; most importantly, they all treated conviction risk as exogenous.

Some of the most compelling evidence of deterrence because of police involves instances in which a complete or near-complete collapse of police presence occurs. In September 1944, German soldiers occupying Denmark arrested the entire Danish police force. According to Andeneas (1974), crime rates rose immediately but not uniformly. The frequency of street crimes like robbery, whose control depends heavily on visible police presence, rose sharply. By contrast, crimes such as fraud were less affected. See Sherman and Eck (2002) for other examples of crime increases after a collapse of police presence.

From a policy perspective, the important question is not whether the complete or near-complete absence of police will result in a large crime increase. Instead, what is interesting and important is whether marginal changes in police presence or different approaches to mobilizing police can affect crimes rates. Research on the marginal deterrent effect of specific police policies has taken two distinct directions. One set of studies examines the effects of abrupt changes in police presence. A second research program has focused on the crime-prevention effectiveness of different strategies for deploying police. We review these literatures separately.

Several targeted studies have involved changes in police presence as a result of local political and social conditions. Such studies have examined the Cincinnati Police Department (Shi, 2009), the New Jersey State Police (Heaton, in press), and the Oregon State Police (DeAngelo and Hansen, 2008). Each of these studies concludes that increases (decreases) in police presence and activity substantially decrease (increase) crime. By way of example, Shi (2009) studied the fallout from an incident in Cincinnati in which a White police officer shot and killed an unarmed African American suspect. The incident was followed by 3 days of rioting, heavy media attention, the filing of a class action lawsuit, a federal civil rights investigation, and the indictment of the officer in question. These events created an unofficial incentive for officers from the Cincinnati Police Department to curtail their use of arrest for misdemeanor crimes, especially in communities with larger proportional representation of African Americans out of concern for allegations of racial profiling. Shi demonstrated measurable declines in police productivity in the aftermath of the riot and documented a substantial increase in criminal activity. The estimated elasticities of crime to policing based on her approach were −.5 for violent crime and −.3 for property crime.

The ongoing threat of terrorism also has provided several unique opportunities to study the impact of police resource allocation in cities around the world, including the District of Columbia (Klick and Tabarrok, 2005), Buenos Aires (Di Tella and Schargrodsky, 2004), Stockholm (Poutvaara and Priks, 2006), and London (Draca, Machin, and Witt, 2008). The Klick and Tabarrok (2005) study examined the effect on crime of the color-coded alert system devised by the U.S. Department of Homeland Security in the aftermath of the September 11, 2001 terrorist attack to denote the terrorism threat level. The alert system's purpose was to signal federal, state, and local law enforcement agencies to occasions when it might be prudent to divert resources to sensitive locations. Klick and Tabarrok (2005) is especially interesting because of its use of daily police reports of crime for the period of March 2002 to July 2003, during which time the terrorism alert level rose from "elevated" (yellow) to "high" (orange) and back down to "elevated" on four occasions. During high alerts, anecdotal evidence suggested that police presence increased by 50%. Their estimate of the elasticity of total crime to changes in police presence as the alert level rose and fell was −.3.

These police manpower studies mainly speak only to the number and allocation of police officers and not to what police officers actually do on the street beyond making arrests. So, in this sense, they are something of a black box. We now turn to the question of how police are used. Much research has examined the crime-prevention effectiveness of alternative strategies for deploying police resources. This research has been conducted mostly by criminologists and sociologists. Among this group of researchers, the preferred research designs are quasi-experiments involving before-and-after studies of the effect of targeted interventions as well as true randomized experiments. The discussion that follows draws heavily on two excellent reviews of this research by Weisburd and Eck (2004) and by Braga (2008). As a preface to this summary, we draw the theoretical link between the police deployment and the certainty and severity of punishment. For the most part, deployment strategies affect the certainty of punishment through its impact on the probability of apprehension. However, notable examples are available in which severity also might be affected.

One way to increase apprehension risk is to employ police in a fashion that increases the probability that an offender is arrested after committing a crime. Studies of the effect of rapid response to calls for service (Kansas City Police Department, 1977; Spelman and Brown, 1981) found no evidence of a crime-prevention effect, but this outcome might be because most calls for service occur well after the crime event with the result that the perpetrator has fled the scene. Thus, it is doubtful that rapid response materially affects apprehension risk. Similarly, because most arrests result from the presence of witnesses or physical evidence, the general view of the criminology literature is that improvements in investigations beyond conventional canvassing for witnesses and collecting on-site physical evidence are not likely to yield material deterrent effects because, again, apprehension risk is not likely to be affected (National Research Council, 2004).

An alternative way to alter police employment after a crime is to change an officer's discretion as to whether to arrest a wrongdoer. A series of randomized experiments were conducted to test the deterrent effect of rules implementing mandatory arrest for domestic violence. The initial experiment conducted in Minneapolis by Sherman and Berk (1984) found that mandatory arrest rules were effective in reducing domestic violence reoffending. Findings from follow-up replication studies (as part of the so-called Spouse Assault Replication Program, or SARP) were inconsistent. Experiments in two cities found a deterrent effect, but no such effect was found in three other cities (Maxwell, Garner, and Fagan, 2002). Berk, Campbell, Klap, and Western (1992) found that the response to arrest in the SARP data differed across social background. Higher status individuals seemed to be deterred by arrest, whereas the assaultive behavior of lower status individuals seemed to be elevated. The heterogeneity in responses at both the citywide and the socioeconomic level is important because it illustrates a more general point; the response to sanction threats need not be uniform across or within the populations. Sherman (1993) proposed a theoretical explanation called defiance theory to explain the status-based heterogeneity in response to mandatory arrest. We are not aware of any theoretical explanation of the heterogeneity in cross-city effectiveness.

The second source of deterrence from police activities involves averting crime in the first place. In this circumstance, no apprehension takes place because no offense occurred. Thus, as discussed in the section titled Key Concepts, measures of apprehension risk based only on enforcement actions and crimes that actually occur, such as arrests per reported crime, are seriously incomplete because such measures do not capture the apprehension risk that attends criminal opportunities that were not acted on by potential offenders because the risk was deemed too high.

Cohen and Ludwig (2003) studied an example of a policing tactic deployed by the Pittsburgh Police Department that was designed to avert gun crimes from occurring in the first place. The tactic involved assigning additional police resources to selected high-crime communities within the city. These patrols were relieved from responding to citizen requests for service (911 calls) to work proactively to search for illegally carried guns. Police contacts were initiated mainly through traffic stops and "stop-and-talk" activities with pedestrians in public areas. Carrying open alcohol containers in public and traffic violations were frequent reasons for initiating contact. These targeted patrols were directed to two of Pittsburgh's five police zones that had unusually high crime rates. Cohen and Ludwig found that this heightened enforcement activity was associated with significant declines in shots fired and assault-related gunshot injuries.

Two other examples of police deployment strategies that have been shown to be effective in averting crime in the first place are "hot spots" policing and POP. Weisburd and Eck (2004) proposed a two-dimensional taxonomy of policing strategies. One dimension is "level of focus," and the other is "diversity of focus." Level of focus represents the degree to which police activities are targeted. Targeting can occur in a variety of ways, but Weisburd and Eck gave special attention to policing strategies that target police resources in small geographic areas (e.g., blocks or specific addresses) that have high levels of criminal activity—so-called crime hot spots.

The idea of hot spots policing stems from a striking empirical regularity uncovered by Sherman, Gartin, and Buerger (1989). Sherman et al. found that only 3% of addresses and intersections ("places," as they were called) in Minneapolis produced 50% of all calls to the police. Weisburd and Green (1995) found that 20% of all disorder crime and 14% of crimes against persons in Jersey City, New Jersey, originated from 56 drug crime hot spots. In a later study in Seattle, Washington, Weisburd and Eck (2004) reported that between 4% and 5%

of street segments in the city accounted for 50% of crime incidents for each year during a 14-year period. Other more recent studies finding comparable crime concentrations include Brantingham and Brantingham (1999), Eck, Gersh, and Taylor (2000), as well as Roncek (2000). Just like in the liquor store example, the rationale for concentrating police in crime hot spots is to create a prohibitively high risk of apprehension and thereby to deter crime at the hot spot in the first place.

The first test of the efficacy of concentrating police resources on crime hot spots was conducted by Sherman and Weisburd (1995). In this randomized experiment, hot spots in the experimental group were subjected to, on average, a doubling of police patrol intensity compared with hot spots in the control group. Declines in total crime calls ranged from 6% to 13%. In another randomized experiment, Weisburd and Green (1995) found that hot spots policing was similarly effective in suppressing drug markets, and Weisburd et al. (2006) found no evidence that hot spots policing simply displaced crime to nearby locations.

Braga's (2008) informative review of hot spots policing summarized the findings from nine experimental or quasi-experimental evaluations. The studies were conducted in five large U.S. cities and in one suburb of Australia. Crime-incident reports and citizen calls for service were used to evaluate impacts in and around the geographic area of the crime hot spot. The targets of the police actions varied. Some hot spots were generally high-crime locations, whereas others were characterized by specific crime problems like drug trafficking. All but two studies found evidence of significant reductions in crime. Furthermore, no evidence was found of material crime displacement to immediately surrounding locations. On the contrary, some studies found evidence of crime reductions, not increases, in the surrounding locations—a "diffusion of crime-control benefits" (Weisburd et al., 2006: 549) to non-targeted locales. We also note that the findings from the previously described econometric studies of focused police actions (e.g., in response to terror alert level) buttress the conclusion from the hot spots literature that the strategic targeting of police resources can be effective in reducing crime.

The second dimension of the Weisburd and Eck (2004) taxonomy is diversity of approaches. This dimension concerns the variety of approaches that police use to affect public safety. Low diversity is associated with reliance on time-honored law enforcement strategies for affecting the threat of apprehension (e.g., by dramatically increasing police presence). High diversity involves expanding beyond conventional practice to prevent crime. One example of a high-diversity approach is POP, which comes in so many different forms that (like pornography) it is regrettably hard to define, but the essence of POP is devising strategies for increasing the apprehension risk or for reducing criminal opportunities that are tailored to address the crime problem at a specific location (e.g., open-air drug market) or a specific type of activity (e.g., adolescents being victimized coming and going from school).

Weisburd, Telep, Hinkle, and Eck (2010) conducted a review of the POP evaluations and reported overwhelming support for its effectiveness. Although most evaluations are of low quality—little more than before-and-after studies—they identified ten studies with credible designs (i.e., randomized experiments or quasi-experiments with credible control comparisons). Eight of the ten studies reported statistically significant reductions in crime. Koper and Mayo-Wilson (2006) reviewed the evidence on the effectiveness of police crackdowns on illegal gun carrying and reported consistent evidence of the effectiveness of these efforts in reducing gun crime.

These findings are notable for our purposes. First, effect sizes vary considerably across interventions, which is a finding that reinforces our argument that police-related deterrent effects are heterogeneous; they depend on how the police are used and the circumstances in which they are used. A second and related point is that two interventions involved monitoring of probationers to avert probation revocation resulting from reoffending or from a violation of conditions of parole. This highlights the point that the police can be used effectively to deter crime not only at high-risk locations but also among high-risk individuals.

The observation that police can be used to affect the criminality of a high-risk individual brings us to another relevant literature—field interventions in which sanctions are focused specifically on high-risk groups. Like POP tactics, all interventions are multifaceted, but deterrence-based tactics are a core feature of each. In all cases, the deterrence component of the intervention involved an attempt to make sanction risk certain and salient to a selected high-risk group. In our judgment, these interventions deserve special attention because they provide a useful perspective on the promise and uncertainties of such focused deterrence-based interventions.

We begin by summarizing the findings of an underappreciated randomized experiment by Weisburd, Einat, and Kowalski (2008) that tested alternative strategies for incentivizing the payment of court-ordered fines. The most salient finding involves the "miracle of the cells," namely, that the imminent threat of incarceration is a powerful incentive for paying delinquent fines. The common feature of treatment conditions involving incarceration was a high certainty of imprisonment for failure to pay the fine. However, the fact that Weisburd et al. labeled the response the "miracle of the cells" and not the "miracle of certainty" is telling. Their choice of label is a reminder that certainty must result in a distasteful consequence, namely incarceration in this experiment, for it to be a deterrent. The consequences need not be draconian, just sufficiently costly to deter proscribed behavior.

The deterrence strategy of certain but non-draconian sanctions has been applied with apparently great success in Project Hope, an intervention heralded in Kleiman (2009), Hawken and Kleiman (2009), and Hawken (2010). Project Hope is a Hawaii-based probation enforcement program. In a randomized experiment, probationers assigned to Project Hope had much lower rates of positive drug tests, missed appointments, and most importantly, were significantly less likely to be arrested and imprisoned. The cornerstone of the Hope intervention was regular drug testing, including random tests, and certain but short punishment periods of confinement (i.e., 1–2 days) for positive drug tests or other violations of conditions of probation. Thus, both the Weisburd et al. (2008) fine experiment and Project Hope show that highly certain punishment can be an effective deterrent to those for whom deterrence previously has been ineffective in averting crime.

The strategy of certain punishment is also a centerpiece of field interventions in Boston, Richmond, and Chicago that are aimed specifically at reducing gun violence. However, unlike Project Hope and the fine-paying experiment, the certain punishment is far more draconian—a lengthy prison sentence. For descriptions of the Boston intervention called Operation Ceasefire, see Kennedy, Braga, Piehl, and Waring (2001); the Richmond intervention called Project Exile, see Raphael and Ludwig (2003); and the Chicago-based intervention, see Papachristos, Meares, and Fagan (2007). A common feature of each intervention was commitment to federal prosecution for gun crimes that, on conviction, allowed for lengthy prison sentences. Notably, concerted efforts also were made to communicate the threat of certain and severe punishment to selected high-risk groups (e.g., members of violent gangs). All interventions claimed to have substantial success in reducing gun crime, but at least for Boston and Richmond, questions have been raised about whether the declines preceded the intervention or were no different than other comparable urban centers (Cook and Ludwig, 2006; Raphael and Ludwig, 2003). These concerns notwithstanding, each of these interventions illustrates the potential for combining elements of both certainty and severity enhancement to generate a targeted deterrent effect. Additional evaluations of the efficacy of this strategy should be a high priority.

Taken as whole, the literature on the preventive effect of policing contains much persuasive evidence that police prevent crime. It also makes clear that the effects of police on crime are heterogeneous. Not all methods for deploying police are comparably effective in reducing crime; indeed some deployment strategies seem to be completely ineffective. Thus, policy recommendations for increasing police resources to prevent crime are incomplete without more elaboration on how they should be used. We are thus sympathetic with the intellectual tradition in the police deployment literature of testing the effectiveness of alternative strategies for using police resources. We return to this observation in the conclusions.

Policy Implications and Future Research

The key empirical conclusions of our literature review are that at prevailing levels of certainty and severity, relatively little reliable evidence of variation in the severity of punishment having a substantial deterrent effect is available and that relatively strong evidence indicates that variation in the certainty of punishment has a large deterrent effect, particularly from the vantage point of specific programs that alter the use of police. In this section, we discuss how to translate these two general findings into policy recommendations. We divide these recommendations into the following categories: general and specific.

With respect to broad conclusions, we believe that it is reasonably clear that lengthy prison sentences particularly in the form of mandatory minimum statutes such as California's three strikes law are difficult to justify on a deterrence-based, crime-prevention basis. They might be justifiable based on either incapacitation benefits or along retributive lines. Although we have not surveyed the evidence on incapacitation, we are skeptical of the incapacitative efficiency of incarcerating aged criminals. The empirical evidence on the negative relationship between crime and age is strong (Farrington, 1986; Hirschi and Gottfredson, 1983). Although we certainly recognize that a subset of the population persists for which incapacitation is appropriate, a crude law such as three strikes does not provide a plausible screening mechanism for identifying these individuals. For the general incarceration of aged criminals to be socially efficient, it must have a deterrent effect on younger criminals, and the theoretical arguments we have made on discounting as well as the evidence we have presented on severity call such a deterrent effect into question. Simply no reliable evidence is available that such an effect is sufficiently large to justify the costs of long prison sentences. Furthermore, we are skeptical that a convincing ethical argument can be advanced for imposing a 25-year or more prison sentence for even a third-strike offense unless it is serious. Thus, we conclude that mandatory minimum statues requiring lengthy sentences for repeat offenders either be repealed or greatly narrowed in terms of applicable offenses so that the sanction is reserved for repeat offenders who also commit serious crimes involving violence or large property losses. See Tonry (2009) for an extended discussion of this conclusion.

If one takes the total resources devoted to crime prevention as fixed, then our conclusions about the marginal deterrent effects of certainty and severity suggest that crime prevention would be enhanced by shifting resources from imprisonment to policing. In 2006, nationwide expenditures on police and corrections totaled $168 billion with policing receiving 59% of this total (BJS). Our analysis does not provide specific guidance on how much the police share should be increased, but it is a realistic possibility that even a modest shift in resources away from imprisonment could reduce both crime and imprisonment. This conclusion follows from a shift of resources toward policies that exploit the high values of e_p and away from policies associated with the low values of e_L. Another possible candidate beneficiary beside the police for a crime-reducing resource shift are enhanced probation and parole supervision services along the lines of Project Hope. According to a 2009 BJS report by Bonczar and Glaze, for the year 2008, nearly 4.3 million individuals were on probation and more than .8 million were on parole. The failure rates among these individuals were high. Glaze and Bonczar reported that in 2008 approximately 400,000 probationers and 200,000 paroles were admitted to state prisons or local jails for probation/parole violations or for new crimes. Thus, probation and parole monitoring systems that are effective in reducing failure rates potentially could result in large reductions in crimes committed by probationers and parolees and in jail and prison admissions.

However, even such apparently self-evident conclusions might be difficult to translate into a defensible operational plan beyond a strong recommendation against any additional escalation of sentence length for initially high sentences. We mention this because our recommendations leave open many questions about the way the resources should be used in the pursuit of high e_p policies. In the context of our discussion, a shift of resources toward policing can lead to a range of changes, including more police, better logistics, and so on. The statistical literature on police resources and crime rates provides little guidance on how those resources should be used. Likewise, no demonstration has been given that probation/parole-monitoring systems designed along the lines of Project Hope can be replicated generally in settings outside the small island state of Hawaii. The success of the monitoring system clearly depends on the support and coordinated efforts of judges, parole/probation officers, and the police. The failure of intensive supervision probation to reduce recidivism rates is an object lesson in the difficulties of designing effective probation/parole-monitoring systems (MacKenzie, 2002; Petersilia, 1998)[15] and should lead to circumspection in claiming that Project Hope can be extrapolated to the rest of the United States.

Our caveat on the difficulty of providing general policy advice from the existing literature is no deeper than the recognition that the details of any policy changes that simultaneously reduce sentences and shift the resource savings to policing, probation, and parole supervision matter. The literature on the crime-prevention effects of different strategies for mobilizing the police makes it clear that the way police resources are allocated is of first-order importance. This literature has assembled an impressive body of evidence that the so-called standard model of policing, which involves the non-strategic use of preventive patrols, rapid response to calls for service, and improved investigation methods, is not effective in deterring crime (National Research Council, 2004; Weisburd and Eck, 2004). A range of strategic uses of police (e.g., hot spot policing) have been shown to be effective. Also, certain forms of so-called POP have shown promise. At the same time, substantial heterogeneity in the specific policies that have been studied as well as the substantial heterogeneity is found in the effects of particular policies that the existing research has examined. This finding means that one cannot make a recommendation about the expansion of police resources that is as general as our recommendation that lengthy sentences be reduced and that large changes in penalties at the age of majority are undesirable. We thus close with a discussion of the type of research that in our judgment will be most effective in delineating the details of a policy that will achieve this policy objective.

We preface this discussion with an important caveat concerning our emphasis on identifying high-elasticity sanction policies, particularly those in which $e > 1$. Ultimately, a criminal justice policy, assuming it passes a priori justice considerations, should be judged

---

15. In addition, the question of the mechanism by which the resources would be transferred has not been addressed. As mentioned, imprisonment is, by and large, a state and federal function, whereas policing is, by and large, a local function.

on whether its benefits exceed its costs, including broad social conceptions of the costs of imprisonment. Policies with elasticities less than 1 might pass a benefit–cost test even though they increase prison population. Likewise, policies with elasticities greater than 1 that are costly to implement might fail the benefit–cost test even though they reduce prison populations. Still, in terms of policy evaluation, the message that these theoretical conditions are meant to convey is that high-elasticity polices are, other things being equal, more desirable than low-elasticity policies and that in principle no logical requirement exists that lower crime means higher imprisonment. The latter is important because of widespread concerns about the social costs of mass incarceration. So, in conjunction with the evaluation of policy effects on crime and imprisonment, clear delineation is needed of the overall costs of the policy.

We are skeptical that large numbers of $e_L > 1$ severity policies exist and that many high-elasticity severity policies exist even if this threshold is not met. In contrast, we are optimistic that viable police deployment strategies might produce $e_p > 1$ and strongly believe that the empirical evidence indicates high-elasticity, certainty-based policies exist. The identification of high-elasticity police deployment strategies thus should be a top priority. Although we know of no research that identifies policing strategies for which $e_p > 1$, the paucity of evidence does not imply the nonexistence of such policies. One issue might be research design. Assuming the postapprehension probability of imprisonment remains unchanged, a policing strategy that is effective in reducing both crime and imprisonment will reduce both the per capita crime rate and the per capita arrest rate. Police deployment research routinely measures effectiveness by the former measure but never measures effectiveness by the latter measure. Future research should measure both. Finally, we reiterate a point we made earlier; even if policing strategies with elasticities greater than 1 are scarce, substituting higher elasticity policing strategies for lower elasticity severity policies will reduce both crime and imprisonment.

What types of deployment strategies are good candidates for high-elasticity policies? We speculate that strategies that result in large and visible shifts in apprehension risk are the most likely to have deterrent effects that are large enough to reduce not only crime but also apprehensions. Hot spots policing might have this characteristic. More generally, the types of POP described and championed by Kennedy (2009) and by Kleiman (2009) have the common feature of targeting enforcement resources on selected high-crime people or places. Also, the multimodal approach to preventing crime among high-risk groups that combines deterrent and reintegration tactics described in Papachristos et al. (2007) is a creative example of a "carrot-and-stick" approach to crime prevention. Although the effectiveness of these strategies for focusing police and other criminal justice resources has yet to be demonstrated, priority attention should be given to their continued evaluation, particularly as they relate the "carrot" component of the intervention. Sanction-related interventions do not have to consist entirely of negative incentives. Interventions can include opportunities for job training as in Papachristos et al. (2007) or for reduced monitoring as a reward

Durlauf and Nagin

for compliance with program requirements in Project Hope. The effectiveness of positive incentives is an understudied topic. Also, as noted, a thorough evaluation of adaptations of the Project Hope program for probation-monitoring settings outside of Hawaii and for parole monitoring should be a similarly high priority.

Research on targeted enforcement tactics also should focus on intangible costs. A heightened police presence might aggravate long-standing grievances of community residents with the police if the tactics involve more aggressive policing tactics such as "stop and frisk" and more generally create tension and suspicion between the police and the residents.[16] Not only are such social costs important in their own right, but over the long term, they might erode any crime-control benefits that the tactics might induce initially. We also note that although little evidence indicates that increased severity is an effective deterrent, the literature is small and mostly focused on severity increments to already lengthy sentences. It is thus important to understand the circumstances better in which severity can be an effective deterrent. As we have noted, the fine payment experiment conducted by Weisburd et al. (2008) and the Project Hope experiment made it clear that the imminent threat of incarceration is a powerful incentive for paying delinquent fines or for conforming with conditions of probation even for populations who have not been deterred previously by the threat of punishment. These experiments suggest that the sanction need not be draconian to deter proscribed behavior. As we discussed, a non-linear relationship might exist between the magnitude of deterrent effects and sentence lengths. Sentence lengths in Western European countries tend to be far shorter than in the United States. For example, more than 90% of sentences in the Netherlands are less than 1 year (Nieuwbeerta, Nagin, and Blokland, 2009). Research based in European data on the deterrent effect of shorter sentence length should be a priority.

Another dimension of international research that potentially might be useful involves the identification of countries that have been successful in achieving a low crime rate and a low imprisonment equilibrium based at least in part on the strategic use of policing. Important issues that should be addressed are the ways in which police are used to achieve this equilibrium. Are proactive efforts made to reduce police–citizen frictions when more aggressive tactics are used? To what degree do police attempt to mobilize informal sources of social control within the community to prevent crime?[17]

We have made brief reference to a large literature on sanction risk perceptions. As emphasized in Nagin (1998), deterrent effects ultimately are determined by perceptions of sanction risk and severity. The literature on sanction risk perceptions shows that little correspondence takes place between perceptions and reality. For at least two reasons, this is

---

16. See, for example, a recent newspaper account of tensions created by the New York City Police Department's stop-and-frisk tactics in a high rate neighborhood (Rivera, Baker, and Roberts, 2010).

17. We thank an anonymous reviewer for this suggestion.

not surprising. First, for most people, knowledge of actual sanctions is not relevant because, for moral, social, or economic reasons, they are not even remotely close to the margin of committing crime. Second, sanction risks and severity are not posted like most market prices. Instead, for the criminally inclined, they must be learned from experience or by word of mouth. This is why the work of Lochner (2007), Hjalmarsson (2009), as well as Anwar and Loughran (2009) on Bayesian updating of sanction risk perceptions based on experience with detection and non-detection for crimes committed is so important and should be extended. Likewise, a small body of research examines how criminal opportunity characteristics affect sanction risk perceptions (Klepper and Nagin, 1989a, 1989b). This type of work should focus particularly on how police deployment tactics affect perceptions of apprehension risk. As emphasized in the section titled The Interrelationship of the Crime and Imprisonment Rates, the rate at which police apprehend the actual perpetrators of crime is an incomplete signal of the overall risk of apprehension posed by the police because it does not measure the apprehension risk the police pose for criminal opportunities that were not acted on because the perceived risk of apprehension was deemed too high. To understand better the mechanism by which police presence might deter, innovative approaches for how police tactics affect perceptions of apprehension risk are required. Ethnographic research methods might be helpful in doing this research, but the development of quantitative approaches also should be a high priority.

We also recommend additional research on the determinants of criminal decision making. Although much work has been done on the formation of beliefs by criminals, as far as we know, no studies exist of whether criminals or non-criminals near the margin of a criminal choice are described better by nonexpected utility decision making than by the standard expected utility theory. In Durlauf and Nagin (in press), we discussed the relevance of nonexpected utility models to studying deterrence. At the risk of oversimplifying a complex body of work, considerable evidence exists that many individuals tend to overweight small probabilities and underweight large probabilities relative to standard expected utility calculations. Furthermore, this probability weighting follows an inverse S shape, which means that larger changes are found in the weights for large and small probabilities than for others. This finding suggests that an additional candidate explanation for the relatively robust evidence that increases in certainty of punishment lower crime in contexts such as hot spot policing is that such policing tactics are being implemented in a circumstance in which standard policing practice projects only a small probability of apprehension, so although the probability might be overweighted, changes in the probability lead to relatively large changes in behavior. Berns, Capra, Moore, and Noussair (2007) found evidence of this type of behavior in an experiment in which the "rewards" were electric shocks, which suggests the relevance of this theory for adverse outcomes (i.e., punishments). These types of findings matter because they suggest that the way in which the probability of apprehension p affects crime choices might be more complicated than it seems in specifications such as the one described in footnote 3.

Research on the deterrent effect of sentence length and more generally on the effects of changes in sentencing statutes on crime rates and imprisonment rates seriously is hampered by the lack of data on the distribution of sentence lengths and time served by different types of offenders across states. Such evidence is crucial for studying the deterrent and incapacitative effects of prison sanctions and for projecting impacts on crime rates and imprisonment rates of changes in prison sanction policies. Such data can be assembled for selected states from prison census data. Prison census data should be expanded to include all 50 states and should be made available in an easily accessible and manipulable format.

Nagin et al. (in press) lay out key elements of a research program on the effects of the experience of imprisonment on reoffending. These elements include the following: (a) measuring the dose–response relationship between the length of imprisonment and the reoffending rate and between the number of times imprisoned and the reoffending rate; (b) understanding how the experience of punishment affects perceptions of sanction risk; (c) analyzing the mechanisms by which the experience of imprisonment might be criminogenic; and (d) estimating the effect on reoffending of different non-custodial sanctions. This program also should be an integral part of an overall policy-oriented research program of sanction effects on crime.[18]

We would add to Nagin et al.'s (in press) list two additional elements. First, policy research should be more sensitive to heterogeneity and move away from the idea that policy effects are constant across jurisdictions. Although one can name many studies that relax homogeneity assumptions, we believe this relaxation should be the norm. Evidence that a given policy is efficacious in one jurisdiction but not in another is not a mark against the policy. Rather, such evidence means that local context matters for policy efficacy. In our judgment, research should identify a portfolio of policies that have been demonstrated to be effective in well-defined sets of circumstances. The local actors in the criminal justice system possess information not available at a more aggregated level; this information should be exploited in the choices of particular policies because they will have superior information on local context. This outcome raises a second additional point. In our view, a neglected area of policy evaluation concerns the incentives of local actors such as the police and prosecutors under alternative criminal sanction policies. In other words, the design of sanction policies needs to ensure that the incentives of the police and others are such that they act in a way to maximize policy effectiveness. For example, the evidence amassed in Loftin et al. (1983) and Loftin and McDowell (1981, 1984) that sentence add-ons for gun use did not seem to

---

18. One example of the relevance of this sanction experience research agenda for the policy conclusions of this article is that if the potentially criminogenic effects of imprisonment are mostly a result of sentence length, then this finding would reinforce our arguments for shorter sentences. However, if it is mostly a result of stigma, not sentence length, then this finding would call into question a policy of short but certain sentences. At this time, the empirical evidence is not sufficient to distinguish each of these two plausible alternative explanations for criminogenic effects.

increase sentence lengths suggests that judges and prosecutors for some reason were resistant to their application.

A final area where more research is needed concerns the sanction effect we have not addressed—incapacitation. As we have emphasized repeatedly, deterrence effects are necessary for it to be possible for a sanction policy to reduce both crime and punishment. This conclusion, however, does not imply that crime prevention by incapacitation does not have a role to play in crime-control policy. Furthermore, incapacitation, if strong enough, can lead to policy changes that reduce crime at the cost of greater imprisonment and so work against the spirit of our argument.

However, the fact that incapacitation might be appropriate for some criminals does not mean that imprisonment needs to be nearly so widespread as it is. An efficient use of incapacitation requires the technical capacity for prospectively identifying high-rate offenders based on legally defensible characteristics. We believe that the mass incarceration found in contemporary America is mixing prisoners with different sensitivities to deterrence, in particular, and with different crime proclivities, in general; hence, incapacitation can go hand in hand with a reduction of crime and imprisonment via an effective use of deterrence. Justice also requires that the identification technology not produce unacceptably large numbers of false positives. The incapacitation of false-positive, high-rate offenders not only wastes prison resources but also is a source of social injustice. To our knowledge, no proven technology exists for the ex ante identification of high-rate offenders with acceptable false-positive rates. However, this does not mean that such a technical capacity might not be feasible; recent work by Berk, Sherman, Barnes, Kurtz, and Ahlman (2009) is an example of efforts to use sophisticated statistical methods to achieve accurate predictions. Thus, we also recommend that more research be done on developing this prediction capacity. In addition, effective incapacitation policies will involve fairly intricate considerations of the sentencing structure so that sentence lengths efficiently use information on recidivism probabilities. It is not clear that such subtlety can be made operational. Nevertheless, we emphasize that any policy adjustments designed to reduce crime and imprisonment via deterrent effects should account for possible incapacitation effects. We believe these effects are implausible in the context of long sentences. But we could imagine that incapacitation might undermine a deterrent-based argument to reduce sentences for young offenders.

Although sound empirical evidence must be a core element of a crime-control policy based on science, policy cannot be based on empirical evidence alone. It also must be based on sound theory because, just as in medicine in which evidence on treatment effectiveness cannot cover all medical contingencies, evidence on sanction effectiveness cannot cover all crime contingencies related to sanction policy. Physicians must make judgments about treatment recommendations based both on evidence and on their theoretical knowledge of the functioning of the human body. Similarly, crime-control policy as it relates to criminal sanctions and the deployment of the criminal justice system (CJS) must combine discrete pieces of empirical evidence with theory on the response to the sanction threats created by the CJS. To this end, in Durlauf and Nagin (in press), we laid out several proposals for generalizing the economic model of crime to account for psychological and sociological aspects of criminal behavior. Thus, we urge the reverse of this form of disciplinary generalization for noneconomic models of crime, namely that they incorporate aspects of the choice-based focus of the economic model.

Implementation of our policy and research recommendations poses significant institutional challenges. One concerns devising a system for transferring resources from corrections, which is primarily a state-level function, to policing, which is primarily a local-level function. Although states routinely make state-to-local-level transfers for other functions such as education, transportation, and community development, a transfer from corrections to policing poses some special challenges. In most states, variations in crime rates across local police jurisdiction are large. Thus, devising a politically feasible mechanism for transferring resources to the highest need locales likely will be difficult. A related problem is devising a mechanism for monitoring the use of the transfers to ensure that resources are used effectively to reduce crime. Designing such a system of monitoring is difficult both because of the large gaps in knowledge about what constitutes effective use and the importance of honoring local independence.

A second institutional challenge concerns research infrastructure. The research agenda that we outline is ambitious and will require the type of sustained and substantial resource commitment that only the federal government can provide. The National Institutes of Health are the model we have in mind for the way this research program should be administered. The obvious candidate for taking on this responsibility is the National Institute of Justice (NIJ). However, for the NIJ to manage such a research program effectively along the lines of an NIH institute, it is incumbent that it adopt the reforms outlined in the recently released National Research Council report *Strengthening Scientific Research and Development at the National Institute of Justice*. We, thus, lend our full support to the report's recommendations.[19]

Finally, we emphasize the importance of recognizing the limits to knowledge faced by policy makers. To some degree, gaps in empirical knowledge can be filled by more complete theory. However, even with better theory, substantial and irreducible empirical uncertainties will remain. In our judgment, far too many proposals for crime amelioration take a single study as their basis or use a subset of studies from a broader literature. Instead, we believe that policy recommendations should be based on cumulative evidence from statistically and scientifically sound research and should place particular value on evidence of the effectiveness of specific crime-control treatments. This emphasis has a strong analogy to the medical literature in which evidence of the efficacy of a particular drug regimen or a specific preventive measure is of the highest value. We also would conjecture that more

---

19. In the interest of full disclosure, one of the authors (Nagin) was a member of the National Research Council committee responsible for this report.

attention should be paid to the effects of policies on particular types of crimes. Again, in the spirit of the medical analogy, policies that are effective for one type of crime might have little effect on others. For example, hot spots policing is unlikely to be effective in reducing crimes such as domestic violence or other crimes that generally occur in non-public places (most homicides occur outdoors). Our argument is that just as in medicine in which a portfolio of treatments is required to address a heterogeneous range of diseases, a well-designed crime-control policy requires a portfolio of crime-control treatments to address diversity in the type of crimes and in the people who commit them.

References

Andenaes, Johannes. 1974. *Punishment and Deterrence*. Ann Arbor: University of Michigan Press.

Anwar, Shamena and Thomas Loughran. 2009. *Testing a Bayesian Learning Theory of Deterrence among Serious Juvenile Offenders*. Unpublished manuscript, School of Public Policy and Management, Carnegie Mellon University, Pittsburgh, PA.

Apel, R. and Daniel S. Nagin. 2009. Deterrence. In (James Q. Wilson and Joan Petersilia, eds.), *Crime*, 4th Edition. Oxford, U.K.: Oxford University Press.

Avio, Kenneth L. and C. Scott Clark. 1974. *Property Crime in Canada: An Econometric Study*. Toronto, Ontario, Canada: Toronto University Press.

Becsi, Zsolt. 1999. Economics and crime in the states. *Federal Reserve Bank of Atlanta Economic Review*, First Quarter: 38–49.

Becker, Gary S. 1968. Crime and punishment: An economic analysis. *Journal of Political Economy*, 78: 169–217.

Berk, Richard A., Alec Campbell, Ruth Klap, and Bruce Western. 1992. The deterrent effect of arrest in incidents of domestic violence: A Bayesian analysis of four field experiments. *American Sociological Review*, 57: 698–708.

Berk, Richard A., Lawrence Sherman, Geoffrey Barnes, Ellen Kurtz, and Lindsay Ahlman. 2009. Forecasting murder within a population of probationers and parolees: A high stakes application of statistical learning. *Journal of the Royal Statistical Association, Series A*, 172: 191–211.

Bernburg, Jon Gunnar and Marvin D. Krohn. 2003. Labeling, life chances, and adult crime: The direct and indirect effects of official intervention in adolescence on crime in early adulthood. *Criminology*, 41: 1287–1318.

Berns, Gregory S., C. Monica Capra, Sara Moore, and Charles Noussair. 2007. A shocking experiment: New evidence on probability weighting and common ratio valuations. *Judgment and Decision Making*, 2: 234–242.

Blume, Lawrence E., William A. Brock, Steven N. Durlauf, and Yannis M. Ioannides. In press. Identification of social interactions. In (Jess Benhabib, Alberto Bisin, and Matt Jackson, eds.), *Handbook of Social Economics*.

Blumstein, Alfred, Jacqueline Cohen, and Daniel Nagin. 1978. *Deterrence and Incapacitation: Estimating the Effects of Criminal Sanctions on Crime Rates*. Washington, DC: National Academies Press.

Blumstein, Alfred and Daniel S. Nagin. 1978. On the optimal use of incarceration. *Operations Research*, 26: 381–405.

Bonczar, Thomas and Lauren Glaze. 2008. *Adults on Parole, Federal and State-by-State, 1975–2008*. Washington, DC: Bureau of Justice Statistics.

Borghans, Lex, Angela Duckworth, James Heckman, and Bas ter Weel. 2008. The economics and psychology of personality traits. *Journal of Human Resources*, 43: 972–1059.

Braga, Anthony A. 2008. *Police Enforcement Strategies to Prevent Crime in Hot Spot Areas*. Crime Prevention Research Review (No. 2). Washington, DC: Office of Community Oriented Policing, U.S. Department of Justice.

Brantingham, Patricia L and Paul J. Brantingham. 1999. Theoretical model of crime hot spot generation. *Studies on Crime and Crime Prevention*, 8: 7–26.

Bureau of Justice Statistics (BJS). 2008. *Sourcebook of criminal justice statistics Online*. Retrieved April 23, 2010 from http://www.albany.edu/sourcebook/pdf/t6282008.pdf, Table 6.28.2008.

Carr-Hill, R. A. and Nicholas Stern. 1973. An econometric model of the supply and control of recorded offenses in England and Wales. *Journal of Public Economics*, 2: 289–318.

Clear, Todd R. 2007. *Imprisoning Communities: How Mass Incarceration Makes Disadvantaged Neighborhoods Worse*. Oxford, U.K.: Oxford University Press.

Cohen, Jacqueline and Jens Ludwig. 2003. Policing gun crime. In (Jens Ludwig and Philip J. Cook, eds.), *Evaluating Gun Policy*. Washington, DC: Brookings Institution Press.

Cook, Philip J. 1979. The clearance rate as a measure of criminal justice system effectiveness. *Journal of Public Economics*, 11: 135–142.

Cook Philip J. and Jens Ludwig. 2006. Aiming for evidenced-based gun policy. *Journal of Policy Analysis and Management*, 25: 691–735.

Corman, Hope and H. Naci Mocan. 2000. A time-series analysis of crime, deterrence, and drug abuse in New York City. *American Economic Review*, 90: 584–604.

Cullen, Francis T. 2002. Rehabilitation and treatment programs. In (James Q. Wilson and Joan Petersilia, eds.), *Crime: Public Policies for Crime Control*. Oakland, CA: ICS Press.

DeAngelo, Greg and Benjamin Hansen. 2008. *Life and Death in the Fast Lane: Police Enforcement and Roadway Safety*. Unpublished manuscript, Department of Economics, UC Santa Barbara, Santa Barbara, CA.

Di Tella, Rafael and Ernesto Schargrodsky. 2004. Do police reduce crime? Estimates using the allocation of police forces after a terrorist attack. *American Economic Review*, 94: 115–133.

Doob, Anthony N. and Cheryl M. Webster. 2003. Sentence severity and crime: Accepting the null hypothesis. In (Michael H. Tonry, ed.), *Crime and Justice: A Review of Research*, Vol. 30. Chicago, IL: University of Chicago Press.

Donohue, John. 2009. Assessing the relative benefits of incarceration: The overall change over the previous decades and the benefits on the margin. In (Stephen Raphael and Michael A. Stoll, eds.), *Do Prisons Make Us Safer? The Benefits and Costs of the Prison Boom*. New York: Russell Sage Foundation.

Draca, Mirko, Stephen Machin, and Robert Witt. 2008. *Panic on the Streets of London: Police, Crime and the July 2005 Terror Attacks*. IZA Discussion Paper no. 3410. Bonn, Germany: Institute for the Study of Labor.

Durlauf, Steven F. and Daniel S. Nagin. In press. The deterrent effect of imprisonment. In (Philip J. Cook, Jens Ludwig, and Justin McCrary, eds.), *Controlling Crime: Strategies and Tradeoffs* Chicago, IL: University of Chicago Press.

Durlauf, Steven N., Salvador Navarro, and David A. Rivers. 2008. On the interpretation of aggregate crime regressions. In (Arthur S. Goldberger and Richard Rosenfeld, eds.), *Crime Trends*. Washington, DC: National Academy of Sciences Press.

Durlauf, Steven F., Salvador Navarro, and David A. Rivers. In press. Understanding aggregate crime regressions. *Journal of Econometrics.*

Eck, John E., Jeffery Gersh, and Charlene Taylor. 2000. Finding crime hot spots through repeat address mapping. In (Victor Goldsmith, Phili G. McGuire, John H. Mollenkopf, and Timothy A. Ross, eds.), *Analyzing Crime Patterns: Frontiers of Practice*. Thousand Oaks, CA: Sage.

Evans, William N. and Emily G. Owens. 2007. COPS and crime. *Journal of Public Economics*, 91: 181–201.

Farrington, David P. 1986. Age and crime. In (Michael H. Tonry and Norval Morris, eds.), *Crime and Justice: An Annual Review of Research*, Vol. 7. Chicago, IL: University of Chicago Press.

Freeman, Richard B. 1996. Why do so many young American men commit crimes and what might we do about it? *Journal of Economic Perspectives*, 10: 25–42.

Garland, David. 2001. *The Culture of Control: Crime and Social Order in Contemporary Society*. Chicago, IL: University of Chicago Press.

Greenwood, Peter and Angela Hawken. 2002. *An Assessment of the Effect of California's Three-Strikes Law*. Working Paper. Toronto, Ontario, Canada: Greenwood Associates.

Glueck, Sheldon and Eleanor Glueck. 1950. *Unraveling Delinquency*. New York: The Commonwealth Fund.

Hagan, John and Alberto. Palloni. 1990. The social reproduction of a criminal class in working-class London 1950–1980. *American Journal of Sociology*, 96: 265–299.

Hawkins, Gordon. 1976. *The Prison: Policy and Practice*. Chicago, IL: Chicago University Press.

Hawken, Angela. 2010. Behavioral triage: A new model for identifying and treating substance-abusing offenders. *Journal of Drug Policy Analysis*, 3: 1–5.

Hawken, Angela and Mark Kleiman. 2009. *Managing Drug-Involved Probationers with Swift and Certain Sanctions: Evaluating Hawaii's HOPE*. NCJ 229023. Washington, DC: National Institute of Justice.

Heaton, Paul. In press. Understanding the effects of anti-profiling policies. *Journal of Law and Economics.*

Heckman, J., L. Malofeeva, R. Pinto, and P. Savelyev. 2010. *Understanding the Mechanisms Through Which an Influential Early Childhood Program Boosted Adult Outcomes*. Chicago, IL: University of Chicago.

Helland, Eric and Alexander Tabarrok. 2007. Does three strikes deter? A nonparametric estimation. *Journal of Human Resources*, 42: 309–330.

Hirschi, Travis and Michael R. Gottfredson. 1983. Age and the explanation of crime. *American Journal of Sociology*, 89: 552–584.

Hjalmarsson, Randi. 2009. Crime and expected punishment: Changes in perceptions at the age of criminal majority. *American Law and Economics Review*, 7: 209–248.

Horney, Julie and Ineke Haen Marshall. 1992. Risk perceptions among serious offenders: The role of crime and punishment. *Criminology*, 30: 575–593.

Irwin, John. 2005. *The Warehouse Prison: Disposal of the New Dangerous Class*. Los Angeles, CA: Roxbury Press.

Jolliffe, Darrick and David P. Farrington. 2009. A systematic review of the relationship between childhood impulsiveness and later violence. In (Mary McMurran and Richard C. Howard, eds.), *Personality, Personality Disorder, and Violence*. New York: Wiley.

Kansas City Police Department. 1977. *Response Time Analysis*. Kansas City, MO: Author.

Kennedy, David M. 2009. *Deterrence and Crime Prevention: Reconsidering the Prospect of Sanction*. New York: Routledge.

Kennedy, David M., Anthony A. Braga, Anne M. Piehl, and Elin J. Waring. 2001. *Reducing Gun Violence: The Boston Gun Project's Operation Ceasefire*. Washington, DC: National Institute of Justice.

Kessler, Daniel P. and Steven D. Levitt. 1999. Using sentence enhancements to distinguish between deterrence and incapacitation. *Journal of Law and Economics*, 42: 343–363.

Klepper, Steven and Daniel S. Nagin. 1989a. The deterrent effect of perceived certainty and severity revisited. *Criminology*, 27: 721–746.

Klepper, Steven and Daniel S. Nagin. 1989b. The anatomy of tax evasion. *Journal of Law, Economics and Organization*, 5: 1–24.

Kleiman, Mark A. R. 2009. *When Brute Force Fails: How to Have Less Crime and Less Punishment*. Princeton, NJ: Princeton University Press.

Klick, Jonathan and Alexander Tabarrok. 2005. Using terror alert levels to estimate the effect of police on crime. *Journal of Law and Economics*, 48: 267–279.

Koper, Christopher S. and Evan Mayo-Wilson. 2006. Police crackdowns on illegal gun carrying: A systematic review of their impact on gun crime. *Journal of Experimental Criminology*, 2: 227–261.

Lee, D. and J. McCrary. 2009. *The Deterrent Effect of Prison: Dynamic Theory and Evidence*. Unpublished manuscript, Department of Economics, Princeton University, Princeton, NJ.

Levitt, Steven D. 1996. The effect of prison population size on crime rates: Evidence from prison overcrowding legislation. *Quarterly Journal of Economics*, 111: 319–352.

Levitt, Steven D. 1997. Using electoral cycles in police hiring to estimate the effect of police on crime. *American Economic Review*, 87: 270–290.

Levitt, Steven D. 1998. Juvenile crime and punishment. *Journal of Political Economy*, 106: 1156–1185.

Levitt, Steven D. 2002. Using electoral cycles in police hiring to estimate the effect of police on crime: Reply. *American Economic Review*, 92: 1244–1250.

Levitt, Steven D. 2006. The case of the critics who missed the point: A reply to Webster et al. *Criminology & Public Policy*, 5: 449–460.

Liedka, Raymond, Anne Piehl, and Bert Useem. 2006. The crime-control effect of incarceration: Does scale matter? *Criminology and Public Policy*, 5: 245–276.

Liptak, Adam. 2008. American exception: Inmate count in U.S. dwarfs other nations. *New York Times*. Retrieved April 23, 2010 from nytimes.com/2008/04/23/us/23prison.

Ljungvist, Lars. 2008. Lucas critique. In (Steven N. Durlauf and Lawrence E. Blume, eds.), *New Palgrave Dictionary of Economics*, Revised Edition. London, U.K.: Palgave MacMillan.

Lochner, Lance, 2007. Individual perceptions of the criminal justice system. *American Economic Review*, 97: 444–460.

Loftin, Colin, Milton Heumann, and David McDowall. 1983. Mandatory sentencing and firearms violence: Evaluating an alternative to gun control. *Law & Society Review*, 17: 287–318.

Loftin, Colin and David McDowall. 1981. "One with a gun gets you two": Mandatory sentencing and firearms violence in Detroit. *Annals of the American Academy of Political and Social Science*, 455: 150–167.

Loftin, Colin and David McDowall. 1984. The deterrent effects of the Florida felony firearm law. *Journal of Criminal Law and Criminology*, 75: 250–259.

MacKenzie, Doris L. 2002. Reducing the criminal activities of known offenders and delinquents: Crime prevention in the courts and corrections. In (Lawrence Sherman, David P. Farrington, Brandon C. Welsh, and Doris L. MacKenzie, eds.), *Evidence-Based Crime Prevention*. London, U.K.: Routledge.

Marvell, Thomas B. and Carlise E. Moody. 1994. Prison population growth and crime reduction. *Journal of Quantitative Criminology*, 10: 109–140.

Matsueda, Ross. 1992. Reflected appraisal, parental labeling, and delinquency: Specifying a symbolic interactionist theory. *American Journal of Sociology*, 97: 1577–1611.

Maxwell, Christopher D., Joel H. Garner, and Jeffrey Fagan. 2002. The preventive effects of arrest on intimate partner violence: Research, policy and theory. *Criminology & Public Policy*, 2: 51–80.

McCrary, Justin. 2002. Using electoral cycles in police hiring to estimate the effect of police on crime: Comment. *American Economic Review*, 92: 1236–1243.

McDowall, David, Colin Loftin, and Brian Wiersema. 1992. A comparative study of the preventive effects of mandatory sentencing laws for gun crime. *Journal of Criminal Law and Criminology*, 83: 378–394.

Moffitt, Terrie E. 1993. Adolescence-limited and life-course persistent antisocial behavior: A developmental taxonomy. *Psychological Review*, 100: 674–701.

Nagin, Daniel S. 1998. Criminal deterrence research at the outset of the twenty-first century. In (Michael H. Tonry, ed.), *Crime and Justice: A Review of Research*, Vol. 23. Chicago, IL: University of Chicago Press.

Nagin, Daniel S., Francis T. Cullen, and Cheryl Lero Jonson. In press. Imprisonment and re-offending. In (Michael H. Tonry, ed.), *Crime and Justice: A Review of Research*, Vol. 38. Chicago, IL: University of Chicago Press.

Nagin, Daniel S. and Raymond Paternoster. 1994. Personal capital and social control: The deterrence implications of individual differences in criminal offending. *Criminology*, 32: 581–606.

Nagin, Daniel S. and Greg Pogarsky. 2003. Cheating as crime: An experimental investigation of deterrence. *Criminology*, 41: 167–194.

Nagin, Daniel S. and Joel Waldfogel. 1995. The effects of criminality and conviction on the labor market status of young British offenders. *International Review of Law and Economics*, 15: 109–126.

Nagin, Daniel S. and Joel Waldfogel. 1998. The effect of conviction on income through the life cycle. *International Review of Law and Economics*, 18: 25–40.

National Research Council. 2004. *Fairness and Effectiveness in Policing: The Evidence.* Washington, DC: National Academies Press.

Nieuwbeerta, Paul, Daniel S. Nagin, and Arjan Blokland. 2009. The relationship between first imprisonment and criminal career development: A matched samples comparison. *Journal of Quantitative Criminology*, 25: 227–257.

Papachristos, Andrew V, Tracey L. Meares, and Jeffrey Fagan. 2007. Attention felons: Evaluating project safe neighborhoods in Chicago. *Journal of Empirical Legal Studies*, 4: 223–272.

Petersilia, Joan. 1998. *Community Corrections: Probation, Parole, and Intermediate Sanctions.* New York: Oxford University Press.

Pew Center for the States. 2010. *Prison Count 2010: State Population Declines for the First Time in 38 Years*. Retrieved July 22, 2010 from pewcenterforthestates.org.

Piquero, Alex R., David P. Farrington, Brandon C. Welsh, Richard Tremblay, Wesley Jennings. 2009. Effects of early family/parent training programs on antisocial behavior and delinquency. *Journal of Experimental Criminology*, 5: 83–120.

Polinsky, A. Mitchell and Steven Shavell. 1999. On the disutility and discounting of imprisonment and the theory of deterrence. *Journal of Legal Studies*, 28: 1–16.

Poutvaara, Panu and Mikael Priks. 2006. *Hooliganism in the Shadow of a Terrorist Attack and the Tsunami: Do Police Reduce Group Violence?* Unpublished manuscript, Department of Economics, University of Helsinki, Finland.

Raphael, Steven. 2006. The deterrent effects of California's Proposition 8: Weighing the evidence. *Criminology & Public Policy*, 5: 471–478.

Raphael, Steven and Jens Ludwig. 2003. Prison sentence enhancements: The case of project exile. In (Jens Ludwig and Philip J. Cook, eds.), *Evaluating Gun Policy: Effects on Crime and Violence*. Washington, DC: Brookings Institution Press.

Rincke, Johannes and Christian Traxler. In press. Enforcement spillovers. *Quarterly Journal of Economics.*

Rivera, Ray, Al Baker, and Janet Roberts. 2010. A few blocks, 4 years, 52,000 police stops. *New York Times*. July 10.

Roncek, Dennis. 2000. Schools and crime. In (Victor Goldsmith, Philip G. McGuire, John H. Mollenkopf, and Timothy A. Ross, eds.), *Analyzing Crime Patterns: Frontiers of Practice*. Thousand Oaks, CA: Sage.

Sampson, Robert J. and John H. Laub. 1993. *Crime in the Making: Pathways and Turning Points Through Life*. Cambridge, MA: Harvard University Press.

Shepherd, Joanna M. 2002. Fear of the first strike: The full deterrent effect of California's two- and three-strikes legislation. *Journal of Legal Studies*, 31: 159–201.

Sherman, Lawrence. 1993. Defiance, deterrence, and irrelevance: A theory of the criminal sanction. *Journal of Research in Crime and Delinquency*, 30: 445–473.

Sherman, Lawrence and Richard A. Berk. 1984. The specific deterrent effects of arrest for domestic assault. *American Sociological Review*, 49: 261–272.

Sherman, Lawrence and John E. Eck. 2002. Policing for prevention. In (Lawrence Sherman, David P. Farrington, and Brandon C. Welsh, eds.), *Evidence Based Crime Prevention*. New York: Routledge.

Sherman, Lawrence, Patrick R. Gartin, and Michael Buerger. 1989. Hot spots of predatory crime: Routine activities and the criminology of place. *Criminology*, 27: 27–55.

Sherman, Lawrence. 1993. Defiance, deterrence and irrelevance: A theory of the criminal sanction. *Journal of Research in Crime and Delinquency* 30: 445–473.

Sherman, Lawrence and David Weisburd. 1995. General deterrent effects of police patrol in crime "hot spots": A randomized study. *Justice Quarterly*, 12: 625–648.

Shi, Lan. 2009. The limits of oversight in policing: Evidence from the 2001 Cincinnati riot. *Journal of Public Economics*, 93: 99–113.

Sjoquist, David Lawrence. 1973. Property crime and economic behavior: Some empirical results. *American Economic Review*, 63: 439–446.

Spelman, William. 2000. What recent studies do (and don't) tell us about imprisonment and crime. In (Michael H. Tonry, ed.), *Crime and Justice: A Review of Research*, Vol. 27. Chicago, IL: University of Chicago Press.

Spelman, William. 2005. Jobs or jails? The crime drop in Texas. *Journal of Policy Analysis and Management*, 24: 133–165.

Spelman, William. 2008. Specifying the relationship between crime and imprisonment. *Journal of Quantitative Criminology*, 24: 149–178.

Spelman, William and Dale K. Brown. 1981. *Calling the Police: A Replication of the Citizen Reporting Component of the Kansas City Response Time Analysis*. Washington, DC: Police Executive Research Forum.

Steffensmeier, Darrell and Jeffrey T. Ulmer. 2005. *Confessions of a Dying Thief*. New Brunswick, NJ: Aldine/Transaction.

Stolzenberg, Lisa and Stewart J. D'Alessio. 1997. "Three strikes and you're out": The impact of California's new mandatory sentencing law on serious crime rates. *Crime & Delinquency*. 43: 457–469.

Tonry, Michael H. 2004. *Thinking About Crime: Sense and Sensibility in American Penal Culture*. New York: Oxford University Press.

Tonry, Michael H. 2009. The mostly unintended effects of mandatory penalties: Two centuries of consistent findings. In (Michael H. Tonry, ed.), *Crime and Justice: A Review of Research*, Vol. 38. Chicago, IL: University of Chicago Press.

Useem, Bert and Anne M. Piehl. 2008. *Prison State: The Challenge of Mass Incarceration*. New York: Cambridge University Press.

Waldfogel, Joel. 1994. The effect of criminal conviction on income and the "trust reposed in workman." *Journal of Human Resources*, 29: 62–81.

Webster, Cheryl, Anthony Doob, and Franklin E. Zimring. 2006. Proposition 8 and crime rates in California: The case of the disappearing deterrent. *Criminology & Public Policy*, 5: 417–448.

Weisburd, David and John E. Eck. 2004. What can police do to reduce crime, disorder, and fear? *Annals of the American Academy of Political and Social Science*, 593: 42–65.

Weisburd, David, Tomer Einat, and Matt Kowalski. 2008. The miracle of the cells: An experimental study of interventions to increase payment of court-ordered financial obligations. *Criminology & Public Policy*, 7: 9–36.

Weisburd, David and Lorraine Green. 1995. Policing drug hot spots: The Jersey City drug market analysis experiment. *Justice Quarterly*, 12: 711–735.

Weisburd, David, Cody W. Telep, Joshua C. Hinkle, and John E. Eck. 2010. Is problem oriented policing effective in reducing crime and disorder? *Criminology & Public Policy*, 9: 139–172.

Weisburd, David, Laura A. Wyckoff, Justin Ready, John E. Eck, Joshua C. Hinkle, and Frank Gajewski. 2006. Does crime just move around the corner? A controlled study of the spatial displacement of and diffusion of control benefits. *Criminology*, 9: 549–591.

Wellford, Charles F., John Pepper, and Carol V. Petrie. 2005. *Firearms and Violence: A Critical Review*. Washington, DC: National Academy Press.

Western, Bruce. 2002. The impact of incarceration on wage mobility and inequality. *American Sociological Review*, 67: 526–546.

Western, Bruce. 2007. *Punishment and Inequality in America*. New York: Russell Sage Foundation.

Western, Bruce, Jeffrey R. Kling, and David F. Weiman. 2001. The labor market consequences of incarceration. *Crime & Delinquency*, 47: 410–427.

White, Jennifer L., Terrie E. Moffitt, Avshalom Caspi, Dawn Jeglum Bartusch, Douglas J. Needles, and Magda Stoutheimer-Loeber. 1994. Measuring impulsivity and examining its relationship to delinquency. *Journal of Abnormal Psychology*, 103: 192–205.

Williams, Kirk R. and Richard Hawkins. 1986. Perceptual research on general deterrence: A critical overview. *Law & Society Review*, 20: 545–572.

Wilson, James Q. and Richard J. Herrnstein. 1985. *Crime and Human Nature: The Definitive Study of Causes of Crime*. New York: Simon & Shuster.

Zimring, Franklin E., Gordon Hawkins, and Sam Kamin. 2001. *Punishment and Democracy: Three Strikes and You're Out in California*. New York: Oxford University Press.

Steven N. Durlauf is Kenneth J. Arrow and Laurits R, Christensen Professor of Economics at the University of Wisconsin at Madison. He is a Fellow of the Econometric Society and a Research Associate of the National Bureau of Economic Research. Durlauf has worked extensively on methodological issues involving inequality, social determinants of behavior, and policy evaluation.

Daniel S. Nagin is Teresa and H. John Heinz III University Professor of Public Policy and Statistics in the Heinz College, Carnegie Mellon University. He is an elected Fellow of the American Society of Criminology and of the American Society for the Advancement of Science and is the 2006 recipient of the American Society of Criminology's Edwin H Sutherland Award. His research focuses on the evolution of criminal and antisocial behaviors over the life course, the deterrent effect of criminal and non-criminal penalties on illegal behaviors, and the development of statistical methods for analyzing longitudinal data.

[4]

The Case for Retributive Sentencing

Richard L. Lippke

In the previous chapter, the retributive aim of punishment employed in this book was developed and defended. Although I conceded that crime reduction is also a justifying purpose of punishment, I claimed that efforts to reduce crime must be shaped by the constraints of retributivism that aims at equalizing censure. These constraints require that we inflict proportionate legal sanctions only on those found guilty through fair legal procedures. It was also claimed that crime reduction considerations are of limited usefulness in constructing an account of sentencing and justified prison conditions. This chapter begins with a defense of that claim. I argue that our knowledge of which sanctions optimally reduce crime is limited. Our knowledge of which prison conditions do so is shown to be more limited still. I also contend that we should doubt our ability to weigh and evaluate the many costs and benefits of punishment, as well as the alternatives to it, as required by the crime reduction approach. I hope to thereby demonstrate that elaboration of a retributive sentencing scheme is sorely needed.

Some features of such a sentencing scheme were hinted at in the previous chapter. This chapter fills in more of the details. It thus takes us closer to the central concerns that occupy us in succeeding chapters—the justifiable conditions of prison confinement. Yet there are formidable challenges to be faced in articulating and defending a retributive sentencing scheme. First, we need accounts of harm and culpability and how to combine them in appropriate ways to produce a scale of crime seriousness. Second, we must construct a scale of sanction severity, including a specifically retributive account of imprisonment as a sanction for certain types of crime. Third, we must find a way to link the crime and sanction scales, to ensure that the sentences imposed on offenders inflict losses and deprivations on them that are commensurate with the seriousness of their offenses.

This chapter attempts no more than a sketch of a retributive approach to sentencing. Numerous important challenges to and problems with such a sentencing scheme will go unaddressed, ones that would have to be discussed further in a comprehensive defense of retributivism. My aim is to say enough to motivate the retributive account of imprisonment and prison conditions that occupy us in subsequent chapters, and specifically to prepare the way for my discussion of imprisonable offenses in the next chapter.

Crime Reduction and Sentencing

Legal punishment, I have conceded, is partly aimed at reducing crime, and thereby at stabilizing a system of equal rights that ensures for all citizens decent lives shaped by their autonomous choices. Yet I have suggested that crime reduction considerations can play only a limited role in developing a theory of sentencing—that is, a theory about sentence types, their duration, and, where imprisonment is appropriate, justifiable conditions of confinement. Usually, retributive opposition to crime reduction sentencing approaches is based on concerns about whether they can justify sanctions that punish individuals proportionately to the seriousness of their offenses. There is, it seems, little reason to believe that sanctions with optimally crime-reducing impact will turn out to correspond with the gravity of offenses, especially across the entire range of offenses. Although I concur with this worry about crime reduction accounts of sentencing, I believe that there are also reasons to doubt whether we can construct a crime reduction sentencing scheme in the first place. It will be puzzling to some why I do not make more use than I do of crime reduction considerations in my normative account of prison conditions. I therefore need to explain in some detail why I do not believe that we can make much use of them in determining sanctions.

The crime reduction approach suggests a general formula for determining sanctions, one that might be used to identify types of sentences, sentence lengths, and (where imprisonment is justified) conditions of confinement. This formula tells us to sanction the various types of crime in ways that will produce the most utility—or more broadly, the most good consequences and least bad ones.[1] Yet if we are to employ this formula, we require two things that, I contend, there is little reason to believe we possess at present or are likely to possess in the foreseeable future. First, we need enormous amounts of credible information about the crime reduction tendencies of the sanctions we might employ in relation to the various types of crimes. Since sanctions vary considerably with regard to the kinds of losses or restrictions they impose, for how long they impose them, and in what ways, we need information about the crime reduction tendencies of many different possible combinations of these factors. We also need detailed information about the costs and burdens these sanctions impose on offenders, their families, and the public as a whole, as well as about the alternatives to punishment (including detailed information about their crime reduction benefits and costs). Second, we need computational abilities of formidable sorts, ones that will allow us to take all of this information and weigh it judiciously to determine optimal sentences for

---

[1] The classic formula is Jeremy Bentham's in *An Introduction to The Principles of Morals and Legislation*, P Wheelwright (ed), (Garden City, NY: Doubleday, Doran & Company, 1935) 129–139.

all types of crime and optimal prison conditions for serious ones. We need, in short, to be 'archangels' of the sort described by Richard Hare, beings endowed with superhuman capacities for practical reasoning.[2]

The first shortcoming, lack of credible information about the precise crime reduction tendencies of sanctions, can be elaborated by considering what we do know about the effects of legal punishment. On the crime reduction approach, legal punishment is alleged to reduce crime in three distinct ways—by deterring it, incapacitating offenders, or rehabilitating them. Criminologists have systematically gathered and weighed evidence about all three of these effects for the last 40 years. Probably the safest thing we can say about their conclusions is that, at this point, we know depressingly little about any of these effects of legal punishment. This is not to say that we do not know anything about its deterrent, incapacitant, or rehabilitative effects, but it is to say that we do not know enough to take a crime reduction sentencing program very far. Moreover, the limited information we have is information about how offenders in existing societies react to the threat or reality of legal punishment. Since such societies are often less than ideal, it is not clear to what extent such information could be used to construct a punishment scale for people whose equal rights to decent lives shaped by their own choices were adequately secured. People in reasonably just societies might react very differently to legal punishment and it is about their reactions that we would need information were we to develop an A-level scheme of criminal sanctions.

Consider, first, the deterrent effects of legal punishment. Not surprisingly, it does seem reasonably clear that the criminal justice system as a whole deters crime. There is debate about how much it does so, but that it does so is not much in dispute. If the criminal justice system as a whole suddenly disappeared, assaults on persons and their property would gradually, if not dramatically, increase. Unfortunately, this proposition about what Daniel Nagin terms 'absolute' deterrence is so general as to be of little use in setting up an optimal crime reduction sanctioning scheme.[3] For that we need information about what Nagin terms 'marginal' deterrence.[4] We need, in other words, information of the sort that tells us that if we institute an X% increase (or decrease) in sentence lengths for crimes of a certain type, we will get a Y% decrease (or increase) in those offenses. But our knowledge about marginal deterrence in relation to any given crime, let alone in relation to the wide array of crimes, is exceedingly thin.

In investigating deterrence, criminologists distinguish between the certainty of punishment and its severity. The former is concerned with offenders' perceptions of the likelihood that they will be apprehended for their crimes. There is evidence of a positive association between offenders' perceptions that they are more likely

---

2 RM Hare, *Moral Thinking: Its Levels, Method, and Point* (Oxford: Clarendon Press, 1981) 44.
3 DS Nagin, 'Deterrence and Incapacitation', in M Tonry (ed), *The Handbook of Crime and Punishment* (New York: Oxford University Press, 1998) 345, 359.   4 Ibid, 359.

to be apprehended and their willingness to desist from crimes.[5] Whether the correlation between certainty of punishment and crime reduction persists over time is less well established. For instance, increased policing activity in a given area seems to deter offenses temporarily. It does not follow that it will do so over the longer term, since those who wish to continue offending may adjust by shifting the locus of their offending. The certainty of punishment can be increased by greater or more intense policing activity or by changes in the technology used to detect or apprehend offenders. Although this correlation is important, it bears only indirectly on determining sanction types and their duration.

With regard to sanctions, it is the relation between severity of sentence and crime reduction that matters. Yet here the empirical evidence does not suggest any positive correlation between sentence severity (typically construed in terms of sentence length) and marginal reductions in crime. The cautious conclusion to draw from the empirical analyses is that we simply have failed to confirm (or disprove) that there is a correlation between sentence severity and marginal deterrence. This is consistent with its nonetheless existing and someday being confirmed. Anthony Doob and Cheryl Webster have urged the bolder conclusion that it is time to entertain seriously the 'null hypothesis' with regard to sentence severity and deterrence.[6] The null hypothesis says that there is no correlation between the two. This, they argue, is the reasonable conclusion to draw for three reasons. First, 40 or so years of failure by empirical research to confirm an association between the two supports the hypothesis. Second, once we understand what would have to be true about offenders in order for there to be such an association, we can see why its existence is unlikely.[7] For instance, if we increase sentence lengths, this will marginally deter offenders only if they are aware of the relevant changes in sentencing policy. Yet it is far from clear that most would-be offenders, or most citizens generally, track changes in sentencing policy with any regularity. Even on the somewhat unrealistic assumption that would-be offenders are aware of such changes, sentence increases will only deter them if offenders believe they are likely to be apprehended and receive the enhanced sentences. Also, such enhancements must be deemed by offenders to be significant enough to make a difference in the economy of their deliberations. In short, a number of things must all be true of offenders if more severe sentences are to increase marginal deterrence effects, and there is little reason to believe that all of them are true very often (or even that most of them are). Third, interviews with prison inmates about their offending reveals that very few of them think

    [5] A von Hirsch, AE Bottoms, E Burney, and PO Wikstrom, *Criminal Deterrence and Sentence Severity: An Analysis of Recent Research* (Oxford: Hart Publishing, 1999) 47; DS Nagin, 'Criminal Deterrence Research at the Outset of the Twenty-First Century', [1998] 23 *Crime and Justice: A Review of Research* 1, 9.

    [6] AN Doob and CM Webster, 'Sentence Severity and Crime: Accepting the Null Hypothesis', [2003] 30 *Crime and Justice: A Review of Research* 143–195.

    [7] Ibid, 181–184. See also von Hirsch, Bottoms, Burney, and Wikstrom (n 5 above) 7.

ahead of time about the sentences they are likely to receive if they are convicted.[8] Most do not believe that they will get caught or anticipate what will happen to them if they are apprehended and convicted. They act impulsively or from strongly felt needs. If they do worry about getting caught, this might only affect how they commit crimes, not whether they do so.[9]

Whether we accept the null hypothesis urged by Doob and Webster, or the more cautious conclusion that no correlation between sentence severity and deterrence has yet to be established, does not matter much for our purposes. Why not? Because there is little reason to believe that we will, in the near future, have reliable and specific information about sentence severity and marginal deterrence across a suitably wide range of offenses. Again, such data would, at most, give us indirect information about how to develop a sanctioning scheme for more ideally just societies. Furthermore, even if we had such data regarding sentence lengths, this would tell us little about the main topic of this book, the types of deprivations and restrictions we may justifiably impose on those serious offenders who are sentenced to prison. Length of confinement is one thing, its conditions are another. Conditions of confinement can vary from extremely harsh to relatively humane, with numerous possibilities in between. If we are to employ a crime reduction approach to determining sanctions, part of what we need is precise and credible information about which combination of sentence lengths and prison conditions would reduce crime optimally for each of the various types of serious offense. Since sentence lengths and prison conditions vary independently, there would be a large number of possible permutations about which we would need such information. Another complication is that there is no *a priori* reason to believe that the kinds of prison conditions that would optimally deter some serious crimes would optimally deter others. This raises the possibility that different types of serious offender would have to be kept under different sets of prison conditions if we were to obtain optimal (or even satisfactory) levels of deterrence.

Yet if the empirical study of sentence severity and deterrence is in its relative infancy, then the study of prison conditions and marginal deterrence (let alone the study of prison conditions, sentence length, and marginal deterrence) has yet to be conceived.[10] There appear to be no empirical studies focused on variations in prison conditions and marginal changes in deterrence. Granted, philosophers (and occasionally criminologists) refer to *specific* deterrence, by which they mean the deterrent effects of punishment on those who have actually experienced it (as opposed to individuals who have not yet experienced it but who might generally be deterred by the prospect of punishment). However, there has been little

[8] Doob and Webster (n 6 above) 183.

[9] von Hirsch, Bottoms, Burney, and Wikstrom cite a study where burglars acknowledged efforts to shorten the time they spent inside buildings in order to reduce their chances of being apprehended (n 5 above) 36.

[10] In a footnote, von Hirsch, Bottoms, Burney, and Wikstrom state that 'the degree of onerousness of the prison regime . . . is seldom addressed in the research . . . ' (n 5 above) 6.

empirical study of specific deterrence.[11] Also, any comprehensive crime reduction approach to sentencing would require us to gather information not only about how variations in prison conditions affect the propensity to reoffend, but also about how such variations affect general deterrence. We cannot begin to develop a crime reduction approach to prison conditions without information about how more or less harsh conditions of confinement affect the willingness of would-be offenders to commit crimes. But we altogether lack such information for existing societies, let alone for more just ones.

When we turn to what we know about legal punishment's incapacitation effects, things are hardly more encouraging. The logic of incapacitation initially seems straightforward enough. By incarcerating serious offenders, we render them less able to commit crimes, especially against members of civil society. But do we thereby reduce crime in the larger community? Criminologists have discovered that the answer to this question is less clear than it might seem. A substantial amount of crime—up to one-half of street crimes like robbery and burglary—is committed by offenders acting in concert with others.[12] This means that if some of the members of an offending group are arrested, convicted, and punished, the rest of the group might continue offending, yielding little, if any, net reduction in crime. They might also recruit new members to replace those who are now imprisoned. Not only might crime in the community therefore not decrease, it could conceivably increase if the new recruits are more motivated or capable offenders. With some types of crimes, there is also a replacement effect. Where there is a well-known market for illegal goods and services, new offenders may come forward to supply the demand when the individuals who formerly supplied them are arrested and imprisoned. Thus, even if all of the individuals originally supplying certain illegal goods and services are taken out of circulation by the criminal justice system, there may be, in some cases, little reduction in overall crime.

This is not to say that imprisoning offenders utterly fails to reduce crime. No doubt it does so to some extent, especially in cases where the law apprehends individuals who would continue to offend, lack co-offenders, or are not likely to be replaced. Crime would be reduced more if we could selectively incapacitate high-rate offenders who act alone and are likely to persist in their offending. Yet there are well-known moral and epistemological difficulties with selective incapacitation strategies;[13] and even high-rate offenders tend to 'age out' in their thirties or forties.[14] Since, on average, offense rates decline throughout individuals' adult years, this means that imprisoning them for lengthy periods in order to reduce crime has diminishing marginal utility. What all of these complications suggest is

---

[11] A Ashworth notes that in the modern debate about crime reduction, 'relatively little is heard of individual deterrence as a specific aim of sentencing . . . .' See his 'Deterrence', in A von Hirsch and A Ashworth (eds), *Principled Sentencing: Readings on Theory and Policy* (2nd edn, 1998) 44, 45.

[12] FE Zimring and G Hawkins, *Incapacitation: Penal Confinement and the Restraint of Crime* (New York: Oxford University Press, 1995) 53.   [13] Ibid, 62.

[14] Nagin, 'Criminal Deterrence' (n 3 above) 364.

that there is a significant and unpredictable gap between imprisoning serious offenders and reducing crime in the community.

Again, this is what we know about incapacitation in existing, less than reasonably just societies. To what extent this information is useful in constructing a sentencing scheme for reasonably just societies is anyone's guess. We might plausibly believe that the incentives to commit crimes in reasonably just societies would be greatly reduced, on the assumption that more legitimate opportunities for advancing everyone's interests would exist. This might produce lower levels of offending overall, and mean that those who did offend would less often be replaced or substituted for. But beyond these few vague conjectures, it seems we have little basis for determining the optimal duration of prison sentences if our aim is to reduce crime by incapacitating offenders. Indeed, there seems scant reason to believe that we have much empirical evidence to help us determine sentence lengths in existing societies. It seems doubtful, for instance, that we can effectively reduce crime by imposing sentences of roughly similar lengths on those who commit similar types of offense. Some offenders within such a group may never reoffend, some may do so for a time shorter than the duration of their sentences, and some may do so for a longer period than the duration of their sentences. Depending on the type of crime in question, we might get substantial reductions of crime in the community from sentences of some determinate duration, or we might get little reduction. Nothing in the empirical literature on incapacitation comes close to suggesting optimal sentence lengths for the various types of serious offense.

When we turn to incapacitation and the question of prison conditions, we have little empirical evidence to draw on. The evidence that we have about the incapacitation effects of imprisonment focuses on its effectiveness as a crime reduction strategy in relation to the broader community. In this respect, all imprisonment has roughly the same prospects for reducing crime (though as we have just seen, that is consistent with its failing to do so). All imprisonment tends to remove and isolate offenders from the broader community. Of course, it might be argued that less restrictive kinds of imprisonment would marginally increase the probabilities of escape, and escapees might victimize members of the public. Or, if we envisaged prison regimes that allowed some inmates work or family visitation furloughs, these too would marginally increase the probability of crime in the community. But if less restrictive prisons were well run, and if furlough programs were properly overseen, then the risks of crime they would pose toward the larger community would be minimal.

Discussion of incapacitation and prison conditions might usefully focus on internal prison security—the risks to guards, prison officials, and other inmates posed by more or less restrictive prison conditions. Here again, matters are exceedingly complex and we have limited empirical information to help us. Ideally, we would examine the internal-to-prison crime reduction effects of a range of more and less restrictive conditions and search for those that tended to minimize prison violence and other disturbances. Yet it would be a mistake to infer that what reduces prison disorder also reduces crime in the communities from which offenders come and to which they are likely to return. It could be, for instance, that fairly restrictive conditions minimize disorder within prisons, but that such conditions are less likely to prepare inmates to live law-abiding lives once they are released. Surely, reducing crime in the larger community ought to be our overriding concern. But this means that variations in the internal-to-prison crime reduction tendencies of different prison regimes would have to be weighed and balanced against variations in the external-to-prison crime reduction tendencies of such regimes. To say the least, this would be a complex task.

It seems fair to say that we only have limited information about the internal-to-prison crime reduction tendencies of a fairly narrow range of prison regimes. Those who study prison order must take what they find, and what they mostly find are prisons that vary along limited parameters.[15] Additional study of a broader range of prison conditions would be required, though its usefulness in determining optimal prison regimes in more nearly just societies would be open to debate. Furthermore, we have hardly any information about how the internal-to-prison crime reduction tendencies of various prison regimes are related to crime reduction in the larger communities to which most prisoners will eventually return. If we lack this information in existing, imperfect societies, then we can do little more than guess at what prison conditions are optimally crime-reducing in reasonably just social orders.

With regard to punishment's rehabilitative effects, the state of our knowledge is only slightly better. As before, the empirical literature examines the rehabilitative effects of various correctional treatment programs in existing societies. Rehabilitation is usually construed in this literature in terms of the impact of prison programs on reducing offender recidivism. It is important to keep in mind that in many existing societies, serious offenders come from socially deprived communities and, once released from prison, return to them. It is thus very difficult for researchers to gauge the rehabilitative effects of prison rehabilitation programs. Some types of correctional treatment program may actually help inmates acquire the skills, attitudes, or dispositions conducive to their desisting from further crime, yet ex-prisoners soon find themselves back in devastated communities with few prospects for legitimately advancing their interests. What might look like a failure at rehabilitation may be something very different. Still, if some ex-prisoners who undergo correctional treatment return to their former communities and do better at refraining from further offending than other ex-prisoners who do not undergo such treatment, this is useful information for anyone hoping to devise penal sanctions that reduce crime. With this in mind, it can safely be said that criminological evaluations of correctional treatment programs range from those that regard all such programs with skepticism, to those that are more optimistic

---

[15] A useful summary of the research in this area is provided by AE Bottoms, 'Interpersonal Violence and Social Order in Prisons', [1999] 26 *Crime and Justice: A Review of Research* 205–282.

about the rehabilitative tendencies of certain types of treatment program.[16] Even the optimists would probably admit that any rehabilitative effects are, at best, mild to moderate and are most reliably found in relatively small-scale programs that are adequately funded and appropriately staffed. They would also admit that much more careful study of these programs is needed.

In their comprehensive and cautiously optimistic overview of adult correctional treatment programs, Gerald Gaes and his co-authors provide the following useful summary of their findings:

Most correctional treatments for adult prisoners probably have modest positive effects. Juvenile interventions seem to have stronger effects. Behavioral and cognitive skills training seems to hold the most promise. Interventions in combination (multimodal treatments) probably work better than those in isolation . . . Intensive in-prison drug treatment programs for adults seem to work; however, they also seem to require extension of treatment into the community, both during supervision and, in some cases, after supervision has ended. Work, vocational training, and education have modest effects on adult postrelease behavior; however, these programs also seem to have salutary effects on behavior in prisons while prisoners are participating in them.[17]

For the sake of argument, suppose that Gaes and his co-authors are substantially correct about the state of our empirical knowledge regarding prison correctional treatment. There is, it should be admitted, some useful information here, information that I will subsequently draw on during my own discussion of prison conditions. But it should be apparent that this information is too tentative and incomplete to help much in developing a crime reduction approach to either sentence length or prison conditions, especially if we are to do so for reasonably just social orders. First, it is mostly information about what we might try to do with serious offenders during their imprisonment, rather than information that will allow us to determine the duration of their imprisonment. Second, this information about how to reduce crime via rehabilitation would have to be weighed against considerations of general deterrence and incapacitation. It could be, for instance, that prison conditions that focus on rehabilitating offenders are not as effective at reducing crime from the standpoint of general deterrence, since they might not be deemed sufficiently 'less eligible' by would-be offenders.[18] On a crime reduction approach, the key is finding the right combination of sentence length and prison conditions to optimally reduce crime overall. Knowing a little about what reduces

---

[16] The skeptics include T Mathiesen, *Prison On Trial* (2nd edn, Winchester, UK: Waterside Press, 2000) 27–54, and A von Hirsch and L Maher, 'Should Penal Rehabilitation Be Revived?' in von Hirsch and Ashworth (n 11 above) 26. More optimistic assessments are provided by GG Gaes, TJ Flanagan, LL Motiuk, and L Stewart in 'Adult Correctional Treatment', [1999] 26 *Crime and Justice: A Review of Research* 361, and by the various authors in AT Harland (ed), *Choosing Correctional Options That Work: Defining the Demand and Evaluating the Supply* (Thousand Oaks, Cal: Sage, 1996). [17] Gaes, Flanagan, Motiuk, and Stewart (n 16 above) 361–362.

[18] The notion that punishment must make offending 'less eligible' than non-offending is elaborated in D Garland, *Punishment and Modern Society: A Study in Social Theory* (Chicago: University of Chicago Press, 1990) 93–94.

recidivism in existing societies does not get us very far, even if we assume that what reduces it in such societies would likewise reduce it under more ideal conditions. For such information must be integrated into a comprehensive approach to sanctions that takes deterrence and incapacitation into account. And as we have seen, we know relatively little about what sentence lengths and prison conditions optimally reduce crime via general deterrence or incapacitation.

To this point, I have highlighted the severe limitations on what we know about how to sanction offenders in order to reduce crime. It might be argued that our knowledge in this area will improve, at least in relation to existing societies. Those who favor the crime reduction approach can articulate, at least in a very general way, an ambitious research program that will enable them to gather the information they need to fill out the details of a sanctioning scheme. I doubt that the information they need to accomplish this will be available any time soon. But suppose I am wrong about this. Suppose that we were able to say with some confidence that sentences of a certain length for each type of serious crime, combined with prison conditions of a certain kind, would optimally (or at least effectively) reduce such crimes in existing societies. Suppose also that, with some appropriate adjustments, we were able to envisage changes in each that we could say with some confidence would effectively reduce crime in more reasonably just societies. Would this be enough to demonstrate the practical feasibility of a crime reduction approach to sentencing and prison conditions?

Not yet, for given the underlying logic of the crime reduction approach, the many negative consequences of punishment in general, and of building, maintaining, and operating prisons to punish serious offenders in particular, would have to be taken into account. The ultimate aim is not simply to reduce crime, but to do so in ways that do not create more costs or burdens than the benefits of doing so. More accurately, on the crime reduction approach, we must find that elusive combination of sentence lengths and prison conditions for serious offenders that produce the most good consequences and least bad ones.

The bad consequences produced by legal punishment, and in particular by imprisonment, are many and diverse. Prisons are extremely costly to build and operate. More humane and rehabilitation-oriented prisons are likely to be still more costly to operate, at least in the short term. Building and operating prisons have opportunity costs that may themselves bear on crime rates. For instance, if communities spend more on building and operating prisons, they might have less to spend on schools, providing appropriate recreational opportunities for juveniles, or job-training programs for teenagers. Yet we have some reason to believe that social deficiencies in these and other areas are apt, over the long term, to produce delinquency that may eventually escalate into more serious crime. Imprisonment also significantly affects the families of offenders in ways that researchers are only beginning to catalog and estimate.[19] The impoverishment of

---

[19] J Hagan and R Dinovitzer, 'Collateral Consequences of Imprisonment for Children, Communities, and Prisoners', [1999] 26 *Crime and Justice: A Review of Research* 121.

spouses and children when a primary breadwinner is sent to prison, along with the critical loss of help in child rearing, has dire effects on families. In some cases these effects may extend to the production of further crime and delinquency. Communities are also negatively affected by imprisonment, especially when many of their members are imprisoned and released, bringing back into communities the sometimes violent and perverse culture of prison life. Independently of this, communities that have many of their members sent off to prisons lose potentially productive citizens and taxpayers. Younger members of such communities may become demoralized, believing that entanglement with the criminal justice system is part of their lot in life, or worse, a badge of honor. Last but not least, imprisonment has very negative effects on inmates themselves, even if we imagine more humane prison conditions that focus on rehabilitating them. There is, it must be admitted, some debate about how profoundly imprisonment affects most offenders, but few believe that its effects are insignificant.[20] For many offenders, the emotional scars of imprisonment are permanent and the impact on their prospects for decent jobs, let alone rewarding careers, is profound.

These and other negative effects of imprisonment must be thoroughly investigated, thus compounding the magnitude of the information-gathering tasks facing a crime reduction approach to determining sanctions. But more than this, they must be assigned some negative value and brought onto a scale that will permit them to be aggregated and compared with the positive effects punishment has on reducing crime. Given the large number and diverse character of the consequences (both good and bad) of legal punishment, those who hope to develop the crime reduction approach face a daunting, if not Herculean, task. Suppose that we set aside the worry that the relevant good and bad consequences may be incommensurable—that there is no plausible way of getting all of them onto a scale that will permit us to compare and weigh them against one another. The challenge will still be to find that combination of social expenditures on policing, legal punishment (including prisons), alternative crime-reducing social programs, sanction types and sentence lengths for the various kinds of offense, and prison conditions (in the case of more serious offenses) that would have the best overall consequences. We might lower the target for such an analysis, saying that it should aim at finding an overall set of policies that keeps crime at 'acceptable' (whatever that means) levels at 'reasonable' (whatever that means) cost. Nonetheless, the demands on our ability to consider all of the relevant information, and weigh all of the relevant good and bad consequences, appear overwhelming. Even if we were to focus more narrowly on determining optimal sentence types, sentence lengths, and (in the case of serious offenses) prison conditions, holding everything else constant, there would still be a very large number of possible combinations of these, each with its own set of good and bad effects, that would have to be

---

[20] An overview of the debate surrounding imprisonment's effects on inmates is provided by A Liebling, 'Prison Suicide and Prisoner Coping', [1999] 26 *Crime and Justice: A Review of Research* 283.

compared and evaluated. One important bit of evidence that such a task is beyond our ken is that there appear to be no serious attempts by anyone who favors the crime reduction approach even to attempt it, let alone make some substantial progress toward completing it.

The problems with the crime reduction approach to sentencing stem from the uncertainties and complexities of the future consequences of punishment (or other crime reduction strategies) combined with the logic of consequentialism, which requires us to search for criminal justice policies that maximize overall good consequences. Given that logic, it is not enough to locate crime reduction strategies that will do more good than harm—though locating these would be hard enough. We must discern which strategies optimally reduce crime while producing the least bad consequences. More realistically, we must decipher which strategies will substantially reduce crime at not too great a cost. But as we have seen, the obstacles in the way of our doing so are formidable. Having surveyed the nature and extent of these obstacles, it should be more apparent than ever why there is little reason to believe that a crime reduction approach will yield sentences for crimes that are commensurate with their seriousness. It would be nothing short of miraculous if, in most cases, optimal crime-reducing sentences turned out to be ones that reflected the seriousness of the various kinds of offenses.

Granted, these problems with the crime reduction approach do not, by themselves, demonstrate the superiority or even feasibility of a retributive approach. There are, as we will see, many difficult problems that a retributive approach to sentencing must address. But one advantage of the retributive approach is its narrower focus. It requires us only to compare the impact of various sanctions on offenders' capacities to live decent, autonomous lives with the effects on victims' lives of the different types of offense. We need some empirical information to make this comparison effectively and good judgment to decipher its implications for sentences in relation to the range of offenses. But we do not need information of the elusive and detailed kind, or superhuman powers of judgment to sort through and weigh it, required by the crime reduction approach.

Crime Seriousness: Harm and Culpability

According to censuring equalization retributivism, the most serious crimes are those that with a high degree of culpability inflict (or threaten to inflict) substantial harms on their victims. To fill in the details of what such an approach implies about sentencing, I must explain how harm and culpability are to be understood and gauged, and how they are to be combined into a scale of crime seriousness. I must then explain the ways in which criminal sanctions are 'equalizing'—how they impose losses or restrictions on offenders that are roughly comparable to the harms that crimes inflict on victims. We do have some intuitive grasp of how to measure the harms resulting from crimes of various kinds, as well as the ways in which culpability for producing those harms is to be determined. We can also make reasonable estimates of the ways in which criminal sanctions are apt to affect the lives of those on whom they are inflicted. The task is to integrate these elements into a coherent sentencing scheme.

Criminal harm is typically a function of both the weight of the right-designated interests invaded and, where such interests can be interfered with to a greater or lesser degree, the extent to which they were invaded. A comprehensive account of harm would therefore require a substantive theory of the moral rights of individuals. Such a theory would tell us which rights they possess, their relative weights, and the appropriate scope for enjoyment of them. In lieu of providing such a theory, I will rely on a more intuitive understanding of harms, one that pays attention to the extent to which actions destroy or impede the abilities of victims to live decent lives shaped by their autonomous choices. Accordingly, loss of life is the gravest harm, followed by such things as severe physical or psychological debilitation, loss or destruction of property on which individuals depend to supply their needs, and substantial loss of liberty, dignity, or privacy. Obviously, there is no fixed order to the severity of harms once we get beyond loss of life, which is all or nothing. Some interferences with liberty, property, or dignity can be more harmful than some kinds of physical or psychological debilitation. Some types of debilitation can come close to death in their effects on individuals. A single crime can inflict multiple harms on a single victim or single or multiple harms on multiple victims. As Andrew von Hirsch and Nils Jareborg make clear in their illuminating discussion of the harm component of crime seriousness, the assessment of harm to victims involves both empirical and value judgments about which disagreement is possible.[21] There are empirical judgments in determining which interests crimes intrude upon and to what extent. There are value judgments involved in determining how significant the intrusions are in relation to the ability of persons to live decent lives shaped by their autonomous choices. Although there is room for disagreement in making such judgments, we can anticipate a general, if somewhat rough, ranking of offenses based on the harms cited above.

One question that emerges at this point is whether we should measure harm by reference to the standard harms the various types of offense cause their victims, or by examining the actual harms offenses cause in each instance. The latter, more individualized approach would require us to investigate victim losses in each case to determine the seriousness of offenses. The former approach would focus on the harms the various types of offense typically cause victims, with less attention to the specific details of each offense. Von Hirsch and Jareborg suggest a plausible compromise, where criminal harm is gauged by reference to the standard harms caused by the various kinds of offense, while permitting the introduction of

---

[21] A von Hirsch and N Jareborg, 'Gauging Criminal Harm: A Living-Standard Analysis', [1991] 11 OJLS 1, 14. For some recent refinement of this account, see A von Hirsch and A Ashworth, *Proportionate Sentencing: Exploring the Principles* (Oxford: Oxford University Press, 2005), 186–219.

aggravating or mitigating factors in specific cases that either raise or lower assessments of the extent of harm.[22] This implies that legislators ought to assign a limited sentence range for each offense category, allowing the courts to make the final determination of the sanctions to be imposed in particular instances. Doing so would satisfy the twin retributive desiderata of maintaining ordinal proportion in sentencing and providing would-be offenders with prior notice of the sanctions they face for lawbreaking.[23]

The second component of crime seriousness is offender culpability. Again, there are important differences between those who harm others deliberately and those who do so out of negligence.[24] Those who inflict deliberate harm attempt to see to it that all of the necessary conditions for its production are satisfied. The harm that results can be directly traced to their agency in the sense that the harms were conceived, intended, and produced by the individuals in question, with comparatively little left to chance. Those who negligently harm others, by contrast, act in ways that they should realize elevate the probabilities that others will suffer harm. But the negligent do not intend the harms nor undertake efforts to effectuate them with a high degree of probability. If they are lucky, no harms result. In this sense, any harms that do result depend partly on factors over which the agents in question exercised no control (though some of them may have been factors over which they could and should have exercised more control). In between those who deliberately harm and those who negligently harm are those who knowingly or recklessly harm. The former do not intend to harm, but recognize that their actions will, with a high degree of probability, cause harm. The reckless also do not intend to harm and may not know that their actions will eventuate in harm. They act in ways that foreseeably raise the probabilities of harm to others, but without the minimal (though inadequate) degree of due care that the negligent exhibit.

Agent culpability will be a greater factor in gauging crime seriousness with regard to some offenses than others. George Fletcher distinguishes between 'crimes of harmful consequences' and 'crimes of harmful actions'.[25] The former include offenses such as homicide, battery, and arson, where there is a conceptual gap between the action and the consequence such that it is possible to cause death, injury, or burn down buildings in numerous ways—deliberately, recklessly, negligently, or accidentally. How such harms are brought about will determine the blameworthiness of those who produce them. With crimes of harmful actions, such as rape, larceny, or burglary, it is typically not possible to commit them

---

[22] von Hirsch and Jareborg (n 21 above) 4–5.

[23] Ordinal proportion requires that individuals convicted of crimes of comparable seriousness receive punishments of comparable severity, while those convicted of crimes of differing seriousness receive punishments that are correspondingly more or less severe. See A von Hirsch, 'Proportionality in the Philosophy of Punishment', [1992] 16 *Crime and Justice: A Review of Research* 55, 76.

[24] Here, I draw on H Gross, *A Theory of Criminal Justice* (New York: Oxford University Press, 1979) 77–88.   [25] GP Fletcher, *Rethinking Criminal Law* (Boston, Mass.: Little, Brown, 1978) 113.

negligently or accidentally.[26] Here the crimes are defined as actions with certain types of intentions, and so culpability with regard to the harms they produce will be uniformly high. The seriousness of such offenses will thus be a function of the harms they tend to cause their victims.

With crimes of harmful consequences, we might begin the task of factoring culpability into a determination of their seriousness by comparing cases where agents inflict similar harms but are distinguished by the extent of their blameworthiness in doing so. With harms caused purposefully, the seriousness of the offense will be a straightforward function of the magnitude of the relevant harms. Death will be the most serious harm, followed by serious debilitation, loss of liberty, significant loss of property, and so on. Next, consider agents who knowingly inflict such harms but without intending them. The difference in culpability between such agents and agents who deliberately cause harm seems slight. Those who knowingly cause harm are aware that potential victims stand in the paths of their dangerous conduct and do nothing to avert the harms their actions are likely to produce. Although such agents do not intend the resulting harms, it would not be unusual for observers to wonder how they could have acted as they did without intending to cause them. Such a degree of indifference to the harms they threaten is hard to understand without supposing such agents to have been actively malevolent. Hence, though we may believe it appropriate to discount the seriousness of offenses where harm is knowingly rather than purposefully produced, the discount should not be a very large one. Perhaps knowingly causing harms is only 70–90 per cent as serious as purposefully causing them, but it is surely more than 30–50 per cent as serious.

The next step would be to compare those who knowingly cause harms with those who recklessly do so. Then we would have to compare those who recklessly do so with those who negligently do so. It may be that the differences in culpability between each of these pairs is not constant—that there is, for instance, a larger difference between those who negligently and recklessly cause harms than there is between those who knowingly and purposefully cause them. All of this would have to be explored further in working out a comprehensive theory of sentencing. But it does not seem implausible to believe that we could eventually arrive at some rough scale of crime seriousness that could be used to assist legislators in the task of assigning sentences to those who inflict similar harms with differing degrees of culpability.

Sentence Severity

A censuring equalization approach to retributivism also provides valuable insights into the sanction scale. Most modern legal systems utilize a range of criminal sanctions, assigning the most severe ones to offenses above a certain level of seriousness. This seems entirely appropriate on my account, given the various ways in which

---

[26] Although as Fletcher notes, there can be mistaken thefts or sexual penetrations: ibid, 114.

and degrees to which crimes harm victims (when they harm them at all). I have suggested that we conceive of the impact of criminal sanctions in terms of the extent to which they diminish the abilities of offenders to live decent lives shaped by their autonomous choices. Fines, required community service, and victim restitution typically impose relatively minor burdens on offenders, allowing them to go on with their lives while having to devote modest personal resources to completing their sentences. So-called intermediate sanctions, which include electronic monitoring, home confinement, and requirements to report to probation officers or other officials on a regular (even daily) basis, are more disruptive to offenders' lives. They can make it difficult for offenders to find and hold jobs, or limit their abilities to travel, associate freely with others, and live as they please without interruption or intrusive surveillance. Minimal and intermediate sanctions can, of course, be combined. Collectively, sanctions short of imprisonment might be very burdensome to offenders. They might interfere with offenders' abilities to live decent lives on their own terms as much if not more so than relatively short jail sentences. This suggests that there is unlikely to be a sharp line on the sanction scale between imprisonment and lesser sanctions.

With regard to imprisonment, it is natural to think first of its role in reducing crime. Imprisonment of any sort seems likely to have substantial deterrent effects, and where it fails to deter, it will at least incapacitate those who have committed serious offenses for some period of time. It is less clear how those who defend punishment on retributive grounds support imprisonment. Retributivists cannot cite the social benefits of detaining serious offenders or dissuading individuals tempted to commit harmful acts. I do not believe that we imprison serious offenders solely for the purpose of censuring their crimes and imposing equalizing sanctions on them. But given the leading role I claim censuring equalization must play in a comprehensive theory of punishment, and the epistemological problems we face in determining which sanctions optimally reduce crime, it is important to show how imprisonment can be construed as performing an equalizing function. I hinted at such an account in Chapter 1. Here I develop it in more detail.

I contend that imprisonment should be understood as an attempt by the state to reduce the quality of offenders' lives in ways that are commensurate with the harmful effects of their crimes on their victims. Typically, the victims of serious crimes have their capacities for decent, autonomous lives diminished, sometimes drastically so. Property that they depend on for their livelihood or comfort is stolen or destroyed, grave physical or psychological damage is inflicted on them, their abilities to work or enjoy their social relations with others are undermined, or in extreme cases, they lose their lives. These reductions in the quality of victims' lives can be mimicked, albeit imperfectly, by imprisoning those who have been found responsible for the crimes that produced them. The length of imprisonment should be determined by reference to the extent and duration of the harms inflicted and the culpability of offenders. There is no precise or easy way to determine the lengths of custodial sentences. In extreme cases where victims are killed and the culpability of offenders is high, lengthy prison terms seem warranted. Again, the retributive intuition that such offenders' lives cannot go on as before, but must be substantially diminished by legal punishment is, in such cases, quite powerful. With regard to other crimes and the harms they inflict, some attention might be paid to empirical studies of the ways and extent to which victims of various crimes suffer. Those tempted to assert that the difficulties here are insurmountable should keep in mind that the most likely alternative approach to determining sentence lengths—one that focuses on crime reduction—has been shown to be beset with grave problems.

Other penalties that might be proposed for serious offenders would not, in most cases, inflict appropriate kinds of losses on them, or would be impractical or inconsistent with treating them as beings capable of comprehending their wrongs and the justice of their punishment. For instance, banishing offenders, in addition to being impractical, would only disrupt their lives if they were assigned to locales where living decent lives on their own terms would be difficult. Another option, corporal punishment, might not inflict commensurate losses if it were relatively brief in duration. If it went on for longer periods of time or was repeated on numerous occasions, its long-term effects might so traumatize offenders as to exceed proportionality limits. There is also Jeffrie Murphy's contention that corporal punishment does not treat offenders as moral beings because, for the duration of its infliction, they are reduced to little more than suffering animals.[27] Another option, public condemnation, would only disrupt offenders' lives if they were sensitive to social perceptions of their conduct. Although we can imagine societies where public denunciation alone would be devastating to the life prospects of serious offenders, most of us do not live in such societies. Many offenders in contemporary societies would simply go on about their business indifferent to state pronouncements about their conduct. Or they would move to new locales where their fellow citizens were unaware of their past misconduct.

Importantly, retributivists need not insist that imprisonment of serious offenders is the only sanction that imposes appropriate kinds of losses on them. If there are sanctions that would function in comparable ways to diminish the abilities of such offenders to live decent lives on their own terms, then retributivists should be open to their use. They need make only the more modest claim that imprisonment is one type of sanction that serves the requisite equalizing purpose of punishing serious offenses. At present, it is probably the only one that can do so in many cases.

Still, objections of various kinds might be raised against this retributive account of imprisonment. First, it might be argued that the effects of many crimes on the abilities of victims to live decent, autonomous lives are apt to be quite different from the effects of imprisonment on offenders. For instance, rape victims

---

[27] JG Murphy, 'Cruel and Unusual Punishments', in MA Stewart (ed), *Law, Morality, and Rights*, (Dordrecht: D. Reidel, 1983), 373, 387.

suffer not only assaults on their bodily integrity and dignity, but also the fears, anxieties, and inability to trust others that result from severe victimization. These harms stunt or deform victims' lives in myriad ways for lengthy periods. It might reasonably be asked how imprisoning rapists inflicts any sort of equivalent losses on them. Keep in mind, however, that the losses imposed by punishment need not, on my account, be strictly equivalent to those suffered by victims. It is enough if the effects interfere in comparable ways with the abilities of offenders to live decent lives of their own choosing. Arguably, imprisonment does this, especially if its duration is appropriate. Prison deprives offenders of significant control over their lives, even their bodies. It also puts them in circumstances where they are apt to experience fears about their safety and future, anxieties about how others will perceive or react to them, and the loss of connection with those who love and care about them. In these and other ways, what prisoners experience is not unlike that which is experienced by many crime victims.

It might be objected that many victims of serious crimes suffer lifelong reductions in their capacity for decent, autonomous lives, yet lengthy prison sentences will only be appropriate, on my account, for the most serious offenses. True enough, but the impact of imprisonment on serious offenders' lives will typically extend somewhat beyond the duration of their prison term. Imprisonment, even under the best of conditions, scars and traumatizes offenders, and likely impedes their ability to get on with their lives. This might be unfortunate, and something we might hope to minimize, but it does suggest that the effects of imprisonment are not wholly unlike those of crimes on their victims.

Another objection to this retributive account of imprisonment will be that there is no typical way in which confinement affects offenders. Instead, its impact will depend on the physical, psychological, or other characteristics of offenders.[28] Young, first-time offenders, for instance, are likely to experience the losses and deprivations of imprisonment very differently from hardened, repeat offenders who are sentenced for similar crimes. It is therefore not clear how imprisonment can serve as any kind of equalizing sanction if its effects vary with factors that are independent of the seriousness of offenses.

There is, it seems to me, no use denying that there is some truth to this objection. There will always be some variation in how criminal sanctions affect offenders, regardless of whether imprisonment or other sanctions are employed. Fines for speeding, for instance, are apt to affect the poor differently than they affect the wealthy. Criminal sanctions must be set with an eye toward the typical case. There seems little doubt that imprisonment imposes substantial losses and restrictions that most offenders will experience in somewhat similar ways. The differences between prison life and life in reasonably just societies are patent, and it is those differences that are crucial in developing a normative defense of imprisonment as

---

[28] N Christie, *Why Punish? Theories of Punishment Reassessed* (Oxford: Oxford University Press, 1991), 99–100.

an equalizing sanction. The fact that some offenders will experience those differences more or less profoundly is, it seems to me, something we just have to accept. We cannot practically design legal sanctions that are entirely sensitive to such differences in offenders. Besides, those who defend imprisonment on crime reduction grounds would also have to countenance differences among offenders. Some will be easier to deter than others, for complicated reasons, and some will be more in need of incapacitation or rehabilitation than others. It seems highly unlikely that these differences will simply track the severity of crimes committed by offenders. Crime reductionists may also have to gloss over such differences if they are to avoid sentencing schemes that are highly individualized.

In addition, we could design prison programs that were more responsive to the differences among offenders. For instance, psychologically more fragile inmates might be provided access to enhanced mental health care that other inmates do not need. And less restrictive prisons of the sort I defend in subsequent chapters might reduce some of the disparities in how prison affects inmates. I contend that prisoners should be provided access to work and ample visitation from outsiders. If that is correct, then prisoners with families and dependents would not be quite so devastated by confinement, especially when compared to their counterparts who lack such ties and responsibilities. Granted, some differences among prisoners' lives will remain no matter what we do to structure prisons differently. But not all of those differences are attributable to prisons themselves; some depend on choices individuals have made or responsibilities that they have taken on.

A further objection begins with the observation that the effects of crime on victims tend to taper off over time. Most victims eventually resume their lives and are progressively less debilitated by their victimization. Yet it might be argued that imprisonment and its effects are more 'all or nothing'. Its debilitating effects do not taper off, at least as long as offenders are behind bars. Hence, the argument continues, imprisonment debilitates more than crime does and so cannot convincingly be cast as an equalizing sanction. This objection ignores the ways in which the punishment of serious offenders can also be made to taper off. Those imprisoned for their crimes can gradually be granted more privileges or opportunities within prisons, be assigned to work release programs or to halfway houses, or be released on parole. In these and other ways they too can be eased back into circumstances where they regain greater control over their lives and access to improved living conditions.

Connecting the Crime and Sanction Scales

A sentencing scheme requires more than that crimes be ranked according to their seriousness and that sanctions be ranked according to the harshness of the losses and restrictions they impose. It also requires that the 'spacing' between crimes and sanctions on their respective scales be appropriate.[29] One type of crime might be deemed more serious than another, which is, in turn, deemed more serious than a third. Yet the first might be much worse than the second, whereas the second might be only slightly worse than the third. The sanctions assigned to these three crimes should reflect these differences in their respective degrees of seriousness. More importantly, a sentencing scheme requires that the crime and sanction scales be appropriately linked. Von Hirsch refers to this as the 'anchoring' problem.[30] Once it is determined that a given type of crime merits a sanction of a given type and duration, considerations of ordinal proportion can be employed to ensure that lesser crimes receive lesser sanctions and more serious crimes are allotted harsher ones. But how do we determine the sanction merited by a given type of crime so that considerations of ordinal proportion can be put to use?

Von Hirsch holds that there is no single preferred way to link the crime and sanction scales. Social conventions, he contends, play some role in solving this problem since they determine how much censure is expressed by a sanction.[31] In some societies, relatively short prison sentences might convey strong censure for crimes; in others they might not. Still, von Hirsch is reluctant to let social conventions alone anchor the sanction scale, since he admits that they might yield sanctions that do not comport with the gravity of offenses. Yet von Hirsch's theory of punishment lacks the conceptual resources to explain his reservations or properly limit the role social conventions might play. The censuring component of legal punishment does not supply these limits, as he admits. And punishment's subsidiary role in providing prudential reasons to desist from crime is unlikely to help.[32] Censuring equalization retributivism, with its focus on the victims of crime, suggests a way to address this problem. Sanctions should impose losses or restrictions on offenders that are commensurate in their impact with the harms the victims of crime suffer (setting culpability aside for the moment). If social conventions demand more or less than this, especially much more or less than this, then they should be ignored. This is not to deny, of course, that they might play some role in determining sanctions. Also, I would concede that whether sanctions are commensurate in their effects on offenders is not something that we can determine with great precision.

Still, how does censuring equalization retributivism suggest that we should anchor the crime and sanction scales? The clearest place to begin is at the top. We might focus initially on crimes that, with a high degree of culpability, cause death. First degree murder, for instance, wholly deprives victims of their abilities to live decent lives shaped by their autonomous choices, and those who commit it are fully culpable for inflicting this harm. Here, it seems to me, censuring equalization

---

[29] A von Hirsch, *Censure and Sanctions* (Oxford: Clarendon Press, 1993) 18.
[30] Ibid, 22.   [31] Von Hirsch, ibid, 19, and 'Proportionality' (n 23 above) 83.
[32] Von Hirsch notes the unavailability of the empirical information we need to gauge the deterrent effects of criminal sanctions: 'Proportionality' (n 23 above) 84.

retributivism must be pretty uncompromising, at least at the A-level of analysis. The only sanctions that appear commensurate with first degree murder are the death penalty or very lengthy prison sentences, for only such severe penalties come close to equalizing the harm such deliberate murders produce. If there is a retributive case to be made for the death penalty, it is in relation to crimes like this that culpably take everything from their victims.[33] As we move from the deliberate causation of death to its knowing, reckless, or negligent causation, censuring equalization retributivism implies that the sanctions imposed on offenders should be reduced accordingly.

Importantly, when we turn to serious offenses that cause harms other than loss of life, the retributive case for lengthy prison terms is weaker. Crimes like rape or aggravated assault cause their victims significant, long-term physical and psychological injuries that impair their ability to live decent lives of their own choosing. But even minimally restrictive imprisonment will impose significant losses on offenders. It is hard to see how, in most cases, prison sentences of more than five to ten years would be needed to impose commensurate losses on those guilty of such crimes. In some cases, sentences of that length might even be excessive. As we move away from personal crimes to property offenses, the retributive case for lengthy imprisonment is weaker still. Many victims of property crimes seem likely to recover from the harms inflicted on them in relatively short periods of time, even if we include other harms resulting from such offenses, such as invasion of privacy or emotional trauma. Except in special circumstances, it is hard to see how imprisonment for anything more than brief periods would be needed to impose commensurate losses on those who commit property crimes. In many cases, the imposition of intermediate sanctions should suffice. In the next chapter, I consider further the kinds of crimes for which imprisonment is an appropriate sanction, comparing the implications of my retributive approach with what we can glean from the crime reduction literature concerning imprisonable offenses.

Goldman's Worry

Alan Goldman has argued that retributive approaches to sentencing which aim at rough equality between criminal harm and penal sanctions (setting aside considerations of culpability) are unlikely to deter many who are tempted to commit property crimes.[34] Approximately half of all such offenders are never apprehended and many are fairly desperate individuals with little to lose. Goldman doubts that intermediate sanctions or short prison sentences will suffice to keep such offenses

---

[33] There are, of course, other grounds on which retributivists might reject the death penalty. My remarks here should not be taken as an endorsement of executions.

[34] AH Goldman, 'The Paradox of Punishment', [1979] 9 *Philosophy and Public Affairs* 42, 48–50. Also, his 'Toward a New Theory of Punishment', [1982] 1 *Law and Philosophy* 57, 62.

within tolerable limits. If he is right about this, then retributivists must either agree to sentences that, in some cases, exceed retributive limits or concede that their approach is disturbingly indifferent to the consequences of legal punishment. In light of the arguments of this chapter, we are now in a position to address Goldman's concerns.

It should first be noted that Goldman's worry takes as its point of departure existing, somewhat unjust societies—something he makes clear in addressing various anticipated responses by retributivists.[35] He concedes that the problem he sees with retributively just sentences may not be as worrisome in reasonably just societies. In such societies, individuals will less often be desperately poor, deprived of legitimate opportunities to advance their interests, or alienated from the social order. Yet I am not convinced that Goldman's argument is persuasive given what we currently know about offenders in less than reasonably just societies. He assumes that such societies contain a substantial number of offenders who will not be deterred by retributively just sanctions but who will be deterred by sanctions that somewhat exceed retributive limits. But is that something we have any reason to believe? As we have seen, many offenders appear to pay little attention to the severity of sanctions they face. It could be argued that if we increased sentence lengths dramatically, we would be sure to get their attention. Yet it is not clear that Goldman is prepared to endorse draconian sentences in order to keep property crimes in tolerable bounds. Hence, the relevant comparison may be between retributively just sanctions and ones that exceed them by some moderate amount. The question then is whether we have any reason to believe that the number of potential offenders deterred by the latter would substantially exceed those deterred by the former. Given the underwhelming character of the evidence linking sentence severity and marginal deterrence, I suspect that we do not. Also, keep in mind that any benefits from the longer sentences would have to be weighed against their numerous negative consequences. Once this has been done, it is far from clear that a compelling case for exceeding retributive limits has been made.

But are there no conceivable cases where crime reduction considerations might trump retributive limits on sentencing? What if we had the information needed to employ crime reduction considerations in certain specific instances? One worrisome kind of case is this: suppose that we had clear and convincing evidence that certain types of offender persist in committing serious crimes after they have been retributively punished for previous ones. Then suppose that we had relatively precise ways of identifying the persistent offenders in question. Should we not at least entertain the idea of selectively incapacitating such offenders (thereby reducing their subsequent offenses)? Notice that this is not a case where, based solely on predictions of future offending, we are prepared to restrain those whom we reasonably fear will at some point offend but who have not yet offended. In such cases, the retributive constraint against punishment of the innocent should be

---

[35] Goldman, 'The Paradox of Punishment' (n 34 above) 58.

accorded its full weight. Even crime reduction theorists argue against punishment of the innocent, on the grounds that giving authorities the power to selectively incapacitate those they deem dangerous, but who have not yet committed any offense, would cause widespread distrust of the criminal justice system.[36]

The harder cases are those where the individuals in question have previous criminal histories of a disturbing kind and where we have compelling evidence that they will continue to offend. In such cases, the public might be more sanguine about permitting the authorities to extend sentences at their discretion, especially if it appeared that there were well-established criteria to guide the judges and correctional officials who would be involved in making such decisions. Some individuals involved in organized crime might satisfy these criteria, as might some unrepentant terrorists. Is this not a point where retributive constraints on legal punishment might yield to considerations of crime reduction?

Perhaps, though I believe that this possibility is of more theoretical than practical interest.[37] Even if we had the relevant kind of information, we might be wary about giving authorities the power to use it—effectively to declare some individuals incapable of self-restraint with regard to the law.[38] Instead, we might first insist that the authorities demonstrate that no other means exist to protect the public from such offenders. Also, we might explore the possibility of some type of non-punitive confinement for such offenders, assuming the feasibility of such an option.[39] In short, though I can conceive of cases where we might be persuaded, at least in theory, to qualify the priority of retributive over crime reduction considerations, I shall ignore them for the most part and simply assume that priority in succeeding chapters.

Concluding Remarks

Some readers will remain skeptical about the kind of retributive approach to sentencing developed in this chapter. I have argued that such an approach is needed given the severe deficits in our knowledge and computational abilities, ones that plague efforts to develop a crime reduction sentencing scheme. Again, it is one thing to believe, as I do, that considerations of crime reduction must play some role in the justification of legal punishment. It is quite another to believe that we have at our disposal detailed information about the kinds and lengths of sentence

---

[36] A point made by J Rawls, 'Two Concepts of Rules', [1955] 64 *Philosophical Review* 3, 11–12, though Rawls defended a mixed theory of punishment. See also J Braithwaite and P Pettit, *Not Just Deserts: A Republican Theory of Criminal Justice* (Oxford: Clarendon Press, 1998) 74.

[37] Here I am indebted to von Hirsch's discussion of hybrid sentencing theories (n 23 above) 85–89.

[38] See JG Murphy's concern about allowing the state to label certain offenders criminal psychopaths, in his 'Moral Death: A Kantian Essay on Psychopathy', reprinted in JG Murphy, *Retribution, Justice, and Therapy* (Dordrecht, Netherlands: D. Reidel, 1979) 128, 139.

[39] Some discussion of this possibility is provided by D Wood, 'Dangerous Offenders, and the Morality of Protective Sentencing', [July 1998] Crim LR 424.

that will optimally reduce crime, or that we could utilize that information in ways that a crime reduction sentencing scheme requires. These problems are independent of the standard objection to crime reduction sentencing approaches—that they only contingently yield proportional sentences.

Censuring equalization retributivism implies that criminal sanctions should be keyed to the harms inflicted on victims, taking into account the degree of culpability offenders exhibited in acting. There are, as we have seen, many difficult problems to be faced in developing such an approach to sentencing. It too requires us to gather information about the effects of crimes on victims, as well as the effects of sanctions on offenders. It also requires us to perform a series of complex judgments to produce a scale of crime seriousness, a ranking of sanction severity, and link the crime and sanction scales. I hope to have said enough to indicate the feasibility of such an endeavor, even if not to demonstrate its likely success. In the next chapter, censuring equalization retributivism is employed to develop an account of the kinds of crimes for which imprisonment is an appropriate sanction.

[5]

The Place of Public Opinion in Sentencing Law

By Stephen Shute*

Senior Lecturer in Law, University of Birmingham

Summary: *This article addresses the question of the extent to which sentencing law allows or requires first instance sentencers to take public opinion into account when passing sentence.*

In his judgment on a motion for a required finding of not guilty at the end of Louise Woodward's highly-publicised 1997 Massachusetts homicide trial, Judge Hiller B. Zobel made the following oft-quoted remark:

> "The law, John Adams told a Massachusetts jury while defending British citizens on trial for murder, is inflexible, inexorable, and deaf: inexorable to the cries of the defendant; 'deaf as an adder to the clamours of the populace.' His words ring true, 227 years later. Elected officials may consider popular urging and sway to public opinion polls. Judges must follow their oaths and do their duty, heedless of editorials, letters, telegrams, picketers, threats, panelists, and talk shows. In this country, we do not administer justice by plebiscite. A judge, in short, is a public servant who must follow his conscience, whether or not he counters the manifest wishes to those he serves; whether or not his decision seems a surrender to the prevalent demands."[1]

While Judge Zobel's prose (like that of Adams) owes as much to its rhetorical force as it does to its logical structure, some of his propositions are relatively easy to accept. Elected officials are, as Judge Zobel opines, largely free to take into account popular urgings and public opinion polls.[2] Indeed in most cases it would be foolhardy for them to do otherwise since politicians who persist in turning their backs on the views of their electorates risk doing irreparable damage to their chances of re-election. Equally, it is a legal commonplace that judges are bound both by their judicial oaths and by a wide range of other moral and legal duties, many of which

---

* This article, a revised and expanded version of a shorter piece which appeared in the *Federal Sentencing Reporter*, was written during a period of leave funded jointly by the Faculty of Law at the University of Birmingham and by an award from the British Academy under its Research Leave Scheme. The author is grateful to both institutions for their support.

[1] *Commonwealth v. Louise Woodward, Memorandum and Order*, November 19, 1997. Judge Zobel was well acquainted with the work of John Adams having published (with L.K. Roth) a three-volume collection of his papers (*The Legal Papers of John Adams* (1965, Harvard University Press)) as well as a book entitled *The Boston Massacre* (1970, Norton).

[2] For a special case where this is not true, see Part 3 of this article (discussing the Home Secretary's role in setting a "tariff" for "mandatory lifers").

are unique to the adjudicative process.[3] However, Judge Zobel's concluding remark that a judge must follow his conscience even when that runs counter to "the manifest wishes of those he serves" takes him into much less certain territory. Neither the meaning of this statement nor its intended scope is free from difficulty. The purpose of the present article is to investigate the nature of such claims. In particular the article seeks to determine whether, if at all, English law permits or requires judges to consider public opinion when determining an appropriate sentence.

The article is divided into four parts. Part 1 raises some foundational issues. Part 2 considers a selection of cases decided by the Court of Appeal (Criminal Division) that have broached the question of whether the law allows trial judges to take public opinion into account when passing sentence. Part 3 extends the discussion to the law of murder, where sentencing is as much in the hands of a senior politician as it is in the hands of the sentencing judge. The final section attempts to draw together the various themes so as to arrive at some conclusion about the prevailing legal position.

1. The nature of the investigation

Before embarking upon a detailed examination of our topic, it is necessary to say a few general things about English sentencing. Unlike some other legislatures, the British Parliament has shown little appetite for extensive intervention in sentencing matters. Throughout most of the twentieth century its role has been confined to setting maximum penalties and dispensing nebulous admonitions against the use of custody[4]; and even now England still has nothing which resembles the American Sentencing Reform Act of 1984.[5] But it would be a mistake to conclude from this that the law leaves sentencing judges with a largely unfettered discretion. In fact, English common law has over the years developed a complex web of legal rules, principles, standards, and norms that govern sentencing practice. The focus of this article is whether, and to what extent, these rules, principles, standards and norms affect the legitimacy of sentencers taking public opinion into account when passing sentence.

The guidance offered by the law could take a number of different forms. At one extreme the law might outlaw trial judges from taking any account of public opinion when passing sentence: *mandatory exclusion*. At the other extreme the law might require sentencers to factor public opinion into every sentencing decision they make: *mandatory inclusion*. In between lie two permissive options. *Partial permission* requires trial judges to consider the relevance of public opinion whenever they pass a sentence but allows them to deny it any influence on the outcome of a particular case if that seems appropriate in the circumstances. *Full permission*, in contrast, gives

---

[3] It is interesting to ask whether the practice of requiring judges to swear an oath before taking office adds anything to their judicial duties. Would any of the duties that currently bind the judiciary cease to apply if an Act of Parliament were introduced abolishing the practice of oath giving?

[4] See, for example, s.20(1) of the Powers of Criminal Courts Act 1973. In the nineteenth century the legislature was much more inclined to intervene: see L. Radzinowicz and R. Hood, *The Emergence of Penal Policy in Victorian and Edwardian England* (1990), Chap. 22.

[5] Although over the last 16 years Parliament has shown greater willingness to intervene in sentencing matters: see, for instance, the Criminal Justice Act 1982, the Criminal Justice Act 1991, and the Crime (Sentences) Act 1997.

sentencers a free hand whether they consider the relevance of public opinion or not.

In addition to these variations, the law might also have something to say about the weight sentencers ought to attach to public opinion. It might, for example, permit or mandate them to take public opinion into account yet deny them the right to let it have the last word. Equally, the law might regulate the circumstances in which it is appropriate for a sentencing judge to take public opinion into account and the methods by which the public's views are to be gauged. Each of these possibilities will have to be borne in mind during the course of the investigation that follows.

2. Public opinion and the law of sentencing

With these thoughts in mind, can we specify what role sentencing law allows for considerations of public opinion? Although a number of authoritative books have been written on sentencing, only one—Nigel Walker and Nicola Padfield's *Sentencing: Theory, Law and Practice*[6]—offers a firm view on this matter. There, in a section headed "Public attitudes", the authors make the following claim:

> "In theory sentencing decisions are influenced only by officially approved considerations, whether embodied in statute, practice direction, case law or Whitehall circular. In real life most sentencers admit to having some regard to what they believe to be public opinion."[7]

Brief though this passage is, its implications are plain: public opinion is not on the list of officially approved considerations and so ought not to influence sentencing judges. Put another way, Walker and Padfield's suggestion is that the law of sentencing adopts an approach to the relevance of public opinion that I dubbed mandatory exclusion. But how accurate is that as a description of the current state of English law?

Two factors introduce an element of doubt as to its veracity. First, mandatory exclusion requires us to accept that most sentencers break the law by taking into account a prohibited factor. While this consideration does not in and of itself establish that the theory is false—there have, after all, been other occasions where sentencers have played fast and loose with their legal obligations[8]—it should introduce a note of caution into the analysis. Secondly, the fact that no legal authority is offered to support the claim should also make us wary of accepting it. To be sure, one must search carefully for any authoritative discussion of the issue at all. No guidance on the issue has been forthcoming from the legislature[9] and no appellate decision addresses the point directly. We are therefore forced to rely upon

[6] 2nd ed. (1996).

[7] *ibid.* at para. 6.18. One might question whether a Whitehall circular is a legally recognised source of sentencing law.

[8] See, for instance, Elizabeth Burney's research into the effects of the Criminal Justice Act 1982 (*Sentencing Young People: What Went Wrong With The Criminal Justice Act 1982?* (1985)) which revealed that many magistrates were breaking the law by failing to follow the statutory sentencing formula and by failing to record reasons as the statute required.

[9] Compare 28 U.S.C., 1988, s.994(c)(4)–(5) which requires the United States Sentencing Commission to determine the relevance of "the community view of the gravity of the offense" and "the public concern generated by the offense" when establishing its guidelines. For a discussion, see D. Golash and J. Lynch, "Public Opinion, Crime Seriousness and Sentencing Policy" (1995) 22 Am. J. Crim. L. 703.

468 **Criminal Law Review** **[1998]**

the few cases where the Court of Appeal (Criminal Division) has, almost in passing, been willing to express some views on the matter. But, when we do so, we find that the issue is considerably more complex than the mandatory exclusion theory would suggest.

Perhaps the most well-known case discussing the relationship between public opinion and the law of sentencing is *Sargeant*.[10] Decided by the Court of Appeal in 1974, *Sargeant* is familiar to most criminal lawyers as one of the few instances where the judiciary has engaged in an extended analysis of the justifications for punishment. The judgment of the Court was delivered by Lawton L.J. who told trial judges that they ought always to have four classical principles in mind when passing sentence. Elaborating on the nature of these principles—which he identified as retribution, deterrence, prevention and rehabilitation[11]—Lawton L.J. then made the following observation about the place of public opinion in sentencing:

> "There is, however, another aspect of retribution which is frequently overlooked: it is that society, through the courts, must show its abhorrence of particular types of crimes, and the only way in which the courts can show this is by the sentences they pass. The courts do not have to reflect public opinion. On the other hand the courts must not disregard it. Perhaps the main duty of the court is to lead public opinion."[12]

The most striking aspect of this passage is its assertion that sentencers are duty-bound not to disregard public opinion. Such an approach clearly rules out a theory based on mandatory exclusion: judges cannot at one and the same time be under a duty to ignore the views of the public and under a duty to take their views into account. It also rules out full permission: if sentencers are under a duty not to disregard public opinion they cannot also have a free hand whether to consider it or not. However, Lawton L.J.'s comment leaves open whether sentencers are required to factor public opinion into every sentence they pass (mandatory inclusion) or merely required to consider its relevance (partial permission).

A second significant feature of Lawton L.J.'s remarks is his claim that the courts "do not have to reflect public opinion". This gives some indication of the weight to be attached to issues of public opinion by sentencing judges. Irrespective of whether judges are mandated or merely permitted to factor public opinion into sentencing, Lawton L.J.'s position is that sentencers should not give public opinion an overriding weight in their deliberations: sentencers must not become its slaves. That view is then further reinforced by Lawton L.J.'s claim that one important duty of the court, perhaps even its main duty, is to lead public opinion.[13]

A final feature of Lawton L.J.'s remarks is that he links the legitimacy of judges taking public opinion into account in sentencing with retributive theories of punishment. Not all writers, of course, would agree with that association. Rupert

---

[10] (1974) 60 Cr. App. R. 74.

[11] *ibid.* at p.77.

[12] *ibid.*

[13] For an experiment testing the possible effect of sentences on the public's disapproval of defendants' behaviour, see N. Walker and C. Marsh, "Does the severity of sentences affect public disapproval? An experiment in England", included in Walker and Hough (eds), *Public Attitudes to Sentencing: Surveys from Five Countries* (1988).

Cross and Andrew Ashworth, for example, have argued that denunciatory justifications of punishment theory are best viewed as "a kind of long-term deterrence".[14] For them, the chief virtue of maintaining a balance between sentence severity on the one hand and the degree of popular abhorrence for certain kinds of crime on the other is to reinforce public attitudes towards those offences, which in turn should reduce the numbers of people tempted to commit them.[15] For Lawton L.J., in contrast, the justification for taking public opinion into account is not forward-looking and utilitarian but backward-looking, Kantian, and retributive.

Fifteen or so years after *Sargeant* an even more explicit clarification of the relationship between public opinion and sentencing was offered in a second case, *Broady*.[16] The defendant, Broady, had pleaded guilty to two counts of inflicting grievous bodily harm, contrary to section 20 of the Offences Against the Person Act 1861. His victim was his baby son, Craig. At first instance the trial judge, His Honour Judge Lee, imposed concurrent terms of three years' imprisonment on each of the counts. Broady appealed against the severity of that sentence but his application was dismissed by the Court of Appeal which said that the crime was a bad one of its kind and, given all the circumstances of the case, the trial judge's sentence could not be validly criticised. The Court also agreed "entirely"[17] with the following remarks made by His Honour Judge Lee when he passed sentence:

" . . . Judges are not here to gain approval or avoid disapproval from the public, and thus decide their sentences perhaps, on the basis of the lowest common denominator of public opinion. But at the same time, public abhorrence of behaviour like the defendant's should not be, and must not be, disregarded by the courts, who also have a duty to the public to pass judgment in a way which is generally acceptable amongst right-thinking, well-informed persons. There are matters of public interest and public policy here which I have to consider, which others do not. I am afraid I regard a custodial sentence as wholly inevitable."[18]

Now that they have the *imprimatur* of the Court of Appeal, these observations rank alongside Lawton L.J.'s judgment in *Sargeant* as one of the few authoritative judicial statements concerning the legitimacy of taking public opinion into account in sentencing. Like *Sargeant*, they claim that sentencers have a duty not to disregard public opinion. They therefore rule out both mandatory exclusion theory and a fully permissive alternative. They also follow Lawton L.J. in suggesting that public opinion must not necessarily be allowed to have the last word in sentencing decisions. Such a view is implicit in Judge Lee's comment in *Broady* that judges must not decide sentences on the basis of the lowest common denominator of public opinion and in his comment that judges must not be afraid to do what they think is

---

[14] Rupert Cross and Andrew Ashworth, *The English Sentencing System* (3rd ed. 1981), p.145. Contrast the views of D. Golash and J. Lynch, "Public Oinion, Crime Seriousness and Sentencing Policy" *op. cit.*, n.9.

[15] This theory has both positive and negative aspects: the former emphasises the need to build up public abhorrence of the prohibited activity; the latter emphasises the need to ensure that public disapproval of the prohibited activity does not diminish or perhaps even disappear.

[16] (1988) 10 Cr. App. R. (S.) 495.

[17] *ibid.* at p.497, *per* Watkins L.J., who gave the opinion of the Court.

[18] *ibid.* at p.498.

right, even if they know that this course of action will meet with strong disapproval from the public.

However, where *Broady* parts company with *Sargeant* is in offering guidance on how public opinion is to be factored into the equation. Sentencing judges, Judge Lee tells us, owe a duty to the public "to pass judgment in a way which is generally acceptable amongst right-thinking, well-informed persons". Although this duty is expressed in positive terms, the negative corollary must be that if a judge were to pass a sentence which was not acceptable to right-thinking and well-informed members of the community, that sentence would, as a matter of law, be flawed. *Broady* thus appears to envisage sentencers engaging in a two-stage reasoning process. Stage one requires the sentencing judge to reach a provisional conclusion as to sentence after taking into account all the relevant considerations of fact and law and giving each its appropriate weight. Stage two requires sentencers to check their provisional conclusions against the views of right-thinking and well-informed persons. If the proposed sentence is consistent with those views, no change is required. But if it is not, the sentence must be adjusted until right-thinking and well-informed persons would find it generally acceptable.

Appealing to the views of right-thinking, well-informed people may have seemed to the *Broady* court like a simply way of circumventing some of the obstacles that traditionally confront those who wish to rely on the notion of public opinion in sentencing: problems of definition and measurement on the one hand and problems created by the public's pervasive lack of knowledge on sentencing matters on the other.[19] In fact, by turning to this solution the Court of Appeal merely substituted one set of intractable problems for another.

The first of the new difficulties is that neither the adjective "well-informed" nor the adjective "right-thinking" is easy to fathom. A "well-informed" person in the present context must at a minimum be fully conversant with all the material facts considered by the sentencing judge. But a more demanding interpretation would require the well-informed person to have in addition some (perhaps even full) knowledge of the complex web of legal rules, principles, standards and norms that govern sentencing. The term "right-thinking" is similarly riddled with ambiguity. One suggestion is that a close synonym for "right-thinking" is "reasonable", thus aligning the right-thinking person with the reasonable person so beloved by English law.[20] The problem with this suggestion, however, is that the expression "reasonable person" is often used to refer to the ordinary person (or, as the common law sometimes quaintly puts it, the person on the Clapham omnibus). But as we all know, ordinary people are not always right-thinking. So assimilating the right-thinking person to the reasonable person risks driving a wedge between the our normal understandings of the term right-thinking and the view taken by the law.

---

[19] See, *e.g.* Andrew Ashworth and Mike Hough, "Sentencing and the Climate of Opinion" [1996] Crim.L.R. 776, at p.785 (the two "major difficulties" with the concept of public opinion are (i) that "members of the public have insufficient knowledge of actual sentencing practices"; and (ii) that "there is a significant but much-neglected distinction between people's sweeping impressions of sentencing and their views in relation to particular cases of which they know the facts"). See also Julian Roberts and Michael Hough, "Public Attitudes Towards Sentencing In Britain" (1998) 10 Fed. Sent. R. 291.

[20] For a discussion of this possibility in the context of the custody threshold embodied in s.1(2)(a) of the Criminal Justice Act 1991, see Andrew Ashworth and Andrew von Hirsch, "Recognising Elephants: The Problem of the Custody Threshold" [1997] Crim.L.R. 187.

An alternative approach, one that avoids straining the natural meaning of the term right-thinking, is to regard the right-thinking person as a kind of ideal type against which a judge's reasoning and conclusions can be tested. On this view the right-thinking person is not a real person or even an amalgamation of real people. Rather the right-thinking person is a hypothetical person who embodies sound moral values and sound principles of rationality. An objectivised standard of that kind has some superficial attractions. It obviates the need to take into account the views of cranks, bigots, racists, sexists, and other fanatics. It also keeps at bay those who would have sentencers attend to evidence drawn from opinion polls. But these advantages are only achieved at the cost of stripping the second stage of the *Broady* inquiry of much of its independent role. This is especially apparent if we stipulate (as *Broady* does) that the right-thinking person is also well-informed. Since a well-informed person is at a minimum someone who is fully conversant with all the material facts of the case, the hypothetical person is now someone who knows everything pertinent about the case, has the correct moral values, and is able to exercise sound principles of rationality when arriving at a decision on sentence. But when we ask why the views of such a person might be important, the answer can only be that they reflect matters which every good sentencer should consider when passing sentence. Yet, if that is true, they ought already to have been taken into account at the first stage of the sentencing inquiry. For at that stage sentencers are duty bound to consider all relevant considerations of fact and law and give each its appropriate weight. So the inevitable consequence of adopting a fully objectivised standard at the second stage of the sentencing inquiry is to leave that stage with no autonomous role. It can act as an *aide-mémoire* or double-checking device, but nothing more.

Apart from *Broady* and *Sargeant*, it is hard to find any other case in which the Court of Appeal (Criminal Division) has made a serious attempt to analyse the nature of the relationship between public opinion and sentencing. What comments there are have been confined to rather bland statements emphasising the importance of sentencers bearing in mind public concern about sentence levels without further elaboration on how this ought to be achieved.[21] The majority of these pronouncements have appeared in cases in which the Attorney-General has referred a sentence to the Court of Appeal on the ground of its alleged undue lenience. Not untypical examples are:

Attorney-General's Reference Nos 17 and 18 of 1994 (Patrick Chamberlain and Toby Chamberlain), *per* Lord Taylor C.J.:

> "If it were only a question of what was best for the two offenders, and what was enough to teach them a lesson not to do this again, we would readily accept what has been said on their behalf. But we have a duty to the public. Anyone sitting in this Court must know that the courts are constantly being scrutinised in what they do regarding crimes of violence. The public is rightly concerned that serious violence should be properly punished. There is a danger that if violence is not properly punished, then people will take the law into their own

---

[21] See, for example, *Harvey* [1997] 2 Cr.App.R.(S.) 306, at p.308, *per* Clarke J.: " . . . in considering whether a sentence of five years' imprisonment was manifestly excessive, we must take account not only of the factors relevant to this appellant . . . but also the wider considerations which reflect the justifiable public concern about the supply of ecstasy which has been emphasised in a series of cases."

hands. This is what this case was about, people taking the law into their own hands. It has to be stopped."[22]

Attorney-General's Reference No. 47 of 1996 (Ivan Williams), *per* Lord Bingham C.J.:

"The court must always be mindful of the personal interests of the offender, the surrounding family circumstances, employment prospects and so on. But the court must be even more mindful of the interests of the public and is conscious that there is justified public indignation when school children, often going to and from school, or paperboys delivering newspapers, are waylaid, set upon, threatened and obliged to hand over money, jewellery or other possessions. It is, in the judgment of this Court, important if confidence in the rule of law and the administration of justice is to be maintained that offenders committing this kind of offence are, and are seen to be, severely punished by the courts. Such offenders do not ordinarily fall into the category of those who can appropriately be made subject to a community penalty."[23]

Attorney-General's Reference No. 60 of 1996 (Michael Hartnett), *per* Lord Bingham C.J.:

"We feel bound to conclude that the trial judge was overimpressed by the personal factors relating to the offender. It is of course right that trial judges should have regard to, and seek to reflect, personal considerations in the sentences which they pass, but it is important also to bear in mind prominently another dimension: the growing menace of serious and wholly unjustified violence in public places. That is a source of acute public concern. While the courts should not be unduly swayed by such concern, nor, in our judgment, should they be indifferent to it. It is necessary that the courts should, and should be seen and understood to, punish such conduct severely. In our judgment the sentence imposed by this judge on these facts did not do so."[24]

While the sentiments contained in these passages are certainly under-analysed by the judiciary, they and other similar passages[25] provide further evidence that the

---

[22] (1995) 16 Cr.App.R.(S.) 418, at p.421. In this case the Court increased sentences imposed on two offenders for causing grievous bodily harm with intent from nine months' to two years' imprisonment. The victim, the boyfriend of the first offender's daughter, had been attacked because he had assaulted the daughter, causing bruising to her face and body.

[23] [1997] 2 Cr.App.R.(S.) 194, at p.197. Here a two-year probation order that had been imposed on a 17-year old youth for robbery was quashed and replaced by a sentence of nine months' detention in a young offender institution.

[24] [1997] 2 Cr.App.R.(S.) 198, at pp.201–202. A six-month sentence for wounding with intent to cause grievous bodily harm imposed on a defendant who, during the course of a violent altercation, bit the ear of his victim down to the cartilage was increased by the Court of Appeal to two years' imprisonment.

[25] See also *Attorney-General's Reference Nos 21, 22 and 23 of 1993 (Venables, Churms and Ashcroft)* (1994) 15 Cr.App.R.(S.) 741, at p.744, *per* Lord Taylor C.J.; *Attorney-General's Reference No. 30 of 1993 (Saunders)* (1995) 16 Cr.App.R.(S.) 318, at p.321, *per* Ognall J.; *Attorney-General's Reference No. 34 of 1995 (George Williams)* [1996] 1 Cr.App.R.(S.) 386, at p.388, *per* Auld L.J.; *Attorney-General's Reference Nos 17 and 18 of 1996 (Wardle and Iseton)* [1997] 1 Cr.App.R.(S.) 247, at p.250, *per* Lord Bingham C.J.; and *Attorney-General's Reference No. 45 of 1996 (Humphries)* [1997] 1 Cr.App.R.(S.) 429, at p.433, *per* Kennedy L.J.

Court of Appeal (Criminal Division) regards public opinion as, at the very least, an entirely legitimate consideration for sentencing judges. What is more there are no signs that the judiciary has felt inhibited in this respect by the enactment of sections 2(2)(a) and 6(2)(b) of the Criminal Justice Act 1991 which stipulate that sentences must be "commensurate with the seriousness of the offence, or the combination of the offence and one or more offences associated with it". The passages also suggest two additional justifications for taking the public's views into account (although no advice is offered as to how these views are to be identified): the first justification is the danger that the public will take the law into its own hands if its opinions are ignored; the second is the need to maintain public confidence in the rule of law and the administration of justice.

3. Mandatory life imprisonment and the role of the Home Secretary

The cases discussed in the previous section give some insight into the law's view of the proper relationship between public opinion and sentencing. But it is a deep irony that the most extensive judicial discussion of this topic to date has taken place not in the context of appeals against sentences passed by judges but in the context of a sentencing decision made by the Secretary of State for the Home Department. The Home Secretary is, of course, a politician, and many (this author included) consider it anomalous that the law allows any sentencing decision to be taken by such a person.[26] Nevertheless, as things currently stand, it is he and he alone who has the power to decide how long a murderer will spend in prison before becoming eligible for parole.

The procedures work in the following way. When an offender is convicted of murder, the trial judge must impose a sentence of life imprisonment.[27] However, few "mandatory lifers" spend the whole of their lives behind bars and most can at some stage expect to be released on parole. A lifer becomes eligible for parole once he has served sufficient time to satisfy the demands of retribution and deterrence: a period generally known as "the tariff" or "the punitive term". While the length of a discretionary lifer's[28] tariff is decided by the sentencing judge at the time of the trial, the length of a murderer's tariff is decided by the Home Secretary some time after the trial has been concluded. The judiciary (in the form of the trial judge and the Lord Chief Justice) are always consulted before a firm conclusion is reached. But their views are not decisive and Home Secretaries retain the right to depart from the judicial view if they deem it appropriate do so.

Given the advisory status of the guidance offered by the trial judge and the Lord Chief Justice, it should be no surprise that the Home Secretary's decision on a murderer's tariff is not subject to appeal on the merits. It is, however, open to challenge by way of judicial review, and a recent case of this kind brought to the fore

---

[26] See, for example, House of Lords Select Committee, *Report of the Select Committee on Murder and Life Imprisonment*, H.L. 78, 1988–1989; House of Commons Home Affairs Committee, *Murder: The Mandatory Life Sentence*, H.C. 111, 1995–1996, and *Murder: The Mandatory Life Sentence (Supplementary Report)*, H.C. 412, 1995–1996; Prison Reform Trust, *Report of the Committee on the Penalty for Homicide*, 1993; Lord Windlesham, "Life Sentences: The Case for Assimilation" [1996] Crim.L.R. 250; and Louis Blom-Cooper and Terence Morris, "The Penalty for Murder: A myth exploded" [1996] Crim.L.R. 707.

[27] See s.1(1) of the Murder (Abolition of the Death Penalty) Act 1965. Those aged under 18 when the offence was committed are detained at Her Majesty's pleasure.

[28] That is, those sentenced to life imprisonment for a crime other than murder.

the question of the proper relationship between public opinion and sentencing.[29] The action turned on a decision taken by Mr Michael Howard, the then Home Secretary, to set at 15 years the tariff for two young boys, Jon Venables and Robert Thompson, who had been convicted in November 1993 of the murder of two-year-old James Bulger.[30] At the time public interest in the case had reached fever pitch. A petition signed by nearly 6,000 people demanded that the boys serve a minimum of 25 years in prison and a second petition, signed by a further 278,300 people (together with 4,400 letters of support), took an even more draconian line. It urged the Home Secretary to ensure that the two boys be kept in prison for the rest of their natural lives. That view was also supported by 21,281 coupons taken from *The Sun* newspaper and by 1,357 other letters and small petitions.[31]

The Home Secretary did not try to hide the effect these communications had had on his thinking. In his letters to the two boys informing them of their tariffs he explained that his decision to depart from the recommendations of the trial judge—who had favoured an eight-year tariff—and the Lord Chief Justice—who had proposed a 10-year tariff—had in part been based on the "petitions and other correspondence" he had received. However, in the litigation that followed, a majority of the House of Lords[32] held that the Home Secretary had acted unfairly in taking such matters into account. In reaching this conclusion the House drew an analogy between the position of the Home Secretary and the position of a trial judge when passing a determinate sentence. The judgments, therefore, can be read as a general statement about the relevance of public opinion to the sentencing decision and merit particularly close attention.

Of the three Law Lords in the majority, two unequivocally accepted the *Sargeant* view—although the case was not referred to by either judge—that public opinion is

---

[29] *R. v. Secretary of State for the Home Department, ex parte Venables and Thompson* [1997] 3 W.L.R. 23. In March 1998 Venables and Thompson were granted permission by the European Commission of Human Rights to challenge their trial and sentencing in the European Court of Human Rights: see *The Times*, March 7, 1998. One of their allegations was that the public nature of the trial together with the intense publicity it attracted and the fact that it was held in an adult court constituted "inhuman and degrading treatment" and so contravened Art. 3 of the Convention. It was also alleged that the Home Secretary's right to set a murderer's tariff breached Art. 6 of the Convention. This guarantees any citizen whose civil rights and obligations are being determined, or who has a criminal charge brought against him, "a fair and public hearing within a reasonable time by an independent and impartial tribunal established by law".

[30] The Home Secretary let it be known in the *Bulger* case that, if the two offenders had been adults, he would have been likely to set the tariff at 25 years. As Venables and Thompson were 10 years old when the murder was committed, they were sentenced to be detained during Her Majesty's pleasure (see n.27 above). Being detained at Her Majesty's pleasure was, at that time, very little different to being sentenced to life imprisonment. However, following a recent adverse ruling from the European Court of Human Rights (see *Hussain v. United Kingdom* (1996) 13 E.H.R.R. 1), the government has been forced to change the law. The result is s.28 of the Crime (Sentences) Act 1997 which assimilates the position of lifers detained during Her Majesty's pleasure with that of discretionary life sentence prisoners and detainees.

[31] The Home Secretary received only 33 letters which agreed with the judicial view or asked for a lower tariff to be set.

[32] Lord Steyn, Lord Hope of Craighead, and Lord Goff of Chieveley formed the majority. Lord Lloyd of Berwick (dissenting) came close to saying that the Home Secretary would have been in breach of his duty if he had *not* taken the petitions and letters into account once they had been placed in his hands: mandatory inclusion. The fifth judge—Lord Browne-Wilkinson—declined to offer a final opinion on the point but his sympathies clearly lay with Lord Lloyd's dissent and not with the majority.

always a relevant factor whenever a sentence is passed. However, both then added flesh to *Sargeant*'s bones by elaborating further on the nature of the relationship between sentencing and public opinion. Following the lead provided by Lord Woolf M.R. in the Court of Appeal, Lord Goff of Chieveley drew a distinction between public clamour that a particular offender be marked out for severe punishment and public concern of a more general nature. The latter, he said, was always a legitimate consideration for any sentencing authority; the former was not.[33] In a similar vein, Lord Steyn argued that sentencers were perfectly entitled to take into account general considerations of "public confidence in the criminal justice system", as well as more specific features of the case such as "public concern about the severity or lack of severity of sentences imposed on children for crimes of violence." But they were not entitled to take into account a "high voltage atmosphere" created by a newspaper campaign or a public demonstration. Such material, said Lord Steyn, was "worthless and incapable of informing [sentencers] in a meaningful way about the true state of informed public opinion", which (following the least demanding of the two possible interpretations of that phrase discussed above) he defined as "public opinion formed in the knowledge of all the material facts of the case."[34]

In contrast to these views, the position taken by Lord Hope of Craighead, the third Law Lord in the majority, is much less easy to divine. Lord Hope clearly agreed with Lord Goff and Lord Steyn that neither a Home Secretary nor a sentencing judge ought to pay heed to public petitions. However, since no explicit distinction was drawn between these and other aspects of public opinion, it is hard to be certain that he was not also attracted to a full-blooded mandatory exclusion theory. On balance, though, there are enough indications in his speech to suggest that he too would be willing to allow public opinion some, albeit limited, role in sentencing.[35]

4. Conclusion

Where do these cases leave the law of sentencing? Plainly, there is now a considerable body of evidence to suggest that mandatory exclusion theory is not a true description of the current state of the law. All the judgments we have examined indicate that sentencing judges are at the very least duty-bound to consider the relevance of public opinion (partial permission) and possibly even required to factor that consideration into any sentence they pass (mandatory inclusion).[36] There is

---

[33] [1997] 3 W.L.R. 23 at 41. By contrast, in his dissent, Lord Lloyd doubted the feasibility of differentiating between material "which is directed to penal policy in general" and material which is "directed to a particular case" (at 66). Similarly, Lord Browne-Wilkinson described (at 53) the distinction between "discovering public feeling generally" and taking into account "distasteful public reactions in a particular case" as "too narrow . . . to be workable in practice".

[34] [1997] 3 W.L.R. 23 at 74.

[35] See, for example, his statement that "*some* measure of detachment from the pressure of public opinion is essential" ([1997] 3 W.L.R. 23 at 76 (emphasis added)) which indicates that the detachment need not be complete.

[36] See also *Brewster and Others* [1998] 1 Cr.App.R.(S.) 181 at 184, where Lord Bingham C.J. said that the very sharp rise in the use of custody by English sentencing judges that had occurred since 1993 (in 1996 the use of immediate custody in the Crown Court for all offences reached 60 per cent—the highest level since the early 1950s) was probably a response not just to legislation but "to certain highly publicised crimes . . . ministerial speeches and intense media pressure."

also good evidence that the common law requires sentencers to handle the concept of public opinion with care. Sentencers must not, for example, fall into the temptation of allowing public opinion an overriding weight in their deliberations. Nor, following the *Bulger* action, must they listen to campaigns or lobbying concerning the particular case at hand.[37]

Some wisdom lies in this approach. On the one hand, there are obvious dangers in overstepping what Walker and Hough have called the "limits of public tolerance".[38] So, despite the formidable stumbling blocks of definition and measurement,[39] it is understandable that the judges should want to find some space for public opinion in sentencing law. On the other hand, public opinion is just one amongst a myriad of other factors that need to be taken into account. So it is also right that public opinion should not be allowed to take pride of place.

By the same token, the House of Lords should be commended for setting its face against mass campaigns targeted at individual defendants. One of the foremost principles of justice is that the law ought to be administered even-handedly—like cases ought to be treated alike—and if a sentencing judge were to yield to a concerted campaign targeted at an identified individual, that principle would be violated.

Nevertheless, three unresolved weaknesses must be set against these strengths. First, until an appellate court addresses the question directly, there will always be an element of doubt surrounding the standing of the existing authorities.[40] Secondly, the law's attempts to rise above the problems of definition and measurement that inevitably confront those wishing to appeal to public opinion have, as we have seen, brought new problems in their wake. Particularly troublesome is the fact that it is still far from clear whether, over and above the two limits mentioned above, the law also expects sentencers to ensure that when they refer to public opinion they do not

[37] See also the views of Lord Bingham C.J. expressed extra-judicially in a lecture to the Police Foundation: "In determining a sentence, the judge should close his or her ears to public and media clamour concerning *that* case." (*The Times*, July 11, 1997 (emphasis added)). A further insight into Lord Bingham's position is provided by the following comment made in a recent interview conducted by Professor Andrew Rutherford for the *New Law Journal*: "Any judge or any magistrate who is provoked by public clamour into passing a severe sentence in a particular case is really abdicating his or her duty. On the other hand, people passing sentence have to be alive to the climate of the society in which they live up to a point. If the judges and magistrates are routinely castigated in the press and on political platforms for not doing their job or for undermining confidence in criminal justice and so forth I don't think they should shut their ears to that and even if they should I don't think they can. If the climate of opinion has to be altered it won't happen by chance and this requires effective leadership, education and explanation." ((1998) 148 N.L.J. 726 at 726).

[38] See "Introduction: developments in methods and perspectives" in Walker and Hough (eds), *Public Attitudes to Sentencing: Surveys from Five Countries* (1988), p.13.

[39] Problems of identification and measurement are a very real impediment to anyone who wishes to factor public opinion into sentencing law (either through mandatory inclusion or full or partial permission) and nothing in this article should be taken as indicating otherwise.

[40] It remains to be seen whether the House of Lords will have more to say about the relationship between public opinion and sentencing when it hears an appeal in *R. v. Secretary of State for the Home Department, ex parte Myra Hindley, The Times*, December 19, 1997. Despite accepting that Ms Hindley (one of the notorious "Moors Murderers") felt herself to be "hostage to public opinion", the Court of Appeal was able to sidestep this issue because Ms Hindley had not accused the Home Secretary of taking into account an irrelevant or improper consideration when setting her tariff. In the absence of such an allegation, the Court concluded that it was unnecessary for it to consider the extent to which, if at all, the Home Secretary was entitled to factor public opinion into his decision.

stray beyond: (i) the views of informed people or (ii) the views of right-thinking, well-informed people. Certainly, Lord Steyn's remarks in the *Bulger* case indicated that he thought the first restriction ought to apply.[41] The *Broady* court, in contrast, endorsed the second. Finally, if an appeal to public opinion is to be limited in these (or other) ways, not only should the limitations (like the appeal to public opinion itself) be properly justified but the terms used to express the limitations (such as "well-informed" or "right-thinking") must be properly explained. To leave these terms vague or, worse still, wholly undefined introduces an element of uncertainty into English sentencing which ill befits a legal system that purports to stand four-square behind the values protected by the rule of law.

[41] A similar view was expressed by judges interviewed in a pilot study into Crown Court sentencing which was conducted from the Oxford Centre for Criminological Research by A. Ashworth, E. Genders, G. Mansfield, J. Peay and E. Player (see *Sentencing in the Crown Court: an Exploratory Study* (1984), p.31). The participating judges stressed that only "informed public opinion" should be taken into account. However, the majorty claimed (perhaps not surprisingly) that "informed public opinion" and their own opinions were synonymous!

Part II
Sentencing Guidelines and the Model Penal Code

[6]

THE UTILITY OF DESERT

*Paul H. Robinson and John M. Darley**

* Paul H. Robinson is Professor of Law, Northwestern University School of Law. John M. Darley is Dorman T. Warren Professor of Psychology, Princeton University. The authors wish to acknowledge the contributions of Dan Kahan, George Fletcher, Dick Craswell, Tom Tyler, Robert Boeckmann, and the participants of a faculty workshop at Northwestern University School of Law, and of the Justice, Authority, and Legitimacy Seminar at the University of California, Berkeley.

NORTHWESTERN UNIVERSITY LAW REVIEW

Criminal punishment can be justified on two broad grounds. The first is utilitarian (sometimes called "consequentialist"): Punishment for a past offense is justified by the future benefits it provides. Characteristically, the future benefit is to avoid, or at least to reduce, future crimes. The other ground of justification is anchored in the past: Punishment that gives an offender what he or she deserves for a past crime is a valuable end in itself and needs no further justification (such as a showing of a future benefit). This is typically referred to as the "retributivist" or "just deserts" view. The arguments of these two positions are generally considered irreconcilable: Consequentialist grounds are justified on the basis of utility, desert grounds on the basis of fulfilling a deontological moral mandate. In this Article, we argue that, while the underlying rationales of the two views may be irreconcilable, their practical applications, properly done, suggest similar distributions of liability and punishment. More specifically, while we argue that society ought to assign criminal punishments on essentially just desert grounds, our arguments are based on purely utilitarian considerations. We argue that, because it promotes forces that lead to a law-abiding society, a criminal law based on the community's perceptions of just desert is, from a utilitarian perspective, the more effective strategy for reducing crime. While much empirical work remains before we fully understand the dynamics of the forces that we cite as suggesting this conclusion, we can say, at very least, that utilitarians must include in their policy calculations the likelihood of a significant cost to crime control in any deviations from a desert distribution.

The debate over the justification for punishing criminals has been deeply confused, and the confusion has a long and honorable history. In the late eighteenth century, Jeremy Bentham argued that "general prevention ought to be the chief end of punishment, as it is its real justification."[1] From this, Bentham went on to develop the classic formulation of the deterrence rationale for punishment. Thus, tautologically to him (but not tautologically to utilitarians who think rehabilitation could minimize crime, for example) an offender's punishment ought to be set not according to the amount deserved, but rather according to the amount needed to deter future instances of the offense. "If the apparent magnitude, or rather value of [the] pain be greater than the apparent magnitude or value of the pleasure or good he expects to be the consequence of the act, he will be absolutely prevented from performing it."[2] Immanuel Kant, a contemporary of Bentham, summarized an opposing "just deserts" rationale. "[P]unishment can never be administered merely as a means for promoting another good . . . ."[3] Punishment ought to be "pronounced over all criminals proportionate to their internal wickedness . . . ."[4] Of course, the history of justifications goes back further; Kant was giving a particular formulation of the Aristotelian view that criminals should be given punishments and penalties, not rehabilitation.[5] Plato weighed in with a justification for punishment that foreshadows the modern rehabilitation justification, arguing that punishment ought not be inflicted for vengeance, but rather to make the offender a better person.[6] The debate between the desert justification and the various utilitarian justifications such as deterrence, incapacitation, and rehabilitation has continued to divide criminal law thinkers to this day.[7] Perhaps more importantly, it has divided practitioners. In the history of incarceration in this country we have seen repeated confusions in what we might call the "public philosophy of punishment," the reasons claimed for the justification of criminal sanctions by policy-makers and legislators.

---

[1] JEREMY BENTHAM, *Principles of Penal Law*, *in* 1 THE WORKS OF JEREMY BENTHAM 396 (John Bowring ed., 1962).

[2] *Id.*

[3] IMMANUEL KANT, THE SCIENCE OF RIGHT (W. Hastie trans.), *reprinted in* GREAT BOOKS OF THE WESTERN WORLD: KANT 397, 446 (Robert M. Hutchins ed., 1952).

[4] *Id.* at 447.

[5] ARISTOTLE, NICOMACHEAN ETHICS (W.D. Ross trans.), *reprinted in* GREAT BOOKS OF THE WESTERN WORLD: ARISTOTLE II 335, 359, 383 (Robert M. Hutchins ed., 1952).

[6] PLATO, THE LAWS 241 (A.E. Taylor trans., 1960). Rothman reminds of us of an historical fact that it is extraordinarily hard to remember given our modern perceptions of penitentiaries as grim, grey places of brutal convict violence: a rehabilitationist philosophy motivated the development of the modern penitentiary, a place in which the convict would be incarcerated until private contemplation showed him the error of his ways, until, in other words, he became "penitent" for his wrongs and could be discharged a better man. DAVID J. ROTHMAN, THE DISCOVERY OF THE ASYLUM: SOCIAL ORDER AND DISORDER IN THE NEW REPUBLIC 79-108 (1971).

[7] For a discussion of the rationales-of-punishment debate and its historical roots, see Matthew A. Pauley, *The Jurisprudence of Crime and Punishment from Plato to Hegel*, 39 AM. J. JURIS. 97 (1994); *see also* JAMES Q. WILSON & RICHARD J. HERRNSTEIN, CRIME AND HUMAN NATURE (1985).

NORTHWESTERN UNIVERSITY LAW REVIEW

Recently, the confusion has seemed to accelerate; the last decades have seen a rapid oscillation among these rationales for the distribution of criminal liability. The rehabilitationist approach, popular in the 1960s, has lost credibility. Deterrence, grounded in a theory of rational conduct, has ceased to command much confidence among thoughtful criminologists, for a number of reasons that we shall show. Incapacitation, currently popular in the form of "three strikes and you're out" laws, can also be expected to run into difficulties for reasons we shall explain. Part I of this article details the limitations of the standard utilitarian theories. Those limitations mean that policy-makers and legislators, not just academics, should be interested in examining our claim that the greatest utility in controlling crime is found in doing justice.

As we signalled, we argue for a just desert allocation of liability, although a particular and unusual form of desert-based liability: one based upon the community's shared principles of justice rather than on those developed by moral philosophers. Our arguments for this system are, as far as we know, unique: The major claim for our desert-based liability assignment system lies in its advantages in promoting future law-abiding behavior. We give, in other words, a utilitarian justification for the only non-utilitarian system for allocating punishment.

The desert-based liability system that we advocate is one that normally assigns liability and punishment according to the principles of justice that the community intuitively uses to assign liability and blame. We ought to mark here that this is a sufficiently heretical variation on desert theory that it is likely that those who argue for a more standard desert theory, Kantians and others working from philosophical perspectives, will find it repugnant, first because it derives liability assignments from community sentiments rather than a reasoned logical system, and second because our arguments for a desert-based system are blatantly utilitarian.

Our goal then is to persuade those who determine rules of criminal liability and punishment—criminal law theorists, code drafters, legislators, and judges—that a criminal law that assigns punishment in ways that closely reflects the community's intuitions about appropriate condemnation and punishment has a number of hitherto unrecognized advantages over alternative systems. Specifically, a distributive theory that tracks the community's perceived principles of justice has a greater power to gain compliance with society's rules of lawful conduct. Therefore, we suggest, those who base criminal liability on the traditional utilitarian considerations—whether deterrence-based, rehabilitationist, or incapacitationist—run the considerable risk of causing a net drop in the law's effectiveness in controlling crime.

456

91:453 (1997)

Here is a brief summary of our argument as detailed in Part II of this Article: The real power to gain compliance with society's rules of prescribed conduct lies not in the threat or reality of official criminal sanction, but in the power of the intertwined forces of social and individual moral control. The networks of interpersonal relationships in which people find themselves, the social norms and prohibitions shared among those relationships and transmitted through those social networks, and the internalized representations of those norms and moral precepts cause people to obey the law.

Next, the core of our argument, set out in Part III: The law is not irrelevant to these social and personal forces. Criminal law, in particular, plays a central role in creating and maintaining the social consensus necessary for sustaining moral norms. In fact, in a society as diverse as ours, the criminal law may be the only society-wide mechanism that transcends cultural and ethnic differences. Thus, the criminal law's most important real-world effect may be its ability to assist in the building, shaping, and maintaining of these norms and moral principles. It can contribute to and harness the compliance-producing power of interpersonal relationships and personal morality.

The criminal law can have a second effect in gaining compliance with its commands. If it earns a reputation as a reliable statement of what the community, given sufficient information and time to reflect, would perceive as condemnable, people are more likely to defer to its commands as morally authoritative and as appropriate to follow in those borderline cases in which the propriety of certain conduct is unsettled or ambiguous in the mind of the actor. The importance of this role should not be underestimated; in a society with the complex interdependencies characteristic of ours, an apparently harmless action can have destructive consequences. When the action is criminalized by the legal system, one would want the citizen to "respect the law" in such an instance even though he or she does not immediately intuit why that action is banned. Such deference will be facilitated if citizens are disposed to believe that the law is an accurate guide to appropriate prudential and moral behavior.

The extent of the criminal law's effectiveness in both these respects—in facilitating and communicating societal consensus on what is and is not condemnable, and in gaining compliance in borderline cases through deference to its moral authority—we argue is to a great extent dependent on the degree of moral credibility that the criminal law has achieved in the minds of the citizens governed by it. Thus, we assert, the criminal law's moral credibility is essential to effective crime control, and is enhanced if the distribution of criminal liability is perceived as "doing justice," that is, if it assigns liability and punishment in ways that the community perceives as consistent with the community's principles of appropriate liability and punishment.

NORTHWESTERN UNIVERSITY LAW REVIEW

Conversely, the system's moral credibility, and therefore its crime control effectiveness, is undermined by a distribution of liability that deviates from community perceptions of just desert. In Parts IV, V, and VI, we discuss how past reforms have hurt the criminal law's moral credibility, and we propose reforms by which its moral credibility might be enhanced.

We begin the argument for our position by criticizing all of the alternatives. That is, before we detail the case for enhancing the criminal law's moral credibility, we comment on the other utilitarian theories for distributing criminal liability and the difficulties that each face. Our conclusion is not that these standard utilitarian mechanisms for controlling crime have no effect in reducing crime, but rather that they have only a limited benefit that is outweighed by their cost in undercutting the law's crime control power by reducing its moral credibility. Remember that sentences based upon desert do provide the opportunity for rehabilitation, incapacitation, and deterrence. In arguing for a desert distribution, then, we need show only that the *additional crime control benefit* that the standard utilitarian analysis claims by *deviating from a desert distribution* is outweighed by the additional cost that such deviation incurs as it inevitably undercuts the criminal law's moral credibility. The optimum distributive principle, we argue, is one that rehabilitates, incapacitates, and deters, but only through the use of liability and punishment that tracks the community's principles of perceived desert.

I. LIMITATIONS OF THE STANDARD UTILITARIAN THEORIES FOR DISTRIBUTING CRIMINAL LIABILITY

A. *Deterrence*

Social scientists have increasingly suspected that the threat of official punishment by the criminal justice system is of modest effect in limiting crime. One reason for its limited effect is the low risk of punishment an offender faces for the contemplated offense. Consider the many ways that an offender can routinely escape punishment for an offense.

An astounding number of serious offenses are never reported to police (*e.g.*, 21% of rapes, 40% of burglaries), either out of embarrassment or fear of reprisal or from a belief that the police are impotent or unwilling to do anything.[8] Of the offenses reported, clearance rates (the rate at which police identify and arrest a suspect for reported

---

[8] Phillip J. Cook, *Punishment and Crime: A Critique of Current Findings Concerning the Preventative Effects of Punishment*, 41 LAW & CONTEMP. PROBS. 164, 172 (1977). *Compare* Table 1, Personal and household crimes, 1990, 1990 CRIMINAL VICTIMIZATION IN THE UNITED STATES 16 (1992), *with* Table 3.122, Estimated number and rate of offenses known to police, 1990, 1992 SOURCEBOOK OF CRIMINAL JUSTICE STATISTICS 357 (1993).

91:453 (1997)   *Utility of Desert*

offenses) have been steadily dropping for decades. The homicide clearance rate nationwide, which was 93% in 1955, has steadily declined to a current 67%. Rape has declined from 79% to 52%. Burglary went from a not very high 32% to a sad 13%.[10] And, of course, getting arrested is a far cry from punishment. The overall conviction rate of those arrested for the most serious offenses—homicide, rape, robbery, burglary, aggravated assault—is 30%.[11] Further, less than half of those convicted of a felony are sentenced to prison.[12]

The cumulative effect of the many escape hatches leaves a deterrent threat that looks like this: Homicide offers a 44.7% chance of being caught, convicted, and imprisoned for that offense. A person contemplating a rape faces a 12% chance of going to prison for that offense. Robbery presents a 3.8% chance. Assault, burglary, larceny, and motor vehicle theft are each a 100-to-1 shot.[13] To put it mildly,

---

9 The chart statistics are drawn from the following sources:

Column (a): Table 1, Personal and household crimes, 1990, 1990 CRIMINAL VICTIMIZATION IN THE UNITED STATES 16 (1992).

Column (b): Table 3.122, Estimated number and rate of offenses known to police, 1990, 1992 SOURCEBOOK OF CRIMINAL JUSTICE STATISTICS 357 (1993).

Column (c): Table 4.2, Number and rate of arrests, 1990, 1991 SOURCEBOOK OF CRIMINAL JUSTICE STATISTICS 424 (1992).

Column (d): Federal figures from Table 5.15, Defendants convicted in U.S. District Courts, 1990, 1992 SOURCEBOOK OF CRIMINAL JUSTICE STATISTICS 486 (1993); State figures from Table 5.49, Felony convictions in state courts, 1990, *id.* at 528.

Column (e): Federal figures from Table 5.19, Offenders sentenced to prison in U.S. District Courts, 1990, *id.* at 490; State figures from Table 5.52, Felony sentences imposed by state courts, 1990 (figures determined by converting percentage incarcerated back to totals through Table 5.49), *id.* at 529.

10 *Compare* 1955 statistics from: Table 15, Offenses known, cleared by arrest, and persons charged - 1955, 27 UNIFORM CRIME REPORTS FOR THE UNITED STATES 48 (1956) with 1991 statistics from: Table 4.19, Offenses known to police and percent cleared by arrest, 1991, 1992 SOURCEBOOK OF CRIMINAL JUSTICE STATISTICS 450 (1993); *see also infra* note 13.

11 *See supra* note 9 and accompanying text; Table 4.5, Arrests, by offense charged, 1992 SOURCEBOOK OF CRIMINAL JUSTICE STATISTICS 429 (1993); Table 5.15, Defendants convicted in U.S. District Courts, *id.* at 486; Table 5.50, Most serious offense of felony offenders convicted in State courts, *id.* at 528.

12 *See supra* note 9 and accompanying text; Table 5.52, Felony sentences imposed by State courts, 1992 SOURCEBOOK OF CRIMINAL JUSTICE STATISTICS 529 (1993) (this figure does not include the many offenders who, before or after conviction, may spend several months in local jails). Of those actually sentenced to prison, the median time served ranges from 5.5 years for murder to 2.2 years for kidnapping to 1.4 years for arson. Table 6.125, First releases from prisons in 35 states, 1988, 1991 SOURCEBOOK OF CRIMINAL JUSTICE STATISTICS 693 (1992). Even these short terms of imprisonment seriously overestimate the typical length of time served because these figures include only those offenders who are sentenced to prison. In reality more violent offenders are sentenced to jail than to prison, and for property offenses twice as many criminals are sentenced to jail. *See* Table 5.57, Sentences received in 14 States, 1988, 1991 SOURCEBOOK OF CRIMINAL JUSTICE STATISTICS 549 (1992).

13 *See supra* text accompanying note 9, col. (d). Note that the calculation gives the chance of being caught and convicted for that offense. No doubt many offenders will be caught and con-

NORTHWESTERN UNIVERSITY LAW REVIEW

our potential offender may not be entirely cowed by these threats. Table 1 summarizes the relevant statistics.

Even these risks of punishment, however, may tend to overstate the effectiveness of the deterrent threat. As one review remarked,

> From an empirical perspective, the existing literature seeking to estimate the expected utility model of criminal choice calls the model into question. . . . A number of laboratory and survey studies . . . of criminal choice provide possible explanations of the poor predictive performance of expected utility models . . . . These studies have found that probabilities used in decision making tend to be subjective rather than objective.[14]

As this suggests, if the task of the criminal justice system is the Bentham-Beccaria notion of deterrence,[15] then it is not the abstract "objective" probabilities that we want to examine, but the representations of these probabilities contained in the heads of potential offenders, and the disutilities that these persons place on the possible prison sentence. We want, in other words, to consider psychological theories of deterrence. A psychological theory of deterrence is a specific case of a "subjective expected utility theory," in which both the estimates of the probabilities of events and the utilities of those events are estimated for the individual about whom the predictions of actions are being made.

The result is worse from the point of view of those who wish to rely on deterrence to prevent crime. Many, if not most, offenders may be unrealistically optimistic about the precautions they take to avoid being caught, or the simple likelihood of being caught, and thus may underestimate that probability.[16] At the same time, just as people notoriously place high discounts on rewards that exist far in the future, so also do they on punishments.[17] The punishment of the prison term

---

victed of a lesser offense. But of course this effect exaggerates the success of the system in capturing and convicting for lesser offenses.

[14] Pamela Lattimore & Ann Witte, *Models of Decision Making Under Uncertainty: The Criminal Choice, in* THE REASONING CRIMINAL: RATIONAL CHOICE PERSPECTIVES ON OFFENDING 129, 131 (Derek Cornish & Ronald Clarke eds., 1986) [hereinafter THE REASONING CRIMINAL].

[15] *See supra* note 7.

[16] Floyd Feeney's interviews with robbers suggest that first-time robbers feel a good deal of fear and apprehension, while more experienced robbers were much less tentative and fearful while committing robberies. Floyd Feeney, *Robbers as Decision-Makers, in* THE REASONING CRIMINAL, *supra* note 14, at 53, 65-66.

[17] In general, people discount future events a great deal. The research method to determine this involves offering a person a choice of, say, $100 now or $200 after some delay and asking them to set the delay length so that they would be indifferent between the two choices. The typical delay time was around 31 days. One way of putting this result is that people were demanding a very high annual interest rate, far higher than available at banks, for keeping their money invested for that 31 days. George Anslie & Nick Haslam, *Hyperbolic Discounting, in* CHOICE OVER TIME 69 (G. Loewenstein & J. Elster eds., 1992). For pain, the case is less clear. If a future pain, such as an unavoidable electric shock, is certain, people often choose to get it

TABLE 1[9]

Type of offense	(a) Number Committed	(b) Number Reported (% of col. a)	(c) Number Arrests (% of col. a)	(d) Number Convictions (% of col. a)	(e) Prison Sentence (% of col. a)	(f) (Months) Sentence Imposed	(g) 1989 Time Served
Total	26,122,820	14,475,630 55.4%	2,313,247 8.9%	379,292 1.5%	279,909 1.1%	Fed=61.4 State=91.0	Fed=36.23 State=35.9
Murder and Non-Negligent Manslaughter	NA	23,440 —	18,298 78.1%	Fed=133 State=10,895 47%	Fed=124 State=10,350 44.7%	Fed=134.7 State=233.0	Fed=53.3 State=83.0 6.9 years
Rape	130,260	102,560 78.7%	30,966 23.8%	Fed=149 State=18,024 14.0%	Fed=120 State=15,500 12.0%	Fed=78.9 State=128.0	Fed=NA State=55.0 4.6 years
Robbery	1,149,710	639,270 55.6%	136,300 11.9%	Fed=1,337 State=47,446 4.2%	Fed=1,313 State=42,701 3.8%	Fed=100.7 State=97.0	Fed=58.6 State=41.0 3.4 years
Assault	4,728,810	1,054,860 22.3%	376,917 8.0%	Fed=455 State=53,861 1.1%	Fed=282 State=38,780 0.8%	Fed=34.8 State=52.0	Fed=41.9 State=23.0 1.9 years
Burglary	5,147,740	3,073,900 59.7%	341,192 6.6%	Fed=99 St.=109,250 2.1%	Fed=83 State=82,313 1.6%	Fed=34.4 State=61.0	Fed=26.0 State=22.0 1.8 years
Larceny-Theft	12,975,320	7,945,700 61.2%	1,241,236 9.6%	Fed=2,709 St.=113,094 0.9%	Fed=940 State=73,511 0.6%	Fed=18.8 State=33.0	Fed=16.3 State=14.0 1.2 years
Motor-Vehicle Theft	1,967,540	1,635,900 83.1%	168,338 8.6%	Fed=275 State=21,065 1.1%	Fed=200 State=13,692 0.7%	Fed=27.6 State=33.0	Fed=21.3 State=13.0 1.1 years

461

NORTHWESTERN UNIVERSITY LAW REVIEW

in our criminal justice system is well understood to exist far in the future, if it exists at all. Further, newspaper articles frequently report on prisons as "revolving doors"; thus, possibilities of early discharge may be exaggerated in the potential offender's mind. Still further, time in prison may not be as hateful for a person living poorly in the present, thus diminishing its deterrent value.[18]

Finally, recent work tends to suggest that the threat of prison is less than one might expect in other ways. For instance, research on the recollection of painful experiences suggests that the duration of the experience is less important than the peak of the pain felt during it, and that the level of discomfort felt at the *end* of the experience is overweighed in recollection. Kahneman points out what that might mean for recidivism:

> [T]he well being of prison inmates is likely to improve in the course of their sentence, as they gain seniority and survival skills. . . . Suppose . . . that prisoners apply a Peak and End rule in retrospective evaluations of their prison experience. The result would be a global evaluation that becomes steadily less aversive with time in prison, implying a negative correlation between sentence length and the deterrence of individual recidivism. This is surely not a socially desirable outcome.[19]

It surely also suggests that lengthy prison terms are not a particularly useful method of increasing deterrence effects on those who experience them.

All of these effects, factored into a perceptual deterrence theory, make the effects of prison term as deterrent less potent than they are in the objective calculations described above.[20] Consider the implica-

---

over with quickly, probably to avoid anticipatory dread and anxiety. *See* George Loewenstein, *Anticipation and the Valuation of Delayed Consumption*, 97 ECON. J. 667 (1987). But, of course, as we have shown, prison terms are by no means certain, or even likely. Elster and Loewenstein suggest a relationship between probability and dread that probably fits the present case. "At very low probability levels, below a threshold of conceivability, . . . dread will be nil. Beyond this threshold, we would expect a sudden jump and then low marginal sensitivity over a wide range of probabilities beyond that point . . . ." Jon Elster & George Loewenstein, *Utility from Memory and Anticipation, in* CHOICE OVER TIME, *supra*, at 213-34.

18 Feeney quotes one robber as saying, "I don't really have any fear of prisons or things like that. I always sort of felt like I was going back someday . . . ." Feeney, *supra* note 16, at 59.

19 Daniel Kahneman, *New Challenges to the Rationality Assumption*, 150 J. INST. & THEORETICAL ECON. 18, 33-34 (1994).

20 A review of the empirical evidence on perceptual deterrence theories confirms what this suggests. The theories predict an inverse relationship between perceived severity and certainty of punishment and crime. But the earlier empirical studies of the theory, which were done using cross-sectional survey study methods, generally found that perceived certainty of punishment deterred crime but the perceived severity did not. In a cross-sectional design, a respondent is asked, for example, about his or her perceptions of the severity and certainty of punishment and arrest record at the same time. These perceptions, reported after experiencing arrest, are assumed to be identical with those held before the arrests, obviously a questionable assumption. Longitudinal, or panel study methods, measure respondent perceptions at time one, and determine respondent arrest records at time two, a better design from the point of view of establishing

tions of this for designing a deterrence-based system that might actually have a significant effect. The logic of a deterrence-based system drives toward the adoption of a fixed "quantum" of punishment for an offense, set according to the stake that society has in lowering the rate of that offense. Inexorably, then, as the probability of arrest or conviction is reduced, and the time of the onset of the already problematic prison term is pushed into the distant and discountable future, one can achieve the fixed quantum of punishment only by increasing the magnitude of the prison sentence or the severity of the conditions under which it is served.

Refer to our earlier figures to see why longer prison terms can have only a limited effect in deterring crime: If a robber faces a 3.8% chance of going to prison, why should it matter to him whether the likely sentence is 2 years or 10 years? The impact of this difference in prison terms on the total disutility score is trivial.[21] If we wished to make it non-trivial, look what we would have to do. If, for instance, we thought that a real threat of a four year sentence was needed to deter burglary, and noticed that only 1.6% of those committing burglary eventually went to prison for their offense, would we wish to impose a 250 year sentence, to keep the quantum of anticipated punishment around that of the 4 year sentence? No. As a practical matter, the community is likely to be morally offended by the suggestion. As one reviewer has remarked, observing the current high levels of crime that are not being deterred by threat of punishment:

> If we cannot live with this, we must lower our ethical standard as the amount of pain we are willing to inflict on others if necessary, and we must considerably tighten police control. . . . If we want to change this,

causality. Later studies, using more sophisticated panel study methods, generally found no evidence of a deterrence effect for either perceived severity or certainty of punishment. Daniel Nagin & Raymond Paternoster, *The Preventive Effects of the Perceived Risk of Arrest: Testing an Expanded Conception of Deterrence*, 29 CRIMINOLOGY 561, 570-72 (1991). None of this is encouraging for those arguing for a deterrence-based system of crime prevention.

The analysis can be made to get worse from the perspective of one wishing to rely on deterrence. Lately in social science there has been increasing skepticism about the validity of the subjective expected utility model that forms the core of perceptual deterrence models. Decision models are being substituted that more closely follow empirical evidence about people's actual representations of events, outcomes, and probabilities. Prospect theory is one contender to replace subjective expected utility theory, and Lattimore and Witte develop a version of Kahneman and Tversky's prospect theory for application to the prediction of criminal behavior. Lattimore & Witte, *supra* note 14, at 137-44. In summary, it does not lead to any more optimistic views on criminal sanction as a successful deterrent of criminal acts. It does not, in other words, rescue a deterrence theory of crime prevention.

[21] Assume that we think that 10 years is a reasonable deterrent sentence for a robbery, as long as it is certain and swift and served in full. In other words, we wanted a deterrence value of 10 for robbery. The simple deterrence value of a 10 year sentence with a 3.8% chance of going to jail, then, is 0.38, of a 2 year sentence, 0.076. Neither deters. *See supra* note 9 and accompanying text.

NORTHWESTERN UNIVERSITY LAW REVIEW

there is a terrible price to pay: a police state operating a brutal criminal justice system.[22]
Realistically and happily, we are not going to pay this price; as a concomitant of that, the deterrence approach to preventing criminality is gravely weakened.

B. Rehabilitation

The rehabilitationist approach to sentencing has lost credibility, based on the findings of numerous studies indicating that criminal rehabilitation programs, as practiced, do not produce impressive, or often even detectable reductions in recidivism of those who have participated in the programs. As Cook comments, a number of true experiments on rehabilitation were conducted, and "[t]he failure of these studies to demonstrate efficacy in reducing recidivism rates has been a major impetus in the current trend away from indeterminant sentencing and the 'rehabilitative ideal.'"[23] Further, "[i]t is safe to conclude that correctional rehabilitation programs, taken collectively, have had a small effect on crime rates in the past, and that a number of notable programs failed completely."[24]

C. Incapacitation

Incapacitation, particularly of repeat offenders, is currently attracting a good deal of popular and legislative attention. Part of the reason for its popularity, we suspect, lies in its apparent realism. An incapacitation-based sentencing system implicitly gives up on rehabilitative possibilities and on the possibilities of deterring the specific criminals to which it is applied. It prevents crime in only one way: by preventing the specific criminal from committing crimes during the duration of his sentence. (Actually, it does not even do that; it prevents the commission of crimes outside, but not inside, the prison.)

The attractiveness of incapacitation stems from the belief that an enormous number of crimes are committed by a relatively small group of repeat offenders.[25] If one locks these offenders away, then crime rates will be greatly decreased. However, several assumptions intervene between the fact of repeat criminality and the postulated success of incapacitation, and these assumptions need to be examined. The possibility exists that we are entering a period of unexamined enthusi-

---

[22] Hans F. M. Crombag, *When Law and Psychology Meet, in* CRIMINAL BEHAVIOR AND THE JUSTICE SYSTEM: PSYCHOLOGICAL PERSPECTIVES 1, 11 (Hermann Wegener et al. eds., 1989).

[23] Cook, *supra* note 8, at 166.

[24] *Id.* Cook goes on to point out that if one or more specific rehabilitation programs can be shown to work, then rehabilitation deserves consideration in that specific instance.

[25] A Rand Corporation study was highly influential in establishing this fact and making the case for an incapacitation-based system. For this study, see PETER W. GREENWOOD, SELECTIVE INCAPACITATION (1982).

asm for incapacitation that will lead to an uncritical adoption of sentencing programs based on it, followed by its rejection, if it produces less than its proponents claim for it.

The central task of an incapacitationist system is to identify those offenders who are likely to commit repeated offenses in the future. By assigning long sentences to those offenders, an incapacitation-based system will have its differential success rate over other sentencing systems. In other words, the system depends on predicting "dangerousness," with dangerousness defined as a high likelihood of committing future crimes, defined, in other words, as recidivism.

Those who have reviewed the empirical status of the prediction of dangerousness do not claim the accuracy rates that would provide confidence in an incapacitation-based system. Schmidt and Witte report a careful and statistically sophisticated study, the conclusions of which are not encouraging for an incapacitation strategy. First, they demonstrate that the accuracy of the prediction of recidivism is highly dependent on the statistical system that one uses to model it.[26] Second, their best model predicts recidivism in a way that is too inaccurate, in their view, to be used in assigning people to such important fates as prison or freedom.[27] That is, the predictions are not entirely inaccurate, but they are too inaccurate for the purposes to which we wish to put them.[28] Specifically, the system falsely identified 47% of those predicted to recidivate; that is, 47% of those predicted to recidivate did not in fact do so in their study.[29] As they remark:

> Our predictions for individuals were reasonable. However, they suffered from a high false positive rate. We were not able to accurately identify a group of career criminals that might be selectively incapacitated. Our false negative rate was lower (28%) and in that sense we were able to identify a group that usefully might be considered for fewer restrictions on their freedom. . . .
>
> A policy of selective incapacitation would be far easier to market if there were some "objective" scientific evidence of one's power to identify a particularly crime-prone group of individuals. We have been able

---

[26] Peter Schmidt & Ann Witte, Predicting Recidivism Using Survival Models 158 (1988).

[27] The model does meet one set of criteria for success, suggested by David Farrington, *Predicting Individual Crime Rates*, 9 Crime and Justice: An Annual Review of Research 53 (1987). He suggests that a successful predictive system should have less than a 50% false positive rate and less than a 50% false negative rate. What this means is that, of each 100 people predicted to recidivate, at least 50 should do so, and of each 100 people predicted to not commit further crimes, at least 50 should not do so. The reader will notice that this set of criteria do not seem highly rigorous, and yet it has proved in practice quite hard for recidivism prediction systems to reach it.

[28] Schmidt & Witte, *supra* note 26, at 160.

[29] A false positive rate of 47% and a false negative rate of 28% are better than those obtained in other studies of a similar sort. Schmidt & Witte review the rates from other studies. *See* Schmidt & Witte, *supra* note 26, at 142.

NORTHWESTERN UNIVERSITY LAW REVIEW

> to identify such a group only with a level of error that we feel is unacceptable. . . .
>
> We find the false positive rates too high to use current methods as models for selecting individuals for harsher treatment than they would receive otherwise.[30]

Other studies have suggested that available models are less successful, showing false positive rates of nearly 80%.[31]

It is reasonable to suppose that predictor systems could improve by reducing their error rates, but there are real limits to any prediction of a particular person's future behavior. This means that, in an incapacitation-based system, some people will receive long sentences because they are falsely predicted to be repeat offenders, and others will receive short sentences because they are not predicted to be dangerous but will prove to be repeat offenders on release. With the first sort of error, we will confine for lengthy sentences many people who do not in fact require such treatment, crowding the prison system and increasing its already substantial cost. However, the fact that many of those incarcerated would have committed no crimes were they out of prison cannot become visible because they are in prison. With the second sort of error, we will fail to confine some who will offend again on discharge, and that fact will become highly, publicly visible. Among those who look to incapacitation as a panacea for what they see as crime out of control, this is likely to lead to a dynamic in which, seeking to avoid letting out of prison those who offend again, we increasingly move to assign incapacitative sentences to those for whom the prediction of dangerousness is weaker and weaker, a fact that arouses concerns for justice in many who think about the issue.

Consider also the ethical issues in an incapacitation strategy. Taking a position similar in some respects to our own, Morris and Miller suggest that an increase in penalties based on predictions of future recidivism is moral only if it does not increase the punishment beyond what would be assigned from a just desert perspective.[32] Gottfredson and Gottfredson are willing to use predictive equations to select those for deinstitutional treatments, but not for selecting those who should receive longer sentences.[33] Consider also what variables are likely to appear in the prediction of dangerousness equations. Certainly race will appear there; certainly also gender, as crimes are disproportionately committed by men, not women. Age also is a remarkably strong predictor of crimes. All of these predictors

---

[30] *Id.* at 149.

[31] John Monahan, *Violence Prediction: The Last 20 and the Next 20 Years, in* 23 CRIM. JUST. & BEHAV. 107 (1996).

[32] Norval Morris & Marc Miller, *Predictions of Dangerousness*, 6 CRIME AND JUSTICE: AN ANNUAL REVIEW OF RESEARCH 1, 35 (1985).

[33] Stephen D. Gottfredson & Don M. Gottfredson, *Accuracy of Predictive Models, in* 2 CRIMINAL CAREERS AND "CAREER CRIMINALS" 212, 280 (A. Blumstein et al. eds., 1986).

emerge as significant.[34] What these predictors will lead to, if they are used, is a remarkably strong tendency to incarcerate, for a long sentence, a young, African-American male who commits one crime.

There is an obvious ethical dilemma here; these are attributes that the individual was born with, and many would object to using them as indicators that a person should be sentenced to a longer prison term. The report of the National Panel on Research on Criminal Careers comments that "[c]haracteristics such as race, ethnicity and religion are especially unacceptable as candidate predictors because they have no relationship to blameworthiness . . . and their use affronts basic social values . . . ."[35]

A different sort of objection is found in the failure of the terms of incarceration to match their rationale. The conditions of prison life can be quite harsh; to go to prison in the United States in 1996 can mean exposure to a debased, mind-numbing environment, including significant possibilities of forcible rape, contracting AIDS, and contracting a virulent strain of tuberculosis. The conditions of confinement upon commitment under the criminal justice system are conditions of punishment. Yet, the justification for confinement under an incapacitation strategy is not punishment but prevention, akin to the system of preventive detention that we use for those with infectious diseases or mental illness that is likely to lead to violent behavior. Systems of preventative detention are morally ambiguous, but certainly we are most comfortable with them when they involve detention conditions that are not punitive in nature, involve "treatment" efforts that attempt to remove the elements in the individual that cause the presumed dangerousness, and continually reassess the dangerousness of the individual who is incarcerated. This is not a good description of the workings of the prison system in the United States. Indeed, the current trend toward increased use of a dangerousness rationale is accompanied by a trend to increase the harshness of prison life and to abolish periodic review.

To us, the most severe criticism of an incapacitation-based sentencing system is that it requires a distribution of liability very different from what the community regards as just punishment for the

---

[34] SCHMIDT & WITTE, *supra* note 26, ch. 8.

[35] Joseph G. Weis, *Issues in the Measurement of Criminal Careers, in* 2 CRIMINAL CAREERS AND "CAREER CRIMINALS", *supra* note 33, at 8-12. There is certainly a desire on the part of the community to protect itself from crime, and a willingness to consider incapacitation as one of the least objectionable options for preventing crime. This has led one of us to suggest that an incapacitation system should exist, but that such a system should be located within the civil rather than the criminal commitment system. The system there will be more familiar with the assessment of the continuing dangerousness of the individual and more able to provide detention conditions that are non-punitive in nature. *See* Paul H. Robinson, *Foreword: The Criminal-Civil Distinction and Dangerous Blameless Offenders*, 83 J. CRIM. L. & CRIMINOLOGY 693, 706-14 (1993).

NORTHWESTERN UNIVERSITY LAW REVIEW

offense committed. First, it assigns sentences of very different lengths to two individuals who have committed exactly the same crime, where one is predicted to be a repeat offender and the other is not. Further, the predicted repeat offender is being punished for an action that he has not yet done, or perhaps even thought of: the future offense. If he is one of the 47% of those predicted from the current best predictor system to commit another offense who would not, the "false positives," he is being punished for an offense that he never would have committed. Finally, an incapacitation strategy assigns liabilities based on considerations that do not figure into the community's perceptions of the appropriate sentences for the crime committed, such as the strong predictors of race, gender, and age. This brings us to what will become our familiar argument: an incapacitation-based sentencing system undercuts the moral credibility of the criminal law and thus the system's ability to produce voluntary compliance with its mandates.

D. Summary

To summarize our arguments about the standard utilitarian-based punishment systems: Rehabilitation-based systems, formerly popular, rarely worked and are now rarely under active consideration as a sentencing strategy. Incapacitation-based systems, currently generating a great deal of interest, have a number of difficulties that are likely, at best, to make them less attractive than they seem and, at worst, to cause intolerable injustice on a broad scale. A system centered on deterrence also has a number of difficulties, most prominently the remarkably low detection and conviction rates on many crimes and conflict with the upper limits on sentences that people consider just. This suggests that a system that would truly deter would be regarded as excessively draconian by the community. The evidence suggests that the fear of arrest and incarceration in prison is not effective in causing people to obey the law. This confronts us with the question: Why, then, do people obey the law? Perhaps if we understood better the dynamics of these forces, we might discover ways in which law-abiding behavior could be enhanced.

II. WHY DO PEOPLE OBEY THE LAW?

Given the weak deterrent threat facing people, why do the vast majority of those free in society still act in a way consistent with the law? Social scientists have a preliminary answer: More than because of the threat of legal punishment, people obey the law (1) because they fear the disapproval of their social group if they violate the law, and (2) because they generally see themselves as moral beings who want to do the right thing as they perceive it. In social science, these two factors are referred to as (1) compliance produced by normative social influence, and (2) behavior produced by internalized moral standards and rules.

These informal sources of behavioral control function in a variety of ways. The normative pressures from other people, generally experienced as an external force by the actor, function like the more formal deterrence mechanisms were thought to function. People obey the social norms of their groups because those groups have rewards to give for doing so and sanctions for failing to do so. Three classes of "informal sanctions" are usually identified and can be incurred when one's group judges that one has transgressed: "commitment costs," in which past accomplishments are in jeopardy; "attachment costs," involving the loss of valued relationships with others; and "stigma," discreditation in the eyes of others.[36] These sanctions may follow arrest for a crime, but if the harm-doing act becomes known or suspected within one's community, even if one is not arrested, informal sanctioning processes may occur.[37] The social costs to the offender may extend beyond the offender's friends and family. If one is thought to have committed a crime, one may lose one's job, ability to borrow money, ability to command trust from others, and possible business partners.[38]

People's own moral rules and action proscriptions are generally experienced as internal forces; people recognize that they come from the moral rules that they have adopted. Phenomenologically, we all have experienced this sense of obligation to act in a certain way, to avoid harm to another, or to fulfill some commitment we have made.

These two barriers to deviant behavior—social sanctions and internal moral sanctions—are analytically and often experientially separable, but in the longer term they converge. Children are trained by a powerful socialization process into internalizing the beliefs represented in the social norms of the culture to which they belong. People come to hold the moral standards of the cultures in which they are

---

[36] Exactly what loss counts in what category is not perfectly resolvable; loss of marriage prospects is often listed as a commitment cost, while loss of an existing relationship with a significant other is an attachment cost. Stigma may be feared because it causes others to be unwilling to enter attachments with the stigmatized individual, hire that individual, and so on. The point is that a good many informal sanctions may be risked when one transgresses, and the initial application of some sanctions may lead to further ones.

[37] Anonymity, often thought to be a cause of crime in cities, works by severing the informal social sanctions from the individual.

[38] Nagin & Paternoster, *supra* note 20, at 562; Kirk R. Williams & Richard Hawkins, *Perceptual Research on General Deterrence: A Critical Review*, 20 LAW & SOC'Y REV. 545, 565-66 (1986). For an examination of the effect of criminal conviction on an offender's future earning potential, see John Lott, Jr., *An Attempt at Measuring the Total Monetary Penalty from Drug Convictions: The Importance of an Individual's Reputation*, 21 J. LEGAL STUD. 159 (1992); John Lott, Jr., *Do We Punish High Income Criminals Too Heavily?*, 30 ECON. INQUIRY 583 (1992).

NORTHWESTERN UNIVERSITY LAW REVIEW

raised; internal moral standards and external norms generally label the same actions right or wrong.

What is the evidence concerning crime prevention due to fear of social sanction or fulfillment of moral obligation? It is scattered but supportive. Since many of the studies that provide evidence for the operation of social sanctions also report evidence about the role of internalized moral control in inhibiting criminal acts, we review evidence for both forces simultaneously.[39]

Harold Grasmick and his associates have done the most sustained work documenting the role of the informal determinants of law-abidingness. Their research consistently finds that fear of social disapproval and moral commitment to the law both inhibit the commission of illegal activity.[40] They comment that their "findings highlight the importance of internal control in producing conformity to the law."[41] Other researchers reach similar conclusions. Paternoster and Iovanni conclude that "the greatest effects on delinquent involvement are those from informal forces of social control."[42] Meir and Johnson conclude: "despite contemporary predisposition toward the importance of legal sanction, our findings are . . . consistent with the accumulated literature concerning the primacy of interpersonal influence" over legal sanction.[43] Tom Tyler's review of existing studies con-

---

[39] In a study measuring the frequency of property and drug offenses committed by juveniles, it was found that offense frequency was predicted by whether the actor perceived that his friends would approve of the delinquent actions, and negatively predicted by possession of a set of conventional moral beliefs that delinquent acts are wrong. Nagin & Paternoster, *supra* note 20, at 574. (Some evidence was also found for an effect of certainty of arrest on delinquent acts.) Commitment but not attachment or stigma costs were measured in this study.

[40] Harold Grasmick & Donald Green, *Legal Punishment, Social Disapproval and Internalization as Inhibitors of Illegal Behavior*, 71 J. CRIM. L. & CRIMINOLOGY 325 (1980).

[41] Harold Grasmick & Robert Bursik, *Conscience, Significant Others, and Rational Choice*, 24 LAW & SOC'Y REV. 837, 854 (1990). They came to this conclusion based on the repeated discovery that those who reported that certain actions were immoral, wrong, bad, or seen by others about whom they cared as wrong, were less likely to engage in those actions.

[42] Raymond Paternoster & Lee Ann Iovanni, *The Deterrent Effect of Perceived Severity: A Reexamination*, 64 SOCIAL FORCES 751, 769 (1986). They came to this conclusion based on the correlation between an individual reporting that certain actions would be disapproved of by others who were significant to that individual, for instance friends or peers, and the individual's comparatively low rate of committing those actions. One is less likely to commit actions of which those around him will disapprove.

[43] Robert Meir & Weldon Johnson, *Deterrence as Social Control: The Legal and Extralegal Production of Conformity*, 42 AM. SOC. REV. 292, 302 (1977). Here the authors are commenting both on their review of the related literature and their own findings. Characteristically, these studies have some assessment of a person's judgment that certain actions are right or wrong, moral or immoral, of concerns about what sanctions that people in his social networks would inflict on him if he did those actions, and of concerns about what sanctions such as arrest, conviction, and jail term the legal system would inflict on him if he did those actions. The power of each of these classes of variables to predict whether he actually commits the actions is tested. The first two sets of variables to predict criminal actions are characteristically demonstrated in this research, and their predictive power is often higher than that of the fear of legal sanctions.

cludes, "Testing the ability of each of the attitudinal factors . . . to predict variance in compliance . . . the most important incremental contribution is made by personal morality . . . ."[44]

III. CRIMINAL LAW'S INFLUENCE ON THE SOCIAL FORCES OF COMPLIANCE

The evidence reviewed suggests that the influences of social group sanctions and internalized norms are the most powerful determinants of conduct, more significant than the threat of deterrent legal sanctions. But, we argue, the law is not irrelevant to the operation of these powerful forces. Criminal law in particular can influence the norms that are held by the social group and that are internalized by the individual. Criminal law's influence comes from being a societal mechanism by which the force of social norms is realized and by which the force of internal moral principles is strengthened. That is, the law has no independent force, the way social group norms and internalized norms do. It has power to the extent that it can amplify and sustain these two power sources; it has power to the extent that it influences what the social group thinks and what its members internalize.

A. *The Criminal Law's Ability to Facilitate the Creation of Shared Norms*

Our first claim is that the criminal law influences the powerful social forces of normative behavior control through its central role in the creation of shared norms. The norms at issue here are of a limited sort, of course. Criminal law ought to and does have little interest in norms that influence everyday matters of style, dress, speech, manners, etc. Cutting in line, being rude, or wearing revealing clothing may be annoying to some people, but it generally is not and ought not be criminal. Even if such violations of norms were frowned upon by most people, the conduct ought not be criminal because it fails to reach the level of seriousness that deserves the condemnation of criminal liability, which is typically and properly limited to the violation of

---

This is not inconsistent with finding that the fear of criminal sanctions has some deterrent effect in some of the studies.

[44] TOM R. TYLER, WHY PEOPLE OBEY THE LAW 60 (1990). In a subset of studies that Tyler reviews, respondents reported on whether they considered certain actions moral or immoral, on other reasons for committing or not committing those actions, and on the frequency with which they committed those actions. Consistently, "personal morality," the degree to which the individual regarded those actions as right or wrong, predicted the frequency with which those actions were engaged in, and predicted this frequency more strongly than did the other possible predictors.

norms against violence and dishonesty.[45] As Gottfriedson and Hirshi have remarked, the criminal law is about force and fraud.[46]

    1. The Educative Function of Criminal Law Adjudication and Legislative Debate.—As to norms against force and fraud, social science suggests that the criminal law builds and maintains societal norms in several related ways. First, criminal law enforcement and adjudication activities send daily messages to all who read or hear about them. Every time criminal liability is imposed, it reminds us of the norm prohibiting the offender's conduct and confirms its condemnable nature.[47] The public condemnation expressed in reaction to the offense supports and encourages the efforts of those who have resisted temptation and continued to remain law-abiding. Having avoided breaking that law, people can regard themselves favorably, which in turn reinforces their moral commitment to the norm expressed in the offense.

    Further, every adjudication offers an opportunity to confirm the exact nature of the norm or to signal a shift or refinement of it. Thus, an endangerment or manslaughter prosecution of a polluter points out that some instances of polluting can violate the norm against endangering others. The publicity surrounding an adjudication can teach all people about the consequences of certain kinds of polluting and, therefore, that it ought to be avoided. Kai Erikson's studies point out the role of criminal law in marking the limits between allowable, although perhaps regrettable, conduct and criminal conduct: The prosecution of a deviant brands the deviant as a criminal and casts a bright light on the exact location of a boundary that previously might have been obscure to the community.[48]

    Further, people are likely to attend to the comparative liabilities that are assigned by sentencing provisions of legal systems; people intuit that more morally serious offenses should command greater penalties. As Cook remarks, "The legislated (and actual) severity of penalty for a particular offense may influence the public's feeling for the seriousness or moral repugnance of this offense."[49] In the long run, for those crimes in which "moral inhibition" plays an important

---

    [45] There are some exceptions, however. Eating human flesh and bestiality, for example, remain criminal because the norms against such conduct remain strongly and widely felt.

    [46] Michael R. Gottfriedson & Travis Hirschi, A General Theory of Crime 4 (1990).

    [47] At the same time, regular non-enforcement or a declination to prosecute or to convict tends to undermine the norm prohibiting the conduct. Thus, adultery may remain on the books but a policy of not prosecuting it takes away the criminal law's support of any norm against such conduct that may have existed.

    [48] Kai Erikson, The Wayward Puritans: A Study in the Sociology of Deviance (1966).

    [49] Cook, *supra* note 8, at 177.

91:453 (1997)   *Utility of Desert*

role, announcing high severity of punishment may be an important communication; more important than ensuring high probability of punishment, which we have argued is generally not possible.

The criminal adjudication process is not the only forum for public discussion and announcement. Legislative proposals for criminalization or decriminalization, or increased or decreased punishment, also provide an occasion for public debate that can help build norms, with the conclusion of the debate announced by legislative action or inaction. The public discussion about the problem of hate speech and proposals to criminalize it, for example, help strengthen the shared public understanding that such conduct is condemnable. When one seeks to criminalize an act, the debate should say why that act endangers others, or otherwise fits the case of those things we are willing to criminalize. In our complex, interdependent society, this can be usefully instructive. If lawmakers argue that an act should not be criminalized, or should be decriminalized, then they should be able to say why it does not resemble the sorts of things that are now criminalized.

2. The Relationship Between Criminal Law and Community Norms.—Notice that we said that laws can *contribute* to the formation and change of community norms and individuals' moral reasoning; laws cannot themselves compel community acceptance. Passing a law cannot itself create a norm, and not passing a law against certain conduct cannot make that conduct morally acceptable to the community. The passage and subsequent failure of National Prohibition shows the law's limited ability to change norms even when the change is supported by a significant portion of the public.[50] Some would argue that the continuing controversy over our "war on drugs" raises a similar issue.[51] The law is, rather, a vehicle by which the community debates, tests, and ultimately settles upon and expresses its norms. The passage of criminal legislation more often reflects a critical level of support for an incipient norm. The act of criminalization sometimes nurtures the norm, as does faithful enforcement and prosecution, and over time the community view may mature into a strong consensus. The criminal law is not an independent player in that process, but it is a contributing mechanism by which the norm-nurturing process moves forward.

We have seen the process at work recently in enhancing prohibitory norms against sexual harassment, hate speech, drunk driving, and domestic violence. It has also been at work in diluting existing norms

---

[50] In December of 1933, the repeal of the Eighteenth Amendment was completed by the adoption of the Twenty-First Amendment. It was, "[i]n hindsight . . . the legal outcome of a foolish, unpopular reform." DAVID E. KYVIG, REPEALING NATIONAL PROHIBITION 3 (1979).

[51] *See, e.g.*, Anthony Lewis, *Prohibition Folly*, N.Y. TIMES, Feb. 12, 1996, at A13.

NORTHWESTERN UNIVERSITY LAW REVIEW

against homosexual conduct, fornication, and adultery. While it is difficult to untangle how much the criminal law reform followed and how much it led these shifts, it seems difficult to imagine that these changes could have occurred without the recognition and confirmation that comes through changes in criminal law legislation, enforcement, and adjudication.

Perhaps more than any other society, ours relies on the criminal law for norm-nurturing. Our greater cultural diversity means that we cannot expect a stable pre-existing consensus on the contours of condemnable conduct that is found in more homogeneous societies. We require more public debate and discussion to reconcile conflicting views and more public education on the refinements and consensuses that result. Unlike many other societies, we share no religion or other arbiter of morality that might perform this role. Our criminal law is, for us, the place we express our shared beliefs of what is truly condemnable.

B. The Criminal Law's Compliance Power as a Moral Authority in Unanalyzed Cases

The discussion above describes the criminal law's role as a forum and communicator in the process by which moral norms are reinforced, established, or diluted. The criminal law also has a second effect in shaping conduct, specifically in gaining compliance with its demands. If it has developed a reputation as a reliable statement of existing norms, people will be willing to defer to its moral authority in cases where there exists some ambiguity as to the wrongfulness of the contemplated conduct.

1. Evidence of the Criminal Law's Power as a Moral Authority.—There is evidence, largely collected and analyzed by Tyler, that people are inclined to accept the law as a source of moral authority that they themselves should take seriously. This is referred to in social science as informational influence—influence produced by the information transmitted by a specific institution, in which one accepts the validity of the definition of right and wrong behavior conveyed by that institution, internalizes that definition, and expects other people to have internalized it as well. Tyler reviews the literature that relates a person's belief that a law reflects a valid moral rule to obedience to that law, and finds them to be quite strongly related.[52] He notes: "This high level of normative commitment to obeying the law offers an important basis for the effective exercise of authority by legal officials. People clearly have a strong predisposition toward following the

---

[52] TYLER, *supra* note 44, at 37.

law. If authorities can tap into such feelings, their decisions will be more widely followed."[53]

Tyler reviews a number of studies that suggest that the level of commitment to obey the law is proportional to what Tyler calls the law's perceived "legitimacy," by which he means a community's perceptions that, first, the law instantiates their moral beliefs, and, second, that the law came into being via fair procedures conducted by the appropriate authorities.[54] Tyler reasons that, if one regards the law as a legitimate source of rules, if it has what we have called "moral credibility," then one should be more likely to regard the law's judgments about right and wrong actions as an appropriate input to one's own moral thinking; in turn, one should be more likely to obey the law. Further, one should be more likely to support the authorities that promulgated the law. To test this contention he reviews a number of studies that examine individual differences in perceptions of the law's legitimacy and relate those differences to differences in support for legal authorities and felt obligations to obey the law.

> Six studies . . . address the question of whether feelings of [the law's] legitimacy lead to behavioral compliance with the law and legal authorities, regardless of whether those feelings are expressed as support for the authorities or as an obligation to obey . . . . These studies suggest that those who view authority as legitimate are more likely to comply with legal authority, whether the legitimacy is expressed as obligation or as support . . . .[55]

Also as one would expect, those who perceive the political authority that governs them to be less legitimate are more likely to engage in acts of social or political protest, some of which are illegal. More research on this issue is obviously needed, but we conclude that the current research supports our claim of a connection between perceptions of the law's moral credibility and obedience to the law.

2. Actions That Are Not Obviously Harmful.—Notice that, as a matter of common sense, the law's moral credibility is not needed to tell a person that murder, rape, or robbery is wrong. The criminal law's influence as a moral authority has effect primarily at the border-

---

[53] *Id.* at 60. In another study, Grasmick and Green conclude: "[E]ach of the three independent variables [of deterrence by threat of legal punishment, social disapproval, and personal moral commitment] makes a significant independent contribution to the explained variance [i.e., the rate of criminal behavior]." Grasmick & Green, *supra* note 40, at 326.

[54] *See* TYLER, *supra* note 44, at 64-68; studies listed in Tables 3.1, 3.2, and 3.3, *id.* at 32-37.

[55] *Id.* at 31. Tyler suggests that the law gains legitimacy in two ways, only one of which we emphasize in our argument. First, and the element we emphasize, the law gains legitimacy because it is seen as being in accord with the moral rules of the community. Second, it gains legitimacy because it is the product of processes such as legislation and judicial debate, which are the processes that society has agreed are the appropriate ones to enact such laws. In other words, the laws are the products of legitimate authority. We agree that procedural fairness is an important additional element producing moral credibility for the law.

NORTHWESTERN UNIVERSITY LAW REVIEW

line of criminal activity, where there may be some ambiguity as to whether the conduct really is wrong.

How does this ambiguity arise? Historically, scholars have distinguished between two kinds of "crimes": crimes that are *mala in se* and those that are *malum prohibitum*; crimes that are wrong in themselves and actions that are crimes because they are prohibited by law. This distinction gained use because of the possibilities of remote consequences that arise in modern, complexly interdependent societies. We all may take actions that are harmful in ways that may not be immediately obvious. The harm may be to specific others or to society as a whole or to society's institutions. If these harms are reasonably predictable from certain kinds of conduct, and of sufficient magnitude, then it is appropriate to criminalize the conduct. Driving faster than the speed limit, driving while intoxicated, or insider trading are all examples of this class of conduct.

To be maximally effective, the legal system must publicize why these kinds of conduct lead to outcomes that are sufficiently damaging to be criminalized. But realistically, the legal system cannot constantly generate public understanding of why each specific prohibited act is wrong, and its ability to discourage the conduct shifts to its general reputation for being a reliable judge of what is sufficiently objectionable to merit the condemnation of criminal conviction. If the law has a good reputation, people are more likely to defer to its judgement. If it has a bad reputation, people are more likely to discount its prohibition as one more example of a criminal law focused on something other than imposing liability for wrongs that deserve condemnation.

C. Summary

Internalized moral rules and social norms that are enforced by community sanctions are important sources of compliance with the moral prohibitions of the community. Criminal law rules can contribute to normative forces; they can shape, alter, and guide those forces, but only if the community accepts the law as a legitimate source of moral authority. If the law has this acceptance, debates over legislative proposals or publicity about criminal prosecutions can educate the public about what actions are sufficiently serious to deserve criminal condemnation. If the law has moral authority, it can be a reliable guide in shaping conduct for those cases in which the moral justifications for its prohibitions are not immediately obvious. In an increasingly complex and interdependent society, there may be many cases of this sort, conduct that on analysis proves to be harmful, but is not immediately apparently so. Public conviction and condemnation of an inside trader, for example, can help spread the word that the conduct really is condemnable. Public conviction and condemnation of one who kills another while driving drunk can and probably has helped to spread the word that driving while drunk is morally reprehensible because of its potential to kill.

But the criminal law can only hope to shape moral thinking or to have people follow its rules in ambiguous cases if it has earned a reputation as an institution whose focus is morally condemnable conduct and is seen as giving reliable statements of what is and is not truly condemnable. A criminal law that is seen as having a different criterion for criminalization—such as criminalization whenever the greater penalties of criminal law can provide useful deterrents—is not likely to gain such a reputation. How the law gains—and loses—its reputation as a reliable moral guide is the topic with which we deal next.

IV. The Determinants of Criminal Law's Moral Credibility

Our central point is this: The criminal law's power in nurturing and communicating societal norms and its power to have people defer to it in unanalyzed cases is directly proportional to criminal law's moral credibility. If criminalization or conviction (or decriminalization or refusal to convict) is to have an effect in the norm-nurturing process, it will be because the criminal law has a reputation for criminalizing and punishing only that which deserves moral condemnation, and for decriminalizing and not punishing that which does not. If, instead, the criminal law's reputation is one simply of a collection of rules, which do not necessarily reflect the community's perceptions of moral blameworthiness, then there would be little reason to expect the criminal law to be relevant to the societal debate over what is and is not condemnable and little reason to defer to it as a moral authority. What then are the requirements for a criminal law system to gain this credibility? How can this credibility be lost?

A. A Central Concern for Doing Justice

Enhancing the criminal law's moral credibility requires, more than anything, that the criminal law make clear to the public that its overriding concern is doing justice. Therefore, the most important reforms for establishing the criminal law's moral credibility may be those that concern the rules by which criminal liability and punishment are distributed. The criminal law must earn a reputation for (1) punishing those who deserve it under rules perceived as just, (2) protecting from punishment those who do not deserve it, and (3) where punishment is deserved, imposing the amount of punishment deserved, no more, no less. Thus, for example, the criminal law ought to maintain a viable insanity defense that excuses those who are perceived as not responsible for their offense, ought to avoid the use of

NORTHWESTERN UNIVERSITY LAW REVIEW

strict liability (imposing liability in the absence of a culpable state of mind), and ought to limit the use of non-exculpatory defenses.[56] In other words, it ought to adopt rules that distribute liability and punishment according to desert, even if a non-desert distribution appears in the short-run to offer the possibility of reducing crime.

The point is that every deviation from a desert distribution can incrementally undercut the criminal law's moral credibility, which in turn can undercut its ability to help in the creation and internalization of norms and its power to gain compliance by its moral authority. Thus, contrary to the apparent assumptions of past utilitarian debates,[57] such deviations from desert are not cost free, and their cost must be included in the calculation when determining which distribution of liability will most effectively reduce crime.

The law's moral credibility also may depend upon procedural and institutional reforms, as one of us has suggested elsewhere.[58] Some of these include less use of the exclusionary rule to exclude reliable evidence, less plea bargaining for reasons unrelated to genuine factual disputes, less restriction on police power where affected citizens want more, and insistence that non-incarcerative sanctions have sufficient punitive bite to inflict the amount of punishment deserved. Such reforms also would include increased protection of inmates against prison violence, decreased use of dangerousness as a criterion in setting prison terms, and more vigorous police training, discipline, and leadership to bring greater respect and restraint by police in dealing with citizens.

---

[56] It is not feasible to eliminate some non-exculpatory defenses, such as diplomatic immunity, but others can be narrowed if not eliminated. The length of statutes of limitation can be increased to avoid barriers that frustrate prosecutions that the society remains interested in. *See* PAUL H. ROBINSON, 2 CRIMINAL LAW DEFENSES 465-66 (1984). The entrapment defense can be eliminated or, at least, limited to cases of overwhelming coercion. *See* Christopher D. Moore, Comment, *The Elusive Foundation of the Entrapment Defense*, 89 Nw. U. L. REV. 1151, 1187-88 (1995).

[57] Consider Shavell's assertion: "Whether or not a party will actually commit an act . . . depends on his perception of the possibility that he will suffer a sanction, either monetary or nonmonetary. A party will commit an act if, and only if, the expected sanction would be less than the expected private benefits. If he decides not to commit an act, he will be said to be deterred." Steven Shavell, *Criminal Law and the Optimal Use of Nonmonetary Sanctions as a Deterrent*, 85 COLUM. L. REV. 1232, 1235 (1985). Certainly if one believes, as Shavell does, that only the threatened sanction affects a person's decision whether to commit an offense, then the extent to which the distribution of sanctions deviates from that perceived as deserved is irrelevant to the calculations. But one may also discount the importance of a distribution of perceived desert if one thinks that the effects of deviation are minor. For the discussion of the danger of any deviation, see *infra* Part VI.

[58] Paul H. Robinson, *Moral Credibility and Crime*, THE ATLANTIC MONTHLY, Mar. 1995, at 72.

B. The Detrimental Effect of Blurring the Criminal-Civil Distinction

The single most important structural reform may be a resharpening of the criminal-civil distinction, which has grown increasingly muddled over the past two decades. Civil law has been "criminalized" with the increased use of punitive damages.[59] But, of greater concern to us, is the "civilization" of the criminal law; the tendency to criminalize actions that are not those that the community would conceive of as condemnable conduct. As Jack Coffee has noted, there is a strong trend toward the criminalization of regulatory offenses, leading to the astounding number of some 300,000 federal "crimes."[60] The problem with this, from our point of view, is that current law has extended criminalization beyond even the domain of traditional *malum prohibitum* offenses, to criminalize conduct that is "harmful" only in the sense that it causes inconvenience for bureaucrats. Thus, most federal regulations are now routinely converted to federal crimes to give the regulators greater leverage in enforcement. Of similar effect is the increased use of strict liability and vicarious liability,[61] common features of civil law but out of place in a criminal system.

Examples of concrete cases will make our point clear. As is well known, individuals and organizations are required to provide large amounts of information to federal, state, and local governments. Providing false information is sometimes a criminalized regulatory offense. If false information knowingly is supplied to evade pollution regulations, taxes, or safety precautions, then the community will agree that this is conduct worthy of criminalization. However, if erroneous information is provided unwittingly or if such information has little bearing on matters of importance, then the community is not likely to see the action as criminal. Or consider a case in which an employer inadvertently fails to put all required information in a federally-required report (as opposed to knowingly putting false information in the report). This may arguably hurt society in some sense, but it is hard to see how; and even if it does, the degree of the injury is so infinitesimal that no one—even those who have full information about the need for the reporting requirement—would think that the failure

---

[59] Punitive damages at civil law may well have been created for a different reason than to mimic criminal liability, and might properly be maintained for this different reason, even in a system that returned to a sharp criminal-civil distinction. Specifically, one might speculate that in cases of intentional wrongdoing, which is where punitive damages typically are imposed, the harm of the violation to the victim is actually greater than where the harm is caused negligently. Note, for example, that the sting of discrimination often lies in its intentionality. The victim of the discrimination suffers more when the motive is clear than where the actions might be accidental. The introduction of punitive damages in cases of intentional torts may well have been out of recognition of this great harm.

[60] John C. Coffee, Jr., *Does "Unlawful" Mean "Criminal"?: Reflections on the Disappearing Tort/Crime Distinction in American Law*, 71 B.U. L. Rev. 193, 216 (1991).

[61] *See id.* at 210-15.

rises to the level of harm that deserves the moral condemnation traditionally associated with criminal conviction. If an adult-appearing twenty-year-old, with high-quality forged ID papers, buys an alcoholic beverage from a harassed bartender, the community has trouble seeing the action as criminal, although a strict liability statute holds the bartender liable and a vicarious liability statute holds the absent bar owner criminally liable.

The law, we suggest, cannot have moral credibility outside of a system with a clear criminal-civil distinction for several reasons. Much of civil law is governed by principles unrelated to desert. While there is some disagreement on the issue, one might well justify, for example, a tort system that uses forms of strict liability or vicarious liability. Even if fairness were adopted as the primary distributive principle for tort liability, no one would claim that tort liability ought to be limited to cases where moral condemnation is appropriate. A mixed criminal-civil system, then, will inevitably have some cases where the result is driven by moral desert and others where it is not. It would be difficult, if not impossible, for such a system to build a reputation with the public as a system devoted exclusively to judging moral blameworthiness. Every instance of liability based upon non-desert criteria would undercut the system's moral credibility, and the "criminal" label could not be used as a clear signal that moral condemnation is deserved. In the cases where the criminal system wishes to wave the red flag of moral condemnation, it would have only an ambiguous pink flag at its disposal. The separation of the two systems, into criminal and civil, enables for the criminal law to focus exclusively on desert and, perhaps more importantly, to make clear to the public that it is so focused. It allows the "criminal" label to be a red flag.[62]

To our minds, the current trend toward blurring the distinction is particularly foolish because it can provide little or no long term gain, even with respect to the very cases brought within the expansion. First, cases of regulatory offenses, strict liability, and vicarious liability are just the cases where the likelihood of a prison sentence is remote;[63] the sentences typically are fines and restitution, the sanctions that are available at civil law. Thus, by criminalizing these offenses, we do not effectively access more severe sanctions.

---

[62] *See* Paul H. Robinson, *The Criminal Civil Distinction and Dangerous Blameless Offenders,* 83 J. CRIM. L. & CRIMINOLOGY 693 (1993); Paul H. Robinson, *The Criminal-Civil Distribution and the Utility of Desert (Symposium on the Intersection of Crime and Tort),* 76 B.U. L. REV. 201 (1996).

[63] The majority of regulatory offenses are misdemeanors, for which a serious prison term is not authorized. Even for the most egregious forms of these offenses, where danger to life or property is created, the likelihood of an incarcerative sentence is not high. In 1989, the number of convicted federal regulatory violators sentenced to prison was: 37 agricultural, 22 antitrust, 2 labor, 24 food and drug. Table 5.17, Sentences imposed in cases terminated in U.S. District Courts, 1992 SOURCEBOOK OF CRIMINAL JUSTICE STATISTICS 488 (1993).

But, of course, access to more severe sanctions is not the reason that many have argued for the extension of the criminal sanction to these cases. More severe sanctions could be provided within the civil system. The arguments for such criminal expansion often focus upon the possibility for the moral stigmatization that criminal liability brings that civil liability does not.[64] Obviously, given our previous discussion, we agree that stigmatization can have a substantial effect in shaping the conduct of potential offenders. But this attempted use of stigmatization is likely to be ineffective because it offends rather than educates the moral code of the community. Passing a statute that criminalizes new conduct does not itself cause that conduct to be perceived as immoral. As the previous discussion suggests, law does not create norms but only acts as a participant in the process by which consensuses are built. Making a regulatory violation a "crime" is not in itself likely to do much to cause people to attach stigma to liability for the violation. Making 300,000 regulatory violations "crimes" makes it even less likely that people will take the resulting liability as evidence that moral condemnation is deserved.[65] Similarly, criminalizing actions that are offenses only from a strict or vicarious liability perspective fails to bring the stigmatization of criminality to bear on those violations. Far from being an independent and respected source of moral authority, a collection of laws of this sort becomes a pettifogging caricature.

More important to us, the expansion of criminal law to punish these various violations is not only ineffective but destructive. The more criminal law's stigmatizing effect is sought to be applied to non-condemnable conduct, the less stigmatizing effect there exists to apply. With each additional non-blameworthy use, the meaning of "criminal liability" becomes incrementally less tied to blameworthiness and incrementally less able to evoke condemnation. As each strict liability case, or vicarious liability case, or case of innocent or trivial conduct is criminalized—such as the woman charged with a criminal offense for picking an eagle feather from the floor of a cage

---

[64] *See* John C. Coffee, Jr., *"No Soul to Damn: No Body to Kick": An Unscandalized Inquiry Into the Problem of Corporate Punishment*, 79 Mich. L. Rev. 386, 424-34 (1981); Brent Fisse, *The Use of Publicity as a Criminal Sanction Against Business Corporations*, 8 Melb. U. L. Rev. 107 (1971); Ernest Gellhorn, *Adverse Publicity by Administrative Agencies*, 86 Harv. L. Rev. 1380, (1973). *But see* Michael K. Block, *Optimal Penalties, Criminal Law and the Control of Corporate Behavior*, 71 B.U. L. Rev. 395 (1991).

[65] We understand that it is sometimes appropriate to apply greater sanctions to regulatory violations. Serious deterrent sanctions can and ought to be imposed but they can as easily and effectively be imposed under an administrative system that is distinct from criminal law and that carries a non-criminal label, perhaps "violation," as many European countries do. Note the similarity to the situation regarding preventive detention—it may be that dangerous people need to be detained, but it is best that the criminal system not be the device for doing it, for to do so carries with it a false claim that these people deserve punishment, which they do not, and this false claim in turn hurts the criminal law's moral credibility.

NORTHWESTERN UNIVERSITY LAW REVIEW

and using it in a piece of art work that she then sold[66]—more and more people will conclude that the criminal law is being used not to reflect community notions of desert but rather as a tool of a powerful government to intervene destructively in the lives of ordinary people. Expanding the criminal law beyond the bounds of perceived desert initially weakens the stigmatizing effect that that expansion seeks to enlist. Finally, it destroys the stigmatizing effect; criminal penalties for non-condemnable conduct cause the public to sympathize with the person charged, and to despise the legal system that brings the charge. And it is the credibility of the criminal law in general that may be destroyed. Criminal conviction for a violation that the community sees as non-condemnable conduct affects not just the meaning of liability imposed for those offenses but the condemnatory message for all criminal convictions. More on this in Section D, "The Generalization of Disrespect."

C. The Problem of Moral Divisions Within the Community

Our thinking predicts a set of circumstances in which the law's moral credibility will be at risk regardless of the criminalization policy that it chooses. When a society contains groups with a strong and deeply felt moral disagreement, as ours does at this time on the morality of abortion, for example, the situation is destructive of the law's moral credibility and thus its power to gain compliance. More critically, one side will feel that the law is immoral, either because it criminalizes an innocent act, or because it fails to criminalize a morally abhorrent act—in this case fails to criminalize what is seen as a particular kind of murder. Our thinking predicts the destructive consequences that this conflict has. Specifically, it suggests that the "losing" side, at this moment those who wish abortion to be criminal, will lose respect for the legislative process, for the courts that enforce the laws, and eventually, for the legitimacy of the entire criminal law system.[67]

When one thinks that the law does not prohibit murder, one is inclined to "take the law into one's own hands," and we have seen anti-abortion people do this. Note the sequence of steps in what we might call the radicalization of the "pro-life" individual. Perhaps it begins with picketing the abortion clinic and then moves toward more coercive forms of picketing that are arguably legal violations of the rights of others. For some, it moves toward spraying noxious sub-

---

66 *They Swooped*, The Economist, Aug. 19, 1995, at 27.

67 Perspective also predicts that a more diverse society, with its less total agreement on norms, will have more crime, all other things being equal. If this is true, the dramatic difference in crime rates between the United States and Japan, for example, has little to do with criminal justice policies and more to do with the extent of community consensus on norms for condemnable conduct.

91:453 (1997)   *Utility of Desert*

stances into the clinics at night—a line has been crossed to committing an undeniable and more substantial legal offense. The next step is setting fire to the abortion clinic, perhaps at night so "no one will get hurt," but certainly this is an act of arson and possibly life-risking. Then death threats and finally the murder of a doctor or nurse who does abortions.

A similar destructive tension exists in Britain at this time. Those who are convinced that animals deserve more humane treatment are outraged at what one is allowed to do to animals under Common Market laws. They protest, seeking to block animal-transporting lorries before they cross the channel. As a recent article comments, for the activists, "[t]he issue is radicalizing . . . . It begins as a protest against abuse of animals. But if the law permits outrages, can it claim moral legitimacy? And if the police protect atrocities, are they not complicit?"[68] Again notice the radicalizing dynamic at work here. The people in question begin as classically law-abiding citizens, typically middle class, middle aged, conservative individuals, but some become willing to commit illegal acts because they regard those acts as morally required. What we have called the process of radicalization occurs most easily and dramatically when there is a group of individuals who are morally opposed to the content of some aspect of the criminal law, but also can occur for a single individual who opposes a law.

D.   *The Generalization of Disrespect*

One might discount the danger of such moral disagreements on the ground that people who disapprove of a particular law—be it Prohibition or giving a right to an abortion—can distinguish this "bad" law from the remainder of the system. But we think the possibility for such compartmentalization of disrespect is limited; more likely is what we might call "the generalization of disrespect." Consider the psychological processes that are begun when, for instance, a constitutional amendment prohibiting the use of alcohol is put in place. Examine the situation from the perspective of a person whose cultural traditions have a place for alcohol consumption on certain occasions, and whose individual opinion supports such use.

A law that criminalizes an activity, such as drinking, that I consider not immoral, may initially seem to me to be an isolated and aberrant one, and only the moral validity of that specific law will be denied by me. However, I cannot deny that it was a criminalization action taken by the same authorities that produced the entire criminal code, and I must now be willing to entertain doubts about the moral correctness of the criminalizing of the other activities that those authorities have chosen to sanction. By a process that is easily under-

---

68 *Also a part of Creation*, THE ECONOMIST, Aug. 19, 1995, at 21.

stood psychologically, if not logically, when the police apprehend me for violation of the drinking laws, I have a revelatory experience canceling the equation of all police actions with the apprehension of wrong-doers, and if the court system convicts, the hypocrisy that I feel that this court manifests is a candidate for generalization to other courts. If I become aware of another instance of the code violating my moral sensibilities, then all these generalizations, and others, are likely to occur. There is a natural process of spreading generalization of disrespect that the reader can intuit here.

The potential for the generalization of disrespect is even greater where the disapproval does not concern a particular controversial law. Where the system generates objectionable case results because of a highly publicized and controversial position, as with Prohibition or the right to an abortion, there is at least the potential to limit the system's discredit to the controversial law. But it is much more frequently the case that the cause of an objectionable result is not so apparent, and in these cases the compartmentalization of disrespect is essentially impossible. The criminal law may conflict with community views in an endless number of ways in its definition of offenses or general principles of liability. An objectionable definition of rape or a counterintuitive rule governing offense culpability requirements, accomplice liability, or causal accountability for a harmful result, or any of a wide range of the general rules relied upon in most cases, can generate an objectionable result. Yet, the specific source of the perceived error will not be apparent to the observer, just the improper result. Without a segregable and visible "bad" law to blame, the observer can do little other than be suspicious of the entire enterprise.[69]

What are the consequences of a generalized discontent with the criminal law and the criminal justice system? Johannes Andenaes remarks that "a certain degree of respect for the formal law is probably essential for the smooth functioning of society. Where it is lacking, law enforcement agencies play a role similar to that of an occupying

---

[69] We would suggest that the dimensions along which generalizations of disrespect occur for legal codes and criminal justice institutions is an urgent topic for psychological research to address. One available example is Jeffrey Kaplan, *Absolute Rescue: Absolutism, Defensive Action and the Resort to Force*, J. TERROR. & POLIT. VIOL. 128 (1993). He uses interview and archival techniques to trace the evolution among the pro-life constituency of a deviant subgroup that has come to accept the use of illegal violent tactics, including killing of abortion workers, to further their aims. To give an example from his work that connects with our argument, it is often the encounter of the pro-lifer with some specific evidence that convinces him of the immorality of abortion—perhaps the sight of an aborted fetus. When that evidence is presented by the pro-lifer to the public, and the legal authorities, and they do not react by outlawing abortion, the moral judgment of the legal authorities is destroyed. Further, encountering the police as the demonstrators were arrested in clinic demonstrations produced more radicalization. "If indifference was the first step in the disillusionment of rescuers with American society, the experience of violence at the hands of those that the civics texts of the 1950's and 1960's held to be the guardians of order was the next great shock." *Id.* at 132.

army in foreign territory . . . ."[70] World War II helped create a popular view that violently opposing the rules imposed by an occupying army is not only not immoral; it is highly moral. A set of laws that is not seen as just is likely to be seen as unjust. When a criminal law offends the moral intuitions of the governed community, the power of the entire criminal code to gain compliance from the community is risked. That there exists such unavoidable sources of injury to the criminal law's moral credibility means that it is that much more important that the criminal law be formulated to maximize its moral credibility in all those respects that are within the control of law makers.

E.   Persuasion v. Contempt

The previous discussion in Parts III and IV enable us to clarify a potential ambiguity in our claims. We claim that sometimes the law can convince persons that they should respect and obey the provisions of the criminal code, and internalize those prohibitions as part of their own moral code. But at other times, a conflict between the legal code and individual moral intuitions can lead people to persevere in their own judgements and move toward contempt for the legal code. In this subpart, we specify the conditions under which one or the other outcome will occur, when the code will be persuasive, and when it well be rejected. The psychological literature on persuasion and attitude change provides a basis for doing so.

Social science research suggests that two factors are particularly relevant: the credibility of the source that is attempting to persuade the individual who is the target of the message and the certainty or strength with which the target holds his or her own opinion. Intuition, as well as research, makes clear that the two factors interact as follows: the higher the credibility of the source, the more likely the source's message is to persuade the target;[71] the more strongly or cer-

---

70 JOHANNES ANDENAES, PUNISHMENT AND DETERRENCE 34 (1974).

71 The credibility of a source of communication is generally thought to be a joint function of the source's expertise on the communication topic and the source's trustworthiness as a communicator. One reviewer concludes, "Few areas of research in social psychology have produced results as consistent as the findings that sources high in expertise and/or trustworthiness are more persuasive than those low in these qualities." Glen Hass, *Effects of Source Characteristics on Cognitive Responses and Persuasion, in* COGNITIVE RESPONSES IN PERSUASION 141 (Richard Petty et al., eds. 1981). In a major recent review of the attitude literature, the review authors reach the same conclusion: "[S]ubjects typically exhibited greater agreement with the beliefs and attitudes recommended in persuasive messages when the source of these messages were portrayed as higher in expertise [and] trustworthiness." ALICE EAGLY & SHELLY CHAIKEN, THE PSYCHOLOGY OF ATTITUDES 429-30 (1993). McGuire, another leading figure in attitude research, suggests that both expertise and trustworthiness must be jointly present for persuasion to take place. William McGuire, *Attitudes and Attitude Change, in* HANDBOOK OF SOCIAL PSYCHOLOGY 233 (Gardiner Lindzey & Elliot Aronson, eds., 3d ed. 1985).

tainly held the original opinion, the less likely the target is to be persuaded to change his or her opinion.[72]

The application of these factors to the present case is fairly direct. The source of the message is the legal code and the intentions and motivations of the drafters who stand behind it.[73] The message is, in essence, that this or that action ought to be criminalized, is wrong, and deserves the specified level of punishment. When will the legal code, as source, be regarded as credible? Much of our argument up to now has been directed to answering this question. We conclude that the legal code is credible to the extent that it has what we have called moral credibility. For the present discussion, we note two components of this credibility. First, the law's credibility is a function of the trustworthiness of its judgement. The code gains trustworthiness by assigning punishment in accord with the principles of justice of the person it is attempting to convince. Second, the law's credibility is a function of its perceived expertise, relevant in this instance when the code asserts that some conduct that is not obviously harmful should be treated as such because the conduct has less apparent but real harmful consequences. The law is saying, in essence, "Trust those of us who drafted the code. We have thought this through. This action is sufficiently harmful or evil that it deserves to be criminalized."

The other factor that influences whether the law will persuade or will draw contempt is the strength of the original opinion on the issue. When are individuals relatively certain of their opinions in the domain of criminal law? People are likely to be certain about the criminality of actions such as killing, arson, and theft—those offenses that historically have been referred to as *malum in se*, "actions that are wrong in and of themselves." Different people may have somewhat different mappings here; as we noted in our section on cultural descensus— abortion and animal cruelty are held to be wrong with great certainty

---

72 EAGLY & CHAIKEN, *supra* note 71, reviews the theories that link attitude strength with resistance to change, and the evidence that supports those theories. Theoretically, people are motivationally linked to their strongly held attitudes. They have strong convictions about their rightness and often have publicly committed themselves to this view. Further, strongly held attitudes are generally connected to the values and beliefs that people hold, as well as other attitudes. To change that attitude would require the change in linked values, beliefs, and other attitudes. For both of these theoretical reasons, then, strongly held attitudes can be expected to be resistant to change. Eagly & Chaiken concludes, "we believe that few researchers would disagree with the idea that [the strength of] people's prior attitudes represent an important source of the resistance to attitude change." *Id.* at 589.

73 McGuire's analysis indirectly supports our extension of the concept of trustworthiness from individuals to institutions and gives a sense of where, among institutions, the trustworthiness of the judicial system might be found: "[I]nstitutional as well as individual sources differ in trustworthiness: Science, medicine, and academic groups tend to elicit a high degree of confidence; the military, police and judiciary somewhat less; followed by business and media leaders, with political officeholders and labor union officials trusted still less." McGuire, *supra* note 71, at 63.

by some. People in general can be expected to be less certain on the actions historically referred to as *malum prohibitum* and may have quite differential certainties produced by past personal histories. A parent whose child has been killed by a drunk driver is likely to hold, with a high degree of certainty, that drunk driving is a serious wrong.

Thus, the social science literature suggests five generalizations, most of which reaffirm conclusions developed in earlier sections. First, the credibility of the legal code depends on it being perceived as a trustworthy guide to assigning liabilities according to the community's perception of which actions are moral, which are immoral, and how severely the immoral actions should be punished. Second, the higher the credibility of the code (that is, the greater its reputation for assigning liabilities according to perceived desert), the more persuasive it will be in convincing people of the correctness of its judgement, and thus, the more they will be inclined to behave in compliance with the code and internalize its judgements as morally appropriate. Third, since people are likely to be relatively less certain about *malum prohibitum* offenses, the code will be more likely to convince people with regard to those offenses. Fourth, when a legal code condemns an action that a person is certain is not morally condemnable, or fails to condemn an action that a person is certain is morally condemnable, its credibility is, at minimum, put at risk, normally lowered, perhaps eventually destroyed, by the spreading processes of radicalization that we have suggested. Fifth, when the criminal law, asserting its expertise, criminalizes an act that is not obviously harmful, if people later discover that the act does not lead to the consequences that they generally regard as properly criminal, the law loses credibility, although not as decisively as in the fourth conclusion above.

Suppose that code drafters wish to adopt a specific proposal that is known to be in conflict with the moral intuitions of the community or a section of the community. They face a difficult but not impossible task; they must convince the community that the community's intuitions are wrong and that justice would be better served by distributing liabilities according to the new principle. From our point of view, they must engage in this persuasive task directly and forcibly and assess the success of their efforts. If they do not succeed in convincing the community, they then risk lowered credibility if they nonetheless adopt the proposal. When, as sometimes happens, the code provisions are adopted without this sort of educational debate, the potential for community contempt for the code has been established, and that potentiality is likely to become an actuality when the first publicized prosecution for violation of the new provision takes place.

NORTHWESTERN UNIVERSITY LAW REVIEW

F. Summary

We have every reason to think that, more than any other body of law, criminal law plays a central role in the creation of new norms, and that the criminal law can have a direct effect in gaining compliance when it is seen as a moral authority. And both of these sources of influence by the criminal law—in building and maintaining norms and in gaining compliance through moral authority—depend upon the criminal law's moral credibility with the community. The criminal law's moral credibility with the community, we argue, requires a distribution of liability that follows the community's perceptions of principles of deserved punishment and requires a separate and distinct criminal justice system, a system which can demonstrate its exclusive focus on blameworthiness and can effectively convey the special condemnation of criminal conviction. This credibility is risked when the legal system criminalizes actions that the community regards as not criminal or does not criminalize actions that the community regards as serious moral violations that deserve criminal condemnation. A society that contains groups in deep disagreement about what should count as a criminal offense is a society in which the moral authority of the criminal law is in tension and at risk.

V.   Determining Community Perceptions of Desert

A.   Code Drafting to Community Standards

We have argued for a criminal law based upon principles of desert, specifically, principles of desert as shared by the community. We need to say more about how such a distribution of liability would be determined. We need to distinguish our view of such a law-drafting system from some of the caricatures of it that could be advanced. Basing the criminal law on community standards does not mean resolving individual cases as the public or press see them in the heat of the moment. We know that the public and the press can lose perspective when buffeted by the biases and prejudices inspired by the facts of any particular case. The tendency of people to be more sympathetic to defendants more like themselves is well documented.[74] Nor does our position support legislators' hastily passing laws driven by public reactions to some recent court case that outrages public opinion.

We envision code-drafting being done by commissions of lawyers, criminal law experts, and social scientists. They would seek community input by means of research studies in which respondents make judgments of cases that elicit their principles for the just distribution of liability. Community judgments on the minimal requirements for

---

[74] *See, e.g.*, Jeffrey T. Frederick, The Psychology of the American Jury 166-67 (1987).

91:453 (1997) *Utility of Desert*

criminalization of conduct, on the justification of conduct that otherwise would be criminal, on the conditions under which wrongful conduct should be excused, and on the grading of offenses would, at a minimum, have claims on the code drafters' attentions. The code drafters would incorporate such shared community intuitions into the code, unless they had well-worked-out reasons not to do so. If they had such reasons, they would make clear what they were, and attempt to educate the community on their validity. The commission's deliberations would be public, and the maximum attention of the community would be sought.

The output of the commission, of course, would be submitted to the legislature, which is the institution to which our constitutional system grants standing to make laws. Many if not most of the commission's recommendations would be non-controversial, especially because they will generally track community views. But where there is disagreement among the community, the commission will have no consensus to report, and it will be in these instances of disagreements that it will be left primarily to the legislature itself to sort out the position that the law will take. Given our general account, we cannot deny the problems inherent in such cases, although we suspect that their existence is rare. Some benefits may arise when the general public sees genuine moral disagreement on one or two of these issues, but these are the truly difficult cases, in which the potential for the radicalization of some segment of the community is present.

We stress the importance of the moral intuitions of the community as a valued beginning for code drafting, followed by a process of code drafting done in public with an eye to educating and involving the community. The establishment of public understanding of the criminal law provides the best chance of a code gaining the respect of the community, and surviving the occasional case of deep community disagreement.

We do not underestimate how complex a task it is to determine liability rules that will capture such shared community intuitions of justice. But, as we show in our recent book, *Justice, Liability, and Blame: Community Views and the Criminal Law*, it is a feasible undertaking given the state of current social science methodology,[75] and it is also an important undertaking. Over the long term, it is by this means that the system will earn its moral credibility with the community.

---

[75] PAUL H. ROBINSON & JOHN M. DARLEY, JUSTICE, LIABILITY, AND BLAME: COMMUNITY VIEWS AND THE CRIMINAL LAW 217-28 (1995).

NORTHWESTERN UNIVERSITY LAW REVIEW

B.   The Content of a Community-Based Code

Based on our preliminary research, a community-based criminal code would retain most of the foundational principles on which current criminal law doctrine is based: a focus on a person's level of culpability, the extent of the harm attempted or risked, the degree to which that harm actually came about, and the presence of any justifying or excusing conditions.

There seems a strong consensus, for example, that the degree of an offender's liability should follow to a considerable degree the person's level of culpability toward the conduct constituting the offense. However, for most offenses other than homicide, current codes set a minimum level of culpability, frequently recklessness, and assign a constant degree of liability once that minimum level is reached. The respondents in our research studies generally imposed higher degrees of liability as the culpability level of the offender increased above the minimum required for liability. A person who commits a crime purposefully, rather than recklessly, receives a stiffer prison sentence from our respondents, and this seems reasonable to us.[76]

Our respondents also recognized and granted validity to many of the excusing conditions that are recognized in criminal law. Specifically, they judged that the effects of mental dysfunction could exculpate a person, and they based their judgments of whether to grant an insanity defense on the degree of cognitive and control dysfunction, as do most legal codes.[77] Our respondents similarly recognized and gave validity to the broad notion of justification defenses—defenses that approve of and therefore exculpate a person for normally unlawful conduct in certain circumstances, such as self-defense or citizen's arrest to prevent commission of a crime.[78]

But our research suggests that a community-based code would differ from current codes in some important respects. Systematic disagreements between the criminal law and our community of respondents were not uncommon. Our respondents disagreed with the Model Penal Code's treatment of various kinds of rape. For instance, where forcible rape has occurred, the Code gives a mitigation to the rapist if the victim had been "a voluntary social companion" of the rapist who had "previously permitted him sexual liberties" or if the victim is the rapist's spouse.[79] Our respondents do not.[80]

Similarly, our respondents do not agree with the Model Penal Code's assertion that a substantial step toward committing a crime

---

[76] *Id.* at 169-73.

[77] *Id.* ch. 5.

[78] *Id.* ch. 3.

[79] MODEL PENAL CODE § 213.1(1), .1(1)(d)(ii).

[80] ROBINSON & DARLEY, *supra* note 75, at 160-69.

alone ought to be sufficient grounds for punishment. And, even for very advanced attempts, they disagree with the Code's grading attempts the same as the completed offense.[81]

Our book gives a more complete characterization of the code that would emerge if one took community intuitions as a basis for criminal sentencing practices. Here we have only described enough to give the reader some sense of what the law would look like and to dispel any notions that it would be excessively savage, excessively lenient, or in marked deviation from the general outlines of existing criminal laws.

C. *Apparent Deviations from Deserved Punishment: Amount, Method, and Forgiveness*

Would the liability and sentencing practices we recommend ever deviate from strict reliance on just desert? Our preferred answer is "no," but this need not mean that considerations of rehabilitation or incapacitation need never enter into decisions about the fate of specific criminals. While the amount of punishment to be imposed must match the amount required by community perceptions of desert, the method of inflicting that punishment is generally irrelevant to the goal of desert.[82] Thus, once judges ensure that the total amount of punishment is the amount deserved, they are free to select a sanctioning method that will maximize rehabilitation or incapacitation (or deterrence or any other worthwhile crime reduction strategy) without fear that their selection of method may endanger the criminal law's moral credibility. To do this, the judge need only take account of the "punishment bite" of each sanctioning method used and ensure that the total "bite" of all sanctions add up to the amount deserved, not noticeably more or less.[83] We have recently published research on public perceptions of the punitive bite of alternative sanctioning methods that can serve as a guide to judges in constructing sentences.[84] It shows that non-incarcerative sentences frequently can be used to inflict the punishment deserved, even for many non-minor offenses.

A second possibility exists, which we do not favor. In some cases, in which the possibility of rehabilitation of the criminal is thought to be high (preferably documentably high), the sentencing system may decide to assign a rehabilitative course of treatment to the criminal

---

[81] *Id.* Study 1.

[82] *See* Paul H. Robinson, *Desert, Crime Control, Disparity, and Units of Punishment, in* PENAL THEORY AND PRACTICE: TRADITION AND INNOVATION IN CRIMINAL JUSTICE 93 (Antony Duff et al. eds., 1994). *But see* Dan Kahan, *What Do Alternative Sanctions Mean?*, 63 U. CHI. L. REV. 591 (1996).

[83] *Id.* at 593.

[84] Robert Harlow et al., *The Severity of Intermediate Penal Sanctions: A Psychophysical Scaling Approach for Obtaining Community Perceptions*, 11 J. QUANTITATIVE CRIMINOLOGY 71 (1995).

NORTHWESTERN UNIVERSITY LAW REVIEW

that does not meet the just desert criterion. What the system is doing
here is essentially deciding to forgive the individual (by forgoing the
deserved punishment for the crime) because it is thought that this increases the possibility of making that person less likely to commit
crimes in the future.

Because it deviates from a desert-based system, we do not favor
this option. However, it at least begins with recognizing the desert-
based considerations and deviates from them openly, giving reasons
for doing so. That is, it acknowledges that there is something to be
forgiven; it acknowledges the offender's blameworthiness. This might
well be a tenable system if it were limited to cases in which research
suggested that shared community notions might support such a show
of forgiveness while nonetheless agreeing that the offender was
blameworthy. For example, research might show that a genuine feeling of great remorse, evidenced by acts of restitution performed
before arrest, was one of several preconditions to forgiveness. If that
were so, one could limit the damaging effect on such a forgiveness
program by limiting it to such cases.

D.   Desert and Dangerousness

A desert-based system such as we advocate would not disguise
lengthy incarceration based on predictions of dangerousness as legitimate punishment. However, it could include more severe sentences
for second-time offenders. Andrew von Hirsch has developed an account of why repeat offenses may justify higher sentences under a desert theory.[85] Community intuitions may mirror his reasoning. Thus,
the system might give a "first offense discount" in many, even most
cases, on the theory that the absence of any prior offense suggests that
this conduct may be an aberration and may not truly reflect the offender's free choice, but rather a response to the pressures of the pe-
culiar situation—a kind of mini-mitigation for coercion, extreme
emotional disturbance, or the like. Alternatively one could conceive
of the harsher sentence for a second-time offender as giving an extra
slap on the wrist to an offender who has previously been reprimanded
and nonetheless committed another violation, thumbing his nose at
the society's law, as it were. We will be more inclined to support an
increase in sentence for a second-time offender only after research
suggests that the public has these intuitions.

Obviously, a reliance upon these theories might seem to generate
a distribution of liability that keeps more dangerous offenders (that is,
repeat offenders) in jail longer. It might well have that effect, but the
likelihood of future criminality would be only a useful coincidence; it

---

[85] *See* Andrew von Hirsch, *Desert and Previous Convictions in Sentencing*, 65 MINN. L. REV.
591 (1981).

would play no role in the distribution of liability. Note also that these two desert-based theories would not operate for all dangerous offenders but only for some; each would apply only to a specific set of cases that logically followed from the rationale. Finally, note that the amount of adjustment in sentence, even for cases where both theories are relied upon, would be rather modest; neither the first-offense discount nor the nose-thumbing penalty concerns factors that are of central concern in determining desert. They certainly would not support the kinds of dramatic increases for apparent dangerousness that we see in current practice.[86]

We should note that we do not think that a society must stand defenseless in the face of dangerous offenders. Our point is simply that it is bad policy to pretend that incarceration based upon a prediction of future criminality can be justified as "punishment," because to do so undercuts the law's moral credibility in assigning deserved punishment for past offenses. Society does and should detain people who are shown to be dangerous. Sometimes that showing, that prediction, is based on an assessment of mental state, sometimes it is based on criminal records. However, we ought to be open about what we are doing, and we ought to structure that incarceration to match the rationale. Specifically, incarceration based upon a claim of dangerousness ought to be under conditions consistent with its non-punitive purpose, much like the conditions of confinement of a person with a contagious disease that we confine for our protection. This does not describe current prisons. Even more importantly, such confinement ought to be subject to regular reviews to confirm the confinee's continuing dangerousness, a practice abandoned under the current "three strikes and you're out" legislation that provides for life imprisonment without possibility of parole.[87]

A recent program in the State of Washington, which civilly commits sexual predators if they are judged to remain dangerous after the expiration of their prison term, follows the course we suggest, and we

---

[86] It has been argued that people, often in their function as jurors, use the prison system as a means of locking up dangerous people, and that this suggests that people may conceive of dangerousness as contributing to an actor's blameworthiness and as grounds for deserved punishment. We agree that people under the current system often imprison (or impose the death penalty) on defendants who they think are dangerous. It does not follow, however, that people are ignorant of or indifferent to the difference between imprisonment as punishment for a past crime and incarceration to prevent a future crime. That the distinction is widely recognized is shown by the nearly universal practice of having a separate civil commitment system, distinct from criminal commitment. People are willing to use criminal commitment to protect society against defendants perceived as dangerous because the current system—with its limitations on the use of civil commitment—gives them no alternative means of protection. If they were given the choice, we think lay persons would elect civil commitment rather than criminal if they thought a defendant was dangerous but did not deserve punishment. The issue can be resolved by empirical research.

[87] *See* Robinson, *supra* note 35, at 714-16.

note that it is much maligned. Obviously, it is difficult to generate a method of holding sexual predators in custody that does not have punitive elements, and those making the predictions of dangerousness may be swayed by considerations of what would happen if they predicted non-dangerousness for a predator who then offended again. Still, the proposal almost certainly makes the situation better for those incapacitated for "dangerousness" than when they are instead sentenced to long terms or life terms of punitive confinement in prisons, with no right of review for dangerousness. We suspect that some of the criticism of this admittedly imperfect system of preventive detention comes from people who do not realize how rampant is the use of dangerousness in current practice as the primary justification for lengthy prison sentences.[88]

VI. Attempts at Justifying Deviations from Desert

In the previous section we considered some possible deviations from a liability and punishment system based on just desert, and showed how those deviations are more apparent than real: Greater use of non-incarcerative sanctions is not necessarily inconsistent with a distribution of punishment according to perceived desert; and forgiveness of some offenders is not necessarily detrimental to the criminal law's moral credibility. In this section we consider some deviations from just desert that may seem attractive but that we regard as undesirable.

Some utilitarians apparently believe that only the threat of sanction or lack thereof determines whether a person will commit an offense.[89] But other utilitarians might agree with our claim that personal morality and interpersonal relations have effect and that the operation of these forces can be influenced by altering community perceptions of the criminal law's moral credibility. They nonetheless may be tempted by a system that intentionally and regularly deviates from a distribution of criminal liability according to perceived desert.[90] They might argue that the crime-control value of one or another deviation from desert outweighs the incremental loss in the criminal law's moral credibility.[91]

---

[88] Notice how a consistent focus on just desert and blameworthiness clarifies issues. If one does not focus on the proper proportionality between blameworthiness and punishment, then it is not apparent that the current sentencing practices are as disproportionate as they are, and that they create sentences that the community would perceive as unjust.

[89] *See, e.g.*, Shavell, *supra* note 57.

[90] To do this, they would have to overcome the objections to the utilitarian approaches that we describe in Part I of this article.

[91] For a discussion of how such a hybrid distributive principle might operate, see Paul H. Robinson, *Hybrid Principles for the Distribution of Criminal Sanctions*, 82 Nw. U. L. Rev. 19 (1987).

Such a system of selective deviations would be an improvement over our current state in which little regard is paid to the effect of deviations from desert. Nonetheless, we suggest that the utilitarian be cautious here. If we had perfect data on the dynamics of the forces at work and their relative effects, the cost-benefit analysis would be clear. We do not, of course, and are not likely to have even a crude understanding of the dynamics in our lifetimes. We can only speculate about the relative effects. Let us explain why we think we should err on the side of caution in deviating from the principles of perceived desert.

A.   The Problem of Attributions to the Criminal Justice System: Reputation and Motive

How will deviations from desert affect the criminal justice system's reputation for doing justice? The general principle that we shall appeal to here is referred to psychologically as an attributional principle. Those studying persons perception have realized that the task that perceivers take on, when they are examining the actions of others, is to determine the dispositions of the other, the abilities the other possesses, the personality, and the immediate or long-term intentions. Dispositional perception of this sort is referred to as "attributional perception."[92] One not only makes attributions to individuals, but to institutions set up by persons; we all can make sense of the question of whether a legal system is "fair." The specific attributional problem here is one of making sense of the cumulative meaning of actions that seem to deviate from the announced purposes of that institution. What conclusions are drawn, what attributions are made, if the system seems to operate by a set of rules (punishment according to just desert) or claims to operate by the set of rules but occasionally deviates from those rules? What conditions determine when those who observe the system conclude that the system does not, in fact, live by the set of rules that it professes? When, in other words, does it lose its "reputation"?

One attributional rule involves whether the deviations are repeated. All of us are aware that there are many reasons that a system could occasionally come to a wrong outcome; rare deviations do not signify. However, repeated ones do signify, especially when the deviations seem to point to the same underlying cause; regular deviations that fall in a regular explanatory pattern, even if they are minor, could

---

92 The seminal publications on attribution theory are: Edward Jones & Keith Davis, *From Acts to Dispositions, in* 2 ADVANCES IN EXPERIMENTAL SOCIAL PSYCHOLOGY 219-66 (L. Berkowitz ed., 1965) and Harold Kelley, *Attribution Theory in Social Psychology, in* 15 NEBRASKA SYMPOSIUM ON MOTIVATION 192-238 (D. Levine ed., 1967).

do much to hurt the system's reputation.[93] This would be true even if the number and extent of the deviations were small in comparison to the system's overall output of decisions.[94]

This reflects the fact that a large part of preserving the reputation of a person or an organization is to cause others to see that the person or organization is genuinely motivated to "play by the rules" that it espouses. An error can be forgiven if it is seen as "out of character." This is true of personal reputations; we suggest that it is also true of the reputations of larger entities.[95] People know that they cannot know what all aspects of the criminal justice system are doing at all times. Their view of the system is likely to be governed by what they think the system is trying to do, by what they see as its motivation to do justice. The criminal law's reputation may depend on its public commitment to never intentionally deviating from the principles of perceived desert, while conceding that inadvertent deviations are unavoidable. To admit a policy that intentionally authorizes failures in administering liability and punishment according to desert is to render the system suspect in all its workings.

B.   The Advantages of a Morally Credible System

Not only is it easy to underestimate the detriment of intentional deviation from desert, it also is easy to underestimate the benefit of maintaining the system's moral credibility. Unlike the threat of legal punishment, the sources of compliance discussed here are not dependent on the effectiveness of the system in arresting, convicting, and punishing offenders. The real sources of compliance power—a person's family or friends and the person's own conscience—can know of an offender's violation even if the authorities do not or cannot prove it. Thus, harnessing the compliance powers of social group and personal morality can reduce current crime levels even if policing and prosecuting functions cannot be made more effective.

Note as well that these sources of compliance power do not have the staggering costs of increased enforcement, adjudication, and imprisonment that would be required if reduced crime were to be achieved through deterrence (or incapacitation or rehabilitation). Again, their power comes not from catching and punishing every

---

[93] Harold Kelley, *Causal Schemata and the Attribution Process, in* ATTRIBUTION: PERCEIVING THE CAUSES OF BEHAVIOR 151-74 (Edward E. Jones et al. eds., 1971).

[94] In the case of sentences handed out by the criminal justice system, this process is exacerbated by mass media reports that focus on what they see as system failures. Lay persons tend not to see the larger picture and rarely are able to put mass media reports in perspective. (The more cynical observation is that news is more "newsworthy" when it exaggerates the significance and extent of a failure of justice.).

[95] *See* BERNARD WEINER, JUDGMENTS OF RESPONSIBILITY: A FOUNDATION FOR THE THEORY OF SOCIAL CONDUCT 212-14 (1995).

criminal but rather from the system's moral power in obviously trying to do justice. That educational and symbolic function can be served in the adjudication of whatever cases are brought to the system, even if many are not. Nor does crime reduction through these mechanisms require the increased intrusions of privacy that more effective crime investigation would require or the increased errors in adjudication that easier prosecution rules would require. In other words, harnessing the social and personal forces of compliance offers the possibility of better compliance at lower cost.

We have argued that a criminal law based on community principles of perceived desert can enhance the law's compliance power and that a criminal law that is seen systematically to deviate from those principles reduces that power. Here we should point out that our account of the role of criminal law assigns it a less powerful role in producing law-abiding behavior than do the traditional theories. One reason for the attractiveness of deterrence theory, for instance, lies in its claims of having great power to autonomously produce compliance. (We have shown the moral and empirical fallaciousness of that possibility earlier in Part II.) We make no such claim for the legal code; its role is secondary and contributive rather than primary and determinative of law-abiding behavior. This seems to us to be an accurate representation of the true state of affairs, and if adopted, might have the useful function of removing from public debate some of the unrealistically high expectations about what can be accomplished by the manipulation of criminal liability and punishment.

VII. SUMMARY AND CONCLUSION

The evidence is reasonably clear that the power of interpersonal relationships and internalized norms to prevent crime is dramatically greater than that of official sanctions. The ability of the law to harness these forces is less clear. Studies suggest that increasing the law's moral credibility can enhance its compliance power, but the studies are preliminary and many important questions remain unanswered. Will research confirm our speculations about the mechanisms by which a morally credible criminal law can increase compliance? Will research confirm our speculations about the practices that most undercut the system's moral credibility and those that would most enhance it?

It will take some time for social scientists to answer these questions, but we need not wait for those answers before we make some changes in what we do. Most importantly, it is clear that a utilitarian calculus in determining the rules for the distribution of criminal liability and punishment must take account of real-world costs that come from deviating from the community's principles of deserved punishment. The costs and benefits of moral credibility may be more diffi-

NORTHWESTERN UNIVERSITY LAW REVIEW

cult to measure than those of the factors typically taken into account by utilitarian calculations in the past, but if they are more powerful in their effect than the other factors, to ignore them risks rendering the calculation meaningless.

While we do not know with any certainty the degree of importance of the criminal law's moral credibility, we can be reasonably sure that it has some. Thus, a corollary to the above is that we ought not tolerate any deviation from desert, or any other measure that may undercut moral credibility, without a clear and significant benefit. And even then, we counsel a close examination of long-term as well as short-term effects. This suggests a number of reforms, which we have mentioned.

Where have we left the long-running debate between desert and utilitarian justifications for punishment? We have used essentially utilitarian reasoning to argue for a desert-based system of criminal law. More specifically, we have argued that people obey the law not so much because they are fearful of being apprehended by the criminal justice system, but because they care about what their social group thinks of them and because they regard obedience as morally appropriate. Criminal laws based on community standards of deserved punishment enhance this obedience. We conclude that desert distribution of liability happens to be the distribution that has the greatest utility, in the sense of avoiding crime. Thus, utility theorists ought to support liabilities assigned according to such a desert-based system.

If our arguments are accepted, we have, in some sense, united two groups of criminal justice philosophers that have characteristically been thought to be at hopeless odds. Desert-based punishment proponents assert that what matters in liability and sentencing is doing justice; utilitarians require an analysis of the consequences of a liability assignment system to justify it, characteristically a showing of how the system is maximally effective in avoiding crimes in the future. We suggest that while these two sides do not agree on the reasons for imposing punishment, if they agree with our analysis, they can, incredibly enough, agree on how punishment should be distributed.

We have, perhaps, united utilitarians and just desert thinkers, but we may have united them in opposition to our recommendations. Liability and punishment should be distributed according to a desert-based distribution system, but the advocate for desert-based punishment systems may not be greatly pleased by this. Our desert-based system is importantly different from the standard one. In the standard desert-based system, what a criminal actually deserves is derived from some underlying systematization of moral principles; in our analysis, desert is not derived from any philosophically-based, coherently-reasoned systematization, but rather is patterned on the principles the community uses in assessing blameworthiness.

Has the utilitarian won the battle if our recommendations are accepted? In one sense, yes; we have used utilitarian arguments to justify our desert-based liability and sentencing scheme. However, the results of that analysis install the kind of liability distribution system that the utilitarians have argued against for decades. Worse, from their point of view, they cannot reject our arguments on principle, as they have rejected desert arguments in the past. If future investigations support the power we claim for the law's moral credibility, there is a powerful utilitarian argument for the adoption of a desert-based criminal law.

If our recommendations are adopted, the utilitarian criminal justice system is in some ways constrained in its distribution of liability, but it is freed from another constraint. During the past decades of the standard utilitarian approach, some criminal justice systems and institutions have had their charters set to a strictly utilitarian purpose, which seemed to exclude considerations of desert.[96] Our thesis suggests that a charge to prevent crime is, as a practical matter, a charge primarily to do justice—to consider just desert—for that will reduce crime more than distributive criteria that ignore desert. Thus, our thesis not only allows these systems and institutions to take account of desert but in fact demands it.

The central point that we seek to make is this—there is practical value, not just "philosophical" value, in maintaining the criminal law's focus on moral blameworthiness. What we have in the past taken to be instances of injustice imposed by the criminal justice system on some individual, when the just desert principle is violated, we ought to understand now as instances of injustice imposed on us all, since each such instance erodes the criminal law's moral credibility and, thus, its power to protect us all.

---

[96] *See, e.g.*, Alaska Const. art. I, § 12; State v. Chaney, 477 P.2d 441 (Alaska 1970); G.A. Res 152, U.N. GAOR, 46th Sess. Supp. No. 49, at 12, U.N. Doc. A/152 (1992) (establishing UN Commission on Crime Prevention).

[7]

THE DISUTILITY OF INJUSTICE

PAUL H. ROBINSON,* GEOFFREY P. GOODWIN** &
MICHAEL D. REISIG***

For more than half a century, the retributivists and the crime-control instrumentalists have seen themselves as being in an irresolvable conflict. Social science increasingly suggests, however, that this need not be so. Doing justice may be the most effective means of controlling crime. Perhaps partially in recognition of these developments, the American Law Institute's recent amendment to the Model Penal Code's "purposes" provision—the only amendment to the Model Code in the forty-eight years since its promulgation—adopts desert as the primary distributive principle for criminal liability and punishment.

That shift to desert has prompted concerns by two groups that, ironically, have been traditionally opposed to each other. The first group—those concerned with what they see as the over-punitiveness of current criminal law—worries that setting desert as the dominant distributive principle means continuing the punitive doctrines they find so objectionable, and perhaps making things worse. The second group—those concerned with ensuring effective crime control—worries that a shift to desert will create many missed crime-control opportunities and will increase avoidable crime.

The first group's concern about over-punitiveness rests upon an assumption that the current punitive crime-control doctrines of which it disapproves are a reflection of the community's naturally punitive intuitions of justice. However, as Study 1 makes clear, today's popular crime-control doctrines in fact seriously conflict with people's intuitions of justice by exaggerating the punishment deserved.

The second group's concern that a desert principle will increase avoidable crime exemplifies the common wisdom of the past half-century that ignoring justice in pursuit of crime control through deterrence, incapacitation of the dangerous, and other such coercive crime-control programs is cost-free. However, Studies 2 and 3 suggest that doing injustice has real crime-control costs. Deviating from the community's shared principles of justice undermines the system's moral credibility and thereby undermines its ability to gain cooperation and compliance and to harness the powerful forces of social influence and internalized norms.

The studies reported here provide assurance to both groups. A shift to desert is not likely either to undermine the criminal justice system's crime-control effectiveness, and indeed may enhance it, nor is it likely to increase the system's punitiveness, and indeed may reduce it.

---

* Colin S. Diver Professor of Law, University of Pennsylvania Law School. The authors thank John M. Darley, Princeton Psychology Department, for his valuable contributions to this project and Sean Jackowitz and Matthew Majarian, University of Pennsylvania Law School Classes of 2012 and 2011, respectively, for their outstanding research assistance.

** Assistant Professor, Department of Psychology, University of Pennsylvania.

*** Professor, School of Criminology and Criminal Justice, Arizona State University. Professor Reisig contributed Study 3 to the project.

INTRODUCTION

The past half-century has seen a continuing debate between "retributivists," who view deserved punishment as a value in itself that does not require further justification, and "utilitarians" (or "instrumentalists"), who see punishment as justified only if it brings about a greater good—typically the avoidance of future crime. Utilitarian avoidance of crime has traditionally been sought through the mechanisms of general and special deterrence, incapacitation of the dangerous, and rehabilitation. Some academics and researchers have recently suggested that, in addition to these traditional coercive crime-control mechanisms, punishment can work to avoid future crime by engaging the powers of social and normative influence.[1] Such normative crime control is possible, however, only if the criminal law has earned a reputation as a moral authority. It is difficult for criminal law to do so if it distributes criminal liability and punishment in ways that conflict with the community's shared intuitions of justice, which are based on moral blameworthiness, not utilitarian factors such as dangerousness or deterrence.[2]

That instrumentalist crime control benefits may be gained by tracking individuals' intuitions of justice suggests that instrumentalist

---

[1] *See* Paul H. Robinson, *Empirical Desert*, *in* CRIMINAL LAW CONVERSATIONS 29, 29–31 (Paul H. Robinson et al. eds., 2009) [hereinafter Robinson, *Empirical Desert*] (suggesting that aligning distribution of punishment with empirical desert strengthens law's moral credibility); Paul H. Robinson & John M. Darley, *Intuitions of Justice: Implications for Criminal Law and Justice Policy*, 81 S. CAL. L. REV. 1, 18–31 (2007) [hereinafter Robinson & Darley, *Intuitions of Justice*] (arguing that concurrence of empirical desert and criminal law is optimal).

[2] *See* Robinson & Darley, *Intuitions of Justice*, *supra* note 1, at 18–31.

and retributivist distributions of punishment may not be as incompatible as has been traditionally assumed. Empirical research shows that laypersons look primarily to moral blameworthiness as a guide to the imposition of criminal liability and punishment,[3] just as the retributivists do. However, the crime-control benefits of the law's moral credibility flow not from following the moral philosopher's view of desert—what one might call "deontological desert"—but rather from following the community's shared intuitive views of justice—what one might call "empirical desert."[4] These two conceptions of desert may differ in important ways.[5] Nonetheless, recent appreciation for the practical value of doing justice suggests some concurrence of interest between the previously warring retributivist and instrumentalist camps.

A.   The Recent Shift to Desert

The long-running debate between retributivists and instrumentalists came to the forefront of criminal law policy recently, when the American Law Institute amended the Model Penal Code for the first time in the forty-eight years since its enactment. Since 1962, the Code has been the model for the codification of criminal law in three-quarters of the states and, for the most part, has represented the epitome of instrumentalist thinking. The Code's original Section 1.02 made clear its preventive focus. While the Code was not entirely indifferent to the offender's moral blameworthiness, it did not explicitly tie liability and punishment to desert:

---

[3] *See* Kevin M. Carlsmith & John M. Darley, *Psychological Aspects of Retributive Justice*, *in* 40 ADVANCES IN EXPERIMENTAL SOCIAL PSYCHOLOGY 193, 233–34 (Mark Zanna ed., 2008) (presenting empirical study showing that people primarily react to crime descriptions emotionally and favor proportional just deserts, and noting that "[c]ontempt will develop when the sentencing practices of the society are importantly out of synchrony with the citizens' rank orderings of the blameworthiness of crimes"); Kevin M. Carlsmith, John M. Darley & Paul H. Robinson, *Why Do We Punish? Deterrence and Just Deserts as Motives for Punishment*, 83 J. PERSONALITY & SOC. PSYCHOL. 284, 295 (2002) (presenting empirical study demonstrating that people assess punishment based upon desert criterion, rather than upon factors relevant to deterrence); John M. Darley, Kevin M. Carlsmith & Paul H. Robinson, *Incapacitation and Just Deserts as Motives for Punishment*, 24 L. & HUM. BEHAV. 659, 676 (2000) (presenting empirical studies finding that people assess punishment based upon desert criterion, rather than upon factors relevant to dangerousness).

[4] *See* Paul H. Robinson, *Competing Conceptions of Modern Desert: Vengeful, Deontological, and Empirical*, 67 CAMBRIDGE L.J. 145, 152–53 (2008) (contrasting conceptions of desert and their effectiveness in crime control).

[5] For a discussion of the practical differences between deontological and empirical desert, see PAUL H. ROBINSON, DISTRIBUTIVE PRINCIPLES OF CRIMINAL LAW: WHO SHOULD BE PUNISHED HOW MUCH? 138–40 (2008) [hereinafter ROBINSON, DISTRIBUTIVE PRINCIPLES].

(1) The general purposes of the provisions governing the definition of offenses are:

(a) to *forbid and prevent conduct* that unjustifiably and inexcusably inflicts or threatens substantial harm to individual or public interests;

(b) to *subject to public control* persons whose conduct indicates that they are disposed to commit crimes;

(c) to safeguard conduct that is without fault from condemnation as criminal; . . .

(e) to differentiate on reasonable grounds between serious and minor offenses.

(2) The general purposes of the provisions governing the sentencing and treatment of offenders are:

(a) to *prevent the commission* of offenses;

(b) to promote the *correction and rehabilitation* of offenders;

(c) to safeguard offenders against excessive, disproportionate or arbitrary punishment; . . . .[6]

This "purposes" provision is not only of intellectual interest, revealing the principles that guided the Code's drafters, but it is also of practical importance because it offers direction to judges in how to interpret and apply the Code's provisions, as well as in how to exercise their discretion in sentencing.

The new Model Penal Code "purposes" section is significantly different. It now sets the primary distributive principle for criminal liability and punishment to desert—that is, the blameworthiness of the offender. Alternative distributive principles such as deterrence, incapacitation, or rehabilitation may be pursued only to the extent that they remain within the bounds of desert:

(2) The general purposes of the provisions on sentencing, applicable to all official actors in the sentencing system, are:

(a) in decisions affecting the sentencing of individual offenders:

(i) to render sentences in all cases within a range of severity proportionate to the gravity of offenses, the harms done to crime victims, and *the blameworthiness of offenders*;

(ii) when reasonably feasible, to achieve offender rehabilitation, general deterrence, incapacitation of dangerous offenders, restoration of crime victims and communities, and reintegration of offenders into the law-abiding community *provided that these goals are pursued within the boundaries of sentence severity permitted in subsection (a)(i)*; and

(iii) to render sentences no more severe than necessary to achieve the applicable purposes in subsections (a)(i) and (ii); . . . .[7]

---

[6] Model Penal Code § 1.02 (Proposed Official Draft 1962) (emphasis added).
[7] Model Penal Code § 1.02 (Tentative Draft No. 1, 2007) (emphasis added).

This rather dramatic turnabout is in part the result of a growing recognition of the weaknesses and limitations of the traditional mechanisms of coercive crime control. Deterrence may work under the right conditions, but those conditions may be the exception rather than the rule.[8] Rehabilitation is effective only occasionally and, even then, commonly generates only modest crime-control effects when used as a distributive principle.[9] Incapacitation of the dangerous clearly does work but generally can be achieved more effectively and with fewer detrimental side effects when done through mechanisms outside of the criminal justice system, such as through civil commitment.[10] However, the Model Penal Code's turn to desert also may reflect a growing appreciation that doing justice is an attractive distributive principle for both retributivist *and* instrumentalist reasons.

The common wisdom of the past half-century has been that deviations from desert are essentially cost-free. It was felt that a legislature could adopt whatever coercive crime control principle it thought effective, without regard to whether the punishment that was generated conflicted with the offender's deontological or empirical blameworthiness. For example, the drafters of the Model Sentencing Act, under which the defendant's potential threat in the future determines punishment, boast that the sentence will have "a minimum of variation according to the offense"[11]—an approach guaranteed to create

---

[8] *See* ROBINSON, DISTRIBUTIVE PRINCIPLES, *supra* note 5, at 48–49 (arguing that deterrence is effective only if following conditions are satisfied: potential offender is aware of legal rule, foresees meaningful chance of punishment, evaluates costs of violating law as outweighing benefits of doing so, and is able to bring information about relevant net costs to bear on her behavior); Paul H. Robinson & John M. Darley, *Does Criminal Law Deter? A Behavioural Science Investigation*, 24 OXFORD J. LEGAL STUD. 173, 173 (2004) (arguing that deterrent effect of criminal law is not typical); Paul H. Robinson & John M. Darley, *The Role of Deterrence in the Formulation of Criminal Law Rules: At Its Worst When Doing Its Best*, 91 GEO. L.J. 949, 951 (2003) (arguing conditions necessary for deterrence to work are not typical in modern societies).

[9] *See* ROBINSON, DISTRIBUTIVE PRINCIPLES, *supra* note 5, at 99–108 (evaluating effectiveness of rehabilitation as both deterrent and distributive principle).

[10] *See id.* at 130–33 (arguing that civil commitment of dangerous offenders would be both more efficient and effective for community protection and fairer to offenders than would using criminal justice system for such preventive detention, as now occurs); Paul H. Robinson, *Punishing Dangerousness: Cloaking Preventive Detention as Criminal Justice,* 114 HARV. L. REV. 1429, 1454–56 (2001) [hereinafter Robinson, *Punishing Dangerousness*] (same).

[11] Council of Judges of the Nat'l Council on Crime and Delinquency, *Model Sentencing Act: Second Edition*, 18 CRIME & DELINQ. 335, 341 (1972).

> The . . . Act diminishes [differences in] sentencing according to the particular offense. Under [the Act] the dangerous offender may be committed to a lengthy term; the nondangerous defendant may not. It makes available, for the first time, a plan that allows the sentence to be determined by the defendant's make-up, his potential threat in the future, and other similar factors, with a minimum of variation according to the offense.

regular and serious conflict with desert. As one can imagine, the Model Penal Code amendments represent a dramatic shift from almost ignoring desert, as the common wisdom of the past half-century would do, to holding desert inviolate.

B. *Two Opposing Concerns About the Shift to Desert, and a Preview of a Response to Each*

Not everyone has applauded the Model Penal Code's shift giving dominance to desert. Two sorts of concerns drive opposition by two quite different groups. The first group—those concerned with what they see as the over-punitiveness of current criminal law—worries that setting desert as the dominant distributive principle means continuing the punitive doctrines that they find so objectionable, and perhaps even making things worse. They reason that current crime control doctrines are a product of the community's views of justice and decry "populist punitiveness."[12] Giving formal deference to that sense of justice, they worry, will only exacerbate the situation. The second group—those concerned with ensuring effective crime control—worries that a desert distributive principle will create many missed crime-control opportunities and will increase avoidable

---

Id. The commentary to the Model Sentencing Act is openly hostile to desert. *See id.* at 344–45 ("[S]entencing on the basis of the offense does not satisfactorily provide public protection . . . . Vengeance or punishment is not a proper motive for a sentence."). The Council even argues that exceeding the minimum sentence required for public safety (which may be, and often is, in serious conflict with desert) "is a disservice to the entire penal system." *Id.* at 363. Additional discussion of the Model Sentencing Act can be found in Robinson, *Punishing Dangerousness, supra* note 10, at 1440–41.

Perhaps the best evidence of the common wisdom that there is no crime-control cost in deviating from the community's conception of desert is shown in Table 4 and Figure 1 in Part II, *infra*, which demonstrate how the most popular modern crime-control doctrines described in Part I, *infra*, seriously conflict with those community conceptions.

[12] Anthony Bottoms, *The Philosophy and Politics of Punishment and Sentencing, in* THE POLITICS OF SENTENCING REFORM 17, 39–41 (Christopher M.V. Clarkson & Rodney Morgan eds., 1995) (defining "populist punitiveness" as overtly political phenomenon). Similarly, David Garland decries this attention to community views and holds it accountable for the draconian sentences and policies of current law:

> A few decades ago public opinion functioned as an occasional brake on policy initiatives: now it operates as a privileged source. The importance of research and criminological knowledge is downgraded and in its place is a new deference to the voice of "experience," of "common sense," of "what everyone knows." . . . [T]he ruling assumption now is that "prison works"—not as a mechanism of reform or rehabilitation, but as a means of incapacitation and punishment that satisfies popular political demands for public safety and harsh retribution.

DAVID GARLAND, THE CULTURE OF CONTROL: CRIME AND SOCIAL ORDER IN CONTEMPORARY SOCIETY 13–14 (2001) (footnote omitted).

crime.[13] In other words, this is a continuation of the classic retribu-tivist-instrumentalist dispute along traditional lines.

The first group's concern about the Model Penal Code amend-ment's shift to desert—that it risks making modern crime-control doc-trines even more punitive—rests upon two assumptions: one probably true, the other clearly false. First, they assume that the distributive principle of desert to which the Model Code refers is that of empirical desert rather than deontological desert—that the Code looks to com-munity views of justice rather than to philosophers' views. As a prac-tical matter, the group's analysis is probably correct, although it is not beyond debate. Deontological desert is difficult to operationalize, if for no other reason than that moral philosophers disagree with one another about many (if not most) things, and there is no authoritative method by which one can easily determine the superiority of one deontological position to another.[14] In contrast, empirical desert has a clear standard and an easy means of determination. One need only test the intuitions of the members of the community that is to be gov-erned by the code. Perhaps more importantly, the Model Code's notion of desert may be empirical rather than deontological because many modern moral philosophers give strong deference to people's shared intuitions of justice in determining what constitutes deontolog-ical desert. In other words, many modern philosophers see little mean-ingful difference between the two.[15]

The first group's concern about punitiveness also rests upon a second assumption: that the current punitive crime control doctrines of which they disapprove are a product and manifestation of the com-munity's intuitions of justice. This assumption, however, is wrong. As Study 1 (reported in Part II) shows, current crime control doctrines seriously conflict with individuals' intuitions of justice by exaggerating the punishment deserved. Thus, a distribution of liability and punish-ment that tracks lay intuitions of justice would significantly reduce the injustice now present. As Part III explains, the modern crime control

---

[13] *See, e.g.*, Louis Kaplow & Steven Shavell, *Fairness Versus Welfare*, 114 HARV. L. REV. 961, 1009 (2000) (arguing that assessment of law enforcement policies should depend exclusively on their effects on individuals' welfare and accord no independent weight to conceptions of fairness in order to maximize crime control); Erik Luna, *Punishment Theory, Holism, and the Procedural Conception of Restorative Justice*, 2003 UTAH L. REV. 205, 225–27 (describing argument that using empirical desert as distributive principle may result in increase of crime that might not be measurable ex ante).

[14] For a discussion of these issues, see Paul H. Robinson, *The Role of Moral Philosophers in the Competition Between Philosophical and Empirical Desert*, 48 WM. & MARY L. REV. 1831, 1838–43 (2007).

[15] *See id.* at 1839–40 (describing and criticizing philosophical attempts to harmonize popular intuitions into "reflective equilibrium").

doctrines are not a product of the community's sense of justice but rather a product of the distortions inherent in American crime politics.

There also is a persuasive response to the concern of the second group that a desert distributive principle will increase avoidable crime. The common wisdom of the past half-century has been that the system is free to ignore doing justice in pursuit of crime control through deterrence, incapacitation of the dangerous, and other such coercive crime control programs—that there is no crime control cost incurred in deviating from desert. This common wisdom is dangerously wrong. There is disutility in injustice, and the crime control costs of deviating from desert must be taken into account when designing an effective crime-control program. Indeed, in the long run, doing justice may be the most effective means of fighting crime.[16]

To telegraph our findings, Studies 2 and 3 (reported in Parts IV and V, respectively) support the arguments we have made elsewhere that doing justice, at least as the community perceives it, increases the law's moral credibility and thereby harnesses the crime-control powers of social and normative influence. Deviating from desert undermines the criminal justice system's moral credibility and thereby undermines its crime-control effectiveness. Specifically, it undermines its power of stigmatization, increases the chances of vigilantism, promotes resistance and subversion rather than the cooperation and acquiescence required by the criminal justice system, undermines compliance in borderline cases where the condemnatory nature of the offense may be ambiguous, and reduces the criminal justice system's influence in the public conversation by which societal norms are shaped. Studies 2a and 2b suggest that changes in the system's moral credibility can have these kinds of effects. Study 3 suggests that the dynamics shown in these laboratory experiments also can be seen in the datasets of existing national surveys.

We believe the studies reported here will assure both groups concerned about a change to desert as the distributive principle for criminal liability and punishment. The shift to a desert distribution—specifically, empirical desert—will not seriously undermine the criminal justice system's crime-control effectiveness, and indeed may enhance it, and is not likely to increase the system's punitiveness, and

---

[16] *See* ROBINSON, DISTRIBUTIVE PRINCIPLES, *supra* note 5, at 210–12 ("[A] charge to prevent crime is, as a practical matter, a charge primarily to do justice—to consider just desert—for that will reduce crime more than distributive criteria that ignore desert."); Robinson, *Empirical Desert*, *supra* note 1, at 29–31 (arguing that use of empirical desert as distributive principle strengthens law's moral credibility); Robinson & Darley, *Intuitions of Justice*, *supra* note 1, at 18–31 (same).

indeed is more likely to reduce it. This shift better tracks the community's shared intuitions of justice.

I

THE MOST POPULAR MODERN CRIME-CONTROL RULES

Do the community's shared intuitions of justice lead to draconian punishments? Described below are seven of the most common and politically popular criminal justice doctrines expressly based upon instrumentalist coercive crime-control strategies—usually those of deterrence and incapacitation. These are not necessarily the statistically most common applications of these doctrines, but neither are they aberrant applications by a rogue judge. Each instance is an expected and intended application by the terms of the doctrine, and many, if not most, have been reviewed and approved on appeal— some by the United States Supreme Court. These are the legal doctrines against which individuals' intuitions of justice are tested in Study 1, as reported in Part II.

A.   Three Strikes and Other Habitual Offender Statutes

The case of William James Rummel is not unusual.[17] In 1964, the twenty-one-year-old Texan uses his employer's credit card to pay $80 for four new tires without permission. He later pleads guilty to felony fraud. In 1969, Rummel forges a check for $28.36 to pay rent at a hotel, another felony. Over a course of years, Rummel is convicted of similar frauds four more times. On a hot August day in 1972, Rummel enters a bar in San Antonio and notices that the air conditioner is broken. He tells the bar's owner that the unit needs a new compressor, and offers to fix it for free if the owner will pay for the necessary part. The owner gives him $120.75 for the compressor, but Rummel never returns to the bar. After the owner decides to press charges, Rummel is arrested.[18] Rummel is found guilty of felony theft,[19] which typically would receive a sentence of two to ten years.[20] However, because this is Rummel's third felony conviction, he is charged under a Texas recidivism statute and receives a sentence of

---

[17] *See* Rummel v. Estelle, 445 U.S. 263, 285 (1980). For more details on the *Rummel* case, see PAUL H. ROBINSON, WOULD YOU CONVICT? SEVENTEEN CASES THAT CHALLENGED THE LAW 28–32 (1999) [hereinafter ROBINSON, WOULD YOU CONVICT].

[18] PAUL H. ROBINSON, CRIMINAL LAW CASE STUDIES 28 (4th ed. 2010).

[19] ROBINSON, WOULD YOU CONVICT, *supra* note 17, at 32.

[20] *Id.* at 29.

life imprisonment.[21] His sentence is affirmed by the Fifth Circuit Court of Appeals and by the United States Supreme Court.[22]

In another case, fifty-nine year old Charles Almond becomes frustrated by the constant arguing of his two adult sons (who still live at home) over which television program to watch. He picks up a .22 caliber revolver that his oldest son had left on the table, and shoots out the television's screen. Thirty years earlier, Almond had been convicted of burglarizing an unoccupied building, and twenty-five years earlier, he was convicted both of throwing "a missile" (a rock) at an automobile driven by his father-in-law and of breaking and entering an office. Because of Almond's decades-old felony convictions, a sentence of fifteen years is imposed in the television-shooting case for "possession of a firearm as a felon" combined with a "career offender" statute.[23]

Such "three strikes" and other habitual-offender legislation commonly impose long prison terms on offenders who have committed previous crimes. The underlying rationale for these statutes is typically incapacitative.[24] Advocates of such statutes reason that the offender's past recidivism shows that he cannot be deterred from future crime and that incapacitation may be the most effective means of preventing future offenses.[25]

Similar habitual-offender statutes, which became common in the 1990s,[26] typically set high mandatory sentences for felonies committed after the offender has been convicted of two prior felonies.[27] The most common form of such statutes requires the two previous felonies to be

---

[21] *Id.* at 32. According to Texas penal law and practice at the time, Rummel may have been eligible for parole after serving twelve years of his sentence with good behavior. *Rummel*, 445 U.S. at 280; *see also* Brief for the Respondent, Rummel v. Estelle, 445 U.S. 263 (1980) (No. 78-6386), 1979 WL 199781, at *16–17 (explaining Texas's parole system and suggesting that Rummel would be eligible to serve twelve years with good conduct or even ten if he earned "trusty status").

[22] *Rummel*, 445 U.S. at 285; Rummel v. Estelle, 587 F.2d 651, 654 (5th Cir. 1978) (en banc), *vacating* 568 F.2d 1193 (5th Cir. 1978).

[23] Almond v. United States, 854 F. Supp. 439, 445 (W.D. Va. 1994); PAUL H. ROBINSON & MICHAEL T. CAHILL, LAW WITHOUT JUSTICE: WHY CRIMINAL LAW DOESN'T GIVE PEOPLE WHAT THEY DESERVE 132–33 (2005) [hereinafter ROBINSON & CAHILL, LAW WITHOUT JUSTICE].

[24] See authorities and examples collected in Robinson, *Punishing Dangerousness*, *supra* note 10, at 1429 n.2.

[25] *See id.* at 1429 n.7 (explaining incapacitation rationale for habitual offender statutes).

[26] *See* BUREAU OF JUSTICE ASSISTANCE, U.S. DEP'T OF JUSTICE, 1996 NATIONAL SURVEY OF STATE SENTENCING STRUCTURES 16–17 & exhibit 1-9 (1998), *available at* http://www.ncjrs.gov/pdffiles/169270.pdf (noting in 1996 that twenty-four states had enacted two- or three-strikes laws and that "overwhelming majority" of such laws had been passed between 1993 and 1995).

[27] Note that the number of "strikes" in recidivist statutes is not always three. It is sometimes two (North Dakota, South Carolina), and sometimes four (Georgia, Maryland). N.D.

of a violent nature.[28] Some jurisdictions allow the inclusion of other felonies, such as drug-trafficking violations.[29] Other jurisdictions have habitual-offender statutes other than the famous "three strikes" laws.[30]

B. Drug Offense Penalties

In another relatively typical case, Anthony Papa is asked by a bowling partner to deliver an envelope containing cocaine to a town in upstate New York in exchange for $500. The courier who gives him the envelope is an undercover drug enforcement officer, and Papa is arrested when he delivers the envelope, which contains 4.5 ounces of cocaine. Under the controlling statute, the court imposes the required sentence of fifteen years to life.[31]

Similarly, in the case of *Harmelin v. Michigan*,[32] Harmelin is driving through Detroit in the early morning when he makes an illegal U-turn through a red light. After Harmelin is pulled over, he is arrested for marijuana possession, and a police search uncovers 672 grams of cocaine in the car's trunk—an amount approximately equal in size to one-and-a-half soda cans. Harmelin, who has no prior police record, is convicted under a Michigan drug statute and is sentenced to a mandatory term of life in prison without the possibility of parole—a sentence that the United States Supreme Court upholds as constitutional and not in violation of the Eighth Amendment prohibition against cruel and unusual punishments.[33]

CENT. CODE § 12.1-32-09 (1997); S.C. CODE ANN. § 17-25-45 (2003); GA. CODE ANN. § 17-10-7 (2008); MD. CODE ANN., CRIM. LAW § 14-101 (LexisNexis 2002).

[28] *E.g.*, 18 U.S.C. § 3559(C) (2006); N.M. STAT. ANN. § 31-18-23 (LexisNexis 2009); VA. CODE ANN. § 19.2-297.1 (2008).

[29] *E.g.*, GA. CODE ANN. § 17-10-7 (2008) (requiring two strikes for violent felonies, four strikes for others); N.D. CENT. CODE § 12.1-32-09 (1997) (allowing for habitual offender sentence when offender has two prior convictions for felonies of Class C or above, which may include out-of-state felony convictions punishable by maximum prison terms of five years or more); S.C. CODE ANN. § 17-25-45 (2003) (requiring life imprisonment without possibility of parole for offenders with two or more convictions for "most serious offense[s]," including certain nonviolent crimes, or upon conviction of three or more "serious offenses," including drug trafficking felonies).

[30] *E.g.*, ALA. CODE § 13A-5-9 (2005) (imposing enhanced penalty for felonies where defendant was previously convicted of felony); ALASKA STAT. § 12.55.125 (2008) (specifying sentence ranges for certain felonies by first-time, second-time, and third-time offender status); S.D. CODIFIED LAWS § 22-7-7 (2006) (enhancing sentence for principal felony if defendant was previously convicted of one or two felonies).

[31] *See* Rebecca Tuhus-Dubrow, *Talking with Anthony Papa*, THE NATION, Dec. 27, 2004, http://www.thenation.com/doc/20041227/tuhusdubrow. Papa serves twelve years of his sentence before being granted clemency. *Id.*

[32] 501 U.S. 957 (1991).

[33] *Id.* at 995–96.

In *United States v. Prince*,[34] Leroy Prince rents a room from Sydney Griffith, the owner of a nearby furniture store. Prince frequently helps move furniture from the house to Griffith's business. In exchange, Griffith agrees to provide furniture when Prince moves into an apartment, as he is planning to do. On one occasion, at Griffith's request, Prince helps unload boxes at the house where Prince rents a room. He smells marijuana during the unloading and confirms its presence by partially opening a box. He continues to help with the unloading but insists that the marijuana boxes be stored in a place other than the house where he lives. He helps move the boxes to the basement of a nearby grocery store. Customs inspectors later seize forty-seven boxes, containing a total of 1169 kilograms of marijuana. After being given downward adjustments under the U.S. Sentencing Guidelines due to his minor role in the offense, his lack of knowledge of the drug's presence beforehand, and his guilty plea, Prince is sentenced to five years' imprisonment without the possibility of early release.[35]

Though they are traditionally governed only by state law, drug-related crimes have increasingly come under federal jurisdiction in recent decades.[36] In an attempt to increase deterrent effects, federal sentencing for drug crimes has become quite harsh.[37] The average federal sentence for drug-related crimes in 2005 was 85.7 months. If marijuana-related crimes are ignored, that average rises to 98.9 months. As a point of comparison, the average federal sentence for all violent crimes is 95.2 months. Homicide has an average sentence of 118.3 months—less than 20% higher than the average sentence for non-marijuana drug offenses.[38] Harsher federal penalties mean that an ever-increasing number of cases that could be brought in state courts are being prosecuted in federal court.[39]

---

[34] 110 F.3d 921 (2d Cir. 1997).

[35] The U.S. Sentencing Guidelines range after those adjustments is fifty-one to sixty-three months. *Id.* at 926.

[36] *See, e.g.*, Edward L. Glaeser et al., *What Do Prosecutors Maximize? An Analysis of the Federalization of Drug Crimes*, 2 AM. L. & ECON. REV. 259, 259–60 (2000) (stating that since 1970s, Congress has expanded federal jurisdiction over drug crimes, and noting that "virtually any drug crime can now be prosecuted federally").

[37] The U.S. Sentencing Guidelines suggest 0 to 6 months for possession, and 0 months up to a maximum of 293 months for possession with intent to manufacture, import, export, or traffic. *See* U.S. SENTENCING GUIDELINES MANUAL §§ 2D1.1(c), 2D2.1(a) (2006).

[38] All sentencing statistics are taken from Bureau of Justice Statistics, U.S. Dep't of Justice, *Defendants Sentenced in U.S. District Courts: By Offense, and Type and Length of Sentence, Fiscal Year 2005*, *in* Sourcebook of Criminal Justice Statistics tbl.5.25.2005, http://www.albany.edu/sourcebook/pdf/t5252005.pdf (last visited Aug. 27, 2010).

[39] *See* Glaeser et al., *supra* note 36, at 260 (noting that expansion of federal jurisdiction and harsher federal penalties could implicate deterrence and equity considerations).

C. *Adult Prosecution of Juveniles*

It is no longer unusual for prosecutors to try juveniles as adults, even if this results in long prison terms.[40] Nathaniel Brazill, thirteen years old, is upset about being suspended from school for ten days just before summer vacation for throwing water balloons. He returns to the middle school to say good-bye to friends. When told by a seventh grade teacher (with whom he has a good relationship) that he has to leave, he pulls out a pistol and points it at the teacher. The gun discharges, hitting the teacher in the head and killing him. After being tried and convicted as an adult, he is sentenced to twenty-eight years in prison without the possibility of parole.[41]

In another case, Zachary Eggers, a sixteen-year-old, is given two natural-life terms for killing his parents.[42] Witnesses testify that Eggers was upset at his parents because he considered them to be too strict.[43] His attorney suggests that Eggers was intoxicated at the time of the killings.[44]

As of the end of the 1990s, all jurisdictions in the United States allow, in at least some cases, juveniles to be transferred to criminal court and tried as adults.[45] Transfers can be by discretionary, presumptive, or mandatory waiver of juvenile court jurisdiction, as well as by specific statutory criteria, and can be limited to specific offenses. The lowest age for which transfer is allowed differs by jurisdiction. Some jurisdictions do not list any minimum age for transfer.[46] Others allow transfer as early as age ten[47] or age fourteen.[48] Some jurisdic-

---

[40] *See infra* notes 45–49; *cf.* Roper v. Simmons, 543 U.S. 551, 578–79 (2005) (holding it unconstitutional to impose capital punishment for crimes committed by defendant under age eighteen).

[41] *See* Kate Randall, *Another Florida Teenager Receives Harsh Adult Prison Sentence*, WORLD SOCIALIST WEB SITE (Aug. 3, 2001), http://www.wsws.org/articles/2001/aug2001/flor-a03.shtml.

[42] Kim Smith, *Teen Gets Life for Killings of His Parents*, ARIZ. DAILY STAR, Sept. 23, 2005, at B4.

[43] Mitch Tobin, *Teen Guilty in 2 Killings*, ARIZ. DAILY STAR, Aug. 25, 2005, at B1.

[44] *Id.* When detectives searched his house, they found marijuana in Eggers's room. Appellee's Answering Brief at 3, State v. Eggers, No. 2 CA-CR 05-0320 (Ariz. Ct. App. 2005).

[45] *See* PATRICK GRIFFIN ET AL., U.S. DEP'T OF JUSTICE, TRYING JUVENILES AS ADULTS IN CRIMINAL COURT: AN ANALYSIS OF STATE TRANSFER PROVISIONS 1 (1998).

[46] *E.g.*, ME. REV. STAT. ANN. tit. 15, § 3101 (West Supp. 2009).

[47] *E.g.*, IND. CODE ANN. § 31-30-3-4 (LexisNexis 2007) (only for murder); VT. STAT. ANN. tit. 33, § 5506 (2001).

[48] *E.g.*, ALA. CODE § 12-15-34.1 (2005); MINN. STAT. ANN. § 260B.125 (West 2007); N.J. STAT. ANN. § 2A:4A-26 (West Supp. 2010).

tions retain a somewhat higher age for transfer, such as fifteen or sixteen, and several retain this higher age with very limited exceptions.[49]

D. Abolition or Narrowing of the Insanity Defense

Eric Clark was a typical teenager until mental illness took over his life. He is diagnosed with paranoid schizophrenia, a subtype of schizophrenia characterized by delusions and hallucinations. He will not drink tap water because he is fearful of lead poisoning. He believes that alien life forms from another planet are after him. Clark sets up a fishing line with beads and wind chimes throughout his home as an alarm system for alien invasions. He also starts to keep a bird in his car to warn him of any airborne poison. He sometimes circles the neighborhood, blaring loud music in an attempt to keep the aliens away. Clark thinks that the aliens are commonly disguised as government agents.

After neighbors call the police to report the excessive noise he is making, Clark is pulled over by a police officer. Believing the policeman to be an alien, and not wanting to be abducted or killed, Clark shoots and kills the officer. Clearly, Clark is dangerous in his current state and needs to be civilly committed for as long as he remains so. Yet it seems difficult to assess his blameworthiness without taking account of his serious mental illness. The Arizona statutes, however, have so narrowed the availability of defenses and mitigations related to mental illness that his disease is essentially legally irrelevant to Clark's criminal case.[50] He is convicted of first degree murder and sentenced to life imprisonment.[51] The Supreme Court upholds as constitutional the Arizona Supreme Court's *Mott* rule, which precludes the use of evidence of diminished capacity caused by mental illness to negate the mens rea elements of a crime.[52]

Consider, similarly, the case of Andrea Yates.[53] She, her husband, and their four young boys live in a renovated bus. They are deeply

---

[49] *E.g.*, D.C. CODE § 16-2307 (LexisNexis 2008) (at least fifteen, with one exception of no minimum age for illegal possession of firearm within 1000 feet of school or day care center); OR. REV. STAT. §§ 419C.349, .352 (2010) (fifteen, with no minimum-age exceptions for certain cases of murder, rape, sodomy and unlawful sexual penetration); TENN. CODE ANN. § 37-1-134 (2005) (sixteen, no exceptions); WASH. REV. CODE ANN. § 13.40.110 (West Supp. 2009) (sixteen, no exceptions).

[50] Arizona law does not allow evidence of mental illness to be introduced to negate specific intent elements for any crime. State v. Mott, 931 P.2d 1046, 1051 (Ariz. 1997). The State does allow a general insanity defense, but only one that is narrow in scope and that puts the burden on the defendant to prove "by clear and convincing evidence" that he was insane. ARIZ. REV. STAT. § 13-502(A)–(C) (LexisNexis 2008).

[51] Clark v. Arizona, 548 U.S. 735, 746 (2006).

[52] *Id.* at 779.

[53] Yates v. State, 171 S.W.3d 215 (Tex. Crim. App. 2005).

religious, often praying together, and want as large a family as possible. Unfortunately, Andrea increasingly manifests signs of mental illness. On one occasion, she attempts to commit suicide by swallowing pills. Though given prescriptions for multiple medications, including anti-psychotics, Andrea does not often take them. She often shakes, fails to feed her children, mutilates herself, and claims that there are cameras in the ceilings. Her husband Rusty stops a second, nearly successful, suicide attempt, but does not report the incident to her physicians. The Yates are warned against having more children because of Andrea's precarious mental state, but they soon have a fifth child, a baby girl. The family moves from the bus into a house. Andrea's condition initially improves, but the improvement is short-lived. Andrea is soon cutting herself again and refusing to feed her children. She worries that her mental illness renders her a bad mother and that, as their minister preaches, her children will then be doomed to eternal torment in hell. One morning, after Rusty leaves for work, Andrea fills the bathtub with water, then drowns each of her children. Her son Noah tries to run, but Andrea grabs him and holds him under the water as he struggles to escape. She believes that by killing her children she is saving them from a horrifying existence of eternal torment.

Again, one would think that her serious mental illness would significantly reduce or eliminate her blameworthiness. Yet she is convicted of capital murder and sentenced to life imprisonment (though the conviction is later overturned because of questionable testimony by a state witness).[54] Yates did not qualify for an insanity defense in Texas because the state limits it to individuals who, owing to mental illness, do not know that their conduct is criminal.[55] Presumably, Yates did know that her conduct was in violation of the state's rules, even though she thought she was doing the right thing in order to save her children.

Today, two jurisdictions do not allow an insanity defense, although they do allow evidence of mental illness to be used more narrowly to negate the culpability requirements of an offense.[56] Another thirty allow an insanity defense based only upon a cognitive

---

[54] *Id.* at 216–22.

[55] The Texas Penal Code provides: "It is an affirmative defense to prosecution that, at the time of the conduct charged, the actor, as a result of severe mental disease or defect, did not know that his conduct was wrong." TEX. PENAL CODE ANN. § 8.01(a) (West 2003). "Wrong" in this sense is interpreted under Texas law to mean "illegal." Ruffin v. State, 270 S.W.3d 586, 592 (Tex. Crim. App. 2008).

[56] Montana, MONT. CODE ANN. § 46-14-214 (2007); Utah, UTAH CODE ANN. § 76-2-305 (LexisNexis 2008).

dysfunction; no defense is allowed for a control dysfunction no matter how severe the impairment.[57] The remaining nineteen allow an insanity defense for either a cognitive or a control impairment.[58]

E. Strict Liability

It is now common for even serious offenses, like statutory rape, to be treated as strict liability offenses. Under such a regime, a culpable state of mind need not be proven with respect to a sexual partner's age. Consider the case of Raymond Garnett,[59] a twenty-year-old mentally retarded man with an IQ of fifty-two. He is introduced to Erica, who says that she is sixteen—a fact confirmed by her friends. Garnett and Erica talk on the phone on and off—he enjoys talking to someone who does not make fun of him. One night, at around 9:00 p.m., he is stranded without a ride home, but notices Erica's house nearby. As he

---

[57] United States, 18 U.S.C. § 17 (2006); Alabama, ALA. CODE § 15-16-2 (LexisNexis 2008); Alaska, ALASKA STAT. § 12.47.010 (2008); Arizona, ARIZ. REV. STAT. ANN. §§ 13-502(A)–(B) (2008); Arkansas, ARK. CODE ANN. § 5-2-312 (2008); California, People v. Drew, 583 P.2d 1318 (Cal. 1978); Colorado, COLO. REV. STAT. §§ 16-8-101(1), -104, -105(2) (2007); Delaware, DEL. CODE ANN. tit. 11, §§ 304a, 401 (2007); Florida, FLA. R. CRIM. P. § 3.217; Illinois, 720 ILL. COMP. STAT. ANN. 5/6-2 (LexisNexis 2008); Indiana, IND. CODE ANN. §§ 35-41-3-6, -4-1(b) (West 2004); Kansas, State v. Roadenbaugh, 673 P.2d 1166 (Kan. 1982) and State v. Grauerholz, 654 P.2d 395 (Kan. 1982); Louisiana, LA. REV. STAT. ANN. § 14:14 (2007); Maine, ME. REV. STAT. ANN. tit. 17-A, § 39 (2006); Minnesota, MINN. STAT. ANN. § 611.026 (West 2009); Mississippi, Herron v. State, 287 So. 2d 759 (Miss. 1974); Missouri, MO. ANN. STAT. § 552.030 (West 2009); Nebraska, NEB. REV. STAT. § 29-2203 (2009); Nevada, Poole v. State, 625 P.2d 1163 (Nev. 1981); New Hampshire, State v. Plummer, 374 A.2d 431 (N.H. 1977); New Jersey, N.J. STAT. ANN. § 2C:4-2 (West 2005); New York, N.Y. PENAL LAW § 40.15 (Consol. 2008); North Carolina, State v. Vickers, 291 S.E.2d 599 (N.C. 1982); Oklahoma, Munn v. State, 658 P.2d 482 (Okla. 1983); Pennsylvania, 18 PA. CONS. STAT. ANN. § 315 (West 1998); South Carolina, S.C. CODE ANN. § 17-24-10 (2007); South Dakota, State v. Kost, 290 N.W.2d 482 (S.D. 1980); Tennessee, State v. Clayton, 656 S.W.2d 344 (Tenn. 1983); Texas, TEX. PENAL CODE ANN. §§ 2.04, 8.01 (West 2003); Washington, WASH. REV. CODE ANN. § 10.77.030(2) (West 2002).

[58] Connecticut, CONN. GEN. STAT. § 53a-13(a) (2007); District of Columbia, Bethea v. United States, 365 A.2d 64 (D.C. 1976); Georgia, GA. CODE ANN. § 16-3-3 (2007); Hawaii, HAW. REV. STAT. § 704-400 (2009); Idaho, State v. White, 456 P.2d 797 (Idaho 1969); Iowa, IOWA CODE ANN. § 701.4 (West 2003); Kentucky, KY. REV. STAT. ANN. § 504.020 (West 2008); Maryland, MD. CODE ANN., CRIM. PROC. § 3-109 (LexisNexis 2008); Massachusetts, Commonwealth v. McHoul, 226 N.E.2d 556 (Mass. 1967); Michigan, MICH. COMP. LAWS ANN. § 768.21(a) (West 2008); New Mexico, N.M. STAT. ANN. § 31-9-3 (LexisNexis 2009); Ohio, State v. Anders, 277 N.E.2d 554 (Ohio 1972); Oregon, OR. REV. STAT. § 161.295 (2009); Rhode Island, State v. Johnson, 399 A.2d 469 (R.I. 1979); Vermont, VT. STAT. ANN. tit. 13, § 4801 (2009); Virginia, Godley v. Commonwealth, 343 S.E.2d 368 (Va. Ct. App. 1986); West Virginia, State v. Lockhart, 490 S.E.2d 298 (W. Va. 1997); Wisconsin, WIS. STAT. ANN. § 971.15 (West 2007); Wyoming, WYO. STAT. ANN. § 7-11-304 (2009).

[59] Garnett v. State, 632 A.2d 797 (Md. 1993). For further facts, see PAUL H. ROBINSON, CRIMINAL LAW: CASE STUDIES AND CONTROVERSIES 114 (2d ed. 2008) [hereinafter ROBINSON, CRIMINAL LAW: CASE STUDIES] and ROBINSON & CAHILL, LAW WITHOUT JUSTICE, *supra* note 23, at 63–65.

approaches the house, Erica opens her upstairs bedroom window and invites him in, directing him to use a nearby ladder. They talk for a long time, have consensual intercourse, and Garnett leaves at about 4:30 a.m. When Erica gives birth eight-and-a-half months later, her parents contact the police, who arrest Garnett for statutory rape. Erica was thirteen years old at the time of their intercourse. Garnett is charged with second-degree rape. Because the offense is one of strict liability, he is not allowed to introduce evidence at trial showing that his mistake as to her age was a reasonable one for him to make.[60]

In another case, nineteen-year-old Ras Haas lets two runaway girls stay at his apartment. They tell him they are eighteen years old, and at different times have consensual intercourse with him. He is later arrested and charged with two counts of sexual assault of a child because the girls, in fact, are fourteen and fifteen years old. At trial he is not allowed to present evidence that he reasonably believed the girls were over the age of sixteen, which is the age of consent required by state law. Because the offense is one of strict liability, such reasonableness is irrelevant. He is sentenced to twenty to thirty years imprisonment for each count, with the terms to be served consecutively.[61]

Roswold Adkins has consensual intercourse with a fourteen-year-old girl who intentionally misrepresents her age. During deliberations, the jury, apparently concerned about the issue, asks the judge about taking the intentional misrepresentation into account in assessing liability and is told that it is irrelevant to liability because even a reasonable mistake is no defense. Adkins is convicted of two counts of criminal sexual conduct and sentenced to two concurrent terms of six-and-a-half to twenty-two years.[62]

Most jurisdictions reject even a reasonable mistake as to age as a defense to statutory rape.[63] While other serious offenses, such as

---

[60] Garnett's prison sentence is suspended, and he is put on probation. *Garnett*, 632 A.2d 799, 803–04.

[61] State v. Haas, No. A-05-804, 2006 WL 996535, at *5 (Neb. Ct. App. Apr. 18, 2006).

[62] People v. Adkins, No. 257845, 2006 WL 142120, at *1 (Mich. Ct. App. Jan. 19, 2006).

[63] *See* Catherine L. Carpenter, *On Statutory Rape, Strict Liability, and the Public Welfare Offense Model*, 53 Am. U. L. Rev. 313, 385–91 (2003) (categorizing each state's approach as among true crime, strict liability, and hybrid, with majority employing strict liability). For states that employ a strict liability approach, see, for example, Fla. Stat. Ann. § 794.021 (West 2007), N.J. Stat. Ann. § 2C:14-5(c) (West 2005), and Wis. Stat. Ann. § 939.43(2) (West 2005). For states that allow for a mistake defense, see, for example, Ind. Code Ann. § 35-42-4-3(c) (LexisNexis 2009), Mo. Rev. Stat. § 566.020 (2000), and W. Va. Code Ann. § 61-8B-12 (LexisNexis 2005). The federal approach is a hybrid, with strict liability only for sexual contact with children under the age of twelve. 18 U.S.C. § 2441(d) (2006).

driving under the influence, can be ones of strict liability,[64] the bulk of strict liability offenses are more minor, such as "public welfare offenses,"[65] speeding and other vehicular offenses, and liquor, narcotics, and food regulation infractions.[66] A few state courts have invalidated the use of strict liability for offenses that impose significant prison sentences or create an unreasonable expectation of knowledge in the offender.[67] The Model Penal Code attempts to restrict the use of strict liability to "violations" rather than crimes,[68] although it too imposes strict liability for the serious felony of aggravated statutory rape.[69]

F. Felony Murder

The felony-murder doctrine punishes as murder all deaths caused in the course of a felony, no matter how accidental the killing, and applies such murder liability not just to the person causing the death but to all accomplices in the underlying felony.[70] The case of Jerry Moore is not unusual. Moore agrees to help Montejo (an acquaintance) burglarize a house while the house's owner is away. Neither man is armed. When the resident returns unexpectedly, Moore is surprised to see Montejo shoot and kill the owner with a gun he apparently found in a nightstand. Moore is convicted of murder for Montejo's shooting of the homeowner and is sentenced to life imprisonment at hard labor without the possibility of parole.[71]

In the case of Forrest Heacock, the defendant supplies cocaine to people at a "drug party" that he attends. He and three other people inject the cocaine; one of them overdoses and dies. Heacock is convicted of felony murder and is sentenced to forty years imprisonment.[72]

---

[64] See Leocal v. Ashcroft, 543 U.S. 1, 8 n.5 (2004) (listing states where driving under the influence is treated as strict liability offense).

[65] See, e.g., Morissette v. United States, 342 U.S. 246, 255 (1952) (comparing nature of "public welfare offenses," which involve neglect or inaction with regard to duty of care, to accepted classifications of common law offenses, which involve "positive aggressions or invasions"); Francis Bowes Sayre, *Public Welfare Offenses*, 33 Colum. L. Rev. 55, 84–88 (1933) (listing state cases involving public welfare offenses with no mens rea requirement).

[66] Wayne R. LaFave, Criminal Law 272 n.1 (4th ed. 2003).

[67] Id. at 279.

[68] Model Penal Code § 2.05(1)(a) (Proposed Official Draft 1962).

[69] Id. § 213.6(1).

[70] See LaFave, *supra* note 66, at 744–65 (providing general overview of felony murder rule).

[71] State v. Moore, No. 2006-KA-1979, 2007 WL 914637, at *1 (La. Ct. App. Mar. 28, 2007).

[72] Heacock v. Commonwealth, 323 S.E.2d 90, 93 (Va. 1984). Heacock's sentence is actually eighty years imprisonment, but forty years of the sentence are suspended.

The most popular version of the rule, used by forty jurisdictions, allows only inherently dangerous felonies (such as arson or drug trafficking) to trigger the rule's use.[73] Ten jurisdictions allow the commission of any felony to be used.[74] Two jurisdictions have abolished the felony murder rule.[75]

G. Criminalization of Regulatory Violations

Robert Blandford and two other seafood importers are arrested, tried, and convicted in federal court for violating the Lacey Act, which criminalizes the importation of wildlife in violation of a U.S. *or* foreign law.[76] In this instance, the importation was in violation of a Honduran law requiring the use of cardboard box–shaped containers

---

[73] United States, 18 U.S.C. § 1111(a) (2006); Alabama, ALA. CODE § 13A-6-2(a)(3) (2009); Alaska, ALASKA STAT. § 11.41.110(a)(3) (2008); Arizona, ARIZ. REV. STAT. ANN. § 13-1105(A)(2) (2010); California, CAL. PENAL CODE § 1-8-1-189 (West 2008); Colorado, COLO. REV. STAT. ANN. § 18-3-102(1)(b) (West 2009); Connecticut, CONN. GEN. STAT. ANN. § 53(a)-54(c) (West 2007); District of Columbia, D.C. CODE § 22-2101 (LexisNexis 2010); Florida, FLA. STAT. ANN. § 782.04 (West 2007); Idaho, IDAHO CODE ANN. § 18-4003(d) (2004); Illinois, 720 ILL. COMP. STAT. ANN. 5/9-1(a)(3) (West 2002); Indiana, IND. CODE ANN. § 35-42-1-2, -3 (West 2004); Iowa, IOWA CODE § 707.2.2-.3 (2007); Kansas, KAN. STAT. ANN. § 21-3401(b) (2007); Louisiana, LA. REV. STAT. ANN. § 14:30(A)(1) (2007); Maine, ME. REV. STAT. ANN. tit. 17-A, § 202(1) (2006); Maryland, MD. CODE ANN., CRIM. LAW § 2-201(a)(4) (LexisNexis 2002); Massachusetts, MASS. ANN. LAWS ch. 265, § 1 (LexisNexis 2008); Michigan, MICH. COMP. LAWS ANN. § 750.316(1)(b) (West 2004); Minnesota. MINN. STAT. ANN. § 609.185(a)(2)-(3) (West 2009); Mississippi, MISS. CODE ANN. § 97-3-19(1)(c) (2005); Montana, MONT. CODE ANN. § 45-5-102(1)(b) (2009); Nebraska, NEB. REV. STAT. § 28-303(2) (2009); Nevada, NEV. REV. STAT. § 200.030(1)(b) (2009); New Jersey, N.J. STAT. ANN. § 2C:11-3.a(3) (West 2005); New York, N.Y. PENAL LAW § 125.25(3) (Consol. 1998); North Carolina, N.C. GEN. STAT. ANN. § 14-17 (West 2000); North Dakota, N.D. CENT. CODE § 12.1-16-01(1)(c) (1997); Ohio, OHIO REV. CODE ANN. § 2903.01(B) (West 2006); Oregon, OR. REV. STAT. § 163.115(1)(b) (2009); Rhode Island, R.I. GEN. LAWS § 11-23-1 (2002); South Carolina, S.C. CODE ANN. § 16-3-20(c)(a)(1) (2003); South Dakota, S.D. CODIFIED LAWS § 22-16-4(1) (2006); Tennessee, TENN. CODE ANN. § 39-13-202(a)(2)–(3) (2006); Utah, UTAH CODE ANN. § 76-5-203(2)(d) (LexisNexis 2008); Vermont, VT. STAT. ANN. tit. 13, § 2301 (2009); Virginia, VA. CODE ANN. § 18.2-32 (2009); West Virginia, W. VA. CODE ANN. § 61-2-1 (2005); Wisconsin, WIS. STAT. ANN. § 940.03 (West 2005); Wyoming, WYO. STAT. ANN. § 6-2-101(a) (2009).

[74] Arkansas, ARK. CODE ANN. § 5-10-102(a)(1) (2006); Delaware, DEL. CODE ANN. tit. 11, § 636(a)(2) (2007); Georgia, GA. CODE ANN. § 16-5-1 (2007); Missouri, MO. REV. STAT. § 565.021.1(2) (1999); New Hampshire, N.H. REV. STAT. ANN. § 630:1-b (2007); New Mexico, N.M. STAT. ANN. § 30-2-1-A(2) (2004); Oklahoma, OKLA. STAT. ANN. tit. 21, § 701.7(B) (West 2002); Pennsylvania, 18 PA. CONS. STAT. § 2502(b) (1998); Texas, TEX. PENAL CODE ANN. § 19.02(b)(3) (West 2003); Washington, WASH. REV. CODE ANN. § 9A.32.030(1)(c), -.050(1)(b) (2009).

[75] Hawaii, HAW. REV. STAT. § 707-701 (1996); Kentucky, KY. REV. STAT. ANN. § 507.020 (LexisNexis 2008).

[76] 16 U.S.C. § 1372 (2006).

for seafood exports. The plastic bags used by Blandford did not violate U.S. law. The men are sentenced to eight years in prison.[77]

In another case, Tom Lindsey, twenty-six, takes his brother and six friends on a rafting and camping trip in the popular Hell's Canyon National Recreation Area, a park created and regulated by federal law.[78] Lindsey acquires the necessary permits to both raft and camp in the area but does not strictly follow the relevant regulations. In order to fish in the mornings, Lindsey and his friends launch their raft at 7:00 a.m., instead of waiting until 9:00 a.m., as the regulations require. Additionally, they camp below the high-water mark of the river, which is technically state and not federal land, in order to evade a federal regulation forbidding campfires during the summer. Forest Service agents arrest Lindsey and his brother. They later send Lindsey a letter informing him that his permits have been revoked. Lindsey and his brother are indicted on felony charges of camping without a permit and building a campfire without a permit.[79]

The federal criminal code in particular has seen "unprecedented expansion" in recent years.[80] Between 1980 and 2004, there was a thirty percent increase in federal offenses that are subject to criminal penalties.[81] Many of these new laws criminalize behavior typically handled through civil regulatory actions, including the expansion of

---

[77] United States v. McNab, 324 F.3d 1266 (11th Cir. 2003); Tony Mauro, *Lawyers See Red Over Lobster Case*, LEGAL TIMES, Feb. 18, 2004, *available at* http://www.law.com/jsp/article.jsp?id=1122023117263&hbx. The Honduran courts subsequently invalidated one of the regulations serving as the basis for the violation of Honduran law—the requirement that tails be no shorter than 5.5 inches. However, even though the laws were declared void retroactively, the Eleventh Circuit Court of Appeals upheld the defendants' convictions, stating that the District Court was able to determine on its own whether the law was valid at the time the offense was committed. Thus, even though the defendants could not be found liable for a violation under Honduran law, they were held liable for violation of the Lacey Act. *Id.*

[78] *See* ROBINSON & CAHILL, LAW WITHOUT JUSTICE, *supra* note 23, at 187 (discussing facts).

[79] United States v. Lindsey, 595 F.2d 5, 6 (9th Cir. 1979); ROBINSON & CAHILL, LAW WITHOUT JUSTICE, *supra* note 23, at 187–89. Before being indicted, Lindsey shows the agents a stipulation in the legislation creating the Hells Canyon Recreation Area that states that permits are not required to camp below the high-water mark. A district court judge dismisses the case for lack of jurisdiction. *Lindsey*, 595 F.2d at 6. However, the Ninth Circuit Court of Appeals rules that the federal government has the power to regulate conduct on state land when necessary to protect adjacent federal land. *Id.* The case is remanded to the District Court, but the prosecutor does not pursue it further. ROBINSON & CAHILL, LAW WITHOUT JUSTICE, *supra* note 23, at 192.

[80] Sara Sun Beale, *The Many Faces of Overcriminalization: From Morals and Mattress Tags to Overfederalization*, 54 AM. U. L. REV. 747, 755 (2005).

[81] *Id.* at 754.

criminal liability for copyright infringement,[82] environmental offenses,[83] and fiduciary irresponsibility.[84]

The phenomenon is not limited to federal law, although the continuing expansion of state criminal codes has taken place in a much longer time frame than has the federal code expansion. The Illinois Criminal Code is a particularly striking example. In 1856, the Code contained 131 crime definitions; by 1951 this number had ballooned to 460.[85] Perhaps more telling is the expansion of Illinois's modern code: Though seventy-two pages long in 1961, the Code had expanded to 1200 pages by the year 2000.[86] Such rapid expansion is not unique to Illinois, and in most cases it is the result of a number of factors, including the continuous adoption of "designer offenses" covering actions already made illegal by more general statutes, the passage of laws covering "crimes *du jour*" that garner heavy news coverage and public outrage, and other forms of ad hoc code amendments tending to expand the range of criminal statutes.[87]

II
TESTING THE PERCEIVED JUSTICE OF MODERN CRIME-CONTROL RULES: STUDY 1

The goal of this study is to compare subjects' treatment of cases involving the crime-control doctrines described in Part I to the law's treatment of those cases. Subjects were asked to rank and then assign a specific punishment to the cases, and these rankings and assigned punishments were then compared to the rankings and punishments that the law gives the cases.

We also examined subjects' treatment of a set of "milestone" cases, which did not engage the various crime control doctrines of interest, and we compared subjects' responses to these cases with their responses to the crime-control cases. We predicted that for the crime-control cases, the subjects' sentences would be much less punitive than those of the law. In contrast, although we expected that there might

---

[82] *E.g.*, 17 U.S.C. § 101 (2006); *id.* § 1204.

[83] *E.g.*, 33 U.S.C. § 1319(c) (2006).

[84] *E.g.*, 7 U.S.C. § 2009 (2006); *see also* United States v. Ntshona, 156 F.3d 318 (2d Cir. 1998); United States v. Goldstein, 883 F.2d 1362 (7th Cir. 1989).

[85] *See* William J. Stuntz, *The Pathological Politics of Criminal Law*, 100 MICH. L. REV. 505, 513 (2001) (discussing rise in number of offenses).

[86] In 2000, Governor George Ryan issued an Executive Order ordering the creation of a Criminal Code Rewrite and Reform Commission whose purpose was to study existing criminal law and create clearer and more coherent standards. *See* 24 Ill. Reg. 7755 (May 4, 2000).

[87] Michael T. Cahill & Paul H. Robinson, *Can a Model Penal Code Second Save the States from Themselves?*, 1 OHIO ST. J. CRIM. L. 169, 170–73 (2003).

be some discrepancies between subjects' sentences and the law's for the milestone cases, we predicted that these would be much smaller and less systematic than the discrepancies for the crime-control cases.

A. *"Milestone" Scenarios*

While people tend to agree on the proper rank order of cases on the punishment continuum, at least for the kind of core harms at issue here, some people tend to be harsh in their "sentencing," while others are lenient. To be able to account for these personal differences in general sentencing severity, subjects were first asked to rank in order, and then to assign specific punishments to a collection of twelve cases that ranged along the punishment continuum. These twelve cases provided "milestones" for the subject's punishment continuum, against which the twelve "crime-control" cases embodying the crime-control doctrines could be compared.

The "milestone" scenarios were taken from a 2007 study by Paul H. Robinson and Robert Kurzban.[88] In that study, subjects rank-ordered twenty-four crime scenarios according to the amount of punishment deserved by the described offender. Most researchers would consider this a quite demanding task, perhaps asking for more concentration and effort than most subjects are willing or able to provide. The task was also quite complex, requiring subjects to compare the deserved punishment for each scenario to that for each of the other twenty-three scenarios. Yet the researchers found that the subjects had little difficulty performing the task and, indeed, displayed an astounding level of agreement in the ordinal ranking of the scenarios across demographics.[89]

A statistical measure of concordance, which measures the degree of agreement between different subjects (in this instance, agreement on rank ordering), is produced by Kendall's W coefficient of concordance; a Kendall's W of 1.0 indicates perfect agreement, and 0.0 indicates no agreement. In the study just described, the Kendall's W was .95 (with $p < .001$). This is a strikingly high level of agreement. One might expect to get this high a Kendall's W if subjects were asked to judge the relative brightness of different groupings of spots, for example.[90] In the context of more subjective or complex comparisons,

---

[88] Paul H. Robinson & Robert Kurzban, *Concordance and Conflict in Intuitions of Justice*, 91 MINN. L. REV. 1829, 1867 (2007).

[89] *Id.*

[90] *See* Charles M.M. de Weert & Noud A.W.H. van Kruysbergen, *Assimilation: Central and Peripheral Effects*, 26 PERCEPTION 1217, 1219–21 (1997) (describing experiment in which subjects were asked to judge brightness of black and white patterns, yielding high Kendall's coefficient of concordance).

such as asking travel magazine readers to rank the attractiveness of eight different travel destinations, one gets a much lower Kendall's *W* of .52.[91] When asking economists to rank the top twenty economics journals according to quality, one study found a Kendall's *W* of .095.[92]

In the present study, we used only twelve of the original twenty-four scenarios. Table 1 shows the control cases that were used as "milestone markers." The text of each of these twelve "milestone" scenarios is reproduced in Appendix A. As is apparent, this collection of cases represents the full punishment continuum, from cases where subjects impose no liability (scenarios 1 and 2), to cases of common minor offenses, such as petty theft, to cases of common serious offenses, such as first-degree murder. As it happens, each of the scenarios represents a different legal offense from the others, named in the second column. The differences in seriousness perceived by the subjects in Robinson and Kurzban's earlier study generally match the differences in offense grade assigned by typical American criminal codes (based, as they often are, upon the Model Penal Code),[93] as is noted in the third column. The ranking of those subjects also corresponds, in a general way, to the average sentences given to state offenders, listed in the fourth column, and to the sentencing of federal offenders provided by the federal sentencing guidelines, listed in the last column.

---

[91] *See* Baruch Fischhoff et al., *Travel Risks in a Time of Terror: Judgments and Choices*, 24 RISK ANALYSIS 1301, 1303 (2004) (illustrating results of study designed to elicit attitudes regarding travel risks).

[92] Kostas Axarloglou & Vasilis Theoharakis, *Diversity in Economics: An Analysis of Journal Quality Perceptions*, 1 J. EUR. ECON. ASS'N 1402, 1422 (2003) (examining perceptions of journal quality among American Economic Association (AEA) members, and finding that these perceptions vary widely across AEA subgroups).

[93] One might note that an exception here is the case of burglary, which is graded more seriously by the criminal code than it is ranked by the subjects. This disparity is probably due in large part to the problem of "combination offenses" (burglary is simply a combination of one offense, such as theft, and the offense of criminal trespass). For general discussion of the problem of combination offenses, see ROBINSON, CRIMINAL LAW: CASE STUDIES, *supra* note 59, at 812–15, and Paul H. Robinson et al., *Codifying Shari'a: International Norms, Legality, and the Freedom To Invent New Forms*, 2 J. COMP. L. 1, 39 (2007).

TABLE 1

CONTROL SCENARIOS—"MILESTONE MARKERS"

Scenario	Offense	Model Penal Code Grade[94]	Average State System Term[95]	USSC Guideline Sentence[96]
12. Ambush shooting	First Degree Murder	Felony—death eligible (§§ 210.2(1)(a), 210.6(3)(h))	10.5 years*	Life (§ 2A1.1)
11. Stabbing	Second Degree Murder	Felony 1st degree (§2 10.2(1)(a))	10.5 years*	19.5–24.5 years (§ 2A1.2)
10. Accidental mauling by pit bulls	Manslaughter	Felony 2d degree (§ 210.3(1)(a))	4.7–8.4 years	2.25–2.75 years (§ 2A1.4(a)(2)(A))
9. Clubbing during robbery	Aggravated Robbery	Felony 2d degree (§ 222.1(1)(b))	4.3 years	6.5–8 years (§ 2B3.1(b)(2)(D), (3)(B))
8. Attempted robbery at gas station	Attempted Robbery	Felony 2d degree (§ 222.1(1)(b))	(<4.3 years*)	4.25–5.25 years (§ 2B3.1(b)(3)(B))
7. Stitches after soccer game	Aggravated Assault	Felony 2d degree (§ 211.1(2))	2.6 years	3.75–4.75 years (§ 2A2.2(b)(2)(B), (3)(B))
6. Slap and bruising at record store	Assault	Misdemeanor (§ 211.1(1)(a))	(<2.6 years*)	4–10 months (§ 2A2.3(b)(1)(A))
5. Microwave from house	Burglary	Felony 3d degree (§ 221.1(1))	2.4 years	2–2.5 years (§ 2B2.1(a)(1))
4. Clock radio from car	Theft	Misdemeanor (§ 223.1(2)(b))	1.5 years	0–6 months (§ 2B1.1(a)(2))
3. Whole pies from buffet	Petty Theft	Petty offense (§ 223.1(2)(b))	–	–
2. Wolf hallucination	Assault—insanity defense	No liability (§ 4.01(1))	–	–
1. Umbrella mistake	Theft—culpability defense	No liability (§2.02(1))	–	–

* National data are not available for this distinct category of offense.

Note that the data in each of the last three columns deviates slightly from the order of scenarios as they appear in the table, which is the order in which lay persons almost universally rank them.[97] This suggests that current state sentencing practice and the federal sen-

---

[94] MODEL PENAL CODE (Proposed Official Draft 1962).

[95] Bureau of Justice Statistics, U.S. Dep't of Justice, *First Releases from State Prison: Sentence Length, Time Served, and Percent of Sentence Served, By Offense*, in NATIONAL CORRECTIONS REPORTING PROGRAM (2003), *available at* http://bjs.ojp.usdoj.gov/index.cfm?ty=pbdetail&iid=2045.

[96] U.S. SENTENCING GUIDELINES MANUAL (2008).

[97] Robinson & Kurzban, *supra* note 88, at 1868.

tencing guidelines are not based strictly upon the community's shared intuitions of justice.[98] On the other hand, some of the inconsistency between the community's view and the rankings by average sentence and guideline sentence no doubt arises from the fact that the state sentencing average and the guideline sentence include a range of cases—sentences for burglary, for instance, vary depending on whether it was more or less aggravated. Thus, the last two columns only give a general sense of the range in which such cases would normally fall.

B. *"Crime-Control" Scenarios*

In the present study, after considering the twelve "milestone" scenarios, subjects were provided with twelve additional "crime-control" scenarios and asked to include them in their ranking exercise. Each of these "crime-control" scenarios summarizes the basic facts of one of the specific real-world cases used to illustrate the operation of the seven crime-control doctrines discussed in Part I. Table 2 shows the real-world case upon which each scenario is based, the crime-control doctrine that it illustrates, and the actual sentence imposed under that doctrine, in order of subjects' rankings.[99] The text of each of these "crime-control" scenarios is reproduced in Appendix B.

---

[98] Federal and state sentences typically are a product of the exercise of judicial discretion or crime-control policymaking. *See* Stephanos Bibas et al., *Policing Policies at Sentencing*, 103 Nw. U. L. Rev. 1371, 1377 n.24 (2009) (collecting studies of how judges' different sentencing philosophies influence sentencing outcomes); Max M. Schanzenbach & Emerson H. Tiller, *Reviewing the Sentencing Guidelines: Judicial Politics, Empirical Evidence, and Reform*, 75 U. Chi. L. Rev. 715, 720 n.30 (2008) (finding in empirical studies that policy preferences of judges influence sentencing and that judges selectively use adjustments and departures to enhance or reduce sentences); *see also* Dissenting View of Commissioner Paul H. Robinson on the Promulgation of Sentencing Guidelines by the United States Sentencing Commission, 52 Fed. Reg. 17,915, 18,121–22 (May 1, 1987) (arguing that federal sentencing guidelines as promulgated lacked coherent organizing principle).

[99] While offenders typically may be required to serve the entire sentence imposed, they also may be released from prison to parole supervision, subject to reimprisonment for a parole violation. These are the actual prison terms served by those offenders for whom information is available: Yates, whose life sentence was overturned on appeal due to questions regarding the proof of the underlying facts, has been held in a state mental hospital for three years with no release date currently set. *Woman Not Guilty in Retrial in the Deaths of Her 5 Children*, N.Y. Times, July 27, 2006, at A20. Brazill has a scheduled release date in 2028, which would mean a term served of almost twenty-seven years. Fla. Dep't of Corr., Inmate Population Information Detail, http://www.dc.state.fl.us/Active Inmates/detail.asp?Bookmark=2&From=list&SessionID=486501272 (last visited Oct. 27, 2010). Clark, who has served six years as of this writing, has no release date set. Ariz. Dep't of Corr., http://www.azcorrections.gov/inmate_datasearch/results.aspx?Inmate Number=180165&LastName=CLARK&FNMI=E&SearchType=SearchInet (last visited Oct. 27, 2010). Rummel's conviction was overturned after eight years in prison, on a claim of incompetent representation, after which an agreement was struck for a sentence of time

TABLE 2

"CRIME-CONTROL" SCENARIOS

Scenario	*Case Name*	*Offense*	*Crime-Control Doctrine*	*Actual Court Sentence*
L. Accidental teacher shooting	*Brazill*	Murder	Adult Prosecution of Juveniles	28 years without parole
K. Drowning children to save them from hell	*Yates*	Murder	Narrowing Insanity Defense	Life
J. Accomplice killing during burglary	*Moore*	Felony murder, burglary	Felony Murder	Life at hard labor without parole
I. Killing officer believed to be alien	*Clark*	Murder	Narrowing Insanity Defense	Life
H. Cocaine overdose	*Heacock*	Felony murder, unlawful distribution of controlled substance	Felony Murder	40 years
G. Cocaine in trunk	*Harmelin*	Complicity in unlawful distribution of controlled substance	Drug Offense Penalties	Life without parole
F. Air conditioner fraud	*Rummel*	Petty fraud	Three Strikes	Life
E. Sex with female reasonably believed overage	*Haas*	Statutory rape	Strict Liability	40 to 60 years
D. Underage sex by mentally retarded man	*Garnett*	Statutory rape	Strict Liability	5 years
C. Marijuana unloading	*Papa*	Unlawful possession of controlled substance	Drug Offense Penalties	8 years
B. Shooting of TV	*Almond*	Unlawfully discharging firearm	Three Strikes	15 years without parole
A. Incorrect lobster container	*Blandford*	Violation of importation regulations	Criminalizing Regulatory Violations	15 years to life

served. *S.A. Man Finally Free After 8-Year Ordeal*, SAN ANTONIO EXPRESS NEWS, Nov. 15, 1980, at 2-A C. Haas has a projected release date in 2035, which would mean a term served of just under thirty years. NEB. DEP'T OF CORR. SERVS., NEBRASKA INMATE DETAILS, http://dcs-inmatesearch.ne.gov/Corrections/InmateDisplayServlet?DcsId=62184 (last visited Oct. 27, 2010). Blandford has a release date in 2011, which would mean a term served of eight years. FED. BUREAU OF PRISONS, INMATE LOCATOR, http://www.bop.gov/iloc2/InmateFinderServlet?Transaction=NameSearch (last visited Oct. 27, 2010). Almond was released from prison in 2006, after having served thirteen years. FED. BUREAU OF PRISONS, INMATE LOCATOR, http://www.bop.gov/iloc2/InmateFinderServlet?Transaction=Name Search (last visited Oct. 27, 2010). Papa served twelve years. Tuhus-Dubrow, *supra* note 31.

We do not suggest that these cases are the statistically most common application of these crime-control doctrines. However, neither are they aberrant applications by a rogue judge. Each is an application of the doctrine as intended by its drafters and, in most cases, as specifically approved on appeal as a proper application in several instances by the United States Supreme Court. It only takes a few objectionable cases to undermine the system's moral credibility in peoples' minds. What we know about making and keeping reputations tells us that intention counts enormously: Accidental or unavoidable injustices or failures of justice may be forgiven if the system appears to be committed to trying to do justice.[100] When revealed, deviations from desert are intended by the system. When they are planned and predictable applications of the criminal law's rules, as with the modern crime-control doctrines examined here, then even a single telling case can have detrimental consequences.

C. *Study 1 Design and Methodology*

1. *Study Design*

The study was administered and funded by the National Science Foundation's Time Sharing Experiments in the Social Sciences (TESS). The 317 subjects were recruited broadly from across the United States and were demographically heterogeneous, representing a wide range of socioeconomic, racial, and religious backgrounds.[101]

---

[100] *See* Paul H. Robinson & John M. Darley, *The Utility of Desert*, 91 Nw. U. L. Rev. 453, 496 (1997) [hereinafter Robinson & Darley, *Utility of Desert*] ("An error can be forgiven if it is seen as 'out of character.' [People's] view of the system is likely to be governed by what they think the system is trying to do, by what they see as its motivation to do justice.").

[101] TESS relies on a company called Knowledge Networks, which recruits samples from a panel that is representative of the entire U.S. population. To create this panel, Knowledge Networks utilizes probability-based sampling methods, using both random-digit dialing and address-based sampling. Panel members do not need to be current web users, as Internet access and hardware are provided as needed. The random-digit dialing method incorporates both listed and unlisted telephone numbers as well as cell phone numbers. Panel members are all randomly selected, and unselected volunteers are not able to join. For a more complete description of this method, see KNOWLEDGE NETWORKS, KNOWLEDGEPANEL DESIGN SUMMARY (2010), *available at* http://www.knowledgenetworks .com/knpanel/docs/KnowledgePanel(R)-Design-Summary-Description.pdf.

Forty-three subjects were excluded from our data analysis for not completing the initial ranking task. The remaining 317 subjects had the following demographic characteristics: Age: 18-29, 24%; 30-44, 27%; 45-59, 28%; 60+, 20%. Gender: male, 51%; female, 49%. Marital status: married, 60%; divorced or separated, 12%; widowed, 2%; living with partner, 5%; never married, 21%. Race: white, 80%; black, non-Hispanic, 7%; Hispanic, 9%; other, 4%. Education: some college, 24%; two-year college degree, 10%; four-year college degree, 25%; Master's degree, 9%; professional or doctorate degree, 3%. Median household income: $60,000-$74,999. Employment status: currently employed, 61%; retired, 14%; not working (laid off, looking for work, disabled, other), 25%. Political views:

1968 *NEW YORK UNIVERSITY LAW REVIEW* [Vol. 85:1940

In the first part of the task, subjects were given the twelve "mile-stone" scenarios and were asked to rank order them in terms of their relative degree of seriousness—that is, in terms of the relative blame-worthiness of the main character in each case. The cases were presented in a new random order for each subject. Following this, sub-jects were then given the twelve "crime-control" cases and were asked to perform the same task. However, the transition between the two blocks of cases was seamless for the subjects. They were not aware of any difference between the two sorts of cases, and instead had the experience of ranking twenty-four cases in turn. The twenty-four cases are reproduced in Appendices A and B.

In the second part of the task, subjects indicated what they thought was an appropriate level of punishment for each case. The instructions asked subjects to report their own judgments about the amount of punishment deserved in each case (if any), not what they thought the law or other persons would assign. They indicated the spe-cific amount of punishment they would give to the offender in each of the twenty-four cases by using the punishment continuum response scale reproduced in Appendix B. In the third part of the task, subjects were asked to respond to ten questions which asked for their general impressions about the American criminal justice system.

2. Procedure

The task was computerized and run over the Internet using a sample of subjects that were recruited by TESS. In the first part of the task, subjects were presented with a vertical array on the left side of the screen, which was labeled "Most serious case (person most blame-worthy)" at the top, and "Least serious case (person least blame-worthy)" at the bottom. A description of each new case was presented on the right side of the screen. Each case had a brief title, followed by a short paragraph describing the circumstances of the case. Subjects read the description of each case and then dragged the case with a mouse cursor to a point on the vertical array corresponding to its rela-tive rank order of blameworthiness. They were then presented with the next case. Once a case had been dragged over to the vertical array, only its title was visible. However, by dragging the mouse over the title, the full description of the case would be visible in a pop-up window. If they wanted to make adjustments to their ordering, sub-jects were able to subsequently move each case by dragging it to a new position with the mouse cursor. Once subjects had ranked all twenty-

---

extremely liberal, 2%; liberal, 16%; slightly liberal, 14%; moderate, 30%; slightly conserva-tive, 15%; conservative, 20%; extremely conservative, 4%.

four cases, they were prompted to review and finalize the order they had constructed.

Subjects then assigned exact punishment amounts to the twenty-four cases they had previously rank ordered. Each case was displayed on the right side of the screen in the rank order that the subject had previously decided upon. Only the title of each case was visible to subjects without further action, but as in the first part of the procedure, subjects could reveal the full description of a case by dragging the mouse cursor over its title. On the left side of the screen was a sentence table which contained slots corresponding to different punishment amounts. The subjects' task was to drag each case to a punishment amount that they felt was appropriate given the blameworthiness of the offender. As shown in the Appendix, the sentence table contained slots corresponding to no punishment, including a "liability but no punishment" option, as well as a "no liability" option. Each punishment amount was capable of taking up to seven cases, so that several cases could be assigned the same sentence if the subjects so chose.

Subjects could assign punishments in any order they chose. However, the program was structured such that they were not able to violate their initial rank ordering in assigning punishment amounts. That is, punishment amounts had to follow a descending order from the case judged most blameworthy to the case judged least blameworthy, allowing ties for cases that were rated adjacent to one another in blameworthiness. This was done to ensure intra-subject consistency between the rankings of blameworthiness and the punishment amounts, as demanded by the deserved punishment assessment that subjects were instructed to impose.

Finally, in the third part of the study, subjects responded to ten questions on nine- and seven-point scales which assessed their general attitudes toward the American criminal justice system. These questions are not of primary relevance in interpreting the present results, so we do not discuss them further.

D. *Study 1 Results and Discussion*

Table 3 below sets out the subjects' mean ranking for each scenario. The "milestone" scenarios are in bold, and the crime-control cases are in italics. The rank order among the "milestone" scenarios matches that of the previous study from which they were taken.[102] Together they present a continuum of blameworthiness along which the modern "crime-control" scenarios, in italics, can be placed. Con-

---

[102] *See* Robinson & Kurzban, *supra* note 88.

sistent with previous research, subjects tended to agree very strongly on the rank ordering of the "milestone" cases (Kendall's $W = .86, p < .001$). There was also moderate agreement on the rank ordering of the "crime-control" cases (Kendall's $W = .52, p < .001$). Table 3 lists the scenarios in the order in which they were ranked by the subjects on average.

TABLE 3
SUBJECTS' MEAN RANKINGS OF SCENARIOS

Scenario	Legal Analysis	Mean Rank
12. Ambush shooting	**First Degree Murder**	**23.3**
11. Stabbing	**Second Degree Murder**	**22.0**
10. Accidental mauling by pit bulls	**Manslaughter**	**19.0**
L. Accidental teacher shooting	*Murder - by juvenile*	*18.8*
K. Drowning children to save them from hell	*Murder - mental illness*	*18.4*
J. Accomplice killing during burglary	*Felony murder, burglary*	*17.9*
9. Clubbing during robbery	**Aggravated Robbery**	**17.3**
8. Attempted robbery at gas station	**Attempted Robbery**	**16.0**
I. Killing officer believed to be alien	*Murder - mental illness*	*15.6*
H. Cocaine overdose	*Felony murder, unlawful distribution of controlled substance*	*14.7*
7. Stitches after soccer game	**Aggravated Assault**	**13.9**
6. Slap and bruising at record store	**Assault**	**11.8**
G. Cocaine in trunk	*Complicity in unlawful distribution of controlled substance*	*11.5*
F. Air conditioner fraud	*Petty fraud - prior record*	*10.6*
5. Microwave from house	**Burglary**	**10.1**
E. Sex with female reasonably believed overage	*Statutory rape - lack of culpability*	*9.0*
4. Clock radio from car	**Theft**	**8.7**
D. Underage sex by mentally retarded man	*Statutory rape - lack of culpability*	*7.8*
C. Marijuana unloading	*Unlawful possession of controlled substance*	*7.2*
B. Shooting of TV	*Unlawfully discharging firearm - prior record*	*6.4*
3. Whole pies from buffet	**Petty Theft**	**6.2**
A. Incorrect lobster container	*Violation of importation regulations*	*5.8*
2. Wolf hallucination	**Insanity Defense**	**5.6**
1. Umbrella mistake	**Culpability Defense**	**2.2**

Perhaps the most striking feature of Table 3 is the locations of the modern "crime-control" scenarios. Recall from Table 2's last column that most of the cases were given very high sentences: The top eight (E–L) were given sentences comparable to that of murder—life imprisonment or its equivalent. If the subjects' rankings had followed the law's treatment of these cases, they would have been ranked at the top of the list, above or between the "milestone" murder scenarios of twelve and eleven. Instead, the top three "crime-control" cases were ranked as being less serious than the "milestone" manslaughter case involving an accidental killing by dogs. The next two "crime-control" cases are ranked as being even less serious—between the "stitches after soccer game" and "attempted robbery at a gas station" scenarios. The next two "crime-control" cases (both of which the law treats as comparable to murder), are ranked by subjects between the "stealing a microwave from a house" and the "slap and bruising at the record store" scenarios. The last case treated by the law as similar to murder is ranked somewhere between "stealing a radio from a car" and "stealing a microwave from a house." The same dramatic disparity is also seen in the remaining four "crime-control" cases, for which the modern crime-control doctrines give sentences of five to fifteen years or more. The subjects, in contrast, treated the cases as almost trivial violations—more like "taking pies from an all-you-can-eat buffet," but less serious than "taking a radio from a car." It seems indisputable that the modern crime-control doctrines are treating cases in ways that dramatically conflict with laypersons' intuitions of justice.

The same serious disparity is evident when comparing the sentences that the subjects gave the scenarios to the actual sentences that courts gave the "crime-control" cases, as set out in Table 4 below.[103] As before, the scenarios are listed in the order in which they were ranked by the subjects.

---

[103] Subject responses of "death" were coded as fifty years, and subject responses of "life" were coded as forty years. Using these values, the mean sentences for Scenarios 12 and 11 were 44.5 and 38.9 years, respectively.

TABLE 4

SUBJECTS' MEAN SENTENCES FOR SCENARIOS COMPARED
TO ACTUAL SENTENCES

Scenario	Subjects' Mean Sentence	Actual Court Sentence
12. Ambush shooting	**Between life and death**	
11. Stabbing	**Essentially life**	
10. Accidental mauling by pit bulls	**20.6 years**	
L. Accidental teacher shooting (juvenile)	19.2 years	28 years without parole
K. Drowning children to save them from hell (insanity)	26.3 years	life
J. Accomplice killing during burglary (felony murder)	17.7 years	life at hard labor without parole
9. Clubbing during robbery	**12.0 years**	
8. Attempted robbery at gas station	**9.1 years**	
I. Killing officer believed to be alien (insanity)	16.5 years	life
H. Cocaine overdose (felony murder)	10.7 years	40 years
7. Stitches after soccer game	**5.0 years**	
6. Slap and bruising at record store	**3.9 years**	
G. Cocaine in trunk (drugs)	4.2 years	life without parole
F. Air conditioner fraud (3 strikes)	3.1 years	life without parole
5. Microwave from house	**2.3 years**	
E. Sex with female reasonably believed overage (strict liability)	2.9 years	40 to 60 years
4. Clock radio from car	**1.9 years**	
D. Underage sex by mentally retarded man (strict liability)	2.3 years	5 years
C. Marijuana unloading (drugs)	1.9 years	8 years
B. Shooting of TV (3 strikes)	1.1 years	15 years without parole
3. Whole pies from buffet	**8.3 months**	
A. Incorrect lobster container (regulatory)	9.7 months	15 years to life
2. Wolf hallucination	**1.1 years**	
1. Umbrella mistake	**1.8 months**	

The data is graphically presented in Figure 1 below. The solid lines show the subjects' punishment decisions—dark for the "mile-stone" cases and lighter for the "crime-control" cases. The dotted lines show the law's actual sentences.

FIGURE 1

COMPARISON OF SUBJECTS' AND LAW'S "CRIME-CONTROL"
CASE SENTENCES

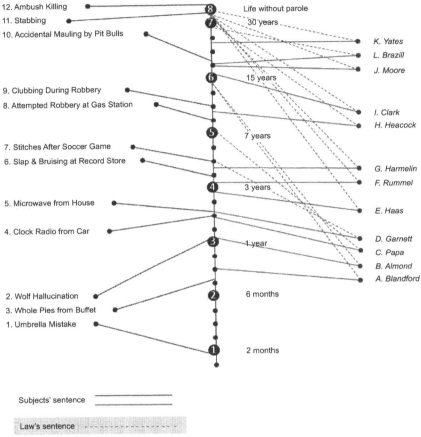

The difference in the slope of the solid versus dotted lines for the same case shows the extent of the disparity between the subjects and the law for the crime-control cases. Note that the punishment scale is exponential rather than linear (to reflect the way American criminal codes define offense grades and the way lay people think about punishment differences[104]); moving up the scale from one large dot to the next may in fact reflect a doubling or tripling of the punishment. Thus,

---

[104] For a more detailed explanation of the scale, see PAUL H. ROBINSON & JOHN DARLEY, JUSTICE, LIABILITY, AND BLAME: COMMUNITY VIEWS AND THE CRIMINAL LAW 8 (1995).

the differences in slope that the graphic shows actually represent enormous disparities.[105]

Within this sampling, the crime-control doctrines most divergent from community views include drug offense penalties, three-strikes (habitual offender) doctrines, strict liability offenses, and felony murder. The differences between community intuitions and legal treatment are sometimes astonishing: 40–60 years instead of 2.9 years (*E*, strict liability), life without parole instead of 3.1 years (*F*, three strikes), 40 years instead of 10.7 years (*H*, felony murder), and life without parole instead of 4.2 years (*G*, drug offense).[106]

These differences appear even though our TESS Internet sample of subjects seems quite punitive. Indeed, they are considerably more punitive than the criminal courts typically are when dealing with cases such as those represented by the "milestone" scenarios. The sentences that the subjects imposed in these cases (see Table 4, column 2, bold entries) are often double or triple the punishment imposed in real-world practice (compare Table 1, columns 4 and 5).[107] (The TESS results are also quite a bit more punitive than any of our pilot test's samples, which were drawn from University of Pennsylvania under-

---

[105] Subjects' sentences were less severe than the law's for each test case considered on its own, all *p*s < .001. And the subjects' sentences for the crime-control cases were, on average, twenty years less severe than the sentence actually handed down in the case, a difference that is highly significant ($t (307) = 78.81$, $p < .001$). *P*-values represent the probability of obtaining the data given that the null hypothesis of no difference between the means is true. The *p*-values yielded by this *t*-test represent the probability of obtaining the observed data given that the null hypothesis of no difference between subjects' sentences and those of the law's is true.

[106] The two insanity cases, *I* and *K*, were given two of the highest rankings and sentences among the "crime-control" cases (although not nearly as high as the courts gave). Those mean rankings and sentences are the result of a bimodal distribution (the only two cases of the twenty-four to have such), and both stood out as having the highest standard deviations (6.1 and 6.3, respectively, for rankings, and 16.7 and 19.0, respectively, for sentences) of the twenty-four cases. As earlier studies have suggested, lay intuitions are quite sympathetic to mitigations and excuses for seriously mentally ill offenders. *See infra* text accompanying note 128.

[107] This comparison between subjects' sentences and time served in state systems is appropriate because our subjects imposed the terms of imprisonment that they wanted to be served, without procedures for early release that some state systems permit. The federal system requires offenders to serve eighty-five percent of the sentence imposed. *See* Sentencing Reform Act of 1984, Pub. L. No. 98-473, 98 Stat. 1988 (codified as amended at 18 U.S.C. § 3624 (2006)) (stating that prisoner may receive credit toward sentence of up to fifty-four days at end of each year of prisoner's sentence for satisfactory behavior, resulting in fifteen percent reduction of sentence, or eighty-five percent of sentence imposed).

graduates.[108]) Despite this punitiveness of the TESS sample, the modern crime-control doctrines still produced sentences that dramatically exceeded those of the subjects.

While the sentences generated by the crime-control cases far exceed the subjects' sentences, for the milestone cases, in contrast, the law's sentences are generally less than the subjects' sentences.[109] Thus, in the subjects' view, the law in the milestone cases is doing no injustice to offenders whatsoever (indeed, if the subjects have a complaint, it is that the law is not punishing the offenders enough).

E. Previous Studies

The previous studies that touch on these matters are consistent with the results reported here.

Three Strikes and Habitual Offender Statutes. The available studies suggest that people do see subsequent offenses as being slightly more blameworthy than equivalent first-time offenses but that they do not support the dramatic increases common in American habitual offender statutes.[110] That the political position differs so

---

[108] Comparison of Punishment Assessments: TESS Sample Versus Pilot Sample (University of Pennsylvania undergraduates, N = 46):

Scenario	Offense	TESS Sample	Pilot Sample
12. Ambush shooting	First Degree Murder	44.5 years	39.4 years
11. Stabbing	Second Degree Murder	38.9 years	34 years
10. Accidental mauling by pit bulls	Manslaughter	20.6 years	15.1 years
9. Clubbing during robbery	Aggravated Robbery	12.0 years	7.8 years
8. Attempted robbery at gas station	Attempted Robbery	9.1 years	4.8 years
7. Stitches after soccer game	Aggravated Assault	5.0 years	1.7 years
6. Slap and bruising at record store	Assault	3.9 years	11.5 months
5. Microwave from house	Burglary	2.3 years	8.4 months
4. Clock radio from car	Theft	1.9 years	5.5 months
3. Whole pies from buffet	Petty Theft	8.3 months	6 days
2. Wolf hallucination	Assault - insanity defense	1.1 years	2.8 months
1. Umbrella mistake	Theft - culpability defense	1.8 months	No punishment

[109] Compare the law's sentences for the milestone cases as shown by the average state sentences on Table 1, column 4, to the subjects' sentences shown on Table 4, column 2, in bold. Only in milestone case 5 (microwave from house) does the law's average sentence exceed the subjects' average sentence (2.4 years versus 2.3 years, respectively). On average, the milestone cases did not produce nearly as much deviation from the law as did the crime-control cases (t (307) = 87.08, $p < .001$).

[110] *See, e.g.*, Brandon K. Applegate et al., *Assessing Public Support for Three-Strikes-and-You're-Out Laws: Global Versus Specific Attitudes*, 42 CRIM. DELINQ. 517, 526 tbl.3 (1996) (illustrating disparity between respondents' disfavor of leniency and support for life sentences for three-time offenders). Other studies in the area have examined the effect of

markedly from the lay intuitive view of justice is shown in a study comparing the two. Subjects given a survey in Ohio were asked whether they supported or opposed passing a "three strikes and you're out" law in their jurisdiction.[111] Of all respondents, 88.4% answered that they would support such a measure.[112] The same set of subjects was then presented with a vignette, identified as a passage from a newspaper story, in which the story's imaginary subject committed a serious felony after having committed two previous crimes in the state (the point being that under a three-strikes regime, the punishment would be life imprisonment). Respondents were asked to assign an appropriate punishment on a scale ranging from "no punishment at all" to "life in prison, with no possibility of being released."[113] Whereas true support for habitual-offender statutes would seem to predict a majority of answers in the "life in prison" range, only 16.9% of respondents gave this answer.[114] More tellingly, only 11.1% of those who chose a sentence of less than thirty years in prison (a group that includes 86.4% of *all* subjects) had answered that they opposed three-strikes legislation.[115] Respondents simply did not sentence according to their reported beliefs. Though there is widespread political support for habitual-offender statutes, lay intuitions of justice significantly contravene the reported public sentiment.

Drug Offenses. The available empirical evidence suggests that, while many people see drug offenses as serious, they typically are not viewed as being nearly as blameworthy as current sentences would suggest. In one study, subjects ranked the offense of marijuana possession as a rather minor offense, comparable to, at most, a minor theft.[116] Possession of cocaine was deemed a bit more serious but still only about as blameworthy as a slightly more serious theft.[117] A conviction for dealing cocaine was seen as being considerably more

---

multiple offenses all committed before the offender is caught and punished for any of the offenses. Generally, sentencing for multiple past offenses shows a *decrease* in added punishment amount for each additional offense, rather than an increase. *See* PAUL H. ROBINSON & JOHN M. DARLEY, JUSTICE, LIABILITY, AND BLAME: COMMUNITY VIEWS AND THE CRIMINAL LAW 189–97 (1995) [hereinafter ROBINSON & DARLEY, JUSTICE, LIABILITY, AND BLAME] (discussing theories and patterns of multiple-offense sentencing).

[111] *Id.* at 522 tbl.2.

[112] *Id.*

[113] *Id.* at 523–24.

[114] *Id.* at 525.

[115] *Id.*

[116] *Compare* Robinson & Kurzban, *supra* note 88, at 1885 tbl.6 (illustrating mean rank of 7.4 assigned to marijuana possession in Study 3), *and id.* at 1888 tbl.8 (illustrating mean rank of 2.2 assigned to marijuana possession in Study 4), *with id.* at 1869 tbl.1 (showing mean rank of 6.8 assigned to short-changing in Study 1), *and id.* at 1876 tbl.3 (showing no offense with mean rank comparable to 2.2 in Study 2).

[117] *Id.* at 1885.

blameworthy—more akin to breaking into a car or robbery.[118] Importing cocaine was seen as more serious still, similar in seriousness to burglary or assault.[119]

Other studies come to similar conclusions. The National Sample Survey of Public Opinion on Sentencing Federal Crimes asked nationwide respondents to assign a sentence to crimes, presented as vignettes.[120] Marijuana possession was assigned a mean sentence of 0.98 years; heroin possession received a mean of 2.7 years; cocaine possession received a median of 3 years, and possession of crack was assigned a median sentence of 3 years.[121] Trafficking in drugs was punished significantly more severely; trafficking marijuana, for example, garnered a mean sentence of 15.3 years.[122]

Adult Prosecution of Juveniles. The available studies suggest that people dramatically mitigate punishments for children, even for the most serious offenses. In one study, a youth was described as committing the horrific offense of pouring gasoline on a sleeping companion and setting him on fire. Although the offense generates high liability and punishment judgments when committed by an adult, it generated quite limited punishment when the offender was described as young: When the offender was described as fourteen years old, 23% of the subjects would impose no liability, and the average sentence was 5.4 years. When the offender was described as ten years old, 47% of the subjects would impose no liability, and the average liability was 11 months.[123]

Another recent study attempted to measure public sentiment regarding prosecution of juveniles by describing an offender and showing a videotape of that offender committing a robbery.[124] Subjects were then asked to rate various aspects of the subject's culpability—but different test subjects were told that the subject was a

---

[118] *Id.*

[119] *Id.* Note that the subjects in the study with the larger, more demographically diverse subject pool (Study 2) treated these four drug offenses as significantly less serious than those in the smaller, more narrow pool of Study 1. Compare the mean rankings found in Table 6 (Study 3) to those of Table 8 (Study 4), which suggests that the text here may overstate the seriousness with which the population generally sees drug offenses. *Id.* at 1885–88.

[120] U.S. SENTENCING COMM'N, NATIONAL SAMPLE SURVEY: PUBLIC OPINION ON SENTENCING FEDERAL CRIMES 25 (1997), *available at* http://www.ussc.gov/nss/jp_exsum. htm.

[121] *Id.* at 49.

[122] *Id.* at 47.

[123] ROBINSON & DARLEY, JUSTICE, LIABILITY, AND BLAME, *supra* note 110, at 141 tbl.5.5.

[124] Elizabeth S. Scott et al., *Public Attitudes About the Culpability and Punishment of Young Offenders* 7 (Columbia Law Sch. Pub. Law & Legal Theory Working Paper Grp., Paper No. 07-135, 2007), *available at* http://ssrn.com/abstract=959635.

different age (twelve, fifteen, or twenty), and the voice in the video and picture presented were altered to fit the test age.[125] The study's preliminary results have found that though age is not a factor in subjects' beliefs about the offender's potential for rehabilitation, it is a significant predictor of perceptions of responsibility for the crime and of whether the offender should be tried as an adult.[126] Subjects indicated that the twelve-year-old was significantly less responsible for the crime than the other two ages and were less likely to answer that the twelve-year-old offender should be tried in adult criminal court.[127]

Abolition of Insanity. The available evidence suggests that people do indeed hold mentally ill offenders blameless when they either do not understand the criminality of their conduct or, if they do understand it, have a substantially impaired capacity to control their conduct. In one study, the vast majority of subjects (66% to 92%, depending upon the facts of the case) imposed no liability in such cases, and even those who did impose liability significantly mitigated the punishment even for a serious offense.[128]

Strict Liability. Available research suggests that people generally do not impose liability in the absence of some level of culpability for a violation. For example, in one study, offenders who made reasonable mistakes about whether a sexual partner was underage were given no punishment by 88% of the subjects, with substantial mitigation of punishment by those few subjects who imposed any.[129]

Felony Murder. The available empirical evidence suggests that peoples' intuitions of justice do not support either the aggravation of culpability or the complicity aspect of the felony murder rule. In one study, for example, subjects aggravated culpability for an accidental killing during a felony but only to the level of manslaughter, not murder.[130] The accomplice in the felony is punished at an even lower level than manslaughter,[131] reflecting a common tendency of people to discount the liability of accomplices even though the legal doctrine typically treats the two as having identical liability.[132]

---

[125] *Id.* at 8–9.

[126] *Id.* at 13–14.

[127] *Id.*

[128] *See* ROBINSON & DARLEY, JUSTICE, LIABILITY, AND BLAME, *supra* note 110, at 132 tbl.5.2 (illustrating respondents' desires to impose civil commitment in cases involving serious offenses).

[129] *See id.* at 89 tbl.4.1 (showing respondents' negligible imposition of punishment in light of negligent mistake).

[130] *See id.* at 172–73 tbl.6.3, 179–80.

[131] *Id.* at 180 ("[W]hile the [felony murder] doctrine treats the accomplice exactly like a murderer, the subjects impose liability somewhat less than they would for manslaughter.").

[132] *Id.* at 36 tbl.2.9, 208–10 (dichotomous-continuous discussion). Norman Finkel analyzed the responses of study subjects to felony-murder hypothetical cases, among others.

III

How Can a Democratic Process Produce Liability Rules that the Community Sees as Unjust?

By this point, one central question must have struck the reader: How can freely elected and presumably accountable legislators enact criminal justice provisions that are responsive to public sentiment regarding crime but are in conflict with the community's shared intuitions of justice? The concept itself seems to be a contradiction in terms. Indeed, politicians often cite public demand as the prime motivation behind enactments of strict criminal law provisions, indicating that they at least publicly believe themselves to be fulfilling their democratic function.[133]

There is no short answer to be found, except that the seeming conflict here is real and can be at least partially explained by a number of factors that shape society, community perceptions, and the mechanisms of local and national legislation. Though no one factor is responsible on its own for the enactment of popularly supported policies that in fact conflict with empirical desert, a number of complex processes play a role in leading legislatures to criminalize actions that

---

NORMAN J. FINKEL, COMMONSENSE JUSTICE 164–71 (1995). His data are hard to interpret because he placed his subjects in the roles of juror and appellate judge, so it is difficult to tell whether their decisions enforcing felony-murder rules reflected their own intuitions of justice or reflected their carrying out of their assigned role to apply the existing law as they believed it to be. In a hypothetical case involving a robbery victim dropping dead of a heart attack, 63% were willing to find first-degree murder (even though the law requires this in only a few jurisdictions), and 60% were willing to uphold such a verdict as constitutional. *See id.* at 166. About 50% of the subjects held accomplices of the gunman guilty of first-degree murder. *Id.* at 167–68.

[133] Though politicians frequently claim that their enactments are driven by public demand, it is often the case that they are in fact the motivation behind the public opinion itself. *See infra* Part III.B (describing studies identifying government as major source of information for crime-related media coverage that shapes public perception about criminal law). However, it is incontrovertible that they at least make the claim. *See, e.g.,* KATHERINE BECKETT, MAKING CRIME PAY: LAW AND ORDER IN CONTEMPORARY AMERICAN POLITICS 12 (1997) [hereinafter BECKETT, MAKING CRIME PAY]; David Schultz, *No Joy in Mudville Tonight: The Impact of "Three Strike" Laws on State and Federal Corrections Policy, Resources, and Crime Control*, 9 CORNELL J.L. & PUB. POL'Y 557, 568 (2000) (discussing public demand for "three strikes" laws in early 1990s and subsequent enactments championed by lawmakers acting in interests of those demanding stricter laws); Stuntz, *supra* note 85, at 509 ("Voters demand harsh treatment of criminals; politicians respond with tougher sentences . . . and more criminal prohibitions."). For an expansive treatment of the numerous factors that can cause the public to support harsh crime measures (and politicians to support them as well), see generally Sara Sun Beale, *What's Law Got To Do With It? The Political, Social, Psychological and Other Non-Legal Factors Influencing the Development of (Federal) Criminal Law*, 1 BUFF. CRIM. L. REV. 23, 28–29, 31–32 (1997) [hereinafter Beale, *What's Law Got to Do With It?*].

the citizens do not feel are criminal, or to assign excessively lengthy sentences to crimes.[134]

A good deal of scholarship on the topic suggests that voter views are a major force behind increases in criminal sentence lengths.[135] Social scientists reviewing public opinion studies on criminal justice matters comment that "[t]he influence of the public on policy in the area of sentencing and parole should not be under-estimated. Many sentencing commissions and judges are to some degree affected by public pressure to make sentences harsher."[136] Sentencing commission recommendations often must be enacted or approved by legislatures, and legislators voting on these enactment bills are aware of voter opinions.

Interestingly, however, another line of thinking regarding popular concern for crime issues argues that, while there may be some latent crime-control concerns present in the public consciousness, it would be erroneous to conclude that public pressures often lead to harsher criminal law enactments. Rather, it may be such that the reverse is true: Expressed concern over and attention paid to crime issues by politicians seems to spur public interest in the issue, thereby making it seem as if voter demand has caused certain legislative enactments when, in fact, the public may have been merely "riding the wave" of concern actuated by a politician's previous comments.[137]

Notwithstanding *how* they arrive at their desires, it seems clear at first glance that voters *do*, in fact, desire higher sentences. Polling studies frequently ask citizens some variation on the question of whether they think sentences for crimes are too lenient, too harsh, or about right. Consistently, those polled think that current sentences are

---

[134] *See generally* Beale, *What's Law Got To Do With It?*, *supra* note 133 (explaining how increase in crime rates during U.S. civil rights era led political campaigns to focus on crime control by following public perception of crime skewed by media coverage and cognitive errors such as overgeneralization of trends, overconfidence in opinions formed from minimal information, and availability of uniquely horrific cases to stand out as general examples of crimes); Doron Teichman, *The Market for Criminal Justice*, 103 MICH. L. REV. 1831, 1847 (2005) (arguing that increased sentence lengths may be effort to displace criminal activity by offering relatively harsher punishments compared with nearby jurisdictions).

[135] *See, e.g.*, Rachel E. Barkow, *The Political Market for Criminal Justice*, 104 MICH. L. REV. 1713, 1718 (2006) (arguing that legislators increase criminal sentencing lengths to appear responsive to demands of voters and interest groups); Schultz, *supra* note 133, at 558 (stating that intense public support for "three strike" laws led to their passage in twenty-two states and federally over two-year period).

[136] JULIAN V. ROBERTS & LORETTA J. STALANS, PUBLIC OPINION, CRIME, AND CRIMINAL JUSTICE 197 (2000).

[137] *See* BECKETT, MAKING CRIME PAY, *supra* note 133, at 78 (arguing that media reproduction of official views on crime generates increased public support for punishment-focused crime policies).

too lenient and wish them to be harsher.[138] Furthermore, citizens report that a politician's position on sentencing affects their vote: About eighty percent of voters surveyed report that if a candidate advocates tougher sentencing policies, they are more likely to vote for that candidate.[139]

The results of these polls are widely reported; thus it would be easy to conclude that politicians feel that they are doing the will of the people when they vote for longer sentences for various crimes. It is also the case that by doing so, they are avoiding being charged by election-year opponents as "being soft on crime." Still, this is not a complete picture of the factors that shape public opinion regarding criminal law, all of which combine to cause enactments that seem to have popular support but for a number of reasons do not reflect the actual preferences of the community. We will discuss a selection of these factors in order to shed light on this conflict.

A.   *Media Omission of Facts Vital to Understanding Sentences*

Current research suggests that there is a complex story behind "what voters want." It is often the case that voters are only informed about the duration of sentences assigned in specific cases through media reports, whether in print, on television, or via the Internet. In one study, researchers asked Canadian and U.S. citizens to read sentencing stories printed in newspapers, and then asked the study subjects to judge the sentence given in each case.[140] Large majorities of readers reported that the sentences assigned in the cases were too lenient and were quite confident in their ratings.[141] The researchers noted that most of the crime stories in newspapers were relatively brief; the stories commonly reported the sentence given but generally omitted or glossed over the reasoning underlying the assigned sentences.[142] The study found that "the modal reaction to these stories was to regard the criminal sentences reported in them as too lenient,"[143] finding such a result in thirteen of the sixteen stories. Furthermore, in spite of the fact that in the stories "[l]ittle information

---

[138] Francis T. Cullen et al., *Public Opinion About Punishment and Corrections*, 27 CRIME & JUST. 1, 26–27 (2000).

[139] Michael J. Hindelang, *Public Opinion Regarding Crime, Criminal Justice, and Related Topics*, 11 J. RES. CRIM. & DELINQ. 101, 107–08 & tbl.4 (1974).

[140] Julian V. Roberts & Anthony N. Doob, *News Media Influences on Public Views of Sentencing*, 14 L. & HUM. BEHAV. 451, 454–56 (1990).

[141] *Id.* at 456–57.

[142] *Id.* at 464.

[143] *Id.* at 456. Generally speaking, "the sentences reported by the newspapers . . . confirmed the a priori view held by most respondents that sentences are generally too lenient." *Id.*

was conveyed on which to base a reasoned evaluation of the appropriateness of the sentence," the respondents reported a high degree of confidence in their view that the sentences were too lenient.[144]

These findings are consistent with other studies. It appears likely that media accounts of crimes are the source that voters generally use to form their judgments on courtroom sentencing. By reading the newspaper or watching television news accounts—which cover a disproportionately high number of violent, as opposed to routine, crimes, and which generally do not highlight extenuating circumstances or the judge's reasoning—readers and viewers quickly come to the conclusion that the sentences assigned are too lenient. Reading further news reports strengthens this conclusion. In fact, over ninety percent of respondents in one study reported that media reports were their most important source of information regarding the crime problem in America today.[145]

This should make it clear that the media holds the central role in shaping the public's perception that sentencing is too lenient. Realizing this, Julian V. Roberts and Anthony N. Doob examined how the public would perceive sentences if they had a different source of accounts of the cases.[146] These researchers derived an account of the newspaper case from the official courtroom records, creating a summary from actual quotes from the proceedings or paraphrasing actual documents. Importantly, the summary included much information that is generally not found in news reports—the offender's previous convictions, a brief description of the offense, the defense's and prosecution's arguments regarding sentencing for the offender, a summary of the presentence reports, and the final comments offered by the judge.[147]

The study proceeded by separating the subjects into two groups: One received a copy of the "court documents" account including all relevant information, and a second matched sample of the subjects received a newspaper account of the same crime. The two groups' reactions to the material were vastly different. Whereas 63% of the newspaper group thought that the sentence was too lenient,[148] only 19% of the "court documents" group thought the sentence too

---

[144] *Id.* at 457. "[I]n 58% of the ratings, subjects indicated that they were 'very confident' of their evaluations. In an additional 35%, subjects indicated they were 'somewhat' confident. In only 7% were subjects 'not at all confident.'" *Id.*

[145] RAY SURETTE, MEDIA, CRIME, AND CRIMINAL JUSTICE: IMAGES AND REALITIES 197 (2d ed. 1998).

[146] Roberts & Doob, *supra* note 140, at 461.

[147] *Id.*

[148] *Id.* at 462.

lenient—while 52% thought it too harsh.[149] Perhaps unsurprisingly, those who read the "court documents" account evaluated the offense as less serious and the offender as a better person than did subjects who had read the newspaper story.[150]

Shari S. Diamond reports conceptually similar results.[151] Studying members of the public called for jury duty, she asked them to assign sentences to hypothetical defendants whose crimes were presented in some detail—again, unlike presentations given by the news media alone.[152] She found that the sentences given by these better-informed subjects were very similar to the sentences recommended by practicing judges who responded to the same material.[153] The takeaway point from these studies is that at least part of the reason why the public at large reports a desire for stricter criminal law is because they are, in fact, underinformed about the actual nature of most crimes and offenders. The nature of news reporting is in some ways antithetical to disclosure of the whole fact pattern that leads to any particular criminal sentence. After all, what is newsworthy is the sentencing itself, not the actual cause therefor. With limited space in which to print or report (coupled with a not-insignificant desire to simplify the news for cross-demographic comprehension), news outlets end up leaving gaps in the "whole story" behind any particular sentencing decision. These gaps often cause people to assume that the sentence imposed was simply too light, which, if it happens in enough cases, can entice society at large to believe that a harsher set of sentencing guidelines (or any other proposed legislation *du jour*) is necessary in order to rectify the "problem" in criminal law.

B. Media Coverage of General Crime Issues with the Government as an Information Source

As mentioned previously, the news media are the primary sources of information that people rely on when judging the operation of the criminal law. This would not be problematic if the news media were able to provide a truly neutral and inclusive picture of the criminal law. Unfortunately, this is not the case. As shown in the previous subsection, the news media commonly skew perceptions of sentences in individual criminal cases by not providing all of the relevant information. Perhaps more significant, however, is the news media's cov-

---

[149] *Id.* at 462–63.

[150] *Id.* at 463.

[151] *See* Shari S. Diamond, *Using Psychology To Control Law: From Deceptive Advertising to Criminal Sentencing*, 13 L. & HUM. BEHAV. 239, 247–48 (1989).

[152] *Id.*

[153] *Id.*

erage of general criminal issues, illustrated by specials highlighting the "war on drugs" or by breaking news reports delivered whenever a study reports an uptick in the crime rate. This coverage (and the innumerable examples of similar reports on other issues) is not by itself problematic; it is the function of the news to report on what is important and relevant to society. Rather, the larger issue in terms of the media's role in shaping public perceptions of the criminal law is traceable to the sources delivering the news to the media in the first place. Though we often assume that the democratic process follows a pattern beginning with news reports, which then shape public opinion, which itself then shapes governmental action, studies have shown that this is often not the case.

In fact, governmental actions are often the prime motivation behind change in public opinion, spurred by popular news reports. The ability of governmental sources "to supply frequent and conveniently formatted 'news' meant that the use of state sources also satisfied the organizational needs of news workers," concludes Katherine Beckett.[154] Her study of news "packages" promoted to news agencies by official sources found that, during four time periods in which all crime-related stories printed in the *New York Times*, the *Los Angeles Times*, and the *Washington Post* were analyzed for content, sixty-five percent of all "packages" (that is, defined issues presented in certain ways) reflected state sponsorship—reliance on a governmental agent as the source of the news contained therein.[155] An additional study analyzing the sources behind drug-related television news reports in the 1980s came to an even more striking conclusion: Seventy-six percent of all news stories containing identified "packages" of information about drugs and related criminality were attributable to state sources.[156]

These studies, however, only tell half of the story. That the state is a source of news is not shocking; it is perhaps not even surprising that more than half of all crime-related news coverage is in some way attributable to the government. Such involvement in newsmaking is only relevant to a discussion of popular opinions regarding criminal sentencing and policy if it can be shown that the news does not, in fact, reflect preexisting concerns held by society as a whole. It is assumed that legislators are responsive to the desires of society; the reasons why this is so in a democracy are outside the scope of this discussion. We cannot assume, however, that those societal desires are organic.

---

[154] BECKETT, MAKING CRIME PAY, *supra* note 133, at 65.

[155] *Id.* at 75.

[156] *Id.* at 76.

We know that people on the whole are influenced by, and shape their opinions according to, what is presented by the media. However, if the picture painted by the media is itself a creation of the very legislators who work to enact stricter criminal law, then they themselves are the force behind those laws, not the demanding public. In other words, we can conclude that governmental influence on the media contributes to the enactment of legislation that deviates from community notions of desert if we can show that public interest in the crime-related problems reported by the media lags behind the news reports—thus showing that the government-provided information has a hand in causing said interest—rather than preceding them.

In many instances, this is in fact the case. While we cannot conclude that a media report can cause any particular change in the opinions of the public, "it is undoubtedly a crucial component of the context in which political opinions are formed. It is quite likely that the media's reproduction of the official view of crime and drugs played an important role in generating support for crime and drug policies" that were advocated by politicians in power at the time of the study.[157] Between 1964 and 1974 (the first timeframe analyzed in the Beckett study), political initiatives and media coverage were strongly correlated with public concern about crime—and the concern only arose *after* the political moves were initiated.[158] In contrast, the actual crime rate was not correlated with public concern.[159] In the second analyzed time frame (1985–1992), the study found that political initiatives regarding drug laws were strongly correlated with public concern over the drug problem—but that the actual rate of drug use was not.[160]

We must be careful not to make too much of these studies, however. Politicians and the media are not the only factors influencing public opinion, and it certainly is not the case that politicians always lead the public by the nose—public opinion and the actions of politicians are more likely mutually reinforcing,[161] and the demands of elections will generally make political actors at least try to do what the public demands. Still, the evidence is striking: In June 1993, only 7% of respondents in a national poll identified crime as the nation's most important problem; by August 1994, this percentage had increased to 52%.[162] Amazingly, this increase contradicted the crime trends at the

---

[157] *Id.* at 78.
[158] *Id.* at 21.
[159] *Id.*
[160] *Id.* at 22.
[161] *Id.* at 23.
[162] *Id.* at 25.

time; victimization studies indicated that most types of crime decreased in prevalence over that time frame. However, then-President Clinton's January 1994 State of the Union address spent significant time addressing the crime problem in the country,[163] and—most importantly—one of the country's most significant crime-control bills, the Violent Crime Control and Law Enforcement Act of 1994,[164] was debated in Congress and passed that year. There is no doubt that these political events contributed significantly to the rise in public concern over crime policy that occurred between 1993 and 1994.

In sum, it is clear that the media are prime motivators of public opinion. While it is often assumed that the media reports objective fact and unbiased information, this may not always be the case. It is problematic, then, to assume that politicians are strictly responsive to the will of the people. Though public opinion may seem to demand stricter crime-control laws, it may simply be that it has been shaped by the very politicians claiming merely to follow public opinion. The previous sections noted that public opinion regarding individual instances of sentencing would be significantly different if the public were able to consider the entire set of facts behind the decision. It is not too far a leap to conclude that public demands regarding stricter criminal laws would be different if the public were given similarly inclusive and unbiased accounts of the more general criminal statutes and proposals in force at any given time. Finally, while politicians claim to be responsive to public demands by enacting harsher criminal penalties, this may be less than true. Evidence exists to show that public interest in crime policy follows rather than causes legislative activity. To unequivocally state that harsher criminal enactments are simply a response to public demand, therefore, is to mischaracterize the situation.

C. *Assuming Headline Crimes To Be Paradigmatic*

As mentioned previously, the media are the chief sources upon which the public bases its opinions regarding criminal law. Another related reason why citizens tend to think that criminal sentences are too lenient involves the ways citizens imagine the crime when they answer the opinion poll asking "whether penalties for crimes are too

---

[163] President William J. Clinton, *Address Before a Joint Session of the Congress on the State of the Union* 126, 127, 133–35 (Jan. 25, 1994), *available at* http://frwebgate.access.gpo.gov/cgi-bin/getdoc.cgi?dbname=1994_public_papers_vol1_text&docid=pap_text-64.pdf.

[164] Violent Crime Control and Law Enforcement Act of 1994, Pub. L. No. 103-322, 108 Stat. 1796; *see also* Cornell W. Clayton & J. Mitchell Pickerill, *The Politics of Criminal Justice: How the New Right Regime Shaped the Rehnquist Court's Criminal Justice Jurisprudence*, 94 Geo. L.J. 1385, 1407–08 (2006) (describing Act as "the largest single crime bill in history").

lenient, too severe, or about right." Recall that the majority of citizens choose the "too lenient" answer to this question. Evidence suggests that when asked this question, people bring to mind violent crimes, and this is disproportionately done by those who give the "too lenient" answer.[165] One cause for this distortion is the reality that only the most heinous or most significant crimes receive significant news coverage.

When a citizen thinks about the appropriate sentence for a crime, he calls to mind a prototype or exemplar of the crime. The citizen does not do what the legislative system must do, which is to consider the necessary and sufficient conditions for having committed that crime. That is, the law must specify what counts as, for instance, murder or rape. If the citizen is judging whether "life" is an appropriate prison sentence for "murder," she will imagine her prototype of a violent murder and report that, indeed, life is the appropriate sentence. Yet that does not mean that she thinks that life in prison is the just sentence for a person who brings to an end the life of her terminally ill husband who is in terrible pain, for example. In fact, the citizen would be shocked at the severity of the sentence in that instance, despite it being an example of "murder."

There is a systematic distortion here, because the prototype of the crime that the citizen brings to mind is the clear, unqualified case of deliberate murder, and not the cases of murder that would require qualifying descriptions about how they occurred. In other words, when thinking of murder cases, the citizen does not consider mercy killings or killings done under provocation. Such distortions of the content of specific offenses occur for other crimes besides murder, as well. The dynamic is exacerbated by the fact that news coverage presents a somewhat misleading perspective of the frequency with which such dramatic crimes occur. In one analysis, 25% of media crime stories were about murder, yet murder is involved in less than 1% of crimes.[166]

Additionally, this "over-broadening of the category" can occur when a certain sort of law is passed. The most salient example is found in the expansion of sex-offender laws. When a terrible incident occurs, such as a child being kidnapped, sexually molested, and perhaps eventually killed, legislators may feel that public opinion demands a hardening of the criminal penalties that can be mobilized if similar incidents occur in the future. Further, some continuation of confinement for "mentally-ill offenders" is often mandated after sexual

---

[165] Roberts & Doob, *supra* note 140, at 464–65.
[166] *Id.* at 452.

offenders have completed their prison terms[167]—and once committed, offenders are almost never released.[168] Finally, laws may be enacted to prohibit the freed offender from living within various distances of spots where children may congregate.[169]

The prototype of the sexual offense—the kidnapping and rape of a child—that comes to mind when people think of the sexual offender may justly warrant the sentence just described. However, the sexual offender laws, as they are currently written, often criminalize a number of actions that are morally quite distant from the prototype. For example, in New Jersey, a teenage person who has sexual intercourse with another teenage person who is just under the legal age of consent has committed a sexual offense.[170] In this instance the offense is "criminal sexual contact," because the victim is a minor. Despite the striking dissimilarity between this crime and the paradigmatic sex offense, both will be referred to as such under the law.

However, news media reporting of the legislature's movement toward passing sexual offender laws, not surprisingly, continues to invoke the actual case that triggered the legislature into action. The reports pay much less attention to other, less offensive cases that would also fall under the scope of the law. Therefore, the public does not focus on whether the scope of the proposed laws will be overly broad and inflict too-severe sentences on persons who commit less

---

[167] Jenny Roberts, *The Mythical Divide Between Collateral and Direct Consequences of Criminal Convictions: Involuntary Commitment of "Sexually Violent Predators,"* 93 MINN. L. REV. 670, 703 (2008) ("In 1990, Washington became the first state to pass a modern law allowing for involuntary commitment of 'sexually violent predators.' Other states quickly followed suit, and there are currently twenty states with some version of an SVPA [Sexually Violent Predators Act]."). For an example of statutes authorizing civil confinement post-sentence-completion, see Adam Walsh Child Protection and Safety Act, 18 U.S.C. § 4248 (2006); Sexually Violent Persons Commitment Act, 725 ILL. COMP. STAT. ANN. 207 (West 2008) (invalidated by United States v. Comstock, 551 F.3d 274 (4th Cir. 2009), but upheld as constitutional by United States v. Tom, 565 F.3d 497 (8th Cir. 2009)); KAN. STAT. ANN. § 59-29 (West Supp. 2009) (amended 2010).

[168] Eric S. Janus, *Sexual Predator Commitment Laws: Lessons for Law and the Behavioral Sciences*, 18 BEHAV. SCI. & L. 5, 10 (2000).

[169] Consider this description of the relevant Georgia state law:

The law, described when it was adopted in 2006 as the nation's toughest restriction on sex offenders, prohibited them from living within 1,000 feet of schools, churches or any other place that children might congregate, including more than 150,000 school bus stops in the state. The ban applied even when a school, a church or the like opened in an area where an offender was already living.

Brenda Goodman, *Georgia Justices Overturn a Curb on Sex Offenders*, N.Y. TIMES, Nov. 22, 2007, at A26 (referencing GA. CODE ANN. § 42-1-15 (West Supp. 2009), which was held unconstitutional in Mann v. Georgia Department of Corrections, 653 S.E.2d 740, 745 (2007), to extent that it permits taking of property without just compensation).

[170] N.J. STAT. ANN. § 2C:14-3 (West 2005).

morally repugnant crimes. The unjust consequences of these new laws are downplayed and thereby hidden from public view.

What emerges is an account of sentencing policies that is much more complicated than it seems at first glance. The standard account holds that the legislatures are doing "the will of the people" when they pass "harsh measures" against crimes. The real mechanisms involved are much more nuanced. Social and political scientists suggest that when citizens are asked relatively simple questions about crimes, they respond in terms of their momentary interpretations of the question. To answer, they think of the crimes that they have seen in the media, which are usually violent crimes presented in dramatic and one-sided terms. They use their answers about sentence duration to make the point that crime is bad and deserves sanction. However, when the question set gives the citizens the opportunity to give a more tempered and nuanced view of what to do about crimes, they take that chance.[171] A more nuanced presentation of the crime at hand inevitably leads to a more nuanced liability judgment by the person asked.

To summarize, a third dynamic arises from citizens' tendencies to think about crimes using the prototypes of crimes that are quickly and automatically recalled when a crime category is discussed. Here, the prototype is generally a "perfect" version of the category—a murder, for example, is a highly deliberate killing of an innocent victim, and not the more complex mix of intention, provocation, and human error that is the case with many nonparadigmatic murders. By conceptualizing the question about penalty severity as an inquiry into the appropriate severity of penalties that should be assigned to the prototype versions of a crime, citizens tend to signal a desire for more severe penalties in general. This masks the fact that a citizen is really only expressing a desire for relatively severe penalties being assigned to the "perfect" (and thus most severe) instances of these crimes. Yet, the resulting sentencing statutes allow for those harsher sentences to be assigned for much lesser forms of the offense, and the public remains unaware.

D. Public Fear

People's opinions about the sentences required for proper criminal punishment fluctuate as a function of their current perceptions of the threat of crimes and, more generally, their state of fear. If, as the news media can make happen, people feel that the threat of crime is

---

[171] Dena M. Gromet & John M. Darley, *Restoration and Retribution: How Including Retributive Components Affects the Acceptability of Restorative Justice Procedures*, 19 Soc. Just. Res. 395, 421 (2006).

high, they will report that criminals need to be locked away to reduce that threat. Long sentences are a way to reduce the threat of crime. People express a desire for crime to be controlled when they answer that sentences are too lenient, and, at the moment they answer, they perceive increasing the duration of sentences as one way of achieving that end.[172]

The point here is that people take different perspectives in answering the questions that they are asked in surveys depending on their perceptions of crime rates, whether or not their perceptions are actually correct. Perhaps more importantly, people tend to generalize their feelings toward crime overall when answering questions about specific crimes. If they are asked these questions when they are primarily concerned with conveying the message that they want more attention paid to crime prevention, then they will answer *all* questions about actions that they perceive as having a crime prevention component favorably. Thus, they may report that they support "harsher prison sentences" but would think, if they were to stop and reflect, that some of the specific examples of harsh sentences are actually unduly harsh and thus unjust. However, this is not the question they perceive themselves as answering. Instead, they see themselves as expressing approval of policies that incapacitate criminals by incarcerating them or policies that seek to deter criminal conduct among the general population.

Further, studies have demonstrated that people report support for deterrence and incapacitation as crime control practices.[173] Here, we are making an importantly different argument than in other sections. In the previous sections, we generally suggested that the public was in some sense being misled, often by mass media reports, into supporting sentences that would be unjust. Now, we suggest that the public sometimes construes questions concerning sentencing practices as questions about their favorability toward achieving crime control overall, without factoring in their own judgments about appropriate sentence durations or their sense of the injustice of draconian sentences. Put simply, if any person has a general desire for more "crime control," he will tend to consistently answer that crimes should

---

[172] *See* Roger G. Noll & James E. Krier, *Some Implications of Cognitive Psychology for Risk Regulation*, 19 J. Legal Stud. 747, 771–79 (1990) (arguing that politicians will endorse policies because of public preference formed from miscalculations of risk); Rachel E. Barkow, *Federalism and the Politics of Sentencing*, 105 Colum. L. Rev. 1276, 1292 (2005) ("[T]he public's fears of crimes will be fueled by the media, and they will perhaps place greater stock in incarceration policies that promise to deal with their fears in the most immediate fashion.").

[173] Kevin M. Carlsmith, *On Justifying Punishment: The Discrepancy Between Words and Actions*, 21 Soc. Just. Res. 119, 133 (2008).

have stricter punishments, without stopping to consider that perhaps some current punishments are already strict enough—or too strict.

Another related effect of high levels of public fear or concern is the passage of "designer laws" designed to address very specific events that have been widely reported or that enter the popular consciousness. Imagine, for example, a brutal attack on a mother and child, committed by polo-clad youths pretending to practice their golf swings in a public park. Media coverage is unrelenting, saturating the airwaves with updates on the case and with other reports of intimidation by nine-iron. Though the vast majority of teenagers merely want to work on their short game, concerned citizens demand legal action to counter the heavily publicized threat. Out of concern for the sensibilities of the public (and wanting to look "tough on crime"), legislators "view these incidents with alarm" and criminalize possession of a golf club or other "weaponized sporting equipment" inside of certain "safety zones," such as within a half-mile of any school or public park. The penalty for possession, of course, is severe—in fact, many demand that all instances of "criminal possession of a golf club" be punished as severely as was the assault that triggered the public's outrage in the first place. Sadly, this scenario is less farfetched than it seems. Legislatures have passed numerous harsh criminal statutes as direct responses to fear based on coverage of a crime that captures the public consciousness[174]—often disregarding prior legislative enactments that already criminalize the covered activity. The consequences of such new, fear- or panic-driven legislation are often disastrous.[175]

---

[174] For instance, Garland notes:

> Many of the laws passed in the 1990s—Megan's law, Three Strikes, sexual predator statutes, the reintroduction of children's prisons, paedophile registers, and mandatory sentences . . . are designed to be expressive, cathartic actions, undertaken to denounce the crime and reassure the public. . . . Typically these measures are passed amidst great public outrage in the wake of sensational crimes of violence, often involving a disturbingly archetypal confrontation between a poorly controlled dangerous criminal and an innocent, defenceless middle-class victim.

GARLAND, *supra* note 12, at 133.

[175] Many of these sorts of ad hoc additions to criminal laws, generated in haste in response to a perceived public demand, criminalize actions that are already criminalized in the general sections of the criminal code and do so in ways that are inconsistent with the penalties set for the acts in the general codes, thereby generating considerable legal complexities. *See* Paul H. Robinson & Michael T. Cahill, *The Accelerating Degradation of American Criminal Codes*, 56 HASTINGS L.J. 633, 637–38 (2005) (describing how pressure from interest groups leads to criminalization of offenses already covered by general provisions and arguing that redundant offenses make code interpretation confusing for public and law enforcement alike); *see also* GARLAND, *supra* note 12, at 103–38 (describing recent change in correctional policy and factors behind these new penalogical aims).

E. Next-Election Vulnerability

During the 1970s and 1980s, a powerful, specific version of the law and economics perspective emerged and quickly gained adherents. It is called the "public choice perspective," and it helps illuminate why legislators in general will sometimes vote for measures that they know are bad ones from a public policy standpoint and, specifically, will vote for draconian sentencing legislation.[176] The basic assumption of the public choice perspective, applied to legislators, is that legislators, like any political actor, will rationally maximize their own self-interest.[177] In other words, when we elect a legislator, we have not created a saint who will consistently work for the public good; we have instead positioned a personally ambitious person into a seat in the legislature from which he or she will keep a keen eye on his or her own personal interests.[178]

As indicated by public choice theorists, one such interest is in getting re-elected. The legislator faces the need to raise money for increasingly expensive re-election campaigns and to take legislative stands that will attract voter support in later elections. The fact that campaigns are expensive can be useful for the incumbent legislator, since it provides a high barrier to entry for candidates running against the incumbent. Therefore, one task of the incumbent is to cast votes that do the bidding of various interest groups. The interest groups' task is to "pay off" the legislator for a favorable vote. The payoffs can be campaign contributions, votes that the interest group can mobilize for the candidate, or implicit promises of future campaign contributions[179] (and sometimes—a current favorite—a promise of a lobbying position in the interest group organization or in lobbying firms the interest group controls after the politician leaves office).[180]

---

[176] To get a sense of the public choice position, see BRIAN Z. TAMANAHA, LAW AS A MEANS TO AN END: THREAT TO THE RULE OF LAW 193–95 (2006). As Tamanaha remarks: "The primary objective of politicians is to ensure their own reelection." *Id.* at 193.

[177] *Id.*

[178] *Id.* at 194.

[179] *Id.* at 193–94 ("A great deal of legislation . . . involves legally imposed and sanctioned transfers of wealth secured by well-financed and organized interest groups at the expense of hapless groups or the unorganized in society. Legislators are paid by beneficiaries of the legislation they produce . . . .").

[180] The eventual ability to transition from a legislative position to a more secure and better-paid position as a functionary in the network of organizations whose interests the legislator has served is important here. It provides security well past that experienced by legislators who have to be re-elected at intervals, and it also provides a monetary return that compensates the former legislator for a number of years receiving a merely adequate public salary. The classic example involves the legislator voting for ultra-expensive defense projects that would benefit the different defense contractors with plants in his legislative district.

Commonly, a legislator's primary goal is to remain in office. Even when considering a post-legislature career, the legislator will be more valuable to an interest group if he has served several terms in the legislature. So, not surprisingly, the successful legislator is alert to occasions or actions that might derail his ability to accumulate campaign funds or attract votes in coming elections. Votes on criminal codes and sentence durations have the possibility of causing such derailment.

We have already mentioned one way of stating the problem: allowing an opponent to cast one's voting record as "soft on crime." The dynamic that links citizens' apparent support of harsh sentencing, detailed above, to legislative increases in prison sentences is the legislators' concern in being perceived as "soft on crime" and thus vulnerable to attack by opponents during election cycles.[181] Negative campaigning involving distortions of the meaning of incumbents' voting patterns is a well-known political phenomenon, and it would make sense for a politician to go to considerable lengths to avoid leaving any voting record that could make him or her vulnerable to such charges—after all, no politician wants to be seen as supporting the "crime lobby."[182] How often these negative attacks happen in practice is not clear, but the knowledge of their possibility may be enough for many politicians to be leery of associating with crime legislation that does anything else but treat crime harshly.[183] This fear of being seen as "soft on crime" is a self-perpetuating cycle—if no party is willing to risk such a label, sentencing standards will only spiral

---

[181] Hindelang, *supra* note 139, at 108.

[182] *See, e.g.*, Douglas Husak, Overcriminalization: The Limits of the Criminal Law 16 (2008) (describing political parties' competition to appear hard on crime). The commonly cited example of this kind of campaign is the "Willie Horton" ads that associated Governor Dukakis (who, at the time, was running for President against eventual winner George H.W. Bush) with the prison furloughing of a criminal who committed a murder while on release. *See generally* Steve Takesian, Willie Horton: True Crime and Its Influence on a Presidential Election (2002).

[183] This fear of looking "soft on crime" has implications even outside of crime policy proper; that is, politicians may *want* to vote against crime bills because they are bad policy, or because of some other concern, such as constitutionality—but the fear of attack is too salient to allow such a vote.

> [A] federal officeholder who votes against a federal car-jacking law will likely be characterized by the officeholder's opponent as soft on crime. Although the officeholder might respond to the attack ad with a discussion of how the vote was motivated by federalism concerns, the officeholder may rightly be concerned that the defense may be too nuanced to be effective in a thirty-second sound bite. The officeholder may legitimately want to avoid the risk of having to expend scarce campaign funds in responding to such an ad altogether.

See, e.g., William Marshall, *American Political Culture and the Failures of Process Federalism*, 22 Harv. J.L. & Pub. Pol'y 139, 152 (1998).

upward, whether or not that outcome is in accord with community views.[184]

A second force is also operating. Politicians planning to seek re-election are often wary of crossing "single issue voters." In general, the current perception of the average voter is as one who does not closely attend to the politician's pattern of voting on the multitudes of individual bills that they consider. Some voters are "single issue" voters—whether or not they vote for any particular candidate depends wholly on that candidate's stance on one issue alone. For instance, voters who think that abortion is murder will tend to vote against any candidate who fails to support the various proposals for laws that limit, restrict, or otherwise move toward making abortions impossible. In this instance, the situation for the legislator may be symmetric in that there also may be voters who will vote against any candidate who supports bills restricting abortions.

F. Summary

The reader should by now realize that public opinion is subject to the influence of many factors, none of which can be definitively identified as primary but all of which have some effect. Unfortunately, as a result, the true feelings of the population are not always reflected in legislative activity or even in public opinion polls. The influence of the media in shaping public opinion often causes people to profess opinions that they would not hold if given all of the information in any particular case. People's generalization of crime opinions, and their construction of crime archetypes upon which they base their sentencing judgments, often simplify their thinking to the point that, because only the worst crimes are reported and come to mind, they, when polled, often want to impose only the worst punishments. As such, any particular legislator can look to this flawed public opinion and conclude that the majority support harsher crime laws, when in fact they do not.

Another reason for the passage of legislation that can conflict with desert is the nature of the democratic process on the whole. The media's crime reporting is often based on information provided by the government—and, as discussed, public concern about crime often *follows* legislative consideration of crime issues, rather than being the cause of said action. Additionally, the legislators' self-preservation

---

[184] For a general discussion of the upward spiral that characterizes American criminal law enactments, see Stuntz, *supra* note 85, at 509. *See also* Erik Luna, *The Overcriminalization Phenomenon*, 54 AM. U. L. REV. 703 (2005) (discussing trend of increased criminalization as abuse of criminal justice system).

interest dictates that they not put themselves in a position that could be vulnerable to attack by a rival—a situation that can be brought about by advocating sentencing reduction or opposing harsher penalties, even if such reforms would be in accord with empirical desert.

The takeaway point here is this: Although we cannot pinpoint one single reason why the democratic legislative process produces crime laws that conflict with the intuitions of justice of the community, we can point to a number of factors that work together to cause such results. These outcomes do happen. Laws passed are often not in accord with the community's sense of justice, as Study 1 reported in Part II makes clear. Knowing some of the reasons why this happens, however, may help us to avoid such deviant enactments in the future. Doing so would harness more of the benefits of keeping the law in accord with shared community perceptions of justice and would reduce the harmful consequences of deviations from desert.

IV

TESTING THE CRIMINOGENIC EFFECTS OF INJUSTICE:
STUDIES 2A AND 2B

As we have argued elsewhere, there are good arguments to suggest that there is significant utility in distributing liability and punishment according to people's shared intuitions of justice—perhaps greater than the utility of distributing liability and punishment in the traditional utilitarian manner (to optimize deterrence, rehabilitation, or incapacitation).[185] We will briefly summarize these "utility of desert" arguments.

First, some of the system's power to control conduct derives from its potential to stigmatize violators. With some potential offenders this is a more powerful, yet essentially cost-free, control mechanism when compared to imprisonment. Yet the system's ability to stigmatize depends upon its moral credibility with the community. That is, for a conviction to trigger community stigmatization, the law must have earned a reputation for following the community's view on what does and does not deserve moral condemnation. Liability and punishment rules that deviate from a community's shared intuitions of justice undercut this reputation.

Second, the effective operation of the criminal justice system depends upon the cooperation, or at least the acquiescence, of those involved in it—offenders, judges, jurors, witnesses, prosecutors,

---

[185] For a fuller account of the argument, see ROBINSON, DISTRIBUTIVE PRINCIPLES, *supra* note 5, at 175–210, Robinson & Darley, *Intuitions of Justice*, *supra* note 1, and Robinson & Darley, *Utility of Desert*, *supra* note 100.

1996 *NEW YORK UNIVERSITY LAW REVIEW* [Vol. 85:1940

police, and others. To the extent that people see the system as unjust—as in conflict with their intuitions about justice—acquiescence and cooperation are likely to fade and be replaced with subversion and resistance. Vigilantism may be the most dramatic reaction to a perceived failure of justice, but a host of other less dramatic (but more common) forms of resistance and subversion have shown themselves. Jurors may disregard their jury instructions. Police officers, prosecutors, and judges may make up their own rules. Witnesses may lose incentives to offer their information or testimony. And offenders may be inspired to fight adjudication and correctional processes rather than participate in and acquiesce to them.

Perhaps the greatest utility of desert comes through a more subtle but potentially more influential mechanism. The real power to gain compliance with society's rules of prescribed conduct lies not in the threat of official criminal sanction but in the influence of the intertwined forces of social and individual moral control. The networks of interpersonal relationships in which people find themselves, the social norms and prohibitions shared among those relationships and transmitted through social networks, and the internalized representations of norms and moral precepts control people's conduct. The law is not irrelevant to these social and personal forces. Criminal law, in particular, plays a central role in creating and maintaining the social consensus necessary for sustaining moral norms. In fact, in a society as diverse as ours, the criminal law may be the only society-wide mechanism that transcends cultural and ethnic differences. Thus, the criminal law's most important real-world effect may be its ability to assist in the building, shaping, and maintaining of shared norms and moral principles. Criminal law can contribute to and harness the compliance-producing power of interpersonal relationships and personal morality but will only be effective in doing so if it has sufficient credibility.

Finally, the criminal law can gain compliance with its commands through another mechanism as well: If it earns a reputation as a reliable statement of what the community perceives as condemnable, people are more likely to defer to its commands as morally authoritative and as appropriate to follow in those borderline cases in which the propriety of certain conduct is unsettled or ambiguous in the mind of the actor. The importance of this role should not be underestimated; in a society with the complex interdependencies that characterize ours, a seemingly harmless action can have destructive consequences. When the action is criminalized by the legal system, one would want the citizen to respect the law, even though he or she does not immediately intuit why that action is banned. Such deference will be facilitated if citizens believe that the law is an accurate guide to appropriate prudential and moral behavior.

The extent of the criminal law's effectiveness in all these respects—in bringing the power of stigmatization to bear, in avoiding resistance and subversion to a system perceived as unjust, in facilitating, communicating, and maintaining societal consensus on what is and is not condemnable, and in gaining compliance in borderline cases through deference to its moral authority—is to a great extent dependent on the degree to which criminal law has gained moral credibility in the minds of the citizens governed by it. Thus, criminal law's moral credibility is essential to effective crime control and is enhanced if the distribution of criminal liability is perceived as "doing justice"—that is, if it assigns liability and punishment in ways that the community perceives as consistent with its shared intuitions of justice. Conversely, the system's moral credibility, and therefore its crime-control effectiveness, is undermined by a distribution of liability that deviates from community perceptions of just desert.

Studies 2a and 2b were designed to test for evidence that reduced moral credibility in the criminal justice system produces disillusionment that in turn could undermine the deference described above. Specifically, these studies examine whether knowledge of the extent to which existing criminal law doctrines deviate from ordinary intuitions of justice can affect people's general respect for the law, as well as their intention to cooperate, support, and comply with it. We hypothesized that, where criminal law doctrines deviate dramatically from ordinary intuitions about justice, such awareness of the law's predictable injustices would indeed negatively affect people's attitudes toward the law, as well as weaken their behavioral intentions to cooperate, support, and comply with it.

A.   *Study 2a Design and Methodology*

We ran two studies to test this hypothesis. In Study 2a, 59 subjects (34 female, 25 male; age range of 18–77) were recruited to participate in a short web survey by two separate means. An invitation to go to a website to participate in the study was circulated to the University of Pennsylvania Law School community and other acquaintances, with a request that people in turn send the invitation to their acquaintances. (Students were excluded from participation.) Eventually, 26 subjects from this source took the online survey. None of these people knew of the study beforehand, its goals or its design, nor who was involved in its design. (As reported below, the results from these subjects did not differ in any significant way from the results obtained from other sub-

1998 *NEW YORK UNIVERSITY LAW REVIEW* [Vol. 85:1940

jects.) The remaining 33 subjects were recruited via Amazon.com's Mechanical Turk system[186] and were paid $0.95 for their participation. This system coordinates a large pool of paid volunteers who perform tasks over the Internet (including many other tasks besides surveys) for a wide range of requesters. All subjects were assured that their data would be kept anonymous.

Study 2a used a simple pre-post design. Subjects were first asked a series of questions to assess their general attitudes and behavioral intentions with regard to the criminal justice system. Their responses to these questions comprised the baseline responses. They were then exposed to a set of cases in which the criminal justice system in a hypothetical jurisdiction gave liability and punishment that was unjust—either too high or too low. All cases and results were real but were not from any single jurisdiction. Subjects were then asked the same set of questions regarding their views to be answered on the assumption that they lived in that hypothetical jurisdiction. The question of interest was whether subjects' answers to the questions based on living in the hypothetical criminal justice system would differ from their earlier baseline answers under the current criminal justice system.

The eight questions of greatest interest for present purposes are reproduced in Table 5 below. A subset of these questions—Questions 1, 2, and 3—examines the extent to which people regard the criminal law, whose norms they are likely to internalize, as a reliable source of moral authority. A second subset—Questions 4, 5, and 6—examines people's willingness to cooperate with and assist in the operation of the criminal justice system. For instance, these questions shed light on how willing people are to report conduct deemed criminal, even though it may not seem particularly condemnable to them. A third subset—Questions 7 and 8—examines people's intentions to comply with the criminal law's rules in morally grey areas.[187] All questions were to be answered on a 9-point scale, which asked subjects to rate their level of agreement with each statement, ranging from 1: "strongly disagree" to 9: "strongly agree," with interim points for "disagree," "agree," and "unsure." As is typical with such scales, most

---

[186] Mechanical Turk is an online system run by Amazon that enables researchers (as well as other entities) to recruit individuals to perform various tasks for payment. The tasks that can be performed include, but are not limited to, surveys such as the one we conducted. *See* AMAZON MECHANICAL TURK, https://www.mturk.com/mturk/welcome (last visited Oct. 18, 2010).

[187] We also asked four other questions that pertained to similar issues. However, these were not affected by the manipulation in that they did not show any pre-post stimulation differences, so we do not discuss them further.

subjects avoided the extremes and answered within the range of 3: "disagree" to 7: "agree." The questions were presented at the beginning of the survey in a new random order for each subject.

TABLE 5
QUESTIONS ON THE EFFECT OF THE CRIMINAL JUSTICE
SYSTEM'S MORAL CREDIBILITY

Question: Agree or Disagree?
1. Life sentence means offense conduct must be heinous   You see a story on the evening news about a prisoner who was sentenced to life in prison. Based on his extremely harsh sentence, you would conclude that the person must have committed a heinous crime, and believe that he deserves the punishment that he got.
2. Law prohibition means posting false comments must be condemnable   You learn from a newspaper story that posting false negative comments on another person's online profile site (e.g. Facebook) can count as an act of criminal libel. Based on the criminal law's prohibition of this act, you would consider it to be condemnable.
3. High sentence for financial maneuver means condemnable   Your newspaper reports that a particular financial maneuver on taxes has just been made a crime and that the law has assigned it a very serious sentence of 28 to 32 years. Because the law assigns such a high sentence, you would conclude that the conduct must be morally condemnable and probably deserves such a sentence.
4. Report removal of arrowhead   You learn of a person in your town who has illegally taken an arrowhead from an important historical site which they visited. It is illegal to take anything from the site. You would report the removal to the relevant authorities.
5. Give found handgun to police   You are walking through an alley and find a hand gun next to a sewer drain. You think it might not be safe for children to leave it there, but you worry that picking it up and carrying it to police might create problems for you. No one is around to see what you are doing. You would pick up the gun and take it to the police.
6. Report dog violation to authorities   Your neighbor is a dog lover. He recently got three more dogs, for a total of six. The law only allows 3 dogs in a single home. You might report the neighbor's new dogs to the relevant authorities.
7. Go back and report your mistake to gas station   While on vacation, in a place that is distant from the one you live in, you drive off from a gas station without paying. You realize this later, but you also know that the employees could have no knowledge of your identity, and that you would not be traceable. You have the possibility to turn back and report your mistake, but you are somewhat concerned that this act itself would lead to some penalty. You would turn back or attempt to contact the gas station to correct for your mistake.
8. Go back and report your mistake to restaurant   While on vacation, in a place that is distant from the one you live in, you drive off from a restaurant without paying. You realize this later, but you also know that the employees could have no knowledge of your identity, and that you would not be traceable. You have the possibility to turn back and report your mistake, but you are somewhat concerned that this act itself would lead to some penalty. You would turn back or attempt to contact the restaurant to correct for your mistake.

Having responded to these questions to establish a baseline, subjects were then presented with seven real-world cases, for which pilot testing had shown that the liability or sentence actually given in the case deviated dramatically from ordinary intuitions. The cases are described in Appendix C in the order in which they were presented. Several of these cases engage the crime-control doctrines described above. Subjects were instructed truthfully that all of the cases and sentences were real. They read each case and assigned a sentence that they thought was appropriate, if any, from a drop-down menu of sentences.[188]

The actual sentences assigned to these cases were then revealed to the subjects,[189] with instructions reminding them that these sentences had all come from real-life cases. It was not explicitly revealed to subjects that all of the cases had in fact occurred within the American criminal justice system. Instead, subjects were instructed to assume that all of the cases had come from a single, hypothetical criminal justice system, and that they should try to form an impression of this system as a whole.

Out of the seven cases, five (cases 1, 3, 4, 5, and 7 in Appendix C) had real-world sentences much more severe than most people judged appropriate, whereas the remaining two (cases 2 and 6) received no sentence, though most people answered that a serious sentence should be imposed. For each case in turn, the computer program that administered the survey (Qualtrics) revealed the actual sentence to subjects, as well as the sentence that the subject had previously assigned. Subjects were asked to calculate the difference between the two sentences and to enter it on the screen. This exercise was meant to focus the subjects' attention on the difference between their own intuitions and the sentences actually imposed in the hypothetical system.

Subjects next responded to the same set of questions that were asked in the first part of the survey, set out in Table 5, which assessed their general attitudes and intentions towards the criminal justice system (this time in a new random order). They were instructed to respond to these questions as if they were living in the hypothetical criminal justice system which had assigned the liability and sentences they had just seen.

Our specific hypothesis was that learning about the injustices created by the current criminal justice system (described to subjects as a hypothetical system), including those created by current crime-control doctrines like those tested in Study 1, would undermine the system's moral credibility and have the detrimental effects on attitudes rele-

---

[188] The options presented to subjects were as follows: Death, Life, 30 years, 26 years, 22.5 years, 19 years, 15 years, 13 years, 11 years, 9 years, 7 years, 6 years, 5 years, 4 years, 3 years, 2.5 years, 2 years, 1.5 years, 1 year, 10.5 months, 9 months, 7.5 months, 6 months, 5 months, 4 months, 3 months, 2 months, 6.5 weeks, 5 weeks, 3.5 weeks, 2 weeks, 11 days, 1 week, 4 days, 1 day, Liability but no punishment, No punishment.

[189] *See* Column 4 of Appendix C.

vant to crime control described above. We predicted that when responding to questions about how they would think and act if they were living in the hypothetical system, subjects would be less inclined to defer to the criminal law and less inclined to cooperate and comply with it.

The hypothetical system framing was derived from recent research on the "hypothetical society paradigm."[190] We framed our study in this way because we surmised that most people have strong existing beliefs about the justness of their own criminal justice system, having lived within that system for many years; thus, experimenters could not reasonably expect to change such beliefs in a few minutes. Moreover, owing to a desire to respond consistently, most individuals would probably be reluctant to indicate that their own beliefs and intentions had changed in the course of a single survey session. The hypothetical system framing is useful in liberating subjects to express what is more likely to be an accurate appraisal of their own beliefs and intentions with full knowledge of the conditions described in that system (which happens to be the current one).

At the conclusion of the survey, subjects responded to a series of standard demographic items. They also responded to two general questions (on a 9-point scale) about the hypothetical criminal justice system. The first of these asked: "Do you think that the hypothetical criminal justice system whose cases you have just seen gives people the punishment that they deserve, no more, no less?" where 1 was: "Not at all—the criminal law in that system does very badly," the midpoint, 5, was: "The criminal law in that system does neither well nor badly," and 9 was: "To a great extent—the criminal law in that system does very well." The second general question asked subjects to indicate their agreement with the following statement: "The hypothetical criminal justice system does a reliable job of doing justice and would have credibility with the citizens it governs," where 1 was "strongly disagree," 3 was "disagree," the midpoint 5 was "unsure," 7 was "agree," and 9 was "strongly agree."

B. *Study 2a Results and Discussion*

The two subject pools were somewhat different demographically. The first group (the emailed invitation sample) was consistently older, better educated, and wealthier than the Mechanical Turk sample.

---

[190] Gregory Mitchell & Phillip E. Tetlock, *Experimental Political Philosophy: Justice Judgments in the Hypothetical Society Paradigm*, in EXPLORATIONS IN POLITICAL PSYCHOLOGY (Jon A. Krosnick & I-Chant A. Chiang eds.) (forthcoming May 2011), *available at* http://papers.ssrn.com/sol3/papers.cfm?abstract_id=912981.

There were no statistically significant differences in political views, belief in a God, or in the gender composition of the two samples. Most importantly, the two groups did not differ in their response to learning about the unjust sentencing outcomes of the hypothetical system— there was no reliable variation in pre-post stimulation differences when comparing the two groups. Hence, we collapse the two groups in the following analyses.

As Appendix C shows, the average sentences imposed by subjects were dramatically different from the actual sentences imposed by the criminal justice system for each of the seven cases.[191] Reflecting this, responses to the two general questions which asked about the hypothetical system showed that people generally thought this system did a poor job of administering justice. In response to the first question— whether the system assigned deserved punishments—the average response, 3.41, was significantly lower than the scale midpoint of 5.[192] The same was true for the average on the second question about the credibility of the system, for which the mean was 3.97.[193] Evidently, having learned about the unjust punishments given by this system, subjects' impressions of it were markedly negative.

The data that are critical for the study's main hypothesis concern the differences between the pre-stimulation and post-stimulation responses to the questions that asked about intentions and attitudes with regard to the criminal justice system. As Table 6 shows, subjects' attitudes and behavioral intentions post-stimulation shifted noticeably from what they had been at the pre-stimulation baseline. For seven of the eight questions, responses moved in the direction of decreased reliance on, and decreased willingness to comply and cooperate with, the criminal law. For Question 2, this decrement was only marginally reliable. Moreover, these shifts occurred with respect to each of the three areas of interest we investigated: deference to the law in drawing conclusions about condemnability of conduct relevant to shaping norms, intention to cooperate with and assist the system, and intention to comply with it. The eight questions on which these shifts occurred, and the means for both time points, were as follows (significance values are reported for one-tailed, paired-samples *t*-tests).

---

[191] Paired sample *t*-tests, all $p < .001$. Paired sample *t*-tests are used to determine whether there are statistically significant differences between the means from two separate variables, i.e., between the same subjects' responses to two separate questions. *See* David C. Howell, STATISTICAL METHODS FOR PSYCHOLOGY 182 (4th ed. 1997).

[192] One-sample *t*-test, t (58) = -5.02, $p < .001$.

[193] One-sample *t*-test, t (58) = -3.72, $p < .001$.

TABLE 6

STUDY 2A PRE- AND POST-STIMULATION AVERAGES

Question	Baseline average	Post-stimulation average	Significance
1. Life sentence means offense conduct must be heinous	6.46	5.14	p<.001
2. Law prohibition means posting false comments must be condemnable	6.14	5.76	p<.07
3. High sentence for financial maneuver means condemnable	5.25	4.63	p<.02
4. Report removal of arrowhead	5.93	5.14	p<.01
5. Give found handgun to police	6.66	5.56	p<.001
6. Report dog violation to authorities	5.15	4.59	p<.01
7. Go back and report your mistake to gas station	7.05	5.69	p<.001
8. Go back and report your mistake to restaurant	7.15	5.71	p<.001

The size of these shifts was predicted by subjects' responses to the first general question about whether the hypothetical system assigned deserved punishments. For each of the eight items, the degree to which subjects saw the hypothetical system as assigning unjust punishments correlated with the size of their attitude shift from pre- to post-stimulation.[194] These correlations are important because they show the link between individuals' general beliefs about the justness of the hypothetical criminal justice system and their more specific attitudes and intentions with regard to that system.

Study 2a shows how knowledge that a criminal justice system produces systematic injustices can generate negative attitudes toward that system. It also suggests that those negative attitudes can lead to diminished intentions to defer to, cooperate with, and comply with the law. The systematic changes in attitude and intentions that we observed occurred even with a relatively small sample size ($N < 60$), suggesting that the effects may be quite substantial. However, the "within-subjects" design of Study 2a is open to a possible criticism concerning demand characteristics—that by asking the same questions twice, there may have been an implicit suggestion perceived by some subjects that the experimenters expected them to change their responses. While acknowledging this point, we note that our subjects were participating in a web survey, and that they were entirely anonymous, which, in contrast to a laboratory setting, should diminish the implied

---

[194] Pearson correlation coefficients ranged from $r = -.22$ to $r = -.37$, all $ps < .05$, one-tailed. The Pearson correlation coefficient indicates the strength and direction of any linear relationship between two variables; it ranges between -1 and +1, where -1 is a perfect negative correlation and +1 is a perfect positive correlation.

pressure to respond in a way that is perceived to be desired by the researcher. The fact that the "disillusioning cases" moved in both directions—with some sentences that were too harsh and some too lenient—also made it less than obvious what change in responses the experimenters might be expecting. However, to more conclusively rule out this possibility, we ran Study 2b, which employed similar measures to those used in Study 2a, but with a "between-subjects" manipulation in which each subject was asked the questions only once.

C. *Study 2b Design and Methodology*

Two hundred and seven subjects (137 female, 70 male) were recruited via Amazon.com's Mechanical Turk system and were paid $0.75 for their participation. The design of the study was straightforward. Subjects were randomly assigned by the survey program (Qualtrics) to one of two groups. The experimental or "high-disillusionment" group ($N = 108$) was presented with the same series of seven real-world cases that were presented in Study 2a (see Appendix C), in which the actual sentencing outcome deviates dramatically from ordinary intuitions. Subjects read each case in turn and assigned a sentence that they thought was appropriate, if any. The actual sentences assigned to these cases were then revealed, alongside subjects' own sentences. As in Study 2a, subjects were instructed that these cases and sentences were all real and had been handed down by a variety of legal jurisdictions but that they should assume that the sentences had all been given by a single, hypothetical criminal justice system. Subjects then responded to the same eight questions that were asked in Study 2a (see Table 5), which were presented in a new, random order for each subject.

The control "low-disillusionment" group ($N = 99$) followed the same procedure, except that the seven cases being "sentenced" by subjects were chosen so that the actual sentences given by courts in the cases accord more closely with ordinary lay intuitions[195]—that is, none of the cases engaged the application of one of the modern crime-control doctrines described in Part I. These cases, along with their sentences, are shown in Appendix D. The cases for the high-disillusionment group were presented in the order shown in Appendix

---

[195] The cases were taken from an earlier study. *See* Robinson & Kurzban, *supra* note 88, at 1894–98 (presenting twenty-four cases used in study). The sentences reported to subjects corresponded to the sentences that might commonly be given in the criminal justice system. In fact, for each case, the sentence described corresponded to the sentence handed down in a very similar actual case. The sentences also very closely matched the average sentences given by forty-six University of Pennsylvania undergraduates who participated in an earlier pilot study. *See supra* note 108.

C; the cases for the control low-disillusionment group were presented in this order for each subject: 7, 1, 2, 3, 6, 5, 4 (see Appendix D).

Our hypothesis was that exposure to the injustices created by the criminal justice system, including those created by current crime-control doctrines, would undermine the system's moral credibility and have the same detrimental effects documented in Study 2a. Thus, we predicted that when reporting how they would think and act in the hypothetical criminal justice system, the high-disillusionment group would report a lessened inclination to defer to the criminal law and to cooperate and comply with it than the low-disillusionment group. The procedures in the high- and low-disillusionment conditions resembled each other as closely as possible, therefore allowing us to test for the specific causal effect of disillusionment.

As in Study 2a, at the conclusion of the survey, subjects responded to a series of demographic items, as well as the same two questions that were asked of Study 2a subjects regarding their general impressions of the hypothetical criminal justice system.

D.   Study 2b Results and Discussion

The results of both the low and high disillusionment groups are reported in Table 7. As a check on the manipulation, and as Appendix C shows, subjects' average sentences in the high-disillusionment condition were dramatically different from the actual sentences imposed by the criminal justice system for each of the seven cases.[196] In contrast, for the low-disillusionment condition, the degree of discrepancy between subjects' sentences and the law's was much lower (see Appendix D). Three out of the seven cases produced statistically significant discrepancies, and these were of much smaller size than those in the high-disillusionment condition. Subjects' average sentences for the "wolf hallucination" case were lower than the law's sentence (seven days vs. three months[197]), whereas their sentences for the "clock radio" case were on average higher than the law's (eleven months, five days vs. five months[198]), as were their sentences for the "slap and bruising at record store" case (nineteen months, ten days vs. twelve months[199]). However, although they were significant, these differences were quite small in terms of sentence duration in comparison with the discrepancies for the high-disillusionment condition. Reflecting the differences between the conditions of the two groups,

---

[196] Paired sample t-tests, all ps < .001.

[197] t (98) = 12.64, p < .001.

[198] t (98) = 2.53, p < .02.

[199] t (98) = 2.47, p < .02.

responses on the two general questions which asked about the hypothetical system showed that subjects in the high-disillusionment condition thought the system did a much poorer job of administering justice
than did subjects in the low-disillusionment condition. The high-
disillusionment group thought the system did a worse job of assigning
deserved punishments (3.04 vs. 5.85 on the 9-point scale[200]), and also
thought the system would have less credibility with its citizens (3.44 vs.
5.96[201]). For both questions, the mean for the high-disillusionment
group was significantly below the scale midpoint of 5, whereas the
mean for the low-disillusionment group was significantly above the
scale midpoint. The manipulation was thus sufficient to produce more
negative attitudes about the hypothetical system among those in the
high-disillusionment group.

Our main question of interest, though, was whether these negative general attitudes would translate into specific decreases in willingness to defer to this hypothetical criminal justice system. As predicted,
the subjects in the high-disillusionment group showed less deference
to and less willingness to assist or cooperate with the criminal justice
system than did subjects in the low-disillusionment group when
responding to the test questions. Six of the eight questions produced
differences that were statistically significant in the predicted direction
at the $p < .05$ level (one-tailed, paired-sample t-tests). That is, the
probability of obtaining these data, assuming that the null hypothesis
of no difference between the means is true, was less than .05 for six of
the eight questions.

Table 7 compares these results to the baseline results for the subjects in Study 2a, who responded to the same eight questions at the
start of Study 2a before any disillusionment.[202] The mean response
scores for this no-disillusionment group were statistically significantly
different from the high-disillusionment cases in seven of the eight
instances, and the difference was marginally significant for the

---

[200] t (205) = 10.29, $p < .001$.

[201] $p < .001$.

[202] The comparison between the Study 2a baseline means and the Study 2b means is not
ideal because the subjects were not randomly assigned to the studies. However, the two
Mechanical Turk surveys were run only ten days apart, and analyses revealed that there
were very few differences between the groups. The Study 2a subjects were significantly
older than those in Study 2b, but there were no other significant differences across other
demographic variables, including gender, political views, annual income, belief in God, and
highest education completed. Critically, there were no significant differences between the
sentences handed out by the Study 2a subjects and those handed out by the Study 2b high-
disillusionment group, and there was only one significant difference between these two
subgroups on the post-disillusionment questions. We conclude that it is highly unlikely that
a cohort difference compromises the comparison between the Study 2a baseline and the
Study 2b subjects.

remaining item (Question 2, $p < .07$). Table 7 suggests that the greater the disillusionment, the less likely that people are to cooperate with the criminal justice system and to defer to it as a moral authority that shapes societal norms and their internalization of those norms.

TABLE 7
STUDY 2A BASELINE AND STUDY 2B RESULTS[203]

Question *(for full text of questions, see* supra *Table 5)*	Study 2a baseline *No Disillusionment*	Study 2b *Low Disillusionment*	Study 2b *High Disillusionment*
1. Life sentence means heinous	6.46[a]	6.59[a]	5.35[b]
2. Posting condemnable	6.14[a]	5.38[b]	5.59[a,b]
3. Financial move condemnable	5.25[a]	5.16[a]	4.34[b]
4. Report arrowhead	5.93[a]	5.65[a]	4.95[b]
5. Turn in hand gun	6.66[a]	5.40[b]	4.32[c]
6. Report dogs violation	5.15[a]	4.75[a,b]	4.43[b]
7. Return to gas station	7.05[a]	6.63[a]	5.63[b]
8. Return to restaurant	7.15[a]	6.47[b]	5.84[c]

What conclusion should we draw from these results in relation to the crime-control costs of doing injustice? They would seem to suggest that there are clear benefits to be found in doing justice: greater assistance and cooperation with the criminal justice system, upon which the system critically depends, and greater ability to harness the powerful forces of social influence and the internalization of norms to gain compliance in borderline cases and to shape norms where needed.

However, it might be argued, given what has been said in Part III about the distortions and imperfections inherent to public perceptions of crime and punishment, that instances of injustice and failures of justice by the system may not be immediately and fully appreciated by the community. The fog of media errors and inaccuracies may protect the system's reputation even when it does not deserve it and, thus, deviating from desert might not result in a loss of moral credibility and its consequent detrimental effects.[204]

---

[203] Where two cells on a row do not share the same letter, their values are statistically different. That is, if three adjacent cells have the superscripts: "a," "a,b," "b," it means that the first cell is significantly different from the third cell, but that the second cell is not significantly different from either the first or third cell.

[204] The reverse is also possible: Distorted media coverage may create the impression that the criminal justice system is deviating from desert when it is not. This is a potential problem especially when, as is currently the case, the media tend to focus on the absolute amount of punishment imposed rather than upon the relative amount of punishment among different cases. That is, when a sentence is reported in isolation, which is the traditional news coverage approach, it may seem inappropriate, yet an examination of a fuller collection of cases may suggest that it is indeed just the sentence this offender deserves,

Unfortunately, it seems unlikely that the fog of media reporting will so completely insulate the system that it can freely do injustice and fail to do justice without concern that these imperfections will be revealed and undermine its moral credibility. Indeed, what seems likely is that, just as crime is news (thereby exaggerating the rate and nature of crime), so too are injustice and failure of justice news.[205] Even if the nature of the news coverage hides some portion of the deviations from desert, the more frequently and more seriously the system deviates from desert, the greater the chances that such deviations will come to light.

Worse, even a very few disclosures have the potential to undermine the system's credibility. As discussed previously, what we know about making and keeping reputations tells us that the system's intention regarding doing justice counts enormously.[206] While accidental or unavoidable injustices or failures of justice may be forgiven when the system seems committed to trying to do justice, if revealed deviations from desert are intended by the system—when they are planned and predictable applications of the criminal law's rules, as with the modern crime-control doctrines examined in Parts I and II—then even a single telling case can have detrimental consequences. The system's only protection is to indeed try to do justice as best it can, admitting that there are some limitations on how perfect it can be in practice.[207]

E. *Limitations and Future Research*

In the studies reported here we relied on self-report measures of individuals' attitudes and of their willingness to take various actions. How well these sorts of self-report measures predict actual behavior might be questioned. Considerable research has shown that the extent

---

given his relative blameworthiness and the spread of the punishment continuum. A useful part of the agenda for future research may be to understand how to encourage less distorting media reporting. Some of this will come naturally if the system moves formally to desert as a distributive principle—something likely to promote public discussion and improve public understanding of the nature of shared intuitions of justice and the central role of relative blameworthiness. However, special efforts to improve news reporting may be a good investment for the long-term success of the criminal justice system.

[205] Indeed, especially if the system formalizes and publicizes the importance of doing justice, such as by adopting desert as the system's distributive principle in the way that the Model Penal Code drafters have done, deviations from desert will attract more press attention, not less.

[206] *See* Robinson & Darley, *Utility of Desert*, *supra* note 100, at 495–96 (discussing impact of doing injustice on reputation of criminal justice system).

[207] For an analysis of the various doctrines by which the criminal justice system regularly and intentionally deviates from desert and a critique of the justifications offered in support of each doctrine of deviation, see generally ROBINSON & CAHILL, LAW WITHOUT JUSTICE, *supra* note 23.

to which such measures of attitude and intention predict behavior varies greatly, depending on whether they specifically capture the context and circumstances in which the relevant behaviors will be enacted.[208] It is well established that very general attitudinal measures are poorer predictors of behavior than more specific measures that capture individuals' "behavioral intentions" to act and to do so in certain ways.[209] Accordingly, the self-report measures that we used in the present studies were quite specific in describing the context and circumstances in which the behaviors of interest would occur. Because of this, we suspect that they have some predictive value with regard to whether people will cooperate with the law (as examined in Questions 4, 5, and 6, *supra* Table 5). One might of course look to what people actually do, and this would provide better evidence of lack of cooperation and assistance. For example, one might look at data on the actual rates of crime reporting, witness cooperation, or jury nullification in different areas where there are divergent levels of confidence in the moral authority of the criminal justice system. The United States, for instance, could be compared with other countries with noticeably less just criminal justice systems—which may include most of the countries in the world. Unfortunately, such data are very difficult to find and expensive to collect.

---

[208] *See generally* Icek Azjen & Martin Fishbein, Understanding Attitudes & Predicting Social Behavior (1980) (discussing how measures of attitude and intention can be used to predict behavior, correspondence between measures of attitude and measures of behavior, and application of measures in six case studies of socially relevant behavior).

[209] Ajzen and Fishbein's "theory of reasoned action" originated the term "behavioral intention." This theory has been critical in shedding light on the conditions under which attitudes predict behavior. *See id.* at pt. 1 (outlining theory of reasoned action, including construct of behavioral intention as way to predict behavior from attitudes). Much research originating from this theory (and leading up to it) has corroborated the importance in predicting behavior of asking questions that gauge people's intentions to perform the specific behaviors of interest. *See generally* Icek Ajzen, *Attitudes, Traits, and Actions: Dispositional Prediction of Behavior in Personality and Social Psychology, in* 20 Advances in Experimental Social Psychology 1, 1–63 (1987) (providing theoretical treatment of when and how general dispositions predict specific behaviors); Alice H. Eagly & Shelly Chaiken, The Psychology of Attitudes 155–218 (1993) (providing integrative review of accumulated research on attitudes including their relation to behavior); Martin Fishbein & Icek Ajzen, Belief, Attitude, Intention, & Behavior: An Introduction to Theory & Research (1975) (presenting conceptual framework for theory of reasoned action and model of behavior prediction based on argument that behavioral intention is function of attitude toward specific behavior and subjective norms); A.R. Davidson & J.J. Jaccard, *Variables that Moderate the Attitude-Behavior Relation: Results of a Longitudinal Survey*, 37 J. Personality & Soc. Psychol. 1364, 1364–76 (1978) (investigating how attitudes predict specific behaviors of having children and using oral contraceptives, showing that closer correspondence between attitude measures and behaviors correlates to stronger predictive relation).

It is not as clear that there is better evidence than this self-report data when one considers the issue of shaping societal norms and promoting the internalization of norms (Questions 1, 2, and 3). Whether these influences will exist is a function of the extent to which people find the criminal law to be a reliable moral authority, which is what is measured in these three questions.

The third effect of disillusionment—compliance with the criminal laws' commands (Questions 7 and 8)—could also be measured more directly than by relying upon the self-reporting done here. However, we suspect that there is a limit to what one will find. For much conduct, the impropriety is clear, and nothing that the criminal justice system can do will change that fact. Societal forces, such as deeply held existing attitudes, can maintain a norm without much help from the criminal justice system. Other forces can establish the condemnability of certain conduct, especially that at or near the core of wrongdoing, even without the help of the criminal law.[210] Even extreme disillusionment, then, is not likely to undermine social norms with regard to this type of conduct. We would expect the extent of the law's moral credibility to have more of an effect in borderline cases, where the condemnability of conduct is not as clear.[211]

The issue of compliance is further complicated because the criminal justice system can potentially affect rates of compliance through multiple causal routes. As we have argued, the moral credibility of the system likely exerts some causal effect on compliance. For instance, a person may remain stopped at a deserted red light purely as a function of internalized norms, rather than any cost-benefit analysis. And these norms, as we have previously argued, are shaped by the moral credibility of the criminal justice system. But compliance is also affected by more local cost-benefit analyses, including, for example, concerns about a highly arbitrary and punitive criminal justice system. Such a system can produce a variety of unpredictable and perverse effects. For example, a system perceived as being arbitrary and highly punitive may encourage people to avoid acts that potentially entangle them in the system. This might have negative effects, as in dissuading people from reporting crime to the police or being a witness in court. Indeed,

---

[210] *See* Paul H. Robinson, Robert Kurzban & Owen D. Jones, *The Origins of Shared Intuitions of Justice*, 60 VAND. L. REV. 1633 (2007) (arguing that matters on which there is high agreement across demographics cannot easily be manipulated, whether due to human predisposition to holding such intuitions or to universal social learning conditions).

[211] *See* Robinson & Darley, *Intuitions of Justice*, *supra* note 1, at 29–31 (arguing that criminal justice system will command more deference in borderline cases if perceived to be morally authoritative); Robinson & Darley, *Utility of Desert*, *supra* note 100, at 475–77 (discussing how criminal law's moral authority has effect in cases where ambiguity exists as to whether conduct is wrong).

this sort of perverse effect may be what accounts for the shift in subjects' responses to the gas station and restaurant items in Studies 2a and 2b: The perceived injustice of the system discourages people from returning to pay the bill they forgot to pay. However, under the right circumstances, such a reputation for arbitrariness also might produce beneficial effects, such as helping to discourage people from committing crimes. On the other hand, few people would want to live in a society whose program for avoiding crime is to be particularly arbitrary or unjust in its treatment of suspected violators.[212]

F.   Previous Studies

The conclusions reached here are consistent with previous studies suggesting that conflicts between the criminal law's dispositional rules and the community's shared intuitions of justice have the sorts of detrimental effects described above. As discussed below, a number of studies have confirmed the existence of the relationship between an individual's disbelief in the morality of a particular law and his or her willingness to obey that law. Studies also show that the degree to which people report that they have obeyed a law in the past and plan to obey it in the future correlates with the degree to which they judge that law to be morally valid. Some studies also go further in showing how perceptions of injustice might lead to more generalized flouting of the law.

Several studies have focused on how beliefs about the morality of a particular law can affect compliance with it. In one such study by Grasmick and Green, a random sample of 400 adults was selected

---

[212] As previously mentioned, a possible criticism of the Study 2a design is that it introduces a demand to respond in ways that the subject perceives that the researcher expects. *See supra* Part IV.B. Study 2a is more vulnerable to this criticism than is Study 2b because it used a within-subjects design. The lack of face-to-face contact between the researcher and subject diminishes the concern, although perhaps not entirely. But the results of Study 2b, which was performed between subjects, cast more doubt on the existence of any such demand effect. Subjects, of course, perceived a relation between the two parts of Study 2b, but it is unlikely that this exerted pressure on them to respond in a particular way. The expected effect was not necessarily obvious to subjects in the disillusionment condition, since the sentences were both overly punitive and overly lenient. We thus think it unlikely that subjects were able to reliably divine the hypothesis under investigation. Indeed, one potential hypothesis they might have entertained, entirely contrary to the one that was supported, is that the researchers wanted them to respond in more moral and law-abiding ways in the high-disillusionment condition, since a reliance on personal morality comes to the fore when the legal system is doing a poor job. Finally, the manipulation was also produced by allowing whatever differences existed between subjects' sentences and the law's to emerge naturally, and it did not rely on any explicit statements about the quality of the legal system by the researchers; subjects had to draw their own inferences about this issue. In sum, we conclude that the worry about "experimenter demand" is insubstantial.

2012   *NEW YORK UNIVERSITY LAW REVIEW*   [Vol. 85:1940

from the Polk City Directory and subsequently interviewed.[213] Information was gathered about the subjects' involvement in eight illegal activities—theft of property worth less than $20, theft of property worth more than $20, gambling illegally, cheating on tax returns, intentionally inflicting personal injury, littering, illegal use of fireworks, and driving under the influence.[214] The respondents were then asked to estimate the perceived certainty of arrest, the perceived severity of punishment, and their moral commitment to adhering to the given legal rule.[215] The researchers summarized their results by saying that "three independent variables—moral commitment, perceived threat of legal punishment and threat of social disapproval—appear to constitute a concise and probably exhaustive set of factors which inhibit illegal behavior."[216]

Similarly, in another study, Jacob suggests a greater relation between compliance and a law's perceived moral correctness than between compliance and the perceived likelihood of punishment for violating it. He interviewed 176 people over the age of eighteen from Evanston, Illinois by allowing a computer to pick random phone numbers. The respondents were interviewed regarding whether they sped on highways, had smoked marijuana, and would shoplift a $50 item if no one was looking.[217] Marijuana smokers were the most numerous, followed by speeders, followed by potential shoplifters. Two-thirds of respondents thought the fifty-five mile-an-hour speed limit was right, three-quarters agreed that the laws against shoplifting were correct, but only one-quarter thought the law against marijuana was correct. The results showed that for those who think the speeding laws are right, 62.3% comply, while only 9.8%, who think it is wrong, comply. Of those who think the marijuana law is just, 85% do not smoke marijuana. Contrastingly, only 36% of those respondents who think that the law is wrong complied with its ban on smoking. There was no statistical difference in shoplifting, which is evidence of high agreement that shoplifting is wrong.[218] The researchers conclude that "[t]he relationship between compliance and legitimacy appears to be consider-

---

[213] Harold G. Grasmick & Donald E. Green, *Legal Punishment, Social Disapproval and Internalization as Inhibitors of Illegal Behavior*, 71 J. CRIM. L. & CRIMINOLOGY 325, 329 (1980) (describing research procedures).

[214] *Id.* at 330 (explaining research procedures).

[215] *Id.*

[216] *Id.* at 334.

[217] *See* Herbert Jacob, *Deterrent Effects of Formal and Informal Sanctions*, 2 L. & POL'Y Q. 61, 64–67 (1980) (presenting outcomes of Illinois phone survey comparing effects of perceived cost of violating law and perceived legitimacy of law on imputed compliance).

[218] *Id.* at 70 (presenting results regarding legitimacy of law and compliance).

ably stronger than the one between compliance and perceptions of severity or certainty of sanctions."[219]

Matthew Silberman conducted a similar study of 174 undergraduates at a small private university.[220] The students responded to whether they had ever committed certain moral or legal violations, such as assault, use of hard drugs, petty theft, vandalism, shoplifting, drunk and disorderly conduct, premarital sex, marijuana use, and drinking under age. The students then responded to questions regarding the morality of the act, the certainty of punishment, the severity of punishment, and peer involvement. One proposed hypothesis that Silberman tested was that "[t]he higher the degree of moral support for the legal regulation of an offense or offenses, the lower the probability that the offense or offenses will be committed . . . ."[221] After reviewing the data, Silberman concluded that "[w]hen public sentiment in general disapproves [of] a given offense, it is relatively unlikely to occur. Similarly, serious criminal activity is less likely to occur among those who show a high degree of moral commitment, even though these individuals might commit less serious offenses," thus validating his hypothesis.[222]

The previous studies demonstrate that perceptions of the moral legitimacy of particular laws can affect compliance with them. Other studies have gone further in showing how perceptions of the immorality of a particular law, or of some act of the criminal justice system, can lead to more generalized effects on compliance. Janice Nadler's recent series of studies looked at how knowledge of injustices created by the criminal justice system can affect intentions to comply with the law.[223] In the first study, subjects read mock newspaper stories describing legislation that was perceived as either highly just or highly unjust. Subjects in the unjust condition later reported greater intentions to engage in minor acts of law-breaking which were unrelated to the content of the unjust legislation, such as parking illegally or making illegal copies of software.[224] In a second study, conducted over

---

[219] *Id.* at 70; *see also* Robert F. Meier & Weldon T. Johnson, *Deterrence as Social Control: The Legal and Extralegal Production of Conformity*, 42 AM. SOC. REV. 292, 301 (1977) (stating that "[t]he belief that marijuana use is immoral . . . functions to inhibit marijuana use," while "legal threat . . . shows a measurable, but essentially trivial influence on marijuana use/nonuse").

[220] Matthew Silberman, *Toward a Theory of Criminal Deterrence*, 41 AM. SOC. REV. 442 (1976).

[221] *Id.* at 457.

[222] *Id.*

[223] *See* Janice Nadler, *Flouting the Law*, 83 TEX. L. REV. 1399 (2005) (providing experimental evidence in support of idea that perceived legitimacy of one law influences compliance with other laws).

[224] *Id.* at 1410–15 (discussing results of Experiment 1).

the Internet, subjects acted as mock jurors and had to render a verdict in a fictional case in which the evidence pointed to a guilty verdict.[225] Prior to this, they were exposed to a mock news story of a (real) crime in which the protagonist watched his friend abduct and rape a seven-year old girl in a casino. The story had two versions—one in which the protagonist was described as being appropriately punished (just version), and another in which he was not punished at all (unjust version). In the ensuing mock trial scenario, with unrelated content, subjects who had seen the unjust news story were more likely to engage in juror nullification by rendering a "Not Guilty" decision.

A similar study by Erich J. Greene presented cases including the one described in the Nadler study and also examined their effect on subjects' attitudes.[226] Greene reached similar conclusions to those arrived at by Nadler. More specifically, subjects who had read cases in which the legal system behaved in ways counter to their moral intuitions rated themselves "more likely to take steps aimed at changing the law, . . . less likely to cooperate with police, more likely to join a vigilante or watch group, and less likely to use the law to guide behavior."[227] He further concluded, "Overall, participants appeared less likely to give the law the benefit of any doubt after reading cases where the law was at odds with their intuitions."[228]

These studies affirm the conclusion reached by our Studies 2a and 2b. Nadler's first study is closest to ours and is also her most conclusive. However, whereas Nadler's study only investigated issues of compliance, our studies have extended her result by showing effects not only on compliance, but also on cooperation and moral credibility.[229] The unjust primes in Nadler's studies were also somewhat fictionalized, whereas the primes in our studies were descriptions of real cases. Nadler's studies are thus an important first step that our studies have extended. The conclusion we draw is that knowledge of systemic injustice can negatively affect not only compliance, but also

---

[225] *Id.* at 1416–24 (presenting methodology and findings of Experiment 2).

[226] Erich J. Greene, Effects of Disagreements Between Legal Codes and Lay Intuitions on Respect for the Law (June 2003) (unpublished Ph.D. dissertation, Princeton University) (on file with Mudd Library, Princeton University).

[227] *Id.* at iv.

[228] *Id.* at v.

[229] Nadler's second study, on juror nullification, does investigate cooperation, but its results are not as easily interpreted as those of her first study, nor are they easily assimilated with our own results. The greater proportion of "Not Guilty" verdicts in the unjust condition were accompanied by diminished ratings of the defendant's guilt. Nadler, *supra* note 223, at 1424–25. This suggests that the unjust prime (the defendant who got off) may have produced juror nullification through shifting subjects' thresholds for criminal culpability, rather than through affecting their perceptions of the moral credibility of the criminal justice system.

other relevant variables such as cooperation and moral credibility, and that these effects can be produced simply through knowledge of several current criminal law practices.

A more recent study by Mullen and Nadler shows how the perception of moral illegitimacy in the legal system can increase rates of deviant behavior.[230] During the experimental session, 137 undergraduates read a newspaper article that summarized the legal trial of a doctor who allegedly provided an unlawful late-term abortion. Subjects were randomly assigned to read either that the defendant was found 'Guilty' or 'Not Guilty.' One week prior to this session, subjects had completed a questionnaire that assessed their attitudes about abortion, and these attitudes were used to predict the critical dependent variable, which was whether subjects failed to return (i.e., stole) the pen that was provided to fill out their questionnaire. After subjects completed all the studies, they were instructed to return their pen and an envelope containing their materials to designated boxes. The researchers numbered the identical pens with ink that was only visible under ultraviolet light. Therefore, subjects did not know that their pen was numbered but the experimenter was able to identify the pens that were not returned at the end of each experimental session. The percentage of subjects who did not return the pen was substantially higher for those subjects who had strong pro-choice attitudes and who were exposed to the guilty verdict—that is, those for whom the outcome clashed with their moral principles. The researchers interpreted these results as indicating that exposure to outcomes that are inconsistent with a person's strongly held moral beliefs increases the likelihood of their engaging in deviant behavior.[231]

Finally, people's common compliance with tax law raises interesting issues related to these points. Large numbers of American citizens pay their taxes even though the penalty for tax evasion is not great, the probability of detection is trivial, and the expected sanction, therefore, is quite small.[232] For these reasons, many legal scholars believe that the threat of official sanction does not explain why such large numbers of citizens pay taxes.[233] A survey by Karyl A. Kinsey sheds some light on the underlying forces.[234] When people reported

---

[230] Elizabeth Mullen & Janice Nadler, *Moral Spillovers: The Effect of Moral Violations on Deviant Behavior*, 44 J. EXPERIMENTAL SOC. PSYCHOL. 1239 (2008).

[231] *See id.* at 1243–45 (analyzing results of two studies).

[232] *See* Eric A. Posner, *Law and Social Norms: The Case of Tax Compliance*, 86 VA. L. REV. 1781, 1782 (2000) (posing problem of explaining tax compliance).

[233] *See id.* (discussing alternative explanation for tax compliance).

[234] Karyl A. Kinsey, *Deterrence and Alienation Effects of IRS Enforcement: An Analysis of Survey Data*, *in* WHY PEOPLE PAY TAXES: TAX COMPLIANCE AND ENFORCEMENT 259 (Joel Slemrod ed., 1992) (presenting results of study of effects of enforcement contacts on

that a friend or coworker, after contact with the IRS, had been made to pay more taxes than they properly owed, the people thought the tax laws generally were less fair and were more likely to intend to cheat on their taxes in the future.[235] Nadler, in reviewing the study, comments that "[t]he results of the tax study suggest that exposure to reports of an unjust legal outcome in a particular situation might lead to lower perceived fairness of the law more generally, which in turn can lead to noncompliance with the law in the future."[236] It would appear that one who sees tax law and the IRS as being just is likely to comply even though expected sanctions are small and unlikely.

Taken together, these studies complement our own in suggesting that knowledge of systematic injustice produced by the criminal justice system, particularly when it is intentional, can have a range of deleterious effects on people's attitudes and behavior. People are less likely to comply with laws they perceive to be unjust. They may also be less likely to comply with the law in general when they perceive the criminal justice system to cause injustice. Our studies have shown that these sorts of effects are not limited to compliance, but generalize to cooperation and assistance with the legal system, as well as to perceptions of its moral authority, which can affect its ability to harness the normative forces of social influence and the internalization of norms. The flip side, of course, is that if the criminal justice system reflects ordinary perceptions of justice, it can take advantage of a range of psychological mechanisms that serve to increase assistance, cooperation, compliance, and deference.

V

TESTING THE EFFECTS OF LAW'S MORAL CREDIBILITY: STUDY 3

The studies reported in Part IV suggest that doing injustice and failing to do justice can undermine the criminal justice system's moral credibility, which in turn can lead to citizen reluctance to support, assist, and defer to the system. Those studies were conducted using data collected by the present researchers under controlled conditions. One may wonder whether the same effects might be observed in data from large population samples collected by others.

In this study, we worked with existing national databases to see what, if anything, they might tell us about our hypothesis concerning

---

sanctions perceptions, perceived fairness of tax laws, and intentions of future compliance with tax laws).

[235] *Id.* at 276, 282 (discussing effects of vicarious enforcement contacts on intention to comply in future).

[236] Nadler, *supra* note 223, at 1409–10.

the practical impacts of a system's moral credibility on the effective operation of the criminal justice system. One large national survey involving telephone interviews with Americans presents potentially relevant variables. The database includes people who recently participated in criminal court proceedings. Bivariate and multivariate statistical techniques were used to determine whether the observed results support our research hypothesis: As the moral credibility of the criminal justice system increases, the willingness to defer to the courts to resolve a similar case in the future will also increase. The findings presented below suggest that the dynamics from the experiment reported in Studies 2a and 2b also operate among people who have actual experience with the criminal courts. Put simply, if a person has a high level of confidence in the moral credibility of the criminal justice system, he or she will be more likely to defer to the system in the future.

A. Study 3 Dataset

The study used data from the Survey of Public Opinion on the Courts in the United States, conducted in 2000.[237] That dataset, which is available from the National Archive of Criminal Justice Data at the University of Michigan, consists of 1567 telephone interviews of randomly selected adults in the United States.[238] Interviews were conducted by the Indiana University Public Opinion Laboratory (IUPOL) between March 22, 2000 and May 3, 2000.[239] The survey

---

[237] DAVID B. ROTTMAN, RANDALL HANSEN, NICOLE MOTT & LYNN GRIMES, INTER-UNIVERSITY CONSORTIUM FOR POLITICAL AND SOCIAL RESEARCH, PUBLIC OPINION ON THE COURTS IN THE UNITED STATES, 2000 (2000), http://www.icpsr.umich.edu/icpsrweb/ICPSR/studies/3864?archive=ICPSR& q=public+opinion+on+the+courts+ [hereinafter ROTTMAN DATASET] (search "All Fields" for "ICPSR03864").

[238] Sample characteristics: Gender: Male, 44%, female, 56%; Race/Ethnicity: White, not Hispanic, 52%, African American, 26%, Hispanic, 20%, other minority, 2%; Age: Average = 43 years; Education: Less than high school, 9%, high school graduate, 29%, some college, 35%, college graduate, 27%; Household Income: $20,000 or less, 26%, $20,001 to $40,000, 30%, $40,001 to $30,000, 30%, $80,000 or more, 14%; Marital Status: Married, 50%, living together but not married, 5%, single, never married, 22%, separated, divorced, or widowed, 23%. *See* ROTTMAN ET AL., *Codebook and Data Collection Instrument, in* ROTTMAN DATASET, *supra* note 237, at 1, 31–32 (describing sample characteristics).

[239] The sampling strategy adopted by IUPOL corrected for the common problem of underrepresentation of racial and ethnic minorities in telephone surveys by oversampling African Americans and Hispanics. The survey was administered in English and Spanish. Additionally, the IUPOL took a number of steps to ensure data quality. First, interviewers received at least four hours of training. Most of the interviewers had prior experience conducting telephone surveys. Second, a widely accepted telephone survey sampling technique, random-digit-dialing with quotas, was used to contact potential respondents. Finally, selected telephone numbers were called repeatedly until an interview was successfully completed. Telephone numbers were replaced if the individual who was contacted by the research staff refused to participate on three separate occasions, if the number was discon-

instrument consisted of two sets of questions. The first set, administered to all respondents, asked subjects their perceptions of the courts in general, while the second set, which was administered only to respondents who reported recent experience with the courts, queried respondents specifically about their recent court involvement (e.g., the type of case and their role in it).[240]

The present study focused on a subset of respondents within the larger data file who reported recent significant interaction with the criminal justice system. Specifically, we selected survey respondents who met all of the following criteria: (1) either the respondent or a member of his or her household had involvement in the courts in the last twelve months; (2) the case was a criminal matter (including juvenile offenses); and (3) in the case, the subject or household member was either a juror or a witness, but not a defendant, and thus less likely to have a personal stake in the outcome of the case. Of the 1567 subjects, 146 individuals met these criteria. Of that 146, 141 were suitable for use in the present study.[241]

The subsample consists of nearly equal numbers of men and women. A majority of subjects were white, but racial and ethnic minorities were well represented in the data file. The respondents' ages ranged from eighteen to more than seventy-two years. An overwhelming majority of subjects graduated from high school, and more than one-third had earned a four-year college degree. When asked about their combined household incomes (before taxes), a majority of subjects reported an income exceeding $40,000. As for marital status, over half of respondents were married. Finally, over two-thirds of the subjects who reported experience in recent criminal court cases

---

nected or no longer in service, or if the potential subject was not contacted after twenty attempts. *See* ROTTMAN ET AL., *Description, in* ROTTMAN DATASET, *supra* note 237, at iv (describing survey methodology).

[240] *See* ROTTMAN ET AL., *Codebook and Data Collection Instrument, in* ROTTMAN DATASET, *supra* note 237, at app. A ("Data Collection Instrument") (reproducing questions asked of subjects).

[241] A common problem with using telephone survey data is that some respondents do not answer every question. Missing cases were replaced using Similar Response Pattern Imputation (SRPI). SRPI is a technique that is widely used to impute missing cases. Using a series of matching variables, SRPI searches the data file of interest for "donor cases." Once a similar response pattern is found, the donor's score is used in place of the missing value. When compared to other methods for handling missing cases (e.g., mean imputation and listwise deletion), research shows that SRPI is a superior technique. *See* Gerhard Gmel, *Imputation of Missing Values in the Case of a Multiple Item Instrument Measuring Alcohol Consumption*, 20 STAT. MED. 2369, 2379 (2001) (showing that SRPI, or "hot-deck imputation," is superior relative to other available procedures).

(either personal or vicarious through a household member) served as jurors.[242]

B. Study 3 Variables

Three survey items were used to develop the key predictor (or independent) variable. Interviewers asked respondents "[P]lease tell me how well you think the courts in your community handle each of the following kinds of cases."[243] Subjects were then asked to judge their local courts' handling of cases involving violence, substance abuse, and delinquency on a scale ranging from 1 to 5, with 1 being "the very lowest" and 5 being "the very highest."[244] These scores reflect respondents' judgments about the extent to which local criminal court outcomes, such as whether individuals who deserve it are punished and whether the deserved amounts of punishment are imposed, are consistent with their own ideals. The average responses suggest that the subjects with court experience view the outcomes of criminal cases as most consistent with their intuitions of justice in cases involving violence (3.40), and comparatively less so for cases involving drug abusers or drunk drivers (2.96) and juvenile delinquency (2.74).

Each subject's three answers to the survey items were summed to create the single scale that was used as the predictor variable, which we term "moral credibility." The scale thus ranged from 3 (low moral credibility) to 15 (high moral credibility), with the average subject's score at 9.09. A series of statistical tests confirmed that the moral credibility scale is a valid and reliable measure.[245]

---

[242] Subsample characteristics: Gender: Male, 49%, female, 51%; Race/Ethnicity: White, not Hispanic, 56%, African American, 24%, Hispanic, 17%, other minority, 3%; Age: Average = 41 years; Education: Less than high school, 5%, high school graduate, 22%, some college, 37%, college graduate, 36%; Household Income: $20,000 or less, 17%, $20,001 to $40,000, 24%, $40,001 to $80,000, 41%, $80,000 or more, 18%; Marital Status: Married, 56%, living together but not married, 4%, single, never married, 19%, separated, divorced, or widowed, 21%; Role in criminal court case: Juror, 69%, witness, 31%. When compared to the full sample of survey respondents, the subsample consists of slightly more females, individuals who have received higher levels of formal education, and those with higher household incomes. In terms of race/ethnicity, age, and marital status, the two samples are very similar.

[243] ROTTMAN ET AL., *Codebook and Data Collection Instrument, in* ROTTMAN DATASET, *supra* note 237, at app. A, 1 ("Data Collection Instrument").

[244] *See id.*

[245] Various statistical techniques are used by behavioral and social scientists to evaluate the psychometric properties of multi-item summated scales. To assess the validity of the moral credibility scale, the three survey items are entered into an exploratory factor analysis. This technique is used to determine whether the three survey items tap into the same underlying construct. The factor structure that emerges indicates that the scale is unidimensional (eigenvalue = 2.07; factor loadings > .80). For technical details on factor-

The outcome variable in the study was "willingness to defer to the criminal justice system in the future." There are a number of ways in which this measure is related to real-world behaviors of any particular member of society. High willingness to defer to the system might mean that a person is less likely to take self-help measures, engage in vigilantism, or flee from police, and is more likely to report violations by others rather than ignore them, more likely to turn himself or herself in after an accident, and so on.

A single survey item was used to construct the outcome variable. Survey respondents with criminal court experience were asked, "How likely would you be to go to the courts to resolve a similar dispute you became involved in at some point in the future?"[246] Respondents were asked to select from four responses on a scale ranging from "very unlikely" (coded as 1) to "very likely" (coded as 4). The distribution of responses was: 24.3% "very unlikely," 15.3% "unlikely," 22.2% "likely," and 38.2% "very likely." The average score on the 4-point scale was 2.73.

C. Study 3 Results and Discussion

Following standard practices in the social sciences, we first conducted a relatively lenient test of the research hypothesis where the relationship between moral credibility and willingness to defer to the criminal justice system in the future was analyzed without consideration of potential intervening variables, such as the respondent's race, gender, age, or socio-economic status. This test established whether some relationship exists between the two key variables. To evaluate the relationship between moral credibility and willingness to defer to the system, we employed Pearson's r.[247] The Pearson's r coefficient

---

analytic techniques, see generally MARJORIE A. PETT, NANCY R. LACKEY & JOHN L. SULLIVAN, MAKING SENSE OF FACTOR ANALYSIS (2003) and BRUCE THOMPSON, EXPLORATORY AND CONFIRMATORY FACTOR ANALYSIS (2004). To assess the scale reliability, two common measures of internal consistency are used. The results of these procedures confirm that the scale possesses a high level of reliability (Cronbach's alpha = .78; mean inter-item correlation = .54). For a discussion of coefficient alpha and reliability theory, see generally Jose M. Cortina, *What Is Coefficient Alpha? An Examination of Theory and Applications*, 78 J. APPLIED PSYCHOL. 98 (1993). In sum, the evidence indicates that the moral credibility scale has strong psychometric properties.

[246] ROTTMAN ET AL., *Codebook and Data Collection Instrument, in* ROTTMAN DATASET, *supra* note 237, at app. A, 8 ("Data Collection Instrument").

[247] The linear statistical techniques used in this section are sensitive to the distributional characteristics of the variables included in the analysis. When variable scores resemble a normal distribution (or a bell-shaped curve), we gain confidence that our estimates are unbiased. Statistical tests show that the score distributions for the moral credibility and willingness to defer variables are symmetric (or bell-shaped). Thus, the results from the linear statistical models will not be adversely affected by displeasing variable attributes.

ranges from -1.0 to +1.0. The closer the estimate is to an absolute value of 1 (that is, either -1.0 or +1.0), the stronger the relationship. The correlation between these two key variables we examined is +.283 (significance level = .001).[248]

In other words, when the law's moral credibility is high, people express a greater willingness to defer to the system in the future. This is an important finding because it demonstrates in an existing database the real-world benefits of moral credibility—if those who believe more strongly in the moral credibility of the system are more willing to defer to its authority, the incidence of negative activities such as the use of self-help or fleeing from law enforcement should decrease as moral credibility increases.

We then tested the research hypothesis using multivariate analysis. Ordinary least-squares (OLS) regression was used, which allowed us to rule out concerns that the observed relationship between moral credibility and willingness to defer to the criminal justice system could be explained by potential intervening variables, such as the respondent's race, gender, age, and socio-economic status, thus providing a more stringent test of the effect of moral credibility when compared to Pearson's *r*. Table 8 presents an OLS model where the outcome measure—willingness to defer to the criminal justice system—is regressed onto moral credibility and onto standard subject characteristics that might also have influence.[249] The standardized regression coefficients

---

[248] The study used two-tailed tests of statistical significance. The two-tailed test, also known as a nondirectional test, does not require that the direction of the research hypothesis (i.e., positive or negative) be specified. The one-tailed test is a directional test, commonly used when the research hypothesis is directional in nature. Both tests are appropriate in a variety of situations; however, the two-tailed test requires that a higher threshold be met to achieve statistical significance.

[249] The respondent characteristic variables were coded as follows: gender (1 = male respondent, 0 = female respondent), age (in years), race (1 = white, non-Hispanic respondent, 0 = racial and/or ethnic minority respondent), education (1 = less than fifth grade to 9 = graduate or professional degree), household income (1 = less than $10,000 to 10 = more than $120,000), and marital status (1 = married respondent, 0 = otherwise). According to established guidelines, the sample is sufficiently large to estimate a six-variable OLS model to detect medium effect sizes. *See* Samuel B. Green, *How Many Subjects Does It Take To Do a Regression Analysis?*, 26 MULTIVARIATE BEHAV. RES. 499, 503 (1991) (showing that power-based analyses suggest that seven-variable regression model consists of minimum of 102 cases to show medium effect sizes). Finally, we evaluated the intercorrelations between the independent variables. When correlations are high, say above .80, harmful levels of collinearity may result in biased parameter estimates. *See* Mark H. Licht, *Multiple Regression and Correlation*, *in* READING AND UNDERSTANDING MULTIVARIATE STATISTICS 45 (Laurence G. Grimm & Paul R. Yarnold eds., 1995) (stating that correlations between independent variables in excess of .80 should be considered "very problematic"). Our investigation revealed that none of the bivariate correlations between the independent variables exceeded an absolute value of .41. Results from the model diagnostic tests strongly suggested that collinearity was not a threat. For example, the estimates

are similar to Pearson's *r* estimates in that they range from -1.0 to +1.0.

TABLE 8
OLS REGRESSION MODEL

Variable	Willingness to Defer to the Criminal Justice System in the Future	
	Standardized Regression Coefficient	*Significance Level*
Moral Credibility	.265	.002
Male	−.072	.395
Age	−.128	.148
White	.062	.476
Education	−.134	.144
Household Income	.017	.859
Married	.167	.069

As can be seen in Table 8, the effect of moral credibility is positive and statistically significant, indicating that higher levels of moral credibility correspond to a greater willingness to defer to the criminal justice system. The effect of moral credibility is stronger than any of the other variables in the model, which means that it is more important in predicting deference to the criminal justice system than those other variables.[250] Indeed, it is the only one of the variables that is statistically significant.[251] The importance of this finding is under-

---

from the tolerance tests exceed .70, which is considered a conservative threshold in the social and behavioral sciences.

[250] The formal statistical interpretation of the moral credibility effect is as follows: Each standard deviation increase in the moral credibility scale corresponds to a .265 standard deviation increase in the willingness to defer to the criminal justice system in the future.

[251] A number of model statistics can be used to evaluate the fit of an OLS regression equation. The measure of joint correlation (or *F*-test) for the model presented in Table 8 indicates that the group of independent variables reliably predicts willingness to defer to the criminal justice system in the future ($F = 2.91$, significance level = .01). The coefficient of multiple determination (or R^2) shows that the model explains 13% of the variation about the dependent variable, willingness to defer. We explored whether other variables outside the scope of the theory being tested here also influence whether experienced respondents are willing to assist legal authorities during the criminal court process. Prior research has shown that citizens who perceive police processes as procedurally just report a greater willingness to participate in crime prevention programs. *See* Michael D. Reisig, *Procedural Justice and Community Policing—What Shapes Residents' Willingness To Participate in Crime Prevention Programs*, 1 POLICING: J. POL'Y & PRAC. 356, 364 (2007) (discussing results of survey showing that people who believe police exercise authority fairly are more willing to participate in crime preventon). Based on prior research, we reason that perceptions of procedural justice regarding court processes may also influence willingness to serve as a juror or witness in a criminal court case. When entered into the equation featured in Table 8, the procedural justice scale (a 7-item summated scale, Cronbach's alpha = .889) was a significant predictor (standardized regression coefficient = .303, significance level = .003).

scored by the fact that effective operation of the criminal justice system depends upon such deference from citizens.

To summarize, the study attempted to assess whether there are real-world crime-control benefits to administering justice in a manner that is consistent with the intuitions of justice of the community. After an analysis using both bivariate and multivariate statistical techniques, the results showed that respondents with criminal court experience who viewed their community courts as morally credible in dealing with criminal cases (specifically those involving violence, drugs/alcohol, and delinquency) expressed a greater willingness to defer to the criminal justice system in the future.[252] The results from the study empirically challenge the conventional wisdom that deviations from desert are essentially cost-free. Individuals who perceived failures of the criminal justice system were significantly less likely to say they would defer to the system in the future.[253]

D. *Limitations and Future Research*

Before discussing avenues for future research on the effects of moral credibility, we should note a limitation of the research strategy employed in Study 3. Like many social scientific studies that test directional research hypotheses, Study 3 used cross-sectional survey data from a general population sample. As previously noted, the responses provided by each participant were collected during individual telephone interviews. Cross-sectional data of this type only

---

[252] A potential limitation of the study concerns the use of a non-random subsample to estimate a behavioral outcome. Statistical problems arise when membership in the subsample is not independent from the outcome measure. When this is the case, selection bias becomes a threat. The most frequently employed approach for dealing with sample selection bias is Heckman's two-step correction. *See* Richard A. Berk, *An Introduction to Sample Selection Bias in Sociological Data*, 48 Am. Soc. Rev. 386, 393–96 (1983) (providing empirical application of Heckman's two-step correction using citizen survey data); James J. Heckman, *Sample Selection Bias as a Specification Error*, 47 Econometrica 153, 156–60 (1979) (providing formal demonstration of how two-step Heckman estimator can correct for sample selection bias). This two-step modeling process has several requirements, one of which is the inclusion of exclusion restrictions in the first-stage model (i.e., variables that predict the selection outcome in the first-stage model but are not related to the dependent variable in the second-stage model). Unfortunately, we were unable to construct a first-stage model that included exclusion restrictions that predicted membership in the subsample (i.e., recent personal or vicarious experience as a juror or witness). Accordingly, the extent to which sample selection bias was a problem in this study remains unknown.

[253] We assessed whether the correlation between moral credibility and willingness to defer to the criminal justice system differed between the two groups that make up our subsample—jurors and witnesses. We found that the estimates for jurors and witnesses were nearly identical. Grouping jurors and witnesses into a single subsample increases statistical power. Given the consistent bivariate relationship between the two key variables across these two groups, this approach is empirically justifiable.

allow us to make claims about relationships between key theoretical variables (i.e., moral credibility and willingness to defer) that are correlational in nature. Although the observed effect of moral credibility in Table 8 is consistent with our hypothesis, we cannot claim that the analysis presented above demonstrates a causal link between moral credibility and willingness to defer to the criminal justice system in the future. When considered alongside the results from the controlled experiments from Studies 2a and 2b, however, the weight of the evidence suggests that moral credibility is a salient causal mechanism in determining behaviors among members of the general public that help the criminal justice system function.

We encourage future researchers to investigate whether moral credibility predicts differences in the kinds of measures noted in the introduction to Part IV: the stigmatization effect of criminal apprehension and conviction, vigilantism, the willingness of citizens to assist or at least acquiesce in the system's judgments and directions, to internalize the system's pronouncements about what conduct is truly condemnable, and to defer to its commands in situations of criminalization grey areas.[254] Studies such as these will help determine the explanatory and predictive scope of moral credibility.

Research also needs to be conducted in other countries with criminal justice systems of noticeably different levels of moral credibility than that of the United States. Doing so would help determine whether the findings reported here can be replicated in settings outside the United States. Unfortunately, the general databases that currently exist, nationally and internationally, offer little opportunity for such testing. Ideally, research could examine a measure of moral credibility drawn from different societies with noticeably different levels of moral credibility in their criminal justice systems. One could then compare these two groups as to the predicted resulting attitudes and behaviors of cooperation with and deference to the system. If a

---

[254] Several recent studies have used legal compliance with soft crimes and cooperation with police scales and may prove useful in future studies on the effects of moral credibility. *See* Michael D. Reisig, Jason Bratton & Marc G. Gertz, *The Construct Validity and Refinement of Process-Based Policing Measures*, 34 CRIM. JUST. & BEHAV. 1005, 1014 (2007) (using compliance scale consisting of six minor offenses: "made a lot of noise at night," "bought something you thought might be stolen," "drank alcohol in a place you are not suppose [sic] to," "smoked marijuana," "illegally disposed of trash and litter," and "broke traffic laws"); Jason Sunshine & Tom R. Tyler, *The Role of Procedural Justice and Legitimacy in Shaping Public Support for Policing*, 37 L. & SOC. REV. 513, 541 (2003) (using compliance scale items that asked respondents whether they followed rules about seven types of behavior: "where to park a car legally," "how to legally dispose of trash and litter," "not making noise at night," "not speeding or breaking traffic laws," "not buying possible stolen items on the street," "not taking inexpensive items from stores or restaurants without paying," and "not using drugs such as marijuana").

system's moral credibility is higher, do we see higher levels of citizens reporting crimes to police, agreeing to serve as witnesses, internalizing the law's condemnation of newly criminalized conduct, following the legal instructions given to jurors, and a variety of other effects discussed in Part II?

CONCLUSION

At the start of this Article, we described the concerns of two quite different groups, traditionally opposed to one another, who had found common ground in their opposition to the recent shift toward desert as the primary distributive principle for criminal liability and punishment.[255] The first group—those concerned with what they see as the over-punitiveness of current criminal law—worries that setting desert as the dominant distributive principle means continuing the punitive doctrines that they find so objectionable, and perhaps even making things worse. The second group—those concerned with ensuring effective crime control—worries that a desert distributive principle will create many missed crime-control opportunities and will increase avoidable crime. The evidence we present should give some comfort to both groups that a shift toward desert will not undermine these goals.

The first group's concern about punitiveness rests upon a false assumption that the current punitive crime-control doctrines of which they disapprove are a product of and a manifestation of the community's intuitions of justice. As is clear from Study 1 reported in Part II, however, the reverse is true. The current crime-control doctrines seriously conflict with people's intuitions of justice by exaggerating the punishment deserved. Thus, a distribution of liability and punishment that tracks lay intuitions of justice would significantly reduce the injustice now present. As Part III explains, the modern crime-control doctrines are not a product of the community's sense of justice, but rather of the distortions inherent to American crime politics.

We also provide a persuasive response to the concerns of the second group: that a desert distributive principle will create many missed crime-control opportunities and will increase avoidable crime. Studies 2 and 3 reported in Parts IV and V help refute the common wisdom of the past half-century that it is cost-free for the system to deviate from desert in the pursuit of crime control through deterrence, incapacitation of the dangerous, and other such coercive crime-control programs. There are crime-control costs in deviating from desert that follow from the system's reduced moral credibility within the commu-

---

[255] *See supra* Section B of Introduction.

nity it governs. Those crime-control costs must be taken into account in setting an effective crime-control program. The power of the forces of normative social influence and internalization of norms, and reasons to be increasingly skeptical about the crime-control effectiveness of the traditional mechanisms of coercive crime control,[256] suggest that, in the long run, doing justice may be the most effective means of fighting crime.

In conclusion, we believe that the studies reported here will give assurances to both groups concerned about a shift to desert as the distributive principle for criminal liability and punishment. The shift to a desert distribution—specifically empirical desert—will not seriously undermine the criminal justice system's crime-control effectiveness—and indeed may enhance it—and is not likely to increase the system's punitiveness—and instead is more likely to reduce it—in order to better track the community's shared intuitions of justice.

---

[256] *See* ROBINSON, DISTRIBUTIVE PRINCIPLES, *supra* note 5, at 21 (discussing reason to be skeptical of crime control effectiveness of measures that deviate from desert).

APPENDIX A

TEXT OF STUDY 1'S "MILESTONE" SCENARIOS

1. UMBRELLA MISTAKE – John takes another person's umbrella assuming it to be his own because it is has the same unusual color pattern as his own, a fact that the police confirm.

2. WOLF HALLUCINATION – Another person slips a drug into John's food, which causes him to hallucinate that he is being attacked by a wolf. When John strikes out in defense, he does not realize that he is in fact striking a person, a fact confirmed by all of the psychiatrists appointed by the state, who confirm John could not prevent the hallucination.

3. WHOLE PIES FROM BUFFET – The owner has posted rules at his all-you-can-eat buffet that expressly prohibit taking food away; patrons can only take what they eat at the buffet. The owner has set the price of the buffet accordingly. John purchases dinner at the buffet, but when he leaves he takes with him two whole pies to give to a friend.

4. CLOCK RADIO FROM CAR – As he is walking to a party in a friend's neighborhood, John sees a clock radio on the backseat of a car parked on the street. Later that night, on his return from the party, he checks the car and finds it unlocked, so he takes the clock radio from the backseat.

5. MICROWAVE FROM HOUSE – While a family is on vacation, John jimmies the back door to their house and steps into their kitchen. On the counter, he sees their microwave, which he carries away.

6. SLAP AND BRUISING AT RECORD STORE – A record store patron is wearing a cap that mocks John's favorite band. John follows him from the store, confronts him, then slaps him in the face hard, causing him to stumble. The man's face develops a harsh black and yellow bruise that does not go away for some time.

7. STITCHES AFTER SOCCER GAME – Angry after overhearing another parent's remarks during a soccer match in which John's son is playing, John approaches the man after the game, grabs his coffee mug, knocks him down, then kicks him several times while he is on the ground, knocking him out for several minutes and causing cuts that require five stitches.

8. ATTEMPTED ROBBERY AT GAS STATION – John demands money from a man buying gas at a gas station. When the man refuses, John punches the man several times in the face, breaking his jaw and causing several cuts that each require stitches. He then runs off without getting any money.

9. Clubbing During Robbery – To force a man to give up his wallet during a robbery attempt, John beats the man with a club until he relinquishes his wallet, which contains $350. The man must be hospitalized for two days.

10. Mauling by Pit Bulls – Two vicious pit bulls that John keeps for illegal dog fighting have just learned to escape and have attacked a person who came to John's house. The police tell John he must destroy the dogs, which he agrees to do but does not intend to do. The next day, the dogs escape again and maul to death a man delivering a package.

11. Stabbing – John is offended by a woman's mocking remark and decides to hurt her badly. At work the next day, when no one else is around, he picks up a letter opener from his desk and stabs her. She later dies from the wound.

12. Ambush Shooting – John knows the address of a woman who has highly offended him. As he had planned the day before, he waits there for the woman to return from work and, when she appears, John shoots her to death.

APPENDIX B
TEXT OF STUDY 1'S "CRIME-CONTROL" SCENARIOS

A. INCORRECT LOBSTER CONTAINER – John and two other seafood importers import lobster from Honduras shipped in plastic containers. Honduran law (but not U.S. law) requires that the containers be cardboard. John is convicted of a U.S. federal law that criminalizes the importation of fish or wildlife in violation of foreign law.

B. SHOOTING OF TV – When he was younger, John committed a number of offenses: twice convicted for burglarizing an unoccupied building, once convicted of throwing a rock at a car, and once convicted of stealing electricity. Several decades later, John, now 59, is annoyed by the constant arguing between his two sons about what to watch on television. On this day, he stops the argument by picking up the .22-caliber revolver that his oldest son left on a nearby table and shooting the television.

C. MARIJUANA UNLOADING – John frequently helps move furniture for hourly pay for the man from whom he rents a room. On this occasion, as he is unloading boxes at the house where he lives, he discovers that some contain marijuana. He nonetheless helps with the unloading but insists that the boxes with marijuana be stored other than in the house in which he lives. Some time later, authorities seize 47 of the boxes that contained 1169 kilograms of marijuana.

D. UNDERAGE SEX BY MENTALLY RETARDED MAN – John is a 20-year-old mentally retarded man with an IQ of 52. He is introduced to Jane, who says she is 16, a fact confirmed by her friends. They have several long telephone conversations. On this evening, John is stranded without a ride home and notices Jane's house nearby. From her bedroom window she sees him coming and directs him to use a nearby ladder. They talk for several hours, then have consensual intercourse. John leaves about 4:30 a.m. 8 1/2 months later, Erica gives birth and her parents contact the police. She was only 13 at the time of the intercourse.

E. SEX WITH FEMALE REASONABLY BELIEVED OVERAGE – John, 19 years old, lets a runaway stay in his apartment. She tells him she is 18. He reasonably believes that she is over the legal age of 16 and has consensual intercourse with her several times. He is later arrested because she in fact is 14 years old.

F. AIR CONDITIONER FRAUD – John promises to fix the air conditioner in a local bar where he is having a drink. The bar owner gives him $129 for parts, which he takes, but he has no intention of returning to do the job. He has been previously convicted of committing such frauds more than a half dozen times.

G. Cocaine in Trunk - John runs through a red light in the early morning and is pulled over by police. After arresting John for possession of a small amount of marijuana, the police search his car and find a small package of cocaine in the trunk, two-thirds of a kilo, about the size of a soda can and a half. John has no prior criminal record.

H. Cocaine Overdose – John is asked to bring cocaine to a "drug party." Three of the people at the party and John shoot up with the cocaine. One of them uses too much and overdoses and dies. John is arrested for his homicide.

I. Killing Officer Believed to be Alien – John suffers from paranoid schizophrenia of a subtype characterized by delusions and hallucinations. He believes alien life forms, usually disguised as government agents, are trying to kill him. He keeps a bird in his car to warn of airborne poison. He sets fishing line with beads and wind chimes throughout his house as an alarm system against alien invasion. On this occasion, he circles his neighborhood block blaring loud music in an attempt to keep the aliens away. A policeman comes in response to complaints about the excessive noise. Believing the officer to be an alien who has come to kill him, John shoots and kills the officer.

J. Accomplice Killing During Burglary – John agrees to help another man burglarize a house while the owner is away. Neither man is armed. When the owner returns unexpectedly, John is surprised when the other man shoots and kills the owner with a gun the man apparently found in a nightstand.

K. Drowning Children to Save Them from Hell – Jane and her husband are very religious. With their five young children, they live in a trailer. Jane is mentally ill and has several times attempted suicide, mutilated herself, failed to feed her children, and believes there are cameras in the ceilings. She comes to believe that because she is a bad mother, her children are doomed to eternal torment in hell. In order to save them from this state, she drowns them all in the bathtub.

L. Accidental Teacher Shooting – John, 13 years old, is upset about being suspended from school for ten days just before summer vacation for throwing water balloons. He returns to the middle school to say good-bye to friends. When told by a seventh grade teacher, with whom he has a good relationship, that he must leave, he pulls out a pistol and points it at the teacher. The gun discharges, hitting the teacher and killing him.

APPENDIX C
SENTENCES FOR STUDIES 2A'S AND 2B'S SEVEN "HIGH DISILLUSIONMENT" CASES

Title	Summary Description (The studies used more detailed descriptions.)	Average punishment imposed by subjects in Studies 2a and 2b, respectively	Punishment imposed by court
Case 1. Possession of Weapon By Federal Prison Guard	John, a disabled guard at a federal prison, is prosecuted under a state weapon possession statute that exempts any "guard of any state prison or of any penal correctional institution." John thinks he qualifies.	2 months; 2 months	3 years
Case 2. Convenience Store Murder Inaction	Two women at a convenience store argue. One stabs the other. After the attacker flees, the victim is bleeding profusely but unable to stand up and get help. John steps over her and takes a photograph of her with his cell phone but does not call for an ambulance. If he had anonymously called 911, the victim would not have died.	3.8 years; 2.9 years	No liability— legal rules do not permit liability for such inaction
Case 3. Sex With Female Reasonably Believed To Be Age of Consent	19-year-old John lets two runaways stay at his apartment. The girls tell him they are 18 years old and he reasonably believes them because they look at least 18. Each have consensual intercourse with him. He is convicted of two counts of sexual assault of a child because the girls in fact are under 16.	1.3 years; 2.3 years	50 years
Case 4. Seafood Import	John imports seafood from Honduras. While the law of his state does not require it and while John does not know it, Honduran law requires that cardboard rather than plastic containers be used for the shipment (in order to help the country's lumber industry). John is convicted of violating a law in his state that criminalizes the importation of wildlife in violation of a foreign law.	3.5 months; 6 months	8 years

Case 5. Shooting of TV	30 years ago, John was convicted of burglarizing an unoccupied building and, 5 years later, of throwing a rock at an automobile driven by his father-in-law. Now age 59, John is frustrated by the constant arguing between his two adult sons, who still live at home, over what television program to watch. Using a gun his oldest son left on the table, he shoots out the television set.	9 months; 11 months	15 years imprisonment without possibility of parole
Case 6. Upper East Side Rapist	Jane is followed into her apartment building by John who forces his way into her apartment and, threatening her with a knife, anally rapes her. John does the same thing to ten other women in the area. Jane one day sees John on the street and notifies police, who arrest him.	33.9 years; 32.7 years	No liability— defendant was son of a diplomat
Case 7. Air Conditioner Fraud	Many years ago, the 21-year-old John used his employer's credit card to pay $80 for four new tires without permission. He pled guilty to felony fraud. A few years later, John forged a check for $28.36 to pay rent at a hotel, another felony. On a hot August day, John, now 30 years old, is in a bar and offers to fix the AC unit, which he claims needs a new compressor, for $120.75. The owner gives him the money, but John never returns.	4.4 years; 3.3 years	Life in prison without possibility of parole

APPENDIX D
SENTENCES FOR STUDY 2B'S SEVEN "LOW DISILLUSIONMENT" CASES
(for text of scenarios, see Appendix A)

Title	Average punishment imposed by subjects in Study 2b	Average punishment imposed by courts as reported to subjects
1. Umbrella Mistake	4 days	No liability
2. Wolf Hallucination	7 days	3 months, 10 days
3. Clock Radio from Car	11 months	5 months, 2 days
4. Slap and Bruising at Record Store	19 months	12 months
5. Attempted Robbery at Gas Station	5.7 years	5 years
6. Mauling by Pit Bulls	17.7 years	15 years
7. Ambush Shooting	41 years	Life

[8]

SENTENCING GUIDELINES AT THE CROSSROADS OF POLITICS AND EXPERTISE

RACHEL E. BARKOW[†]

INTRODUCTION

When Minnesota created the first sentencing commission in 1978 and the first sentencing guidelines in 1980, it was hard to predict where the guidelines movement would go. More than three decades

[†] Segal Family Professor of Law and Regulatory Policy, New York University School of Law, and Faculty Director, New York University Center on the Administration of Criminal Law. Portions of this Article are drawn from testimony I gave before the United States Sentencing Commission on the status and future of the Federal Sentencing Guidelines at a regional hearing in New York on July 10, 2009. *See* Rachel E. Barkow, Professor of Law & Faculty Director, Ctr. on Admin. of Sentencing Law, N.Y. Univ. Sch. of Law, Statement Before the U.S. Sentencing Comm'n, Regional Hearings (July 10, 2009), *available at* http://www.ussc.gov/Legislative_and_Public_Affairs/Public_Hearings_and_Meetings/20090709-10/Barkow_testimony.pdf. I thank Kevin Friedl for his excellent research assistance and the participants at the *University of Pennsylvania Law Review* symposium, "Sentencing Law: Rhetoric and Reality." I also owe thanks to the Ford Foundation and to the Filomen D'Agostino and Max E. Greenberg Faculty Research Fund at NYU for their generous support.

and twenty sentencing guideline regimes later,[1] it is still not easy to foresee what will become of sentencing commissions and guidelines. The past decade alone has witnessed tremendous changes in sentencing law and policy that were hard to imagine even just a few years before they occurred. The Supreme Court's landmark sentencing decisions in *Apprendi v. New Jersey*,[2] *Blakely v. Washington*,[3] and *United States v. Booker*,[4] the reform of federal crack cocaine laws, and a financial crisis that has sparked significant sentencing reforms have all been monumental and, to some extent, unexpected developments. These seismic shifts will undoubtedly alter the landscape going forward in similarly unpredictable ways.

As this Symposium looks to the future and what it holds for sentencing guidelines, it is important to proceed with caution and a healthy dose of modesty. None of us really knows what will happen. But one helpful way to approach the future is to reflect on some of the key lessons we have learned in the more than thirty years with sentencing commissions and guidelines. There have been consistent themes and struggles, and there is no reason to believe these core issues will dissipate going forward. In this Article, I highlight these struggles and analyze how they can productively guide the future of sentencing guidelines.

Although I divide this Article into four different topics, they are united under one umbrella: the tension that arises from the fact that sentencing commissions must produce guidelines that are simultane-

---

[1] *See* Rachel E. Barkow & Kathleen M. O'Neill, *Delegating Punitive Power: The Political Economy of Sentencing Commission and Guideline Formation*, 84 TEX. L. REV. 1973, 1994 tbl.1 (2006) (listing eighteen guideline regimes as of publication in June 2006). Alabama's guidelines became effective in the fall of 2006, and the District of Columbia has guidelines as well. *See* Act of Apr. 5, 2006, No. 312, § 2, 2006 Ala. Acts 663, 663 (codified at ALA. CODE § 12-25-34.1 (2006)); D.C. SENTENCING & CRIMINAL CODE REVISION COMM'N, VOLUNTARY SENTENCING GUIDELINES MANUAL (2011), *available at* http://acs.dc.gov/acs/frames.asp?doc=/acs/lib/acs/pdf/2011_Voluntary_Sentencing_Guidelines_Manual.pdf.

[2] *See* 530 U.S. 466, 490 (2000) ("[I]t is unconstitutional for a legislature to remove from the jury the assessment of facts that increase the prescribed range of penalties to which a criminal defendant is exposed. . . . [S]uch facts must be established by proof beyond a reasonable doubt." (first alteration in original) (quoting Jones v. United States, 526 U.S. 227, 252-53 (1998) (Stevens, J., concurring)) (internal quotation marks omitted)).

[3] *See* 542 U.S. 296, 304-05 (2004) (holding a 90-month sentence invalid under the Sixth Amendment where the sentencing scheme required the judge to make additional factual findings beyond the jury verdict to impose that sentence).

[4] *See* 543 U.S. 220, 237 (2005) (applying *Blakely*'s Sixth Amendment analysis to Federal Guidelines cases).

ously reflective of the best empirical and expert knowledge about sentencing and acceptable to political overseers. The battle between expertise and politics is a familiar one for all administrative agencies, but it is particularly fraught for sentencing commissions. This is because the politics of crime is, in William Stuntz's memorable phrasing, "pathological,"[5] and because the expertise involved is less scientific— or at least appears to be less scientific—than in other regulatory fields.[6] Striking the proper balance between these often-competing forces must be the central mission of every sentencing commission as it crafts guidelines. This Article's central inquiry is how commissions manage the tension between expertise and politics given what we know about commissions and guidelines.

Part I begins by considering a topic that provides common ground for both experts and politicians: data. Guidelines are at their best and most effective when they are based on sound empirical data and professional expertise. Achieving that outcome often requires commissions to consider what empirical information most influences political actors. Whether the data represent the fiscal impact of proposed sentencing laws or the effect of sentencing laws on different populations, empirical information has had a profound impact on sentencing law and policy and will undoubtedly continue to do so.

Part II turns to a related empirical question: the relationship between race and sentencing guidelines. A concern with racial disparities was a driving force of the guidelines movement, and it is thus a topic of political importance. Yet we remain uncertain today whether guidelines have eased or exacerbated racial disparities. Sentencing commissions can no longer stand on the sidelines of this question. While commissions cannot make policy calls about what to do with the racial disparities in the criminal justice system, they are ideally placed to study sentencing patterns and practices to better understand the relationship between sentencing guidelines, their enforcement, and the racial composition of the prison population. It should be the goal of every sentencing commission to use its expertise to arm elected representatives with as much data as possible on the question of race and criminal justice so those officials can make decisions informed by facts, not assumptions or inaccurate impressions.

---

[5] William J. Stuntz, *The Pathological Politics of Criminal Law*, 100 MICH. L. REV. 505 (2001).

[6] *See* Rachel E. Barkow, *Administering Crime*, 52 UCLA L. REV. 715, 734-35 (2005) (explaining why legislators might view sentencing as more accessible than more technical fields of regulation).

While Parts I and II focus on the ways in which expertise and politics can come together, Part III confronts the question of what commissions should do when there is a conflict between politics and expertise in crafting guidelines. Commissions must adapt to the political environment in which they operate to achieve real-world change. But commissions should not let politics override the agency's expert mission unless the agency's political overseers demand it and no other viable options present themselves. The relationship between guidelines and mandatory minimums offers an example of this dynamic. Mandatory minimums are often set by legislatures based on political factors that conflict with a commission's expert judgment about how best to set guidelines. This Part argues that guidelines should stay true to expert assessments and that mandatory minimums should trump the guidelines only in cases in which the mandatory minimums are expressly applicable. An entire system of guidelines should not be determined by legislative judgments that are contrary to sentencing expertise unless the legislative body makes it clear that it desires this outcome. Commissions must respond to political will, but that does not mean that they should compromise their professional judgments unless the legislature directly commands them to do so.

Part IV concludes by exploring important limits on what guidelines can accomplish. If we have learned anything from the past that can inform our future expectations, it is that there are limits to what guidelines can do, even when they are based on the best empirical information available. Guidelines must strike the difficult balance between individualization and uniformity. Ultimately, it is critical to recognize that no amount of expertise can fully resolve this tension. Guidelines will never be perfect and comprehensive, and there will always need to be some play in the joints.

Guidelines have been limited in another way: they govern judges, and sometimes parole officials, but they do not address prosecutorial discretion. To be sure, commissions could and should do more to address the relationship between guidelines and prosecutorial power. But here too there are limits to what a commission can accomplish with guidelines, even when armed with all the data in the world. Because some amount of prosecutorial discretion is necessary and inevitable, guidelines must account for that reality.

Finally, it is important for commissions and guidelines not to neglect an often forgotten actor in the criminal justice system: the jury. The jury is the quintessential foil to a model based on expertise, as it is comprised of lay people with no specialized knowledge of crime or punishment. Yet it is important to remember that at the heart of any criminal justice system are questions of morality and justice that are not amenable to charts and data but rather are suited for juries comprised of members of the community. Commissions must be attuned to the jury's role as well.

I. DATA

Although political judgment and expert opinion often conflict, in the sentencing guidelines context they come together through data. Many kinds of data might reflect expert knowledge, yet only certain types of data have currency in political debates over crime. Information on the costs of proposed sentencing reforms is the most effective data sentencing commissions can produce to obtain legislative approval of guidelines.

Nearly every state with a sentencing commission has made a cost projection system a central part of its mission. Minnesota's demonstrated success in pioneering and using fiscal forecasting to maximize the effectiveness of the state's limited resources has led other states to follow suit.[7] These state sentencing commissions and their respective legislatures value cost projection data because the data allow them to allocate efficiently their limited crime-fighting resources to establishing guidelines.[8] State legislators have frequently modified proposed laws in light of expert forecasting by a state sentencing commission. Sometimes states increase sentences in light of cost data, knowing that they can afford the expense. Other times, states decrease sentences for some crimes, often nonviolent crimes, to prioritize scarce prison resources for violent crimes and to reduce crime at a lesser cost. The data thus assist elected officials no matter what their policy goals.

---

[7] *See* Letter from the Ctr. on the Admin. of Criminal Law, N.Y. Univ. Sch. of Law, to the U.S. Sentencing Comm'n 3 (Aug. 29, 2008), *available at* http://www.law.nyu.edu/ ecm_dlv3/groups/public/@nyu_law_website__centers__center_on_administration_of_ criminal_law/documents/documents/ecm_pro_058383.pdf (noting that "virtually every sentencing commission has followed" Minnesota's sentencing commission model, which included cost projections in its mandate).

[8] *See* Barkow, *supra* note 6, at 809 (noting that "[a]lmost every state to adopt a guideline system since the middle of the 1980s has opted to require some version of an impact statement" and that these cost estimates have "proven to be effective in cutting costs by slowing incarceration rates and prison overcrowding"); Letter from the Ctr. on the Admin. of Criminal Law, *supra* note 7, at 3 (arguing that cost projections allow lawmakers to "[a]chieve a more rational and effective criminal justice system that maximizes . . . crime reduction benefits from . . . criminal justice expenditures").

1604   *University of Pennsylvania Law Review*   [Vol. 160: 1599

States that have used these forecasts to maximize their resources have not experienced an increase in crime rates. Indeed, during the last twenty years—the period over which most states have made use of these estimates—crime rates have largely declined or stabilized. Between 1992 and 1999, homicide rates declined to 1960s levels.[9] The national crime rate reached a historic low in 2000.[10] During this period of lower crime rates, states used cost projections to make the most of their limited resources by slowing both the growth of their incarceration rates and the rate of spending on corrections.[11] Indeed, these forecasts have been so useful that the American Bar Association has included the use of cost forecasts as a key recommendation in its proposed Model Sentencing Act.[12] The Act requires an impact analysis on the theory that "it is in every state's interest to coordinate resource and policy decisions."[13]

These forecasts have not only influenced particular sentencing debates, they have also improved the overall political standing of state commissions with their respective legislatures. State commissions that use forecasts "have found that, over time, as their resource projections have been shown to be accurate and objectively-determined, their legislatures have placed ever greater stock in their forecasts, affording the commissions a deepening reputation for credibility, and allowing their research to play a more powerful role in legislative deliberations."[14]

Cost forecasting is particularly important in today's strained economic climate. The states spent $51.1 billion on corrections in 2010, constituting 3.1% of their annual budgets.[15] After a brief dip between 2009 and 2010, state corrections budgets resumed their upward climb last year; early tallies for fiscal year 2011 put the total at $51.7 billion.[16] At the federal level, where the government spends over $5 billion on

---

[9] *See* Alfred Blumstein & Joel Wallman, *The Recent Rise and Fall of American Violence*, *in* THE CRIME DROP IN AMERICA 1, 3-4 (Alfred Blumstein & Joel Wallman eds., 2000).

[10] Emma Schwartz, *Crime Rates Shown to Be Falling*, U.S. NEWS & WORLD REP., June 11, 2008, http://www.usnews.com/news/national/articles/2008/06/11/crime-rates-shown-to-be-falling.

[11] *See* Barkow & O'Neill, *supra* note 1, at 2008-09.

[12] STANDARDS FOR CRIMINAL JUSTICE: SENTENCING § 18-2.3 (1994).

[13] Kevin R. Reitz & Curtis R. Reitz, *Building a Sentencing Reform Agenda: The ABA's New Sentencing Standards*, 78 JUDICATURE 189, 194 (1995).

[14] Kevin R. Reitz, Am. Law Inst., *Model Penal Code: Sentencing, Plan for Revision*, 6 BUFF. CRIM. L. REV. 525, 592-93 (2002).

[15] NAT'L ASS'N OF STATE BUDGET OFFICERS, STATE EXPENDITURE REPORT 2010, at 52 (2011), *available at* http://nasbo.org/sites/default/files/2010%20State%20Expenditure%20Report.pdf.

[16] *Id.*

corrections,[17] these expenditures are rising rapidly. From 1982 to 2003, the federal government increased corrections expenditures by 925%.[18] Moreover, between 1995 and 2004, the federal prison population increased at an annual average rate of 7.8%, compared to an average annual increase of 2.7% in the states.[19] The federal system, which is the largest prison system in the country,[20] exceeds its capacity by 36%.[21] Using cost forecasting, the federal and state governments could realize fiscal rationality and implement better, and more cost-effective, criminal justice policies. And the commissions providing this information could potentially improve their standing and influence with their respective legislatures by providing valuable information on the costs of any policy under consideration.

Because legislative debates often overlook the availability and best use of resources, this enforced cost projection is particularly valuable. The extent to which many sentencing laws require large capital expenditures—such as the maintenance and construction of prison facilities or the hiring of staff—often goes unrecognized. Although the costs of longer terms of imprisonment might be worth it for many offenses and offenders, the money spent on some extended prison terms could be better spent somewhere else: for example, confining more serious offenders, providing alternatives to incarceration for some nonviolent offenders, or making more money available for policing or education. Because the political process does not always reasonably consider how to allocate its resources,[22] commission-provided cost data

---

[17] *See* KRISTEN A. HUGHES, U.S. DEP'T OF JUSTICE, BUREAU OF JUSTICE STATISTICS, BULLETIN: JUSTICE EXPENDITURE AND EMPLOYMENT IN THE UNITED STATES, 2003, at 3, 9, *available at* http://www.bjs.gov/content/pub/pdf/jeeus03.pdf (reporting total federal spending on corrections—defined broadly to include incarceration, community supervision, and rehabilitation programs—at $5.55 billion in 2003). Federal expenditures in 2003 were $2.59 trillion dollars. OFFICE OF MGMT. & BUDGET, EXEC. OFFICE OF THE PRESIDENT, HISTORICAL TABLES, BUDGET OF THE U.S. GOVERNMENT, FISCAL YEAR 2012, at 22 tbl.1.1 (2011), *available at* http://www.gpo.gov/fdsys/pkg/BUDGET-2012-TAB/pdf/BUDGET-2012-TAB.pdf.

[18] *See* HUGHES, *supra* note 17, at 2.

[19] PAIGE M. HARRISON & ALLEN J. BECK, U.S. DEP'T OF JUSTICE, BUREAU OF JUSTICE STATISTICS, BULLETIN: PRISON AND JAIL INMATES AT MIDYEAR 2004, at 2 tbl.1 (2005), *available at* http://bjs.ojp.usdoj.gov/content/pub/pdf/pjim04.pdf.

[20] *Id.* at 1.

[21] PAUL GUERINO ET AL., U.S. DEP'T OF JUSTICE, BUREAU OF JUSTICE STATISTICS, BULLETIN: PRISONERS IN 2010, at 7 (2011) *available at* http://bjs.ojp.usdoj.gov/content/pub/pdf/p10.pdf.

[22] *See* Rachel E. Barkow, *Federalism and the Politics of Sentencing*, 105 COLUM. L. REV. 1276, 1292 (2005) ("The current political process is disproportionately likely . . . to ignore or pay far less attention to the costs of incarceration.").

can focus attention on fiscal concerns and provide politicians with the information they need to ensure that limited government funds are spent wisely.

This vision of a sentencing commission's role comports with the overall place of agencies in government and their ability to use expertise to serve political goals. Cost-benefit analysis is a centerpiece of the modern regulatory state, particularly at the federal level. For example, the Office of Management and Budget engages in a cost-benefit analysis for regulations proposed by executive agencies.[23] The Federal Sentencing Commission is not subject to this oversight, but its Guidelines should be influenced by efficiency concerns all the same. Sentencing policies, like all other government policies, should seek to make government as efficient and effective as possible. States are not as attentive to cost-benefit analysis as the federal government, but in many states, policies are similarly evaluated for their effect on state budgets.[24] It is essential to good governance, at both state and federal levels, to ensure that any proposed policy maximizes welfare at the lowest cost.[25]

The data that unite politics and expertise are not limited to costs. A sound evaluation of sentencing laws must look at not only the costs but also the benefits of these laws. To that end, in addition to producing information on the costs of various sentencing proposals, commissions are well positioned to collect data on the effect various sentencing proposals have on recidivism and crime rates. This information is salient in political debates and can motivate political action.

Some sentencing commissions, including those in Pennsylvania, North Carolina, and Kansas, have explicit mandates to release this kind of information. Pennsylvania empowers its commission to "[c]ollect

---

[23] *See* Exec. Order No. 13,563, 76 Fed. Reg. 3821 (Jan. 21, 2011).

[24] JASON A. SCHWARTZ, INST. FOR POLICY INTEGRITY, 52 EXPERIMENTS WITH REGULATORY REVIEW: THE POLITICAL AND ECONOMIC INPUTS INTO STATE RULEMAKING 87 (2010), *available at* http://policyintegrity.org/files/publications/52_Experiments_with_Regulatory_Review.pdf (noting that "45 states require some form of economic impact analysis" when considering the implementation of new regulations).

[25] *See* STEPHEN HOLMES & CASS R. SUNSTEIN, THE COST OF RIGHTS: WHY LIBERTY DEPENDS ON TAXES 228-29 (1999) (arguing that public deliberation should be focused on, among other things, how much to spend on a given right and "the optimal package of rights, given that the resources that go to protect one right will no longer be available to protect another right"); RICHARD L. REVESZ & MICHAEL A. LIVERMORE, RETAKING RATIONALITY: HOW COST-BENEFIT ANALYSIS CAN BETTER PROTECT THE ENVIRONMENT AND OUR HEALTH 12-13 (2008) (discussing the advantages of cost-benefit analysis in government decisionmaking, even for government regulation motivated by goals other than efficiency, because it achieves more rational government programs, increases accountability and transparency, and structures and channels exercises of discretion by government decisionmakers).

systematically and disseminate information regarding effectiveness of parole dispositions and sentences imposed."[26] In 2006, the Pennsylvania Commission on Sentencing began a multiyear study of sentencing's effect on recidivism.[27] Similarly, North Carolina's commission has a statutory command to collect data and regularly report on both adult and juvenile recidivism.[28] Kansas's mandate to its commission is even broader. Its statute requires the agency to "analyze . . . and make recommendations for improvements in criminal law, prosecution, community and correctional placement, programs, release procedures and related matters including study and recommendations concerning the statutory definition of crimes and criminal penalties and review of proposed criminal law changes."[29]

The Washington State Institute for Public Policy provides the preeminent model for how data collection can improve public policy. The Institute analyzes alternatives to incarceration, measures sentencing laws' effects on recidivism, and assesses the cost effectiveness of criminal justice programs.[30] Created by the state legislature in 1983, the Institute researches a wide array of public policy issues.[31] In the area of criminal law, the Institute works directly with state agencies and lawmakers to provide data and concrete recommendations on specific policies. For example, the Washington Department of Corrections contracted with the Institute to determine best practices for community supervision of offenders,[32] and the state legislature asked for an evaluation of the effects of a 2003 law on recidivism rates.[33]

---

[26] 42 PA. CONS. STAT. ANN. § 2153(a)(11) (West Supp. 2011).

[27] *Effectiveness of Sentencing Project*, PA. COMM'N ON SENTENCING, http://pcs.la.psu.edu/publications-and-research/research-and-evaluation-reports/special-reports/effectiveness-of-sentencing-project (last visited Mar. 15, 2012).

[28] N.C. GEN. STAT. ANN. § 164-48 (West 2007); N.C. GEN. STAT. ANN. § 164-47 (West, Westlaw through S.L. 2012-1 at the 2011 Regular Session of the General Assembly).

[29] KAN. STAT. ANN. § 74-9101 (West Supp. 2010).

[30] *See generally* WASH. STATE INST. FOR PUB. POLICY, http://www.wsipp.wa.gov/default.asp (last visited Mar. 15, 2012).

[31] *Id.*

[32] *See* ELIZABETH K. DRAKE, WASH. STATE INST. FOR PUB. POLICY, "WHAT WORKS" IN COMMUNITY SUPERVISION: INTERIM REPORT 1 (2011), *available at* http://www.wsipp.wa.gov/rptfiles/11-12-1201.pdf (outlining the research questions posed by the Department of Corrections for the Institute's report on community supervision).

[33] *See* ELIZABETH K. DRAKE ET AL., WASH. STATE INST. FOR PUB. POLICY, INCREASED EARNED RELEASE FROM PRISON: IMPACTS OF A 2003 LAW ON RECIDIVISM AND CRIME COSTS, REVISED 1 (2009), *available at* http://www.wsipp.wa.gov/rptfiles/09-04-1201.pdf (providing an overview of the legislature's request and finding that the 2003 law decreased recidivism overall, lowered prison costs, and increased earnings through labor).

To be sure, arguments based on cost-benefit analyses will not always win the day in political debates. The politics of crime remain too heated for that. But when the time is politically right, even once-ignored data can reemerge to influence policy.

Consider in this regard the U.S. Sentencing Commission. Congress has vested the Commission with a research and data collection function, instructing it to "develop means of measuring the degree to which the sentencing, penal, and correctional practices are effective in meeting the purposes of sentencing"[34] and to "collect systematically the data obtained from studies, research, and the empirical experience of public and private agencies concerning the sentencing process."[35] The Sentencing Commission has produced extensive and well-researched reports on issues such as mandatory minimum sentencing laws,[36] the disparity between crack and powder cocaine,[37] alternatives to incarceration,[38] and a host of other topics.[39] Congress has often ignored the Commission's advice and recommendations[40]—as it did when the Commission proposed eliminating the disparity between sentences for crack and powder cocaine in 1995.[41] But Commission reports that Congress and the Executive branch initially ignored have, over time, influenced the debate over sentencing. For example, with the passage of the Fair Sentencing Act of 2010,[42] Congress finally revised its approach to the disparate treatment of crack and powder co-

---

[34] 28 U.S.C. § 991(b)(2) (2006).

[35] *Id.* § 995(a)(13).

[36] *See, e.g.,* U.S. SENTENCING COMM'N, SPECIAL REPORT TO THE CONGRESS: MANDA-TORY MINIMUM PENALTIES IN THE FEDERAL CRIMINAL JUSTICE SYSTEM (1991), *available at* http://www.ussc.gov/Legislative_and_Public_Affairs/Congressional_Testimony_and_Reports/Mandatory_Minimum_Penalties/199108_RtC_Mandatory_Minimum.htm.

[37] *See* U.S. SENTENCING COMM'N, REPORT TO THE CONGRESS: COCAINE AND FEDERAL SENTENCING POLICY (2007), *available at* http://www.ussc.gov/Legislative_and_Public_Affairs/Congressional_Testimony_and_Reports/Drug_Topics/200705_RtC_Cocaine_Sentencing_Policy.pdf.

[38] *See* U.S. SENTENCING COMM'N, ALTERNATIVE SENTENCING IN THE FEDERAL CRIMINAL JUSTICE SYSTEM (2009), *available at* http://www.ussc.gov/Research/Research_Projects/Alternatives/20090206_Alternatives.pdf.

[39] *See generally* U.S. SENTENCING COMM'N, GUIDE TO PUBLICATIONS & RESOURCES (2010–2011), *available at* http://www.ussc.gov/Publications/2010_Guide_to_Publications_and_Resources.pdf (providing a list of reports that the Commission has prepared).

[40] *See* Barkow, *supra* note 6, at 767-70.

[41] *See* U.S. SENTENCING COMM'N, SPECIAL REPORT TO THE CONGRESS: COCAINE AND FEDERAL SENTENCING POLICY (1995), *available at* http://www.ussc.gov/Legislative_and_Public_Affairs/Congressional_Testimony_and_Reports/Drug_Topics/199502_RtC_Cocaine_Sentencing_Policy/index.htm.

[42] Pub. L. No. 111-120, 124 Stat. 2372.

caine offenses, referring to the Commission's research on the subject when it did so.[43]

II. RACE

The emergence of sentencing guidelines is in large measure a story about the desire for racial justice.[44] Unfortunately, even a cursory look at criminal justice in the United States—in states with or without guidelines—demonstrates that questions of racial justice have hardly been answered. The numbers show a widely disproportionate impact on some racial and ethnic minorities. Blacks and Hispanics are disproportionately incarcerated relative to their numbers in the general population. While the American population is 12.6% black and 16.3% Hispanic,[45] blacks comprise 37.9% of the American prison population, and Hispanics 22.3%.[46] Of 216,361 federal prisoners, 81,211 individuals (37.5%) are black and 74,931 (34.6%) are Hispanic.[47] In 2010, 71.4% of federal drug offenders were black or Hispanic.[48] More than 11% of black men under the age of 40 are imprisoned, and more than 20% of black men born since the late 1960s have spent at least a year, and typically two, in prison for a felony conviction.[49] Some cities have 40-50% of their young black men under some form of criminal justice system supervision.[50] "If brought together in one incorporated region,

---

[43] Attorney General Holder referred to the Commission's report on the crack-powder disparity in his speech reaffirming the Department's commitment to seeking an end to that disparity. *See* Eric Holder, Att'y Gen., Remarks for the Charles Hamilton Houston Institute for Race and Justice and Congressional Black Caucus Symposium: Rethinking Federal Sentencing Policy 25th Anniversary of the Sentencing Reform Act (June 24, 2009) [hereinafter Holder Speech], *available at* http://www.justice.gov/ag/speeches/2009/ag-speech-0906241.html.

[44] *See* Barkow, *supra* note 6, at 742 ("The left supported sentencing reform based on a concern . . . that minorities and the poor were being disproportionately penalized."); *cf.* U.S. SENTENCING GUIDELINES MANUAL § 5H1.10 (2011) (stating that race, among other factors, is "not relevant in the determination of a sentence").

[45] U.S. CENSUS BUREAU, OVERVIEW OF RACE AND HISPANIC ORIGIN: 2010, at 4 tbl.1 (2011), *available at* http://www.census.gov/prod/cen2010/briefs/c2010br-02.pdf.

[46] U.S. DEP'T OF JUSTICE, PRISONERS IN 2010, at 26 tbl.12 (2011), *available at* http://bjs.ojp.usdoj.gov/content/pub/pdf/p10.pdf.

[47] FED. BUREAU OF PRISONS, *Quick Facts About the Bureau of Prisons*, http://www.bcp.gov/news/quick.jsp (last visited Mar. 15, 2012).

[48] *See* U.S. SENTENCING COMM'N, SOURCEBOOK OF FEDERAL SENTENCING STATISTICS 2010 tbl.34, *available at* http://www.ussc.gov/Data_and_Statistics/Annual_Reports_and_Sourcebooks/2010/Table34.pdf.

[49] *See* BRUCE WESTERN, PUNISHMENT AND INEQUALITY IN AMERICA 19 tbl.2, 26 (2006).

[50] *See* Alfred Blumstein, *Racial Disproportionality of U.S. Prison Populations Revisited*, 64 U. COLO. L. REV. 743, 744 (1993) (noting that 42% of black men in their twenties in

the black males who are now in prison would instantly become the twelfth-largest urban area in the country."[51] Almost one-third of black men can expect to be incarcerated during their lifetimes under current trends. Black children are more than seven times more likely to have a parent in prison than white children.[52]

Some states have begun to investigate why the numbers are so disproportionate. For example, in 2008, Iowa was the first state in the country to pass legislation requiring a minority impact statement for any proposed criminal law.[53] Both parties overwhelmingly endorsed the law—the Iowa House voted unanimously in favor of it, and the Senate approved the law 47-2.[54] The law requires that all new criminal laws be examined before they are passed to determine how they will impact minorities.[55] The minority impact statement requirement allows Iowa legislators to anticipate disparities and, where possible, pursue an alternative path to accomplishing its goals to avoid those disparities.

Connecticut and Illinois have also recently passed legislation that mandates a legislative evaluation of the racial and ethnic impact of certain criminal justice legislation. Connecticut requires racial impact statements as part of a broader statute that creates remedies for wrongfully convicted individuals.[56] It passed overwhelmingly in the House (126-11) and unanimously in the Senate, and was signed into law in June 2008.[57] Illinois followed suit a few months later when Governor Rod Blagojevich signed Senate Bill 2476 into law.[58] The bill as

---

Washington, D.C., and 56% in Baltimore are "under the control of the criminal justice system on any day").

[51] DERRICK BELL, SILENT COVENANTS: BROWN V. BOARD OF EDUCATION AND THE UNFULFILLED HOPES FOR RACIAL REFORM 183 (2004).

[52] THE SENTENCING PROJECT, INCARCERATED PARENTS AND THEIR CHILDREN 2 (2009), *available at* http://www.sentencingproject.org/Admin/Documents/publications/inc_incarceratedparents.pdf. This problem promises to become only more acute because "[e]thnic and racial minorities will comprise a majority of the nation's population in a little more than a generation, according to new Census Bureau projections." Sam Roberts, *A Generation Away, Minorities May Become the Majority in U.S.*, N.Y. TIMES, Aug. 14, 2008, at A1.

[53] Act of Apr. 17, 2008, 2008 Iowa Acts 312 (codified at IOWA CODE § 2.56 (2009)).

[54] *See* H. JOURNAL, 82nd Gen. Assemb., Reg. Sess., at 897-98 (Iowa 2008), *available at* https://www.legis.iowa.gov/docs/pubs/hjweb/pdf/March%2025,%202008.pdf#page=27; S. JOURNAL, 82nd Gen. Assemb., Reg. Sess., at 869 (Iowa 2008), *available at* https://www.legis.iowa.gov/docs/pubs/sjweb/pdf/March%2031,%202008.pdf#page=19.

[55] 2008 Iowa Acts 312.

[56] *See* 2008 Conn. Acts 489 (Reg. Sess.).

[57] *Id.*

[58] *See* Commission to Study Disproportionate Justice Impact Act, Pub. Act 095-0995, 2008 Ill. Laws 3698.

introduced mandated legislative racial impact reports;[59] the form that eventually passed instead created a panel to study the problem.[60] This commission disbanded after issuing its report in December 2010, which included a recommendation that lawmakers reconsider racial impact statements.[61]

In Wisconsin, Governor Jim Doyle did not wait for legislative action to mandate racial impact statements for agency regulations. In May 2008, he issued an executive order that required all state agencies to track the racial impact of their policies and created a Racial Disparities Oversight Commission.[62] The panel was not empowered to issue racial impact statements per se but was tasked with reducing racial disparity across the criminal justice system.[63]

Some sentencing commissions have also explored the impact of the guidelines on different racial groups.[64] Even before Iowa's legislature mandated racial impact statements, Minnesota's sentencing commission was the first body actually to provide such estimates. It began doing so on its own initiative in early 2008.[65] The U.S. Sentenc-

---

[59] S.B. 2476, 95th Gen. Assemb., Reg. Sess. (Ill. 2007–2008).

[60] Commission to Study Disproportionate Justice Impact Act § 5, 2008 Ill. Laws at 3699.

[61] *See* ILL. DISPROPORTIONATE JUSTICE IMPACT STUDY COMM'N, FINAL REPORT 42-43 (2010), *available at* http://www.centerforhealthandjustice.org/DJIS_FullReport_FINAL.pdf (recommending that disproportionate minority contact with the justice system should be addressed through state-level policy, statutory changes, additional funding, and the reduction of the harmful long-term effects of conviction).

[62] *See* Wis. Gov. Exec. Order No. 251 (May 2008), *available at* https://docs.legis. wisconsin.gov/code/executive_orders/2003_jim_doyle/2008-251.pdf (noting that the Commission on Reducing Racial Disparities in Wisconsin "was created to determine whether discrimination is built into the criminal justice system at each stage of the criminal justice continuum").

[63] *See id.* (ordering the Commission "to exercise oversight and advocacy concerning programs and policies to reduce disparate treatment of people of color across the spectrum of the criminal justice system"). In early 2010, Governor Scott Walker disbanded the Commission as part of a broader austerity program. Alex Ebert, *State Cuts Poet Laureate Board; He'll Keep Job*, WISCNEWS.COM, Mar. 8, 2011, 11:45 PM, http://www.wiscnews.com/portagedailyregister/news/article_6d75a0bc-4a11-11e0-9255-001cc4c002e0.html.

[64] For general overviews of noncommission research on the relationship between race and sentencing, see JOHN H. KRAMER & JEFFERY T. ULMER, SENTENCING GUIDE-LINES: LESSONS FROM PENNSYLVANIA 90-101 (2009), which surveys research on Pennsylvania's sentencing disparities, and Cassia C. Spohn, *Thirty Years of Sentencing Reform: The Quest for a Racially Neutral Sentencing Process*, 3 CRIM. JUSTICE 427, 429 (2000), which lists studies in this area.

[65] *See* MINN. SENTENCING GUIDELINES COMM'N, REPORT TO THE LEGISLATURE 14 (2009), *available at* http://www.msgc.state.mn.us/data_reports/jan_leg_report/leg_report_jan09.pdf; Marc Mauer, *Racial Impact Statements: Changing Policies to Address Disparities*, 23 CRIM. JUSTICE, Winter 2009, at 16, 17 (naming Iowa as the first state to pass a law mandating such considerations).

1612   *University of Pennsylvania Law Review*   [Vol. 160: 1599

ing Commission has also studied the relationship between the federal guidelines and race.[66] The sentencing commissions in Maryland and North Carolina have both mounted comprehensive investigations into racial disparity and sentencing in the past,[67] though neither has returned to the issue in detail in recent years.[68] Depending on the institutional design of a state's sentencing commission, the commission may be the best-placed agency not only to investigate potential racial disparities in sentencing but also to apply what it learns to its future policy choices.

But more should be done. Given the critical role guidelines play in jurisdictions where they exist, it is crucial to understand the effect guidelines have on defendants of different races. Exploring this question falls within the statutory mandates of most sentencing commissions, as they are often charged with avoiding unwarranted

---

[66] *See, e.g.,* U.S. SENTENCING COMM'N, DEMOGRAPHIC DIFFERENCES IN FEDERAL SENTENCING PRACTICES: AN UPDATE OF THE *BOOKER REPORT*'S MULTIVARIATE REGRESSION ANALYSIS 23 (2010) (analyzing the disparity in sentences between different racial and ethnic groups over time); U.S. SENTENCING COMM'N, FIFTEEN YEARS OF GUIDELINES SENTENCING: AN ASSESSMENT OF HOW WELL THE FEDERAL CRIMINAL JUSTICE SYSTEM IS ACHIEVING THE GOALS OF SENTENCING REFORM 113-35 (2004) [hereinafter FIFTEEN YEAR REVIEW] (providing an in-depth analysis of the Guidelines' racially disparate effects and identifying the sentencing rules that create the most significant adverse impacts on African Americans). For a criticism of the Sentencing Commission's 2010 Report, see Jeffery T. Ulmer et. al, *Racial Disparity in the Wake of the* Booker/Fanfan *Decision: An Alternative Analysis to the USSC's 2010 Report,* 10 CRIMINOLOGY & PUB. POL'Y 1077 (2011).

[67] *See* DEBORAH DAWES ET AL., N.C. SENTENCING & POL'Y ADVISORY COMM'N, SENTENCING PRACTICES UNDER NORTH CAROLINA'S STRUCTURED SENTENCING LAWS 4 (2002), *available at* http://www.nccourts.org/courts/crs/councils/spac/documents/disparityreportforwebr_060209.pdf (attempting to establish the presence of sentencing disparities in North Carolina); CLAIRE SOURYAL & CHARLES WELLFORD, REPORT TO THE MARYLAND COMMISSION ON CRIMINAL SENTENCING POLICY, AN EXAMINATION OF UNWARRANTED SENTENCING DISPARITY UNDER MARYLAND'S VOLUNTARY SENTENCING GUIDELINES 9-22 (1997), *available at* http://www.msccsp.org/Files/Reports/Souryal%20and%20Wellford%20(1997)%20An%20Examination%20of%20Unwarranted%20%E2%80%A6.pdf (evaluating the prevalence of racial disparities in sentencing in Maryland).

[68] North Carolina's commission does issue annual reports with sentencing statistics that include breakdowns based on race. *See, e.g.,* AMY CRADDOCK & TAMARA FLINCHUM, N.C. SENTENCING & POL'Y ADVISORY COMM'N, STRUCTURED SENTENCING STATISTICAL REPORT FOR FELONIES AND MISDEMEANORS: FISCAL YEAR 2009/10, at 9 fig.D (2011), *available at* http://www.nccourts.org/Courts/CRS/Councils/spac/Documents/statisticalrpt_fy09-10.pdf. The most recent treatment of this issue by Maryland's Commission on Racial and Ethnic Fairness in the Judicial Process was in a 2004 study based on the experiences of actual litigants, witnesses, and jurors and their perceptions of bias in the criminal justice system, but the study did not focus on sentencing. REPORT OF THE MD. COMM'N ON RACIAL & ETHNIC FAIRNESS IN THE JUDICIAL PROCESS (2004), *available at* http://www.courts.state.md.us/publications/racialethnicfairness04.pdf.

disparities.[69] These data will undoubtedly be enormously important to elected officials. If a legislator knows that a proposed sentencing law will disproportionately affect a particular group, he can consider alternatives that achieve the same goals without the disparate effects.

More research is also needed on the relationship between prosecutorial discretion, sentencing, and race. The work of the Vera Institute of Justice provides a helpful model. The Institute has been working with district attorneys in Milwaukee, San Diego, and Mecklenburg County, North Carolina as part of its Prosecution and Racial Justice initiative.[70] The pilot program uses statistical indicators and empirical evidence in an attempt to increase transparency and uniformity in prosecutors' charging decisions by alerting them when their offices' aggregate decisionmaking appears to exhibit racial or ethnic biases.[71]

The goal of all this research is to unearth the causes of the striking disparities we see in the population under penal supervision and understand how shifts in sentencing policy could ameliorate these disparities.

III. WHEN POLITICS AND EXPERTISE CONFLICT

Although there will be many opportunities for commissions to use expert data in a way that influences political overseers, inevitably there will be conflicts. Legislative sentencing determinations are a mixed lot. Some determinations are the product of deliberation and consideration of relevant data. Others—perhaps most—are the product of political posturing based on little-to-no research.[72] The question for commissions is how this latter type of legislative judgment should affect the formulation of guidelines. Many times, the answer is clear because the legislature has left no role for the commission. This happens when

---

[69] *See, e.g.,* 28 U.S.C. § 991(b)(1)(B) (2006) ("The purposes of the United States Sentencing Commission are to . . . establish sentencing policies and practices for the Federal criminal justice system that . . . provide certainty and fairness in meeting the purposes of sentencing, *avoiding unwarranted sentencing disparities* among defendants with similar records who have been found guilty of similar criminal conduct . . . ." (emphasis added)).

[70] *See Prosecution and Racial Justice,* VERA INST. JUST., http://www.vera.org/project/prosecution-and-racial-justice (last visited Mar. 15, 2012) (describing a pilot program designed to identify evidence of racial or ethnic bias among district attorney's offices).

[71] *Id.*

[72] *See, e.g.,* Brief of Amicus Curiae Center on the Administration of Criminal Law, New York University School of Law, Supporting Petitioners at 6-10, Dorsey v. United States & United States v. Hill, at *5-10, Nos. 11-5683 & 11-5721 (consolidated) (U.S. Feb. 1, 2012), 2012 WL 362807 (detailing the absence of research to support Congress's decision to create the 100-to-1 crack/powder ratio in cocaine sentencing).

a legislature passes a statute demanding a particular guideline amendment or enacts a sentencing law that trumps a guideline.

In other situations, however, there may be a political judgment that is at odds with the commission's judgment. Then there is an open question for the commission to resolve: should the commission extend the political judgment into a related area or limit the political decision to its sphere and take it no further? In this context, the best approach for a commission—unless the legislative body explicitly orders otherwise—is to accept legislative judgments based on political factors but not to extend them further than the legislature commands if doing so would conflict with the commission's expert judgment.

The relationship between sentencing guidelines and mandatory minimum sentences set by legislatures without careful study provides a prime illustration of this point. If the mandatory minimum is not the product of careful study or research, then keying all guidelines to that minimum exacerbates the harms of a failure to reflect on the consequences and goes against an agency's mission to base its decisions on empirical information and studies.

The U.S. Sentencing Commission's treatment of mandatory minimums for drug crimes provides a cautionary tale. When the Commission developed its initial set of sentencing guideline ranges for drug trafficking, it incorporated statutory mandatory minimum sentences into the federal sentencing grid so that the trafficking guidelines, like mandatory minimum laws, were driven largely by the drug quantity involved.[73] Moreover, the sentences for all quantities have been set based on the sentences Congress selected for mandatory minimums.[74] Thus, offenses involving five or more grams of crack cocaine, as well as all other drug offenses carrying a five-year mandatory minimum penalty, were assigned a base offense level of 26, which corresponded to a guideline range of 63-78 months for a defendant in the lowest criminal history category.[75] Likewise, drug offenses carrying a ten-year mandatory minimum penalty were assigned a base offense level of 32, which corresponded to a sentencing guideline range of 121-151 months for a defendant in the lowest criminal history category.[76]

---

[73] *See* FIFTEEN YEAR REVIEW, *supra* note 66, at 15, 48-49 (noting that "statutory minimum penalties" drove drug trafficking guidelines and that the minimums were often "triggered" by the weight of the substance containing the drug, not just the amount of the pure drug found).

[74] *Id.* at 49.

[75] *Id.*

[76] *Id.*

"[N]o other decision of the Commission," the Commission has noted, "has had such a profound impact on the federal prison population."[77] Indeed, this initial set of judgments accounts for much of the increase in the federal prison population and for a large measure of the racial disparities in its composition.[78] Judges have widely condemned these Guidelines as too harsh.[79] And yet the Commission has offered little to defend this choice. The Commission did not explain at the time this fundamental decision was made what was the motivating rationale.

So why did the Commission take this path? Most likely, it was trying to be respectful of its political overseers. Once Congress set these sentences, the Commission seems to have wanted to respect the role of mandatory minimums in the overall sentencing landscape and avoid "cliffs" in sentencing, where offenders find themselves with vastly different penalties depending on whether they reached the mandatory minimum threshold or fell just below it.[80] The discussion at one of its regional hearings suggested that the Commission might have taken this approach to comply with 28 U.S.C. § 994, which requires the Commission to issue guidelines "consistent with all pertinent provisions of any federal statute," including mandatory minimum sentencing statutes.[81]

There are, however, several problems with the Commission's decision to give mandatory minimum laws such a broad influence on the Federal Guidelines. First, a particular sentencing statute, such as a statute requiring mandatory minimums, is often at odds with other

---

[77] *Id.*

[78] *See id.* at 76 ("Given that drug trafficking constitutes the largest offense group sentenced in the federal courts, the two-and-a-half time increase in their average prison term has been the single sentencing policy change having the greatest impact on prison populations."); *see also id.* at 132 ("This one sentencing rule contributes more to the differences in average sentences between African-American and White offenders than any possible effect of discrimination.").

[79] *See id.* at 52 (discussing a 2002 survey that found that 31% of district judges ranked "drug sentencing as the greatest or second greatest challenge for the guidelines in achieving the purposes of sentencing" and that "73.7% of district court judges and 82.7[%] of circuit court judges rated drug punishments as greater than appropriate to reflect [their] seriousness").

[80] *See id.* at 50. Another explanation posited in the Commission's *Fifteen Year Review* is that the Commission imposed these mandatory minimums because the quantities are reasonable measures of harm. *See id.* at 49-50. But the report goes on to note, "Drug quantity has been called a particularly poor proxy for the culpability of low-level offenders, who may have contact with significant amounts of drugs, but who do not share in the profits or decision-making." *Id.* at 50.

[81] 28 U.S.C. § 994(a) (2006).

general statutory commands that a commission must follow. This situation holds true for the U.S. Sentencing Commission, which is required under 28 U.S.C. § 991(b)(1)(A) to establish guidelines that meet the sentencing purposes set out in 18 U.S.C. § 3553(a)(2).[82] These purposes include providing punishments that "reflect the seriousness of the offense," "promote respect for the law," and "provide just punishment."[83] The Commission would violate the command of § 3553(a)(2) by using mandatory minimums to set other sentences if those mandatory minimums did not fulfill one of the statute's goals. This conclusion is consistent with § 994 because the Guidelines can set sentences tied to drug quantities without reference to mandatory minimums while emphasizing that relevant mandatory minimums will trump a different Guidelines sentence. Indeed, this is the only approach that reconciles § 3553(a)(2) and § 994, and it justifies any cliffs that this sentencing scheme would create.

Further these types of cliffs are hardly new to criminal law. At common law, the line between grand larceny and petit larceny rested on whether the value of the property stolen exceeded twelve pence.[84] If the stolen amount was above this threshold, the larceny was a capital offense. But stealing any amount below twelve pence received a punishment of only a forfeiture and a whipping.[85] A sentencing scheme in which applicable mandatory minimums would trump sentences otherwise set by guidelines would not create such dramatic differences in punishment. Moreover, any time the legislature opts to set mandatory penalties on the basis of bright-line thresholds, it anticipates that cliffs will result. Thus, there is no reason for commissions to focus on avoiding these disparities in sentencing at the expense of their expert judgments about where sentences should be set.

More fundamentally, although allowing mandatory minimums to trump guidelines sentences would create some disproportionate sentences, the alternative approach of keying sentences to mandatory minimums leads to even greater disproportionality[86] and undercuts the value of using empirical information and expertise to establish sentences. Neither solution results in perfect sentencing across the board, so the best a commission can do is create a sentencing regime that is based as much as possible on its expert judgment. In the case

---

[82] *See id.* § 991(b)(1)(A).

[83] 18 U.S.C. § 3553(a)(2)(A).

[84] ROLLIN M. PERKINS & RONALD N. BOYCE, CRIMINAL LAW 335 (3d ed. 1982).

[85] *Id.*

[86] *See supra* notes 73-79 and accompanying text.

of the U.S. Sentencing Commission, statutory commands make this preference for expertise explicit. The Commission's guidelines must "reflect, to the extent practicable, advancement in knowledge of human behavior as it relates to the criminal justice process."[87] The Commission cannot ignore its statutory mandate to create a just sentencing regime based on knowledge and expertise and simply accept Congress's view about the sentence for one particular offense as the appropriate baseline for every other similar offense.

Congress did not consult the Commission in setting its mandatory minimums, and it did not base them on "advancement in knowledge of human behavior."[88] While mandatory minimums are binding, Congress has never explicitly stated that these minimums were meant to replace the Commission's expertise in setting all other guidelines sentences for which there are no mandatory minimums. Congress's failure to provide a simple directive indicating otherwise suggests that it left the question of appropriate sentences for offenses without mandatory minimums to the Commission's judgment.

There are good reasons to adopt a presumption that limits statutes based on political judgments to their narrowest interpretation unless there is evidence to the contrary. First, because legislators obtain valuable information from commissions, narrow interpretations of legislative enactments allow legislatures to update their policies in light of a commission's conclusions. If, for instance, a commission's expert judgment reveals that drug sentencing should vary from the legislative mandatory minimums, the legislature may use that information to revise its own approach to sentencing. Under the U.S. Sentencing Commission's current approach, in contrast, the legislature would not receive that feedback because its mandatory minimums would be accepted and incorporated wholesale into the guideline structure without the Commission's independent analysis. This wide application of legislative judgments stifles dialogue between the Commission and the legislature and fails to capitalize on the value of the expert assessments.

The Supreme Court's decision in *Kimbrough v. United States*[89] lends further support to this view. In *Kimbrough*, the Supreme Court held that federal district judges could deviate from a guidelines sentence based on a policy disagreement with the disparate treatment of crack

---

[87] 28 U.S.C. § 991(b)(1)(C).

[88] *Id.*

[89] 552 U.S. 85 (2007).

and powder cocaine.[90] In reaching this conclusion, the Court pointed to the Commission's own research disagreeing with the disparity.[91] The Court rejected the notion that federal statutes mandating minimum sentences that treated crack and powder differently "'[i]mplicit[ly]' require[] the Commission and sentencing courts" to treat the drugs differently.[92] The Court observed that the "statute, by its terms, mandates only maximum and minimum sentences," but "says nothing about the appropriate sentences within these brackets."[93] Consistent with the argument here, the Court "decline[d] to read any implicit directive into that congressional silence," especially when "Congress has shown that it knows how to direct sentencing practices in express terms."[94]

The Court further intimated that the Guidelines merit greater respect when they are based on the Commission's institutional expertise than when they are not. Because the guidelines addressing crack and powder cocaine were not based on empirical data but were solely tied to the congressional mandatory minimums, the Court noted that variances from those guidelines would not amount to an abuse of discretion if a district court concluded that adhering to them would yield a sentence greater than necessary to achieve the purposes of sentencing laid out in 18 U.S.C. § 3553(a).[95] Some lower courts have agreed that guidelines based on expertise and empirical data deserve more respect than those that are not.[96] It is likely that regardless of the standard of

---

[90]   *Id.* at 110.

[91]   *Id.* at 97-100 (citing Sentencing Guidelines for United States Courts, 72 Fed. Reg. 28,558, 28,571-72 (May 21, 2007); Amendments to the Sentencing Guidelines for United States Courts, 60 Fed. Reg. 25,074, 25,075-77 (May 10, 1995); U.S. SENTENCING COMM'N, *supra* note 37, at 8-10; U.S. SENTENCING COMM'N, REPORT TO THE CONGRESS: COCAINE AND FEDERAL SENTENCING POLICY, at iv, viii, 93-94, 96, 100-03 (2002); U.S. SENTENCING COMM'N, REPORT TO THE CONGRESS: COCAINE AND FEDERAL SENTENCING POLICY 2 (1997); and U.S. SENTENCING COMM'N, *supra* note 41, at 66-67, 174).

[92]   *Id.* at 102 (first and second alterations in original) (quoting Brief for the United States at 32, *Kimbrough*, 552 U.S. 85 (No. 06-6330), 2007 WL 2461473, at *32).

[93]   *Id.* at 102-03.

[94]   *Id.* at 103.

[95]   *Id.* at 109-10.

[96]   *See, e.g.*, United States v. Reyes-Hernandez, 624 F.3d 405, 418 (7th Cir. 2010) ("*Kimbrough* instructs sentencing courts to give *less* deference" where the Commission is not acting "'in its characteristic role,' in which it typically implements guidelines only after taking into account 'empirical data and national experience.'" (quoting *Kimbrough*, 552 U.S. at 109)); United States v. Arrelucea-Zamudio, 581 F.3d 142, 150 (3d Cir. 2009) (expressing agreement with the First Circuit's interpretation of *Kimbrough* in *United States v. Rodriguez*); United States v. Rodriguez, 527 F.3d 221, 227 (1st Cir. 2008) ("[G]uidelines and policy statements [not based on empirical data and national experience] deserve less deference . . . ." (citing *Kimbrough*, 552 U.S. at 109-10)). *But see,*

review, judges will have greater respect for guideline sentences grounded in empirical research than for those based on congressional decisions that rest on anecdotal cases instead of a comprehensive review of all relevant facts.

IV. THE LIMITS OF GUIDELINES

Having discussed the role of expertise in setting guidelines, it is important to note the limits of expertise itself when it comes to sentencing. Indeed, perhaps the greatest lesson to take away from the experience with the guidelines is that they can only do so much, even if they are grounded solely in expertise and are uncorrupted by pathological political dynamics. This Part discusses three important limits to any guidelines regime.

A. *Guidelines Cannot Capture All Human Behavior*

Any successful guidelines system must strike a balance between individualization and uniformity.[97] Put another way, guidelines should treat like cases alike but also acknowledge real differences. There is, at the risk of understatement, an inherent tension between these two goals.[98]

The guidelines movement grew out of dissatisfaction with discretionary and indeterminate sentencing regimes that focused too much on individualization and not enough on avoiding unjust disparities.[99]

---

e.g., United States v. Gonzales-Zotelo, 556 F.3d 736, 740-41 (9th Cir. 2009) (holding that *Kimbrough* authorized downward departures if the district court disagreed with the Commission's reasoning behind the Guidelines, not if the court disagreed with congressional policy).

[97] 28 U.S.C. § 991(b)(1)(B), for example, directs the U.S. Sentencing Commission to establish sentencing policies that

provide certainty and fairness in meeting the purposes of sentencing, avoiding unwarranted sentencing disparities among defendants with similar records who have been found guilty of similar criminal conduct while maintaining sufficient flexibility to permit individualized sentences when warranted by mitigating or aggravating factors not taken into account in the establishment of general sentencing practices.

28 U.S.C. § 991(b)(1)(B) (2006).

[98] *See, e.g.*, Eddings v. Oklahoma, 455 U.S. 104, 110 (1982) (explaining that "[s]ince the early days of the common law, the legal system has struggled to accommodate these twin objectives" of individualization and consistency).

[99] *See* FIFTEEN YEAR REVIEW, *supra* note 66, at xviii (citing the perceived unfairness of indeterminate sentencing as a factor behind the adoption of federal sentencing guidelines); Richard S. Frase, *State Sentencing Guidelines: Diversity, Consensus, and Unresolved Policy Issues*, 105 COLUM. L. REV. 1190, 1202 (2005) (describing state sentencing guidelines as "always motivated at least in part by a desire to make sentencing more

Unfortunately, the movement's reaction against the prior regime often placed too much emphasis on uniformity and not enough on individualization.

Exhibit A for this obsessive focus on uniformity is the federal system. The federal system has concentrated almost exclusively on eliminating judicial discretion, too often resulting in the exclusion of remedies that are proportionally based on individual conduct. Congress bears primary responsibility for this lopsided approach. For example, the congressional "25 percent rule" provides that the maximum of a sentencing guidelines range for a term of imprisonment "shall not exceed the minimum of that range by more than the greater of 25 percent or 6 months."[100] This law was meant to promote uniformity and restrict judicial discretion in sentencing.[101]

Congress further sought to limit judicial discretion to individualize sentences by enacting laws that trump the Guidelines. Mandatory minimum laws were the most significant measures aimed at curbing judicial discretion.[102] However, these mandatory minimums have not resulted in greater equality in sentencing because prosecutors retain unreviewable discretion as to whether or not they will charge an individual with an offense bearing a mandatory minimum sentence, a point that the Commission itself has noted.[103] When prosecutors do elect to charge defendants with offenses carrying mandatory minimums, they prevent judges from sentencing defendants proportionately based on individualized factors. Congress has enacted other statutes, like the

---

uniform and to eliminate unwarranted disparities"). *See generally* MARVIN E. FRANKEL, CRIMINAL SENTENCES: LAW WITHOUT ORDER (1973) (describing judicial discretion in sentencing as "terrifying and intolerable").

[100] 28 U.S.C. § 994(b)(2).

[101] *See* S. REP. NO. 98-225, at 168-69 (1983); *see also* U.S. Sentencing Comm'n, The Sentencing Reform Act of 1984: Principal Features (Nov. 1996) (unpublished Simplification Draft Paper), *available at* http://www.ussc.gov/Research/Working_Group_Reports/Simplification/SRA.HTM (reviewing how the Sentencing Commission has interpreted the 25 percent rule, and considering alternative readings to ensure fairness but to permit some discretion).

[102] *See* U.S. SENTENCING COMM'N, SPECIAL REPORT TO THE CONGRESS: MANDATORY MINIMUM PENALTIES IN THE FEDERAL CRIMINAL JUSTICE SYSTEM 8-9 (1991) (tracking the evolution of mandatory minimum laws in the context of the Guidelines).

[103] *See id.* at 89 ("[D]efendants who appear to be similar are charged and convicted pursuant to mandatory minimum provisions differentially depending upon race, circuit, and prosecutorial practices . . . .").

PROTECT Act,[104] that similarly limit judicial discretion to sentence based on individualized factors.

When they were mandatory, the Guidelines themselves prevented judges from achieving proportional punishments in many cases because they dramatically limited the grounds on which judges could depart from the guidelines. Since the Supreme Court's decision in *Booker*,[105] however, the federal system has placed more emphasis on individualizing sentences.[106] *Booker* gives judges some room to adjust sentences based on relevant individual differences in setting punishments by allowing them to deviate from the Guidelines to achieve the purposes of sentencing in 18 U.S.C. § 3553(a).

It is noteworthy that rates of within-guidelines sentences are roughly comparable throughout the country, regardless of whether the guidelines are mandatory or advisory, with most states seeing compliance rates around eighty percent.[107] The post-*Booker* experience in the federal system is consistent with this overall trend.[108] This con-

---

[104] Prosecutorial Remedies and Other Tools to End the Exploitation of Children Today (PROTECT) Act of 2003, Pub. L. No. 108-21, 117 Stat. 650 (codified as amended in scattered sections of 18, 21, 28, 42, and 47 U.S.C.).

[105] United States v. Booker, 543 U.S. 220 (2005).

[106] *See* D. Michael Fisher, *Striking a Balance: The Need to Temper Judicial Discretion Against a Background of Legislative Interest in Federal Sentencing*, 46 DUQ. L. REV. 65, 98 (2007) (*"Booker* has clearly wrought a new era in sentencing. Federal judges . . . again retain discretion to sentence individual offenders based on individual determinations."); Ryan W. Scott, *Inter-Judge Sentencing Disparity After* Booker*: A First Look*, 63 STAN. L. REV. 1, 17 & fig.2 (2010) (noting a gradual but marked increase in the percentage of federal sentences falling outside the Guideline ranges).

[107] *See* Ronald F. Wright, Professor of Law & Assoc. Dean for Academic Affairs, Wake Forest Univ. School of Law, Statement Before the U.S. Sentencing Commission, Regional Hearings Marking the 25th Anniversary of the Passage of the Sentencing Reform Act of 1984: The Power of Information Versus the Power of Enforcement, at 6-7 (Feb. 11, 2009), *available at* http://www.ussc.gov/Legislative_and_Public_Affairs/Public_Hearings_and_Meetings/20090210-11/Wright_statement.pdf (noting that guidance compliance rates for Pennsylvania, North Carolina, and Minnesota guidelines hovered around seventy-five percent despite dramatic differences in their legal force). States with purely advisory guidelines report similar compliance rates. *See, e.g.*, VA. CRIMINAL SENTENCING COMM'N, 2008 ANNUAL REPORT 16 fig.2 (2008), *available at* http://leg2.state.va.us/dls/h&sdocs.nsf/By+Year/RD4152008/$file/RD415.pdf (showing that Virginia's advisory guidelines have a compliance rate of 79.8%); Nat'l Ass'n of Sentencing Comm'ns, *Maryland*, SENTENCING GUIDELINE, Feb. 2009, at 7, *available at* http://thenasc.org/images/2009_February_Issue.pdf (reporting that Maryland's advisory guidelines have a compliance rate of approximately 80%, based on data from fiscal year 2008); David Oldfield, Mo. Sentencing Advisory Comm'n, Using the New Sentencing Tools 5 (June 26, 2006), *available at* http://www.mosac.mo.gov/file.jsp?id=45415 (reporting Missouri's 81.9% compliance rate with its advisory guidelines).

[108] The Commission's most recent quarterly report shows that judges are sentencing outside the guideline range without a government motion in 17.5% of cases. U.S.

sistency in the proportion of cases sentenced within guidelines and those sentenced outside of them reflects the fact that while there is a core of cases that guidelines can capture, there remains a substantial minority of cases that do not fit the grid. That the numbers are consistent across varied jurisdictions suggests that there is a strong pull for individualizing sentences.

The U.S. Sentencing Commission recently recognized this dynamic when it relaxed the limits on considering individual circumstances in sentencing. Before 2010, a defendant's age, mental and emotional conditions, physical condition, and military service were deemed "not ordinarily relevant."[109] Now the Commission's policy statement provides that these factors "may be relevant" in determining whether a departure is permitted if these factors are "present to an unusual degree and distinguish the case from the typical cases."[110] This shift was in many ways a product of judges' reliance on these individualized factors in the wake of *Booker* and of the Commission taking notice of the fact that these factors could be relevant in finding meaningful distinctions between cases.

It is, of course, hard to know where to strike the balance between individualization and uniformity. But a main lesson of the guidelines is that expertise only goes so far in identifying where that line should be drawn.

B. *Acknowledging the Power of Prosecutors*

Discretion in the criminal justice system does not disappear simply because judges are subject to greater control. On the contrary, placing greater limits on judges has led to other actors gaining power. This is the story of sentencing reform: as judges and parole officials have lost discretion, prosecutors have gained it. Once again, the federal story offers the lesson through a negative example. As Professor

---

SENTENCING COMM'N PRELIMINARY QUARTERLY DATA REPORT: 1ST QUARTER RELEASE 1 tbl.1 (2012) [hereinafter 2012 QUARTERLY DATA REPORT], *available at* http://www.ussc.gov/Data_and_Statistics/Federal_Sentencing_Statistics/Quarterly_Sentencing_Updates/USSC_2012_1st_Quarter_Report.pdf

[109] U.S. SENTENCING GUIDELINES MANUAL ch. 5, pt. H, introductory cmt. (2009); *see also id.* §§ 5H1.1, 5H1.3, 5H1.4, 5H1.11.

[110] U.S. SENTENCING GUIDELINES MANUAL ch. 5, pt. H, introductory cmt. (2011); *see also id.* §§ 5H1.1, 5H1.3, 5H1.4, 5H1.11.

Kate Stith has persuasively detailed, federal prosecutors have gained tremendous power since the Guidelines were adopted.[111]

Prosecutorial influence goes far beyond just the plea power. Federal prosecutors have enormous formal powers under the Guidelines through their ability to file substantial-assistance motions that lead to sentence reductions.[112] Government-sponsored motions are the primary reason sentences are set below the Guidelines. This occurs in roughly 26.4% of all cases.[113] This dwarfs all other bases for downward departures, which together amount to 17.5% of all cases.[114]

The Department of Justice often points to the Commission's statistics on sentences imposed within the Guideline range when expressing concern with the post-*Booker* disparities.[115] In a recent speech, Assistant Attorney General Lanny Breuer noted that "since the *Booker* decision, judges have increasingly been sentencing defendants to prison sentences outside the ranges prescribed by the guidelines."[116] As an example, he pointed to the wide disparity between the Southern and Western Districts of Texas, where 71.5% of federal sentences in fiscal year 2010 fell within the Guidelines ranges, and the Southern District of New York, where only 32.6% did.[117] "[M]ore and more," Breuer said, "the length of a defendant's sentence depends primarily on the identity of the judge assigned to the case, and the district in which he or she is in."[118] He went on to note the Commission's finding that racial and ethnic sentencing disparities increased in the wake of *Booker.*[119]

---

[111] *See* Kate Stith, *The Arc of the Pendulum: Judges, Prosecutors, and the Exercise of Discretion,* 117 YALE L.J. 1420, 1425 (2008) (arguing that the Guidelines "provided prosecutors with indecent power relative to both defendants and judges, in large part because of prosecutors' ability to threaten full application of the severe Sentencing Guidelines").

[112] *See* U.S. SENTENCING GUIDELINES MANUAL § 5K1.1.

[113] 2012 QUARTERLY DATA REPORT, *supra* note 108, at 1 tbl.1.

[114] *Id.*

[115] *See, e.g.,* Holder Speech, *supra* note 43 ("The percentage of defendants sentenced within the guidelines has decreased [since *Booker*].").

[116] Lanny A. Breuer, Assistant Att'y Gen., Speech at the American Lawyer/National Law Journal Summit (Nov. 15, 2011), *available at* http://www.justice.gov/criminal/pr/speeches/2011/crm-speech-111115.html.

[117] *Id.*; *see also* U.S. SENTENCING COMM'N, STATISTICAL INFORMATION PACKET: FISCAL YEAR 2010 SOUTHERN DISTRICT OF TEXAS 11 tbl. 8 (2010); U.S. SENTENCING COMM'N, STATISTICAL INFORMATION PACKET: FISCAL YEAR 2010 WESTERN DISTRICT OF TEXAS 11 tbl. 8 (2010); U.S. SENTENCING COMM'N, STATISTICAL INFORMATION PACKET: FISCAL YEAR 2010 SOUTHERN DISTRICT OF NEW YORK 11 tbl. 8 (2010).

[118] Breuer, *supra* note 116.

[119] *See* U.S. SENTENCING COMM'N, DEMOGRAPHIC DIFFERENCES IN FEDERAL SENTENCING PRACTICES: AN UPDATE OF THE BOOKER REPORT'S MULTIVARIATE REGRESSION ANALYSIS 2 (2010), *available at* http://www.ussc.gov/Research/Research_Publications/

However, government officials almost invariably overlook the fact that the vast majority of sentences outside the Guideline range are given at the government's request—because of either the government's fast-track policy or a prosecutor's substantial assistance motion, or for some other reason.

It is therefore simplistic and potentially misleading to suggest there is a problem with judicial discretion based on departure rates without looking into the impetus for those departures. For example, in the districts compared by Lanny Breuer, government-sponsored motions produce the greatest disparity.[120] In addition, districts cannot be meaningfully compared without accounting for differences in the cases that arise in different geographic areas. In the Southern and Western Districts of Texas, roughly 75% of the federal docket consists of low-level immigration and marijuana smuggling—cases where the sentences are relatively low under the guidelines and therefore judges feel no need to depart. The Southern District of New York, in contrast, has a large number of cases on the docket involving long guideline sentences for drug offenses because of the quantity involved that take little account of a defendant's personal culpability.[121] Prosecutors in these districts are therefore bringing different types of cases and filing different departure motions at different rates.

These statistics illustrate the breadth of prosecutorial discretion under the Guidelines. Prosecutors have broad power to dictate sentencing outcomes because they can determine how to charge an individual without facing judicial review of that decision.[122] Federal prose-prosecutors are also the gatekeepers of key departure motions and therefore have additional power to determine whether an individual's sentence should deviate from the Guidelines. Substantial assistance motions are the most common reason for a defendant to receive a sentence outside the Guidelines. Moreover, on average, judges will de-

---

2010/20100311_Multivariate_Regression_Analysis_Report.pdf ("Black male offenders received longer sentences than white male offenders. The differences in sentence length have increased steadily since *Booker*.").

[120] Letter from David E. Patton, Exec. Dir., Fed. Defenders of N.Y., Inc., et al., to Lanny A. Breuer, Assistant Att'y Gen., U.S. Dept. of Justice 2 (Nov. 22, 2011), *available at* http://sentencing.typepad.com/files/letter-to-lanny-breuer-from-defenders.pdf.

[121] *Id.* at 2-3.

[122] *See* FIFTEEN YEAR REVIEW, *supra* note 66, at 85-92 (discussing presentencing techniques used by prosecutors that affect sentencing, such as charging decisions, plea bargaining, and fact bargaining); Stith, *supra* note 111, at 1430 ("[T]he prosecutor, through her discretionary charging authority, effectively determines what the defendant's Guidelines sentencing range will be.").

part from the Guidelines to a "far greater" extent for substantial assistance motions than they will for other reasons.[123] Thus, whether a prosecutor views a defendant as sufficiently cooperative remains the number one basis by which a court distinguishes two defendants guilty of the same crime, and a favorable determination will more likely result in a greater departure from the Guidelines than any other reason.

Yet neither Congress nor the Commission has established guidelines for how prosecutors should assess cooperation for the purposes of sentencing discounts. In fact, all of the evidence suggests that districts differ greatly as to how they evaluate this factor and how they discount sentences for defendants who have provided substantial assistance to prosecutors. Some evidence also suggests that these district-level decisions may be influenced by race and gender—factors that should be irrelevant to the cooperation inquiry.[124] The fast-track program also differs by region,[125] and it too is a common basis for distinguishing among otherwise similarly situated defendants.

As long as guidelines apply only to judges, they will never resolve the disparity in the system and in fact may end up exacerbating the disparity by failing to provide a valuable check on prosecutors. This

---

[123] *See* FIFTEEN YEAR REVIEW, *supra* note 66, at 102-03 (conducting an analysis of sentences imposed in 2001 and noting that "[t]he mean departure length for substantial assistance was 43 months . . . while the mean departure length for other downward departures was just 20 months").

[124] *See* LINDA DRAZGA MAXFIELD & JOHN H. KRAMER, U.S. SENTENCING COMM'N, SUBSTANTIAL ASSISTANCE: AN EMPIRICAL YARDSTICK GAUGING EQUITY IN CURRENT FEDERAL POLICY AND PRACTICE 13-14 & exhibit 9 (1998), *available at* http://www.ussc.gov/ Research/Research_Publications/Substantial_Assistance/199801_5K_Report.pdf (illustrating that nonminorities and women are more likely to receive substantial assistance motions than racial or ethnic minorities and men); Rachel E. Barkow, *Institutional Design and the Policing of Prosecutors: Lessons from Administrative Law*, 61 STAN. L. REV. 869, 900 (2009) (discussing evidence that "personal characteristics" affect prosecutors' decisions about which defendants receive substantial assistance motions). *But see* FIFTEEN YEAR REVIEW, *supra* note 66, at 105 (discussing a reevaluation of the Maxfield & Kramer data that calls into question their findings regarding the role of race and gender).

[125] Alison Siegler, Observations, *Disparities and Discretion in Fast-Track Sentencing*, 21 FED. SENT'G REP. 299, 299-301 (2009) (describing both the regional disparities that result from fast-track sentencing and a circuit split over judges' authority to reduce this disparity); Memorandum from James M. Cole, Deputy U.S. Att'y Gen., on Department Policy on Early Disposition or "Fast-Track" Programs 2 (Jan. 31, 2012), *available at* http://www.justice.gov/dag/fast-track-program.pdf ("The existence of these programs in some, but not all, districts has generated a concern that defendants are being treated differently depending on where in the United States they are charged and sentenced."). In January 2012, the Department of Justice started requiring all districts to offer fast-track programs and implemented "uniform, baseline eligibility requirements for any defendant who qualifies for fast-track treatment, regardless of where that defendant is prosecuted." *Id.*

need for prosecutorial checks is another key lesson illustrating the limitations of guidelines.

C. *Respecting the Role of the Jury*

The Supreme Court has emphasized the jury's central relationship to sentencing since its decision in *Apprendi*.[126] However, its jurisprudence has thus far failed to address one of the starkest threats to the jury's role: sentencing guidelines that require judges to increase sentences on the basis of conduct for which the defendant has been acquitted. Only the Federal Guidelines take this approach, and the Sentencing Commission implemented it without a directive from Congress.

Congress has never specified—either in the Sentencing Reform Act or anywhere else—whether the Guidelines should follow a sentencing model that uses "real" offenses or "charge" offenses. A charge offense system bases the defendant's punishment on the charges for which he was convicted.[127] A real offense sentencing scheme looks to the defendant's actual conduct and is not limited to conduct that the jury finds to be criminal.[128] The original Sentencing Commission adopted a real offense sentencing model for the Guidelines. Therefore, many factors, not just the charged offenses, determine an individual's sentence. Relevant conduct that was not charged—or even relevant conduct that forms the basis of a charge of which the defendant was acquitted—can determine the Guidelines base offense level and can increase the sentence through upward adjustments and departures. In fact, in many cases relevant conduct can outweigh the charged offense in determining the defendant's sentence.[129]

For relevant conduct to have a bearing on the defendant's sentence, the prosecutor need only prove that conduct by a preponder-

---

[126] Apprendi v. New Jersey, 530 U.S. 466 (2000).

[127] *See* Stephen Breyer, *The Federal Sentencing Guidelines and the Key Compromises Upon Which They Rest*, 17 HOFSTRA L. REV. 1, 9 (1988).

[128] *Id.* at 10 (noting that a real offense system "bases punishment on the elements of the specific circumstances of the case").

[129] *See* Pamela B. Lawrence & Paul J. Hofer, *An Empirical Study of the Application of the Relevant Conduct Guideline § 1B1.3*, 10 FED. SENT'G REP. 16, 18 (1997) (relating the results of an empirical study on the vastly different sentencing ranges that can result from "relevant conduct" considerations); Jon M. Sands & Cynthia A. Coates, *The Mikado's Object: The Tension Between Relevant Conduct and Acceptance of Responsibility in the Federal Sentencing Guidelines*, 23 ARIZ. ST. L.J. 61, 71-72 (1991) (describing the importance of relevant conduct in federal sentencing and finding that most courts have held that "any criminal conduct alleged should be factored into the sentence").

ance of the evidence, even if a jury has already examined the evidence and acquitted the defendant of a charge based on that conduct. If the prosecutor meets this burden, the Guidelines instruct judges to increase the defendant's sentence on that basis, regardless of what happened at trial.[130] This instruction can substantially change a defendant's case. For example, the defendant in *United States v. Manor* was charged with one count of conspiracy to distribute 250 grams of cocaine and other distribution counts involving an additional 19 grams.[131] The jury acquitted him on the conspiracy count but convicted him on the intent to distribute 19 grams.[132] The sentencing judge found that the conspiracy to distribute 250 grams was relevant conduct, a finding that tripled the defendant's sentence exposure.[133] The jury's acquittal had no effect because the defendant faced the same punishment range as he would have had he been convicted of the conspiracy charge.

Allowing sentencing courts to consider conduct for which the defendant has been acquitted disregards the constitutional role of the jury. Under our Constitution, it is the defendant's right to have a jury definitively decide, beyond a reasonable doubt, whether or not he is guilty of a crime. When the law instructs a judge to override a jury acquittal based on the judge's own findings, it undermines both the effort jurors put into evaluating cases and the defendant's constitutional rights. Thus, even before the Court's *Apprendi/Booker* line of cases, judges and scholars criticized the Commission's decision to use acquitted conduct to set sentencing ranges.[134]

In *Booker*, the Court found that the Guidelines' mandate to use relevant conduct in sentencing proceedings violated the Constitution's

---

[130] *See* Frank O. Bowman, III, *The Failure of the Federal Sentencing Guidelines: A Structural Analysis*, 105 COLUM. L. REV. 1315, 1325 (2005) (explaining how the relevant conduct inquiry requires judges to consider a defendant's "uncharged, dismissed, and sometimes even acquitted conduct"). *See generally* William W. Wilkins, Jr. & John R. Steer, *Relevant Conduct: The Cornerstone of the Federal Sentencing Guidelines*, 41 S.C. L. REV. 495 (1990) (providing an overview of the rationale behind the relevant conduct rules and describing their practical application).

[131] 936 F.2d 1238, 1242 (11th Cir. 1991).

[132] *Id.*

[133] *See id.* (explaining that the district court's consideration of the conspiracy claim increased the defendant's "base offense level from 12 to 20").

[134] *See* Rachel E. Barkow, *Recharging the Jury: The Criminal Jury's Constitutional Role in an Era of Mandatory Sentencing*, 152 U. PA. L. REV. 33, 94 (2003) (discussing judges and commentators who have criticized the real offense sentencing scheme).

Sixth Amendment jury guarantee.[135] Thus, the Court ruled that judicial consideration of the Sentencing Guidelines would be advisory rather than mandatory.[136] However, *Booker* did not eliminate the consideration of acquitted conduct in determining defendants' sentences. Thus, the Guidelines preserve the problem of acquitted conduct increasing sentences. Advising judges to increase a sentence on the basis of relevant conduct, even when a jury acquitted a defendant of that conduct, may no longer violate the Constitution in fact,[137] but it stands in sharp tension with the jury's constitutional role because judges continue to comply with the Guidelines,[138] and the Guidelines continue to instruct judges to consider relevant conduct in sentencing.[139]

Congress did not command this result, nor is there any evidence in the Sentencing Reform Act's legislative history that suggests Congress even intended this outcome. Instructing judges to consider "real" conduct was a discretionary decision by one set of Commission members who seemed to believe that Guidelines could and should occupy the entire field.[140]

Other commissions have taken a more modest view of how far guidelines should sweep. More than a third of all states now have some form of guidelines, most of which were passed after the federal guidelines.[141] No state has followed the federal approach to real offense sentencing. States have achieved all the same successes with guidelines as the federal system, but without substantially intruding on the jury's function. As in the federal system, states have been able to increase the predictability and uniformity of their sentencing through guide-

---

[135] *See* 543 U.S. 220, 245 (2005) ("[T]he provision of the federal sentencing statute that makes the Guidelines mandatory . . . [is] incompatible with today's constitutional holding.").

[136] *Id.*

[137] *See, e.g.*, United States v. Watts, 519 U.S. 148, 154 (1997) ("[W]e are convinced that a sentencing court may consider conduct of which a defendant has been acquitted."); Witte v. United States, 515 U.S. 389, 406 (1995) (upholding the use of relevant conduct in determining a defendant's sentence within the legislatively authorized punishment range).

[138] *See supra* notes 107-08 and accompanying text.

[139] *See, e.g.*, United States v. Waltower, 643 F.3d 572, 577 (7th Cir. 2011) (upholding, once again, the constitutionality of considering acquitted conduct for sentencing and noting that every circuit to consider the question has ruled the same way).

[140] *See* Breyer, *supra* note 127, at 8-12 (describing the decisionmaking process behind the Commission's choice of a modified "real offense" system).

[141] *See* Barkow & O'Neill, *supra* note 1, at 1994 tbl.1 (listing eighteen states that use sentencing guidelines and their dates of adoption). Alabama joined the list when its sentencing guidelines went into effect in October 2006. Act of Apr. 5, 2006, No. 2006-312, § 2, 2006 Ala. Acts 663 (codified at ALA. CODE § 12-25-34.1 (2006)).

lines. There is no evidence that any state's failure to mandate the consideration of a defendant's acquitted conduct has led to increased
crime rates. Furthermore, many states have experienced decreases in
their incarceration rates since they passed their guidelines.[142]

The states' experiences thus show that a real offense sentencing
scheme is not necessary for maintaining low crime and incarceration
rates. The Commission's rationale that broadly worded federal criminal laws lack sufficient detail to form the basis for a charge offense
system[143] may support the use of uncharged conduct in general, but it
fails to support the use of acquitted conduct to increase sentences.

The Commission's other rationale for adopting the modified real
offense system also fails to excuse the Guidelines' use of a defendant's
acquitted conduct. The Commission justified this approach by arguing that a real offense sentencing scheme would curb the ability of
prosecutors to manipulate sentences through their decisions on charging and their power to hide facts relevant to the case.[144] But that justification does not account for the Guidelines' use of acquitted conduct
because, in cases where acquitted conduct is relevant, prosecutors have
brought the relevant charges out into the open already.   If anything,
the ability to use acquitted conduct bolsters the power of prosecutors
in this framework because it allows them to increase sentences after
trials have taken place, using a lower standard of proof and without
deferring to the rules of evidence. The use of acquitted conduct also
allows prosecutors to avoid the restrictions of the Double Jeopardy
Clause by essentially giving them a second try at inflicting punishment
for the same offense.

Again, the lesson is that guidelines have limits and other actors
must be considered. In our constitutional system, the jury occupies a
place of prominence, and guidelines should respect its role.

---

[142] *See* Barkow & O'Neill, *supra* note 1, at 2009 (explaining that "sentencing commissions act to curb growth rates of incarceration").

[143] *See, e.g.,* FIFTEEN YEAR REVIEW, *supra* note 66, at 25 ("[T]he statute-defined elements of many federal crimes fail to provide sufficient detail about the *manner* in which
the crime was committed to permit individualized sentences that reflect the varying
seriousness of different violations.").

[144] *See id.* ("[T]he Commission remained concerned that the charges to which defendants were subject would continue to depend to some extent on which prosecutors
were assigned to each case or in which district the offense was prosecuted, leading to
unwarranted sentencing disparity.").

CONCLUSION

The future of sentencing guidelines may depend on variables as diverse as the strength of the economy, appointments to the Supreme Court, and fluctuations in crime rates. But if we have learned anything from our experience thus far with guidelines, it is that the future will also continue to present to any sentencing authority the tension between expert assessments based on data and empirical facts, and political judgments based on popular will. This Article seeks to make some modest suggestions for navigating that divide based on what we know so far.

[9]

Departures from the Sentencing Guidelines

Andrew Ashworth*

Vinerian Professor of English Law, University of Oxford

ⓔ Courts' powers and duties; Riot; Sentencing guidelines

Summary

This article explores the 2009 Act's test for departing from sentencing guidelines, in the light of the Lord Chief Justice's judgment in the "riots" case of Blackshaw, *the wording of the statute, and relevant case-law.*

When may a court depart from a relevant sentencing guideline? A court's duty, according to s.125(1) of the Coroners and Justice Act 2009, is to follow the applicable guideline. First, according to s.125(3), the court should identify which of the offence-categories in the relevant guideline most resembles the offender's case (except where none of the categories sufficiently resembles the case at hand). Assuming that the offence-category has been identified, the court should then follow the steps set out in the guideline, taking account of aggravating and mitigating factors, and if some of those factors are particularly strong this may lead the court to move the case into a higher or lower category-range. That, however, does not count as a departure; it is merely a category change. A departure occurs when a court imposes a sentence outside the "offence-range", i.e. either below the floor of the lowest category-range or above the ceiling of the highest category-range indicated in the guideline.[1] If the court is minded to take that exceptional course, then according to s.125(1) it must be satisfied that it would be "contrary to the interests of justice" to impose a sentence within the offence-range. It has a duty to state why it is of that opinion.[2]

What does the duty to "follow" guidelines amount to? The previous statutory requirement was to "have regard to" the guidelines, and a majority of the Gage working group recommended a "more robust" requirement, in the form of a "presumption" that courts "must apply" the guidelines unless it would be contrary to the interests of justice to do so.[3] The legislation uses "follow" rather than "apply". In *Blackshaw* (2011)[4] Lord Judge C.J. began by stating that the word "follow" does not require "slavish adherence", not least because of the presence of the

---

* I am most grateful to Julian Roberts and to Ian Dennis for their comments on an earlier draft.

[1] See the discussion of this provision in A. Ashworth, "Sentencing Guidelines and the Sentencing Council" [2010] Crim. L.R. 389, and in J.V. Roberts, "Sentencing Guidelines and Judicial Discretion" (2011) 51 B.J. Crim. 997, 1006–1010.

[2] Criminal Justice Act 2003 s.174(2)(aa) as amended by Sch.21 para.84 to the 2009 Act.

[3] *Sentencing Commission Working Group, Sentencing Guidelines in England and Wales: an Evolutionary Approach* (2008), para.7.18 and Annex C.

[4] *Blackshaw* [2011] EWCA Crim 2312.

"interests of justice" exception. The main function of guidelines, he stated, is to provide "starting points" for sentencers and thereby to foster consistency of approach, "without sacrificing the obligation to do justice in the individual and specific case." So far, so good. But he then noted that, when referring to the legislative provisions on setting the minimum term for murder in Sch.21 to the Criminal Justice Act 2003, the Court of Appeal had emphasised that those provisions do not require an inflexible approach, and that even if they appeared to be detailed and comprehensive, the overriding obligation of the judge is to "achieve a just result".[5] Lord Judge concluded that the legislation relating to Sentencing Council guidelines could not "impose a more rigid system than that which applies to the statutory sentencing framework created for sentencing in murder cases."

This is a strange and unconvincing way in which to explore the proper meaning of the obligation to "follow", for two reasons. First, if Lord Judge's approach was to consider the 2009 Act in comparison with other sentencing legislation, he ought surely to have taken account of prescribed sentences, which require courts to impose such sentences unless it would be "unjust to do so in all the circumstances"[6] and mandatory minimum sentences such as the five-year minimum for firearms offences, which courts must impose unless they find "exceptional circumstances."[7] The structure of the provisions on prescribed sentences, in particular, is so close to that of the 2009 Act that the judicial interpretation of those provisions ought surely to have been discussed. Secondly, however, to focus on murder sentences (as the Lord Chief Justice did) is to miss the target entirely, because the murder provisions in Sch.21 are stated in the legislation to be only "general principles" to which courts "must have regard" (s.269(5) of the Criminal Justice Act 2003). The duty to "have regard" was the language of the 2003 Act[8] which the 2009 Act was intended to replace. Indeed, in an earlier case the Court of Appeal stated that a judge "is not bound to follow" the principles in Sch.21,[9] an observation which clearly indicates that the statutory murder guidelines cannot properly be used to illuminate the meaning of the word "follow" in the 2009 Act.

What the Court of Appeal in *Blackshaw* should have done is to focus on the actual wording of the 2009 Act: starting from the proposition that "follow" does not require "slavish adherence", the Lord Chief Justice should have given some attention to the scope of the "interests of justice" exception. Nothing was said about this, although obviously in relation to the riot appeals his Lordship must have concluded (although he did not use the statutory wording) that it would be "contrary to the interests of justice" to pass sentences within the applicable guidelines for offences that had to be assessed "within the context of nationwide public disorder." Sentences above the various offence-ranges were therefore upheld for several offenders who committed offences as part of the riots of August 2011.

The purpose of this article is to explore the circumstances in which a court may, under the terms of the Coroners and Justice Act 2009, depart from definitive

---

[5] At [14], quoting from *Height* [2008] EWCA Crim 2500; [2009] 1 Cr. App. R. (S) 117 (p.656) per Lord Judge C.J. at [29]; *Thornley* [2011] Cr. App. R. (S) 62 (p.361) at [13].

[6] Powers of Criminal Courts (Sentencing) Act 2000 ss.110 and 111; Sentencing Council, *Assault: Definitive Guideline* (2011), p.24.

[7] Criminal Justice Act 2003 s.287, amending the Firearms Act 1968.

[8] Criminal Justice Act 2003 s.172(1).

[9] *Sullivan* [2004] EWCA Crim 1762; [2005] 1 Cr. App. R. (S.) 67 (p.308) per Lord Woolf C.J. at [12].

sentencing guidelines. The study draws on a number of decisions of the Court of Appeal responding to claims either that the sentence is outside the relevant guideline when it should not be, or that the sentence should have been outside the guideline when it was not. We then return to the "riots" judgment and re-assess its relationship to the 2009 Act.

Downward departures

Under the scheme of the 2009 Act there are two different senses in which a court may deviate from a guideline. One is where the court, having identified the appropriate category-range for the offence(s) under consideration (s.125(3)), then finds other factors which are thought sufficient to justify moving the case down into the category-range below. An example of this, under the Council's guideline on causing grievous bodily harm,[10] would be a case that the court places in category 2 at stage one of its deliberations, but then lowers to category 3 at stage two when it takes account of certain factors reflecting personal mitigation. As noted in the opening paragraph, this is merely a category change, and does not amount to a departure, so that the "interests of justice" test does not need to be satisfied. It would nevertheless be a ground of appeal that the court placed an offence in the wrong category-range. However, the second form of downward deviation is where the court finds sufficient mitigation to go outside the offence-range for the offence (s.121(4)), that is, it decides on a sentence that lies below the lowest sentence in the ranges established by the guidelines. Returning to the guideline on causing grievous bodily harm, the lowest sentence in the category 3 range is three years' custody. Thus, if the court is minded to impose a sentence below that level, it must find that it would have been "contrary to the interests of justice" to follow the guideline and give three years. Finally, it should be noted that a downward departure is not possible if the floor of the lowest category-range has been set at a discharge, as in common assault.[11] There is simply no lesser sentence that the court can select.

Very few appellate decisions have considered the new law, but it may be instructive to consider the two "prescribed" or presumptive minimum sentences that have existed in English law since 1997. Now consolidated in ss.110 and 111 of the Powers of Criminal Courts (Sentencing) Act 2000, they require a court to pass a minimum sentence of seven years on a third-time class A drug dealer and one of three years on a third-time domestic burglar.[12] In both instances the minimum sentence should be imposed unless it would be "unjust to do so in all the circumstances". The departure test in the 2009 Act, requiring courts to follow the guidelines unless satisfied that "it would be contrary to the interests of justice to do so,"[13] also turns on the concept of justice. It may therefore be relevant to consider how the courts have interpreted the departure test in relation to these two minimum sentences.

The only general discussion of the "unjust to do so" test for departure is that of Lord Woolf C.J. in his guideline judgment on domestic burglary:

---

[10] Sentencing Council, *Assault: Definitive Guideline* (2011), pp.3–6.

[11] Sentencing Council, *Assault: Definitive Guideline* (2011), p.24.

[12] For the many details behind this broad statement, see D.A. Thomas, *Current Sentencing Practice*, A15; and more briefly, A. Ashworth, *Sentencing and Criminal Justice*, 5th edn (Cambridge University Press, 2010), pp.226–228.

[13] Coroners and Justice Act 2009 s.125(1) and Sch.22 Part 4.

> "The [minimum] sentence could be unjust if two of the offences were committed many years earlier than the third offence; or if the offender has made real efforts to reform or conquer his drug or alcohol addiction, but some personal tragedy triggers the third offence; or if the first two offences were committed when the offender was not yet 16."[14]

These examples were intended as no more than indications of how the section might be applied. An illustration of the first circumstance can be found in *McDonagh* (2006), where the Court of Appeal held that it would be unjust to apply the prescribed sentence for drug dealing where the second qualifying offence had been 10 years earlier (although the court also noted a significant delay in bringing the case to trial).[15] An illustration of the second circumstance can be found in *Stenhouse* (2000), where the Court of Appeal held that it would be unjust to apply the prescribed sentence for drug dealing where the offender had made determined efforts to conquer his addiction since arrest (although the court also noted that his second qualifying offence had been considered so venial that only a community sentence had been imposed).[16] The decision in *Turner* (2006)[17] indicates a further circumstance, the Court of Appeal holding that it would be unjust to impose the prescribed sentence where all three qualifying offences were non-commercial, involving the supply of drugs to friends.

How much guidance can be derived from these decisions? The overall sense is that applying a minimum sentence would be unjust if a single strong mitigating factor, which tends to negative a purpose of the minimum sentence, is present. When Lord Bingham C.J. considered prescribed sentences in an early judgment, he said this:

> "The object of the section quite plainly is to require courts to impose a sentence of at least seven years in circumstances where, but for the section, they would not or might not do so. If that were not the intention of the section, it is in our judgment very difficult to see what the intention of the section was."[18]

This emphasis on legislative purpose led Lord Bingham to hold that it would not be enough that the sentence would otherwise be "manifestly excessive": the test of injustice requires a stronger set of mitigating circumstances than merely showing that the prescribed sentence would be higher than the court would otherwise impose.

The rationale for those prescribed sentences is deterrence and/or incapacitation, in relation to repeat drug dealers and repeat burglars. Guidelines have a different function from the prescribed sentences that Lord Bingham was discussing. They are ubiquitous and their principal purpose (as Lord Judge observed in *Blackshaw*) is to bring about consistency of approach to sentencing. So long as a court identifies an appropriate starting-point in the guideline, it ought then to take account of whatever mitigating factors are present in the case—as it would do when sentencing for an offence not covered by a guideline. Often the mitigating factors will not be so great as to take the court below the relevant category-range, or they will be

---

[14] *McInerney* [2002] EWCA Crim 3003; [2003] 2 Cr. App. R. (S.) 39 (p.240) at 251.
[15] *McDonagh* [2005] EWCA Crim 2742; [2006] 1 Cr. App. R. (S.) 111 (p.647) at 651.
[16] *Stenhouse* [2000] 2 Cr. App. R. (S.) 386 at 388.
[17] *Turner* [2005] EWCA Crim 2363; [2006] 1 Cr. App. R. (S.) 95 (p.565).
[18] *Harvey* [2000] 1 Cr. App. R. (S.) 368 at 371.

counterbalanced by aggravating factors (such as previous convictions). But in some cases the mitigating factors will be so strong — or the case will already be on the floor of the lowest category-range—that the court should regard it as "contrary to the interests of justice" to remain within that category-range. In principle, therefore, it is "contrary to the interests of justice" for a court to remain within the offence-range if there is mitigation which is strong and significant, and which the guideline does not take into account.[19]

Before seeking to pursue this reasoning further, it may be instructive to consider cases in which the courts have made radical departures from the guidelines.

Downwards departures: the "mercy" cases

In a number of cases in recent years the Court of Appeal has accepted that it is right to go below the applicable offence range or category range on grounds of "mercy". A reading of these judgments suggests that the court has tended to require a stronger argument for "mercy" than it is likely to require for "the interests of justice". Seven recent cases may be discussed in this connection.

One of the best known is *Schumann* (2007),[20] where a depressed mother jumped off the Humber Bridge holding her two-year-old daughter, then kept the child alive in the water for 45 minutes until rescued. The trial judge imposed an unusually lenient sentence for attempted murder (18 months' imprisonment), pointing to D's depressed state and her successful efforts to save the child's life. Although there were no definitive guidelines on attempted murder in place at the time, Lord Phillips C.J. held that, "the one word that is not contained in the sentencing guidelines is "mercy." There are occasions where the court can put the guidelines and the authorities on one side and apply mercy instead."[21] The court held that this was such a case, and substituted a community sentence. Thus, it is clear that the court would not have followed guidelines even if they had existed; under the current guidelines for attempted murder,[22] the floor of the offence-range is six years, and the court would undoubtedly have held that it would be "contrary to the interests of justice" to follow the guidelines.

In *Attorney General's Reference (No.11 of 2007) (Knox)* (2008)[23] D, with two other women, robbed a neighbour on the street, causing minor injuries but taking little. Although D had 37 previous convictions for thefts and assaults, the judge took note of her guilty plea and of the fact that D's sister was terminally ill with cancer, and imposed a sentence of 12 months' imprisonment. A few days later the sister died, and the judge recalled D and reduced the sentence to six months. The Court of Appeal declined to interfere with the sentence, stating that the trial judge "exercised the right of all judges to extend mercy" by passing a relatively low sentence[24] in view of the mitigation relating to the death of D's sister.

---

[19] Lord Woolf C.J. adopted a similar view in *McInerney* [2003] 2 Cr. App. R. (S.) 39 (p.240) at 251, though without reference to the legislative purpose of prescribed sentences.

[20] *Schumann* [2007] EWCA Crim 569; [2007] 2 Cr. App. R. (S.) 73 (p.465).

[21] *Schumann* [2007] EWCA Crim 569; [2007] 2 Cr. App. R. (S.) 73 (p.465) at 469.

[22] Sentencing Guidelines Council (SGC), *Attempted Murder* (2008), p.7.

[23] *Attorney General's Reference (No.11 of 2007) (Knox)* [2007] EWCA Crim 960; [2008] 1 Cr. App. R. (S.) 6 (p.26).

[24] The robbery guideline does not identify the floor of the range for category 1 offences, stating that the category range is "up to 3 years' custody" (Sentencing Guidelines Council, *Robbery: Definitive Guideline* (2006), 11); this means that this element of the 2009 Act cannot be applied to it.

A well-publicised but intricate case was *Hussain* (2010),[25] where MH had arrived home with his family to be confronted by armed burglars, one of MH's sons managed to escape and alert TH (who lived nearby), MH succeeded in distracting a burglar and breaking free, and then both MH and TH chased one of the burglars until they caught him. They then gave him a severe beating, causing a fractured skull and many other injuries. Both were convicted of causing grievous bodily harm with intent (s.18). TH was sentenced to three years three months' imprisonment and MH to two years six months. In the Court of Appeal Lord Judge C.J. referred to the extreme provocation suffered by MH, to his family's victimisation in the burglary, to subsequent threats to him and his family, and to his impeccable character and voluntary work for the community, and reduced his sentence to 12 months' imprisonment suspended. Lord Judge held:

> "There are some situations which guidelines cannot and do not cover. This is one of them. Today, as ever, the sentence of the court must address and balance the ancient principles of justice and mercy. In this case the call for a merciful sentence is intense."[26]

The sentence for TH was reduced to two years' imprisonment, in recognition of the extreme provocation without the other mitigating factors available to MH. The lowest sentence in the ranges for the offence was then three years,[27] so both sentences were departures from the offence-range and therefore, under the 2009 Act, they would have to be justified on the basis that it would have been "contrary to the interests of justice" to follow the guidelines. No doubt this test would have been held to be satisfied by the unusually strong combination of mitigating factors.

This theme of an accumulation of mitigating factors runs through several other decisions. In *Foster* (2010)[28] D momentarily lost concentration when driving his wife back from a hospital appointment at which they had been told that her motor neurone disease could not be treated further. D's car veered to the wrong side of the road and killed a motorcyclist. D was sentenced to 18 months' imprisonment for causing death by dangerous driving, the judge taking two years as the floor of the lowest range and reducing the sentence to reflect the special circumstances, D's impeccable character and driving record, and his remorse. The Court of Appeal held that this was "a proper case for mercy", not least because D had already spent three months in prison, and reduced the sentence to 12 months suspended.[29] The language of mercy was used where, under the 2009 Act, the "contrary to the interests of justice" test would surely be invoked.

In *Clarke* (2010)[30] D suffered a hypoglycaemic attack when driving, veered on to a footpath and collided with two boys, killing one of them. The judge concluded from expert evidence that D would have been aware of the onset of hypoglycaemia for some moments, and sentenced him to three years' imprisonment for causing death by dangerous driving. The Court of Appeal held that the appropriate

---

[25] *Hussain* [2010] EWCA Crim 94; [2010] 2 Cr. App. R. (S.) 60 (p.399).

[26] *Hussain* [2010] EWCA Crim 94; [2010] 2 Cr. App. R. (S.) 60 (p.399) at 406.

[27] SGC, *Assault and other offences against the person* (2008), p.13; the range applicable to this offence was probably 4–6 years.

[28] *Foster* [2009] EWCA Crim 1184; [2010] 1 Cr. App. R. (S.) 36 (p.219).

[29] The fact that account was taken of the three months D had already spent in prison means that the sentence substituted by the CA gives no indication of what the original sentence should have been.

[30] *Clarke* [2009] EWCA Crim 921; [2010] 1 Cr. App. R. (S.) 26 (p.158).

category-range was four to seven years, but brought the case down below that because D's awareness of his condition (and opportunity to stop the car) would only have been momentary, there were delays in bringing the case to trial, and D suffered from complicated medical conditions which rendered imprisonment particularly onerous for him. The sentence was reduced to 12 months' imprisonment, well below the offence-range (the floor of the lowest category-range is two years),[31] referring to reduced culpability from "highly exceptional circumstances" that took the offence "significantly below" the range.

In *Attorney General's Reference (No.95 of 2009) (Blight)* (2010),[32] D had been struck twice by the blunt end of an axe wielded by his partner's 19-year-old son; D and his partner then shut themselves in the kitchen, but the son began to kick the door down, so D armed himself with a kitchen knife and told the son to drop the axe; as the argument continued D went to strike the son and stabbed him. D pleaded guilty to wounding with intent (s.18) and the trial judge sentenced him to two years' imprisonment suspended.[33] The judge referred to the intent being formed in the most anguished of circumstances, a "desperate situation", by a man of good character severely provoked and fearful. The Court of Appeal added that D had been "goaded beyond endurance" and that "sentencing guidelines do not address cases of such exceptionality." The Court therefore refused the Attorney General's application, and confirmed the sentence of 12 months' imprisonment suspended.[34] As noted in relation to the *Hussain* case, this sentence is well below the offence-range for s.18; the Court of Appeal justified the "humane and justifiably merciful sentence" by reference to the unusually strong mitigation.

Different in its details but similar in its reasoning is *Mooney* (2010),[35] where D (aged 17) had consensual intercourse with a girl of 12 and pleaded guilty to two offences of rape of a child under 13. He had suggested that three girls stayed overnight at his aunt's house rather than walking home in the rain. The girls slept in one room, he in another, but one girl visited him in the night and initiated sex with him. She did the same again the next night. She told her parents, and D readily admitted the sex. It was accepted that the girl had told him she was 14, and he was unaware that it was an offence to have sex with a 14 year old. He was sentenced to 30 months' detention for rape of a child under 13, well below the applicable category-range for an adult (8–13 years). The Court of Appeal held that it would be right to make an even more radical departure from the guideline than the trial judge had done, in view of D's youth, his immediate admissions, his remorse, his ignorance of the law, the absence of any predatory or grooming element, and the strong desire of the girl and her parents not to see D dealt with harshly. The court reduced the detention to 12 months, concluding that custody remained necessary in order to recognise the purpose of the legislation. Under the terms of the 2009 Act, this was well below the offence-range (lowest point, four years), but the strong

---

[31] Sentencing Guidelines Council, *Causing Death by Driving* (2008), p.11.

[32] *Attorney General's Reference (No.95 of 2009) (Blight)* [2010] EWCA Crim 353; [2010] 2 Cr. App. R. (S.) 83 (p.535).

[33] This was an unlawful sentence, as the Court of Appeal noted; only sentences of up to 12 months may be suspended.

[34] The CA took account of the fact that D had spent four and a half months in custody awaiting trial: the fact that account was taken of the three months D had already spent in prison means that the sentence substituted by the CA gives no indication of what the original sentence should have been.

[35] *Mooney* [2010] EWCA Crim 698; [2010] 2 Cr. App. R. (S.) 97 (p.636).

mitigation would have made it "contrary to the interests of justice" to pass a sentence within the offence-range.

None of these cases was decided under the 2009 Act, but it is not thought that the outcome would be different under the new scheme of "follow ... unless ...it would be contrary to the interests of justice to do so." The judges have tended to use the concept of mercy to justify reductions of sentence below the offence-range in two closely related types of case—those where there is an unusually powerful accumulation of mitigating factors (*Hussain, Attorney General's Reference (No.95 of 2009) (Blight),* and *Mooney),* and those where there is an exceptionally strong showing of one or two mitigating factors (*Schumann, Attorney General's Reference (No.11 of 2007)(Knox), Clarke, Foster).*

Insufficient reasons for downward departure

There are other decisions in which attempts to persuade the courts to impose a "merciful" sentence have been unsuccessful. In *DG* (2010)[36] D was charged with aggravated taking of a car, driving with excess alcohol and driving while uninsured. Having been seen crossing a red light, police signalled him to stop but he did not; the police chased him and he crashed the car. He pleaded guilty and was sentenced to 12 months' imprisonment. Account was taken of the aggravating effect of the excess alcohol, but on appeal the defence invited the court to quash the custodial sentence "as an act of mercy" because any custodial sentence would result in D's discharge from the army. The Court of Appeal declined: D's military career should not deflect the court from passing an appropriate sentence for serious offences. In *McDade* (2010)[37] the appellants had pleaded guilty to misconduct in a public office and trying to smuggle prohibited items into prison. They were prison officers, and as a result of a relationship with a prisoner M was about to give birth to their child. M appealed against her sentence of 30 months' imprisonment, arguing that since her motive for the offences was not greed but love she should be treated mercifully. The Court of Appeal held that account had already been taken of the strong personal mitigation and of the effect on the young baby of being separated from its mother, concluding that the sentence was "consciously compassionate" and could not be reduced further.

In these two decisions the question was whether enough "mercy" had been shown, given the personal consequences of the sentences (discharge from the army; separation from a new-born child). The Court of Appeal concluded that in both cases the trial judge had gone as far as possible, but would the decisions have been different if there had been applicable guidelines and if the question had been whether it would be "contrary to the interests of justice" to impose the guideline sentence? In principle, the "interests of justice" may be broader than the concept of mercy employed by the courts, so that a less powerful ground of personal mitigation should suffice for the new test. However, that does not resolve the conflict that sentencers often have to negotiate, between the intrinsic gravity of the offence(s) on the one hand and the strong pull of certain mitigating factors on

---

[36] *DG* [2010] EWCA Crim 2813.
[37] *McDade* [2010] EWCA Crim 249; [2010] 2 Cr. App. R. (S.) 82 (p.530).

the other hand.[38] The Court of Appeal might well decide cases such as *Gibson* and *McDade* in the same way if dealing with offences to which guidelines and the new departure test applied.

If the argument for a downward departure from the guidelines comes from the victim or the victim's family, that should not make it stronger. Indeed, the applicable Practice Direction states that the opinions of the victim or the victim's relatives as to what the sentence should be are "not relevant" and that, if such opinions find their way into the victim personal statement or any other statement to the court "the court should pay no attention to them."[39] It is important to distinguish between this prohibition and the possibility of taking account of the exceptional effect on an offence on the victim or victim's family.[40] Courts do not always follow this Practice Direction.[41]However, if they do break away from it and consider a view expressed by the victim or victim's family, they should focus on the question whether it would be "contrary to the interests of justice" to pass the sentence indicated by the guideline.

Finally, a downward departure from a guideline in "the interests of justice" ought to be regarded as a matter of principle, not an unreviewable exercise of discretion. In *Bernard* (1997)[42] one of the issues was whether a court should adjust the sentence to take account of a serious medical condition that would be difficult to treat while the offender was serving a prison sentence. The Court of Appeal held that:

> "[A]n offender's serious medical condition may enable a court, as an act of mercy in the exceptional circumstances of a particular case, rather than by virtue of any general principle, to impose a lesser sentence than would otherwise be appropriate."[43]

Insofar as this suggests that the proper response to personal mitigation of this kind does not involve an issue of principle, it is surely unacceptable.[44] It is not necessary to put "mercy" and "principle" in opposition to one another. While it would not be possible to specify the precise circumstances in which a serious medical condition would render it "contrary to the interests of justice" to pass the normal sentence, use of the term "exceptional" combined with some indication of the

---

[38] For example, in *Bright* [2008] 2 Cr. App. R. (S.) 102 (p.578), per Sir Igor Judge P. at 591: "In the light of his age, and ill health, and his wife's ill health, some small reduction from the notional maximum might have been allowed as an act of mercy, but the judge was entitled to conclude that in view of the appellant's conduct, he had forfeited any mercy which the Court might otherwise have extended to him."

[39] Consolidated Practice Direction, III.28.2(c).

[40] Two judgments of Judge L.J. bear out this point: in the leading case of *Nunn* [1996] 2 Cr. App. R. (S.) 136 the Court of Appeal made a small reduction of the sentence to take account of the difficulty of the victim's family in coming to terms with the imprisonment of a friend who had caused the death of their son, and similar reasoning may be found in *Attorney General's Reference (No.77 of 2002) (Scotney)* [2002] EWCA Crim 2312; [2003] 1 Cr. App. R. (S.) 111 (p.564).

[41] A recent example of this is *Mooney* [2010] EWCA Crim 698; [2010] 2 Cr. App. R. (S.) 97 (p.636), where the Court of Appeal referred to "the attitude of the mother or parents of the complainant" as a reason for further reducing the sentence, the mother having stated that she thought only some kind of warning to the offender was needed. See also the earlier decision in *Attorney General's Reference No.18 of 1993 (Kavanagh)* (1994) 15 Cr. App. R. (S.) 800.

[42] *Bernard* [1997] 1 Cr. App. R. (S.) 135.

[43] *Bernard* [1997] 1 Cr. App. R. (S.) 135 at 139; for critical appraisal, see A. Ashworth and E. Player, "Sentencing, Equal Treatment and the Impact of Sanctions", in A. Ashworth and M. Wasik (eds), *Fundamentals of Sentencing Theory* (1998), and C. Piper, "Should Impact Constitute Mitigation? Structured Discretion versus Mercy" [2007] Crim. L.R. 141.

[44] When relying on *Bernard* in *Qazi* [2010] EWCA Crim 2579; [2011] 2 Cr. App. R. (S.) 8 (p.32) at 37, Thomas L.J. referred simply to "the principles set out by Rose L.J. in *Bernard*."

degree of the difficulty of treatment for the sufferer during the serving of a prison sentence would be sufficient to bring the matter within the realm of principle and of appellate review.

Upward departures from guidelines

The forms of upward departure mirror those of downward departure. First, a court may deviate from the category-range, in which the appropriate starting point was located, to a higher category-range, if it finds aggravating factors (such as previous convictions) which are sufficiently weighty to justify upward movement. As stated earlier, this is a category change which does not amount to a departure, even if it might provide a ground of appeal. However, where the court finds itself in the highest category-range and decides that the aggravating factors call for an even higher sentence, it may conclude that it would be "contrary to the interests of justice" to keep within the guidelines and it may impose a sentence up towards the statutory maximum sentence. But such an upward departure is not always possible: the architecture of existing sentencing guidelines varies in that, although most guidelines leave a gap between the top of the highest category-range and the statutory maximum sentence (e.g. unlawful wounding, assault occasioning actual bodily harm),[45] there are some guidelines in which the highest category-range goes right up to the statutory maximum (e.g. causing death by dangerous driving[46] and common assault).[47] For guidelines of the latter type, no upward departure is possible. There are some guidelines with a different structure, where the top of the offence-range leaves a considerable gap before the maximum sentence is reached: an example would be domestic burglary, where the offence-range runs up to six years but the statutory maximum is 14 years.[48]

When might a court find that "the interests of justice" indicate a sentence above the ceiling of the offence-range? There is a substantial line of precedents in support of the propositions that the statutory maximum sentence should be reserved for the worst kind of case,[49] and that this should be interpreted as referring to "the broad band of that type" of case[50] or to "cases which in the statutory context are truly identified as cases of the utmost gravity."[51] Thus, as the proposed sentence nears the statutory maximum, the "interests of justice" seem likely to require that the case be in this broad band of cases of the utmost gravity, exhibiting features worse than those specified for the highest category-range, and/or a bad criminal record. However, where (as in domestic burglary) there is a considerable distance between the ceiling of the offence-range and the statutory maximum, there will be cases where the interests of justice might be held to indicate an upward departure, even though the sentence will still be well below the statutory maximum and therefore not required to meet the more demanding common-law test for a sentence approaching the maximum.

[45] Sentencing Council, *Assault: Definitive Guideline* (2011), pp.8 and 12.
[46] SGC, *Causing Death by Driving* (2008), p.13; the same applies to the offence of causing death by driving while unlicensed, disqualified or uninsured (p.17).
[47] Sentencing Council, *Assault: Definitive Guideline* (2011), p.24; also assault on a police constable, p.21.
[48] Sentencing Council, *Burglary: Definitive Guideline* (2011), p.9.
[49] *Harrison* (1909) 2 Cr. App. R. 94.
[50] *Ambler* [1976] Crim. L.R. 266, applied in *Butt* [2006] 2 Cr. App. R. (S.) 59 (p.364).
[51] *Bright* [2008] EWCA Crim 462; [2008] 2 Cr. App. R. (S.) 102 (p.578) at 588.

An example of these principles in operation is provided by *P* (2010),[52] where the appellants had been involved in bringing girls and women to this country and forcing them to work as prostitutes. The relevant sentencing guideline for trafficking has four to nine years as its highest category-range.[53] This leaves a considerable gap beneath the statutory maximum of 14 years, and the guideline indicates that sentence lengths in that gap might be appropriate where aggravating factors such as "a large-scale enterprise involving a high degree of planning, organisation or sophistication, financial or other gain, and the coercion and vulnerability of victims" are present. The sentences imposed here were 11 years for the first appellant and 14 years for the second appellant, who was convicted of offences relating to two women. The Court of Appeal concluded that the cluster of aggravating factors in this case—bringing a girl to this country under false expectations, exploitation of a child prostitute through coercion, commercial operations on a considerable scale—justified sentences above the highest category and therefore outside the offence-range. One assumes that the decision would be the same under the "interests of justice" test.

Another example is the offence of unlawful wounding, contrary to s.20 of the Offences Against the Person Act 1861, where the highest category-range is now two and a half to four years[54]; the statutory maximum sentence is five years. Two implications flow from this—first, that a sentence of longer than four years is only available for a crime that is broadly of the most grave type within the offence definition; secondly, that a judge dealing with an offender who has pleaded guilty may not take a starting point higher than four years unless the offence falls within that exceptional category. It seems that the "interests of justice" would only indicate a sentence in that four to five year range if the facts of the offence, perhaps combined with the criminal record of the offender, indicate that the case falls within that highest band of cases of the "utmost gravity", and if there was no guilty plea.[55] This is difficult to assess because the sentence ranges for the more serious offence of wounding with intent, contrary to s.18 of the same Act, overlap with those for s.20. This very problem was raised in a different context in *Shepherd* (2010),[56] where the offender was sentenced to four years' detention for causing death by careless driving after driving at excessive speed in a car that he knew to have defective brakes and tyres, losing control of the car and killing another driver. Since he had pleaded guilty, this means that the trial judge must have taken the statutory maximum of five years as the starting point. Clearly the judge thought that the more serious offence of causing death by dangerous driving (whose sentence ranges overlap with those for causing death by careless driving) should have been charged. The highest category-range for the offence charged has a ceiling of three years, and, while the Court of Appeal agreed that the driving was bad enough to go above that range, it reduced the original sentence:

> "By placing this case at the statutory maximum, but for the plea, [the judge] left no room for the sort of case which might contain other aggravating

[52] *P* [2009] EWCA Crim 2436; [2010] 2 Cr. App. R. (S.) 2 (p.7).
[53] SGC, *Sexual Offences Act 2003: Definitive Guideline* (2007), p.131.
[54] Sentencing Council, *Assault: Definitive Guideline*, p.8.
[55] Cf. *Collins* [2011] 1 Cr. App. R. (S.) 35 (p.218), where four years was upheld for an offender who had pleaded guilty to a s.20 offence; also *Hurley* [2008] EWCA Crim 2620; [2009] 1 Cr. App. R. (S) 100 (p.568).
[56] *Shepherd* [2010] EWCA Crim 46; [2010] 2 Cr. App. R. (S.) 54 (p.370).

features, or relevant previous convictions. It can be said on the other side of the coin that he cannot have given any weight to the appellant's young age and previous good character."[57]

Thus, the facts were not thought to place the case in the group of cases of "the utmost gravity" for this crime, and that was partly because of the presence of mitigating factors and the absence of previous convictions.

In *Pennant* (2011)[58] the Court of Appeal considered the appropriate sentence for repeated offences of exposure by an offender with previous convictions for the offence. The offence-range for the offence has a ceiling of 26 weeks' imprisonment, but the trial judge had imposed two consecutive sentences of 12 months. The Court of Appeal held that the circumstances of the cases and the offender's criminal record justified an upward departure from the guideline. However, applying a reduction for the guilty plea the Court approved two consecutive sentences of 26 weeks. It seems probable that, if the court had been applying the 2009 Act, it would have taken the same course.

Some cases that have been discussed in terms of departure do not require justification in this way. Thus, in *Turner* (2011)[59] the judge, in sentencing an offender for benefit fraud, decided that the case had so many aggravating features that the starting point should be above the indicated category-range (which was 12 weeks to 18 months custody) , and so the judge took a starting point of two years before allowing for mitigation. The Court of Appeal upheld this: there were good reasons for taking the case into the next higher category-range. This was a category change rather than a departure, since the sentence was still within the offence-range. The same may be said of two recent rape cases, where the ground of appeal (successful in both cases) was that the judge had placed the case in a higher category-range than was justified on the facts.[60] If the cases in this paragraph had been dealt with under the 2009 Act, they would not have involved a departure that required consideration of the "interests of justice" exception: under the terms of the 2009 Act the judges had "followed" the guidelines, even though they had placed it in the wrong category-range, since the sentence was within the overall offence-range.

Conclusions: the departure test and best practice

This article began with some strong criticism of the Lord Chief Justice's approach to interpreting the 2009 Act, before surveying recent decisions that may cast light on how the new departure test may be expected to operate. This leads to four concluding issues—(i) a contrast with other departure tests; (ii) how the 2009 Act's departure test should be interpreted; (iii) the difficulties of the *Blackshaw* decision; and (iv) some "good practice" suggestions in support of the guidelines.

---

[57] *Shepherd* [2010] EWCA Crim 46; [2010] 2 Cr. App. R. (S.) 54 (p.370) at 376.
[58] *Pennant* [2010] EWCA Crim 2117; [2011] 1 Cr. App. R. (S.) 92 (p.551).
[59] *Turner* [2011] 2 Cr. App. R. (S.) 18 (p.102).
[60] See *S.* [2010] EWCA Crim 750; [2011] 1 Cr. App. R. (S.) 9 (p.86), and *Shahjahan* [2011] EWCA Crim 619; [2011] 2 Cr. App. R. (S.) 94 (p.522).

Departures from the Sentencing Guidelines 93

(i)   **Possible departure tests**

When the Gage working group examined possible departure tests, they rejected the test used in the Minnesota guidelines—"substantial and compelling reasons"—as too restrictive.[61] Presumably the same argument led to the rejection of the departure test for mandatory minimum sentences in England and Wales such as the five-year minimum for firearms offences, which must be imposed unless the court finds "exceptional circumstances relating to the offence or to the offender which justify its not doing so,"[62] a test that the courts have interpreted strictly.[63] On the other hand, the Gage working party also rejected the "have regard to" test in the Criminal Justice Act 2003 as not "sufficiently robust to provide the necessary consistency, transparency and predictability." By implication, therefore, Gage rejected the approach of the murder starting points in Sch.21 to the 2003 Act, which employ the "have regard to" test also. This reinforces the claim that Lord Judge was in error when he based his reasoning in *Blackshaw* on the murder starting points.

(ii)   **The interpretation of the 2009 Act**

What, then, should be said about s.125(1) of the Coroners and Justice Act 2009? The obligation to "follow" the guidelines means that courts must faithfully treat the guidelines as establishing appropriate starting-points and ranges for any case that involves an offence for which guidelines exist. This is a stronger obligation than the previous duty to "have regard to" guidelines[64]: the new statutory formula of "must follow" should be taken as requiring courts to apply the guidelines as they stand, unless it would be "contrary to the interests of justice to do so." The fundamental duty, therefore, is to identify the category-range most appropriate to the facts of the case, and then to adopt the step-wise reasoning set out in the definitive guidelines issued by the Sentencing Council (nine steps in the guidelines on assault and on burglary), or formerly by the Sentencing Guidelines Council.[65] That enables the court to give effect to aggravating and mitigating factors in the case; if some of those factors are adjudged sufficient to carry a case into a higher or lower category-range than the category provisionally adopted at step one, this may furnish a ground of appeal but does not constitute a departure. If, however, certain factors have unusual strength in a particular case, either individually or in combination, the court does not have to follow the

---

[61] Gage Sentencing Commission Working Group, *Sentencing Guidelines in England and Wales: an Evolutionary Approach* (2008), para.7.18 and Annex C, paras 7.14–7.21; J.V. Roberts, "Sentencing Guidelines and Judicial Discretion" (2011) 51 B.J. Crim. 997, 1002 and 1003.

[62] Firearms Act 1968 s.51A(2).

[63] The leading case is probably *Rehman and Wood* [2006] 1 Cr. App. R. (S.) 404; for recent examples, see *Attorney General's Reference No.64 of 2010* [2011] 2 Cr. App. R. (S.) 135 and *Shaw* [2011] 2 Cr. App. R. (S.) 376.

[64] Although "must have regard to" was interpreted quite strictly: see Rose L.J. in *Oosthuizen* [2005] EWCA Crim 1978; [2006] 1 Cr. App. R. (S.) 73 (p.385) at 391.

[65] Compare the Sentencing Council, *Assault: Definitive Guideline* (2011), pp.4–6, setting out the steps in some detail, with, e.g. Sentencing Guidelines Council, *Sentencing for Fraud — Statutory Offences: Definitive Guideline* (2009), p.17, setting out a "decision making process" that is far less detailed.

guidelines (i.e. to pass sentence within the offence-range) if satisfied that it would be "contrary to the interests of justice to do so." The court must state why it was of this opinion. The reasons given must demonstrate that the factors are unusually strong, that they go beyond the factors already specified in the guidelines (no double counting), that the appropriate sentence is therefore outside the total offence-range set out in the guideline, and, where a departure takes the court towards the statutory maximum, that the common law test for such sentences is satisfied. This interpretation should not prevent a court from "doing justice in the individual and specific case", as the Lord Chief Justice rightly insisted.[66]

(iii)   **The judgment in Blackshaw**

There is no doubt that the offences that were the subject of these sentencing appeals were aggravated by the extreme public disorder at the time and by the mutual support and encouragement of offenders, in opposition to the police and the emergency services, as Lord Judge stated.[67] However, this statement was not followed by an examination of the reasoning in relevant precedents, such as *Keys*.[68] Instead Lord Judge moved on to the assertion that the sentences "should be designed to deter others from similar criminal activity."[69] The problems with this are well known: there is no evidence that general deterrent sentences of this kind are effective, either in the available research[70] or even in judicial lore.[71] There is certainly no evidence that general deterrent sentences will have an effect on the frequency of riots that begin spontaneously, and only every few years. Moreover, even if a deterrent strategy were being pursued, it would be important to consider what the proportionate sentence would be, and then how much should be added to it in the hope of achieving the deterrent purposes. Unfortunately, when Lord Judge upheld the sentences for the two Facebook offenders, Blackshaw and Sutcliffe, he said nothing about the appropriate starting point, i.e. whether and why it should have been three, four, six or eight years, and how much reduction was appropriate for the guilty pleas. One assumes that the starting point was six years, with a two-year reduction for the early guilty pleas, but this should be spelt out in the judgment and properly justified. The same applies

[66] *Blackshaw* [2011] EWCA Crim 2312 at [14].

[67] *Blackshaw* [2011] EWCA Crim 2312 at [9]. Cf. the findings of the National Centre for Social Research, *The August Riots in England: understanding the involvement of young people* (November 2011), and the standard texts on aspects of behaviour in groups, such as D.R. Forsyth, *Group Dynamics*, 5th edn (Wadsworth Cengage Learning, 2010), Ch.17, discussing the dynamics of collective behaviour, "contagion" and "deindividuation".

[68] *Keys* (1986) 8 Cr. App. R. (S.) 444.

[69] *Keys* (1986) 8 Cr. App. R. (S.) 444 at [4] and [75].

[70] See A. von Hirsch et al, *Criminal Deterrence and Sentence Severity* (Oxford: Hart, 1999), and A. Doob and C. Webster, "Sentence Severity and Crime: Accepting the Null Hypothesis", in M. Tonry (ed), *Crime and Justice: a Review of Research* (2003), 30: 143.

[71] "In my experience, having spent the best part of forty years representing, prosecuting and passing judgment on criminals, I have no doubt that what primarily deters crime is the likelihood of detection." Lord Taylor of Gosforth, "Continuity and Change in the Criminal Law" (1996) 7 King's College L.J. 1, 9; on the next page he adds a quotation that "severe and barbarous punishments are no more effectual than milder ones as deterrent to crime."

to those convicted of handling stolen goods, whose crimes "stemmed from this public disturbance, but [were] not intrinsic to it."[72] Was Lord Judge right to state that the guideline judgment on handling was not at all relevant in these unusual circumstances?[73] What parameters was the Court of Appeal drawing on when it halved the sentences in these three handling cases, but still imposed custody? No clue is given as to how the calculation was made. The riots amounted to serious civil disorder, as Lord Judge rightly emphasised, but when sentences of imprisonment are involved their length must be carefully justified. Section 152(2) of the Criminal Justice Act 2003 restricts custodial sentences to cases where a fine or community sentence cannot be justified; s.153(2) states that custodial sentences "must be for the shortest term ... commensurate with the seriousness of the offence." No reference was made to either provision. In summary, the judgment is significantly flawed by its failure to justify its conclusions on these appeals by reference to the applicable legislation, to relevant guidelines, or to the giving of adequate reasons.

(iv)   **Good practice**

The effectiveness of sentencing guidelines would be enhanced if certain points of good practice were also developed. For example, (a) where a court decides that it would be "contrary to the interests of justice" to sentence within the guidelines, it must not only articulate its reasons for departure but also explain the extent of the departure involved (i.e. why less or more would not be appropriate). Stepping outside a guideline should not mean stepping into an entirely unstructured realm where proper justifications are absent.[74] On the contrary, when a court departs from a guideline it is especially important that it gives reasons for its choice of sentence, and justifies the distance between the sentence imposed and the offence-range in the guideline. The same should apply if there is no relevant guideline or if (under s.125(3)) there is a guideline but no category-range sufficiently resembles the case at hand. Further, although the statute literally requires a court to justify departure only when the final sentence is outside the offence-range, (b) it would be good practice for courts to give reasons where they adopt a starting point that lies outside the offence-range, even if they subsequently (e.g. by making a reduction for a guilty plea) impose a sentence that comes within the offence-range[75]; and (c) both these principles should apply equally to the Court of Appeal. Failure to follow principle (a) was a significant shortcoming of the judgment in *Blackshaw*: once the

---

[72] *Blackshaw* [2011] EWCA Crim 2312 at [140].

[73] *Blackshaw* [2011] EWCA Crim 2312 at [16].

[74] On this point, see the commentary of Dr. D. A. Thomas on *Tokeer Hussain and Munir Hussain* [2010] Crim. L.R. 428, 431.

[75] See *Pennant* [2010] EWCA Crim 2117; [2011] 1 Cr. App. R. (S.) 92 (p.551) and *Shepherd* [2010] EWCA Crim 46; [2010] 2 Cr. App. R. (S.) 54 (p.370) for cases to which this would apply.

Court of Appeal had decided that sentences beyond the guidelines were called for, there was no attempt to explain how great an aggravating effect the context of the riots should have, and no attempt to justify the length of the sentences actually imposed on the principal offenders. This applies *a fortiori* to the sentences for non-domestic burglary (upheld) and those for handling (halved) where there was no engagement with the relevant guidelines. Only if good practices of this kind are adopted will the work of the Sentencing Council be properly supported, even if departures from the guidelines turn out to be relatively rare (because offence-ranges themselves are so broad).[76]

---

[76] The first report of the Sentencing Council's survey records a departure rate of two per cent for assault occasioning actual bodily harm: Sentencing Council, *Crown Court Sentencing Survey* (October 2011), p.3. Cf. the small-scale survey by the Sentencing Guidelines Working Group, *Crown Court Sentencing Survey* (2008), showing that some 48 per cent of sentences for assault fell outside the category-ranges (not the offence-range, as relevant under the 2009 Act); see J.V. Roberts, "Sentencing Guidelines and Judicial Discretion" (2011) 51 B.J. Crim. 997, 1004 and 1005, concluding that previous convictions are often the reason for moving to a higher category-range.

[10]

Sentencing Councils and Victims

Ian Edwards*

This article explores the place victims have, and should have, in bodies that formulate sentencing guidelines, with particular reference to sentencing guidelines in England and Wales and the Sentencing Council's obligation under the Coroners and Justice Act 2009 to have regard to 'the impact of sentencing decisions on victims of offences' when devising guidelines. The issues are situated in political and penological contexts; the place of victims in sentencing commissions or advisory bodies in the USA, England and Australia is analysed and the meaning and significance of the Sentencing Council's obligation towards victims is considered, relating the specific obligation to broader issues concerning the place of victims within bodies that formulate sentencing guidelines. While incorporating victims within sentencing commissions might undermine commissions' aims, it can play an important role in helping to boost public confidence in criminal justice, a touchstone for all western governments' criminal justice policies.

INTRODUCTION

Many jurisdictions now have an agency, often called a sentencing commission or council, that has as one of its aims the production of binding or voluntary sentencing guidelines. There is a range of types of commission with a variety of approaches to composition, aims, functions, criteria, procedures and constitutionality of guidelines production.[1] These mechanisms supplement or replace the role of the jurisdictions' appellate courts in providing sentencing guidelines. They aim to promote consistency and transparency, many have a duty to monitor sentencing practice and some have to ensure some sort of correspondence between sentencing guidelines and available penal resources. In the USA, there is a Federal Sentencing Guidelines Commission and twenty-two states in the USA have a sentencing commission of some type.[2] New Zealand has legislated for a Sentencing Council, although the Sentencing Council Act 2007 is not in force.[3] Similarly, in Scotland Part One of the Criminal Justice and Licensing (Scotland)

---

*Senior Lecturer in Law, UEA Law School, University of East Anglia. Many thanks to Rosemary Pattenden, Julian Roberts and the MLR's two anonymous reviewers for helpful comments on earlier drafts. I take full responsibility for the content, opinions and errors in the article.

1 R. Frase, 'Sentencing Guidelines: Diversity, Consensus and Unresolved Policy Issues' (2005) 105 Colum L Rev 1190, 1191.

2 The following states have such a body, which is called a Sentencing Commission unless otherwise indicated: Alabama, Arkansas, Connecticut, Delaware, District of Columbia, Illinois (Sentencing Policy Advisory Council), Kansas, Louisiana, Maryland (State Commission on Criminal Sentencing Policy), Massachusetts, Minnesota, Missouri (Sentencing Advisory Commission), New Mexico, North Carolina, Ohio (State Criminal Sentencing Commission), Oregon (Criminal Justice Commission), Pennsylvania (Commission on Sentencing), South Carolina (Sentencing Guidelines Commission), Utah, Vermont, Virginia (Criminal Sentencing Commission), Washington (Sentencing Guidelines Commission).

3 W. Young and C. Browning, 'New Zealand's Sentencing Council' (2008) Crim LR 294; 'National to scrap sentencing council' New Zealand Herald 2 August 2008, at http://www.nzherald.co.nz/nz/news/article.cfm?c_id=1&objectid=10524915 (last visited 1 January 2012).

Ian Edwards

Act 2010 provides for the establishment of a Scottish Sentencing Council, although the relevant provisions are not yet in force. In South Africa and Northern Ireland there have been recommendations for some form of guidelines body.[4] Four Australian states (New South Wales, Victoria, Tasmania and Queensland) have advisory councils on sentencing providing advice to the state's Court of Criminal Appeal or Justice Minister about the need for, and content of, guidelines that should be issued. In England and Wales, the Sentencing Council was established by the Coroners and Justice Act 2009 (CJA 2009) and replaces the Sentencing Guidelines Council (SGC) and Sentencing Advisory Panel (SAP).[5] The Council must prepare sentencing guidelines about reductions in sentence for guilty pleas and about the totality of sentences.[6] It can prepare guidelines about any other matter and revise issued guidelines.[7] The Council must publish a resource assessment of the likely effect of the guidelines on the resources required for the provision of prison places, probation and youth justice services.[8] It must monitor the operation and effect of its sentencing guidelines and consider what conclusions can be drawn from that monitoring.[9] Sentencers must follow the guidelines unless it is contrary to the interests of justice to do so.[10]

Much has been written about mechanisms for structuring sentencing guidelines.[11] Almost nothing has been said, however, about the place of victims within them.[12] Given the practical significance of the Sentencing Council's work for all criminal courts, there has been surprisingly little analysis of its remit or work to

---

4 Sentencing Commission for Scotland, *The Scope to Improve Consistency of Sentencing* (Glasgow: Sentencing Commission for Scotland, 2006); S. Terblanche, 'Sentencing Guidelines for South Africa: Lessons from Elsewhere' (2003) 120 *South African Law Journal* 858–882; Northern Ireland Assembly Research and Information Service, *Comparative Research into Sentencing Guidelines Mechanisms* (2011: Research Paper 66/11) at http://www.niassembly.gov.uk/Documents/RaISe/Publications/Justice/6611.pdf (last visited 1 January 2012). South Korea has introduced guidelines modelled on England. There are similar proposals in Israel: J. Roberts, 'Structured Sentencing: Lessons from England and Wales for Common Law Jurisdictions' (2012) *Punishment & Society* (forthcoming).

5 A. Ashworth, 'Coroners and Justice Act 2009: Sentencing Guidelines and the Sentencing Council' (2010) Crim LR 389; Roberts *ibid*.

6 CJA 2009, s 120(3)(a) and s 120(3)(b).

7 s 120(4) and s 120(9); s 122(6).

8 s 127(1)–(3).

9 s 128(1)–(2).

10 s 125.

11 M. Tonry, *Sentencing Matters* (Oxford: OUP, 1996); A. Freiberg and K. Gelb (eds), *Penal Populism, Sentencing Councils and Sentencing Policy* (Cullompton: Willan, 2008). There are hundreds of articles; among the most important are R. Frase, 'Sentencing Guidelines: Diversity, Consensus and Unresolved Policy Issues' (2005) 105 Colum L Rev 1190 and R. A. Duff, 'Theories and Policies Underlying Guidelines Systems' (2005) 105 Colum L Rev 1162.

12 Debate in each jurisdiction has focused on the place of victims in individual sentencing decisions, on which there is a burgeoning literature: for an overview of the issues see, I. Edwards, 'Victim Participation in Sentencing: The Problems of Incoherence' (2001) 40 *Howard Journal of Criminal Justice* 39 and I. Edwards, 'The evidential quality of victim personal statements and family impact statements' (2009) 13 *International Journal of Evidence and Proof* 293; R. Butler, 'What Practitioners and Judges Need to Know Regarding Crime Victims' Participatory Rights in Federal Sentencing Proceedings' (2006) 19 *Federal Sentencing Reporter* 21–29; limited discussion of victims does appear in Freiberg and Gelb *ibid*.

Sentencing Councils and Victims

date.[13] One important aspect of the Council's remit has not featured in the literature at all: the relationship between the Council and victims. One of the six matters to which the Council must have regard when preparing, reviewing and revising guidelines is 'the impact of sentencing decisions on victims of offences' (the other matters are 'the sentences imposed by courts in England and Wales for offences', 'the need to promote consistency in sentencing', 'the cost of different sentences and their relative effectiveness in preventing re-offending', 'the need to promote public confidence in the criminal justice system' and the results of monitoring the operation and effect of its sentencing guidelines).[14] The inclusion of an obligation to have regard in some way to victims is striking: it is not a factor to which the SGC or SAP had to have regard and as we shall see below virtually no other jurisdiction has such an obligation.[15] What is the relationship between victims and sentencing commissions and what are the implications of an obligation such as the Council's?

First, I situate the issues within two broader contexts: the political emergence of victims and the penological precipitants of sentencing commissions. Second, I consider the ways in which victims can be incorporated in the work of sentencing commissions. Third, I examine the meaning and significance of the Sentencing Council's obligation to have regard to 'the impact of sentencing decisions on victims', situating it in the context of the Council's functions and considering the broader implications of involving victims in commissions. I will argue that including victims might appear to threaten the development of parsimonious and progressive sentencing guidelines but is actually more likely to strengthen the ability of guidelines authorities to propose politically palatable guidelines.

VICTIMS AND SENTENCING COMMISSIONS IN CONTEXT

Victims' relationships with sentencing commissions should be understood against a backdrop of two interrelated contexts. First, victims have emerged as the rhetorical and practical focus of contemporary criminal justice policies in which public confidence is a touchstone of reform. Second, penological and economic contexts have spurred the introduction of structured sentencing mechanisms to promote consistency of approach to sentencing while tempering the demand for prison places. The connections between the two bear directly on the nature and meaning of victims' places within structured sentencing mechanisms.

---

13 See Ashworth, n 5 above; Roberts, n 4 above and 'Sentencing Guidelines and Judicial Discretion: Evolution of the Duty of the Courts to Comply in England and Wales' (2011) 51 BJ Crim 997–1013; J. Roberts and A. Rafferty, 'Structured Sentencing in England and Wales: Exploring the new Guideline Format' (2011) Crim LR 681–690; A. Lovegrove, 'The Sentencing Council, the Public's Sense of Justice and Personal Mitigation' (2010) Crim LR 906; J.V. Roberts, M. Hough and A. Ashworth, 'Personal Mitigation, Public Opinion and Sentencing Guidelines in England and Wales' (2011) Crim LR 524; J. Raine and E. Dunstan, 'How well do sentencing guidelines work? Equity, proportionality and consistency in the determination of fine levels in the Magistrates' Courts of England and Wales' (2009) 48 *Howard Journal of Criminal Justice* 13–36; M. Wasik, 'Sentencing Guidelines in England Wales: State of the Art?' (2008) Crim LR 253–263; J. Cooper, 'The Sentencing Guidelines Council: A Practical Perspective' (2008) Crim LR 277.
14 s 120(11).
15 CJA 2003, s 170(5); Crime and Disorder Act 1998, s 80(3).

Ian Edwards

The political resonance of victims in sentencing

The emergence of victims as a political force has been extensively documented
and victims are now routinely a focal-point of criminal justice policy.[16] Appre-
ciating the key factors behind this development helps us grasp the potential
significance of including victims in sentencing commissions' work. A number of
factors have precipitated this focus on victims since the 1980s. Conceptions of
what constitutes 'public service' and how it is to be delivered have changed
dramatically, which in turn have influenced both the development of criminal
justice policies and the position of victims within them. Public services must now
be responsive, accountable and cost-effective, setting standards by which success
and failure can be judged and service quality assessed. Managerialism pervades
criminal justice, manifested in a growing concern with performance indicators,
cost-efficiency and consumerism.[17] Faced with the seemingly insurmountable
problems of reducing crime, governments adopt 'strategies of adaptation', one of
which is to redefine how to judge success: instead of crime-reduction, the
managerialist ethos defines success partly in terms of maintaining good 'customer
relations'. Victim participation is part of a wider agenda of improving the quality
of public services.[18] Western governments now view victims and witnesses as
consumers of their criminal justice services.[19] Satisfying criminal justice 'consumers' helps maintain public confidence in the criminal justice system. If this
were to collapse, criminal justice 'consumers' might be tempted to take the law
into their own hands and resort to vigilantism.

The criminological retreat from positivism also hastened the decline of a
criminal justice system in which the needs of offenders and understanding
their behaviour had prevailed, heralding a more condemnatory, repressive and
punitive era.[20] Western governments have responded to the difficulties of actually
reducing crime rates (or convincing electorates that they can), by invoking 'tough
on crime' measures. As well as being expressive modes of action, emphasising

---

16 J. Doak, *Victims' Rights, Human Rights and Criminal Justice: Reconceiving the Role of Third Parties*
    (Oxford: Hart, 2008); R. Elias, *The Politics of Victimization: Victims, Victimology and Human Rights*
    (Oxford: OUP, 1986); L. Sebba, *Third Parties: Victims and the Criminal Justice System* (Ohio: Ohio
    State UP, 1996). M. Cavadino and J. Dignan, 'Towards a framework for conceptualising and
    evaluating models of criminal justice from a victim's perspective' (1996) 4 *International Review of
    Victimology* 153. There is a voluminous literature on the problems associated with the term 'victim':
    eg D. Miers, 'Positivist Victimology: a Critique' (1989) 1 *International Review of Victimology* 3; N.
    Christie, 'The Ideal Victim' in E. Fattah (ed), *From Crime Policy to Victim Policy* (Basingstoke:
    Macmillan, 1986) 17–30.
17 J. Raine and M. Willson, 'Beyond Managerialism in Criminal Justice' (1997) 36 *Howard Journal of
    Criminal Justice* 80.
18 B. Williams, 'The Victim's Charter: Citizens as Consumers of Criminal Justice Services' (1999) 38
    Howard Journal of Criminal Justice 384.
19 eg the British Government's 2002 White Paper, *Justice for All* Cm 5563 (2002) 11, pledging to
    'rebalance criminal justice in favour of victims'.
20 D. Garland, *Culture of Control: Crime and Social Control in Contemporary Society* (Oxford: OUP,
    2001); D. Garland, 'The Limits of the Sovereign State' (1996) 36 *British Journal of Criminology* 445;
    D. Garland, 'The Culture of High Crime Societies: Some Preconditions of Recent "Law and
    Order" Policies' (2000) 40 *British Journal of Criminology* 347; D. Garland and N. McCormick,
    'Sovereign States and Vengeful Victims: The Problem of the Right to Punish' in A. Ashworth and
    M. Wasik (eds), *Fundamentals of Sentencing Theory* (Oxford: Clarendon Press, 1998).

Sentencing Councils and Victims

punitive or denunciatory objectives, these measures are populist and politicised and, in support of punitive segregation, routinely invoke images of actual victims and their families as 'righteous figure[s] whose suffering must be expressed and whose security must henceforth be guaranteed.'[21] Public opinion, however defined, has become a privileged driver of policy.[22]

The emergence of sentencing commissions

The history and penological contexts for the emergence of these bodies has been well-documented.[23] Arguably the one unifying factor is pursuit of greater consistency, whether in the name of justice, efficiency, effectiveness or economy.[24] The emergence of such bodies in the USA can be understood as a response to criticism of unfettered discretion in sentencing and parole decisions, as well as an institutional strategy for constraining the use of imprisonment and connecting sentencing guidelines in some way with resources, whether by simply publishing a resource impact assessment alongside the guidelines (as the English Sentencing Council must do) or at the other extreme requiring guidelines to fit a 'capacity envelope'.[25] The Sentencing Council has its roots in Lord Carter's review of the prison system of England and Wales. His report saw the solution to prison population pressures in improving the balance between the supply of prison places and demand for them and called for, amongst other things, 'a structured sentencing framework and permanent Sentencing Commission . . . with judicial leadership, to improve the transparency, predictability and consistency of sentencing . . .'[26] It recommended the Government introduce measures to 'moderate the demand for custody . . . in accordance with the government's strategy to reserve custody for the most serious and dangerous offenders'[27] as well as an expansion of the prison population which it said is 'essential to maintain public confidence in the criminal justice system.'[28] The report called for 'an effective, integrated and transparent planning mechanism that reconciles penal capacity with criminal justice policy' to improve transparency and predictability in the effect of sentencing decisions on penal capacity.[29] The subsequent Report of the Sentencing Commission Working Group examined the advantages, disadvantages and feasibility of a permanent sentencing commission.[30] The report was built around principles of 'transparency, predictability,

---

21 Garland (2000) *ibid*, 350.

22 J. Pratt, 'Penal Scandal in New Zealand' in Freiberg and Gelb, n 11 above, 31.

23 M. Frankel, *Criminal Sentences: Law Without Order* (New York: Hill & Wang, 1973); M. Tonry, *Sentencing Matters* (Oxford: OUP, 1997) 9; Duff, n 11 above.

24 Tonry, n 11 above, 4.

25 Freiberg and Gelb n 11 above, 1.

26 Lord Carter, *Securing the future: Proposals for the efficient and sustainable use of custody in England and Wales* December 2007 at http://www.justice.gov.uk/publications/docs/securing-future.pdf 3 (Carter) (last visited 1 January 2012).

27 *ibid*, 3.

28 *ibid*, 2.

29 *ibid*, 16.

30 Sentencing Commission Working Group, *Sentencing Guidelines in England and Wales: An Evolutionary Approach* (London: HMSO, 2008) (the Gage Report).

consistency and compatibility . . . subject to an overarching commitment to achieve justice in an individual case.'[31] It recommended replacing the SAP and SGC with one body that had the duty and capacity to collect data on sentencing and a responsibility to predict the impact of guidelines and Government sentencing policies.[32]

The desire to boost consumer satisfaction and public confidence seems, at first glance, to conflict with these aims of sentencing commissions. Early normative accounts of sentencing commissions posited the importance of insulating policy development from 'political whimsy'.[33] As Frase argues, independent sentencing commissions are valued not only for their expertise and research capacity but also because they promote a long-term, fiscally responsible perspective and help to insulate sentencing policy development from short-term political pressures driven by sudden shifts in public opinion.[34] An independent commission and a judiciary insulated from political pressure help to provide a policy buffer preventing excessive recourse to 'populist punitiveness'. Some have argued that the absence of public involvement could insulate commissions from public opinion and electoral accountability and promote coherent aims: in Frase's words, 'to apply subject-matter expertise, research and planning capacity, institutional continuity and a long-term perspective to complex public policy issues, while partially insulating controversial issues from direct electoral pressures and short-term swings in public opinion.'[35]

The rise to influence of victims on criminal justice policy has impacted on the work of sentencing commissions. First, victims' increasing influence over criminal justice policy has impelled sentencing policies, including guidelines from sentencing commissions, that acknowledge at some level the experiences of victims and the public. Second, the pursuit of consistency as a principal aim requires public engagement to ensure the authority and legitimacy of commissions, which come not solely from their claims to expertise but from their ability to nurture and counsel the difficult relationship between empirically-grounded research and politically palatable recommendations.[36] Commissions are not insulated from public opinion and ought not to be. Sentencing commissions are, in a sense, post-modern institutions of penality.[37] Ostensibly they work towards specified goals, such as ensuring a fit between supply of and demand for prison places and/or making sentencing more consistent, but may have other primary or subsidiary aims that pull in opposite directions, such as promoting public confidence. Victims can be caught in the maelstrom of aims. In New Zealand for example the Council's proponents invoked victims in its support (victims were said to be the beneficiaries of greater consistency in sentencing) while the National Party has justified non-implementation of the law establishing the

---

31 *ibid*, para 3.5.

32 *ibid*, 20.

33 Tonry, n 11 above, 192.

34 Frase n 1 above, 83.

35 R. Frase, 'Minnesota Sentencing Guidelines' in Freiberg and Gelb, n 11 above, 99.

36 Duff, n 11 above.

37 J. Pratt, 'The Return of the Wheelbarrow Men; or the Arrival of Postmodern Penality?' (2000) BJ Crim 127.

Sentencing Councils and Victims

Council by claiming that victims will be better served by diverting the Council's funding to provide compensation to the victims of serious crimes, particularly victims of homicide or sexual violence.

In England, victims have a somewhat ambiguous and ill-defined relationship with the Sentencing Council. The Coroners and Justice Bill originally contained no reference to victims in the list of factors to which the Council would have to have regard, and victims were barely discussed during Parliamentary debate, unlike the new test for departure from the guidelines and the potential implications of having regard to resources when devising the guidelines.[38] The clause that became section 120(11)(c) (the obligation to have regard to 'the impact of sentencing decisions on victims') was introduced late in the Parliamentary process, and was described without elaboration by the Government minister as a 'straightforward and effective way' to ensure that the Council has regard to victims.[39] Hansard reveals no authoritative ministerial statement as to the Executive's understanding of the meaning and effect of section 120(11)(c).[40] Neither the Carter Review nor Gage Report made any significant mention of crime victims. However, both referenced the need to boost public confidence, such as in Carter's discussion of the inadequacy of early release mechanisms as a means of responding to an increasing prison population, measures which he said, 'inevitably affect confidence and the integrity of sentences and the criminal justice system as a whole.'[41] Despite the lack of explicit reference to victims in decision-making processes, Carter did reference the central importance of public protection, prevention of re-offending and thus prevention of future victimisation.[42] In the subsequent Gage Report there was no discussion of victims or public confidence other than implicitly through the concept of 'transparency', which the Report defined as:

> the ability of Parliament, the public and sentencers to have an understanding, through the existence of clear and comprehensive sentencing guidelines for offences or classes of offence, of how offenders may expect to be sentenced under existing legislation, together with an appreciation of the aggravating and mitigating factors that may be taken into account through judicial discretion.[43]

Neither report envisaged an explicit place for victims' interests in the new guidelines mechanism other than through including a victim's representative, as the Sentencing Guidelines Council had, although Gage did recommend that victims and the public should better understand sentencing processes and outcomes. The lack of a recommended role for victims is not surprising: the overarching purpose of most mechanisms for ensuring structured judicial discretion in sentencing is to promote consistency of approach and to promote a link,

---

38 A misapprehension of many was that the requirement would involve telling judges to consider resources when making individual sentencing decisions.

39 HC Deb vol 712 col 1198 15 July 2009 (Lord Bach).

40 *Pepper* v *Hart* [1993] AC 593.

41 Carter n 26 above, 2.

42 *ibid*, 34.

43 The Gage Report, n 30 above, 8.

Ian Edwards

however loose, between available resources and sentencing decisions.[44] There is no obvious role for victims in achieving these aims. Are victims inevitably just onlookers during guidelines promulgation?

VICTIM PARTICIPATION IN SENTENCING COMMISSIONS

Before turning to analyse the Sentencing Council for England and Wales's specific obligation towards victims, I want to consider the role of victims in the sentencing commissions of other jurisdictions. A review of the enabling legislation for each sentencing commission in the USA, the advisory bodies in Australia and the SAP, SGC and Sentencing Council in England and Wales reveals that victims frequently feature amongst the commissions' members' roles, rarely feature in the aims and purposes of the commission and implicitly feature in the processes by which such bodies should discharge their responsibilities.

Victims in the membership of the commission

The most obvious way in which victims feature in the work of these bodies is in their composition, which typically includes a representative of crime victims. Of the twenty-two American states only three lack this feature: Oregon, South Carolina and Delaware (although there is provision for four members at large '[w]ho by training or experience, possess a knowledge of Delaware sentencing'). Four include a victim or victim's relative in the body's membership (Alabama, Louisiana, Minnesota, Ohio). Four do not make provision for a victim or victims' representative, but do provide for the inclusion of at least one private citizen, who may actually be a victim or victims' representative (Arkansas, DC, Kansas, Missouri). Two include a crime victims' advocate (Connecticut, Massachusetts). Eight include a representative of a victims' organisation or advocacy group (Illinois, Maryland, New Mexico, North Carolina, Pennsylvania (as a non-voting member), Vermont, Virginia and Washington (both of whom also legislate for a victim to be included as an alternative)). Utah's Sentencing Commission includes '[s]omeone who exhibits sensitivity to the needs of victims.' In Australia, victims feature in the composition of the four sentencing advisory bodies. In New South Wales, four of the Sentencing Council's members are to be persons representing the general community, of whom two are to have expertise or experience in matters associated with victims of crime.[45] Victoria's Sentencing Advisory Council must include one member of a victim of crime support or advocacy group and two people with broad experience in community issues affecting the courts.[46] Tasmania's Sentencing Advisory Council includes two community members and Queensland's Advisory Council includes 'victims of crime' among the fourteen constituencies from which the Council's twelve members are

---

44 BBC News Online 'Judge pledges more consistency in assault sentencing' 9 March 2011 at http://www.bbc.co.uk/news/uk-12681250 (last visited 1 January 2012).
45 New South Wales Crimes (Sentencing Procedure) Act 1999, s 100I.
46 Victoria Sentencing Act 1991, as amended, s 108F.

Sentencing Councils and Victims

drawn.[47] In England and Wales, the Sentencing Guidelines Council had to include someone with experience of 'the promotion of the welfare of victims of crime' as one of the four non-judicial members.[48] The Coroners and Justice Act 2009 does not guarantee that the Sentencing Council's composition will include a victims' representative; the legislation lists someone with experience of 'the promotion of the welfare of victims of crime' as eligible for appointment as one of the six non-judicial members of the Council to work alongside the eight judicial members.[49]

What is the significance of including victims or victims' advocates in sentencing commissions? Does it merely threaten to introduce 'populist punitiveness' into sentencing guidelines? This is too simplistic a view for two reasons. First, victims never have a veto over sentencing guidelines, being (usually) only one voting member of the commission (and in the case of Pennsylvania's commission, not even a voting member). Second, as I will discuss later, the accusation that victims bring only punitiveness to the table does not withstand empirical evaluation. Campaigning representatives from particularly strident and implacable victims' groups may seek particularly punitive retribution but others, such as representatives of Victim Support for England and Wales, can adopt moderate and constructive perspectives that facilitate the development of grounded policies.

Given this positive engagement, a more subtle view is that victims' inclusion in commissions can actually promote the latter's aims. First, participatory mechanisms can be better at achieving their aims than bodies that exclude interested parties. The literature on deliberative democracy suggests that citizens' participation is essential because it protects individuals and groups from being subject to arbitrary and capricious rule.[50] Legitimacy and participation are linked in the sense that for decisions to be legitimate they must be the outcome of collective decision-making with the participation of all who will be affected by the decision or their representatives.[51] Second, agencies responsible for sentencing can be more efficacious when they are politically enmeshed and grounded by a range of views. Barkow suggests that US state sentencing agencies' power and significance comes not from their independence and insulation from politics but from their ability to generate politically saleable information.[52] The successful sentencing commission acts, in effect, as an interest group for rational sentencing policy.[53] This is not to say that a *politicised* commission will be the most effective form of administrative agency to regulate sentencing: as Stith and Koh note in their analysis of the history of the federal sentencing guidelines, the dominance of political interests in the make-up of the Federal Sentencing Commission has been a key reason for the failure of the guidelines to keep the

---

47 Penalties and Sentences Act 1992, as amended, s 202.
48 CJA 2003, s 167(4).
49 Schedule 15.
50 D. Held, *Models of Democracy* (Cambridge: Polity, 2ⁿᵈ ed, 1996) 99.
51 J. Elster (ed), *Deliberative Democracy* (Cambridge, New York: Cambridge UP, 1998) 8; J. Dryzek, *Discursive Democracy: Politics, Policy and Science* (Cambridge: Cambridge UP, 1990); D. Galligan, *Due Process and Fair Procedures: A Study of Administrative Procedures* (Oxford: Clarendon Press, 1996) 122.
52 R. E. Barkow, 'Administering Crime' (2005) 52 UCLA L Rev 715, 719.
53 *ibid*, 720.

Ian Edwards

level of incarceration within federal prison capacity.[54] But by including victims, a democratic deficit within insulated commissions can be filled and politically palatable guidelines can be developed.[55]

Victims' interests as an explicit factor in commissions' aims and purposes

In the USA, only three enabling statutes mention victims explicitly in the aims and purposes of the particular commission. The Louisiana Sentencing Commission must formulate recommendations for amendments to state sentencing law that will maximise uniformity, certainty, consistency, and adequacy of a sentence structure having regard in particular to three factors: punishment aligned with the seriousness of the offence; the protection of the public through deterrence and rehabilitation; and to ensure that 'appropriate consideration is accorded to the victims of the offence, their families, and the community.'[56] The North Carolina Sentencing Commission has two specific obligations: to classify offences into categories based on their severity and to 'recommend structures for use by a sentencing court in determining the most appropriate sentence to be imposed in a criminal case'. In discharging those obligations, the Commission must consider *inter alia* 'the rights of the victims'.[57] Among the numerous obligations of the Massachusetts Sentencing Commission is one to 'promote truth in sentencing, in order that all parties involved in the criminal justice process, including the prosecution, the defendant, the court, the victim and the public, are aware of the nature and length of the sentence and its basis.'[58]

Explicit mention of victims in the aims raises four issues. First, what interests do victims have in the promulgation of guidelines? While the Massachusetts obligation to promote 'truth in sentencing' is clear, the wording of the clauses in Louisiana and North Carolina relating to victims gives little indication about how and to what extent the process of formulating guidelines should be influenced by victims' interests, however those are defined. North Carolina's obligation to consider the 'rights of victims' relates to the process of determining the appropriate category of seriousness into which each felony and misdemeanour should fall. In deciding each offence, the Commission has to consider also 'the nature and degree of harm likely to be caused by the offense, including whether it involves property, irreplaceable property, a person, number of persons, or a breach of the public trust; the deterrent effect a particular classification may have on the commission of the offense by others; [and] the current incidence of the offense in the State as a whole.'[59] In deciding on the suggested range of punishment for each offence the Commission has to take into consideration, 'the current range

---

54 K. Stith and S. Koh, 'The Politics of Sentencing Reform: The Legislative History of the Federal Sentencing Guidelines' (1993) 28 Wake Forest L Rev 223.

55 House of Commons Justice Committee, *Sentencing Guidelines and Parliament: Building a Bridge* HC 715 (2009) at http://www.publications.parliament.uk/pa/cm200809/cmselect/cmjust/715/71502.htm (last visited 1 January 2012).

56 Louisiana Statutes 15-321-G.

57 North Carolina Statutes 164-41 & 164-42.

58 Massachusetts General Laws Chapter 211E, section 2.

59 North Carolina Statutes § 164-41.b.

Sentencing Councils and Victims

of punishment for each offense.'[60] It is unclear what 'rights' of victims are in this context and how they are relevant to this process. Louisiana's statute does not explain what it might mean to give 'appropriate consideration' to victims, there is no policy statement on its meaning and no court has had to interpret it.

Second, the inclusion of such an aim does not mean that a commission is therefore 'victim-centred' and must privilege victims' interests (however defined). For example, the overarching aim of Louisiana's Sentencing Commission is to recommend legislation 'to achieve a uniform sentencing policy that ensures public safety and the imposition of appropriate and just sentences in terms that are clear and transparent and which make the most efficient use of the correctional system and community resources.'[61] This multiplicity of aims inevitably means that protecting victims' interests, whatever they may be, must exist alongside other objectives. Third (and conversely) the lack of reference to victims in a commission's aims does not mean that no account is taken of victims in the commission's work. Neither the Sentencing Advisory Panel nor the Sentencing Guidelines Council were explicitly obliged to have regard to victims' interests yet the former conducted research on victims' experiences and the latter built into its guidelines references to victims' experience of offences.[62] Fourth, in the states that mention victims in their commissions' aims there is no research examining how those aims have been interpreted by the commission and what their impact has been. Nor are there official policy statements in those jurisdictions setting out what the obligation entails for the work of the particular commission. Further research is needed to understand how those obligations are interpreted by commissions in those jurisdictions and how those obligations interrelate with the other factors that must be taken into account. However, there are methodological problems in trying to isolate the impact of one factor from a plethora of criteria to which a commission must have regard: only a detailed analysis of the process by which each guideline (or the body of guidelines in states that have developed guidelines in one exercise) has been formulated will reveal how, and to what the extent, the members of the commission have factored in victims' interests as a relevant consideration.

Victims as information providers to assist the commission in discharging its obligations

There is another important place for victims in the work of commissions. Rational, structured sentencing mechanisms, whether narrative or grid-based, definitive or voluntary, must coherently embed cardinal and ordinal proportionality within the guidelines. Offence seriousness cannot be determined *a priori*. Aggregate information about victims is needed to develop guidelines based on offence seriousness. We need insight into the experiences of those affected by the

---

60 North Carolina Statutes § 164-41.c.
61 Louisiana Statutes 15-321-D.
62 eg Sentencing Advisory Panel, *Advice to the Sentencing Guidelines Council: Sentencing for Domestic Burglary* (London: HMSO, 2010); Sentencing Guidelines Council, *Consultation Paper on Sentencing for Fraud Offences* (London: SGC, 2007).

Ian Edwards

type of offence which is the subject of the guideline in order to ground proportionate sentences. One factor in ensuring this coherence is the inclusion of
aggregated information about victims' harm as one element of offence seriousness, alongside culpability. For example, Von Hirsch and Jareborg's 'living standard
analysis' shows how sentencing could be structured to reflect standardised rather
than individualised harm, setting out principles for assessing the gravity of harms
to provide a guide for measuring one aspect of offence seriousness.[63]

Such an approach is evident in the development of Minnesota's guidelines. Its
Sentencing Commission decided it was important from the outset to articulate
the general principles of the guidelines, including establishing the 'ground rules'
for determining what the severity level ranking principles should be. First,
the Commission evaluated whether the interests invaded by each offence were
personal (most serious) through misuse of drugs, property, down to institutional
integrity/governmental process (least serious). The second principle was that the
actual harm, the threat of harm, or the potential for harm as defined by the statute
would be the primary determinant of crime severity within each interest group.[64]
The third principle was that culpability would be the secondary determinant
of crime severity within each crime grouping, with different levels of 'offender blame' associated with individual crimes that affect the overall seriousness of
the crime.

The Sentencing Council has to take account of victims in a similar way,
although it is not trying to develop a grid-based system of guidelines such as the
one in Minnesota. The Council needs information about victims to discharge its
duty under section 120(1) to set out 'different categories of case . . . which
illustrate in general terms the varying degrees of seriousness with which the
offence may be committed'.[65] In assessing offence seriousness the Council must
have regard to 'the harm caused, or intended to be caused or which might
foreseeably have been caused, by the offence'. Aggregating and standardising
harm can be used to situate victims' experiences within a seriousness-based
framework.[66] Survey data addressing the rating of seriousness by the general
public or by victims themselves could be used, or commissions could use
victimological studies of the type and degree of injury actually associated with
different offences.[67] Of course, victims' harm is not the sole factor determining
the appropriate sentence ranges or starting points. The Council must also have
regard to offenders' culpability and any other factors that it considers particularly

---

63 A. Von Hirsch and N. Jareborg, 'Gauging Criminal Harm: a Living-Standard Analysis' (1991) 11
    OJLS 1, 4.

64 Minnesota Sentencing Guidelines Commission, *Severity Level Ranking Principles* (Minneapolis:
    MSGC, 1994).

65 CJA 2009, s 121(2); The SGC's was to ensure that sentencing guidelines included 'criteria
    for determining the seriousness of the offence or offences, including (where appropriate) criteria
    for determining the weight to be given to any previous convictions of offenders' (CJA 2003,
    s 170(7)).

66 D. Hall, 'Victims' Voices In Criminal Court: The Need For Restraint' (1991) 28 *American
    Criminal Law Review* 233.

67 M. Wolfgang and T. Sellin, *The Measurement of Delinquency* (New York: Wiley, 1964); R. Sparks,
    H. Genn and D. Dodd, *Surveying Victims: A Study of the Measurement of Criminal Victimization*
    (London: Wiley, 1977).

Sentencing Councils and Victims

relevant.[68] However, the process of taking account of victims' harm is an important way in which victims' experiences feature in the guidelines process. For example, the Council's draft guideline on burglary drew on Mawby's research on burglary victims, the British Crime Survey and the SAP's research on public attitudes to burglary.[69] The Council states it has 'sought to have full regard to the impact of burglary on victims' which should be taken into account in two stages of the sentencer's decision-making process under the guidelines: step one (deciding what category the offence falls into) and step two (considering relevant aggravating and mitigating factors).[70] The Council's definitive guideline for assaults provides a second example; it specifies a number of aggravating and mitigating factors which allow the court to take account of victims: '[f]or the varying degrees of assault, victims may suffer a wide range of harm from physical injury, damage to health or psychological distress. Injuries caused to victims may not be particularly significant, but humiliation endured by a victim can increase the offender's culpability.'[71] At the level of individual sentencing decisions, there are mechanisms to ensure the effect of an offence on the victim is taken into account at sentencing through the Victim Personal Statement Scheme and the obligation on sentencers in section 143(1) when assessing offence seriousness to consider the harm caused, intended to be caused or that might foreseeably have been caused.

THE SENTENCING COUNCIL'S OBLIGATION TO TAKE ACCOUNT OF THE IMPACT OF SENTENCING DECISIONS ON VICTIMS OF OFFENCES

What is the meaning of the new obligation on the Council to have regard to 'the impact of sentencing decisions on victims of offences'? The phrase is undoubtedly poorly drafted. We might dismiss it as an empty political gesture by which the Government can demonstrate solidarity with victims, akin to the frequently heard but conceptually limited claims that the criminal justice system must be 'rebalanced' in favour of victims.[72] A literal interpretation suggests the Council must have regard to victims' affective responses to the effect or impression of sentencing decisions, to their subjective experiences of sentencing processes and outcomes. But victims can be impacted by decisions in different ways: the decisions can affect victims emotionally in terms of whether a decision makes them feel 'better' or 'worse'; the decisions can help them to recover from the offence or make recovery harder; they can make victims feel more or less safer;

---

68 CJA 2009, s 121(3).
69 Sentencing Council, *Burglary Offences Guideline: Professional Consultation* (London: Sentencing Council, 2011) 10 citing R. R. Mawby, *Burglary* (Devon: Willan Publishing, 2011) and Sentencing Advisory Panel, n 62 above.
70 Sentencing Council, *ibid*, 14.
71 Sentencing Council, *Assault Guideline: Professional Consultation* (London: Sentencing Council, 2010) 27–28 at http://sentencingcouncil.judiciary.gov.uk/docs/ASSAULT_Professional_web.pdf (last visited 1 January 2012).
72 I. Edwards, 'An Ambiguous Participant: The Crime Victim and Criminal Justice Decision-Making' (2004) 44 BJ Crim 967–982.

Ian Edwards

the decisions can make victims feel that the decision-maker acknowledges their experiences and takes appropriate account of their suffering. This does not really take us very far though. Why collate such information and what should be done with it?

The clause contains a series of possible interpretations each with significant consequences for victims and the Council, and raising deeper questions that commissions in common law jurisdictions need to address. We can delineate three interpretations of commissions' obligations towards victims, such as that to be found in section 120(11)(c). These reveal different participatory roles for victims *vis-a-vis* the Council, obligations on the Council *vis-a-vis* victims and research priorities for the Council. I delineate these interpretations for their heuristic value rather than as normative explications of the role they *should* have. The three approaches are: first, the Council has to take account of its guidelines' impact on preventing victimisation; second, the Council must take account of victims' confidence as a particular instance of the public's confidence; third, the Council must ensure that particular victims' interests are taken into account as appropriate in individual cases.

Victims, guidelines and crime prevention

First, the clause could oblige the Council to consider the impact of sentencing decisions on preventing offending and thus preventing victimisation. The clause could mean that the Council need not have regard to victims' affective responses to sentencing decisions but instead should consider whether decisions taken by sentencers prevent victimisation (or re-victimisation). This is perhaps the interpretation of the clause closest to the meaning envisaged by its supporters during the debate on the Coroners and Justice Bill; they posited victims and potential victims as the likely beneficiaries of a guidelines structure that could and should prioritise preventing re-offending and victimisation, with restorative justice mentioned as a progressive and effective response to crime. Labour MP Alun Michael called for the Council to have the reduction of re-offending as the principal criterion amongst the matters to which it must have regard, and he invoked the name of victims, who 'want to know, more than anything else, that they will not become victims again in the future.'[73] He criticised the Bill as introduced for not making explicit reference to prioritising re-offending. The emphasis on sentence ranges in the Bill as introduced seemed to preclude the use of interventions outside the prescribed ranges that might prevent re-offending.[74] The Bill would have obliged the Council to delineate categories of offence based on relative seriousness of types of that offence, recommending an appropriate range of sentences for each category. A sentencer would have been obliged to sentence within the category range unless in his or her opinion it would have been contrary to the interests of justice to do so. In the Act itself, the sentencer's obligation is somewhat looser: sentencers must sentence somewhere within the

73 HC Deb vol 487 col 39 (26 January 2009).
74 HC Deb vol 489 col 619-628 (10th March 2009).

Sentencing Councils and Victims

overall offence range, unless it is contrary to the interests of justice to do so.[75] Victims were posited by those who sought greater flexibility in the original Bill's provisions as the likely beneficiaries of a less 'mechanistic view of retribution' that could encourage rehabilitative sentences:

> [V]ictims and concern for them should be at the heart of the criminal justice system, but that must include potential victims. Only by reducing re-offending – most offending is committed by those who have done things in the past – do we genuinely put victims, especially potential victims, at the heart of the system.[76]

Others called for the Council to be given a clear statutory aim, similar to the principal aim of the youth justice system set out in section 37 of the Crime and Disorder Act 1998, namely to prevent offending.[77] Baroness Linklater called for 'effectiveness in reducing reoffending . . . [to] . . . inform all our thinking, planning and practice'. She argued that the clause could facilitate 'the use of effective and robust community sentences . . . In particular, it seems to us that it would also open the door to the greater use of restorative justice . . . which probably has the most direct impact of all for a large number of victims.'[78]

The Sentencing Council does not actually have a primary aim of crime reduction; none of the sentencing commissions do (although it is a factor to which many must have regard). All commissions face the difficult task of reconciling a sentencing guidelines structure based on retribution with the efficacious pursuit of utilitarian, crime control aims. A common way to do this is to devise guidelines based on offence seriousness but allow sentencers to pursue those crime control aims within limits (what Morris calls 'limiting retributivism'[79]), or allow departure from the guidelines when necessary to achieve one or more of those aims. The problem for the Sentencing Council is that its guidelines' sentencing ranges and starting points need to be based on offence seriousness, yet it is obliged to consider non-retributive aims in section 120(11), in particular 'the cost of different sentences and their relative effectiveness in preventing re-offending' (section 120(11)(e)). If the obligation to take account of victims is interpreted as an obligation to develop guidelines that focus on preventing victimisation, the Council's guidelines will need to find a way of accommodating evidence-based intermediate sanctions. For example, 'justice reinvestment' strategies are increasingly finding favour with some policy-makers.[80] These strategies aim to shift resources away from incarceration and towards rehabilitation and

---

75 This change has been criticised by Ashworth: see n 5 above.
76 HC Deb vol 490 col 224 (24 March 2009) David Howarth MP.
77 HC Deb vol 490 col 243 (24 March 2009).
78 HL Deb vol 496 col 1026 (13 July 2009), HL Deb vol 496 col 1200 (15 July 2009), HL Deb vol 492 col 1290-1 (18 May 2009).
79 R. Frase, 'Limiting Retributivism' in A. von Hirsch, A. Ashworth and J Roberts (eds), *Principled Sentencing: Readings on Theory and Policy* (Oxford: Hart, 2009) ch 4.4.
80 R. Muir, T. Lanning and I. Loader, *Redesigning Justice: Reducing Crime Through Justice Reinvestment* (London: IPPR, 2011) at http://www.ippr.org/publication (last visited 1 January 2012)); R. Allen and V. Stern (eds), *Justice Reinvestment: A New Approach to Crime and Justice* (London: ICPS, 2007) at http://www.kcl.ac.uk/depsta/law/research/icps/downloads/justice-reinvestment-2007. pdf (last visited 1 January 2012).

crime prevention. In its 2009 report on justice reinvestment the House of Commons Justice Committee noted, 'A genuinely victim-based approach to crime should . . . go wider and deeper than providing supportive and responsive services for victims . . . and be focused on crime reduction and prevention as well as justice.'[81] It called for the Sentencing Council's role to be that of ensuring that sentencing practice succeeds in reducing offending and re-offending and providing sentencers with more information to understand what works in terms of reducing re-offending: 'Sentencers . . . need data on the cost-effectiveness, and thus the consequences for the taxpayer, of their decisions', as well as promoting awareness of the effectiveness of different non-custodial sentences.[82] The Committee noted that a major shortcoming of the Council is that its research function concentrates only on sentencing rather than the global management of resources to reduce crime.[83]

Restorative justice provides another example of a non-retributive (and ostensibly victim-centred) response to crime sitting awkwardly with a structured approach to sentencing that emphasises offence seriousness and consistency. Some of restorative justice's advocates argue that proportionality and consistency are anathema to the achievement of restorative solutions to offences.[84] Other theorists, such as Dignan, have argued that restorative aims can be reconciled with proportionality constraints.[85] The point is that commissions that are obliged to promote consistency and transparency will inevitably tend to produce guidelines that emphasise proportionality between offence and sentence, and this might preclude the development of guidelines that benefit victims in the sense of preventing re-offending or facilitating restorative outcomes. The academic literature is yet to deal fully with the tensions they face in promoting both consistency and instrumentalist aims.[86] Commissions may be able to incorporate these objectives. The Sentencing Council's first guideline, on assaults, requires a sentencer first to place the offence into one of three categories based on the extent of harm and culpability involved, then to sentence within the offence range unless it is contrary to the interests of justice to do so.[87] This seems to allow sentencers discretion to pursue non-retributive aims. First, the obligation is to sentence within the offence range, not the category range. Second, even a departure from the category range is permissible if to sentence within it would be contrary to the

---

81 House of Commons Justice Committee, *Cutting Crime: The Case for Justice Reinvestment* 2009 at http://www.publications.parliament.uk/pa/cm200910/cmselect/cmjust/94/94i.pdf 7 (last visited 1 January 2012).

82 *ibid*, para 417 and 432.

83 *ibid*, para 432.

84 N. Christie, 'Conflicts as Property' (1977) 17 *British Journal of Criminology* 1; J. Braithwaite, 'Principles of Restorative Justice' in A. von Hirsch, J. Roberts, A. Bottoms, K. Roach and M. Schiff (eds), *Restorative Justice and Criminal Justice: Competing or Reconcilable Paradigms* (Oxford: Hart, 2003).

85 J. Dignan, 'Normative Constraints: Principles of Penality' in A. von Hirsch, A. Ashworth and J. Roberts (eds), *Principled Sentencing: Readings on Theory and Policy* (Oxford: Hart, 3rd ed, 2009) 199–205.

86 Frase, n 1 above, 1208.

87 Sentencing Council, *Assault: Definitive Guideline* (London: Sentencing Council, 2011) at http://sentencingcouncil.judiciary.gov.uk/docs/Assault_definitive_guideline_-_Crown_Court.pdf (last visited 1 January 2012); CJA 2009, s 125.

Sentencing Councils and Victims

interests of justice. Jurisdictions that have adopted a sentencing grid and a narrower test for departure, such as Minnesota, may be less able to accommodate instrumentalist aims.

This tension is complicated further by the obligation on commissions to promote public confidence in sentencing.[88] Public confidence might be best served by ensuring and demonstrating that sentencing is effective in preventing people from being victims rather than resorting by default to punitive sentences. As the House of Commons Justice Select Committee noted in its 2009 report on sentencing guidelines, sentencing policy should not be determined on the presumption that the public find current sentencing too lenient.[89] In this respect victims' confidence is affected by the efficacy of sentencing and not its punitiveness. Thus, this first interpretation of the Council's obligation towards victims, requiring sentencing guidelines to accommodate instrumentalist aims, needs to be seen alongside a second: the Council needs to have regard to victims' confidence as a particular instance of the public's confidence in criminal justice.

Victims and public confidence

When the clause was introduced in Parliament the then Secretary of State, Jack Straw, linked the possibility of an obligation towards victims with public confidence rather than crime reduction:

> I was a little surprised – even though I claim authorship of them – to find that although the purpose of the Sentencing Council was embedded in the clauses, it was not explicitly stated . . . I am happy to consider . . . whether it would not be appropriate specifically to mention the importance of victims . . . where we set out the matters to which the council must have regard. At the moment, we mention . . . 'the need to promote public confidence in the criminal justice system'; by implication, that includes victims, but they are not mentioned explicitly.[90]

Public and community sentiment needs to be incorporated in the work of sentencing commissions; as Roberts argues, there should be some degree of correspondence between the criminal law and the community to which it applies.[91] The guidelines system will lack credibility if it takes no note of the public's and victims' feelings. This has two aspects: first, victims need to understand sentencing guidelines; second, the process of producing them needs to be inclusive to promote legitimacy.

---

88 CJA 2009, s 120(11)(d).
89 House of Commons Justice Committee *Sentencing Guidelines and Parliament: Building a Bridge* HC 715 (2009) at http://www.publications.parliament.uk/pa/cm200809/cmselect/cmjust/715/71502.htm 36 (last visited 1 January 2012).
90 HC Deb vol 490, col 243 (24 March 2009).
91 J. Roberts, 'Sentencing policy and practice: the evolving role of public opinion' in Freiberg and Gelb, n 11 above, 20; the Council will face difficulties in ensuring its work is reported accurately in the media, as is evident from tabloid reaction to draft guidelines on drug offences: 'Off Their Heads' *The Sun* 29 March 2011 at http://www.thesun.co.uk/sol/homepage/news/3496327/Judges-No-jail-for-dealers-caught-with-50-heroin-wraps.html (last visited 1 January 2012).

Ian Edwards

First, if we understand victims' perceptions we know what information victims need to understand the decision-making processes of sentencing, which can help to manage or respond to those experiences. Research has revealed the importance that victims attach to understanding the reasons for sentencing decisions and what a particular type of sentence means in reality.[92] This interpretation of the obligation is evident in the Council's explanation of its assault guideline:

> It is important that victims, and the wider public, gain a better understanding of sentencing through the new guideline. To this end, the Council proposes that new guidelines should better manage the expectations of victims ahead of any sentence being passed. The formulation of a clearer decision making process will aid victims' understanding of how a sentence is likely to be reached and what range of sentences is available to the court when considering individual cases. Following the passing of a sentence, the clarity of the process will further help in understanding what considerations were taken into account and how the final sentence was reached.[93]

The Council's responsibilities are first to recognise that the opacity of sentencing decisions and processes do affect victims and second to anticipate possible negative reactions. The Council clearly is doing and will continue to do this, for example in its rationale for setting out starting points within the guidelines' category ranges. The Council recognised that not specifying starting points 'might negatively impact on the consistency of sentencing' by leaving sentencers with no anchor within the range and make it difficult for legal practitioners to predict what sentence is likely to be passed in individual cases, 'thus impacting on victims as well as public understanding of the sentencing process.'[94] Thus the Council and commissions more generally have an important function in promoting the 'truth in sentencing' that so many victims want.

Second, victims' confidence in the legitimacy of guidelines can be promoted by an open and inclusive consultation process. The Council must consult with victims to test the political acceptability of its guidelines. This is not to say that the Council must seek victims' approval of sentencing guidelines. Few jurisdictions give victims a determinative role in devising sentencing guidelines or in individual sentencing decisions, the effect of which would of course be likely to undermine objectivity, rationality and consistency.[95] At the level of guidelines development and promulgation, to give determinative weight to victims' views would see guidelines becoming disconnected from underlying principles of proportionality informed by both harm and culpability. It would also hamper the development of a body of guidelines made coherent and rational by anchored scales of both cardinal and ordinal proportionality. At the level of individual sentencing decisions, consistent and proportionate treatment of similarly-situated

---

92 eg M. Hough *et al*, *Attitudes to the Sentencing of Offences Involving Death by Driving* Research Report 5 (London: Sentencing Advisory Panel, 2008).

93 Sentencing Council n 71 above, 28.

94 *ibid*, 12.

95 There are instances in Islamic law: M. Bassiouni (ed), *The Islamic Criminal Justice System* (New York: Oceana Publications, 1982); 'Iran Acid Attack Woman "Pardons" Attacker' 31 July 2011 at http://www.bbc.co.uk/news/world-middle-east-14357261 (last visited 1 January 2012).

Sentencing Councils and Victims

offenders would be threatened by giving individual victims determinative influence over the sentence type and length. However, one might conceive commissions' obligations towards victims as involving work with victims' groups to ensure that they understand and accept guidelines so that their confidence can be promoted and the potential tendency towards vengeance shown by victims and communities can be displaced. Commissions must ensure that their integrity and legitimacy are preserved, and consulting with victims and victims' representatives is one means by which it can do this. However, a separate clause is perhaps unnecessary. The consultation process through which the Council's draft guidelines must go is a key mechanism by which victims and victims' groups can feed into the guidelines process.[96] The Lord Chancellor must be consulted, as must such persons as the Lord Chancellor may direct and also the House of Commons Justice Select Committee.[97] The breadth of the Council's consultation is evident in the development of its first definitive guideline, on assaults. A range of victims' organisations and the Commissioner for Victims and Witnesses contributed views on the Council's draft guideline on assault.[98]

In this respect, the Council has to negotiate politically acceptable guidelines and can use research on victims' attitudes to do so. For example, research for the Council on attitudes towards reductions for guilty pleas showed that compared to the general public victims were more likely to express support for reductions for early guilty pleas.[99] Whether victims and witnesses felt a sentence reduction for a guilty plea was acceptable in their case tended to be linked to their attitudes towards the prospect of having to attend court and testify.[100] However, the Council will face the perennial difficulty of ensuring accurate reporting of such research and its implications in the media.[101]

Would an obligation to ensure, in some way, victims' endorsement of guidelines lead commissions to 'ratchet up' sentencing, hampering any attempt to develop parsimonious sentencing policies that could moderate pressures on scarce penal resources for the sake of boosting victims' confidence? This might well be true if commissions are obliged to give weight to what Philip Pettit calls the 'outrage dynamic', the 'populist punitiveness' that research suggests pervades public opinion in this field.[102] However, empirical research provides reasons to doubt whether this will be the actual effect of working with victims in

---

96 Coroners and Justice Act 2009, s 120(6).
97 *ibid*, s 120(6).
98 Sentencing Council, *Assault Guideline: Response to Consultation* 2011 at http://sentencingcouncil. judiciary.gov.uk/docs/Assault_guideline_-_Response_to_the_consultation.pdf 24–25 (last visited 1 January 2012).
99 W. Dawes, P. Harvey, B. McIntosh, F. Nunney and A. Phillips, *Attitudes to Guilty Plea Sentence Reductions* 2011 Sentencing Council Research Series 02/11 at http://sentencingcouncil. judiciary.gov.uk/docs/Attitudes_to_Guilty_Plea_Sentence_Reductions_(web).pdf (last visited 1 January 2012).
100 *ibid*, 19.
101 As became apparent during the vociferous reaction to the Justice Secretary's suggestion of increasing sentencing discounts for guilty pleas: 'Prisons U-Turn: Kenneth Clarke Forced to Bow to Daily Mail Demands' *The Guardian* 21 June 2011 at http://www.guardian.co.uk/society/2011/jun/21/prisons-kenneth-clarke-bows-to-pressure (last visited 1 January 2012).
102 P. Pettit, 'Is Criminal Justice Politically Feasible?' (2002) 5 Buff Crim L Rev 427, 437.

developing guidelines. Members of the public are not as punitive as some polls have suggested; there are well-documented research findings that while members of the public appear to be punitive and highly critical of sentencing and judges, the more information that people have about crime and the available penalties, the more closely their sentencing preferences align with actual sentencing decisions.[103] Research commissioned by the SAP on public attitudes to the principles of sentencing found no appreciable difference between the views of victims and non-victims on the importance of different purposes of sentencing.[104] Many victims wanted criminal justice outcomes to prevent re-offending, focus on rehabilitation and provide 'closure' for victims and witnesses.[105] Victims were more punitive when considering previous convictions, with 74 per cent favouring incarceration compared to 62 per cent of non-victims.[106] There was no significant difference between victims and non-victims in their attitudes to cases near the custody threshold.[107] Victims were more likely to consider a range of aspects as comprising an appropriate sentence than the public generally. For example, victims gave more consideration to changing the behaviour of the offender and preventing re-offending and consequently whether punishment allowed for rehabilitation and support. Some victims of serious crimes emphasised the offender taking accountability for the offence rather than the sentence length.[108] Of course, the 'outrage dynamic' might be more prevalent for some offences than in others and there will inevitably be limits to a sentencing commission's capacity to promulgate guidelines that are acceptable to victims.[109]

Victims' interests and sentencing decisions

A third interpretation would oblige the Council to ensure that guidelines have sufficient flexibility to accommodate victims' preferences and views when appropriate. Rigid adherence to its guidelines might not be what victims in particular cases want. A noteworthy finding from the SAP's research on public attitudes to sentencing was the high percentage of the public who believed that the victim's wish for a community penalty definitely or probably justified the imposition of a community order. Aggregated across two offences, this circumstance was the factor most likely to be cited as justifying a community order rather than a term of custody, a finding which 'reflects the strong appeal of victims' interests to members of the public.'[110] If victims' interests are to be respected and promoted,

---

103 M. Hough and J. Roberts, 'Sentencing Trends in Britain: Public Knowledge and Public Opinion' (1999) 1 *Punishment and Society* 11–26; N. Hutton, 'Beyond Populist Punitiveness' (2005) 7 *Punishment and Society* 243.

104 M. Hough *et al*, *Public Attitudes to the Principles of Sentencing* Research Report 6 (London: Sentencing Advisory Panel, 2009) 16.

105 *ibid*, 18.

106 *ibid*, 30.

107 *ibid*, 52.

108 Dawes *et al*, n 99 above, 14.

109 For example, research on victims' attitudes to 'death by driving' offences revealed anger, shock and disbelief amongst victims' relatives at the sentences imposed, although the research involved only a small cohort of victims: see Hough *et al*, n 92 above, 50.

110 Hough *et al*, n 104 above, 52, 65.

Sentencing Councils and Victims

sentencers should have some discretion to depart from the guidelines when appropriate if the particular victim or victim's family feels that the sentence is not what they want or need. The difficulty of course is in defining when it is 'appropriate' to allow victims' interests to justify departure from guidelines, given that consistency in sentencing needs to be promoted.

One such situation might be where the sentence due under the guidelines is likely to impact adversely on the particular victim(s). In England and Wales the Court of Appeal's decisions and the Lord Chief Justice's guidance on Victim Personal Statements state that victims' opinions are generally not relevant to sentencing decisions, and victims should be advised of this before making a VPS, but there is a minor exception to that broad principle. Whilst courts can never take account of calls for vengeance they can in exceptional circumstances be 'instruments of compassion'.[111] The Court of Appeal has been willing to reduce a sentence on appeal in recognition of the impact that the original sentencing decision was having on the victim or the victim's family. For example, in *R v Matthews* a sentence of five years' imprisonment for the manslaughter of the appellant's brother was reduced to a term of three years and six months to take account of the distress caused by the sentence to other members of the family.[112]

What would it mean for the work of sentencing commissions if victims' interests in this sense had to be incorporated into sentencing guidelines? Would it threaten or compromise the ability of commissions to achieve their aims, particularly promoting consistency? Not necessarily. First, although there are no statistics available, it is likely that there are few cases in which victims call for more lenient sentences than the guidelines will recommend, so the overall impact of allowing victims' interests to be a factor justifying departure on aggregate sentencing levels and resources is likely to be minimal. Second, in response to the criticism that giving weight to victims' interests will compromise consistency, the key point is that the aim of commissions is not to guarantee uniformity of outcome in cases that are different. As Tonry argues, guidelines need to be sufficiently flexible to accommodate ethically relevant considerations.[113] Provided that sentences remain within an overall sentencing framework based on limiting retributivism, there is little sense in which justice will be compromised.

The Sentencing Council actually need do very little in this respect. It is not even necessary to include the limited exception to the principle of giving no weight to victims' opinions in its guidelines given that the Criminal Procedure Rules and guidance from the Court of Appeal in *R v Nunn*[114] and *R v Perks*[115] are clear: where the sentence passed on the offender is aggravating the victim's distress, the sentence may be moderated to some degree.[116] Even though the test for departure from the guidelines has been strengthened, there is still sufficient flexibility to allow sentencers to take account of such factors. Under the CJA

---

111 *Roche* [1999] 2 Cr App R (S) 105, 109 per Lord Bingham.
112 [2002] EWCA Crim 1484.
113 Tonry, n 11 above, 23.
114 *R v Nunn* [1996] 2 Cr App R (S) 136.
115 *R v Perks* [2001] 1 Cr App R (S) 19.
116 For further analysis of the Court's approach to victims' opinions, see I. Edwards, 'The Place of Victims' Preferences in the Sentencing of "Their" Offenders' (2002) Crim LR 689–702.

2003, courts had to 'have regard to' sentencing guidelines but now the strength-ened test for departure in section 125(1) of the CJA 2009 obliges courts to 'follow' them 'unless the court is satisfied that it would be contrary to the interests of justice to do so'.[117] Perhaps the clause in section 120(11)(c) indicates that guidelines should ensure that victims' 'interests', however defined, are included as explicit factors that might allow judges to depart from the guidelines or at least indicate the effect on locating the sentence in the category and offence ranges. It seems clear though from the Court of Appeal's interpretation of the new test for departure that while it is important that sentencers do have regard to the relevant guidelines, they are merely guidelines and the different levels and starting points in them should not be viewed in a purely mechanical or mechanistic way.[118] In *R v Blackshaw and others* (2011) (the conjoined appeals against sentence for ten offenders convicted of offences during the riots of August 2011) the Court reiterated the flexibility that the new test for departure preserves for sentencers.[119] As the Lord Chief Justice stated firmly, the CJA 2009 'does not constrain the proper exercise of individual judgment on the specific facts of the case' and 'does not require slavish adherence' to guidelines.[120] The Court has also made it clear that the weight to be attached to its decisions on sentencing issues or policy is 'undiminished by the issue of guidelines.'[121] Thus, the Court's guidance in *Nunn*[122] and *Perks*[123] on how courts should take account of the impact of sentencing decisions on victims or victims' families remains applicable.

CONCLUSION

What can we learn from the English Sentencing Council's obligations about the appropriate position of victims in sentencing commissions? One view is that victims have no particularly special or distinctive role. From this perspective, an obligation towards victims such as that in section 120(11)(c) imposes no addi-tional responsibilities on commissions, given that victims are members of the public and commissions usually have an obligation to promote public confi-dence; if we boost public confidence, we boost victims' confidence. On this reading, the Sentencing Council is no more obliged to be 'victim-centred' than were the SAP or SGC, both of whom had to have regard to 'public confidence' in discharging their responsibilities.[124] However, there are deeper issues raised by incorporating victims' views and interests in sentencing commissions. At one level, the somewhat ambiguous meaning of the obligation on the Sentencing Council reflects the ambiguity of the role of victims vis-à-vis decision-makers in criminal justice more generally. Elsewhere I have conceptualised four potential

---

117 For full discussion see Roberts (2011), n 13 above.
118 per Beatson J in *Rendell* [2011] EWCA Crim 1438 at [12].
119 *R v Blackshaw and others* [2011] EWCA Crim 2312.
120 *ibid* at [13].
121 per the Lord Chief Justice in *Thornley* [2011] EWCA Crim 153.
122 n 114 above.
123 n 115 above.
124 The SGC, explicitly under the CJA 2003, s 170, and the SAP implicitly through its obligations towards first the CACD in the CDA 1998, s 80-81 and then the SGC under CJA 2003, s 171.

Sentencing Councils and Victims

roles for victims *vis-à-vis* decision-makers in criminal justice: as providers of relevant information; consultees on matters of legitimate interest; permitted expressers of views; and, at the end of a spectrum of participation types, decision-makers.[125] In terms of the potential role of victims in relation to the functions of sentencing commissions, victims appear to have information-providing roles in facilitating the development of guidelines based in large part on offence serious-ness, one component of which is harm. They can be consultees, either through the opportunities provided to the public at large to respond to draft guidelines or through formal membership of commissions. An expressive role can similarly be accorded to victims through the consultation process and commission member-ship, providing opportunities to communicate their experiences even if the commission is not obliged to factor them in to the actual guidelines promulgated. Victims might also be granted determinative influence over the guidelines, but as we have seen this rarely happens. Each potential role raises questions about the principal aims of sentencing commissions and councils, whether they need victims to achieve those aims and whether victims' interests can be acknowledged and protected whilst also achieving those principal aims. The place of victims is not necessarily antithetical to the aims of sentencing commissions. But the increasing prominence of victim-centred interventions such as restorative justice and crime preventive strategies such as 'justice reinvestment' poses a challenge for bodies such as the Sentencing Council, which must address the deeper tension between retributively-based guidelines and instrumentalist aims. In doing so it should continue to recognise that maintaining public confidence means, at least in part, maintaining victims' confidence in justice.

---

125 Edwards, n 72 above.

Part III
Sentencing and Emotions

[11]

Hearing the Voices of Victims and Offenders: The Role of Emotions in Criminal Sentencing*

JONATHAN DOAK

Durham Law School, Durham University

LOUISE TAYLOR

Nottingham Law School, Nottingham Trent University

The place of emotions in the criminal justice system is delineated by a curious paradox. On the one hand, law is imbued with emotion. The criminal law, in particular, is replete with numerous examples of trials concerning crimes of passion, episodes of provocation and inquiries into the general state of mind of the offender.[1] The existence, absence or extent of emotions such as anger, passion, fear, or extreme distress on the part of the accused may well determine the applicability of various defences, such as the loss of control (formerly provocation), diminished responsibility, duress or self-defence. Magistrates, judges and juries are routinely faced with facts that will inevitably trigger emotional responses including anger, disgust, moral outrage and compassion.[2] The collapse of the public/private divide has permitted the penetration of emotions into the public space,[3] where they have become popular currency in an era of 'new punitiveness' and 'moral panics'.[4] In the United States in particular, the increasing tendency to adopt public shaming rituals as part of community-based sentences (such as the wearing of sandwich boards indicating criminality, or undertaking public works whilst wearing orange jumpsuits) are designed in part to assuage public anger whilst simultaneously triggering shame on the part of the offender.[5]

---

* Forthcoming in *Northern Ireland Legal Quarterly* 64(1). Many thanks to Thom Brooks and David O'Mahony, both of Durham Law School, for their insightful comments on previous drafts. Thanks also to the referees for their helpful suggestions.

[1]   S Karstedt, 'Emotions and Criminal Justice' (2002) 6 *Theoretical Criminology* 299.

[2]   See further TA Maroney, 'Emotional Regulation and Judicial Behavior' (2011) 99 *California Law Review* 1481.

[3]   J Brewer, 'Dealing with Emotions in Peacemaking' in S Karstedt, I Loader and H Strang (eds), Emotions, Crime and Justice (Oxford: Hart, 2011).

[4]   See generally, J Pratt, D Brown, M Brown, S Hallworth and W Morrison (eds), *The New Punitiveness: Trends, Theories, Perspectives* (Cullompton: Willan, 2005).

[5]   See further D Kahan, 'What's *Really* Wrong with Shaming Sanctions' (2006) 84 *Texas Law Review* 2075; T Massaro, 'Shame, Culture, and American Criminal Law' (1991) 89 *Michigan Law Review* 1880; 'The Meanings of Shame: Implications for Legal Reform' (1997) 3/4 *Psychology, Public Policy, and Law* 645; M Nussbaum, *Hiding from Humanity. Disgust, Shame and the Law* (Princeton: Princeton University Press, 2004); J Pratt, 'Emotive and Ostentatious Punishment: Its Decline and

Nevertheless, the imprecision and volatility of emotions pose a direct challenge to the presumed rational and measurable nature of the legal realm. In a lawyer-driven system underpinned by adversarial confrontation, there is little room for empathy, or any form of enquiry into emotions other than those which the law deems to be relevant. As Bandes contends, 'the passion for predictability, the zeal to prosecute, and mechanisms such as distancing, repressing and isolating one's feelings from one's thought processes are the emotional stances that have always driven mainstream legal thought.'[6] The fear that victims, witnesses, defendants, lawyers and judges might be anything other than rational actors pervades the law in general[7] and sentencing process in particular.[8] In leaving the door ajar for emotions that are traditionally alien to legal discourse, it is feared that its core normative features of consistency, certainty and fairness would be lost in a maelstrom of emotional outpourings. Emotions of anger, hatred and pain – or indeed of sorrow, understanding and forgiveness – may translate into undue punitiveness or leniency and thereby compromise the normative objectivity of the law. This aversion to emotion is reflected in the structures and processes of the law and magnetises its governance. As such, emotions tend to 'creep in interstitially, as indicators that individual defendants are less bad and so need less deterrence, incapacitation, or retribution'.[9] Remorse, for example, may be directly linked to rehabilitation, insofar as that an offender who realises that his / her actions were wrong is less likely to repeat them in the future. In this way, remorse may also serve to reinforce social norms, denounce public wrongs, and thus contribute to deterrence in the longer run.[10]

Recent years have seen a marked reduction in scepticism toward emotions. Emotions have come to feature prominently in late modernity, with heightened emotional awareness increasingly viewed as quintessentially a 'good thing', comprising 'a critical source of information for problem-solving and learning'.[11] A greater awareness of emotions should enable institutions and decision-makers within them to better predict when negative sentiments

---

Resurgence in Modern Society' (2000) 2 *Punishment & Society* 417; J *Whitman*, 'What is Wrong with Inflicting Shame Sanctions?' (1998) 107 *Yale Law Journal* 1062. Though some commentators have argued that shame in and of itself need not be used in a stigmatic way: see eg J Braithwaite, *Crime, Shame and Reintegration* (Cambridge: Cambridge University Press, 1989); T Brooks, 'Shame On You, Shame On Me? Nussbaum on Shame Punishment' (2008) *Journal of Applied Philosophy* 322; A-M McAlinden, 'The Use of "Shame" with Sexual Offenders' (2005) 45 *British Journal of Criminology* 378; L Walgrave and I Aertsen, 'Reintegrative Shaming and Restorative Justice: Interchangeable, Complementary or Different?' (1996) 4 *European Journal on Criminal Policy and Research* 67.

   [6]   S Bandes, 'Empathy, Narrative, and Victim Impact Statements' (1996) 63 *U. Chi. L. Rev.* 361, p. 369.

   [7]   S Bandes, 'Introduction' in S Bandes (ed), *The Passions of Law* (New York: New York University Press, 1999).

   [8]   See eg DJ Hall, 'Victims' Voices in Criminal Court: The Need for Restraint' (1991) 28 *American Criminal Law Review* 233; Y Buruma, 'Doubts on the Upsurge of the Victim's Role in Criminal Law' in H Kaptein and M Malsch (eds), *Crime, Victims, and Justice, Essays on Principles and Practice* (Aldershot: Ashgate, 2004).

   [9]   S Bibas and RA Bierschbach, 'Integrating Remorse and Apology into Criminal Procedure' (2004) 114 *Yale Law Journal* 85, p. 88.

   [10]   Ibid.

   [11]   William J. Long and Peter Breke, *War and Reconciliation: Reason and Emotion in Conflict* (MIT Press, Boston, 2003), p. 127.

may arise and how best to dissipate them.[12] In doing so, institutions can become better placed to adapt their procedures in such a way so as to perform a more effective regulatory role whilst simultaneously building confidence among the public.[13]

In a widely cited 2002 presidential address to the American Society of Criminology, Lawrence Sherman called for an 'emotionally intelligent' approach to criminal justice,[14] 'in which the central tools will be inventions for helping offenders, victims, communities, and officials manage each other's emotions to minimize harm'.[15] Under this paradigm, the state itself would adopt a rational stance in dealing with the emotions of victims, offenders and communities in order to persuade citizens to comply with the law and repair any harm caused.[16] Sherman envisages such a system working 'like an emotionally intelligent political campaign or product marketing plan, one that is likely to employ disaggregated strategies based on research evidence about what messages or methods work best for each type of audience'.[17]

This article draws on Sherman's vision, and examines the place of emotions within the law and practice of sentencing within England and Wales. In a sense, sentencing can be viewed as the apogee of the criminal process; it is at this juncture that the aims of punishment are given concrete and public expression.[18] We begin by exploring in depth why emotions matter, and, in particular, the benefits that a more emotionally intelligent approach to sentencing might reap. Next, we consider a number of legal and policy developments that have arguably increased the place of emotion in sentencing; particular attention is given in this context to pleas in mitigation and the reception of victim impact evidence. Finally, we move on to evaluate the overall role of emotion within the sentencing framework of England and Wales and proceed to make a number of suggestions to unlock the full potential benefit of emotions.

---

[12] K Murphy, 'Procedural Justice, Emotions and Resistance to Authority' in Karstedt et al, n. 3 above.

[13] See generally D D Welch, 'Ruling With the Heart: Emotion-Based Public Policy' (1997) 6 *Southern California Interdisciplinary Law Journal* 55.

[14] L Sherman, 'Reason for Emotion: Reinventing Justice with Theories, Innovations, and Research — The American Society of Criminology 2002 Presidential Address' (2003) 41 *Criminology* 1. The concept of emotional intelligence itself is generally attributed to Howard Gardner, who proposed an alternative concept of multiple intelligences, which included both *interpersonal intelligence* (our capacity to understand the feelings and motivations of other people) and *intrapersonal intelligence* (our capacity to understand our feelings, our wants and fears, our strengths and weaknesses, and motivations and goals): H Gardner, *Frames of Mind: The Theory of Multiple Intelligences* (New York: Basic Books, 1983). Debate continues as to the precise definition of emotional intelligence, and indeed whether it is a useful concept at all given the lack of consensus as to what constitutes an 'emotion' as opposed to a mood, affect, feeling, cognition, temperament or personality: see generally R Plutchik, 'The Nature of Emotions' (2001) 89 *American Scientist* 344.

[15] Sherman, 'Reason for Emotion', ibid., p. 6.

[16] Ibid., 8.

[17] Ibid., citing D. Massey, 'Presidential Address. A Brief History of Human Society: The Origin and Role of Emotion in Social Life' (2002) 67 *American Sociological Review* 1.

[18] R Henham, *Sentencing and the Legitimacy of Trial Justice* (Abingdon: Routledge, 2012), p. 1.

The Importance of Emotional Narratives

An emotionally intelligent approach as advocated by Sherman would require us to ascertain how the primary participants in the system – victims, offenders and legal actors – think and interact using both their emotional and rational brains.[19] Law and policy would evolve in light of what we learn about the emotional responses of victims, offenders and the community. In particular, we contend that such an approach holds the potential to reap four significant benefits to the sentencing process: (1) strengthening therapeutic jurisprudence; (2) strengthening procedural justice; (3) improving the quality of decision-making; and, finally (4), the transformation of relationships.

Strengthening Therapeutic Justice

Perhaps the most commonly cited advantage of an emotionally intelligent approach to sentencing is the potential for therapeutic benefit. There is considerable overlap between emotional intelligence and therapeutic jurisprudence discourse. Therapeutic jurisprudence posits that lawyers and policymakers can seek to reduce anti-therapeutic aspects of the legal process, whilst simultaneously enhancing its therapeutic effects by studying the emotions and psychological experiences of victims and offenders.[20] While lawyers cannot be expected to act as therapists, and trials cannot provide a substitute for psychological interventions, therapeutic jurisprudence contends that justice processes, and their key players, hold the potential to operate as 'change agents' whereby victims and witnesses are offered respect and space to tell their story and air their emotions.[21]

As far as victims are concerned, their emotions are likely to vary according to the types of crimes committed, the levels of injury or loss experienced, and the diverse life experiences of the individuals concerned as well as their inherent characteristics.[22] Bearing this in mind, care should be taken in navigating a minefield of literature that can be at times prone to adopting generalist and vague concepts such as 'emotional redress / restoration', 'closure', 'healing', 'catharsis', etc. without defining what is specifically meant.[23] Even if emotional expression does lead to such phenomena, it should not be assumed that feelings of closure or catharsis expressed in the aftermath of a criminal hearing will necessarily have any longer-term bearing on clinical diagnoses such as depression, anxiety, post-traumatic stress or recognised psychiatric disorders.

---

[19]   Massey, 'A Brief History', n. 17 above.

[20]   B Winick, 'The Jurisprudence of Therapeutic Jurisprudence' in D Wexler and B Winick. *Law in a Therapeutic Key: Developments in Therapeutic Jurisprudence* (Durham, NC: Carolina Academic Press, 1996).

[21]   D Wexler, 'Therapeutic Jurisprudence and the Rehabilitative Role of the Criminal Defense Lawyer' (2005) 17 *St. Thomas Law Review* 743, p. 748.

[22]   See generally J Shapland and M Hall, 'What do We Know about the Effects of Crime on Victims?' (2007) 14 *International Review of Victimology* 175.

[23]   See further A Pemberton and S Reynaers, 'The Controversial Nature of Victim Participation: Therapeutic Benefits in Victim Impact Statements' in E Erez, M Kilchling and J Wemmers (eds), *Therapeutic Jurisprudence and Victim Participation in Justice* (Durham, NC: Carolina Academic Press, 2011).

However, evidence does suggest that overcoming negative emotions resonates closely with evidence-based strategies to deal with states of distress. There is now a robust body of empirical evidence suggesting that externalising traumatic experiences through verbalisation can be an effective intervention for many people facing major life-changing events, including violent crime.[24] Such verbalisation – which is the lynchpin of contemporary counselling and psychotherapy – can help reduce feelings of anger, anxiety and depression;[25] bolster self-confidence;[26] and even improve physical health.[27] By pinpointing the therapeutic effect through more specific and evidence-based terminology, some of the pitfalls associated with altogether grander claims about the capacity of the criminal justice system to effect 'closure' or 'catharsis' for victims can be avoided.[28]

Although the highly-fragmented nature of story-telling that takes place within the trial is vastly different from the comparatively free-flowing and client-focused nature of most talking therapies,[29] there is evidence that victim impact statements can give certain victims a sense of confidence and control, which can also serve to reduce feelings of anger and retribution.[30] As Erez has argued, '[t]he cumulative knowledge acquired from research in various jurisdictions, in countries with different legal systems, suggests that victims often benefit from participation and input. With proper safeguards, the overall experience of providing input can be positive and empowering'.[31] By the same token, however, it ought to be borne in mind that such therapeutic effects will not be universally experienced by all victims; and indeed there is some evidence that while participation may help victim recovery in certain cases, it may hinder it in others.[32]

---

[24]   J Smyth and J Pennebaker, 'Sharing One's Story: Translating Emotional Experiences into Words as a Coping Tool' in C. Snyder (ed.), *Coping: The Psychology Of What Works*, (Oxford: Oxford University Press, 1999); J Kenney, 'Gender Roles and Grief Cycles: Observations of Models of Grief and Coping in Homicide Survivors' (2003) 10 *International Review of Victimology* 19; M White, *Narrative Means to Therapeutic Ends* (New York: W.W. Norton & Co, 1990). A 2005 study by Zech and Rime did, however, suggest that some of these benefits may be perceived rather than real: E Zech and B Rime, 'Is Talking about an Emotional Experience Helpful? Effects on Emotional Recovery and Perceived Benefits'. (2005) 12 *Clinical Psychology & Psychotherapy* 270.

[25]   T Orbuch, J Harvey, S Davis, and N Merbach, 'Account-Making and Confiding as Acts of Meaning in Response to Sexual Assault' (1004) 9 *Journal of Family Violence* 249.

[26]   J Koenig Kellas and V Manusov, 'What's in a Story? The Relationship Between Narrative Completeness and Tellers' Adjustment to Relationship Dissolution' (2003) 20 *Journal of Social and Personal Relationships* 285.

[27]   R Enright and R Fitzgibbons, *Helping Clients Forgive: An Empirical Guide for Resolving Anger and Restoring Hope* (Washington D.C: American Psychological Association, 2000).

[28]   Pemberton and Reynaers, 'The Controversial Nature', n. 23 above.

[29]   See generally C Feltham, *What Is Counselling? The Promise and Problem of the Talking Therapies* (Sage, London, 1995).

[30]   J C Karremans and P Van Lange, 'Does Activating Justice Help or Hurt in Promoting Forgiveness?' (2005) 41 *Journal of Experimental Social Psychology* 290; H Strang, *Repair or Revenge? Victims and Restorative Justice* (Oxford: Clarendon, 2002).

[31]   E Erez, 'Who's Afraid of the Big Bad Victim? Victim Impact Statements as Victim Empowerment and Enhancement of Justice' [1999] *Criminal Law Review* 545, pp. 550–51.

[32]   C Hoyle, 'Empowerment through Emotion: The Use and Abuse of Victim Impact Evidence' in E Erez, M Kilchling and J Wemmers (eds), n. 23 above.

A further therapeutic benefit for the victim may result from the offender expressing remorse or offering an apology. Although there is strong empirical evidence to suggest that victims desire apologies and feel better in their aftermath,[33] there is also an obvious risk that some expressions of remorse will be feigned in order to secure a lighter sentence. Yet, as Bibas and Bierschbach contend, even false or half-hearted expressions of remorse are better than none at all, as these may still help victims to feel vindicated and may ultimately lead offenders to internalise the awareness that they ought to feel remorse after a period of time.[34]

While the most obvious therapeutic benefits of participation may be self-evident in the case of victims, offenders may also benefit in a similar way. Although there is a dearth of empirical evidence as to the precise nature of offender emotions in the sentencing process,[35] the literature is replete with references to anger, resentment, hatred, anxiety, depression, remorse, defiance and shame.[36] Participation in the justice system might be used as a means of processing the myriad of sometimes conflicting emotions that an offender may experience before, during and after committing the offence. If we accept that rehabilitation and desistance are desirable goals for criminal justice, then we should do everything to encourage verbalisation and the construction of personal narratives. This is, after all, a proven means by which individuals can be encouraged to accept responsibility for their actions, identify reasons for their offending behaviour, and learn practical techniques that may help them to desist in the future.[37]

As with victims, criminal courts cannot and should not be transformed into therapy rooms overnight, and there is little scientific evidence to support the therapeutic efficacy of 'one-shot' forms of expression.[38] However, it still seems sensible to at least explore the ways in which therapeutic potential of sentencing procedures can be maximized through the use of personal narratives, whilst simultaneously taking steps to minimise the risk of any anti-therapeutic effects.

Strengthening Procedural Justice

An increased emphasis on the role of emotion should ensure much improved levels of procedural justice. Basically, the theory of procedural justice stipulates that an individual's

---

[33]   C Fercello and M Umbreit, Client evaluation of family group conferencing in 12 sites in 1st Judicial District of Minnesoto (St. Paul: Center for Restorative Justice & Mediation, 1998); Strang, *Repair or Revenge?*, n. 30 above.

[34]   Bibas and Bierschbach, 'Integrating Remorse', n. 9 above.

[35]   M Proeve, D Smith, and D Niblow, 'Mitigation Without Definition: Remorse in the Criminal Justice System' (1999) 32 *Australia & New Zealand Journal of Criminology* 16.

[36]   For a generally overview, see J Katz, *Seductions of Crime: Moral and Sensual Attractions in Doing Evil* (New York: Basic Books, 1988); D Canter and M Ioannou, 'Criminals' Emotional Experiences During Crimes' (2004) 1 *International Journal of Forensic Psychology* 71; T Scheff and S. Retzinger, *Emotions and Violence: Shame and Rage in Destructive Conflicts*. (Lexington: Lexington Books, 1991); J Braithwaite,) 'Shame and Modernity' (1993) 33 *British Journal of Criminology* 1.

[37]   See eg R Masters, *Counselling Criminal Justice Offenders* (Thousand Oaks, CA: Sage, 2003); S Tarolla, E Wagner, J Rabinowitz and J Tubman, 'Understanding and Treating Juvenile Offenders: A Review of Current Knowledge and Future Directions' (2002) 7 *Aggression and Violent Behavior* 125; A Moster, D Wnuk and E Jeglic, 'Cognitive Behavioral Therapy Interventions With Sex Offenders' (2008) 14 *Journal of Correctional Health Care* 109.

[38]   Pemberton and Reynaers, 'The Controversial Nature', n. 23 above.

sense of justice in any given case is largely dependent on the procedure that led to the decision (as opposed to merely the outcome).[39] Moreover, it has been found that individuals are likely to place more trust in authorities after a negative outcome than they did prior to that outcome, providing that the procedures followed have been perceived as fair.[40] There is thus a clear link between high levels of procedural justice and overall perceptions of legitimacy with the criminal justice system.

There are a number of values and attributes that have come to be associated with high levels of procedural justice, including 'representation, honesty, quality of decision, and consistency, and more generally of participation and esteem'.[41] However, the notion of 'voice" is perhaps one of the most renowned yardsticks for procedural justice.[42] As one recent study suggests, the concept of 'voice' is not just about expressing one's needs but gravitates around communication and the concept of being heard.[43] It is the mechanism used to express oneself, and as such it is indelibly intertwined with our emotions. The ability to exercise 'voice' is critical for victims and offenders alike. Victims of violent crime, in particular, are often beset with negative emotions including fear, helplessness, shame, self-blame, anger and vulnerability that may prevail for some time.[44]

Victims clearly value the opportunity to tell offenders how the offence impacted upon them and have their questions answered.[45] A range of empirical studies confirm that victim participation in the criminal justice process enhances satisfaction with justice by through giving victims a sense of empowerment and official, albeit symbolic, acknowledgement.[46]

---

[39] See generally E Lind and T Tyler, *The Social Psychology of Procedural Justice* (New York: Plenum Press, 1988).

[40] Lind and Tyler, ibid.; E Lind, C Kulik, M Ambrose and M de Vera Park, 'Individual and Corporate Dispute Resolution: Using Procedural Fairness as a Decision Heuristic' (1993) 38 *Administrative Science Quarterly* 224; T Tyler, *Why People Obey the Law* (Princeton, NJ: Princeton University Press, 1990).

[41] Tyler, ibid., p. 175.

[42] See eg R Folger, 'Distributive and Procedural Justice: Combined Impact of Voice and Improvement on Experienced Inequity' (1977) 35 *Journal of Personality and Social Psychology* 108; Lind and Tyler, ibid.; E Lind, R Kanfer, C Earley, 'Voice, Control, and Procedural Justice: Instrumental and Noninstrumental Concerns in Fairness Judgments' (1990) 59 *Journal of Personality and Social Psychology* 952.

[43] J Wemmers and K Cyr, 'What Fairness means to Crime Victims; A Social Psychological Perspective on Victim-Offender Mediation' (2006) 2 *Applied Psychology in Criminal Justice* 102.

[44] J Bisson and J Shepherd, 'Psychological Reactions of Victims of Violent Crime' (1995) 167 *British Journal of Psychiatry* 718; A Lurigio 'Are All Victims Alike? The Adverse, Generalized, and Differential Impact of Crime' (1987) 33 *Crime & Delinquency* 452; P Resick, 'Psychological Effects of Victimization: Implications for the Criminal Justice System' (1987) 33 *Crime & Delinquency* 468.

[45] J Roberts and E Erez, 'Communication in Sentencing: Exploring the Expressive Function of Victim Impact Statements' (2004) 10 *International Review of Victimology* 223. 238; J Shapland, J Willmore, and P Duff, *Victims and the Criminal Justice System* (Aldershot: Gower, 1985); Strang, *Repair or Revenge?*, n. 30 above.; J Wemmers, *Victims in the Criminal Justice System* (Amsterdam: Kugler Publications, 1996).

[46] See eg E Erez, L Roeger, and F Morgan, 'Victim Harm, Impact Statements and Victim Satisfaction with Justice: An Australian Experience' (1997) 5 *International Review of Victimology* 37; E Erez and E Bienkowska, 'Victim Participation in Proceedings and Satisfaction with Justice in the

Without a mechanism for exercising 'voice', procedures may seem fundamentally unbalanced – and thus unfair – given the offender's right to express his or her emotions to the court through a mitigating plea.[47]

Procedural justice and the concept of 'voice' are also important to offenders. Even victim impact evidence may instil a sense of procedural justice among offenders, since it provides a link between the impact of the offence and the imposition of punishment. Of course, offender participation is equally important. A study by Casper et al showed that convicted felons' views as to whether their sentences were heavier than those given to other offenders convicted of the same crime strongly correlated with their sense of whether their overall treatment was fair.[48] Like victims, offenders are the owners of their stories and, as such, should ultimately control the message conveyed to the court on their behalf.[49] The more an offender feels involved in the process, the more that process is likely to be perceived as fair. It might be surmised that being able to explain to the court the emotional turmoil that may have precipitated an offence, or the feelings of shame and remorse that followed in its aftermath, may all contribute to the sense of procedural justice experienced by offenders.

An 'emotionally intelligent' approach to sentencing would thus prioritise the role of 'voice'. Both victims and offenders should be able to relate their emotions to the courtroom directly; in their own words and at their own pace. The more of an opportunity victims and offenders are given to tell their emotional stories, the more likely it is that they will perceive the process as fair even where they are dissatisfied with the actual sentencing decision. Indeed, the criminal justice system as a whole stands to benefit from higher levels of procedural justice given its potential to bolster legitimacy and effective governance. Studies have shown that negative experiences of the criminal processes are likely to deter victims from co-operating in the future.[50] In the same way, procedural justice may be seen to contribute to desistance from future offending by instilling a greater sense of respect for the law, a willingness to remain within its parameters, and a greater sense of legitimacy of its institutions.

Improving the Quality of Decision-Making

An emotionally intelligent approach to sentencing would also carry a third potential benefit, insofar that it may enhance the quality of the decision-making process. In most common law jurisdictions, the question of sentence is resolved primarily by reference to offence seriousness. Determining seriousness is not a precise science; it may depend on any number

---

Continental Systems: The Case of Poland' (1993) 21 *Journal of Criminal Justice* 47; Shapland et al, ibid., J Wemmers, 'Victims in the Dutch Criminal Justice System' (1995) 3 *International Review of Victimology* 323; J Wemmers and K Cyr, 'Victims' Perspectives on Restorative Justice: How Much Involvement Are Victims Looking For?' (2004) 11 *International Review of Victimology* 259.

[47]   P Cassell, 'In Defence of Victim Impact Statements' (2008) 6 *Ohio State Journal of Criminal Law* 611.

[48]   J Casper, T Tyler and B Fisher, 'Procedural Justice in Felony Cases' (1988) 22 *Law & Society Review* 483.

[49]   K Thomas, 'Beyond Mitigation: Towards a Theory of Allocution' (2007) 75 *Fordham Law Review* 2641, p. 2659.

[50]   Shapland, Willmore, and Duff, *Victims*, n. 43 above.

of factors depending on the jurisdiction, although culpability and harm tend to act as common indicators.[51]

Emotions – and the ability to empathise – may be useful to sentencers in providing a more accurate picture of both culpability and harm. As the former US Federal Judge Irving R. Kaufman explained, 'our intuition, emotion and conscience are appropriate factors in the jurisprudential calculus'.[52] Learning about the offender's emotional state prior to, during and after the offence gives way to a truer perception concerning the question of culpability. Anger, hatred and resentment prior to the offence may all give an indication as to motive, which in turn may provide evidence of intention and blameworthiness. Similarly, blameworthiness may be lessened if the offender was depressed, anxious or nervous. Information of this type allows the sentencer to empathise and appreciate the perspective of others and how blameworthy they ought to be in the eyes of the law.[53]

In a similar way, the more sentencers learn about the emotions of victims, the more information they glean about the full extent of the harm that has been caused. Cassell and Erez both cite a number of empirical studies highlighting how sentencers often value the additional information supplied within victim impact evidence.[54] In the context of emotions, this is perhaps most obvious in relation to psychiatric or emotional harm, which is becoming more widely recognised, in addition to harms which are physical or material in nature.[55] Victims would be better placed than anyone else to describe the nature and extent of their emotional and psychological states and, in doing so, sentencers would be granted important new insights into dimensions of the case of which they may not previously have been aware.

However, many opponents of participatory rights for victims maintain that emotional outpourings endanger the objectivity of sentencing and are inherently inappropriate for the courtroom.[56] Susan Bandes, for example, warns that the 'hatred, bigotry, and unreflective empathy' contained within victim impact statements serves to demean the dignity of both victims and offenders.[57] Whilst Bandes' comments were made in the specific context of US capital murder trials, they nonetheless underline the need to carefully consider what emotions victims *actually* convey through their participation in criminal justice. Whilst it may be foolhardy to deny that many victims experience deep-seated feelings of anger, hatred and desire some measure of revenge, studies suggest that victims would seem to be no more

---

[51]   'Seriousness' in England and Wales is determined by the offender's culpability as well as 'any harm which the offence caused, was intended to cause or might foreseeably have caused: Criminal Justice Act 2003, s 143(1).

[52]   I R Kaufmann, 'The Anatomy of Decisionmaking' (1984) 53 *Fordham Law Review* 1, p. 16.

[53]   See further Bandes, 'Empathy', n. 6 above.

[54]   Cassell, 'In Defence', n. 45 above; 'E Erez, 'Who's Afraid of the Big Bad Victim? Victim Impact Statements as Victim Empowerment and Enhancement of Justice' [1999] *Criminal Law Review* 545.

[55]   The English courts have come under some criticism for their failure to attach criminal liability of emotional harm that is unaccompanied by recognised psychiatric injury. See further J Stannard, 'Sticks, Stones and Words: Emotional Harm and the English Criminal Law' (2010) 74 *Journal of Criminal Law* 533. A similar critique has been made of the position in the English civil courts: see R Mulheron, 'Rewriting the Requirement for a "Recognized Psychiatric Injury" in Negligence Claims' (2012) 32 *Oxford Journal of Legal Studies* 77.

[56]   See eg Bandes, 'Empathy' n. 6 above.

[57]   Ibid., p. 394.

punitive than the general public in relation to sentencing attitudes.[58] Moreover, as with offenders expressing remorse, the sentencer is under no obligation to believe the statement or to alter the proposed sentence in response to victim outrage.[59] Therefore we should trust sentencers to use their judgment and discretion appropriately and in the manner in which they have been trained and educated.

Finally, a better understanding of emotions may also assist judges in tailoring the specific nature of a sentence so that it best 'fits' the offender. As Thomas argues, taking close account of how the offender feels, and how he/she is likely to respond to a sentence can help to ensure that the sentence is likely to be beneficial in achieving its goals:

> Having this information could allow judges and other actors in the criminal justice system to develop a more nuanced portrait of defendants. By doing so, these officials may, for example, be better able to develop creative solutions to criminal justice problems or to observe trends in offender characteristics or behaviour.[60]

Using the specific example of shaming-type punishments, Thomas argues that whilst in some cases a punishment involving some degree of public moral condemnation or embarrassment might be acceptable, in other cases it would have a disproportionate effect on the offender's rehabilitation efforts.[61] Similar arguments might also be levied in terms of the impact of imprisonment. In sum, the more detailed and holistic the picture that is offered, the more accurate and proportionate the sentence is likely to be.

Transforming Relationships between Victims and Offenders

A more central role for emotions could also herald new and better opportunities for reconciliation between the victim and the offender. Drawing on Randall Collins' theory of interaction rituals,[62] Sherman and others contend that the dissemination of emotions (which may include anger, compassion, remorse and shame) create a new shared experience and sense of solidarity.[63] This reflects what social psychologists have termed the so-called 'contact hypothesis', which postulates that conflict can be most effectively resolved through direct

---

[58]   See eg M Hough and A Park, 'How malleable are attitudes to crime and punishment ? Findings from a British Deliberative Poll' in J. Roberts and M. Hough (eds), *Changing Attitudes to Punishment.* (Cullompton: Willan, 2002); J Mattinson and C Mirrlees-Black, *Attitudes to Crime and Criminal Justice: Findings from the 1998 British Crime Survey* (London: Home Office, 2000). S Maruna and A King, 'Public Opinion and Community Penalties' in T. Bottoms, S. Rex and G. Robinson (eds), *Alternatives to Prison: Options for an Insecure Society* (Cullompton: Willan, 2004).

[59]   Indeed, arguably most victims already realise this fact and wish to participate notwithstanding: see PG Cassell, 'Barbarians at the Gates? A Reply to the Critics of the Victims' Rights Amendment' (1999) *Utah Law Review* 479.

[60]   Thomas, 'Beyond Mitigation', n. 49 above, p. 2675.

[61]   As illustrated, for example, through the use of 'shaming' practices which are frequently criticized on the ground that they are reflective of the 'punitive turn': see n 3 above.

[62]   R Collins, *Interaction Ritual Chains* (Princeton, MA: Princeton University Press, 2004).

[63]   L Sherman, H Strang, C Angel, D Woods, G Barnes, S Bennett, and N Inkpen, 'Effects of Face-to-Face Restorative Justice on Victims of Crime in Four Randomized Controlled Trials' (2005) 1 *Journal of Experimental Criminology* 367.

and deliberative contact and communication between conflicting parties.[64] In this sense, a previously broken bond may be transformed by the emotional energy into a new social bond, providing a potential platform for repair of broken relationships. Individual narratives of victims and offender can create a coherent story-frame for both victims and offenders, and their interaction can thereby create a new 'co-narrative' which can serve to affirm a new norm, vindicate victims, humanise offenders, and denounce the evil of an act without labelling any person as a villain.[65]

In order for this to happen, sentencing procedure would need to open a more communicative conduit capable of facilitating dialogue between victims and offenders. There is already an abundance of evidence that victims place a high value on receiving apologies,[66] and this prospect is often an important factor influencing their decision to become involved in mediation and restorative justice programmes.[67] A genuine apology should signal to the victim that the offender genuinely regrets his or her behaviour and wishes to make amends. The victim is then empowered to choose whether to accept the apology (thereby restoring a state of equality), or reject it, allowing that moral imbalance to stay in place.[68]

The potential benefits of an apology are not limited to victims. As Etienne and Robbennolt point out, offenders who apologise 'may be able to relieve their guilt and assuage other negative emotions, begin to repair their relationships with their victims and society, improve their reputations, and begin a process of reintegrating into society'.[69] Similarly, encouraging the expression of remorse and/or repentance is something that is potentially valuable to the community, in terms of the offender having acknowledged that communal norms have been breached.[70] It is also highly probably that most people who are remorseful and repentant are less dangerous, and are thereby less likely to reoffend than those who are unrepentant or defiant.[71] This would be particularly true in the case of first-time offenders.[72]

It will be apparent that the four potential benefits outlined above are not necessarily discrete and may overlap. Whilst care should be taken, for example, not to conflate victims' sense of procedural justice with therapeutic benefits, some studies have suggested that such a link exists.[73] In the same way, the expression of an apology or reconciliation during the sentence

---

[64]   See generally WG Stephen, 'Intergroup Contact: Introduction' (1995) 41 *Journal of Social Issues* 1; RJ Fisher, *The Social Psychology of Intergroup and International Conflict Resolution* (Springer: New York, 1990).

[65]   See further J Braithwaite, 'Narrative and "Compulsory Compassion"', *Law and Social Inquiry* 31 (2006): 425–46; Thomas, 'Beyond Mitigation', n. 49 above, pp. 2673–74.

[66]   Fercello and Umbreit, n. 33 above; Strang, *Repair or Revenge?*, n. 30 above.

[67]   Strang, *Repair or Revenge?*, n. 30 above.

[68]   C Petrucci, 'Apology in the Criminal Justice Setting; Evidence for Including Apology as Additional Component in the Legal System' (2002) 20 *Behavioral Science and the Law* 337.

[69]   M *Etienne* and J K Robbennolt, 'Apologies and Plea Bargaining' (2007) 91 *Marquette Law Review* 295, p. 298.

[70]   S Bibas, 'Forgiveness in Criminal Procedure' (2007) 4 *Ohio State Journal of Criminal Law* 329.

[71]   J G Murphy, 'Remorse, Apology, and Mercy' (2007) 4 *Ohio State Journal of Criminal Law* 423.

[72]   J Jacobson and M Hough, 'Personal Mitigation in England and Wales' in J Roberts (ed), *Mitigation and Aggravation at Sentencing* (Cambridge: Cambridge University Press, 2011).

[73]   J Wemmers and C Cyr, 'Can Mediation Be Therapeutic for Crime Victims? An Evaluation of Victims' Experiences in Mediation with Young Offenders' (2005) 47 *Canadian Journal of Criminology and Criminal Justice* 527.

may also significantly increase both procedural satisfaction as well as carrying therapeutic effects. Having outlined a range of purported benefits, the next section proceeds to consider the extent to which emotional intelligence underpins the sentencing process of England and Wales.

The Role of Emotional Narratives in the English Sentencing Process

Since the beginning of the eighteenth century, a process of adversarialisation and lawyerisation of criminal trials has resulted in the silencing of victims and offenders in English criminal justice.[74] This 'appropriation' of private conflicts[75] has turned the trial into a showdown between lawyers representing the State and the defence, with the role of the primary stakeholders being restricted to 'evidentiary cannon fodder' for one side or the other.[76] Whilst the end of the nineteenth century was marked by the emergence of participatory rights for the accused,[77] the latter years of the twentieth century and early years of the twenty-first century have witnessed a drive towards similar participatory rights for victims.[78] In this section we particularly focus on the ways in which the emotional narratives of victims and offenders can be taken into account when determining sentence, with particular reference to the communication of offenders' emotions through pre-sentence reports and pleas in mitigation, and the communication of victims' emotions through Victim Personal Statements (VPS) and Family Impact Statements (FIS).

The Narratives of Offenders

Offenders play a passive role in English criminal trials. Whilst some may testify in their own defence, it is rare for them to speak directly at the sentencing stage. More usually, offenders utilise two main conduits to convey their emotions indirectly to the court, these being the pre-sentence reports (PSRs) and pleas in mitigation.

The use of pre-sentence reports is governed by section 156 of the Criminal Justice Act 2003. The provision stipulates that courts must obtain a PSR and take it into account in determining sentence unless it forms the opinion that a pre-sentence report is unnecessary.[79] Their purpose is to assist the courts 'in determining the most suitable method of dealing with an offender';[80] in other words, they are designed to give the sentencer a better idea of the seriousness of the

---

74   J H Langbein, *The Origins of the Adversary Criminal Trial* (Oxford: Oxford University Press, 2003).

75   N Christie, 'Conflicts as Property' (1977) 17 *British Journal of Criminology* 1.

76   J Braithwaite, 'Juvenile Offending: New Theory and Practice'. Address to the National Conference on Juvenile Justice, Adelaide, Institute of Criminology, September 1992.

77   The practice of permitting the defendant to make an unsworn statement from the dock evolved in the nineteenth century as a means of enabling some form of personal participation by the defendant. It was not until the passage of the Criminal Evidence Act 1898 that defendants were permitted to give evidence on oath. For comparative US perspective, see Thomas, 'Beyond Mitigation', n. 49 above.

78   See generally J Doak, 'Participatory Rights for Victims of Crime: In search of international consensus' (2011) 15 *Canadian Criminal Law Review* 41.

79   Criminal Justice Act 2003, s 156(3).

80   Criminal Justice Act 2003, s158.

offence as well as the offender's suitability to carry out particular types of sentences. While the report may contain a sentence recommendation, the court is not bound to follow it and may deviate from any such recommendation if it chooses to do so.[81]

To this end, PSRs are heavily based on probing interviews with a probation officer.[82] Its precise form and contents are laid down within the National Standards for the Management of Offenders,[83] although it can be noted that interviews will typically cover offending information; analysis of the offences; accommodation; education; training and employability; financial management and income; relationships; lifestyle and associates; drug and alcohol issues; emotional wellbeing; thinking and behaviour including the offender's attitudes towards the victim and the offence.[84] Offenders may be asked by the probation officer about attitudes to the victim and the offence; the level of the awareness of its consequences; the extent to which responsibility is accepted; along with relevant emotional responses as denial, defiance, remorse, shame or a desire to make amends for their actions.[85]

The introduction of PSRs in the early 1990s gave rise to a sense of optimism that this new opportunity for offenders to exercise 'voice' would constitute a welcome departure from the conveyor belt of lawyer-led proceedings.[86] Such an aspiration was expressed by one commentator in a 1992 article in the *Criminal Law Review*:

> The probation officer is requested to interview the defendant in a private, relatively unhurried, in-depth encounter, having some of the ambience of the confessional, encouraging the defendant to be candid, open and trusting. Defendants can welcome this opportunity to speak because they can feel listened to, understood and respected in a way that may be missing from their other encounters with criminal justice professionals.[87]

Notwithstanding the best efforts of many officers, such hopes seem to have given way to a sense of frustration as demands for cost efficiency have impacted on both the number and nature of pre-sentence reports. The introduction of the computerised Offender Assessment System (OASys) in 2001 added considerably to the investment of resources required to complete full reports,[88] which triggered a decision to change the majority of reports to a 'fast-delivery' format based on a 'tick-box' exercise.[89] Interviews for these types of reports tend to be considerably shorter, with less scope for defendants to relay their narratives. 'Full' or 'standard' reports are now restricted to more complex and serious cases where it would not

---

[81] Criminal Justice Act 2003, s 156(4).

[82] Or, in the case of a young offender, by a social worker or a member of a Youth Offending Team.

[83] Ministry of Justice, *National Standards for the Management of Offenders* (London: Ministry of Justice, 2011).

[84] P Whitehead, 'The probation service reporting for duty: court reports and social justice' (2008) 6 *British Journal of Community Justice* 86.

[85] N Stone, 'Pre-Sentence Reports, Culpability and the 1991 Act' [1992] *Criminal Law Review* 558.

[86] PSRs were first introduced by the Criminal Justice Act 1991, s 3.

[87] Ibid., pp. 565–6.

[88] Whitehead, 'The Probation Service', n. 84 above.

[89] However, scope remains to include explanatory written text to expand upon tick box data if required. It is even possible for a simple verbal report to be given if a written report is not considered necessary (see ibid.).

be deemed possible to provide sufficient information to meet the needs of the court within the 'fast delivery' report.[90]

The second means by which the offender may communicate emotions is through the plea in mitigation. This is an oral statement read to the court by the defence advocate and which has traditionally brought a wide range of factors to the attention of the court, including information about the offender and the circumstances of their offence in a bid to reduce the severity of the sentence. Whilst it is not uncommon for offenders to speak for themselves in the United States, this is relatively rare in England and Wales. Nevertheless, it has been suggested that sentencers may place greater emphasis on the plea in mitigation than the pre-sentence report, given that the former may have been prepared some time beforehand.[91] There is also some evidence to suggest that PSRs may be afforded less weight because judges may view them as encroaching upon their 'ownership' of the sentencing process, since they essentially amount to a recommendation by an outsider as to how to perform that role.[92] By contrast, pleas in mitigation are delivered by lawyers, who are insiders to the court and may be seen as having a more legitimate conduit to the judge.

Although PSRs and pleas in mitigation do provide limited channels through which offenders are able to communicate their emotions to the court, it is unclear as to what weight – if any – sentencers ought to attach to such emotions alongside other relevant factors. The starting point for the court is its assessment of the seriousness of the offence. This is undertaken by reference to the culpability of the offender and the harm he or she caused, intended to cause, or might foreseeably have caused.[93] Once the level of seriousness has been determined, the court must take account of any aggravating or mitigating factors as well as any personal mitigation of the offender. It is within this latter context that the Sentencing Guidelines Council has envisaged that the emotions of the offender (specifically remorse) may enter the equation:

> 1.27 When the court has formed an initial assessment of the seriousness of the offence, then it should consider any offender mitigation. The issue of remorse should be taken into account at this point along with other mitigating features such as admissions to the police in interview.[94]

In addition to this generic provision, existing sentencing guidelines make specific reference to offender remorse as a mitigatory factor in relation to assault offences, attempted murder, and burglary.[95] However, none of the Guidelines offer any indication as to the form it ought to

---

[90]   HC Justice Committee, *The Role of the Probation Service*, Eighth Report of Session 2010–12, Vol. 1, p. 16. The Committee also notes that Probation trust budgets were immediately reduced in 2009 on the assumption that standard delivery reports would only be used where use of the fast delivery report would be inappropriate.

[91]   A Ashworth, *Sentencing and Criminal Justice*, 5th ed. (Oxford: Oxford University Press, 2010), p. 381.

[92]   Ibid., p. 379.

[93]   Criminal Justice Act 2003, s 143(1).

[94]   Sentencing Guidelines Council, *Seriousness: Overarching Principles* (London: Sentencing Guidelines Council, 2004).

[95]   Guidelines are issued by the Sentencing Council pursuant to Part IV of the Coroners and Justice Act 2009. Remorse is a factor relevant to personal mitigation in the Sentencing Council's Definitive Guidelines on all of which make clear reference to offender remorse as a mitigating factor. See: http://sentencingcouncil.judiciary.gov.uk/guidelines/guidelines-to-download.htm (accessed 31/07/12). By

take or the weight that odd to be attached to it. The extent to which the sentencer's discretion will be used to consider such information is very much dependant on the subjective view of sentencers as to the relevance of such factors, and the extent to which the offender's legal representative seeks to bring the offender's emotions to the attention of the court in their plea in mitigation.

The variable effect of emotional expressions was confirmed by a study by Jacobson and Hough, who analysed the role of personal mitigation in some 132 cases across five Crown Court centres in 2007.[96] It was found that emotional responses of the accused did bear some influence on the sentencing decision, although mere expressions of remorse alone were unlikely to carry much weight in the minds of the sentencers. Such expressions became much more effective in bringing about sentence reduction where it was accompanied by honest discussion of the circumstances of the offending behaviour or a gesture, such as a letter of apology to the court.[97] Admittedly, determining the extent of remorse was an uncertain exercise; judges spoke of using 'experience and feeling' or 'gut feeling rather than careful calculation".[98] Emotions also entered into sentencing where the sentencer believed that the prosecution process caused the offender to suffer emotionally.[99] Such suffering is sometimes treated as part of the punishment for the crime, thereby lessening the severity of sentence.[100] Emotional stress at the time of the offence was also taken into account as a mitigating factor in a small amount of cases.

In summary then, offenders have limited capacity to provide emotional narratives to the court; the system is structurally conditioned for them to remain passive observers in their own cases. Although some offenders will communicate expressions of remorse through counsel as part of their plea in mitigation, such sentiments are communicated to the court; offenders are not encouraged to provide explanations or apologies directly to victims. A generally remorseful offender has no clear channel to pursue should s/he want to do so, and since such gestures are not generally repaid in the currency of sentencing law, so it is unsurprising that processes are not put in place to facilitate them. While remorse is perhaps the most desirable emotion, it may not be the only one which offenders experience at the point of sentence. While protests of innocence or messages of defiance may not be what the victim, the public or the sentencer want to hear, arguably these stories should also be heard.[101]

---

contrast, the lack of remorse or defiance is not explicitly identified as an aggravating factor, although there is no reason why a judge could not consider it as such in practice.

[96]   J Jacobson and M Hough, *Mitigation: The Role of Personal Factors in Sentencing* (London: Prison Reform Trust, 2007).

[97]   Ibid., p. 24.

[98]   Ibid., p. 48.

[99]   Ibid., p. 28.

[100]   There are a number of studies in the US suggesting significant reducations in sentence for offenders who express contrition of remorse in both state and federal courts: see further Bilbas and Bierschbach, n. 9 above, p. 93.

[101]   See further Thomas, 'Beyond Mitigation', n. 49 above, p. 2665 (citing the example of Nelson Mandela's address to the Rivonia Trial upon being sentenced to life imprisonment in 1964).

The Narratives of Victims

A more controversial question is the extent to which the victim may participate in the sentencing process, for instance by giving some of form of victim impact evidence at the point of sentence. Since October 2001, victims are entitled to submit a Victim Personal Statement (VPS) to the court containing details of how the crime affected them: whether they feel vulnerable or intimidated; whether they are worried about the offender being given bail; whether they are considering a compensation claim; and anything else that they feel may be helpful or relevant.[102] A more advanced version of the VPS scheme also exists for the benefit of relatives bereaved by homicide; the Victim Focus Scheme (VFS) operates in a similar way allowing families to submit a 'Family Impact Statement', which means (unlike the VPS) that the statement will be read aloud in court by the prosecutor or the judge.[103]

Inclusion in the scheme is voluntary and it is possible for all crime victims to participate, with the exception of large retailers and corporations. In line with the Lord Chief Justice's Consolidated Criminal Practice Direction,[104] the police officer transcribing the statement is likely to guide the victim as to the issues they may wish to include such as the financial, emotional, psychological, physical or other impacts that the crime has had upon them. The officer should also advise the victim to avoid the inclusion of their opinion on sentence as this is considered irrelevant to the sentencing decision. Although this may be preferable than leaving victims to their own devices, there is a risk that the more emotional aspects of victim narrative might come to be replaced with a sanitised and innocuous version of events which is less capable of fully conveying to the court the full intricacies of the crime's impact upon the victim.

The VPS is appended to the case papers, but will only be considered by the sentencer as and when a finding of guilt has been reached. Its legal significance is detailed in the Practice Direction as well as the Court of Appeal in *R v Perks*.[105] While both authorities make it very clear that the victim's opinions as to sentence must be disregarded, they also stipulate that the information contained within the VPS should be taken into account in determining offence seriousness. Although the weight that ought to be attached to these factors has never been clarified in precise terms, they appeared to weigh heavily in the Court of Appeal's determination of the appropriate sentence in *R v Saw*,[106] a domestic burglary case. Here Lord Phillips CJ drew attention to the adverse consequences that may follow a burglary. Such effects, he noted, related not only to the emotional consequences of material loss, but also to the aggravating impact of the severe shock that victims often experience, especially the elderly, when intruders are known to have been present in their homes. In the eyes of the court, the emotional effects of burglary on the victim could clearly be taken into account

---

[102] See: http://www.cps.gov.uk/victims_witnesses/reporting_a_crime/victims_personal_statement. html (accessed 30/07/12).

[103] See further Doak, J., Henham, R. and Mitchell, B. 'Victims and the Sentencing Process: Developing Participatory Rights?' (2009) 29(4) *Legal Studies* 651.

[104] Consolidated Criminal Practice Direction (November 2011), Pt III.28. http://www.justice.gov. uk/courts/procedure-rules/criminal/docs/CCPD-complete-text-Oct-2011.pdf (accessed 30/07/12).

[105] [2001] 1 Cr.App.R.(S) 19.

[106] [2009] EWCA Crim 1.

alongside the state's interests in consistency and proportionality or other factors relating to the offender's interest culpability.

The Sentencing Council have now made clear, through their Definitive Guidelines, that the impact of the crime on the victim is a factor affecting sentence severity.[107] Indeed, some make implied reference to the emotional well-being of the victim as an aggravating factor; for example, the Guideline on Assault Offences states that 'ongoing effects upon the victim' can merit an upward adjustment in sentence severity.[108] While this does not specifically mention emotional impact, this can clearly be encompassed within the notion of 'ongoing effects'. The Guideline on burglary similarly makes reference to 'significant trauma to the victim'[109] as an aggravating factor; and again this may encompass the concept of emotional harm.

It is not always, however, the case that the impact of the offence on the victim will constitute an aggravating factor. Indeed, the Court of Appeal has been willing on a number of occasions to reduce a sentence where it was felt that the original decision exaggerated the impact on the victim or on his or her family. A sentence of four years' imprisonment for causing death by dangerous driving was reduced to three years in *R v Nunn*,[110] where the mother and sister of the deceased appellant had given evidence that the length of sentence was adding to their grief. Similarly, in *R v Matthews*,[111] the appellant's five year prison sentence for the manslaughter of his brother was reduced to three years because of concerns about the impact a lengthier sentence would carry on other family members.[112]

This underscores the point that considerable care needs to be exercised in making assumptions about what victims actually seek through participating in the criminal process and, specifically, the extent to which they seek vengeance through doing so. Although content analysis of victim impact evidence is somewhat thin on the ground, research conducted in Staffordshire in 2005 by one of the authors suggests that where a victim chooses to participate in the VPS scheme they are very likely to include an outline of the emotional impact that the crime has had upon them.[113] The content analysis conducted as part of that study found that 88% of the 233 VPS's considered included information outlining the emotional response of the victim to the crime committed against them, with the most often cited emotions being fear, upset and anger.[114] While many of emotional responses would tend towards sentence

---

[107] See http://sentencingcouncil.judiciary.gov.uk/guidelines/guidelines-to-download.htm (accessed 31/07/12).

[108] See: http://sentencingcouncil.judiciary.gov.uk/docs/Assault_definitive_guideline_-_Crown_Court.pdf (accessed 31/07/12).

[109] See the Guideline on Aggravated Burglary, p.5. The Guideline on Domestic Burglary makes a similar reference to 'trauma to the victim, beyond the normal inevitable consequence of intrusion and theft' (at p. 8). The Guideline on Burglary Offences can be accessed at: http://sentencingcouncil.judiciary.gov.uk/docs/Burglary_Definitive_Guideline_web_final.pdf (accessed 31/07/12).

[110] [1996] 2 Cr App R (S) 136.

[111] [2003] 1 Cr App R (S) 26.

[112] See further I Edwards, 'The Place of Victims' Preferences in the Sentencing of 'Their' Offenders' [2002] *Criminal Law Review* 689.

[113] These are the findings from an unpublished study by Louise Taylor analysing the content of 233 VPS taken from Magistrates' Court files for Chase Police Division in 2004.

[114] As a percentage of the total emotions detailed by victims in the study 37% of these related to fear, 26% related to upset, and 9% related to anger.

aggravation there were also limited instances where victims displayed emotional responses such as sympathy and empathy,[115] which could serve to mitigate the offender's sentence. These findings broadly correlate with other studies.[116] In their evaluation of the VPS pilots, Hoyle and others found that, as indicated earlier, 'rather than… encouraging exaggeration, inflammatory statements, and vindictiveness, the opposite appears to apply: they [victim personal statements] tend to understate rather than over-state the impact of offences'.[117] Similarly, an analysis by Chalmers and others of the content of victim statements in Scotland indicated that statements made concerning sentence tended to be unspecific and some even displayed some concern for the offender and requested a lighter sentence.[118] Even where victims do express anger or a desire for vengeance, sentencers have little problem disentangling legally relevant information from that which is inappropriate conjecture or opinion.[119]

It is vital, however, that victims are made fully aware of the purpose of their participation. In particular, they should be advised in very clear terms that they cannot make specific demands as to sentence, and that the effect of the crime upon them is only one of a number of factors which the sentence must consider.[120] A number of studies have identified a real risk that victims may end up frustrated and even more isolated if they feel their expectations have not

---

[115]   Two VPS in the study demonstrated this emotional response which represented 0.5% of the total emotions detailed by victims in the study.

[116]   C Hoyle, E Cape, R Morgan, and A Sanders, *Evaluation of the One Stop Shop and Victim Pilot Statement Projects* (London: Home Office, 1998); Chalmers et al, n. 12 above.

[117]   Hoyle et al, ibid, p. 28.

[118]   J Chalmers, P Duff, and F Leverick, 'Victim Impact Statements: Can Work, Do Work (For Those Who Bother to Make Them)' [2007] *Criminal Law Review* 360, p. 374.

[119]   E Erez and L Rogers, 'Victim Impact Statements and Sentencing Outcomes and Processes: The Perspectives of Legal Professionals' (1999) 39 *British Journal of Criminology* 216; M L Schuster and A Propen, 'Degrees of Emotion: Judicial Responses to Victim Impact Statements' (2010) 6 *Law, Culture and the Humanities* 75; M O'Connell, 'Victims in the Sentencing Process: South Australia's Judges and Magistrates give their Verdict' (2009) 4 *International Perspectives in Victimology* 50; A Sweeting, R Owen, C Turley et al., *Evaluation of the Victims' Advocate Scheme Pilots*, Ministry of Justice Research Series 17/08 (London: Ministry of Justice, 2008).

[120]   Empirical evidence in both the UK and further afield suggests that victim impact evidence rarely influences sentencing decisions to a significant degree: see eg Chalmers et al, n. 118 above; T Eisenberg, S P Garvey, and M T Wells, 'Victim Characteristics and Victim Impact Evidence in South Carolina Capital Cases' (2003) 88 *Cornell Law Faculty Publications* 306; E Erez and P Tontodonato, 'The Effect of Victim Participation in Sentencing on Sentence Outcome' (1990) 28 *Criminology* 451; *R Morgan and A Sanders, The Use of Victim Impact Statements (London: Home Office, 1999)*. See further JV Roberts and M Manikis, *Victim Personal Statements at Sentencing: A Review of Empirical Research* (London: Office of the Commissioner for Victims and Witnesses for England and Wales, 2011), pp. 30–31.

E Erez and L Rogers, 'Victim Impact Statements and Sentencing Outcomes and Processes: The Perspective of Legal Professionals' (1999) 39 *British Journal of Criminology* 216, p. 226.

been met.[121] This is a particularly salient finding given that studies suggest that victim impact evidence rarely influences sentencing decisions to a significant degree.[122]

Although the VPS and VFS do open a channel through which victims can communicate their emotions to the court, the emotional power of their stories is likely to be significantly diminished by the fact that they are unable to address either the defendant or the court in person. Unlike the United States, where victims have a right to make representations in all federal and most state criminal hearings, victims in England and Wales are restricted to exercising their voice indirectly, through a third person. Whilst the VFS was initially intended to give families of victims of homicide the choice between reading an oral statement themselves or leaving that task to counsel, this option has since been withdrawn. In their evaluation of the VFS pilots,[123] Sweeting and others found that a significant minority of victims (22%) had opted to present them in person. This was an opportunity that appeared to be valued by the families who did so, with the husband of one deceased victim telling the researchers that he was 'doing it because I just felt I owed it'.[124] Moreover, the researchers noted that overcoming the fear of speaking in court on such an emotional subject had helped victims to feel empowered and more satisfied with the process. It was also reported that there was a perception among practitioners that family members felt they could have a greater personal impact and 'do more to help' by delivering the evidence themselves. Although self-delivery of the statement tends to involve additional work for all stakeholders, it is regrettable that the emotional potential of the VFS has been curtailed by placing restrictions on the victim's role, rather than seeking to strengthen it.

The Limits of Emotion

There is clearly some scope for victims and offenders to communicate their emotional narratives to court. Certainly, opportunities to do so have increased in recent years. However, by the same token, the room for emotional narratives is still extremely small, and an emotionally intelligent approach to sentencing involves more than victims and offenders expressing their views to the court in a formulaic and mechanistic manner. Evidentiary and procedural rules, and the structure of the trial as an adversarial content mean that victims and offenders can only portray their stories in a way that lies within these stringent parameters. This is particularly true within magistrates' courts; sentencing here has been said to be 'swift to the point of

---

[121] Chalmers et al, 'Victim Impact', n. 118 above; E Erez and P Tontodonato, 'Victim Participation in Sentencing and Satisfaction with Justice' 9 *Justice Quarterly* 393; A Sanders, C Hoyle, R Morgan, and E Cape, 'Victim Impact Statements: Don't Work, Can't Work' (2001) *Criminal Law Review* 437.

[122] See eg Chalmers et al, 'Victim Impact', n. 118 above; T Eisenberg, SP Garvey, and MT Wells, 'Victim Characteristics and Victim Impact Evidence in South Carolina Capital Cases' (2003) 88 *Cornell Law Faculty Publications* 306; E Erez and P Tontodonato, 'The Effect of Victim Participation in Sentencing on Sentence Outcome' (1990) 28 *Criminology* 451; R Morgan and A Sanders, *The Use of Victim Impact Statements* (London: Home Office, 1999). See further JV Roberts and M Manikis, *Victim Personal Statements at Sentencing: A Review of Empirical Research* (London: Office of the Commissioner for Victims and Witnesses for England and Wales, 2011), pp. 30–31.

[123] Sweeting et al, n. 119 above. Note that the VFS was originally known as the Victim Advocate Scheme.

[124] Ibid., p. 21.

abruptness, relying heavily on the speedy delivery of guilty pleas'.[125] Indeed, many victims will opt not to attend such hearings, and will thus not hear any emotions expressed by the offender or his/her lawyer.

As Habermas famously observed, the justice system has become 'colonized' by abstract principles of formal law, drawing the court of law away from the *Lebensweld* or 'lifeworld', this being the typical environment which human beings experience and use as a point of reference in their personal narratives and in their relationships with others.[126] Intimate, informal and direct interactions generally act as precursors and conveyers of apology and forgiveness,[127] and these are a far cry from the world of the criminal court. Here, the formal environment is bipartisan, rigidly structured, ritualistic and dominated by zealous advocates.[128] It is the advocates, rather than victims or offenders, who assume the roles of story-tellers, suppressing individual narrative autonomy, shaping narratives to bring out their maximum adversarial effect,[129] and turning witnesses into 'weapons to be used against the other side'.[130] There is no physical space or procedural mechanism though which victims or offenders might freely communicatetheir own stories in the way that makes sense to them. Bilbas and Bierschbach contend that this explains why apologies, expressions of remorse, and victim acknowledgement or forgiveness are exceedingly rare in US courtrooms:

> Courtrooms are quasi-public settings, where defendants' families and close friends are often present. This setting can humiliate offenders, especially those who prize their reputations most highly (such as white-collar offenders) or who have committed highly stigmatized crimes (such as sex offenders). Sentencing allocutions, moreover, are tightly scheduled, hurried, vague, and often in front of a judge who did not preside over the guilty plea. For most defendants, this is their first real chance to apologize for their crime to victims or the community. It is no wonder that, when apologies do occur at sentencing, they often are stilted, forced, or 'not enough'[131]

It might be added that even those emotions which are successfully communicated to the court are passive and 'locked' in time. Victims may have prepared a VPS many months, or perhaps longer, before sentencing occurs. The emotions contained in that document may no longer reflect how they feel at the point of sentence. The passage of time, counselling, and other

---

[125]   C Tata, 'A Sense of Justice: The Role of Pre-Sentence Reports in the Production and Disruption of Guilt and Guilty Pleas' (2010) 12 *Punishment and Society* 239.

[126]   J Habermas, *The Theory of Communicative Action*, Vol. I (Boston: Beacon Press, 1984), p. 376.

[127]   S Retzinger and T Scheff, 'Strategy for community conferences: Emotions and social bonds' in B Galaway and J Hudson (eds) *Restorative Justice: International Perspectives* (Monsey, NY: Criminal Justice, 1996); J Braithwaite, 'Narrative and "compulsory compassion"' (2006) 31 *Law and Social Inquiry* 425. See also L Hickson, 'The Social Contexts of Apology in Dispute Settlement: A Cross-Cultural Study' (1986) 25 *Ethnology* 283. Not all commentators agree that forgiveness is always the appropriate moral response: see eg. J and J Hampton, *Forgiveness and Mercy* (Cambridge: Cambridge University Press, 1998).

[128]   See further S Szmanua and DE Mangis, 'Finding the Right Time and Place: A Case Study Comparison of the Expression of Offender Remorse in Traditional Justice and Restorative Justice Contexts' (2005) 89 *Marquette Law Review* 336.

[129]   W Pizzi, *Trials without Truth* (New York: NYU Press, 1997), p. 197.

[130]   Ibid.

[131]   Bilbas and Bierschbach, n 3 above, p. 98.

forms of support and assistance may have changed the way the impact of the offence and their feelings towards the offender. Family impact statements prepared under the VFS, and indeed pleas in mitigation, can be more easily tailored to the moment. However, these also represent a very momentary insight into the emotions of victims and offenders. We are unlikely to gain much deeper insights into the life journey of victims and offenders, how they felt about the fairness legal process, and how their emotions might have evolved over time. There is a considerable body of evidence supporting the idea that emotions, as cognitive processes, may fluctuate and are open to change;[132] both victims and offenders may feel an array of complex and potentially contradictory emotions in the aftermath of an offence. Unfortunately, the sentencing system does not offer a means of communicating this fluidity to other stakeholders or the court.

Future Directions: Towards Emotionally Intelligent Practice

A fully-fledged emotionally intelligent model of sentencing may depend on a significant reconfiguration of penal ideology. Such a normative shift remains an indeterminate prospect in the short to medium term. However, it is still conceivable to think of a number of ways in which emotion might usefully play a more central role within the existing normative parameters of the criminal justice system. There are three ways, in particular, by which current sentencing might be better tailored to facilitate the communication of emotions.

The Need for Legal Clarity

First, there is a need to clarify the legal weight that can be attached to the emotions of victims and offenders in sentencing. As a starting point, the Sentencing Council ought to consider providing more detailed guidance concerning their relevance with regard to personal mitigation. As noted above, current guidance offers very little detail as to the weight that sentencers ought to attach to personal mitigation in general, and expressions of remorse in particular. Judges could, for example, be offered guidance as to how remorse might be assessed; whether it might carry more weight if accompanied by an unconditional apology, an offer of reparation or any other step taken to make amends. Bibas proposes that US federal sentencing law should be amended to replace the almost-automatic 35% sentence discount for guilty pleas with a sliding scale that reflects remorse, apology, and forgiveness. It is our contention that the English sentencing system, which also operates a similar automatic discount,[133] may also benefit through the introduction of a similar mechanism.

Clarity is also needed in respect of the function of the VPS and VFS. Although the Lord Chief Justice and the Court of Appeal have attempted to shed light on their potential impact on sentences, there is still no guidance as to the nature of the relationship between (emotional)

---

[132] Bandes, n. 2 above; see also MC Nussbaum, *Love's Knowledge: Essays on Philosophy and Literature* (Oxford: Oxford University Press, 1990); RC Soloman, *The Passions, Emotions and the Meaning of Life* (Indianapolis: Hackett Press, 1993).

[133] See Sentencing Guidelines Council, *Definitive Guideline for Reduction in Sentence for a Guilty Plea*. Available: http://sentencingcouncil.judiciary.gov.uk/docs/Reduction_in_Sentence_for_a_Guilty_Plea_-Revised_2007.pdf (accessed 31/07/12).

harm to victims and offence seriousness. Yet the duty to shed light on the role and function of the VPS and VFS is not limited to the judiciary. Both initiatives were introduced citing a myriad of justifications and objectives,[134] and it is unclear whether they their primary purpose concerns boosting satisfaction levels (and/or therapeutic benefits) among victims, or whether they are simply intended to give the sentencer an improved picture of past events. It would be helpful for both stakeholders and practitioners to know how emotional harm might be specifically weighed alongside other factors in determining the overall seriousness of the offence. As things stand, rates of participation vary considerably across the country and victims seem unsure of the purpose of the schemes.[135] This can lead to later problems insofar as victims may feel dissatisfied if their expectations have remained unmet. To this end, a much clearer system of protocols and guidelines for professionals and information sheets for victims themselves could give victims a better picture of what participation does and does not entail and what they can expect from the process.[136]

The Need for Victim / Offender Interaction

A second emotionally intelligent reform would entail the opening up of communication channels between victims and offenders. As mentioned above, this would not only help to resolve conflicts between individuals, but might also send out a broader message to society concerning the social causes of crime and punishment and how best to address them.[137] Victims and offenders should - if they so choose – have the opportunity to engage in dialogue with each other, rather than talking to the court through lawyers. Under this proposal, victims would be conferred with a direct right of allocution and would be able to prepare and read their own statements in court. They would be given broad remit as to the content, and might also include photographs, drawings or poems as is currently permitted in the Australian state of Victoria.[138] Importantly, victims could also ask questions of the offender; the 'why me?' question, in particular, is one which tends to preoccupy victims of serious crime.[139]

Offenders should also be offered the opportunity to respond to victims' statements, and, indeed challenge them where appropriate. The lawyer-led plea in mitigation would be replaced by the opportunity for the offender to deliver a statement in person. This would take the form of a narrative that would not be confined by the parameters of evidentiary rules as to relevance. Offenders would be free to recount aspects of their life stories and their emotions before, during and after the offence. Such emotions would not only cover the 'acceptable' feelings of shame and remorse but offenders would also be free to make protests of innocence

---

[134] See Doak, Henham and Mitchell, n. 102 above.

[135] J Roberts and M Manikis, 'Victim Personal Statements in England and Wales: Latest (and Last) Trends from the Witness and Victim Experience Survey' (2012) 12 *Criminology and Criminal Justice* [forthcoming].

[136] Ibid. The Ministry of Justice has now recognised the need for such clarity and has recently announced a consultation on reform of the scheme: *Getting it Right for Victims and Witnesses* (London: Ministry of Justice, 2012).

[137] Bandes, 'Empathy', n. 6 above, p. 404.

[138] Ibid.

[139] L Sherman and H Strang, 'Repairing the Harm: Victims and Restorative Justice' (2003) 1 *Utah Law Review* 15.

or defiance. Just as offenders would have a right to challenge aspects of the victim's evidence, so too would victims be empowered to challenge any aspect of the offender's statement. It is, perhaps, self-evident that a risk exists that a dialogue of this nature could quite easily spiral into a freewheeling fracas, or indeed the victim narrative could become dominant, thereby drowning or pre-empting the account of the offender.[140] However, with careful formulated ground rules, close facilitation by the trial judge, and preparation and oversight by legal professionals, such a risk could be substantially reduced.

Integrating Restorative Justice within Sentencing

A more radical step than either of the two proposals set out above would entail the mainstreaming of restorative justice. Restorative justice programmes provide a forum for victims and offenders to exchange views and emotions within a safe environment. In spite of its growing popularity, restorative justice remains a contested concept, which has proved difficult to define in concise terms. One of the more widely accepted definitions is that provided by Tony Marshall, who described it as 'a process whereby all the parties with a stake in a particular offence come together to resolve collectively how to deal with the aftermath of the offence and its implications for the future'.[141] In restorative justice settings, personal narratives are used 'to understand the harms, the needs, the pains and the capacities of all participants so that an appropriate new story can be constructed'.[142] They are typically delivered in the victim's own words, and at his or her own pace. In contrast to the courtroom, a new 'co-narrative' is created to collectively affirm a norm, vindicate a victim, and denounce the evil of an act without labelling any person as a villain.[143]

Research evidence suggests that restorative justice delivers considerably higher satisfaction levels among stakeholders than court. In a meta-study of seven RJ programmes which compared restorative practices with court-based sentencing, Poulson found that almost three quarters (74%) of offenders apologized in RJ settings, around the same proportion (71%) who went through the court process did *not* apologize.[144] In other words, offenders were 6.9 times more likely to apologize to the victim in restorative justice settings than in court. If we accept that emotions matter – but are difficult to channel within the confines of the criminal court – it may be that we ought to look at how the court might make use of restorative justice operating in a different environment.

Traditionally, restorative programmes have often been situated on the periphery of the criminal justice system and have been primarily associated with diverting young offenders before any court process is instituted. However, in recent times commentators and policymakers alike are affording more thought as to how restorative justice might interact and

---

[140]   Bandes, 'Empathy', n. 2 above, p. 386.

[141]   T Marshall, *Restorative Justice: An Overview* (London: Home Office, 1999), p. 5.

[142]   K Pranis, 'Restorative Values and Confronting Family Violence' in H Strang and J Braithwaite (eds), *Restorative Justice and Family Violence* (Cambridge: Cambridge University Press, 2002), p. 31.

[143]   J Braithwaite, 'Narrative and "Compulsory Compassion"' (2006) 31 *Law and Social Inquiry* 425.

[144]   B Poulson, 'A Third Voice: A Review of Empirical Research on the Psychological Outcomes of Restorative Justice' (2003) 1 *Utah Law Review* 167.

dovetail with the established sentencing framework.[145] With appropriate safeguards, court-ordered mediation and conferencing could serve to complement existing sentence practice. Referrals to mediation are becoming increasingly commonplace within continental Europe; Austria and Finland both operate schemes whereby the law provides that certain cases may be diverted away from court at the prosecution stage.[146] While many post-conviction and prison-based schemes exist throughout England and Wales, these operate independently of the formal sentencing process and lie on the periphery of the criminal justice system. They are generally applied in a haphazard fashion and are not currently subject to any form of statutory. However, in a significant move, the Government recently indicated that it intended to introduce an amendment to the Crime and Courts Bill 2012 which would provide a statutory basis by which courts could defer imposing sentence until a restorative activity has taken place.[147] At the time of writing (November 2012), it remains to be seen whether the provision will eventually enter into law, and, if so, whether it might act as something of a precursor to placing restorative justice on a more prominent (and legally certain) footing within the criminal justice system.

Such a mainstreamed framework is already in place in the Northern Irish youth justice system. Here, all young people who plead guilty or who are convicted of an offence are referred to conferencing either by the Public Prosecution Service or by the court (providing they consent to the process).[148] The subsequent agreement is then returned to court for approval by the magistrate to ensure that the sentence is not disproportionate and that the public interest is served. Although careful thought would need to be given to the roll-out of any equivalent scheme for adults in England and Wales – and particularly which offences it might cover – there is no reason in theory or practice why such a system could not be successfully established to offer a more effective approach to sentencing across the Irish Sea.

Conclusions

Emotions have assumed centre stage in various legal and criminological discourses including procedural justice, therapeutic jurisprudence, restorative justice, transitional justice as well as conflict resolution and peace building.[149] Scholars and practitioners in these areas

---

[145] See generally T Brooks, *Punishment* (2012: London, Routledge); J Shapland, 'Restorative Justice and Criminal Justice: Just Responses to Crime?' in A von Hirsch, J Roberts, A E Bottoms, K Roach and M Schiff (eds), *Restorative Justice and Criminal Justice: Competing or Reconcilable Paradigms?* (2003: Oxford, Hart Publishing); D O'Mahony and J Doak, *Criminal Justice and Restorative Justice: Theory, Law and* Practice (forthcoming) (2013: Oxford, Hart Publishing)

[146] See further D O'Mahony and J Doak, ibid.

[147] Providing that such a course of action is opted for by both the victim and the offender: see Crime and Courts Bill 2012, sch 16(2), inserting a new Section 1ZA of the Powers of Criminal Courts (Sentencing) Act 2000.

[148] Justice (NI) Act 2002, Pt IV. Only those offences which carry an automatic life sentence are excluded from the regime. See further D. O'Mahony and C. Campbell, 'Mainstreaming Restorative Justice for Young Offenders through Youth Conferencing: The Experience of Northern Ireland' in J Junger-Tas and S Decker (eds), *International Handbook of Youth Justice* (Amsterdam: Springer, 2006).

[149] See eg Karstedt, 'Emotions' n. 1 above; Brewer, 'Dealing with Emotions', n. 3 above; Nussbaum, 'Hiding from Humanity', n. 5 above; Bandes, 'Empathy', n. 6 above.

acknowledge significant value placed on the role of emotions, and the processes put in place to elicit them. Yet despite the rapid expansion of these concepts, emotions are still regarded with suspicion. The vast majority of sentencing decisions remain within the preserve of the formal legal system and are characterised by formality, legality and a closed system of communication[150] dominated by legal professionals. All this takes place against a normative framework orientated towards retributivism (albeit slightly mottled with occasional allusions to deterrence, incapacitation, rehabilitation and reparation).

Emotions *ex post facto* are largely deemed an irrelevant factor for pure retributivists,[151] and such a narrow focus has led to the social causes of and solutions to conflict being sidelined in discussions concerning how both theory and practice might move forwards. Still, as Bandes has contended, if the lawyers have not been persuaded by the encroachment of emotion, they have certainly felt impelled to respond.[152] As this *special edition* attests, the place of emotion within law is well and truly established as a key theme within legal discourse.

Undoubtedly some relatively recent initiatives, such as the advent of sentencing guidelines and victim impact statements, have increased the flow of emotional information to the court. However, the potential of emotions to enrich our justice system has been simultaneously thwarted by the reluctance of policymakers and practitioners to consider the wider questions concerning how sentencing might be improved by affording a more central role to emotional narratives and the need for deliberative interactions between victims and offenders. As it stands, the sentencing system of England and Wales affords scant attention to the emotions of criminal offenders and victims. Whilst, in the longer term, a considerable amount of theoretical and practical work needs to be done in developing and refining our understanding of emotions – and their precise relationship to the justice system – there are some steps that can be taken in the interim to make criminal sentencing more responsive to human emotions. Our hope is that a timely injection of emotional intelligence may trigger a broader realisation that criminal sentencing ought to perform a wider function than the mere retribution of wrongs.

---

[150] N Luhmann, 'Law as a Social System' (1989) 83 *Northwestern University Law Review* 136.

[151] Clearly emotions such as remorse cannot alter seriousness of crime or culpability of the time of the offence: see further A Von Hirsch, 'Propotionality and Progressive Loss of Mitigation: Further Reflections' in J Roberts and A von Hirsch eds, *The Role of Previous Convictions in Sentencing: Theoretical and Applied Perspectives* (Oxford: Hart, 2010). However, it is also worth noting Chris Bennett's observation that emotions are, in effect, the principle reason for the public engaging with the very concept of retribution through their moral disapproval of criminality: C Bennett, 'The Varieties of Retributive Experience' (2002) 48 *Philosophical Quarterly* 145.

[152] Bandes, 'Empathy', n. 6 above p. 368.

Part IV
Sentencing as Punitive Restoration

[12]

The Arts and Prisoners: Experiences of Creative Rehabilitation

BRIEGE NUGENT and NANCY LOUCKS

Briege Nugent is an Independent Criminologist; Nancy Loucks is Chief Executive, Families Outside

Abstract: The following article presents findings from an ongoing evaluation of arts programmes from Artlink Central taking place in Cornton Vale, which is Scotland's main prison for women. Through a discussion of the findings, and a look to international research on this area, the arts can clearly generate significant rehabilitative benefits for offenders. However, such work has both real and perceived limitations. Ultimately the arts, like other rehabilitative efforts, can be regarded as an 'add on' and, therefore, do not receive the credit or place they deserve in policy and consequently in practice.

Keywords: arts; prison; rehabilitation

This article presents findings from an evaluation of Artlink Central's work over the past two years within HMP & YOI Cornton Vale, which is Scotland's main prison for women. Artlink Central is a registered charity founded in 1988 in the belief that involvement in the arts is life-enhancing and should be available to all. It enables a wide range of marginalised and special needs groups to work with experienced professional artists on high-quality art projects in the Stirling, Falkirk and Clackmannanshire areas of Central Scotland.[1] They have delivered art workshops in prisons in Scotland for the past 14 years and, therefore, have extensive experience in working within the prison environment. The evaluation highlighted the rehabilitative effects that the arts can have within a prison setting as well as the barriers (both real and perceived) to the use of arts with prisoners. At present the arts are not part of the core programme for prisoners.

Female Offenders in Scotland

Prisoner numbers continue to increase in Scotland. On 1 April 2007 the prison population stood at 7,238, but by May 2010 had increased to over 8,000.[2] The number of women going to prison, in particular, has risen at an alarming rate. Over the ten-year period from 1998/99 to 2007/08, the average daily prison population (men and women) increased by 22%. In the same ten-year period, the female prison population increased by 87% – over four times the growth experienced in the male prison population

The Howard Journal Vol 50 No 4. September 2011
ISSN 0265-5527, pp. 356–370

(20%) (Scottish Government 2008). HMP & YOI Cornton Vale was built in 1975 to hold a maximum of 200 women. The Social Work Services and Prisons Inspectorate (1998) recommended that the female population should be limited to 100, yet in 2010 the figures now stand at around 400. This parallels the situation for female offenders in England, where Gelsthorpe (2006) lamented that things were not changing despite countless reports highlighting that sending women to prison was not the answer. Tombs (2006) summarised the situation of women offenders in Scotland as an 'unmet commitment' and called for a coherent plan to reduce the level of inappropriate imprisonment of women to be developed.

Based on figures from 2007/08, each prisoner place costs £32,358 per year (Scottish Prison Service 2008). The prison population in Scotland generally comes from the most deprived backgrounds (Houchin 2005). Many prisoners lack educational attainment, and between 20% and 30% of offenders have learning difficulties or learning disabilities that interfere with their ability to cope within the criminal justice system (Loucks 2007). Research in England shows that many offenders' basic skills are rudimentary, with half of all those in custody at or below Level 1 (the level expected of an eleven-year-old) in reading; two-thirds in numeracy; and four-fifths in writing. These basic skills are required for 96% of all jobs (Social Exclusion Unit 2002) and are likely to be the basic skills required to be able to live a happy and meaningful life on a day-to-day basis. Those with learning disabilities or who have literacy and numeracy problems are often not able to take part fully in the prison regime, such as in courses available in prison, and this exclusion can sometimes lead to isolation (Loucks and Talbot 2007). In short, most people in prison have little current prospects for the future and have often given up on the idea of education.

Research shows that female prisoners such as those in HMP & YOI Cornton Vale are particularly vulnerable, with many having mental health problems, histories of physical and sexual abuse, self-harm and addiction to drugs (see, for example, Loucks 1998; Social Work Services and Prisons Inspectorate 1998; Corston 2007). Andrew McLellan, then the Chief Inspector of Prisons for Scotland, stated in 2004 that: 'This is not a cross section of society: these are very damaged women' (McLellan 2004). This statement is as relevant to today as it was then.

The Benefits of Arts in Prison

A number of studies has shown that the arts have a positive impact on offenders. For example, arts-based projects have been shown to help those with mental health issues, particularly in relation to feelings of empowerment and building of confidence (Matarasso and Chell 1998; Ruskin 2006). The Scottish Prison Service's (2002) *Framework for Promoting Health* recognises that there is a need to 'use the full range of health interventions (not just pharmaceutical aids) to support individuals and groups in discussing and seeking solutions to mental health problems' (p.23). The

The Howard Journal Vol 50 No 4. September 2011
ISSN 0265-5527, pp. 356–370

Framework outlines the importance of recreational activity; however it makes no specific reference to the arts. There is an increasing awareness at policy level about the benefits of the arts for people with mental health issues. Corston (2007) recommends that innovative and creative solutions are used to work with the most vulnerable prisoners; the arts can be a way of doing this, as the ongoing evaluation we describe here suggests. The arts are especially useful as no restrictions or barriers determine who can access them, and the work can be tailored easily to suit individual needs and skills.

The use of drugs and the link to offending, especially for women offenders in Scotland, are irrefutable: at one point, 98% of women in HMP & YOI Cornton Vale were recorded as having a drug addiction (HM Inspectorate of Prisons 2005). Factors that lead women to start taking drugs often include the influence of a partner and a perceived need to use drugs as a coping strategy against abuse (Benda 2005). The arts can help people find different ways of coping and improve mental health and well-being. As the former director of Arts in Corrections, California, commented:

> ... the arts are a low cost, high touch, non threatening intervention that have produced measurable results in the areas of reduction of psychopathological behaviour, reduced incident rates, reduced recidivism, improved educational performance and increased self-esteem. (Cleveland 2003, cited in Hughes 2005, p.37)

Wilson, Caulfield and Atherton (2008) reflect that the arts can be a powerful and highly valuable activity for all prisoners. Allen, Shaw and Hall (2004) found that benefits can be direct, such as improved writing skills, or indirect, through improved social skills such as working as part of a team or increased self-esteem. In their evaluation for the Anne Peaker Centre for Arts and Criminal Justice, Cheliotis and Tankebe (2008) found increased self-esteem, a sense of achievement and improved likelihood to move into education.

The arts can provide routes into learning for those alienated from the formal education system. Miles (2007) pointed out that a dance-led programme with young offenders and young people at risk of offending in Bradford, for example, is seeing the majority of its graduates going on to college or re-engaging with school. In the report *Offenders' Learning Journey for Juvenile Offenders*, the Offender Learning and Skills Department at the Ministry of Justice in England (2004) highlighted the importance of offering young offenders the opportunity to gain qualifications in the arts, if this is something that they would like to pursue. It recommended that service providers should work hard to maintain the learning process from the prison into the community. The report notes that the arts 'provide an opportunity for self-expression and can thereby assist in maintaining good order' (p.2). The Council of Europe Recommendation R. (89) 12 of the Committee of Ministers to Member States on Education in Prison states that:

The Howard Journal Vol 50 No 4. September 2011
ISSN 0265-5527, pp. 356–370

Creative and cultural activities should be given a significant role because these activities have particular potential to enable prisoners to develop and express themselves.

The arts have been shown to be an innovative and effective way of dealing with anger and aggression (Blacker, Watson and Beech 2008). For example, the impact on offending behaviour through the use of arts was evident in the work of the Barlinnie Special Unit, where even the most violent prisoners were said to be calmer as a result. Using arts as a tool for expression, participants can build human capital and begin to see how they could 'make good' for the future, which is important for the process of desistance from crime (Maruna 2005). This transformation is noted in the work of Laing, who was the art therapist at Barlinnie Special Unit. Laing describes how Jimmy Boyle, a notorious prisoner at the time in the unit, reacted to using clay to create models and how it helped him realise that he was talented and more than just a 'hard man':

Two parallel emotions were engulfing him; he was bursting with enthusiasm for ideas he wanted to try with this material which was new to him and he was also experiencing a new concept of the self: the former hard man spending his time working on art. (Carrell and Laing 1982, p.58, cited in Nellis 2010, p.5)

Arts interventions are increasingly credited with enhancing social capital (Williams 1997). The importance of building 'social capital' or creating opportunities is now well established as a key factor in the process of desistance from crime (Farrall 2002; Maruna 2005; Whyte and McNeill 2007). The scant research available into gender differences and social capital suggests that female offenders have particular difficulty generating social capital due to a lack of opportunities for this (Reisig, Holtfreter and Morash 2002). For example, women attempting to get back into work face barriers such as childcare responsibilities, abusive partners and a lack of support (O'Keefe 2003). In a recent evaluation of the Willow Project – an alternative to custody for women in Edinburgh – women who were attending the project as part of their probation order said that they enjoyed being out of the house and meeting others and were glad of the chance to do this (Nugent, Loureiro and Loucks 2010).

Arts programmes in prison could be a useful way for women to meet others from their area and begin to establish a common pro-social interest that could, in turn, lead to mutual support and benefit. Farrall and Maruna (2004) point out that 'social capital' is both an 'enabling' feature of an individual's life, as well as a feature of that which 'is enabled'. Therefore, for those who have been generally excluded, social capital is not easy to generate, and the arts can provide a more accessible and realistic way of achieving this. Whyte and McNeill (2007) stress that social capital requires community support; in this context, taking part in the arts in prison is an opportunity to interact with people, and ideally this work should continue beyond the prison gates.

The emphasis is that the benefits of the arts should not just be internal to the prison but should, and could, transfer to the community. In particular,

The Howard Journal Vol 50 No 4. September 2011
ISSN 0265-5527, pp. 356–370

they can impact positively upon future offending, especially if this means that the prisoner begins to engage in education. In 2003, the Learning and Skills Development Agency conducted a study of participation in education amongst 211 prisoners at four prisons. The results showed that the reconviction rate in the first year after release, for ex-prisoners who had begun a general education course between 2001 and 2002, was 28%, compared with a national average of 44% for all offenders.[3] Criminological research has also found that prisoners who report high levels of self-belief and confidence in their ability to stop offending were also the most successful in desisting from crime when they left prison (Gendreau, Grant and Leipciger 1979; Maruna 2005). Hughes (2005) argues that arts programmes can not just reduce offending behaviour but also help disaffected young people re-engage with education, and sponsor personal and social development.

The arts can, therefore, be a very useful pathway for helping prisoners enter into education and building confidence and self-esteem. It is also, potentially, a multi-faceted way to support offenders both in and out of prison. The recognition of the benefits of the arts in prison is evident by their growing use throughout the world, with well-established theatre and art projects in prisons such as in Italy, America, Germany and Northern Ireland. In Northern Ireland, the Prison Arts Foundation has become part of the core programme of prison activity.[4] In Scotland, a number of different initiatives are taking place such as 'fine cell' work in HMP & YOI Cornton Vale, which culminates in chosen work being shown in an exhibition in London, and the work of Artlink Central. HMP Barlinnie recently held an exhibition about the importance of art in prisoners' lives, one of the central aspects of which was to highlight the work of Theatre Nemo, which has been working in HMP Barlinnie for five years. As the Scottish Prison Service (2009a) highlighted in the publication *The Gallery*, prisoners, as well as visitors who came to the exhibition, were able to see themselves, through the art, in a different light.

This is not an exhaustive list, and many projects have taken place in the past and will, indeed, begin in the future in Scotland and throughout the UK. The use of arts in prison is, therefore, not a new initiative, but the benefits are now gaining both acknowledgement and credibility.

Findings from the Evaluation of Artlink Central

Artlink Central is a registered charity founded in 1988 in the belief that involvement in the arts is life-enhancing and should be available to all. Engaging in professional art requires commitment, concentration, self-discipline, motivation and dedication. The ultimate aim for their work in HMP & YOI Cornton Vale is to help the women be better equipped to make the transition into education, training or employment, both within the prison and on release. The main objectives of the work are to support the women in developing core life skills, increase self-esteem, and improve well-being.

The Howard Journal Vol 50 No 4. September 2011
ISSN 0265-5527, pp. 356–370

Artlink Central has been working in Scottish prisons for the past 13 years with all offenders, including remand, short-term, long-term and even life sentenced prisoners. In the current evaluation discussed, the women taking part were serving a range of sentences and some were on remand. The women either referred themselves onto the course through their residential officer, or in some cases the residential officer approached prisoners whom they felt could particularly benefit from taking part. One restriction to working with both remand and short-term prisoners is that of time, and imaginative ways to deal with this are essential. For example, in North-Rhine Westphalia (NRW) in Germany, any prisoner who begins a programme of education who is serving a short sentence is offered the option of continuing and completing this in the community after release (Wolfgang 2008). In HMP & YOI Cornton Vale this is not happening at present, but Artlink Central hopes that this can be the case in the future, at least in relation to the arts programmes that they offer.

The Scottish Prison Service's multi-disciplinary Integrated Case Management process (similar to sentence planning) and supporting IT system (PR2) should mean that prisoners' information can be shared between prisons and external agencies so that their needs are identified and met. Through their courses, Artlink Central has close contact with prisoners who may not necessarily access other services and could help them, for example those with learning disabilities, to access the help they need.

Artlink Central's work within HMP & YOI Cornton Vale has been independently evaluated since April 2008. During the period of evaluation from April 2008 to April 2010, 32 different courses have taken place, ranging from arts and crafts to more technically-challenging projects such as animation and radio plays. Each course lasts for five days, and at the end, all who have participated are presented with a certificate by one of the directors of Artlink Central or by the governor within the prison. The courses were offered to all prisoners, including those on remand and those serving short sentences, both of which groups often have little or no opportunities for such support (Social Exclusion Unit 2002).

Methods

The findings presented are based on feedback forms filled in by 112 women at both the beginning and the end of the course in which they participated from April 2009 to April 2010. The women filled in these forms by themselves, although residential prison officers or those officers supervising the course offered help when literacy was an issue. The feedback forms mainly consisted of closed questions to find out which aspects of the course they felt to be most useful. They also contained Likert scales to measure self-confidence and self-esteem 'before' and 'after' the course and gave the women an opportunity to add any comments they wished. An independent researcher collated and analysed the data from the forms.

The Howard Journal Vol 50 No 4. September 2011
ISSN 0265-5527, pp. 356-370

In order to provide more developed information on the impact of the course, the researchers also conducted qualitative interviews with 65 women both before and at the end of the courses. The women interviewed were chosen largely at random, although a small number was selected specifically because the responses they had given on the forms merited further exploration. Also, women from different age groups were targeted for interviews to determine whether these courses were responsive to the potential differences in their needs and expectations.

In addition to this, ten prison officers supervising the courses were interviewed, in order to gain their views and sometimes to cross reference or check some of the information given by the women. Prison and Artlink Central managers directly relevant to the setting up and carrying out of the courses were also interviewed.

Part of the evaluation involved trying to measure the potential impact of the courses on the behaviour of the women. Therefore, relevant residential prison officers were requested to fill in an assessment form for each participant before and after the course. This short form was mainly comprised of closed questions and Likert scales rating the women from 'calm' (1) to 'disruptive and difficult' (5). Sixteen forms were returned in total and, although this is a small number in comparison with the full sample, it gave some idea of the impact of the arts projects.

In addition to these forms, four residential officers were interviewed to determine whether the courses appeared to have an impact generally on participants' behaviour. Observational notes were also made by the researcher for five different courses. Information drawn from these sources was analysed using a thematic approach. The current evaluation has the potential for follow-up research to be undertaken with participants. The short timescale for this evaluation limits the evidence of longer-term impact, although other studies indicate the potential for this (Caulfield and Wilson 2010).

Positive Impacts of the Course: Participants' Views

From the feedback forms and the interviews, all of the women reported feeling many positive impacts as a result of taking part in the courses. In line with the original objectives, women believed that they grew in confidence and self-esteem, and a comparison of scales recorded before and after each course showed an improvement in these areas. One of the main findings is that the women enjoyed learning something new and appreciated the opportunity to meet other women, to have a chance to work as a team and to learn new skills. They found the courses relaxing, and a few even said that they had been able to forget that they were in prison during the course; this humanising aspect of the arts in prison is also reflected in other research (Caulfield, Wilson and Wilkinson 2009). The women felt that having professional artists, actors and musicians working with them was empowering, and they valued the experience.

The music and drama workshops are recorded and edited profession-ally, and each woman receives a copy of a DVD or CD of the work, which

The Howard Journal Vol 50 No 4. September 2011
ISSN 0265-5527, pp. 356–370

reinforces their sense of achievement. All of the women interviewed valued having something tangible to take away from the experience. Two women interviewed even said that taking part in the drama and music workshops was one of the best things they had ever done in their lives:

This is the best thing I have done since being in here, it was so so much fun. Drugs robbed me of my life and personality, and this type of thing made me remember what I used to be like and what I can be like.

Before the craft classes, the artists and prison officers plan the work so that the women are allowed to keep the pieces they create. Participants in these classes were pleased that they were able to make something for their room and in many cases also for their children. The women explained that the chance to give something tangible to their children was important and provided a rare opportunity for them to feel proud when their children visited them. Many women said that they had very few belongings when they came to prison, and, therefore, having something that was 'theirs' was really appreciated.

Taking part in the courses can give both the women and prison officers an opportunity to show a different, 'softer' and more approachable side. Prison officers who took part in the courses, either by being actively involved in the making of crafts or playing of instruments, reportedly had a particularly beneficial effect on the atmosphere and overall project. All of the women interviewed felt that they had seen a 'softer' side to the prison staff and respected them more as a result:

Having him [the residential prison officer] involved helped us to join in and you see them as human beings, they let their guard down.

This finding is similar to one of the most important benefits noted of the work in the Barlinnie Special Unit. Their work showed that arts projects spurred communication between prisoners and officers to understand commonalities rather than focusing on difference (Nellis 2010).

Women interviewed also said that they saw a different side to other prisoners, and observation of the courses for the research showed that the women encouraged one another. Two women reconciled their differences as a result of taking part in the course, as they realised that their perceptions of one another had not been correct. The work of Artlink Central used to be a part of a pilot restorative justice scheme within the prison, so the potential for the arts to be used in this way appears to remain.

Prison officers – even those who admitted to being sceptical at first – reported that the courses had a visible positive impact on the women. They felt that those who took part were calmer, more at ease, more confident and less troublesome as a result of taking part in the arts projects.

The evaluation highlighted the potential for the arts to be used as a new and innovative way of looking into, and challenging, offending behaviour. One of the courses was a make-up workshop that included a session dedicated to looking into the many 'faces' we have in our daily lives. The artists felt that this session gave the women an opportunity to discuss the complexities of their lives in an abstract and, therefore, a perceivably

The Howard Journal Vol 50 No 4. September 2011
ISSN 0265-5527, pp. 356–370

less-intrusive way. One interviewee in particular who had convictions for violent offences said she was able to open up about the need to be 'hard' and how difficult this image was to maintain. The women also explored how they viewed each other, and, again, this allowed the women to be open and honest about the complexities of their lives. One woman interviewed said she now realised that everyone felt she was intimidating and that there was no need for her to continue to act in this way. Although this course only took place over a week, the potential for this type of initiative to be expanded was apparent.

The women interviewed appreciated sessions such as the make-up workshop, which was about making the best of yourself. Artlink Central also reported that this course had been oversubscribed and, as a result, they were planning to reschedule another session. One interviewee said this was the first time she had taken time to look after herself and, as a result, she could see a better version of herself, both physically and mentally. Using make-up as a tool for expression, the women were building human capital and beginning to see how they could 'make good' for the future, which is important for the process of desistance from crime (Maruna 2005).

For foreign prisoners, the use of the arts as a way of integration is particularly interesting. Twelve Chinese women had taken part in the courses, and one Scottish woman interviewed observed that up until then they had 'kept themselves to themselves' but were now mixing better with other prisoners. One Chinese woman even started teaching the other women origami in the evenings, and in return they were teaching her English. All felt that, without the arts project, the previous lack of interaction would have continued.

Many of the women spoke about the opportunity to allow their imaginations to be free for a short period of time, which was relaxing and fun. In support of the recommendations of the Corston (2007) report, this use of arts was an easy and accessible way of helping those who were particularly vulnerable. Research generally agrees that prison is not the ideal setting for the treatment of mental health issues (Kupers 1999). Despite this, those who had mental health issues reportedly enjoyed the therapeutic effects of taking part in the courses and pointed out that very few activities of this sort took place within their hall. Two women interviewed said that they were generally problematic in the prison: one woman admitted to 'thrashing' her room regularly but that, during the course, she felt calm and did not feel like causing trouble. Another woman was a prolific self-harmer but explained that, when she was taking part in art, she felt in control and had not harmed herself throughout the week. This small finding supports other research into the positive impact that the arts can have on those who have a history of self-harming (Caulfield, Wilson and Wilkinson 2009), and, therefore, highlights the potential therapeutic effects of arts projects.

Those in the sample with reported mental health issues especially appreciated seeing a result from their work in a relatively short period of time. Women reported feeling shocked and proud of what they were

The Howard Journal Vol 50 No 4. September 2011
ISSN 0265-5527, pp. 356–370

able to achieve. One prison officer had worked with vulnerable prisoners for ten years and said that giving the women even the smallest bit of attention and support paid dividends. She felt that prisoners with mental health issues, more than any other prisoners, were able to benefit from using the arts to build confidence, self-esteem and 'feel good' about themselves.

Many of the women have no formal qualifications, therefore they regarded receiving a certificate from the governor at the end of the course as an important event. Those who took part in the music classes also performed a concert. Most of the women interviewed said that they would like the opportunity to have their family and friends come to the prison to see them perform or show them their completed pieces of work. Based on the attendance and feedback of prisoners and families at art courses in HMP Pentonville in England, Cahillane (2008) reflects that having families view the work helps to reinforce the positive experience. HMP Shotts in Scotland also holds art exhibitions open to family. With these things in mind, the attendance of families to view final work could beneficially be arranged where possible.

Many of the women felt that they would like to extend their learning within the courses to involve a more formal educational element that could lead to a qualification. Artlink Central has now linked up with the college based at the prison to raise awareness of the other activities in which the women could get involved. However, two prison officers felt that the formal education offered in the prison was unlikely to be successful for those who had already given up a 'classroom' style of learning. The ability of Artlink Central to draw women with a range of abilities into their programmes highlights the realities that learning in a more interactive way may be the best way forward. Indeed, this approach is being adopted on an international level as the ideal way to provide education (Hawkins 2010).

Whether the projects will have a long-term impact could not be discerned in any credible way from this evaluation due to the current lack of follow-up available within the timescales. There is an opportunity for follow-up to take place in the future, and other research has been able to show that the arts have the potential to have a long-term impact (Caulfield, Wilson and Wilkinson 2009). One woman interviewed as part of the evaluation pointed out:

It might not help many people long term, but for me it was one of the best experiences of my life and I have not had many of them.

If the projects are able to provide a 'stepping stone' into education, then this is certainly one way in which it can have a lasting impact. Artlink Central can also help women link with work within the community which, in turn, can provide the type of intervention which can make the difference for the future, particularly in relation to the building of social capital. Artlink Central is working in partnership with the prison; their part in highlighting and helping women approach the appropriate services for the support they require could prove invaluable.

The Howard Journal Vol 50 No 4. September 2011
ISSN 0265-5527, pp. 356–370

Barriers to Delivering Arts Projects

The main issue for the delivery of arts projects is that prisons are overcrowded, with the result that officers are overstretched. This is a real barrier to the arts or any other project being run within a prison, as regimes may be limited to ensure safe staff-prisoner ratios. Priority for staffing also goes to the running of core programmes when resources are limited (see, for example, HM Inspectorate of Prisons for Scotland 2009).

The Scottish Prison Service does not currently fund arts projects, and Artlink Central's work exists due to short-term funding from independent sources. In HMP & YOI Cornton Vale, the prison governor and manager of activities are incredibly supportive of the work and can see the positive impact. Overall, the current work is taking place because those who want it to happen are going out of their way to make it happen. This work is not underpinned by strategic policy and sits as an 'add on' to the core delivery objective of security; however, this is not the case in all prisons. For example, in HMP Shotts, art projects from Motherwell College are regarded as part of the core programme for prisoners if they want to take part. An art exhibition also takes place in the prison once a year for a small number of art students. HM Inspectorate of Prisons highlighted this as an example of best practice, with the proviso that more regular events should be held to promote achievement (McLellan 2007). The possibility of inviting families in at the end of each Artlink Central course would, therefore, comply with the Inspectorate's example of best practice, namely the acknowledgement and celebration of achievement on a more regular basis.

The evaluation noted that Artlink Central appears to be making a number of contributions to the Scottish Prison Service's nine Offender Outcomes identified in the Scottish Prison Service Delivery Plan as having a positive impact on reducing offending (Scottish Prison Service 2009b). Specifically, the courses appear to improve mental well-being, attitudes and behaviour and be a step towards improved literacy, employability and access to community support. The courses also have the potential to strengthen prisoners' relationships with families and peers. Overall, the arts can play an important role in the rehabilitation of offenders, but at present this work is happening out of perseverance rather than design.

Certain perceptions also pose significant barriers to the use of arts in prison. Despite the benefits, some commentators believe that prisoners should simply not be allowed to take part in 'fun' activities. For example, Orr (2009) reported in the *Independent* that the London Royal Festival Hall was obliged to remove a sculpture and apologised for displaying it after *The Times* revealed that it was the work of a child sex killer. As Orr pointed out:

The work of the Koestler Trust in nurturing the evidence of human complexity is extremely valuable. The possibility that the organisation is now going to be dogged by investigators bent on finding out whether those who attract its critical attention are 'too evil' to take part is repellent and fatuous.

The Howard Journal Vol 50 No 4. September 2011
ISSN 0265-5527, pp. 356–370

This situation is not usual, and the Koestler Trust is able to show exhibitions without similar controversy, which may be evidence that the public is gradually becoming more open to the benefits of the arts in prison. The Scottish Prisons Commission (2008) pointed out that the public must be engaged and informed on criminal justice matters. The introduction of real evidence rather than simply gut reaction creates a new opportunity for resurrecting and developing the concept of rehabilitation in prisons. In support of Cullen, Cullen and Wozniak (1988), rehabilitation continues to retain 'substantial legitimacy', spawning optimism that the existence of a punitive public may be a 'myth'. One question following the debacle at the London Royal Festival Hall is whether anyone actually asked 'the public' what they thought and, instead, presumed the worst.

The Future of the Arts in Prison

The evidence nationally and internationally, and the findings presented here which are based on the evaluation of the work of Artlink Central, have been able to show that the arts can have a significant positive impact on offenders, especially in building self-confidence, self-esteem and social capital. They can also be particularly useful in working with those who have mental health issues. At present, the arts are used in many prisons, but only a few have included them as part of their core programmes. The Scottish Prison Service works towards the reduction of offending as outlined through their Offender Outcomes, and, therefore, rehabilitation is vital. However, the very 'real' limitations due to overcrowding, understaffing and restrictions in resources mean that this work is often greatly inhibited. One of the main priorities for prisons is security; this alone is demanding enough, and more needs to improve in terms of prison conditions and pressures in order for the Offender Outcomes to have their rightful place.

The arts and rehabilitation overall are currently an 'add on', and, indeed, the work of Artlink Central is reliant on external funders outside of the prison system, but the short- and longer-term benefits are those that would eventually benefit the public. Without adequate support and services, prisoners will continue to reoffend and return to prison; therefore the future of the arts, as part of a core package of programmes for offenders in and out of prison, should be given serious consideration. As the Scottish Prisons Commission (2008) pointed out, the public needs to be engaged in rational debate. Taking on board evidence from Finland, such debate must also include policy makers such as government ministers, legislators, the judiciary, the police and prosecutors and the media (Lappi-Seppala 2006). Until then, the arts and rehabilitation, and the work of Artlink Central, have an uncertain future in which their full potential is never realised. Arguably a presumption of a punitive public is what is driving current criminal justice policy; for the arts, this presumption may be the most significant barrier of all.[5]

The Howard Journal Vol 50 No 4. September 2011
ISSN 0265-5527, pp. 356–370

Notes

1 Available at: *http://www.artlinkcentral.org* (accessed 23 March 2011).
2 Available at: *http://www.sps.gov.uk* (accessed 23 March 2011).
3 Available at *http://www.literacytrust.org.uk/Database/prisonarchive.html* (accessed 23 March 2011). The Learning and Skills Research Centre (LSRC) website has been removed, so this information is not able to be taken from its original source, *http://www.hmie.gov.uk/documents/publication/lsergpsp.html*
4 To read more information about each of these projects in detail, see Allen, Shaw and Hall (2004).
5 *Acknowledgements*: We would like to thank Sarah Chester MBE, from Artlink Central, Christine Scullion of the Robertson Trust, and staff at HMP & YOI Cornton Vale and HMP Shotts. This work was supported by the Robertson Trust, Artlink Central, and the Scottish Prison Service. The Robertson Trust is an independent Scottish grant-making trust (Scottish Charity No: SC002970). Artlink Central is a limited company (No. 109852) and has charitable status with the Inland Revenue SC0 08158.

References

Allen, K., Shaw, P. and Hall, J. (2004) *The Art of Rehabilitation: Attitudes to Offenders' Involvement in the Arts*, London: Rethinking Crime and Punishment, Esmée Fairbairn Foundation.

Benda, B. (2005) 'Gender differences in life course theory of recidivism: a survival analysis', *International Journal of Offender Therapy and Comparative Criminology*, 49(3), 325–42.

Blacker, J., Watson, A. and Beech, A.R. (2008) 'A combined drama-based and CBT approach to working with self-reported anger aggression', *Criminal Behaviour and Mental Health*, 18, 129–37.

Cahillane, M. (2008) 'Jailhouse rocks', in: *Prison Report: Freeing the Spirit: Prison and the Arts*, Summer 2008, Issue 73, 19–21, London: Prison Reform Trust. Available at: *http://www.prisonreformtrust.org.uk/temp/PrisonspReportsp73.pdf* (accessed 14 November 2010).

Carrell, C. and Laing, J. (Eds.) (1982) *The Special Unit, Barlinnie Prison: Its Evolution Through its Art*, Glasgow: Third Eye Centre.

Caulfield, L.S. and Wilson, D. (2010) 'Women and the arts: the impact of a prison music programme on female offenders', *Journal of Social Criminology*, 3, 67–90.

Caulfield, L.S., Wilson, D. and Wilkinson, D.J. (2009) *Continuing Positive Change in Prison and the Community: An Analysis of the Long-term and Wider Impact of the Good Vibrations Project* (Grant Report to Good Vibrations), Birmingham: Birmingham City University.

Cheliotis, L. and Tankebe, J. (2008) *An Evaluation of Learning to Learn, Phase 3*, London: Anne Peaker Centre.

Cleveland, W. (2003) 'A rationale for arts-based programs in youth services' (unpublished).

Corston, J. (2007) *The Corston Report: A Review of Women with Particular Vulnerabilities in the Criminal Justice System*, London: Home Office.

Cullen, F., Cullen, J. and Wozniak, J. (1988) 'Is rehabilitation dead? The myth of the punitive public', *Journal of Criminal Justice*, 16(4), 303–17.

Farrall, S. (2002) *Rethinking What Works with Offenders: Probation, Social Context and Desistance from Crime*, Cullompton: Willan.

Farrall, S. and Maruna, S. (2004) 'Social capital and offender reintegration: making probation desistance focused', in: S. Maruna and R. Immarigeon (Eds.), *After Crime and Punishment: Pathways to Offender Reintegration*, Cullompton: Willan.

The Howard Journal Vol 50 No 4. September 2011
ISSN 0265-5527, pp. 356–370

Gelsthorpe, L. (2006) 'Counterblast: Women and criminal justice: saying it again, again and again', *Howard Journal*, *45*, 421–4.

Gendreau, P., Grant, B. and Leipciger, M. (1979) 'Self-esteem, incarceration and recidivism', *Criminal Justice and Behavior*, *6*, 67–75.

Hawkins, D. (2010) *Using Prevention Science to Promote Healthy Youth Development* (Public Lecture Series on behalf of Scottish Collaboration for Public Health Research and Policy (SCPHRP), Edinburgh, 4 May 2010), Edinburgh: SCPHRP.

HM Inspectorate of Prisons (2005) *HMP & YOI Cornton Vale Inspection: 2–3 February 2005*, Edinburgh: Scottish Executive.

HM Inspectorate of Prisons for Scotland (2009) *Annual Report 2008–2009*, Edinburgh: Scottish Government.

Houchin, R. (2005) *Social Exclusion and Imprisonment in Scotland*, Glasgow: Glasgow Caledonian University.

Hughes, J. (2005) *Doing the Arts Justice: A Review of Research Literature, Practice and Theory*, London: Department for Culture, Media and Sport.

Kupers, T. (1999) *Prison Madness: The Mental Health Crisis Behind Bars and What We Must Do About It*, San Francisco, CA.: Jossey-Bass.

Lappi-Seppala, T. (2006) 'Reducing the prison population: long-term experiences from Finland', in: Council of Europe, *Crime Policy in Europe*, Strasbourg: Council of Europe.

Loucks, N. (1998) *HMP Cornton Vale: Research into Drugs and Alcohol, Violence and Bullying, Suicide and Self-Injury, and Backgrounds of Abuse* (Occasional Paper No 1), Edinburgh: Scottish Prison Service.

Loucks, N. (2007) *No One Knows: Offenders with Learning Difficulties and Learning Disabilities: The Prevalence and Associated Needs of Offenders with Learning Difficulties and Learning Disabilities*, London: Prison Reform Trust.

Loucks, N. and Talbot, J. (2007) *No One Knows: Identifying and Supporting Prisoners with Learning Difficulties and Learning Disabilities: The Views of Prison Staff in Scotland*, London: Prison Reform Trust.

Maruna, S. (2005) *Making Good: How Ex-convicts Reform and Rebuild Their Lives*, Washington, DC.: American Psychological Association.

Matarasso, F. and Chell, J. (1998) *Vital Signs: Mapping Community Art in Belfast*, Stroud: Comedia.

McLellan, A. (2004) *Interim Inspection Report of HMP Cornton Vale* (web only), Edinburgh: Scottish Government. Available at: *http://www.scotland.gov.uk/Publica tions/2004/05/19329/36710* (accessed 1 November 2010).

McLellan, A. (2007) HM *Inspectorate of Prisons: Report on HMP Shotts Inspection, 12–16 February 2007* (web only), Edinburgh: Scottish Government. Available at: *http:// www.scotland.gov.uk/Publications/2007/07/25093202/0* (accessed 14 November 2010).

Miles, A. (2007) 'Give prison arts projects a break', *Guardian*, 8 March. Available at: *http://www.guardian.co.uk/artanddesign/artblog/2007/mar/08/giveprisonartsprojectsabr* (accessed 26 November 2010).

Ministry of Justice (2004) *Offenders' Learning Journey for Juvenile Offenders*, London: Department for Innovation, Universities and Skills.

Nellis, M. (2010) 'Creative arts and the cultural politics of penal reform: the early years of the Barlinnie Special Unit, 1973–1981', *Journal of Scottish Criminal Justice Studies*, *20*, 1–19.

Nugent, B., Loureiro, T. and Loucks, N. (2010) *Evaluation of the Willow Pilot Project*, Edinburgh: Families Outside.

O'Keefe, C. (2003) *Moving Mountains: Identifying and Addressing Barriers to Employment, Training and Education from the Voices of Women (Ex)Offenders*, Sheffield: Sheffield Hallam University Press.

The Howard Journal Vol 50 No 4. September 2011
ISSN 0265-5527, pp. 356–370

Orr, D. (2009) 'This artwork was made by a killer: it is no less valid for that', *Independent* (online), *11 April*. Available at: *http://www.independent.co.uk/opinion/commentators/ deborah-orr/deborah-orr-this-artwork-was-made-by-a-killer-it-is-no-less-valid-for-that-1667286. html* (accessed 16 November 2010).

Reisig, M.D., Holtfreter, K. and Morash, M. (2002) 'Social capital among women offenders', *Journal of Contemporary Criminal Justice*, 18(2), 167–87.

Ruskin, A. (2006) *Mental Health and Social Inclusion: Developing the Evidence Base. Interim Report from Phase 2: Retrospective Analysis of Project Data*, London: National Social Inclusion Programme.

Scottish Government (2008) *Prison Statistics Scotland, 2007/08* (Statistical Bulletin Crime and Justice Series) (web only). Available at: *http://www.scotland.gov.uk/ Resource/Doc/235546/0064616.pdf* (accessed 1 November 2010).

Scottish Prison Service (2002) *The Health Promoting Prison: A Framework for Promoting Health in the Scottish Prison Service*, Edinburgh: Health Education Board for Scotland.

Scottish Prison Service (2008) *Annual Report and Accounts 2007–2008*, Edinburgh: Scottish Prison Service.

Scottish Prison Service (2009a) *The Gallery* (Issue 47), Edinburgh: Scottish Prison Service.

Scottish Prison Service (2009b) *Scottish Prison Service Delivery Plan 2009–2010*, Edinburgh: Scottish Prison Service.

Scottish Prisons Commission (2008) *Scotland's Choice: Report of the Scottish Prisons Commission*, Edinburgh: Scottish Prisons Commission.

Social Exclusion Unit (2002) *Reducing Reoffending by Ex-prisoners*, London: Home Office.

Social Work Services and Prisons Inspectorate (1998) *Women Offenders – A Safer Way: A Review of Community Disposals and the Use of Custody for Women Offenders in Scotland*, Edinburgh: Scottish Office.

Tombs, J. (2006) *Women in Prison in Scotland: An Unmet Commitment*, Glasgow: Scottish Consortium on Crime and Criminal Justice (SCCCJ).

Whyte, B. and McNeill, F. (2007) *Reducing Reoffending: Social Work and Community Justice in Scotland*, Cullompton: Willan.

Williams, D. (1997) *How the Arts Measure Up: Australian Research into the Social Impact of the Arts* (Social Impact of the Arts Working Paper 8), Stroud: Comedia.

Wilson, D., Caulfield, L.S. and Atherton, S. (2008) *Promoting Positive Change: Assessing the Long Term Psychological, Emotional and Behavioural Effects of the Good Vibrations in Prisons Project* (Report for the Firebird Trust), Birmingham: Birmingham City University.

Wolfgang, W. (2008) 'Throughcare and resettlement in Europe' (The European Organisation for Probation (CEP), conference on *Resettling Adult Offenders*, Glasgow, 25–26 April 2008, unpublished).

Date submitted: November 2010
Date accepted: February 2011

[13]

High-Intensity Rehabilitation for Violent Offenders in New Zealand: Reconviction Outcomes for High- and Medium-Risk Prisoners

Devon L. L. Polaschek[1]

Abstract

As the empirical evidence accumulates, so does confidence that carefully designed and delivered rehabilitation approaches can reduce risk. Yet little is known about how to rehabilitate some specialized groups, such as high-risk violent offenders: career criminals with an extensive history of violent behavior. Since 1998, New Zealand's Rimutaka Violence Prevention Unit (RPVU) has provided intensive cognitive-behavioral rehabilitation to violent men. In this evaluation, 112 medium- and high-risk prisoners who entered the program after 1998 are case matched to 112 untreated men. Reconviction outcome data over an average of 3.5 years postrelease show that 10% to 12% fewer program completers were reconvicted for violence compared to their untreated controls. High-risk completers also are less likely to be reconvicted for any offense. Those men who opted out of the study are a slightly higher-risk group than those who completed it, but noncompletion

[1]Victoria University of Wellington, New Zealand

Corresponding Author:
Devon L. L. Polaschek, School of Psychology, Victoria University of Wellington, P. O. Box 600, Wellington, New Zealand.
E-mail: devon.polaschek@vuw.ac.nz

does not further increase their risk. Given the lack of program theory, and formidable practical challenges involved in working with such a high-risk group, these results are very promising.

Keywords

community violence, violence exposure, violent offenders

Correctional policy in several Western nations (e.g., the United Kingdom, Canada, New Zealand) has been significantly influenced by the accumulation of empirical research on effective offender rehabilitation. Based on numerous meta-analyses, leading researchers have distilled this "what works" literature into a series of principles. The best known series is the risk, need, and responsivity principles: (a) programs should be delivered only to higher risk cases, (b) programs should target risk-related factors, and (c) programs should be designed and delivered in a manner that enhances offenders' abilities to respond to them (Andrews & Bonta, 2006). Programs that conform generally to these principles can reduce criminal risk in offenders who complete them (Hollin & Palmer, 2006). Yet within this growing body of knowledge there remain some important offender subgroups about whom relatively little is known. High-risk violent offenders—mainly male offenders with a high risk of future violence and a very high risk of future criminal activity—comprise one of these groups: This article reports recidivism outcomes following rehabilitation in a sample with these characteristics.

In New Zealand—as in other jurisdictions with rehabilitative objectives—current psychological interventions for high-risk violent offenders are the result of a long-term commitment to developing effective rehabilitation of violent offending. During the past at least 25 years, programs targeting violent offending have developed from low-intensity anger management packages into much higher-intensity cognitive-behavioral programs that intervene with multiple criminogenic needs, thus adhering to principles derived from rehabilitation meta-analyses.

Yet these program developments are supported by only a small body of specific outcome evidence that they reduce violence risk. Polaschek and Collie (2004)—in an extensive search of electronic journal databases and websites—found just 9 quasiexperimental studies that examined the impact of some form of rehabilitation on violent reconviction. Of these, most designs had significant methodological weaknesses, and few specifically targeted violent offenders. Just one program reported enough information to determine that it was intensive (i.e., more than 100 hr), intervened with multiple dynamic risk factors, and had an adequate evaluation design (e.g., comparison group matched on risk, outcome data on completers and noncompleters). In this study, with 17 months of follow-up, Berry (2003) found an overall treatment effect for violent recidivism even with an intent-to-treat analysis. After 6 years of follow-up, 58% of the treatment group and 78% of the controls had been reconvicted for a violent offense (Wilson, 2002).

Three recent reports from the Correctional Service of Canada (CSC) also examine reconviction outcomes for men receiving a specialist cognitive-behavioral multiple-target intervention for violent offenders. First, Cortoni, Nunes, and Latendresse (2006) examined recidivism of prisoners in CSC's 190-hr violence prevention program (VPP), using a large-sample, case-matched, untreated comparison group and controlling for prior treatment. At 1-year follow-up postrelease, 8.5% of treatment completers, 24.5% of non-completers, and 21.8% of matched comparisons had been reconvicted for violent offenses. Similar patterns of results were obtained for parole license revocation and other reconviction indices.

The Regional Psychiatric Center (RPC) in Saskatchewan, Canada, hosts the 6- to 8-month aggressive behavior control program (ABC). Di Placido, Simon, Witte, Gu, and Wong (2006) investigated rates of reconviction in four groups of men who had entered the RPC: treated and untreated gang members, and treated and untreated non–gang members *(n* = 40 per group). However, the "untreated" samples contained both assessed-only referrals and treatment noncompleters. They were closely matched to treated men on risk and other relevant variables. Over 2 years of follow-up, men who completed treatment were less likely to be reconvicted of any type of offense than comparison men, whether gang members or not. There were no statistically significant differences for violent reconviction.

The third Canadian report is from the same RPC. Wong, Gordon, and Gu (2007) compared 34 ABC graduate men with a mean PCL-R (The Hare Psychopathy Checklist—Revised) rating of 28.6, and 34 untreated controls matched on PCL-R score, age, past criminal history, and length of follow-up (mean of 7.4 years). No differences were found between the two groups on violent or nonviolent reconvictions, nor time to reconviction. However, treated men subsequently received significantly shorter sentences. The selection criteria for the untreated men are not described.

In short, few studies underpin efforts to develop effective rehabilitation programs for men with index violent offenses, though these men comprise significant proportions of many Western prison populations. Recent evaluations suggest that some programs designed for violent offenders can reduce both violence risk and overall offending risk.

In 1998 New Zealand opened its first intensive custodial program for high-risk violent offenders; the Rimutaka Violence Prevention Unit (RVPU). Recidivism outcomes from this program are presented here. A preliminary evaluation compared the first 22 program completers after 2 years in the community, with the 60 untreated comparison men used by Berry (2003). In this evaluation, Polaschek, Wilson, Townsend, and Daly (2005) found no significant differences in the proportion of each group reconvicted for non-violent offenses or reimprisoned. However, 32% of RVPU completers were reconvicted for violence compared to 63% of the untreated comparisons. Treated violent recidivists took more than twice as long to be reconvicted as control violent recidivists. Although tentatively encouraging results, the methodology of this study is weakened by the very small sample, lack of data on treatment noncompleters, and convenience comparison sample.

The present study is a quasiexperimental investigation of reconviction outcome data from this intensive prison-based rehabilitation program for high-risk violent offenders. There were four objectives for this study. First, the stated aim of the RVPU during the evaluation period was to reduce the risk of further *violent* offending in program completers, and the program informed men that their nonviolent reoffending was not its focus. Therefore, the outcome of most interest was violent reconviction. However, given (a) significant reductions in some previous evaluations in overall offending risk, and (b) the lack of offense specialization evident in high-risk violent offenders' careers (see sample description in the following section), examining effects on overall rates of reconviction was the second objective. Third, Andrews and Bonta's risk principle stipulates that high-intensity programs should be reserved for higher-risk cases. In an extension of that finding, it was expected that the intensive program would be more effective with high-risk than medium-risk offenders. Lastly, because data were available on outcomes for noncompleters, the study sought to examine whether any apparent improvement in completers' subsequent conviction risk was due to selective attrition of higher-risk cases and whether noncompletion itself increased risk.

Method

Description of the RVPU and Program

The RVPU is a purpose-built 30-bed medium-security unit, located at Rimutaka Prison, near Wellington, New Zealand, to which male prisoners nearing release eligibility are referred from all over the nationalized prison system. Over the time period evaluated here, criteria for admission to the program were index violent offense, absence of major barriers to program participation, for example,

668 *Journal of Interpersonal Violence 26(4)*

major *DSM-IV* Axis I mental disorder (*Diagnostic and Statistical Manual of Mental Disorders*, 4th ed., American Psychiatric Association, 1994), major neurological impairment, poor English, and consent to attend. Midway through the evaluated program period, a minimum actuarial risk criterion was introduced, in line with a change in national corrections policy.

The program was delivered to closed groups of 10 men led by two therapists. Therapist pairs usually comprised a psychologist and a rehabilitation worker. In practice, psychologists varied from fully qualified senior clinicians to students in their final year of training. Rehabilitation workers had varied backgrounds and usually quite extensive experience in social services but often had no formal training in criminal psychology or rehabilitation of offenders.

Program intakes commenced about 3 times per year. Treatment intensity was approximately 330 hr of group sessions over 28 weeks. The design of the program content and process conformed broadly to the principles for effective program design in correctional settings (e.g., Andrews & Bonta, 2006; McGuire, 2004). In brief, it was cognitive-behavioral and modular, with content that covered (a) identifying individual risk factors by examining index offense chains, (b) offense-supportive thinking, (c) mood management, (d) victim empathy, (e) moral reasoning, (f) problem solving, (g) communication and relationship skills, and (h) plan for postrelease risk management (see Polaschek, et al., 2005, for more detail). On completing the program, many offenders appeared before the national parole board and were released on parole within days or weeks.

RVPU Treatment Sample

The sample consisted of all men who had entered the program since the unit opened in 1998 and who had been released for at least 12 months when reconviction data were extracted.

The final sample contained 112 men.[1] Their mean age at program entry was 28 years (*SD* = 8.1). More than half (56%) were New Zealand Maori, 31% were New Zealand European, and 11% identified as other Pacific nationals (e.g., Samoan, Tongan). Their mean years of education were 9.8 (*SD* = 1.3). Mean IQ—estimated using the Schonell Reading Test (Ruddle & Bradshaw, 1982)—was 102 (*SD* = 10.4, *n* = 70). Their offense histories suggested they were chronic violent career criminals: mean age of first conviction was 16.4 (*SD* = 2.4), and they averaged 40 previous convictions (*SD* = 31.6), including 7.2 violent convictions (*SD* = 6.2). The most serious index offenses were aggravated robbery (38%), serious assault (e.g., assault with intent to commit grievous bodily harm, injury with intent-to-injure weapon; 27%), murder or attempted murder (6%), other violence (14%), and not recorded (13%).

The *RoC*RoI* (Bakker, Riley, & O'Malley, 1999) is the New Zealand Department of Corrections' tool for actuarial risk assessment, developed on a sample of 24,000 offenders and cross-validated using a second sample of 24,000 offenders. Expressed as a probability, it is an offender's estimated risk of reimprisonment over the next 5 years. Its predictive validity is very good: Bakker et al. reported an AUC of 0.76, and recent research has confirmed a high level of accuracy over 3 years postrelease (Nadesu, 2007). The mean RoC*RoI scores for men in this sample was 0.59 (*SD* = 0.21). The risk range in the sample made it possible to examine separately the effect of the program on medium-risk men, those below the program cutoff of a RoC*RoI of 0.4 implemented partway through the evaluation period.[2]

Selecting the Comparison Sample

For each prisoner in the treatment sample, a matched comparison man was selected from a national computer database of 5,000 men who had served a prison sentence of at least 2 years for a violent offense. Criteria for matching comparison men to treated men were same primary ethnicity (Maori, Pacific, European), RoC*RoI score within 0.05, actual release date within 5 months, and age at release within 5 years. The database did not contain information about whether comparison men had attended human service programs during their sentence; the comparison sample is referred to as "untreated" because other routine program options at that time were unlikely to have been effective. As expected, statistical comparisons of the two groups on the matching variables and a range of other conviction history variables found no significant differences.

Of the 112 program starters, 71% completed the RVPU program. Of the 33 who did not, 18% were removed by staff because of prolonged disruptive behavior; 36% left at their own request without a reason being recorded; 30% were removed because they committed further offenses during the program; and the remainder asked to leave because they were concerned for their safety.

Results

Criminal reconviction data for both samples were extracted in April 2005 from the national conviction records database. Actual reoffense dates were used to calculate survival times; time in the community averaged 3.5 years (range 360 to 2,701 days). Included in the definition of violent reconviction were aggravated robberies and all types of actual physical violence except sexual assaults.[3]

Table 1. Percentage Reconvicted and Days to Reconviction: High-Risk Completers, Noncompleters, and Matched Controls

	TC (n = 56)	TCC (n = 56)		TNC (n = 28)	TNCC (n = 28)	
	% Reconvicted		φ	% Reconvicted		φ
Any reconviction	83	95	.19	93	89	−.06
Reconviction for violence	62	72	.11	71	75	.04
Reimprisonment for violence	43	38	−.05	50	50	0

Days to reconviction/end of follow-up period

	M (SD)	M (SD)	M (SD)	M (SD)
Any reconviction	352 (379)	258 (381)	295 (346)	366 (456)
Reconviction for violence	576 (470)	490 (498)	459 (380)	630 (615)
Reimprisonment for violence	894 (611)	830 (728)	725 (519)	763 (729)

Note: TC = treatment completer; TCC = treatment completer control; TNC = treatment noncompleter; TNCC = treatment noncompleter control.

The minimum risk criterion for program entry—RoC*RoI score of 0.4—was used to divide the sample into medium-risk and high-risk groups. The resulting mean RoC*RoI scores for the two groups (0.27 and 0.68, respectively) were significantly different, $t(222) = 20.7$, $p < .01$.

To reduce the risk of drawing conclusions from artifactual results, several outcome variables were examined (Lösel, 2001). For both high-risk and medium-risk groups, the percentage of men who were reconvicted was calculated for any offense, any violent offense, and any violent offense resulting in reimprisonment. Mean survival times and survival functions also were calculated for the same variables.

High-Risk Sample

Table 1 presents the results for the 86 high-risk men and their untreated counterparts and suggests a small reduction in the proportion of program completers who were reconvicted for violence, with no corresponding increase in violence reconvictions for noncompleters, compared to their controls. The top row of the table shows that 12% fewer treatment completers were reconvicted for any

Table 2. Percentage Reconvicted and Days to Reconviction: Medium-Risk Completers, Noncompleters, and Matched Controls

	TC (n = 21)	TCC (n = 21)	φ	TNC (n = 5)	TNCC (n = 5)	φ
	% Reconvicted			% Reconvicted		
Any reconviction	76	67	−.11	80	40	−.41
Reconviction for violence	33	48	.15	80	20	−.60
Reimprisonment for violence	5	10	.09	40	0	−.50

Days to reconviction/end of follow-up period

	M (SD)	M (SD)	M (SD)	M (SD)
Any reconviction	642 (515)	516 (511)	305 (94)	738 (656)
Reconviction for violence	1129 (665)	937 (606)	564 (484)	1109 (824)
Reimprisonment for violence	1363 (512)	1354 (528)	1042 (714)	1328 (733)

Note: See footnote to Table 1.

offense compared to their controls, whereas noncompleters failed slightly more often than their controls. For reimprisonment for violence, there was a small increase in the proportion of treated failures compared to their controls.

Statistical analyses showed that only the largest difference was significant: high-risk treatment completers versus their controls on any reconviction, $\chi^2(1) = 4.25$, $p = .04$. The effect size data tell a similar story, with small positive effects of treatment completion on the risk of any reconviction and of violence reconviction. However, men who completed the program were no less likely to go back to prison for violence than untreated men. Effect sizes for noncompleters were similarly negligible.

The mean survival times in Table 1 show that completers tended to survive longer and noncompleters to fail faster than their respective comparisons. However, no comparison was statistically significant.

Medium-Risk Sample

Those with RoC*RoI scores below 0.4 comprised a small sample. For completeness, their results appear in Table 2. Statistical comparisons were all nonsignificant for treatment completers compared to the untreated comparison

672   *Journal of Interpersonal Violence 26(4)*

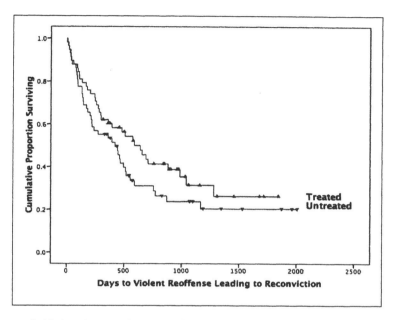

Figure 1. High-risk treated violent offenders versus untreated controls: Survival curves for violent reconviction

men. No analyses were undertaken with the noncompleters. Visual comparison of the outcomes for treatment completers' untreated controls in Tables 1 and 2 suggests the medium-risk participants were— as predicted by the RoC*RoI— generally at lower risk for violence and violent imprisonment than those of the high-risk. However, they were at high risk of any reconviction. The effect-size statistics for Table 2 confirm that treatment completers showed a small increase in the risk of any reconviction, and a small decrease in reconviction for violence compared to their controls. The picture was bleak for the 5 noncompleters: 4 were reconvicted for violence, and 2 returned to prison.

The results in both Tables 1 and 2 suggest that treatment noncompleters— and therefore their risk-matched controls—entered the program at higher risk of serious reconviction than treatment completers. However, statistical analyses support this view only for the high-risk sample. High-risk treatment completers had significantly lower RoC*RoI scores ($M = 0.67$) than noncompleters ($M = 0.71$): $t(170) = 2.3$, $p = .025$, $d = 0.36$. There was no significant difference and a slightly smaller effect in the medium-risk group: completers' $m_{\mathrm{RoC^*RoI}} = 0.26$, noncompleters' $m_{\mathrm{RoC^*RoI}} = 0.30$, $t(50) = 0.8$, $p = .43$, $d = 0.28$.

Intention-to-treat analyses represent the most stringent test of program effects: Treatment starters are compared with their matched untreated controls. Table 3 presents these results. Although reduced, small positive effects

Table 3. Percentage Reconvicted: Men Entering the Treatment Program Versus Untreated Controls

	Program Starters	Untreated Controls	φ
High risk			
Any reconviction	86	93	.11
Reconviction for violence	65	73	.08
Reimprisonment for violence	45	42	−.04
Medium risk			
Any reconviction	77	62	−.17
Reconviction for violence	58	58	0
Reimprisonment for violence	12	8	−.07

Note: $n = 172$ for high risk; $n = 52$ for medium risk.

remain for high-risk men; a smaller proportion of those entering treatment were reconvicted for any offense or a violent offense. There is no evidence that medium-risk men who entered treatment were at reduced risk compared to their controls.

Finally, Kaplan–Meier product-limit survival analyses were used to examine the speed of failure. Just as with data in Tables 1 and 2, survival times were calculated from the actual day of release to the day on which the offense occurred or the end of the follow-up period if there were no relevant convictions. For proportions of men convicted for any offense, the survival functions for high-risk completers and their controls were significantly different: log-rank test of equality = 4.5, $df = 1$, $p = .03$. No other functions were significantly different. As an example, Figure 1 shows the survival curve for the time to violent reoffense, for high-risk treatment completers and their controls. The two curves separate early in the follow-up period, and the treated men consistently fail a little more slowly. The initial slope of the curve is strikingly steep. Even for treated men, 38% of those who failed had done so within 6 months of release.

Discussion

This article presented various outcomes from the RVPU, an intensive cognitive-behavioral rehabilitation program for high-risk violent prisoners. The main research objectives addressed by these data were (a) the effects of program completion on subsequent convictions, especially violent convictions; (b) whether the results for treatment completers—if positive—could be attributed not to treatment, but instead to the selective loss from the program of those most likely to fail; and (c) whether the program was more effective with high-risk versus medium-risk prisoners.

Based on a robust quasiexperimental evaluation design, the results presented here provide some evidence that the program had a positive effect on reconviction risk: fewer high-risk program completers were reconvicted for any offense, or for a violent offense during an average of 3.5 years of postrelease follow-up. Completers' first reoffense of any kind occurred significantly more slowly than for the matched untreated comparison men, and the survival curve for violent reoffending showed a similar pattern. Furthermore, these positive results for high-risk program completers were not offset by the recidivism outcomes of noncompleters. Intent-to-treat analyses—where these men who received only a partial dose of the treatment are treated statistically as if they attended all of the program—also show overall positive results.

Noncompleters were slightly higher-risk cases at the outset. Static risk estimates—which are not affected by program attendance or offenders' efforts to rehabilitate themselves—show that compared to those who completed the program, noncompleters were estimated to be 4% more likely to reoffend seriously at the time they entered the program. However, there is no evidence in their actual outcomes that removal from the program—whether voluntary or enforced—further increased their risk. Noncompleters' rates of recidivism were similar to those of their matched untreated comparisons. Researchers often suggest that offender departures from treatment program increases risk (e.g., Bowen & Gilchrist, 2006). Actually, the question of whether noncompleters have somehow suffered criminogenic harm by entering and then not completing a program can only be examined if completers and noncompleters are compared separately with their own risk-matched controls, not when—as is more common— completers and noncompleters are separately compared with a combined control group (see McMurran & Theodosi, 2007, for a discussion of this issue).

It is worthy of note that attrition did not leave in treatment only low-risk YAVIS (young, attractive, verbal, intelligent, and successful) clients (Wormith & Olver, 2002). Based on the recidivism performances of their matched untreated comparisons, the treated group remained one of the highest risk samples in the published literature.

The final research question was whether outcomes for medium-risk and high-risk prisoners were equivalent: Was the 330-hr program equally beneficial across both bands of risk? RVPU data tentatively support the view that the program was more effective with high-risk than medium-risk men, confirming correctional policy that denied men with less than a 40% risk of serious reconviction referral to the program. This question is of particular interest given Andrews and Bonta's (2006) empirically based conclusions that providing high-intensity services to lower risk offenders generally has no effect or increases risk. The mechanisms underlying risk increases are not clear, but one possibility is "deviancy training" (Dishion, McCord, & Poulin, 1999). Adolescents have been found to show increases in criminality after group interventions, probably as a consequence of peer reinforcement of criminal thinking and behavior (Dishion et al., 1999). The RVPU brings together with a few less-criminal prisoners some of the most violent men in the New Zealand prison system. During this evaluation period, 12 hr each week were spent in structured group therapy; the remainder of the day often comprised unstructured, largely unsupervised contact between prisoners. Criminal modeling and reinforcement processes could easily have a more detrimental effect on lower-risk men in that environment.

Having reviewed the major findings of this study, the final sections consider how to interpret the overall effects of the program on general and violent recidivism and discuss future research directions.

Program Effects on Violent Versus General Recidivism

During much of the evaluation period, the focus of the program-as-designed was on violent offending exclusively. There are good empirical and theoretical reasons for arguing against such a specialized focus for programs for violent offenders (see the following), so it is not particularly surprising that these results do not show that the program was more effective with violence than other types of offending. In fact, only the difference in overall reoffending for high-risk completers versus their controls was statistically significant. The effect sizes for all reoffending—including violence—generally were larger than for violence only.

Interpreting Program Effect Sizes

The plethora of meta-analyses of "what works" with criminal offenders suggests a mean difference of about 10% in favor of the treatment group (e.g., McGuire, 2004) and that cognitive-behavioral programs (Wilson, Bouffard, & MacKenzie, 2005), especially those conforming to risk, need, and responsivity principles, often achieve higher-than-average effects. This program generally did conform to these principles: It was intensive and cognitive behavioral, targeted medium- to high-risk offenders, and the program manual included intervention for a range of needs associated with effective outcomes, including criminal attitudes, anger management, self-regulation, and relapse prevention (Andrews & Bonta, 2006; Dowden & Andrews, 2000). Yet the strongest positive effects found in this evaluation are quite small. Positive phis range from .08 for reconvictions for violence in high-risk program starters to .15 for reconviction for violence in medium-risk completers. Three factors may have contributed to this lower-than-expected effect size: program design, program delivery, and offender risk. Each is discussed in the sections that follow.

Program Model and Design

Program theory for violent offending is still poorly articulated (Polaschek & Collie, 2004). The RVPU program was designed over a decade ago, when even the general information about how to run effective programs was less clearly understood, and the criminogenic needs of repetitively violent offenders were not well established empirically.

The program manual of the time—since overhauled—had several important weaknesses. First, it was based substantially on the relapse prevention model; the program assumed both that men specialized in a single violent offense pattern typified by the index offense and that all of their relevant criminogenic needs would be identified by focusing assessment and treatment on that offense. This approach followed the trend in specialist sexual offender treatment at the time (e.g., Hudson, Wales, Bakker, & Ward, 2002). RVPU research is underway that shows that such specialization is not typical in high-risk violent offenders. A narrow focus may cause important needs to be overlooked, reducing program effectiveness.

Several common criminogenic needs were not well addressed in the program. Cognitive intervention modules used Beck's general approach to cognitive therapy (e.g., Beck & Freeman, 1990) to remediate dysfunctional thinking styles but did not systematically challenge common offense–supportive schema of violent offenders (Polaschek, Calvert, & Gannon, 2009). There was insufficient emphasis on specific techniques for managing impulsive urges, and intervention for problematic drug and alcohol use was limited to educational approaches delivered outside the program. Generally education alone is not effective with offenders (Wormith et al., 2007).

Lastly, the program had no specialized aftercare. Although we have no data to indicate the circumstances in which they reoffended, it can be speculated that at least some men left prison intending not to return and either underestimated how much effort was needed to manage high-risk situations or simply found it was easier to return to crime than to secure attractive employment or find somewhere supportive to live. Parole requirements and services were generic and piecemeal, and the level of support was inadequate to the level of risk. The importance of extending intervention and focused support into the community has been known for some time (e.g., Wormith et al., 2007; Zamble & Quinsey, 1997). The very steep initial gradients of postrelease-survival curves demonstrate that despite intervention, a significant proportion of graduates remained very vulnerable to serious reoffending at the point of release (e.g., Figure 1).

Program Delivery: Integrity and Quality

Second, examination of archival program files revealed that the program had not been delivered uniformly across therapists and time. The program manual had been modified on an ad hoc basis, and there were other signs that the program's quality may have been compromised though formal integrity-monitoring information was not available. Therapeutic integrity—the extent to which a program adheres to its intended design—predicts outcome in correctional programs (Andrews & Dowden, 2005). Given the problems noted earlier, it may be a surprise that this evaluation suggests that the RVPU program is associated with positive effects.

Actually, departures from a highly prescriptive program design are not always antitherapeutic. The current trend is toward prescriptive program documents, and highly vigilant program monitoring (Howells et al., 2001), which give increased confidence that the minimum standard of program delivery has been achieved (McMurran, 2006). Yet a high degree of deliverer compliance and a high *quality* of program are not necessarily synonymous. In fact, skilled therapists may have their effectiveness reduced by high levels of prescriptiveness (McMurran, 2006), as it is based on the assumption that "one version of the program fits all." This view is supported by psychotherapy research showing that achieving high technical adherence can actually damage the therapeutic process (Henry, Strupp, Butler, Schacht, & Binder, 1993).

It is likely that integrity drift at the RVPU comprised a mix of therapeutic and ineffective deviations from the program model. The overall effect remains positive, but it is difficult to be very specific about the content of the program for different cohorts. In conclusion, it is argued here that therapeutic drift—though clearly undesirable—does not necessarily explain the size of the program effect, nor rule out the possible influence of the other factors discussed here.

Effect Size and Risk Level

The final consideration in interpreting the results of this evaluation is in deciding where to locate this study in relation to the meta-analytic research literature on rehabilitation outcome with offenders. One aspect of the risk principle states that intervening with higher-risk cases increases the size of the treatment effect (e.g., Andrews & Dowden, 2006; Lowenkamp, Latessa, & Holsinger, 2006). Yet there is also some acceptance that the highest-risk offenders—such as people with high PCL-R scores—are very difficult to treat (Skeem, Polaschek, & Manchak, 2009). Is there a ceiling on the gains that can be achieved with increasing risk?

There is no universally accepted definition of high risk. The RVPU sample appears to have higher rates of recidivism and violent recidivism than most other studies. Rice and Harris (2005) noted that 25% is a more typical base rate in studies of violent recidivism. The imprisoned psychopath controls in the Oak Ridge study did not achieve as high a rate of violent recidivism as this RVPU sample, even after more than 10 years mean follow-up (Rice, 1997).

Campbell, French, and Gendreau (2007) recently suggested that additional data were needed before meta-analytic findings on the prediction accuracy of risk assessment tools and personality measures with violent reconviction could be generalized to high-risk samples. Similarly, in a meta-analysis of the risk principle, Andrews and Dowden (2006) noted, "The effects of appropriate treatment need to be explored with very high-risk groups such as psychopaths" (p. 98). Interpretation of the RVPU treatment effect in this study depends then with whom they are compared. Alongside large meta-analyses of mainly lower-risk offenders the RVPU effect seems small. If the high-risk RVPU treatment sample is compared with a group of men with high PCL-R scores, the outcome looks more encouraging (Skeem et al., 2009).[4]

Future Directions

The RVPU program has been significantly rebuilt since 2005 and outcome evaluation of the revised program is underway, along with additional analyses of in-program data from this earlier evaluation. However, there are much bigger issues at stake. A number of jurisdictions offer specialist programs like that at the RVPU to repetitive violent offenders. Scant outcome research, and lack of a program theory—especially for high-risk offenders—leaves program designers guessing about whether programs will be effective with one of the most troubling segments of Western correctional populations (Polaschek & Collie, 2004).

Polaschek   **679**

The growth in empirical studies in this domain is very slow: There is just a handful more outcome evaluations than a decade ago. High rates of failure in high-risk offenders render unevaluated programs vulnerable to closure, whether they are more effective or not than the alternatives. If countries like New Zealand—with its very high imprisonment rate—are not simply to warehouse even more offenders, there must be more research.

Outcome evaluations make an important—though quite indirect—contribution to program theory. Alongside such evaluations, more basic research also is needed into the etiology of violence, violent offenders' criminogenic needs, and the measurement of treatment gain. The results presented here contribute to the small but important body of empirical work that presently suggests that rehabilitation can make some difference to risk. The RVPU data show that a program developed without clear guidance from a well-validated program theory, with variation in program integrity, and no substantial aftercare, still reduced recidivism risk in high-risk violent prisoners. The results represent another small step away from the "rehabilitation is a failed experiment" rhetoric. Many more steps are needed.

Acknowledgment

My thanks for assistance and practical support with data collection from Corrections staff, including David Riley, David Wales, Branko Coebergh, Nick Wilson, Alex Skelton, and from research assistants Elizabeth Ross and Paul Oxnam.

Declaration of Conflicting Interests

The author declared that she had no conflicts of interests with respect to their authorship or the publication of this article.

Funding

The author disclosed receipt of the following financial support for the research and/or authorship of this article: This research was supported by funding from the New Zealand Department of Corrections.

Notes

1. Including the 22 treatment completers reported by Polaschek, Wilson, Townsend, and Daly (2005).
2. Although a minimum risk level for program entry was in place for only part of the evaluated period, there were no significant differences in the mean risk level for different time bands within the evaluation. The term "medium risk" is used here in preference to "low risk" (see Dowden, Blanchette, & Serin, 1999): Although low risk in the New Zealand prison system, the reconviction rates of their matched

680   *Journal of Interpersonal Violence 26(4)*

untreated controls indicate that this group would not be considered low risk in typical meta-analyses of program effectiveness.

3. Two men subsequently were convicted of serious sexual assaults. However, in both cases they were convicted of a violent offence concurrently. Therefore, this omission had no practical effect on reported rates of violent reconviction.

4. PCL-R scores currently only are available for 41 men in the RVPU high-risk sample. Their mean is 24.2 (*SD* = 6.7).

References

American Psychiatric Association. (1994). *Diagnoastic and statistical manual of mental disorders* (4th ed.). Washington, DC: Author.

Andrews, D. A., & Bonta, J. (2006). *The psychology of criminal conduct* (4th ed.). Cincinnati, OH: Anderson.

Andrews, D. A., & Dowden, C. (2005). Managing correctional treatment for reduced recidivism: A meta-analytic review of programme integrity. *Legal and Criminological Psychology, 10*, 173-187.

Andrews, D. A., & Dowden, C. (2006). Risk principle of case classification in correctional treatment: A meta-analytic investigation. *International Journal of Offender Therapy and Comparative Criminology, 50*, 88-100.

Bakker, L., Riley, D., & O'Malley, J. (1999). *Risk of reconviction: Statistical models predicting four types of re-offending*. Wellington, New Zealand: Department of Corrections Psychological Service.

Beck, A. T., & Freeman, A. M. (1990). *Cognitive therapy of personality disorders*. New York: Guilford.

Berry, S. (2003). Stopping violent offending in New Zealand: Is treatment an option? *New Zealand Journal of Psychology, 32*, 92-100.

Bowen, E., & Gilchrist, E. (2006). Predicting dropout of court-mandated treatment in a British sample of domestic violence offenders. *Psychology, Crime, and Law, 12*, 573-587.

Campbell, M. A., French, S., & Gendreau, P. (2007). *Assessing the utility of risk assessment tools and personality measures in the prediction of violent recidivism for adult offenders* (No. 2007-04). Ottawa, Ontario, Canada: Department of Public Safety and Emergency Preparedness Canada.

Cortoni, F., Nunes, K., & Latendresse, M. (2006). *An examination of the effectiveness of the Violence Prevention Program* (No. R-178). Ottawa, Ontario, Canada: Correctional Service of Canada.

Di Placido, C., Simon, T. L., Witte, T. D., Gu, D., & Wong, S. C. P. (2006). Treatment of gang members can reduce recidivism and institutional misconduct. *Law and Human Behavior, 30*, 93-114.

Dishion, T. J., McCord, J., & Poulin, F. (1999). When interventions harm: Peer groups and problem behavior. *American Psychologist, 54*, 755-764.

Dowden, C., & Andrews, D. A. (2000). Effective correctional treatment and violent reoffending: A meta analysis. *Canadian Journal of Criminology, 42*, 449-467.

Dowden, C., Blanchette, K., & Serin, R. (1999). *Anger management programming for federal male inmates: An effective intervention* (Research Report R-82). Ottawa, Ontario, Canada: Correctional Service of Canada.

Henry, W. P., Strupp, H. H., Butler, S. F., Schacht, T. E., & Binder, J. L. (1993). Effects of training in time-limited dynamic psychotherapy: Changes in therapist behavior. *Journal of Consulting and Clinical Psychology, 61*, 434-440.

Hollin, C. R., & Palmer, E. J. (Eds.). (2006). *Offending behavior programmes: Development, application, and controversies*. Chichester, UK: Wiley.

Howells, K., Day, A., Bubner, S., Jauncey, S., Parker, A., Williamson, P., et al. (2001). *An evaluation of anger management programs with violent offenders in two Australian states*. Adelaide, Australia: University of South Australia Forensic and Applied Psychology Research Group.

Hudson, S. M., Wales, D. S., Bakker, L., & Ward, T. (2002). Dynamic risk factors: The Kia Marama evaluation. *Sexual Abuse: A Journal of Research and Treatment, 14*, 103-119.

Lösel, F. (2001). Evaluating the effectiveness of correctional programs: Bridging the gap between research and practice. In G. A. Bernfeld, D. P. Farrington, & A. W. Leschied (Eds.), *Offender rehabilitation in practice* (pp. 67-92). Chichester, UK: Wiley.

Lowenkamp, C. T., Latessa, E. J., & Holsinger, A. M. (2006). The risk principle in action: What have we learned from 13,676 offenders and 97 correctional programs? *Crime & Delinquency, 52*, 77-93.

McGuire, J. (2004). *Understanding psychology and crime: Perspectives on theory and action*. Maidenhead, UK: Open University Press.

McMurran, M. (2006). Drug and alcohol programmes: Concept, theory, and practice. In C. R. Hollin & E. J. Palmer (Eds.), *Offending behavior programmes: Development, application, and controversies* (pp. 179-207). Chichester, UK: Wiley.

McMurran, M., & Theodosi, E. (2007). Is treatment non-completion associated with increased reconviction over no treatment? *Psychology, Crime and Law, 13*, 333-343.

Nadesu, A. (2007). *Reconviction patterns of released prisoners: A 36-months follow-up analysis*. Wellington, New Zealand: Department of Corrections Policy Development unpublished report.

Polaschek, D. L. L., Calvert, S. W., & Gannon, T. A. (2009). Linking violent thinking: Implicit theory-based research with violent offenders. *Journal of Interpersonal Violence. 24*, 75-96.

Polaschek, D. L. L., & Collie, R. M. (2004). Rehabilitating serious violent adult offenders: An empirical and theoretical stocktake. *Psychology, Crime and Law, 10*, 321-334.

Polaschek, D. L. L., Wilson, N. J., Townsend, M., & Daly, L. (2005). Cognitive-behavioral rehabilitation for high-risk violent offenders: An outcome evaluation of the Violence Prevention Unit. *Journal of Interpersonal Violence, 20*, 1611-1627.

Rice, M. E. (1997). Violent offender research and implications for the criminal justice system. *American Psychologist, 52*, 414-423.

Rice, M. E., & Harris, G. T. (2005). Comparing effect sizes in follow-up studies: ROC area, Cohen's *d*, and *r*. *Law and Human Behavior, 29*, 615-620.

Ruddle, H. V., & Bradshaw, C. M. (1982). On the estimation of premorbid intellectual functioning: Validation of Nelson & McKenna's formula, and some new normative data. *British Journal of Clinical Psychology, 21*, 159-164.

Skeem, J. L., Polaschek, D. L. L., & Manchak, S. (2009). Appropriate treatment works, but how? Rehabilitating general, psychopathic, and high-risk offenders. In J. L. Skeem, K. Douglas, & S. Lilienfeld (Eds.), *Psychological science in the courtroom: Controversies and consensus* (pp. 358-384). New York: Guilford.

Wilson, N. J. (2002, August). *Montgomery House VPP Re-imprisonment analysis.* Internal memorandum, Department of Corrections Psychological Service, Wellington, New Zealand.

Wilson, D. B., Bouffard, L. A., & MacKenzie, D. L. (2005). A quantitative review of structured, group-oriented, cognitive-behavioral programs for offenders. *Criminal Justice and Behavior, 32*, 172-204.

Wong, S., Gordon, A., & Gu, D. (2007). Assessment and treatment of violence-prone forensic clients: An integrated approach. *British Journal of Psychiatry, 190*(Suppl. 49), 66-74.

Wormith, J. S., Althouse, R., Simpson, M., Reitzel, L. R., Fagan, T. J., & Morgan, R. D. (2007). The rehabilitation and reintegration of offenders: The current landscape and some future directions for correctional psychology. *Criminal Justice and Behavior, 34*, 879-892.

Wormith, J. S., & Olver, M. E. (2002). Offender treatment attrition and its relationship with risk, responsivity, and recidivism. *Criminal Justice & Behavior, 29*, 447-471.

Zamble, E., & Quinsey, V. L. (1997). *The criminal recidivism process.* Cambridge, UK: Cambridge University Press.

Bio

Devon L. L. Polaschek, PhD DipClinPsyc, is an associate professor/reader in psychology at Victoria University of Wellington, New Zealand. Her research interests include theory, intervention, and intervention evaluation with serious violent and sexual offenders, psychopathy, desistance, and experimental approaches to offender assessment.

[14]

Unified theory

Thom Brooks

Introduction

Hybrid theories of punishment attempt to bring together two or more penal goals. They oppose standard views that demand we choose between existing options: for example, either we must side with retributivists or deterrence proponents because there is no middle ground. The common problem for hybrid theories is theoretical coherence. This is because different penal goals may pull in different directions. Retributivist desert may recommend punishments that may be counterproductive to general deterrence. Many have argued that hybrid theories are unstable at best and incoherent at worst.

The unified theory of punishment is a unique attempt to bring together several different principles of punishment within a single and coherent approach.[1] The problem is not that we must choose whether punishment must aspire to ensure offenders receive just deserts or how they might be restored, but how these goals can be satisfied in combination with other penal goals. The unified theory of punishment is ambitious: it aspires to offer a compelling 'grand unifying theory' of punishment bringing together the best elements from each view of punishment without being subjected to standard objections.

This chapter will examine the case for a unified theory and how it might succeed where other theories have failed. I will argue that the unified theory is not only possible, but it is perhaps the most compelling theory of punishment available. Only a unified theory can best address the complexity that confronts theories of punishment and can command widespread support as punitive restoration.

Why a unified theory of punishment?

The philosophy of punishment is at a crossroads. Judges and legal practitioners stand opposed to many academic philosophers and legal theorists. How sentencing is considered in courtrooms is perhaps starkly different from how it is understood in many lecture theatres. Judges and legal

124   *Hybrid theories*

practitioners operate within sentencing guidelines that include references to several different penal goals. One issue is whether punishment is able to address multiple goals within a coherent theory; a second issue is whether a theory of punishment should address multiple goals.

The Model Penal Code continues to have a profound influence on sentencing guidelines in the United States, Canada, Britain, and elsewhere.[2] The Code was originally published in 1962 by the American Law Institute to assist national and state legislative bodies revise and better codify criminal codes. Each legislature had been left to draft individual codes and this led to the problem of divergence across all areas of criminal law. The Code is an attempt to arrive at sentencing principles that might improve coherence across codes.

The Model Penal Code recommends that sentencing guidelines address multiple penal goals. Section 1.02 says:

> (2) The general purposes of the provisions governing the sentencing and treatment of offenders are:
>
> a. to prevent the commission of offences;
> b. to promote the correction and rehabilitation of offenders;
> c. to safeguard offenders against excessive, disproportionate or arbitrary punishment;
> d. to give fair warning of the nature of the sentences that may be imposed on convictions of an offence;
> e. to differentiate offenders with a view to a just individualization in their treatment.

The Model Penal Code recommends that sentencing guidelines address multiple penal goals, such as prevention, rehabilitation, proportionality, desert, and publicity. The Code was later expanded to include the goal of restorative justice as well.[3] Punishment should be preventative and contribute to crime reduction; it should enable offender rehabilitation; punishment should never be disproportionate nor arbitrary; it should be proportionate to the individual case; and punishment should satisfy publicity in being publicly known in advance and avoid retrospective criminalization. The Model Penal Code's multiple penal goals approach was reaffirmed in the Sentencing Reform Act of 1984 creating the United States Sentencing Commission.[4] The Act states:

> The court, in determining the particular sentence to impose, shall consider–
>
> 1   the nature and circumstances of the offense and the history and characteristics of the defendant;
> 2   the need for the sentence imposed–

A to reflect the seriousness of the offense, to promote respect for the law, and to provide just punishment for the offense;

B to afford adequate deterrence to criminal conduct;

C to protect the public from further crimes of the defendant; and

D to provide the defendant with needed educational or vocational training, medical care, or other correctional treatment in the most effective manner.[5]

These sentencing guidelines have exercised a profound influence in the US, UK, and beyond. Most guidelines have since stipulated that sentencing should be determined with reference to multiple penal goals. So, in fact, those who argue that punishment should adopt only one or two goals defend a view of punishment contrary to the guidelines courts use to fix punishments: accepting their less pluralistic conceptions of punishment may lead to a fairly radical and substantial revision of most sentencing guidelines in use today.[6]

Critics argue that the Code suffers from at least two problems. First, the Code is outdated because the criminal code has changed significantly since, which may require substantive revision of the Model Penal Code if it is to be relevant. Standard examples include the omission of various drug offences from the Code and changes to the law that have criminalized marital rape. Critics claim that these changes call for a fundamental rethinking of the Model Penal Code and require us to abandon the existing Code. Note that this criticism does not offer any specific reasons to abandon the view that punishment should address multiple penal goals. Instead, this criticism speaks to how a multiple-goals approach may be better applied to contemporary issues.

Secondly, critics argue that the Code is incoherent. This is because multiple penal goals may come into conflict. For example, a sentence that might best promote offender rehabilitation may not safeguard offenders from disproportionate punishment. Multiple penal goals serve a multitude of ends and cannot be brought together in a unified and coherent theory of punishment. Of course, the Model Penal Code does not attempt to offer any *theory* of punishment and so it does not defend any philosophical account of how punishment can and should adopt multiple goals. Instead, the Code recommends guidelines that incorporate the multiple goals that many criminal codes have already adopted. Even those generally supportive argue that its promise is in helping us reflect on the best distribution of punishment, but 'not about the justification of the institution of punishment'.[7] The multiple penal codes may appear to us as more of a 'laundry list' providing 'more illusion than guidance' in the absence of any clear framework.[8] Nevertheless, the Model Penal Code has found very few philosophers and legal theorists willing to defend it. The widely shared position is that a penal code must ultimately choose between penal goals. We should adopt either retributivism, deterrence, rehabilitation, restorative justice, expressivism, or the negative retributivism of Rawls and Hart because we cannot provide a coherent 'Grand Unifying Theory of Punishment'. Different theories cannot be combined across the board on so large a scale.

I believe this widespread rejection is built upon a mistake. Perhaps we cannot offer a unified theory that unifies retributivism, deterrence, rehabilitation, and so on. But we can defend a theory that unified multiple goals. The problem with the Model Penal Code is that it lacks a more compelling justificatory framework that may show how multiple goals may be brought together in a unified and coherent way.[9] This project is possible and I will present this case here. If we can provide a compelling framework for how multiple goals may coherently work together, then we might offer a major advance in our understanding of punishment and how philosophy may meet the demands of practice. I therefore side with the judges and legal practitioners. It has been noted by others that 'the philosophies of punishment, at least in their traditional form, are based upon a rather idealized and one-dimensional image of punishment'.[10] The unified theory of punishment offers an account of how such problems may be best overcome.

What is the unified theory of punishment?

The unified theory of punishment is a theory that unifies multiple penal goals in a single and coherent theoretical approach. The idea is not that different theories are compatible, but instead that different penal goals are compatible. The argument is that the different penal goals found across different theories of punishment may be combined within a unified framework. The project of the unified theory of punishment is to show how this combination is possible and compelling.

The unified theory of punishment has attracted many defenders.[11] Perhaps the best classic statement is presented by Hegel:

> Punishment, for example, has various determinations: it is retributive, a deterrent example as well, a threat used by the law as a deterrent, and also it brings the criminal to his senses and reforms him. Each of these different determinations has been considered the *ground* of punishment, because each is an essential determination, and therefore the others as distinct from it, are determined as merely contingent relatively to it. *But the one which is taken as ground is still not the whole punishment itself.*[12]

This cryptic passage may be understood to present at least two philosophical positions. The first is that retribution, deterrence, and rehabilitation need not be considered in opposition to each other. Instead, we should conceive them as different components of one unified theory of punishment that brings them together. The second position is that retribution, deterrence, and rehabilitation fit together in an unequal way. A unified theory of punishment will have a 'ground' that will provide a foundation, but not serve as 'the whole punishment itself'.[13] Hegel is the first to offer a unified theory of punishment where we attempt to bring coherent unity to multiple penal goals within a new framework. Our task is to provide a compelling view of how to structure this framework to unify multiple penal goals.

There have been several different proposals for how we might construct a unified theory of punishment since Hegel and most notably by British Idealists, including Bernard Bosanquet, F. H. Bradley, T. H. Green, and James Seth.[14] Each builds on Hegel's idea that punishment can and should bring together multiple penal goals in a unified theory. For example, Green says: 'It is commonly asked whether punishment according to its proper nature is retributive or preventative or reformatory. The true answer is that it is and should be all three'.[15] Green and the British Idealists reject the idea that different penal goals are mutually exclusive.[16] More importantly, they help us conceive of a compelling framework that can successfully unify multiple penal goals. Let me explain how this framework may be understood.[17]

Punishment is a response to crime. We must understand one in relation to the other. Furthermore, the justification of punishment *requires* the justification of crime. This point is worth highlighting: if we cannot justify a particular criminal act or omission, then we cannot justify its punishment. There can be no just punishment for an unjust crime.[18] If punishment is a response to crime, then criminalization must be justified for the punishment of crimes to be justified. Penal justice is linked with just criminalization within a just legal system.

Laws are necessary for the continuation of any political community.[19] This is because there will be inevitable conflicts between community members over time. These conflicts will require some agreed procedures for future conflict resolution.[20] These procedures form a legal system. Note that legal systems are not necessary because people are naturally antagonistic per se, but instead because conflicts are inevitable over time in any political community. This is the fact of member disagreement. A legal system is a necessary, but not sufficient, condition for future political stability. While every political community requires a legal system to resolve member disagreement over time, good laws alone may be insufficient for this purpose.

The criminal law aims at the protection of individual *legal rights*. Our legal rights are substantial freedoms worthy of protection for each member.[21] Each person possesses rights in virtue of their recognized political membership. This idea is based upon 'a political conception of justice that all citizens might be reasonably expected to endorse' and which 'can serve as a basis of public reason and justification'.[22] While the legal system aims to protect individual rights, not all rights have equal value. This is because some rights represent more substantial freedoms than others. For example, the right to life free from murder is linked to a more substantial freedom than the right to private property. If we were murdered, then we cannot choose to exercise private property rights. Some rights are more central to the protection of our substantial freedoms than others.

This is not to say there is any trade-off between rights such that we should tolerate less of some rights to enjoy more of others. Instead, all rights demand protection because rights give expression to substantial freedoms. However, some rights may have more central importance because the freedoms they safeguard make possible other rights. Again, the right to life free from murder makes possible further rights, such as liberty of conscience.[23] All rights have importance although some are more centrally important than others.

The protection of individual rights is conducted within a legal system, and it is a *system*. Laws are often enacted in a piecemeal fashion. Any legal system will lack full coherence, but every system seeks greater coherence. Where there is inconsistency or incoherence, we clarify our understanding of law and its application through political and judicial bodies to resolve these shortcomings.[24] Some rights may be more central to the protection of individual rights within the context of a legal system. This system does not exist for its own sake as some 'end-in-itself'.[25] Instead, legal systems exist fundamentally for the protection of the individual rights of its members. Community members must find satisfaction in their community and the legal system employed to assist the community's future continuity.

Crimes are rights violations that threaten the substantial freedoms protected by law.[26] Punishment is the response to crime. Punishment aims at the protection of individual legal rights threatened by crime.[27] The goal of punishment is not to make people morally good, but rather to provide for the protection of individual legal rights.[28] Punishment is about the protection of rights.[29]

This view of punishment is not unique to British Idealism. For example, John Stuart Mill argues that, for each of us, laws are 'the rules necessary for the protection of his fellow creatures, individually or collectively'.[30] Mill says:

> The only right by which society is warranted in inflicting pain upon any human creature, is the right of self-defence ... But our right to punish, is a branch of the universal right of self-defence; and it is a mere subtletly to set up any distinction between them.[31]

Punishment aims to protect us from crimes in a form of legal self-defence. Crimes present us with threats that punishment attempts to overcome. Mill's understanding of punishment has many substantial differences from unified theories of punishment.[32] However, his position is worth noting to highlight how others have similarly accepted some version of the view that punishment serves a protective aim.

Nevertheless, the British Idealists more specifically understand crimes as threats to individual rights that may require punishment to best protect these rights and safeguard the public from 'criminal conduct'.[33] Thus, Green argues that 'the justice of the punishment depends on the justice of the general system of rights' and 'the proper and direct object of state-punishment [is] ... the general protection of rights'.[34] Green says:

> a violation of a right, requires a punishment, of which the kind and amount must depend on the relative importance of the right and of the extent to which its general exercise is threatened. Thus every theory of rights in detail must be followed by, or indeed implies, a corresponding theory of punishment in detail.[35]

Punishment is only required where rights have been violated by crime. Crimes are punished differently, if at all, in relation to the importance of the right violated. Crime is a necessary, but not sufficient, condition for punishment. Crime must present some threat to our rights in order for punishment to become justified. Rights, criminalization, and punishment are interconnected.

Furthermore, punishment expresses a specific form of disapproval. Green says:

> [Punishment] is a disapproval founded on a sense of what is necessary for the protection of rights ... It is founded essentially on the outward aspect of a man's conduct, on the view of it as related to the security and freedom in action and acquisition of other members of society.[36]

Punishment is an expression of disapproval, but its character is distinct from expressivist theories of punishment. This is because unified theories understand disapproval in terms of 'penal right' and not 'penal morality'.[37] We punish in view of 'what is necessary for the protection of rights, not on a judgment of good and evil'.[38] The unified theory of punishment rejects legal moralism. We punish crimes because they are legal wrongs that threaten our legal rights. Punishment is about illegality, not necessarily immorality.

This view of punishment is held by other British Idealists. For example, James Seth argues:

> This view of the object of punishment gives the true measure of its amount. This is found not in the amount of moral depravity which the crime reveals, but in the importance of the right violated, relatively to the system of rights of which it forms a part ... The measure of the punishment is, in short, the measure of social necessity; and this necessity is a changing one.[39]

130   *Hybrid theories*

Several key features are highlighted in this compelling position. First, rights
are substantial freedoms that are protected by criminalizing their violation.
Second, punishment is a response to crime that is proportionate to the right
violated in view of how best to maintain and protect rights. Some rights
are more central than others. More central rights may require more severe
punishment than less central rights. Third, crime is necessary, but not
sufficient, for punishment. If the protection of rights does not require punishment, then it may be unnecessary. This view of punishment is open to
the possibility of justified pardons where such a condition applies. Seth
correctly argues that 'punishment is not an end-in-itself, but a means of ...
protection'.[40] We never punish for the sake of it, but instead where it
becomes necessary for the protection and restoration of rights. Punishment
must always be 'undertaken in the interest of the ... individual'.[41] Fourth,
we punish crimes as legal wrongs and not moral wrongs. We punish crimes
and not immorality. This is not to say the two never overlap, but it is to
say that our focus is on illegality and rights rather than morality and
wickedness.

Finally, the relation between crime and punishment is not fixed, but it
must be responsive to changing circumstances. This is because the relation
between crime and rights is not fixed either. Our understanding of individual
rights as substantial freedoms has changed over time and so has our view
about crime. Crimes that may have once been subjected to capital punishment may no longer be criminal today. What has changed during this time
is the view of a crime as a potential violation of a particularly central right
that would require the most severe punishment in order to provide the best
source of protection. If an act or omission does not present any threat to
our rights that might require punishment in some form, then it should not
be criminalized.

The unified theory of punishment *unifies* multiple penal goals. First,
punishment is a response to crime. We cannot punish the innocent because
they do not present any threat that may violate our rights as substantial
freedoms. Offenders are deserving of punishment insofar as they must only
be punished for their crimes. The unified theory of punishment adopts a
more restrictive view of desert than retributivism where punishment is
deserved for crimes and not necessarily immorality.[42] Not all moral failures
are criminal and not all crimes are moral failures. Offenders may only
deserve punishment when they have performed crimes.

Secondly, punishment aims to protect rights from criminal violations.
Punishment is proportionate to the violation of right that is criminalized
and gives rise for the need of punishment. Some crimes may require
more severe punishments than others because rights that are more central
are violated or threatened with violation. So punishment has a distinctive
understanding of proportionality in view of rights protection. Punishment
metaphorically may be said to *express* the community's disapproval. The
greater the threat to our rights as substantial freedoms, then the greater

the punishment and the greater our disapproval of such crimes as manifest in the severity of punishment. The most central rights may require the most severe punishments which, in turn, may express in some sense our community's disapproval for such crimes.

Punishment may also address penal goals such as deterrence and rehabilitation within a more robust understanding of restorative justice. Proponents of restorative justice argue that crime damages community relations that should be restored. Community members including any victims engage with offenders in a restorative process to come to a greater collective understanding in an important alternative to sentencing. We have seen that this view suffers from some shortcomings. Restorative justice need not be an alternative to prison only, but a process that may be employed in tandem with imprisonment. Our choice need not be prison or restorative justice, but some combination of the two. Some commentators have argued for the benefits of restorative justice for victims of violent crimes and their offenders in prison environments.[43]

Punishment can and should restore what crime has damaged. Punishment aims at the protection of rights threatened by crimes and their restoration where violated. There are many reasons to believe that restorative conferences may have a positive impact on reducing recidivism with high public confidence and the satisfaction of victims and offenders. While imprisonment may not always be the best environment conducive to effective restoration, there is no reason to believe that it might never play some role. Punishment may best serve the aims of rights protection through incorporating some restorative justice element wherever possible. Instead of an alternative to punishment, we might argue that any punishment should employ restorative conferences as a default and not as an exception. This is not to say that restorative conferences must be used or always relevant, but instead to argue that they should become a standard part of all punishments. Restoration may require that a criminal accepts his punishment as deserved and proportionate.[44] The most effective route to criminal reformation is his ownership of wrongdoing.[45] Restorative conferences should often be one part of any punishment as a response to crime where it may help assist offenders accept responsibility for their crimes and how they should be held accountable.

Restoration may require more than these conferences alone, however, in order to best guarantee the restoration of rights in most cases.[46] Punishment is not justified by deterrence or rehabilitation. However, deterrence and rehabilitation may play some *secondary* role in justified sentencing.[47] If our goal is the protection of rights, then this task may be achieved in different ways depending upon the particular circumstances. We must first confirm that an offender has performed a crime. We then punish in proportion to the rights threatened by the crime. The particular form this punishment should take may address deterrent or rehabilitative penal goals insofar as they might contribute to the restoration and protection of rights within these

132 *Hybrid theories*

proportional limits. Furthermore, the unified theory of punishment defends *punitive restoration*. Punishment aims at the restoration of rights. Restoration may require some punitive element to best secure the restoration and protection of rights, such as community sentencing, a suspended sentence, or imprisonment.

The unified theory of punishment may address desert, proportionality, deterrence, rehabilitation, restoration, and expressivism in a coherent and unified account bringing together these multiple penal aims. The Model Penal Code presents a list of multiple penal goals. The unified theory of punishment offers us a theory about how these different goals may be pursued within a single coherent framework. Crimes are legal wrongs against rights. Punishment aims at the restoration of our rights and this restoration may take multiple shapes to achieve these aims.[48] Punishment is a response to crime that responds best as a unified theory.

Is the unified theory a 'unified' theory?

The unified theory of punishment raises several questions. Perhaps the most pressing is examining how 'unified' the unified theory is, in fact. Is it a *genuinely* unified theory?

One potential criticism is that the unified theory is no more unified than the Model Penal Code. The Code has been described as 'principled pragmatism'. It is principled because it is inclusive of several attractive penal goals. These goals address multiple sentencing principles, such as that punishment should be deserved, proportionate, provide a deterrent, and rehabilitate offenders. The Code is also pragmatic. This is because it recognizes that these different goals may potentially clash. For example, the aim of proportionate punishment may clash with the aim of providing a strong deterrence. The solution is to say that judges should weigh these different goals together in determining sentencing. So is there any difference between this position and unified theories?

The problem with the Model Penal Code is that its principled pragmatism is insufficiently principled: we require coherent pluralism, instead. This is because the multiple penal goals form a list lacking a suitably robust framework that offers a sufficiently clear steer on how these goals relate to one another *within* the framework. Why should *any* of these goals be included? The answer seems to be that each is intuitively attractive on its individual merits. But this fails to address specifically how each might relate. Imagine making a cake combining only those ingredients that you enjoy individually. Following this procedure may not guarantee that all the necessary ingredients for making a cake are included. Nor is there any guarantee that the cake will be edible. Now imagine starting a company by inviting only those persons that you enjoy working with individually. This procedure may not guarantee that all the necessary tasks will be covered. Nor is there any guarantee that the company's members will work together suitably effectively. These examples centre on the problem of justifying a legal practice without sufficient consideration of how the individual parts coherently work together in support of the practice aims. This problem lies at the heart of the Model Penal Code.[49]

The unified theory of punishment overcomes this problem. It addresses desert, proportionality, and other penal goals because they come together within a larger unified framework. So we don't weigh up possible sentences in light of general deterrence versus desert and other penal considerations because we find them intuitively attractive individually. Punishment does not bring together multiple penal goals because it can, but because it should. Punishment is a response to crime that aims at the restoration of rights. Punishment addresses multiple penal goals in serving its aims. The unified theory of punishment is not a mere list, but coherent penal pluralism.

A second potential criticism is that the unified theory may punish to maintain the power of the state at the expense of its citizens. This is a criticism some have levied at other approaches which claim punishment is justified by its ability to maintain political order. For example, one view attributed to Emile Durkheim is that punishment symbolizes and expresses our moral judgements with the purpose of reaffirming some moral order.[50] We punish in order to protect and maintain this moral order that governs us all. Punishment is justified in reference to its 'social necessity'.[51]

The unified theory of punishment overcomes this worry as well. We do not punish to maintain and protect the rights of the state, but the rights of its citizens which demarcate their substantial freedoms. Punishment does not serve the interests of the state at the expense of the interests of citizens. Punishment is only justified insofar as it fulfils its aim of restoring rights from criminal violations and protecting the substantial freedoms of individuals.

The problem of coherence

The unified theory of punishment is a specific variety of a hybrid theory of punishment. Hybrid theories of punishment attempt to offer theories which address two or more penal goals. Unified theories attempt to offer an account that may address multiple penal goals in a unified framework. There are alternative hybrid theories that speak to multiple penal goals.

One alternative states that we should consider various penal goals within sentencing guidelines and we should choose the most severe punishment available. For example, it might be argued that 'the length of the sentence of imprisonment imposed on the defendant by the court shall be the longest of the four sentences derived'.[52] Suppose that desert, deterrence, and other views could each support different prison term lengths where deterrence supported the longest term. This hybrid theory of punishment would endorse deterrence. The idea is that all principles are satisfied where we support the penal goal that is most punitive.

134   *Hybrid theories*

There are at least two problems with this approach. First, we should draw a different conclusion. Why believe all principles are satisfied in choosing the goal that exceptionally supports more punishment than the others? If this hybrid approach is attractive because it shows how multiple goals might support a common position, then we should instead endorse a punishment that all multiple goals support. Justified punishment is punishment that meets some threshold and within a range that multiple goals may endorse. This approach should lead us to a different conclusion. So we should not support the greatest punishment possible from the viewpoint of any single penal goal, but instead any punishment that all penal goals might endorse.

A second problem with this approach is that it lacks unity. It has a view about how we might determine sentences using different penal aims, but it says little about why these aims matter. Moreover, punishment is not determined so to further any particular aim, but rather only to find some – or, indeed, any – support for punishing offenders as much as possible. So it is hybrid in the full sense of being a collection of penal goals without being unified in the sense of offering some clear unifying rationale for why these goals and how they might work together in a coherent approach. This is the problem we found with the Model Penal Code.

Another alternative hybrid approach argues that multiple penal goals should be used to determine punishment within the boundaries of a primary penal goal. One formulation is to say that no criminal should be punished more or less than she deserves. Deserved punishment will typically fall within some range of possibilities. We choose from these possibilities with reference to multiple penal goals. Our theory of punishment is then hybrid insofar as it may address multiple penal goals, but guided by a primary goal. Suppose desert might support a punishment of between two and four years in prison. We then consider how penal aims such as deterrence, rehabilitation, expressivism, restoration might apply in determining a more precise sentence. One worry is that different penal goals may lend support to different outcomes. Thus, deterrence might endorse a longer punishment than restoration. The response to this worry is that this problem does not represent an injustice. If any punishment between two and four years may be said to be 'deserved', then there is nothing unjust about choosing a punishment within this deserved range according to other principles.

The main problem with this view is that it does not offer a coherent unified theory of punishment. Perhaps there is no injustice in selecting any punishment within some range of deserved alternatives. What justifies the relevance of applying other penal goals? Why not flip a coin? This formulation may offer a view that may bring together multiple penal goals, but it lacks a satisfactory account for why multiple goals should figure into a compelling theory of punishment.

A second formulation is to say that punishment should defer to the greatest utility, understood as crime reduction. Different penal goals may conflict when balanced against each other in determining just punishments. We should navigate between them with reference to supporting those punishments that best reduce crime. Broadly speaking, this is a formulation offered by the Model Penal Code. The main problem with this approach is that its declared primary goal is not primary, in fact. For example, the Model Penal Code is governed by 'basic considerations of justice' whereby punishment is not 'excessive, disproportionate or arbitrary'.[53] So punishment must be determined within the bounds of justified desert first and then we consider how we might best enable crime reduction second. Punishment does not defer to the greatest utility in fact, but only within clearly prescribed constraints determined by desert. While this formulation may present itself as a unified theory, it bears close resemblance to negative retributivism as discussed in chapter 5 and with all the problems associated with this approach.[54]

There are two further possible objections. The first is about distinctiveness. How is the unified theory *not* retributivist? The objection might claim the following. The unified theory punishes crimes in proportion to what is deserved. Its understanding of desert may be distinctive, but many retributivist theories differ on their precise understandings of desert. So perhaps there is nothing unique about the unified theory of punishment offering a different view about desert and it is best understood as a retributivist theory. This objection fails because the unified theory punishes crimes in order to restore rights. Punishment is not deserved because a criminal has performed a moral wrong, but because of a crime. Furthermore, retributivists argue that punishment should be proportionate to what is deserved. However, the unified theory does not claim that punishment is proportionate to moral desert, but instead what is required to best enable the restoration of rights. Moral depravity does not determine criminalization or penal proportionality. The unified theory of punishment rejects retributivism because it rejects the idea that punishment must be proportionate to a crime's moral wrongness. The unified theory is both coherent and distinctive; it is not retributivism by another name.[55]

Finally, it must be noted that the unified theory of punishment is not a 'rights forfeiture' theory of punishment. These theories claim that punishment is justified where offenders forfeit their right not to be punished.[56] The unified theory does not claim punishment is justified when offenders 'forfeit' their right against punishment. First, offenders cannot be said to forfeit their rights when their rights are merely suspended and not terminated. If we were to forfeit a game, then we have lost: we have terminated our participation. But we do not terminate our rights, not least any rights against punishment, unless sentenced to death. We do not lose our rights when punished. On the contrary, justified punishment aims to protect and restore our rights. This may include imprisonment, but

136 *Hybrid theories*

only as a last resort where alternatives are unsatisfactory. So offenders do not lose their rights in being punished although certain rights may be suspended where justificatory conditions are satisfied.

Another objection concerns the justificatory aims of punishment. For example, we might accept the complexity that confronts punishment, but reject the possibility that it can have any 'single meaning or a single purpose'.[57] So punishment may speak to different penal goals, but not under any one coherent framework: 'any attempt to build a single theoretical model of the causes, forms, and consequences of penalty would be misconceived'.[58] This objection is correct to claim that a significant problem for most standard theories of punishment is their inability to address the complexity of punishment from their single purpose. However, this criticism is directed only to retributivists, deterrence proponents, and others. It is not a criticism of the more recent and novel unified theory of punishment. We may agree that standard theories have run into this problem, but this is more reason to accept the unified theory precisely because it avoids this objection.

This chapter's presentation of the unified theory shows that this objection is misplaced. It is possible to conceive of a unified theory of punishment that brings together multiple penal goals within a single, coherent framework. Punishment may speak to different penal goals, but we must first establish a new justificatory framework. The unified theory of punishment demonstrates this possibility.

The problem of treating like cases differently

The unified theory of punishment may appear a target for the problem of treating like cases differently. The objection is that the criminal law should not justify different outcomes in broadly similar cases. The unified theory may coherently bring together multiple penal goals, but it cannot guarantee similar treatment in similar cases. For example, two offenders convicted for similar thefts may be punished differently so that the first receives more rehabilitation (e.g. perhaps greater drug and alcohol therapy) and the second more hours of community service. Like cases are not treated alike.

There are two problems with this objection. The first problem is that there is no evidence that punishing two thieves convicted of similar offences differently is a case where like cases have been treated differently. Punishment aims at the restoration of rights violated by crimes. This restoration must be tailored to individual circumstances. Suppose that the first thief engaged in crime to support his drug and alcohol dependency and the second engaged in crime because she did not expect to get caught. The punitive restoration and protection of rights may take different forms to best address these different cases. We should distinguish between crime and its circumstances. The *crimes* in both cases are alike: each thief is supposed to have committed broadly similar offences. The *criminal circumstances* in these cases are not alike. We punish crimes in light of their crime-relevant circumstances. The unified theory of punishment may justify different punishments for these thieves without treating like cases differently. This is because the criminal circumstances are not alike.

For the objection to succeed, it must show that different punishments would be justified for the same criminal circumstances. Of course, no one argues that there is one and only one fixed sentence for the great majority of crimes.[59] We don't say that all arsonists should be punished by eight years and not a minute more or less in every case. The individual circumstances of a case will matter and judges will have some discretion in sentencing to account for these circumstances. Punishment is an imprecise science at best. We should not expect our penal theories to offer any specific recommendations beyond a small range of potentially permissible tariffs.[60] A theory of punishment cannot declare that only one sentence is justified in all cases at all times, but it can claim that sentences within some fixed range are justified, to be determined in light of particular relevant circumstances and open to future revision. Therefore, we should reject the view that punishment should be inflexible. The problem with this is that punishment cannot be so precise in addressing even the same circumstances to say that only eight years in prison is justified for all arsonists in every criminal circumstance. Some difference is permitted within a fixed range to be determined in light of circumstances subject to future revision and judicial review. The unified theory of punishment is not subject to the objection that it fails to treat like cases alike.

The problem of relativism

The unified theory of punishment aims to restore rights violated by crimes. One implication is that crimes may warrant greater or lesser punishment depending, in part, on changing circumstances. Punishment must do more work in societies that are engaged in civil war. Crime may present a different amount of threat to our rights within different contexts. Furthermore, political societies may then punish the same crimes in the same individual circumstances very differently in some part due to possible differences in societal contexts. Crimes and punishments may significantly differ from one political society to the next. The potential objection is that the unified theory of punishment is open to a kind of relativism that is problematic and should be avoided. There should be broad congruence across different political societies on criminalization and punishment.

The unified theory of punishment rejects the necessity of broad congruence across political societies. This is not to argue that broad congruence is impossible or problematic, but rather to argue that it is not necessary for a legal system to be satisfactorily justified. Of course, some minimal conditions concerning the recognition of rights as substantial freedoms protected by law are required. However, different societies may understand this recognition and its protection by law in different ways. We should not expect every political society to converge on all matters of criminal law. Perhaps we might expect this if we believed that all political societies are governed by a particular universal morality that should guide how we criminalize and punish. We have already rejected this strong version of legal moralism. In the absence of a particular universal morality to play such a role, we should expect some differences to emerge between legal systems on criminal justice matters, and this need not be fundamentally problematic.

We have seen that the unified theory of punishment may punish the same crime differently in different circumstances. This does have clear limits. Hegel says:

> The fact that an injury to *one* member of society is an injury to *all* the others does not alter the nature of crime in terms of its concept, but in terms of its outward existence ... [I]ts *danger to civil society* is a determination of magnitude ... This quality or magnitude varies, however, according to the *condition* of civil society.[61]
>
> The very stability of society ... makes crime appear in a milder light, so that its punishment also becomes milder ... Thus, harsh punishments are not unjust in and for themselves, but are proportionate to the conditions of their time; a criminal code cannot be valid for every age ... A penal code is therefore primarily a product of its time and of the current condition of civil society.[62]

Crimes are punished in proportion to their threat to our rights. Crimes will pose a greater threat under some conditions rather than others. Punishment is a response to crime that may vary in severity and application depending upon circumstances. Therefore, the unified theory of punishment rejects the position that there must be any one particular punishment that is always best for any specific crime. This is not so much penal relativism as it is *penal realism*. Punishment must always be considered in context. It matters whether or not the state is in civil war or prosperous times of prolonged peace.

It is worth highlighting that many political societies acknowledge the importance that changing circumstances may have in determining justified punishments. For example, many societies have different penal codes for non-ordinary times where they are at war. Punishments are typically more punitive during times of war than prolonged peace. Punishments may also be modified in response to mass protest. One recent illustration is the case of the London riots that took place during August 2011. Sentences were increased for offenders about 25 per cent, attracting political support across party divisions and supported by public opinion.[63] It makes sense to increase the severity of punishment for crimes committed during mass public disturbances, such as riots, because the threat posed to individual rights becomes much greater than normal. People who might not otherwise offend may attempt to take advantage of the temporary chaos in the hope of not getting caught. Such a likelihood increases during times of public disturbance and so punishment must do more in order to best safeguard and restore our threatened individual rights.

Note that punishment reacts to *perceptions* about threats to rights. There is always the danger that this perception is mistaken. Call this *the problem of penal perception*. This is perhaps an increasing worry given that the public have become increasingly fearful of crime during a period where crime has reached historic lows and prison numbers have hit historic highs. The fact that the public's perception of crime's potential threat to rights may be mistaken is not a reason to reject the role that penal perception should play in helping to determine punishment for crime. Instead, this problem alerts us to the need to endeavour so to ensure that our perceptions about threats to rights are satisfactory and not a product of fear mongering, but rather evidence based.

Judging success

There are at least two potential problems concerning how we might judge the success of the unified theory of punishment. The first problem concerns its success in its own terms. The unified theory of punishment has the aim of the protection and restoration of rights. Those acts or omissions that represent some threat to violating rights may require criminalization. Crimes are punished to the degree that they represent some threat to violating rights. This understanding of crime and punishment best addresses criminal justice. First, it offers a compelling explanation for why the 'standard' class of crimes, such as murder, assault, or theft, should be punished. These crimes represent threats to violation of the rights of others. Our response is greater in proportion to the threat a particular crime represents when considering the full criminal circumstances. The unified theory would normally justify greater punishment for assault than petty theft and greater punishment for murder than either assault or petty theft. It is not the case that most categories of crime need always be punished more or less than others. For example, some thefts may require greater punishment than some assaults in consideration of the full circumstances. This view of criminal justice accounts for the full 'standard' class of crimes we would want to punish and it defends a view of proportionality that is compelling without recourse to legal moralism.

Secondly, the unified theory of punishment also offers a compelling explanation for why the 'non-standard' class of crimes should be punished, such as victimless crimes. These are punished not because they are evil, but because they represent potential threats to rights. Such crimes might include drug and traffic offences as well as prostitution. To be criminal, these must be understood as threats to rights as substantial freedoms. It may be argued

140 *Hybrid theories*

that some drug offences do not pose such a threat. If so, then the unified theory would not justify criminalization or punishment. However, if it is possible to argue that individuals might not only act in ways that may threaten the violation of rights of others, but also of themselves, then this may offer a more compelling explanation for why some victimless crimes should be considered criminal. We do not say that an act is criminal because no one should be able to consent to it. Rather we argue that some acts are criminal because they violate rights. Therefore, slavery is wrong as the violation of individual rights and so consent is irrelevant for determining criminalization. Furthermore, illegal parking may not be wicked. However, where the specific regulations concerning parking are justified as protecting the rights of citizens, perhaps in terms of rights of free movement within practical constraints, then a breach of the law may require some proportional penal response. Traffic offences can and should be criminal where they serve the maintenance and protection of rights. This role may often be relatively minor which explains why these offences are often punished by penalties and overlooked entirely by most considerations of criminal law.

The unified theory of punishment has at least two further merits. Treason is the most severely punished crime in every jurisdiction from antiquity to today.[64] Whatever a society's most severe punishment, it is always and everywhere a possibility for convicted traitors. The question is why? Treason is not clearly immoral or wicked in every case. We may have a moral duty to engage in treason against some states. The best reason for criminalizing treason is that treason is a crime against the state. Again, this may not always be morally wrong. The crucial point is that if rights are maintained and protected by a legal system and treason aims to end this system, then treason represents a threat to all rights within a legal system. Therefore, treason may be punished more than any other crime. The unified theory of punishment can offer the best explanation for why treason may require the greatest punishment. This is not to say that it is always 'best' to punish traitors and to do so more severely than all others. This is because a legal system does not exist for its sake, but instead for the sake of citizens with the aim of maintaining and protecting their rights. Where a legal system fails in these areas, such a system may be deeply flawed and perhaps not fit for its purpose. So one merit of the unified theory of punishment is that it may best account for treason as the most serious crime.

A second merit is its position with respect to persons unfit for trial, but detained in institutions almost as if they were sentenced. Many theories of punishment require the presence of retributivist desert, such as retributivism, expressivism, and other views. They might claim that punishment is justified where it is deserved and there is a problem where persons cannot be held morally responsible for violence. Suppose there is a violent psychopath. He is genuinely suffering from psychopathic delusions that compel him to attempt killing innocent persons without provocation. He lacks culpability for his actions, but these actions present a clear danger to the public.

The unified theory of punishment might argue that the violent psychopath should be incapacitated regardless of culpability. His actions represent real threats to the rights of others. The aim of punishment is to restore and protect rights and so incapacitation may be required. It is unnecessary to convict and sentence the violent psychopath for murder. This is because it is unnecessary for us to say only murderers should be incapacitated to best maintain and protect individual rights.

The unified theory of punishment may be successful when understood in its own terms. It offers a compelling and coherent account of how we might understand criminalization and the punishment of crimes across standard and non-standard cases. The unified theory is successful where it restores and protects rights. Further evidence for its success would consist in its ability to promote crime reduction. We should expect fewer crimes and less serious crimes where crime rates fall. Additional evidence for the success of the unified theory of punishment may arise from the positive endorsements of restorative conference participants. Any theory that aspires to restore and protect rights should command the support of those who have a stake. Victims, offenders, and community members each have a stake in penal outcomes. Where they are satisfied with these outcomes, this is an important benchmark for judging success of the unified theory. If stakeholders are satisfied, then this offers a strong reason why others should also be satisfied with outcomes.

A second potential problem is whether the theory is successful on other terms. For example, one criticism of retributivist desert is that there are many different positions on moral responsibility and it may be very difficult, if not impossible, to determine approximately how much punishment is deserved in proportion to moral responsibility for any crime. Similarly, one criticism of deterrence is that we cannot guarantee that our punishment today will have the effect we predict in reducing future crime. So why think the unified theory does any better?

The unified theory does not run into this problem of *penal indeterminism* to the same degree. Retributivists have more substantial problems with determining punishments in relation to moral responsibility: moral responsibility is not always relevant and may be impossible to know. Likewise, deterrence proponents may never know how many potential crimes were effectively deterred by a penal threat: they can only measure crime reduction and not deterrence itself. The unified theory claims to restore and protect rights. This view holds that rights can be known. We may be mistaken about the identity of rights and no legal system can expect to be free from any criticism. However, if we can have some satisfactory grasp of what our rights are, then this is a more secure foundation than found in rival theories. It will always be a matter of debate and good judgement concerning how punishment might best fulfil its aim of maintaining and protecting rights, but this task – however relatively open-textured – is no less clear than other theories of punishment. Furthermore, we should not expect any theory to

142   *Hybrid theories*

offer any precise determinations. All we might expect is that a theory may offer a more compelling argument than its rivals. So while we may err in how best to protect rights, we could never know if we do not err in punishing criminals retributively or to secure deterrence.

The unified theory of punishment supports punishments that best restore rights violated or threatened with violation by crimes. Note that this view justifies punishment only where necessary: if punishment is unnecessary to restore rights, then it is unjustified. Note further that this view has a clear position on the punishment of criminal attempts. An attempt may be unsuccessful in fulfilling some criminal goal, such as a murder or theft. While an attempt may not succeed in violating rights, punishable attempts must succeed in presenting a sufficiently substantial threat to rights in order to be punishable. This is intuitively compelling. We often punish criminal attempts less, but often lack some clear principle to explain why we punish attempts less in some cases and not others. The unified theory offers us a helpful solution. Where an attempt presents a sufficiently substantial rights threat, then the attempt is punishable. The punishment is proportionate to the threat presented by a criminal attempt. This need not always entail that criminal attempts merit reduced punishment because they failed to succeed in achieving some criminal goal. The unified theory helps us make best sense of cases like these. The unified theory of punishment endorses punitive restoration.

Finally, we should note that the unified theory of punishment supports the use of restorative justice in conjunction with imprisonment and including intensive supervision programmes. Conviction is legal confirmation of personal criminality, but it also is often confirmation that a person requires help *now*. It's often crucial to provide necessary support sooner rather than later. Again, conviction often confirms that a person is in need of help.

This need not entail swift justice as moving too quickly to court which might undermine any fair trial. This is because the overwhelming majority of cases never reach trial. Only about 6 per cent or less (and about 3 per cent in Scotland) receive a full court trial. All others are handled through plea bargaining and alternatives to trial. Time must be granted for all parties to examine the relevant evidence and present their best case in court. But those who accept their criminal guilt should not wait too long. It is essential that criminals come to acknowledge their criminal wrongdoing through taking responsibility by being held accountable. The sooner, the better. For example, intensive supervision programmes enacted early may 'dramatically' improve reducing recidivism rates fourfold.[65]

Another idea is using imprisonment more frequently in shorter sentences. Brief imprisonment may provide criminals with a 'cooling off' period. Of course, brief imprisonment is often believed to be criminogenic, ensuring reoffending is more likely. But this common problem in prison studies often overlooks significant facts that contribute to this specific concern. For example, prisoners may receive little, if any, rehabilitative support during terms of 12 months or less. This support is often directed to offenders with longer sentences instead. It is little wonder that offenders are likely to return to criminal activity post-release when too little is done about them. Over 90 per cent of offenders will avoid trial and most of these accept some form of plea bargain. This is a substantial number of people and we could redesign our criminal justice system to better assist offenders acknowledging their crimes and taking responsibility by being held accountable. We can achieve these goals through punitive restoration by expanding the use of restorative justice conferences as a more common feature of punishments to be used in conjunction with brief imprisonment where this might best enable the restoration of rights and their protection. Early intervention may often serve this goal effectively.

The unified theory of punishment helps us explain this goal has importance and sheds light on how it may be fulfilled. Prison as a cooling off period may serve a useful rehabilitative function by best securing more immediate alcohol and drug treatment as well as perhaps anger management and life coaching where appropriate. This cooling off period might also serve a useful deterrent function in signalling imprisonment as a more likely outcome, but also retributive and expressivist functions by indicating the seriousness with which the public views crimes. Finally, prison may serve a wider restorative function in better securing public confidence through punitive restoration. Prison may be redesigned to better ensure the restoration of rights violated or threatened by crimes.

Restoration need not require the absence of imprisonment, but may require its use on occasion. Prisons are expensive and often poor at reducing reoffending by offenders post-release. The unified theory of punishment does *not* recommend imprisonment where it would fail to best restore and protect rights. However, the unified theory does encourage us to consider new ways of ensuring that prison more effectively serves the aim of best restoring and protecting rights. A likely result is more brief prison terms where offenders receive immediate and intensive support rather than more longer terms in prison. While these brief terms will carry greater costs, they might also contribute to better results and be cost effective in reducing the need for longer prison terms. Brief prison terms might be served in one block or spread over time. One major problem in imprisoning offenders is that it may contribute to a bad situation becoming much worse. Many are unemployed and face financial insecurity. So one option might be to permit non-violent offenders to work during the day, but return to prison at night and perhaps on weekends. Offenders might then retain employment and maintain support networks while securing public confidence that they are being held accountable for their crimes through the loss of personal liberty while in prison. The unified theory helps explain not only why prisons should be avoided where possible, but also how they might become reimagined to better serve the underlying purpose that justifies their use as punitive restoration.

144 *Hybrid theories*

The stakeholder society

The idea of the stakeholder society may play a significant role in any compelling theory of punishment.[66] Many wonder about how to best tackle crime. We have already identified in previous chapters factors that are often associated with criminal behaviour. These factors include drug and alcohol abuse, unemployment, financial insecurity, housing problems, and past offending. There are other important associated factors, such as support networks of friends and family. Many offenders will share one or more of these factors although each case will be very different from the next. Criminal profiling is an imprecise art far removed from detectives depicted on the silver screen.[67] It is an informed guess about more likely findings. Nevertheless, it remains tempting to speculate about the criminal mind. This is relevant because insights into criminality may contribute to reduced crime and less need for punishment. We may further wonder how it is that crime rates have changed over time and how associated factors may have changed, too.

It is easy to overlook a common bond that these risk factors address. Crime is not necessarily a problem of drug abuse or unemployment although these factors may often be present. The unifying thread that brings together these factors concerns the individual's beliefs about his or her relation to others. The primary factor associated with likely criminal behaviour is the failure of individuals to see themselves as having a stake in their political community. Other associated factors become a concern where they contribute to a sense that someone lacks a stake.

The problem of failing to believe someone has a stake in the political community is often understood as a failure of political recognition. This is captured well by Hegel:

> When a large mass of people sinks below the level of a certain standard of living ... that feeling of right, legitimacy, and honour ... is lost. This leads to the creation of a rabble ... Poverty in itself does not reduce people to a rabble; a rabble is created only by the disposition associated with poverty, by inward rebellion against the rich, against society, the government, etc.[68]

Hegel identifies a group, the rabble, united by their shared disposition about how they relate to others. The rabble believes they are disassociated from others in their political community. This disassociation is based upon a sense of injustice: that they lack in some significant share of right, legitimacy, and honour. The rabble are united by the conviction that they are somehow divorced from lawful society; that the rules applying to all somehow don't relate to them because of this sense of political otherness.

Hegel's rabble may often be found amongst those in poverty, but this is not the only associated factor. Hegel is clear that 'an excess of wealth' may also contribute to a rabble.[69] The rabble is a state of mind, a mentality. Not all persons with associated factors will identify with the rabble although many may self-identify. Anyone may adopt the rabble state of mind whether rich or poor. However, the problem is not only how to prevent a rabble from arising in the first place, but how to bring about a change of heart and convert the rabble to believing themselves to have a stake. Hegel famously lacks any clear answer to either question although we might do better.

The idea of the stakeholder society is the idea that each individual citizen believes he or she has some significant stake in the political community and its continuation. This shared sense that I have a stake in the continuation of my political community may lead me to refrain from crime where possible. This is because the stakeholder society is a political community that satisfactorily attracts my interest and concern.[70] People will believe that any problems are best resolved within the system rather than without. Not everyone need be fully satisfied with any current political arrangement or oppose radical reforms. Instead, the essential concern is whether persons identify themselves as having a stake in the political community or not. Some may believe they do not have a shared stake and can 'opt out' in a position we might call political exceptionalism, which is rooted in alienation. Not everyone possesses a palpable sense of social belonging. Our challenge is to convince Hegel's rabble to 'opt in' where they remain unconvinced.[71]

One important route to helping individuals become more conciliatory to their political community is to honour our *recognitional debt* to them. This debt is the political recognition we owe fellow citizens. It is understood in terms of a shared political reciprocity.[72] John Rawls says:

> The least advantaged are not, if all goes well, the unfortunate and unlucky – objects of our charity and compassion, much less our pity – but those to whom reciprocity is owed as a matter of political justice among those who are free and equal citizens along with everyone else.[73]

Our perception is key to changing hearts and minds. Hegel's rabble is best addressed where they are convinced that they are not strangers to be pitied, but fellow citizens who deserve our respect. All members must enjoy some standard of reciprocity in order to best secure acceptance of the self-identity that comes with believing in possessing a stake in society. This is politically and legally realist in taking people as they are and predicting how they will respond to different situations.[74] The political community should ensure that its members do not view themselves as powerless, isolated, and disconnected if only to best guard against crime and the need for punishment.[75] The more members believe they have a stake in society, the less likely crime will occur. We have a responsibility to honour our recognitional debt to all and ensure that our political community is a place where all may share some stake in its present and future.

146 *Hybrid theories*

The idea of the stakeholder society offers an insight into criminality. It claims that failing to see yourself as having a stake is a primary factor associated with crime. If punishment is to be an effective response to crime, then punishment must aim to restore and protect our rights without undermining stakeholding. Offenders should accept responsibility for their crimes while coming to see their having a stake in society. We best reduce crime where all view themselves as belonging to a stakeholder society. There is compelling evidence that criminality is linked with a failing to see one's stake in the political community and its future.[76]

There are several ways we might promote stakeholding. Criminal justice policy must focus on reducing recidivism while improving public confidence. Most offenders will be eventually released if imprisoned. Our view must consider punishment with a view to life post-conviction and post-release.[77] Stakeholding is promoted where key contributing risk factors for social and political disassociation are effectively managed. This raises the importance of behavioural and employability programmes in addressing stakeholding.[78] This may require assistance with accommodation, skill building, financial advice, cognitive therapy, and behavioural support. There must be a more effectively managed post-conviction plan integrating penal management with addressing offender needs.[79]

These efforts may be assisted in several ways. Restorative justice conferences promote stakeholding. Offenders, victims, and community members come together to determine how offenders may restore rights. Each has a stake in the deliberative outcome premised on the offender's acknowledgement of his crime. Unsurprisingly, all parties regularly report high satisfaction with the process and its outcome. Restorative conferences have demonstrated promising crime reduction potential at a fraction of the cost of alternatives without sacrificing public confidence. The key to their success is the promotion of stakeholding where each has a stake in the outcome. These conferences may be reformed to permit more punitive possible outcomes where these may best secure the restoration of rights. Such conferences might be mediated by a magistrate or judge rather than a facilitator, depending upon the circumstances involved.

A second example is so-called 'community pay back', where offenders perform public tasks as part of their punishment. These may include voluntary work at charitable organizations and rebuilding the community. Examples of the latter may include cleaning graffiti, interior decoration of public buildings, and assisting public building maintenance and new construction. These forms of punishment are public and punitive without stigmatization. Offenders are encouraged to see themselves as having a stake in what they help maintain and create for public benefit.

A further example is the Certificate of Good Conduct issued by the US state of New York to reformed criminals.[80] It gives offenders the ability to seek work without automatic disqualification for having a past criminal conviction. The Certificate removes a large barrier that may prevent offenders from securing employment and furthering their stake in society. An alternative idea is to place time limitations for how long some offenders are required to acknowledge past convictions on applications. This might be limited to offenders without previous convictions or no more than two convictions. Or perhaps only relating to conviction for non-violent crimes. Perhaps first non-violent offences need not be acknowledged on applications at all. These measures might retain some obstacles to full future stakeholding, but without closing this possibility off permanently. They address the concern that if an offender must also face obstacles to employment, housing, and other areas for even minor crimes performed long ago in his past the possibility of full restoration may be inhibited and perhaps even denied. Such possibilities provide offenders with hope and a goal to pursue that may better inspire them to see themselves as having a stake in society.

These are only a few recommendations for how we might promote the idea of a stakeholder society. Of course, not everyone will see themselves as having a stake in society. Stakeholding requires individuals to *believe* that they have a stake in society.[81] It may be the case that some hold false beliefs about their relation to others. Call this *the problem of stakeholding beliefs*. This problem is a concern because citizens may be most at risk of criminal engagement. However, while criminal justice policy should aspire to crime reduction, it cannot deliver crime eradication. Moreover, there is no crime in failing to see oneself as having a stake. We punish crimes alone. Our goal must be to reduce crimes, but we cannot end crime without abandoning criminalization itself. If there is a criminal law, then there will be criminals. Our society is characterized by the fact of crime and it cannot be wished to disappear. But we can acknowledge, confront, and reduce crime more effectively. The idea of the stakeholding society paired with the unified theory of punishment offers the best approach to criminal justice.

The idea of the stakeholder society has a central relevance for any penal theory although its complete treatment would require a separate text and my discussion cannot be more than preliminary. The central idea presupposes that the political community is worth having a stake in in the first place. We have already seen that the conception of politics accepted by the unified theory of punishment is the idea that rights are understood as our substantial freedoms. Crime is the violation or threatened violation of our rights. Punishment is a response to crime that aims to restore and protect our rights through punitive restoration. We have also seen that there can be no just punishment for an unjust crime. The restoration and protection of rights is best guaranteed within the political conception of the stakeholder society although the idea of a stakeholder society is not exclusive to the unified theory of punishment.[82] Finally, the promotion of stakeholding must be aimed at all members of a political community. It is not for offenders alone. The central importance for promoting stakeholding to offenders is that it fosters good citizenship, including crime reduction.[83]

Conclusion

We have examined the diversity in strengths and weaknesses for various theories of punishment both general and hybrid. Each contains something of importance. There is something intuitively compelling about a theory of punishment that might bring diverse and attractive penal goals together into a coherent unity. If a theory of punishment could address retributivism, deterrence, rehabilitation, restoration, expressivism, and perhaps more, then such a theory may prove more compelling than alternatives that address only one or two. The problem is how to conceive of such a theory and get the balance right where so many have got it wrong.

The unified theory of punishment proposed in this chapter is an important attempt to offer a compelling hybrid theory of punitive restoration that brings together multiple penal goals into a coherent and unified theory. While its presentation here is novel, its philosophical roots extend to Hegel, the British Idealists, and perhaps even earlier. The unified theory of punishment has been defended in different forms. The form explained and defended here is one of many possible forms.

Not only is a unified theory of punishment theoretically possible, it also makes best sense of our current practices.[84] A major problem of the Model Penal Code is not that it seeks to address multiple goals in sentencing, but its lack of a more robust and attractive theoretical framework that brings unity to its goals and illuminates punishment's primary goal of restoring rights within the context of a stakeholder society. This perspective helps us better understand where current practices might be reformed and conceive of new ways to achieve this end.

Philosophers looking to defend the most compelling theory of punishment that makes best sense of the world as we find it while pointing towards a bold new vision for criminal justice policy and political justice more broadly should accept the unified theory of punishment.

Notes

1 My thanks to Fabian Freyenhagen for first recommending to me that this view of punishment is perhaps best understood as a 'unified' theory of punishment.

2 See the American Law Institute, *Model Penal Code* (Philadelphia: American Law Institute, 1962). See also the Sentencing Council, 'Guidelines to Download', http://sentencingcouncil.judiciary.gov.uk/guidelines/guidelines-to-download.htm.

3 See American Law Institute, *Model Penal Code: Sentencing* § 1.02(2) (T.D. No. 1, 2007) (comment on 2a-b).

4 See Paul H. Robinson, *Distributive Principles of Criminal Law: Who Should Be Punished How Much?* (Oxford: Oxford University Press, 2008): 3–4.

5 The Sentencing Reform Act of 1984, 18 U.S.C. 3553 (a).

6 Few philosophers of punishment appear to appreciate how very different their positions are from how sentencing is determined in courtrooms. Perhaps radical reforms are necessary requiring substantive revisions of current practice. But there is relatively little, if any, recognition of the implications arising from their specific theories of punishment on the criminal law.

7 For example, see Robinson, *Distributive Principles of Criminal Law*, 1. See also ibid. chap. 11.

8 See ibid. 5.

9 There is perhaps little doubt that the Model Penal Code's justificatory framework is under-theorized and this has attracted deserved criticism. For example, its professed illustrations begin from the obvious point that sentencing can never say that any offender should receive 'precisely' a specific punishment, but move towards the view that sanctions are permissible where 'not undeserved'. Essentially, the Code offers multiple goals that should be considered when judges are determining proportionality within existing sentencing guidelines. Moreover, the Code does not presume its stated goals are 'applicable, or appropriate to pursue, in every individual case' without clear specific guidance on how we might make such judgements.

10 David Garland, *Punishment and Modern Society: A Study in Social Theory* (Oxford: Clarendon, 1990): 9.

11 See Samuel Johnson, 'Robert Chambers's Vinerian Lectures on the English Law' [1767], *The Major Works* (Harmondsworth: Penguin, 1984): 570–9 (punishment has a threefold end: to benefit the offender, the suffering party, and the general public).

12 G. W. F. Hegel, *Science of Logic*, trans. A. V. Miller (Amherst: Humanity Books, 1969): 465. On Hegel's theory of punishment, see Brooks, 'Is Hegel a Retributivist?', Brooks, *Hegel's Political Philosophy*, 39–51; and Brooks, 'Hegel and the Unified Theory of Punishment', 103–23.

13 See Hegel, *Science of Logic*, 465.

14 British Idealism flourished in the late nineteenth century and waned with the beginning of the First World War. British Idealists first popularized the work of Kant and Hegel for an Anglo-American audience. Idealists also attempted to offer new contributions that built on compelling insights uncovered in Kantian and Hegelian philosophies. On British Idealism more generally, see David Boucher (ed.), *The British Idealists* (Cambridge: Cambridge University Press, 1997); Thom Brooks, 'British Idealism', *Oxford Bibliographies Online* (2011); and W. J. Mander, *British Idealism: A History* (Oxford: Oxford University Press, 2011). On British Idealism and the unified theory of punishment, see Thom Brooks, 'T. H. Green's Theory of Punishment', *History of Political Thought* 24 (2003): 685–701; Thom Brooks, 'Punishment and British Idealism', in Jesper Ryberg and J. Angelo Corlett (eds), *Punishment and Ethics: New Perspectives* (Basingstoke: Palgrave Macmillan, 2010): 16–32; Thom Brooks, 'Is Bradley a Retributivist?', *History of Political Thought* 32 (2011): 83–95; and Thom Brooks, 'What Did the British Idealists Do for Us?' in Brooks (ed.), *New Waves in Ethics* (Basingstoke: Palgrave Macmillan, 2011): 28–47.

15 Green, *Lectures on the Principles of Political Obligation*, §178.

16 See James Seth, *A Study of Ethical Principles*, 3rd ed. (Edinburgh: William Blackwood and Sons, 1898): 312. Probably no other philosopher or work has

had a more profound effect on my thinking about the philosophy of punishment than this.

17 While there are many significant differences between individual British Idealists, many leading figures accepted a common position and it is this view that I offer. My main aim here is not to provide a scholarly analysis of British Idealists on legal philosophy, but instead to indicate how many of their leading figures contribute to a distinctive theory, the unified theory of punishment, and why this theory is worthy of our attention and further study. See Thom Brooks, 'Rethinking Punishment', *International Journal of Jurisprudence and Philosophy of Law* 1 (2007): 27–34.

18 The use of 'just' found here is shorthand for 'justified' (and not 'morally just'). The unified theory of punishment is not consistent with most versions of natural law nor legal moralism.

19 See Hume, *A Treatise of Human Nature*, 337 [3.2.6]: 'Society is absolutely necessary for the well-being of men; and [laws] are as necessary to the support of society'. See also Beccaria, *Of Crimes and Punishments*, 8.

20 See Johnson, *The Major Works*, 570: 'The first purpose of every political society is *internal peace*'.

21 My understanding of rights is broadly consistent with some versions of the capabilities approach, but note that the view of freedom used here may be consistent with several different theories of freedom. See Thom Brooks (ed.), *Justice and the Capabilities Approach* (Aldershot: Ashgate, 2012); Thom Brooks, 'Capabilities' in Hugh LaFollette (ed.), *International Encyclopedia of Ethics* (Oxford: Blackwell, 2012); Martha C. Nussbaum, *Women and Human Development: The Capabilities Approach* (Cambridge: Cambridge University Press, 2000); and Martha C. Nussbaum, *Creating Capabilities: The Human Development Approach* (Cambridge: Harvard University Press, 2011). This view of rights is also consistent with the view that dignity is the basis of rights. See Jeremy Waldron, 'How Law Protects Dignity', *Cambridge Law Journal* 71 (2012): 200–22, esp. 217–19. On rights more generally, see Wesley N. Hohfeld, *Fundamental Legal Conceptions* (New Haven: Yale University Press, 1964) and Leif Wenar, 'The Nature of Rights', *Philosophy and Public Affairs* 33 (2005): 223–53.

22 Rawls, *Political Liberalism*, 137.

23 For example, see Martha C. Nussbaum, *Liberty of Conscience: In Defense of America's Tradition of Religious Equality* (New York: Basic Books, 2008).

24 This has been a central idea in the legal philosophy of Ronald Dworkin. For example, see Ronald Dworkin, *Law's Empire* (Oxford: Hart, 1998).

25 James Seth, *Essays in Ethics and Religion with Other Papers*, ed. Andrew Seth Pringle-Pattison (Edinburgh: William Blackwood and Sons, 1926): 179.

26 My understanding of crime here includes the idea that crimes are criminal insofar as they violate or threaten to violate rights as substantial freedoms. Crimes may violate rights, but may also pose a threat to violate rights. See Hegel, *Elements of the Philosophy of Right*, §95: 'to infringe the existence of freedom in its concrete sense – i.e., to infringe right as right – is *crime*'.

27 Beccaria argues that the 'only true measurement of crimes is the harm done to the nation'. The unified theory of punishment rejects the idea that harm to the nation per se may demand punishment. Instead, we punish crimes as threats to violate our rights. See Beccaria, *Of Crimes and Punishments*, 16.

28 This view is presented forcefully by Seth, 'Individual and Social Ethics' in *Essays in Ethics and Religion*, 172. See also W. D. Ross, *The Right and the Good* (Oxford: Clarendon, 1930): 60.

29 See John D. Mabbott, 'Punishment', *Mind* 48 (1939): 152–67.

30 Mill, *On Liberty*, 77, see 93.

31 Mill, 'On Punishment', 79.

238 *Notes*

32 See Thom Brooks, 'Was Green a Utilitarian in Practice?' *Collingwood and British Idealism Studies* 14 (2008): 5–15.

33 Seth, *Essays in Ethics and Religion*, 179.

34 Green, *Lectures on the Principles of Political Obligation*, §§189, 204. See W. H. Fairbrother, *The Philosophy of Thomas Hill Green* (London: Methuen and Co., 1896): 151–2.

35 Green, *Lectures on the Principles of Political Obligations*, §177.

36 Ibid. §197.

37 For this distinction, see Brudner, *Punishment and Freedom*, 16.

38 Green, *Lectures on the Principles of Political Obligation*, §197.

39 Seth, *A Study of Ethical Principles*, 305. See H. J. W. Hetherington and J. H. Muirhead (eds), *Social Purpose: A Contribution to a Philosophy of Civic Society* (London: George Allen and Unwin, 1918): 129.

40 Seth, *Essays in Ethics and Religion*, 179.

41 See Seth, *Freedom as Ethical Postulate* (Edinburgh: William Blackwood and Sons, 1891): 337.

42 This distinction shares some similarities with Brudner's distinction between 'legal retributivism' and 'moral retributivism'. See Brudner, *Punishment and Freedom*. See also Thom Brooks, 'Punishment: Political, Not Moral', *New Criminal Law Review* 14 (2011): 427–38.

43 This understanding of restorative justice views restoration as a process that is post-sentencing and not a part of sentencing. Restorative justice is something we engage in after a punishment has been determined in light of some alternative theory of punishment. This view of restorative justice is not of restorative justice *as a theory of punishment*. My argument above is that restorative justice as a theory of punishment fails to acknowledge that our choice need not be either restoration or imprisonment. However, I would also argue that restorative justice understood as not a theory of punishment in the second sense is illuminating, but also too restrictive. Restorative justice can and should be a more ambitious theory of punishment than often argued. The unified theory is one attempt to show how a greater ambition as a view to punitive restoration is possible and compelling.

44 See James Seth, *Freedom as Ethical Postulate*, 336. Seth understands this as the 'private re-enactment of the social judgement' whereby 'the judgement of society upon the man must become the judgement of the man upon himself'.

45 See Seth, *A Study of Ethical Principles*, 314: 'The judgment of society upon the man must become the judgment of the man upon himself, if it is to be effective as an agent in his reformation'.

46 See Hegel, *Elements of the Philosophy of Right*, § Remark: Punishment is 'the restoration of right'.

47 The British Idealist Bernard Bosanquet, who was from the Newcastle upon Tyne area, argues similarly that 'deterrence and reformation are subordinate aspects'. Bernard Bosanquet, *Some Suggestions in Ethics* (London: Macmillan, 1918): 207.

48 One implication is that the question of how much we should punish is not divorced from the question of how we should punish. For example, see Lippke, *Rethinking Imprisonment*.

49 My identification of this problem is more sophisticated than the usual understanding of it. The usual understanding is that the Model Penal Code suffers from incoherence because the multiple goals *do* clash where this is thought inevitable for any hybrid theory of punishment. This objection is unsuccessful because the unified theory of punishment clearly shows that it is possible to conceive of a hybrid theory that may address multiple penal goals within a single, coherent account without such a clash. The new criticism of incoherence

in the Model Penal Code is that it lacks coherence because it does not provide a sufficiently satisfactory justificatory framework that may account for why *these* penal goals and how they are to fit together. So while the old objection ultimately misses its mark, it may be reconsidered from a different perspective which better addresses the problem at the core of the Model Penal Code.

50 See Garland, *Punishment and Modern Society*, 47.

51 See ibid. 58.

52 See Pierce O'Donnell, Michael J. Churgin, and Dennis E. Curtis, *Toward a Just and Effective Sentencing System* (New York: Praeger, 1977): 109.

53 See Robinson, *Distributive Principles of Criminal Law*, 236–7n414.

54 This view of 'negative retributivism' might also be understood as 'limiting retributivism'. See Robinson, *Distributive Principles of Criminal Law*, 240–2. Robinson proposes a view of empirical desert whereby punishment is distributed to those possessing blameworthiness as determined by 'the shared intuitions of justice of the community'. Punishment aspires to 'more effectively control crime' and set about ensuring crime reduction. Robinson admits that 'the greatest weakness of the proposal may be its failure to solve the problem of community blindness to injustice'. This is because he offers guidelines that direct us to reduce crime, but without a view about why we should reduce crime. He does not acknowledge that the justice of punishment is inextricably linked with the justice of the corresponding crime. If this link were recognized and accounted for, then this problem of blindness to injustice might be better overcome. See ibid. 248–9, 254.

55 Nor is the unified theory another name for restorative justice for reasons offered previously. The unified theory addresses more penal goals than this in a theory we might call *punitive restoration*.

56 For example, see Christopher Heath Wellman, 'The Rights Forfeiture Theory of Punishment', *Ethics* 122 (2012): 371–93.

57 Garland, *Punishment and Modern Society*, 17.

58 Ibid. 284.

59 Possible exceptions might include murder and treason.

60 See Aristotle, *Nicomachean Ethics*, in *The Complete Works*, vol. ii, ed. Jonathan Barnes (Princeton: Princeton University Press, 1984): 1730 [1094b22–23]: 'it is the mark of an educated [person] to look for precision in each class of things just so far as the nature of the subject admits'.

61 Hegel, *Elements of the Philosophy of Right*, §218 Remark.

62 Ibid. §218 Addition, Remark.

63 Alan Travis and Simon Rogers, 'Revealed: The Full Picture of Riot Sentences', *The Guardian* (19 August 2011): 1–2.

64 For example, see Beccaria, *Of Crimes and Punishments*, 18.

65 See Eric J. Widahl, Brett Garland, Scott E. Culhane, and William P. McCarty, 'Utilizing Behavioral Interventions to Improve Supervision Outcomes in Community-Based Corrections', *Criminal Justice and Behavior* 38 (2011): 386–405.

66 The idea of stakeholding has a history that includes British Prime Minister Tony Blair and the idea of the stakeholder economy. See Bruce Ackerman, 'Why Stakeholding?', *Politics and Society* 32 (2004): 41–60; Will Hutton, *The Stakeholding Society: Writings on Politics and Economics* (Cambridge: Polity, 1998); John Kaler, 'Morality and Strategy in Stakeholder Identification', *Journal of Business Ethics* 39 (2002): 91–9; John Kaler, 'Differentiating Stakeholder Theories', *Journal of Business Ethics* 46 (2003): 71–83; John Plender, *A Stake in the Future: The Stakeholding Solution* (London: Nicholas Brealey, 1997); Rajiv Prabhaker, 'Whatever Happened to Stakeholding?', *Public Administration* 82 (2004): 567–84; and Stuart White, 'The Citizen's Stake and Paternalism',

240 *Notes*

Politics and Society 32 (2004): 61–78. I have noted previously that my idea of the stakeholder society differs significantly from Ackerman and Alstott, *The Stakeholder Society*. A key difference is that past conceptions of stakeholding have focused almost exclusively on economic considerations, such as business ethics and corporate governance. The idea of the stakeholder society presented here is focused on political and legal justice.

67 On criminal profiling and forensic psychology, see Peter Ainsworth, *Offender Profiling and Crime Analysis* (Portland: Willan, 2001).

68 Hegel, *Elements of the Philosophy of Right*, §244, Addition (modified translation).

69 See ibid. §245. Recent research supports Hegel's position. See Paul K. Piff, Daniel M. Stancato, Stephane Cote, Rodolfo Mendoza-Denton, and Dacher Keltner, 'High Social Class Predicts Increased Unethical Behavior', *Proceedings of the National Academy of Sciences* 109 (2012): 4086–91.

70 See Green, 'Will, Not Force, is the Basis of the State' in *Lectures on the Principles of Political Obligation*, §§113–36.

71 For more on Hegel's proposed solutions to this problem, see Michael O. Hardimon, *Hegel's Social Philosophy: The Project of Reconciliation* (Cambridge: Cambridge University Press, 1994).

72 See Thom Brooks, 'Reciprocity as Mutual Recognition', *The Good Society* 21 (2012): 21–35.

73 Rawls, *Justice as Fairness*, 139. See Thom Brooks (ed.), *Rawls and Law* (Aldershot: Ashgate, 2012).

74 On legal realism, see William M. Fischer III, Morton J. Horwitz, and Thomas A. Reid (eds), *American Legal Realism* (Oxford: Oxford University Press, 1993) and Brian Leiter, *Naturalizing Jurisprudence: Essays on American Legal Realism and Naturalism in Legal Philosophy* (Oxford: Oxford University Press, 2007). The unified theory of punishment is consistent with legal realism, but not exclusively.

75 Citizens become more likely to engage in crime where they feel subjectively alienated from their community. For example, see Catherine E. Ross and John Mirowsky, 'Neighborhood Disorder, Subjective Alienation, and Distress', *Journal of Health and Social Behavior* 50 (2009): 49–64 and S. Saegert and G. Winkel, 'Crime, Social Capital, and Community Participation', *American Journal of Community Psychology* 34 (2004): 219–33.

76 For a recent example, see the Riots Communities and Victims Panel, *After the Riots: The Final Report of the Riots Communities and Victims Panel* (London: Riots Communities and Victims Panel, 2012): 6, 9, 21, 25, 31–2, 74, 80–1, 115, 126, 141.

77 See Robinson, *Distributive Principles of Criminal Law*, 260.

78 For example, see Edward Latessa, 'Why Work is Important, and How to Improve the Effectiveness of Correctional Reentry Programs that Target Employment', *Criminology and Public Policy* 11 (2012): 87–91 and Dora Schriro, 'Good Science, Good Sense: Making Meaningful Change Happen – A Practitioner's Guide', *Criminology and Public Policy* 11 (2012): 101–10.

79 Many argue for more integrated post-release programmes, but most offenders will not be imprisoned yet have a significant impact on crime. This requires greater attention to post-conviction and not only post-release. See Sophie R. Dickson, Devon L. Polaschek, and Allanah R. Casey, 'Can the Quality of High-Risk Violent Prisoners' Release Plans Predict Recidivism Following Intensive Rehabilitation? A Comparison with Risk Assessment Instruments', *Psychology, Crime, and Law* (2012) (DOI: 10.1080/1068316X.2011.640634) and Devon L. Polaschek, 'High-Intensity Rehabilitation for Violent Offenders in New Zealand: Reconviction Outcomes for High- and Medium-Risk Prisoners', *Journal of Interpersonal Violence* 26 (2011): 664–82.

80 See New York State Department of Corrections and Community Supervision, 'Who is Eligible for a Certificate of Relief?' (https://www.parole.ny.gov/certrelief. html). Interestingly, the Certificate of Relief and Certificate of Good Conduct are both designed *explicitly* with a view to 'the restoration of rights'. See New York State Department of Corrections and Community Supervision, 'Restoration of Rights' (https://www.parole.ny.gov/program_restoration.html).

81 Recognition as a stakeholder requires that persons believe themselves to have a stake in society. Poverty and deep inequality may present substantial obstacles for some to have this belief. See Richard Wilkinson and Kate Pickett, *The Spirit Level: Why Equality is Better for Everyone,* rev. ed. (London: Penguin, 2010).

82 For example, other theories of punishment, such as rehabilitation and restorative justice, may also accept the idea of a stakeholder society.

83 See Seth, *A Study of Ethical Principles,* 308–9.

84 It is worth reflecting on the implications that would follow if we accepted alternative penal theories. Each appears to run into significant problems addressing some substantive area of criminal law. For example, many retributivists run into problems with trying to account for strict liability or the criminalization of illegal but not immoral acts or omissions. One merit of the unified theory of punishment is that it avoids these problems while remaining committed to significant reforms of our political and legal institutions. The unified theory does not accept the world as we find it, but it does make best sense of it from a novel and critical perspective. We do not accept the world as we find it, but first bring an improved understanding to better grasp how our world may be better shaped. While they may be principled, theories that are substantially too divorced from practice may run the risk of becoming impractical and unrealistic for the price of conceptual purity.

[15]

Stakeholder Sentencing *

Thom Brooks

Introduction

Recent years have witnessed increasing interest in how to provide new avenues for incorporating a greater public voice in sentencing (see Roberts and Hough 2005; Ryberg 2010). This development is the product of a widely perceived growing crisis concerning the lack of public confidence in sentencing decisions. One important factor is negative media headlines that draw attention to cases that contribute to feeding a culture of sentencing disapproval by the public where punishments are believed to be undeservedly lenient. A second factor is the recognition that victims should have greater involvement in the criminal justice system, including sentencing decisions. But how might we improve public confidence and provide a greater voice for victims without sacrificing criminal justice in favour of mob rule?

These developments concerning the relation of public opinion and punishment raise several fundamental concerns. How much voice, if any, should the public have regarding sentencing decisions? Which institutional frameworks should be constructed to better incorporate public opinion without betraying our support for important penal principles and support for justice?

This chapter accepts the need to improve public confidence about sentencing through improving avenues for the public to posses a greater and better informed voice about sentencing decisions within clear parameters of justice. I will defend the idea of *stakeholder sentencing*: those who have a stake in penal outcomes should determine how they are decided. This idea supports an extension of restorative justice I will call *punitive restoration* where the achievement of restoration may include a more punitive element, including imprisonment. My argument is that the idea of stakeholder sentencing offers a compelling view about public opinion might be better incorporated into sentencing that promotes a coherent and unified account of how punishment might pursue multiple penal goals, including improving public confidence in sentencing.

I. The Problem of the Public

A powerful argument against greater incorporation of public opinion in sentencing decisions is that a larger public voice would contribute to disproportionate punishments. Justice is best served through ensuring punishments are proportionate and not by tailoring outcomes to those more favoured by the public.

---

* Forthcoming in Julian V. Roberts and Jesper Ryberg (eds), *Popular Punishment: On the Normative Significance of Public Opinion for Penal Theory* (Oxford University Press, 2014).

The idea that the public might be more likely to endorse disproportionate punishments, especially overly severe sanctions, is understood to be a compelling reason why the criminal law has endorsed victim displacement. The concern is that punishments would become too harsh and injustices practised if the victims determined the appropriate punishments for their offenders. This runs together separate issues that may bear on how we determine sentencing: the first is the voice of victims and the second is the input by the general public. If the general public should be able to have some input on sentencing, then it is often submitted that victims in particular should have a voice rather than remain silent (O'Hara 2005).

Victims were traditionally displaced from decisions about sentencing in order to best promote justice through a better guarantee of consistency and proportionality:

> we seem to have lost sight of the origins of the criminal law as a response to the activities of *victims*, together with their families, associates and supporters. The blood feud, the vendetta, the duel, the revenge, the lynching: for the elimination of these modes of retaliation, more than anything else, the criminal law as we know it today came into existence (Gardner 1998: 31).[1]

Victim displacement helped end the private pursuit of justice against offenders by private citizens and promote the rule of law. We should not serve as judges in cases where we have an interest in the outcome, for John Locke, because of the danger that victims will be 'partial to themselves and their friends' at the expense of others (2004: 275). Decisions should be impartial to secure justice. This may be best guaranteed by ensuring that those with a special interest in sentencing decisions should not possess much influence over how these decisions are made.

The concern that a greater public voice would contribute to overly severe sanctions is thought to receive support from populist proposals, such as California's so-called 'Three Strikes and You're Out' law where offenders convicted of a third strike-eligible crime face a minimum 25 years in prison (Cullen et all, 2000; Zemring, et al 2001). These proposals have proven counterproductive from the perspective of effective criminal justice policy. Studies have concluded that California has benefited from at best a negligible deterrent effect of 2 per cent or less alongside an explosion in the prison population and associated costs.[2] If this is the kind of criminal justice policy the public most wants, then it may lead to a far more expensive system for little, if any, effect on crime reduction and improved public safety.

But must a greater public voice result only in support for overly harsh sentencing? It is not inconceivable to imagine popular celebrities commanding wide support for a more lenient sentence or perhaps a pardon. The core issue is not that the public might support more punitive sentences, but that sentencing decisions may become more arbitrary and less uniform where similar cases may be treated too differently and, thus, unfairly. The claim that the public are more likely to endorse disproportionate punishments is a statement about the failure of the public to properly account for proportionality more generally. This may be explained by the fact that the public may often have an inaccurate, perhaps even irrational, fear about crime and likely future victimhood (Cook and Lane 2009; Hutton 2005; Lai et al, 2012; Roberts et al 2003). The public is also often mistaken about the potential benefits of more punitive penal policies (Williams 2012). If the public has inaccurate or incomplete

---

[1]   See Doak (2005) and for criticisms see Edwards (2002).
[2]   See Durlauf and Nagin 2011: 28 and also *Brown v. Plata*, 563 U.S. (2011).

information about relevant factors, then it cannot be expected to arrive at any satisfactory judgement in sentencing matters. And yet criminal justice must command public confidence if it is to command satisfactory legitimacy and be effective. Otherwise, the public might turn to 'take the law into their own hands' and undermine the rule of law.

The *problem of the public* is that we must secure public confidence despite the fact that the public possesses deep epistemic problems. A greater public voice might only secure higher confidence at the cost of abandoning evidence-based sentencing policy on how crime reduction and other penal goals might be achieved. How might we achieve public confidence without falling into this trap?

I believe that this trap may be avoided. We should first recognise that the issue is not whether public opinion matters, but rather how much it should matter. This is because the idea that the public should have a voice in sentencing is deeply entrenched in its democratic institutions. The public indirectly exercises its voice on the criminal law through electing political leaders that help shape the future contours of the criminal law and the criminal justice system more generally.[3] The public has a more direct voice as lay magistrates or juries. Many countries have long established practices where the public may participate in sentencing decisions. One example is the use of lay magistrates in the United Kingdom to determine the punishment of less serious criminal offences (Darbyshire 2002, Grove 2003, Roberts et al 2012). Several Continental jurisdictions allow for the sentencing of more serious offences to be determined by lay magistrates sitting alongside professional judges. Additionally, the use of civilian juries to determine monetary awards and offender punishment after a conviction is secured is well established in many jurisdictions as well (Brooks 2004a, 2004b, 2009). Juries are often used in trials concerning more serious offences. Juries in the United States are also entrusted with determining sentences in capital trials, including whether a convicted offender should be executed.[4] Furthermore, judges are increasingly permitted to consider victim impact statements in determining penal outcomes. These statements are presented in court and detail how a crime has affected victims and their relations. Victim impact statements have had an awkward reception by the courts where the impact on victims may be relevant in sentencing, but not normally victim opinions about sentence preferences (Brooks 2012a: 72–3).[5]

These examples confirm that the idea that the public should have a voice about sentencing is widely entrenched through democratic institutions. This fact does not render the idea uncontroversial. The issue is not whether public opinion should be less, but rather whether it

---

[3]   This view supports the observation by Joseph Schumpeter that democracy is not rule by the people, but rather rule by politicians elected by the citizenry (1942: 284–5).

[4]   See *Ring v. Arizona* (2002), 536 U.S. 584, 122 S.Ct. 2428.

[5]   There are exceptions for some US states where victims are permitted to offer sentencing recommendations. On victim rights and US states, see Twist (2003) citing Ala. Const. amend. 557; Alaska Const. art. I, Sec. 24; Ariz. Const. art. II, 2.1; Cal. Const. art. I, 12, 28; Colo. Const. art. II, 16a; Conn. Const. art. I, 8(b); Fla. Const. art. I., 16(b); Idaho Const. art. I, 22; Ill. Const. art. I, 8.1; Ind. Const. art. I, 13(b); Kan. Const. art. 15, 15; La. Const. art. 1, 25; Md. Decl. Of Rights art. 47; Mich. Const. art. I, 24; Miss. Const. art. 3, 26A; Mo. Const. art. I, 32; Mont. Const. art. II, sec. 28; Neb. Const. art. I, 28; Nev. Const. art. I, 8; N.J. Const. art. I, 22; New Mex. Const. art. 2, 24; N.C. Const. art. I, 37; Ohio Const. art. I, 10a; Okla. Const. Art. II, 34; Or. Const. art. I, sec. 42; R.I. Const. art. I, 23; S.C. Const. art. I, sect. 24; Tenn. Const. art. I, 35; Tex. Const. art. I, 30; Utah Const. art. I, 28; Va. Const. art. I, 8-A; Wash. Const. art. 2, 33; and Wis. Const. art. I, 9m.

should be more. It is widely held that public confidence in the criminal justice system is an important source of democratic legitimacy (Bennett 2013). This does not require that every outcome receives popular approval, but rather that the overall system has satisfactory public support. This is because citizens are governed by the rule of law rather than the tyranny of the majority. So the lack of public confidence may represent a problem of legitimacy concerning sentencing outcomes.

While there is no argument for *reducing* the public voice, it is questionable whether it could be less than it is. Relatively few cases ever proceed to trial, perhaps no more than 5–7% (Brooks 2004a: 201). Fewer receive decisions by juries on verdicts. Some populist policies, such as California's 'Three Strikes' law, have become enacted due to popular support. However, it remains unclear how close the link is between public favour and penal policy outcomes. The public may favour more punitive sanctions, but it also supports crime reduction which may be undermined by increasing penal severity. This gap between public favour and public expectation is a problem for politicians trying to win both public support and crime reduction.[6]

Consider attempts to address this gap in the United Kingdom. The British government has planned to implement greater usage of community sentences and restorative justice with tough sounding rhetoric about 'breaking' reoffending cycles and community 'pay back' in an effort designed primarily to generate significant savings as alternatives to hard treatment and its much higher costs (Ministry of Justice 2010, 2012a). These plans are correct to claim public support for criminal justice measures that are effective at crime reduction, but overlook the lack of public support for measures leading to reduced punitiveness (Dawes et al, 2011. These plans are an example where securing public confidence has importance, but it does not drive policy change. This case illustrates how the indirect expression of public opinion on sentencing matters through democratic institutions does not confirm a strong link. So perhaps a reason why there is little argument for *reducing* the public voice in sentencing matters is because the public exercises relatively modest impact.

It does not follow that the public voice should be *increased* to improve public confidence and democratic legitimacy (Thomsen 2013). The most powerful criticism is that further inclusion of public opinion may undermine just punishment. The problem is that public disapproval about sentencing decisions is known to decrease where the public has better information (Roberts et al 2012). One approach to improve public confidence is to increase public knowledge: the problem is not how criminal justice is conducted, but how little the public understands it. We require improved public education about sentencing to overcome the present crisis of low public confidence. So judges should not tailor sentencing decisions to better cohere with public opinion, but the public should be better educated about how these decisions are made in order for the public to support judges and not *vice versa* (De Keijser 2013). So the solution to the problem of the lack of public confidence in sentencing decisions might be found in improved public knowledge. Our task might be to better shape public opinion to support current sentencing decisions rather than to create a larger space for the public voice. Improving public confidence need not require us to increase the influence of

---

6   While some argue that victim impact statements *might* influence juries to support harsher sentences (Myers et al, 2013), there is convincing evidence that sentencing *does not* become more punitive with victim impact statements (Roberts 2009).

public opinion.[7] If successful, this approach might secure greater public confidence without sacrificing consistency and proportionality.

II. In Defence of Public Opinion

Increasing the impact of public opinion on sentencing outcomes faces several important challenges. The first problem is that the public lacks satisfactory information to form a justifiable judgement. The greater influence of public opinion may open the door to disproportionate punishments based upon inaccurate or incomplete relevant knowledge. A second problem is that sentencing decisions might become more arbitrary. Like cases may not be treated similarly if outcomes were less under the control of professional judges and trained lay magistrates. The third problem is that the public may be more likely to support greater sentence severity which may undermine penal goals, such as proportionality, improving crime reduction and offender rehabilitation. Public confidence is important in order to secure legitimacy, but increasing the impact of public opinion on sentencing outcomes presents us with more problems than prospects.

Overcoming these three problems requires institutional reforms where a greater public voice is exercised within clearly set parameters ensuring satisfactory consistency across similar cases. It would also entail the public gaining opportunities to acquire relevant knowledge to better inform their decisions, or what we might call the creation of an 'ontologically thick public opinion' (Dzur 2013). How to avoid arbitrariness while getting the criminal law to better track public opinion?

Restorative justice helps us identify the way forward (Braithwaite 2002, Brooks 2012a: 64–85). Restorative justice is an approach that offers an alternative to the criminal trial. Trials are adversarial and combative. In contrast, restorative justice aspires to create mutual understanding and reconciliation between offenders, their victims and the wider community. Criminal trials take place in courtrooms, but restorative justice is practised through a mediated conference. While trials are thought to produce winners and losers, restorative justice seeks to promote healing and a 'restoration' of damaged relationships.

The restorative justice conference often takes the form of either a meeting between the victim and offender or in some cases inclusive of victims' families and community representatives. Both settings are mediated by a trained facilitator operating under a professional body, such as the Restorative Justice Council. Offenders retain access to legal representation, but must admit their guilt prior to participating in a conference and offenders are expected to speak for themselves. The conference is designed to create a structured dialogue aimed at improving understanding. A standard scenario is that the facilitator begins by clarifying the meeting parameters. The victim next explains the impact a crime has inflicted on her. The offender then accounts for his crimes. This usually includes an apology to the victim. Offenders are believed to benefit from a better understanding about how their crimes have impacted their

---

[7] It is controversial whether or not popular decision-making is likely to lead to unsatisfactory public policy outcomes. For a powerful counterargument, see Estlund (2008). Furthermore, the idea that citizens should devote greater efforts to become better educated about criminal justice matters in order to improve public confidence may rest on an idealistic view about civic participation unlikely to be achieved (Hibbing and Theiss-Morse 2002).

victims and the wider community. Victims are believed to benefit by hearing the offender apologize for his crimes in person (and not through legal counsel), gaining greater clarity about the offender and his reasons for offending and having a voice on the post-conference contract the offender is expected to accept.

Restorative justice is an example about how the problem of the public may be overcome. First, there are clearly set parameters for restorative conferences that help ensure consistency (Ormerod 2012, Restorative Justice Council 2011a). Conferences are facilitated by trained mediators ensuring a structured dialogue where like cases are treated similarly. Restorative conferences have the advantage of greater flexibility over the range of penal options to best fit the specific needs of offenders. Conference participants agree contracts in about 98 per cent of cases (Shapland et al, 2006, Shapland et al, 2007: 27). Standard outcomes include requirements that offenders attend treatment to overcome substance abuse or problems with anger management, training to improve employability and life skills, and participation in community services. These are each believed to promote the 'restoration' of an offender's public status as an equal citizen.[8] If offenders fail to satisfy the terms of their contract, then a more burdensome contract may be offered or the offender can face a possible trial and a potential criminal record.

Secondly, members of the public that participate in restorative conferences are able to acquire relevant knowledge to help inform their decisions about contractual outcomes. Outcome decisions might benefit from operating with a more robust view about specific offences within the terms of the personal and wider 'social context', including a more robust account of desert (Roberts 2013). Desert is often understood within the framework of legal moralism: punishment is justified where offenders are culpable for moral wrongdoing. The more wrong the crime, the greater the deserved punishment. This understanding about desert and morality has received much criticism for its potential arbitrariness and potential incompatibility with the criminal law (Brooks 2012a: 20–26). Desert enjoys central importance for most, if not all, sentencing guidelines. We require a more compelling account that overcomes these problems. One alternative is 'empirical desert', an idea championed by Paul Robinson that identifies 'the community's intuitions of justice' discovered through 'empirical research into those factors that drive people's assessment of blameworthiness' (2008: 149).[9]

Restorative justice is able to provide an account consistent with empirical desert. Conference participants work together to clarify shared intuitions about desert concerning a specific offender. The structured setting of a restorative conference helps avoid the problem of relying on any one contested moral view about an offender might deserve in his restorative contract. Conference participants are also able to avoid the influence of media manipulation concerning relevant facts through direct engagement with the offender.

Restorative justice indicates how the problem of the public may be overcome. The first problem is that the public lacks satisfactory information to form a justifiably informed judgement. This is overcome through the constructive dialogue designed to generate improved understanding between victim, offender and the community. This avoids the concern that outcomes might be based on inaccurate or incomplete relevant knowledge. The

---

[8]   See Ashworth 2002 and Brooks 2012a: chapter 4 for doubts about whether restorative justice achieves its aims.

[9]   See Robinson and Darley1997, 2007; Robinson, et al 2010 and Robinson 2013.

second problem is that sentencing decisions would become more arbitrary if the public voice held greater weight. This problem is overcome through the structured conference setting facilitated by a trained mediator where contracts for the offender are tailored to his particular circumstances. The third problem is the worry that the public, if granted a greater say on outcomes, are more likely to support greater sentence severity that may threaten other penal goals. Instead, this has not been the case with most available studies about restorative justice in practice (Braithwaite 2002; Doak and O'Mahoney 2006).

Restorative justice is an approach that promotes improved public confidence while reducing offending and at reduced costs. Both victims and offenders report high satisfaction with participation in restorative conferences (Sherman, et al 2008: 25–6). It might be likely that further use of restorative conferences will contribute to continued satisfaction by future participants. Restorative justice has also been found to contribute to 25 per cent less reoffending than alternatives while saving £9 for every £1 spent (Shapland, et al 2008, Restorative Justice Council 2011b).[10] If we want to improve public confidence without sacrificing crime reduction efforts and other penal goals, then restorative justice is an approach we must take seriously.[11] Restorative justice indicates how public opinion may be brought back into criminal justice and overcome the problem of the public.

III. Sentencing by Stakeholders

Restorative justice is hamstrung by several limitations. Restorative justice can overcome these challenges without sacrificing its attractiveness through recommended revisions that I will indicate in this section.

The first problem concerns a fundamental question about 'restoration'. Restorative justice aims at the restoration of offenders, victims and the community. The idea is that criminal offending has damaged the relationship between them. We require a process that may help restore the shared bonds of association through constructive dialogue that will yield a mutually satisfactory outcome for the relevant parties. The problem is identifying the relevant community members. Some argue, such as Andrew Ashworth, that 'the concept of restoring the community remains shrouded in mystery, as indeed does the identification of the relevant "community"' (2010: 94).[12] He says elsewhere:

> If the broad aim is to restore the 'communities affected by the crime', as well as the victim and the victim's family, this will usually mean a geographical community; but where an offence targets a victim because of race, religion, sexual orientation, etc., that will point to a different community that needs to be restored (Ashworth 2002: 583).

So the first problem is identifying the community members to be restored through restorative justice.

A second problem with restorative justice concerns conference membership. Restorative justice aims to restore the damaged relationship between victim, offender and the community.

---

[10] See Latimer, Dowden and Muise (2005) on empirical studies confirming the effectiveness of restorative justice practices in reducing reoffending.

[11] See National Offender Management Service (2012).

[12] See Edwards (2006).

Let us suppose each party is known so we do not face the first problem of not knowing the persons to be restored. There remains problems where one or more parties are unable or unwilling to participate in a restorative conference. In practice, these conferences may proceed without the victim where he or she chooses not to attend. This is because, in part, restorative justice requires the active consent of participants: none should be coerced as this would undermine restoration. Conferences may proceed for the additional reason that some positive conclusion may result nonetheless. Perhaps the relation between victim and offender remains damaged, but there may be benefits still where offenders acknowledge their guilt and seek restoration with the community. The problem of who is a relevant member of 'the community' will remain. A related concern is in cases where the victim is murdered and unable to participate. Conference membership has central importance as these are the parties that need to be engaged for restoration to be achieved. It is a serious problem where we cannot identify whose participation is required.

The third problem is limited applicability. Most proponents of restorative justice defend the approach as alternative to imprisonment. Restorative justice as an approach to punishment seeks to engage participants outside the courtroom through constructive dialogue and mutual understanding that will lead to outcomes which avoid hard treatment.[13] The rejection of imprisonment by restorative justice restricts its applicability. The concern is that the public may not support alternatives to imprisonment, such as the use of restorative conferences, for offenders guilty of the more serious violent crimes (Kahan 1996, Khan 2011, Spiranovic, et al 2011). The practice of restorative justice has been generally limited to cases involving youth offenders and minor offences. Its limited applicability raises further questions about whether it can offer a theory of punishment because it may only apply to some, but not all or even most, cases.

These three limitations can be addressed together. The first challenge concerns the problem of identifying the community to be restored. I believe that we should be guided by an important principle of stakeholding: *that those who have a stake in penal outcomes should have a say in decisions about them.* Stakeholding is an idea that originates in the literature about business ethics and corporate governance (Hutton 1998; Plender 1997; Prabhaker 2004). It is meant to offer a model that improves transparency and accountability through shared responsibility and communicative dialogue. Stakeholding has direct relevance for sentencing policy. Stakeholders are those individuals with a stake in penal outcomes. These persons will include victims, if any, their support networks and local community. Each marks himself or herself out as a potential stakeholder in virtue of his or her relative stake. Stakeholders will also include offenders because they, too, have a stake in penal outcomes.

The restorative justice conference setting is a useful model for working out how stakeholding might take shape. Conference proceedings aim to achieve restoration though dialogue and the offender satisfying contractual conditions that participants agree. The idea is that the expression of apology by the offender, improved mutual understanding and completion of specified terms yields 'restoration', but we might better understand this process as promoting

---

[13]   Restorative justice is practised in different ways. My focus is on its use as a view about punishment and not its use post-conviction. See Miller (2011) for an insightful account about restorative justice post-conviction and McGlynn (2012) for an approach more closely related to my defence of punitive restoration below.

stakeholding. Some commentators refer to participants as 'stakeholders' and there is overlap between my account of stakeholder sentencing and standard views about restorative justice (Braithwaite 2002: 11, 50, 55). Nonetheless, the differences are crucial and reveal how restorative justice might be transformed into a more compelling account of punishment that better incorporates public opinion.

A focus on stakeholding clarifies who should be included in conference proceedings: those that have a stake in penal outcomes. This will involve those directly affected, such as the victim and her support network.[14] Stakeholders bear the costs and are most affected by penal outcomes. Together, they should determine what these outcomes are within prescribed limits acceptable to the general public.

It is crucial to highlight that this focus on stakeholder decision-making does not exclude the general public. So while it is clear that members of the public may be stakeholders as victims and offenders, then general public is also a stakeholder. Stakeholding is not about the expression of the general public's judgement nor is this often possible if thought desirable (Brooks 2012a: 10–22; Hart 1968: 161). Stakeholding is instead about giving special attention to those who have a greater stake in outcomes. The general public constrains the actions of stakeholder sentencing by setting the parameters for permissible penal procedures and outcomes. So conferences are mediated by a trained facilitator to ensure procedures are sufficiently robust and offenders are entitled to legal representation as a further guarantee.[15] Furthermore, the general public might also participate as local community members or as members of a victim's support network. Neither the victim, her family or support network, the offender or others have the only say on penal outcomes. Neither does the general public. Stakeholding is about bring these different interests together in a structured way to determine penal outcomes.

If the general public is a relevant stakeholder, then it might be argued that it should have a say. The problem is that this might justify mob rule whereby penal outcomes are determined by popular vote. But not all stakeholders are similarly situated and some have a greater stake than others. For example, victims and those directly affected by crimes and their outcomes will have a larger stake and, thus, should be included in stakeholder conferences. The general public should also be included, but principally through representation, such as a few persons. So the stakeholder conference may somewhat resemble a jury in membership size. It will remain essential that its size is relatively small to better facilitate constructive dialogue and to keep focussed on the needs of those with the largest stakes.[16] This position broadly supports

---

[14]   Other relevant stakeholders will include the offender and any support network. In practice, restorative conferences often include friends and family of the victim and of the offender, respectively, in 73% and 78% of cases examined in one study (Shapland, et al 2007: 20). Interestingly, the same study found that parents were far more likely to attend restorative conferences (50% of offenders and 23% of victims) than partners (3% of offenders and 5% of victims) (Shapland, et al 2007: 20).

[15]   The involvement of legal representation might suggest the need for a judge to serve as an adjudicator. This is not current practice, but my defence of punitive restoration – administered by a trained facilitator – is not inconsistent with the facilitator's role being served by a legal professional.

[16]   The general public has a stake in outcomes and so should exercise a voice. The model advocated here justifies inclusion of persons serving as representatives of the general public perhaps drawn from the local community, a common practice in restorative conferences at present. This permits members of the general public to be included while keeping conference membership to a size that is large enough

the widely used restorative conference model instead of victim-mediation meetings.[17] This is because the latter excludes community representation. The victim may have a larger personal stake than other individuals in penal outcomes, but this does not negate the stake held by the community. Both categories of stakeholders can be accommodated through the restorative justice conference. This model has proven practically workable with the additional benefit that it promotes stakeholding.

The stakeholder model broadens the applicability of the restorative conference model to endorse what I call *punitive restoration*. This is the idea that penal outcomes arising from the conference model need not always exclude imprisonment.[18] While it is clear that incarceration often makes successful crime reduction efforts more difficult, it is also clear that prisons can and should be transformed to improve their disappointing results (Liebling 2006). For example, restorative justice contracts often include an obligation on offenders to engage in developing employability and life skills as well as treatment for any drug and alcohol problems (Brooks 2012a: 66–7, 73–5).[19] There is no reason to accept that these activities could never be successfully delivered within prisons. Perhaps imprisonment should be used sparingly. This is not an argument for never using custodial sentences. It is conceivable and possible that a secure facility, such as a prison, may prove the best environment for some offenders in select cases (Perez and Jennings 2012). Furthermore, prison officers might receive additional training to become Personal Support Officers (Chapman and Smith 2011: 228). These officers have most frequent contact with imprisoned offenders and the trust that builds over time could be put to more effective use where officers provided improved pastoral support. There are then several ways in which the prison might be restructured in ways that would better enable it to foster a more conducive environment for the rehabilitation and restoration offenders than found in most prisons today. These reforms may require additional resources, but they may prove cost-effective over time in the likely, although no means certain, result of improved crime reduction.

The idea that we should make more effective use of prisons does not ignore evidence that prisons often undermine offender rehabilitation. Short-term imprisonment is often linked with high recidivism rates. This is a significant problem because most offenders receive sentences of less than 12 months and about 60% reoffend within weeks of their release.[20] There is no confirmed link between reductions in recidivisms and increased penal tariffs. In the words of Prime Minister's Strategy Unit: 'there is no convincing evidence that further increases in the use of custody would significantly reduce crime' (Carter 2003: 15; see Langan and Levin 2002: 2). The prison has been considered by some to be 'criminogenic' because it may

---

to include persons with largest stakes and representative membership of the general public and small enough in size to best facilitate constructive dialogue.

[17]   For a brief overview of different restorative justice models, see Restorative Justice Council, 'RJ Models: Models of Restorative Justice' (website: http://www.restorativejustice.org.uk/resource/rj_models/).

[18]   Punitive restoration is a revision of restorative justice models that does not rule out the permissibility of incarceration under specified conditions where restoration would not be undermined. Punitive restoration may also be commensurate with further revisions of the mechanics of restorative justice, including improving the therapeutic potential of restorative justice (see Doak 2011).

[19]   See Towl (2006) on prison-based programmes designed to better tackle drug and alcohol abuse.

[20]   See Ministry of Justice (website: http://open.justice.gov.uk/home/).

contribute to more likely criminal activity post-release than if an offender had received an alternative punishment (Tonry 2011: 138, 140–41).

The lack of reformatory efforts for those serving less than 12 months sentences is a major contributing factor to the high recidivism.[21] Brief intensive interventions have been employed to address problems associated with drug use and offenders were found to benefit from 'significant gains in knowledge, attitudes, and psychosocial functioning' (Joe et al 2012). These sessions were corrections-based treatment of moderate (30 outpatient group sessions three days per week) or high intensity (six month residential treatment) has been found to yield cost savings of 1.8 to 5.7 the cost of their implementation (Daley et al 2004). Such policies indicate that prisons may be reformed to better support offender rehabilitation and improve post-release crime reduction efforts without sacrificing cost-effectiveness.

These reforms toward punitive restoration are important. This is because it is possible that the punishment of offenders guilty of more serious crimes may require more punitive outcomes than currently available to most restorative justice conferences. For example, current practice rejects the permissibility of including the threat or imposition of imprisonment in restorative contracts. In contrast, punitive restoration might find offenders in a position where they might agree to treatment and community service plus a suspended sentence that could be imposed if contractual terms are not satisfied. This option would extend the flexibility of restorative justice to address a greater range of offences in a restorative context and bypass the need for a criminal trial. Stakeholder sentencing can then identify how a restorative model might be transformed and overcome the problem of limited applicability.[22]

This transformation might be objected to on the grounds that imprisonment, even for a few days, is a major curtailment of individual liberty. Such a sanction requires special safeguards that only the courtroom can satisfy. The problem with this objection is that the overwhelming majority of offenders, and as high as 97% in Scotland, never go to trial. Most cases end in plea bargains with a judge or magistrate.[23] If it remains acceptable for more serious crimes to be punished after this process, the stakeholder model should be an attractive alternative. This is because punitive restoration would have a trained facilitator not unlike a lay magistrate conducting criminal proceedings, but with the advantages of victims gaining the satisfaction of an apology from their offender, the promotion of greater mutual understanding among stakeholders and penal outcomes better targeted to address the specific needs of offenders. Perhaps it may be contended that facilitators should receive additional training or that their role is performed by magistrates. We should also expect that, if this extension of restoration justice can continue to earn victim satisfaction, it will build and support public confidence, too (Gromet et al 2012). The stakeholder model of punitive restoration can deliver a more satisfactory outcome for victims, offenders and the wider community than the less transparent proceedings that often lead to plea bargaining.

---

[21] The lack of these efforts is a major contributing factor, but I do not suggest that it is the sole or primary factor for unsatisfactory reoffending rates.

[22] The UK's Ministry of Justice has published recent proposals that aim to further embed restorative justice within the criminal justice system includes the aim for greater usage between conviction and sentencing (2012: 5). Punitive restoration can fulfill this aim and provide a means for determining a greater variety of sentencing outcomes.

[23] See Lippke (2011) for an authoritative critique of plea bargaining and Ashworth and Redmayne (2005: 6–7).

It might be objected that punitive restoration has limited applicability even if it may be applied to far more cases than restorative justice. This is because the public will not permit its use in all cases, such as trials for murder, treason or serious sex offences. There is an increasing amount of work that argues in favour of restorative justice in cases like these (McGlynn 2011; Mills 2003). If punitive restoration improves public confidence in the punishment for most, if not all, crimes, then it represents a compelling alternative demanding greater engagement. The evidence already noted may be indicative, but it represents encouraging support for such policies that appear likely to grow as further studies are performed.

It might be further objected that stakeholder sentencing through punitive restoration would fail to treat like cases alike. The concern is that offenders convicted of similar crimes might receive different penal outcomes. If similar cases have different outcomes, then penal justice may be undermined. This objection can be met because stakeholder sentencing is about determining outcomes that better address the needs of stakeholders. There will be differences between similar cases that the restorative conference setting can discover and better target through the greater flexibility available to it. Alternatives appear more consistent at the high price of their inability to address offender needs, for example, with the outcome flexibility of punitive restoration.

Much of my argument for stakeholder sentencing above is that it is compelling because it is an improvement over alternatives. Stakeholder sentencing is also a more powerful view about the justice of punishment. So this model offers not only a compelling way to better incorporate public opinion into sentencing decisions, but also a more compelling view about justice addressing issues of both theory and practice. Thus, stakeholder sentencing may overcome concerns that misinformed public opinion is driving criminal justice policy (Page and Shapiro 1983). Stakeholder sentencing develops an important revision of restorative justice through the restorative conference model that extends its applicability and flexibility of outcomes in a way that is likely to improve public confidence, reduce reoffending and be cost-effective.

Stakeholder sentencing also represents a compelling view about penal justice. Punishment is often justified through its justifying aim or purpose, such as retribution, deterrence or rehabilitation. Philosophers have long disagreed on which principle of sentencing is best although there is general agreement that hybrid theories aiming to endorse two or more principles often suffer from inconsistency (see Brooks 2012a: 89–100). Stakeholder sentencing is one form that a *unified theory of punishment* might take because it is able to pursue multiple penal goals within a unified and coherent account.[24] For example, desert is satisfied because offenders must accept guilt prior to participation. The penal goals of crime reduction (including the goal of protecting the general public) and enabling offender rehabilitation are

---

[24]   There are several ways such a theory might be constructed, but the one I have favoured is to view crime as a harm to individual rights and punishment as 'a response' to crime with the purpose of the protection and maintenance of rights protected by the criminal law. This model rejects the view that penalties and hard treatment have different justificatory foundations, but rather penal outcomes share a common source of justification: the protection of rights (see Feinberg 1970). The model is then able to address the fact that penal outcomes are often multidimensional and include punitive and financial elements. The idea that those who have a stake in penal outcomes should have a say is consistent with this rights-based framework. See Brooks (2012a: 123–48) for a defence of the unified theory of punishment. See Brooks (2010, 2011a, 2011b, 2011c, 2012b) for further discussions of the unified theory of punishment.

achieved through the restorative conference from the available evidence on restorative justice outcomes. Restoration is secured through the high satisfaction of participants in restorative conferences, including both victims and offenders. Stakeholder sentencing, as a unified theory of punishment, need not prioritize one penal goal over others, but it may facilitate the pursuit of several goals together. It must be emphasized that the pursuit of these goals transpires within an overall restorative framework that helps avoid conflict between principles.

Conclusion

Recent years have seen a growing interest in securing a greater incorporation of public opinion in sentencing decisions. This effort is thought to help produce improved public confidence about penal outcomes. This development has alarmed some because of the fear that a greater role for the public's collective voice will lead to disproportionate and overly harsh punishment. While it has been clear that public confidence in the criminal justice system is important to secure and sustain, it is much less clear how this might be achieved without sacrificing important penal principles and the rule of law.

I have argued that this problem of the public may be addressed through stakeholder sentencing. The central idea is that sentencing decisions should be made collectively by those who have a stake in penal outcomes. This model supports a greater incorporation of public opinion within specified parameters that avoid the concerns flagged by critics. Stakeholder sentencing sheds light on one way that public confidence might be secured without undermining the legitimacy of sentencing decisions. This approach is a revised and expanded account of restorative justice in what I have called punitive restoration.

The ideas of stakeholder sentencing and punitive restoration represent an important model for how we might bring the victim and others with a stake in penal outcomes back into the criminal justice system. Nils Christie rightly says: 'The victim is a particularly heavy loser . . . Not only has he suffered, lost materially or become hurt, physically or otherwise . . . But above all he has lost participation in his own case' (1998: 314). Stakeholder sentencing helps correct this unjust imbalance.

If we wish to incorporate a greater voice for the public without sacrificing judicial standards, then the idea of stakeholder sentencing deserves greater attention.[25]

References

Ashworth, Andrew. 2002. 'Responsibilities, Rights and Restorative Justice', *British Journal of Criminology* 42: 578–95.
Ashworth, Andrew. 2010. *Sentencing and Criminal Justice*, 5th ed. Cambridge: Cambridge University Press.
Ashworth, Andrew and Mike Redmayne. 2005. *The Criminal Process*, 3rd ed. Oxford: Oxford University Press.

---

[25]   This chapter benefited enormously from the comments on earlier drafts by fellow contributors to this book, especially Richard Lippke and Paul Robinson. I am further grateful to Julian Roberts and Jesper Ryberg for additional written comments.

Bennett, Christopher. 2013. 'Public Opinion and Democratic Control of Sentencing Policy' in Julian Roberts and Jesper Ryberg (eds), *Popular Punishment: On the Normative Significance of Public Opinion for Penal Theory*. Oxford: Oxford University Press, forthcoming.

Braithwaite, John. 2002. *Restorative Justice and Response Regulation*. Oxford: Oxford University Press.

Brooks, Thom. 2003. 'T.H. Green's Theory of Punishment', *History of Political Thought* 24: 685–701.

Brooks, Thom. 2004a. 'The Right to Trial by Jury', *Journal of Applied Philosophy* 21: 197–212.

Brooks, Thom. 2004b. 'A Defence of Jury Nullification', *Res Publica* 10: 401–23.

Brooks, Thom, ed. 2009. *The Right to a Fair Trial*. Aldershot: Ashgate.

Brooks, Thom. 2011a. 'Punishment: Political, Not Moral', *New Criminal Law Review* 14: 427–38.

Brooks, Thom. 2011b. 'Is Bradley a Retributivist?' *History of Political Thought* 32: 83–95.

Brooks, Thom. 2011c. 'What Did the British Idealists Ever Do for Us?' in Thom Brooks (ed.), *New Waves in Ethics*. Basingstoke: Palgrave Macmillan, pp. 28–47.

Brooks, Thom. 2012a. *Punishment*. New York: Routledge. Brooks, Thom. 2012b. 'Hegel and the Unified Theory of Punishment' in Thom Brooks (ed.), *Hegel's Philosophy of Right*. Oxford: Blackwell, pp. 103–23.

Brooks, Thom and Martha C. Nussbaum, eds. 2013. *Rawls's Political Liberalism*. New York: Columbia University Press.

Brudner, Alan. 2009. *Punishment and Freedom: A Liberal Theory of Penal Justice*. Oxford: Oxford University Press.

Carter, Patrick. 2003. *Managing Offenders, Reducing Crime: A New Approach*. London: Prime Minister's Strategy Unit.

Chapman, Jenny and Jacqui Smith, 'Cutting Crime and Building Confidence: Empowering Victims and Communities' in Robert Philpott (ed.), *The Purple Book: A Progressive Future for Labour*. London: Biteback, 2011, pp. 215–30.

Christie, Nils. 1998. 'Conflicts as Property' in Andrew von Hirsch and Andrew Ashworth (eds), *Principled Sentencing: Readings on Theory and Policy*. Oxford: Hart, pp. 312–16.

Cook, Carrie L. and Jodi Lane. 2009. 'The Place of Public Fear in Sentencing and Correctional Policy', *Journal of Criminal Justice* 37: 586–95.

Cullen, Francis T., Bonnie S. Fisher and Brandon K. Applegate. 2000. 'Public Opinion about Punishment and Corrections', *Crime and Justice* 27: 1–79.

Daley, M., C. T. Love, D. S. Shepard, C. B. Peterson, K. L. White and F. B. Hall. 2004. 'Cost-Effectiveness of Connecticut's In-Prison Substance Abuse Treatment', *Journal of Offender Rehabilitation* 39: 69–92.

Darbyshire, Penny. 2002. 'Magistrates' in Mike McConville and Geoffrey Wilson (eds), *The Oxford Handbook of the Criminal Justice Process*. Oxford: Oxford University Press, pp. 285–309.

Dawes, William, Paul Harvey, Brian McIntosh, Fay Nunney and Annabelle Phillips. 2011. *Attitudes to Guilty Plea Sentence Reductions*. London: Sentencing Council.

De Keijser, Jan W. 2013. 'The Engagement between Penal Theory and Popular Opinion: Imperative, Impossible or Inappropriate?' in Julian Roberts and Jesper Ryberg (eds), *Popular Punishment: On the Normative Significance of Public Opinion for Penal Theory*. Oxford: Oxford University Press, forthcoming.

Doak, Jonathan. 2005. 'Victims' Rights in Criminal Trials: Prospects for Participation', *Journal of Law and Society* 32: 294–316.

Doak, Jonathan. 2008. *Victims' Rights, Human Rights and Criminal Justice: Reconceiving the Role of Third Parties*. Oxford: Hart.

Doak, Jonathan. 2011. 'Honing the Stone: Refining Restorative Justice as a Vehicle for Emotional Redress', *Contemporary Justice Review* 14: 439–56.

Doak, Jonathan and David O'Mahoney. 2006. 'The Vengeful Victim? Assessing the Attitudes of Victims Participating in Restorative Youth Conferencing', *International Review of Victimology* 13: 157–77.

Durlauf, Steven N. and Daniel S. Nagin. 2011. 'Imprisonment and Crime: Can Both Be Reduced?' *Criminology and Public Policy* 10: 13–54.

Dzur, Albert. 2013. 'Repellant Institutions and the Absentee Public: Grounding Opinion in Responsibility for Punishment' in Julian Roberts and Jesper Ryberg (eds), *Popular Punishment: On the Normative Significance of Public Opinion for Penal Theory*. Oxford: Oxford University Press, forthcoming.

Edwards, Ian. 2002. 'The Place of Victims' Preferences in the Sentencing of "Their" Offenders', *Criminal Law Review* (September): 689–702.

Edwards, Ian. 2006. 'Restorative Justice, Sentencing and the Court of Appeal', *Criminal Law Review*, 110–23.

Ellis, Anthony. 2003. 'A Deterrence Theory of Punishment', *Philosophical Quarterly* 53: 337–51.

Estlund, David M. 2008. *Democratic Authority: A Philosophical Framework*. Princeton: Princeton University Press.

Feinberg, Joel. 1970. 'The Expressive Function of Punishment' in *Doing and Deserving: Essays in the Theory of Responsibility*. Princeton: Princeton University Press, 1970, pp. 95–118.

Gardner, John. 1998. 'Crime: In Proportion and in Perspective' in Andrew Ashworth and Martin Wasik (eds), *Fundamentals of Sentencing Theory: Essays in Honour of Andrew von Hirsch*. Oxford: Clarendon, pp. 31–52.

Gromet, Dena M., Tyler G. Okimoto, Michael Wenzel and John M. Darley. 2012. 'A Victim-Centered Approach to Justice? Victim Satisfaction Effects on Third-Party Punishments', *Law and Human Behavior* 36: 375–89.

Grove, Trevor. 2003. *The Magistrate's Tale: A Front Line Report from a New JP*. London: Bloomsbury.

Hart, H. L. A. 1968. *Punishment and Responsibility: Essays in the Philosophy of Law*. Oxford: Clarendon.

Hibbing, John R. and Elizabeth Theiss-Morse. 2002. *Stealth Democracy: Americans' Beliefs about How Government Should Work*. Cambridge: Cambridge University Press.

Hutton, Neil. 2005. 'Beyond Populist Punitiveness?' *Punishment and Society* 7: 243–58.

Hutton, Will. 1998. *The Stakeholding Society: Writings on Politics and Economics*. Cambridge: Polity.

Joe, George W., Kevin Knight, D. Dwayne Simpson, Patrick M. Flynn, Janis T. Morey, Norma G. Bartholomew, Michele Staton Tindall, William M. Burdon, Elizabeth A. Hall, Steve S. Martin and Daniel J. O'Connell. 2012. 'An Evaluation of Six Brief Interventions That Target Drug-Related Problems in Correctional Populations', *Journal of Offender Rehabilitation* 51: 9–33.

Kahan, Dan M. 1996. 'What Do Alternative Sanctions Mean?' *University of Chicago Law Review* 63: 591–653.

Kant, Immanuel. 1996. *The Metaphysics of Morals*, ed. Mary Gregor. Cambridge: Cambridge University Press.

Khan, Sadiq, ed. 2011. *Punishment and Reform: How Our Justice System Can Help Cut Crime*. London: Fabian Society.

Lai, Yung-Lien, Jihong Zhao, and Dennis R. Longmire. 2012. 'Specific Crime-Fear Linkage: The Effect of Actual Burglary Incidents Reported to the Police on Residents' Fear of Burglary', *Journal of Crime and Justice* 35: 13–34.

Langnan, Patrick A. and David J. Levin. 2002. *Recidivism of Prisoners Released in 1994*. Washington, DC: Bureau of Justice Statistics.

Latimer, Jeff, Craig Dowden and Danielle Muise. 2005. 'The Effectiveness of Restorative Justice Practices: A Meta-Analysis', *Prison Journal* 85: 127–44.

Liebling, Alison. 2006. 'Prisons in Transition', *International Journal of Law and Psychiatry* 29: 422–30.

Lippke, Richard L. 2011. *The Ethics of Plea Bargaining*. Oxford: Oxford University Press. Locke, John. 2004. *Two Treatises of Government*, ed. Peter Laslett. Cambridge: Cambridge University Press.

McGlynn, Clare. 2011. 'Feminism, Rape and the Search for Justice', *Oxford Journal of Legal Studies* 31: 825–42.

Miller, Susan. 2011. *After the Crime: The Power of Restorative Justice Dialogues between Victims and Violent Offenders*. Oxford: Oxford University Press.

Mills, Linda G. 2003. *Insult to Injury: Rethinking Our Responses to Intimate Abuse*. Princeton: Princeton University Press.

Ministry of Justice. 2010. *Breaking the Cycle: Effective Punishment, Rehabilitation and Sentencing of Offenders*. London: Her Majesty's Stationary Office.

Ministry of Justice. 2012a. *Punishment and Reform: Effective Community Sentences*. London: Her Majesty's Stationary Office.

Ministry of Justice. 2012b. *Restorative Justice Action Plan for the Criminal Justice System*. London: Her Majesty's Stationary Office.

Myers, Bryan, Allison Roop, Deorah Kalnen and Andre Kehn. 2013. 'Victim Impact Statements and Crime Heinousness: A Test of the Saturation Hypothesis', *Psychology, Crime and Law* 19: 129–43.

National Offender Management Service. 2012. *Better Outcomes through Victim-Offender Conferencing (Restorative Justice)*. London: NOMS.

O'Hara, Erin Ann. 2005. 'Victim Participation in the Criminal Process', *Journal of Law and Policy* 13: 229–47.

Ormerod, David. 2012. 'Editorial: Getting It Right for Victims and Witnesses', *Criminal Law Review* 5: 317–19.

Page, Benjamin I. and Robert Y. Shapiro. 1983. 'Effects of Public Opinion on Policy', *American Political Science Review* 77: 175–90.

Perez, Deanna M. and Wesley G. Jennings. 2012. 'Treatment Behind Bars: The Effectiveness of Prison-Based Therapy for Sex Offenders', *Journal of Crime and Justice* 35: 435–50.

Plender, John. 1997. *A Stake in the Future: The Stakeholding Solution*. London: Nicholas Brealey.

Prabhaker, Rajiv. 2004. 'Whatever Happened to Stakeholding?' *Public Administration* 82: 567–84.

Rawls, John. 1996. *Political Liberalism*, paper edn. New York: Columbia University Press.

Rawls, John. 2001. *Justice as Fairness: A Restatement*. Cambridge: Harvard University Press.

Restorative Justice Council. 2011a. *Best Practice Guidance for Restorative Practice*. London: Restorative Justice Council.

Restorative Justice Council. 2011b. *What Does the Ministry of Justice RJ Research Tell Us?* London: Restorative Justice Council (available at http://www.restorativejustice.org.uk/assets/_ugc/fetch. php?file=21w6_ministry_of_justice_evaluation_of_restorative_justice.pdf).

Roberts, Julian V. 2013. 'Justifying a Role for Public Opinion in Sentencing Policy and Sentencing Practice' in Julian Roberts and Jesper Ryberg (eds), *Popular Punishment: On the Normative Significance of Public Opinion for Penal Theory*. Oxford: Oxford University Press, forthcoming.

Robert, Julian V. 2009. 'Listening to the Crime Victim: Evaluating Victim Input at Sentencing and Parole', *Crime and Justice* 38: 347–412.

Roberts, Julian V. and Mike Hough. 2005. *Understanding Public Attitudes to Criminal Justice*. Maidenhead: Open University Press.

Roberts, Julian V., Mike Hough, Jonathan Jackson, and Monica M. Gerber. 2012. 'Public Opinion Towards the Lay Magistracy and the Sentencing Council Guidelines', *British Journal of Criminology* 52: 1072–91.

Roberts, Julian V., Loretta J. Stalens, David Indermaur and Mike Hough. 2003. *Penal Populism and Public Opinion: Lessons from Five Countries*. Oxford: Oxford University Press.

Robinson, Paul H. and John M. Darley. 2007. 'The Utility of Desert', *Northwestern University Law Review* 91: 453–99.

Robinson, Paul H. and John M. Darley. 2007. 'Intuitions of Justice: Implications for Criminal Law and Justice Policy', *Southern California Law Review* 81: 1–67.

Robinson, Paul H. 2008. 'Competing Conceptions of Modern Desert: Vengeful, Deontological, and Empirical', *Cambridge Law Journal* 67: 145–75.

Robinson, Paul H., Geoffrey P. Goodwin and Michael Reisig. 2010. 'The Disutility of Injustice', *New York University Law Review* 85: 1940–2033.

Robinson, Paul H. 2013. 'The Proper Role of the Community in Determining Criminal Liability and Punishment' in Julian Roberts and Jesper Ryberg (eds), *Popular Punishment: On the Normative Significance of Public Opinion for Penal Theory*. Oxford: Oxford University Press, forthcoming.

Ryberg, Jesper. 2010. 'Punishment and Public Opinion' in Jesper Ryberg and J. Angelo Corlett (eds), *Punishment and Ethics: New Perspectives*. Basingstoke: Palgrave Macmillan, pp. 149–68.

Schumpeter, Joseph A. 1942. *Capitalism, Socialism and Democracy*. New York: Harper Perennial.

Shapland, Joanna, Anne Atkinson, Helen Atkinson, Becca Chapman, E. Colledge, James Dignan, Marie Howes, Jennifer Johnstone, Gwen Robinson and Angela Sorsby. 2006. *Restorative Justice in Practice: The Second Report from the Evaluation of Three Schemes*. Sheffield: Centre for Criminological Research, University of Sheffield (available at http://www.sheffield.ac.uk/ccr.)

Shapland, Joanna, Anne Atkinson, Helen Atkinson, Becca Chapman, James Dignan, Marie Howes, Jennifer Johnstone, Gwen Robinson and Angela Sorsby. 2007. *Restoratice JusticeL The Views of Victims and Offenders*. London: Ministry of Justice.

Shapland, Joanna, Anne Atkinson, Helen Atkinson, James Dignan, Lucy Edwards, Jeremy Hibbert, Marie Howes, Jennifer Johnstone, Gwen Robinson and Angela Sorsby. 2008. *Does Restorative Justice Affect Reconviction? The Fourth Report from the Evaluation of Three Schemes*. London: Ministry of Justice.

Sherman, Lawrence W., Heather Strang and Dorothy Newbury-Birch. 2008. *Restorative Justice*. London: Youth Justice Board.

Spiranovic, Caroline A., Lynne D. Roberts, David Indermaur, Kate Warner, Karen Gelb and Geraldine Mackenzie. 2011. 'Public Preferences for Sentencing Purposes: What Difference Does Offender Age, Criminal History and Offence Type Make?' *Criminology and Criminal Justice* 12: 289–306.

Thomsen, Frej Klem. 2013. 'Why Should We Care What the Public Thinks? A Critical Assessment of the Claims of Popular Punishment' in Julian Roberts and Jesper Ryberg (eds), *Popular Punishment: On the Normative Significance of Public Opinion for Penal Theory*. Oxford: Oxford University Press, forthcoming.

Tonry, Michael. 2011. 'Less Imprisonment is No Doubt a Good Thing: More Policing is Not', *Criminology and Public Policy* 10: 137–52.

Towl, Graham J. 2006.'Drug-Misuse Intervention Work' in G. J. Towl (ed.), *Psychological Research in Prisons*. Oxford: Blackwell, pp. 116–27.

Twist, Steven J. 2003. *Rights of Crime Victims Constitutional Amendment: Hearing on H. J. Res. 48, Before the Constitution Subcommittee of the Committee on the Judiciary, House of Representatives*, U.S. Congress (30 September 2003) (available at judiciary.house.gov/legacy/twist093003.pdf).

Williams, Monica. 2012. 'Beyond the Retributive Public: Governance and Public Opinion on Penal Policy', *Journal of Crime and Justice* 35: 93–113.

Zemring, Franklin E., Gordon Hawkins and Sam Kamin. 2001. *Punishment and Democracy: Three Strikes and You're Out in California*. Oxford: Oxford University Press.

Part V
Sentencing Alternatives

[16]

SETTING STANDARDS FOR RESTORATIVE JUSTICE

JOHN BRAITHWAITE*

Three types of restorative justice standards are articulated: limiting, maximizing, and enabling standards. They are developed as multidimensional criteria for evaluating restorative justice programmes. A way of summarizing the long list of standards is that they define ways of securing the republican freedom (dominion) of citizens through repair, transformation, empowerment with others and limiting the exercise of power over others. A defence of the list is also articulated in terms of values that can be found in consensus UN Human Rights agreements and from what we know empirically about what citizens seek from restorative justice. Ultimately, such top-down lists motivated by UN instruments or the ruminations of intellectuals are only important for supplying a provisional, revisable agenda for bottom-up deliberation on restorative justice standards appropriate to distinctively local anxieties about injustice. A method is outlined for moving bottom-up from standards citizens settle for evaluating their local programme to aggregating these into national and international standards.

Pluralizing State Power

This essay will explore the tensions between restorative justice as a bottom-up social movement and the fact that its philosophical fundamentals require it to exercise power accountably (Roche 2001). Top-down managerialist accountability of an 'audit society' that takes the techniques of the discipline of business accounting into fields to which they are not well adapted (Power 1997) does not have an encouraging history in criminal justice (Jones 1993). Managerialist restorative justice is also anathema to the bottom-up democratic (civic republican) ethos of the social movement. Yet this essay develops two philosophical positions: (a) that top-down accountability of some form is needed with top-down standards that are contestable bottom-up; (b) that human rights must be protected by restorative justice processes (Braithwaite and Pettit 1990). It will be argued that human rights meta-narratives that come from above can be made concretely meaningful by local standards that have contextual relevance to restorative justice programmes. This concrete experience can then generate democratic impulses that can inform the reframing of top-down human rights discourse (Habermas 1996).

In the article Northern Ireland is selected as a least likely case study (Eckstein 1975) for such an approach in Western societies—a case study selected as one where the approach would prove least likely to be feasible. Northern Ireland is a context where political trust is low, where there is a long history of democratic impulses from below being blocked by blood and domination and which has not had an exemplary rights culture. It is of course not as unlikely a case study as Afghanistan, but in the West we can plausibly advance Northern Ireland as a least likely case. If it can be shown that the approach can be

---

* Professor in the Law Program, Research School of Social Sciences, Australian National University, Canberra.

developed in a feasible way in the least likely case, then the methodological idea is that the approach might have prospects of being robustly relevant in many contexts.

One of the reasons restorative justice gathers modest support in reformist politics is that many can identify with a commitment to combating oppressive state structures of inhumane reliance on prisons. It also involves empowering citizens with responsibility for matters that over the past few centuries came to be viewed as state responsibilities. For most restorative justice advocates, restorative justice is consequentialist philosophically, methodologically, and politically. The restorative method is to discuss consequences of injustices and to acknowledge them appropriately as a starting point toward healing the hurts of injustice and transforming the conditions that allowed injustice to flourish. Politically, if citizens can see that there are consequences for offenders in taking responsibility for dealing with all of this, they may see less need for punishment because 'something needs to be done' and punishment seems the natural thing to do with crime. Notwithstanding this consequentialism, many of the limits that retributivists regard as central are also found to be important standards of restorative justice. The article considers what those standards should be and how they should be refined. But if restorative justice is about shifting power to the people, surely reimposing the state to set standards for restorative justice shifts the power back to the state?

It may. And there is certainly a worry here, especially in contexts like Northern Ireland. In Northern Ireland, as in South Africa, Bougainville (Howley 2002) and other post-conflict situations, all sides have their historical reasons for distrusting moves by the state that might disempower their people. Equally, there are historical reasons for the state to distrust paramilitary elements in civil society who they fear will use control of informal justice to sustain an armed tyranny over local communities. So we need state standards to render the empowerment of restorative justice robust. In popular justice throughout the ages we have seen all manner of disempowerment of minorities by majorities, of those without guns by those with guns (Abel 1981, 1982; Nader 1980). State-sanctioned human rights are vital for regulating the tyrannies of informal justice. They are also vital for regulating the tyrannies of the police, of state-sanctioned torture and violence, which in Northern Ireland have been considerable problems.

State standards can enable the deliberative democracy of the people or it can disable it. It all depends on what the standards are and how they are implemented. So we must get down to detail. But before we do that, it is worth mentioning that part of the genius of restorative justice as a policy idea is that many of its most precious ideals are invulnerable to state power. An example is Kay Pranis's (2000) great insight about how empowerment works with restorative justice. Pranis says we can tell how much power a person has by how many people listen to their stories. When the prime minister speaks from his podium many listen; when the pauper on a street corner mutters his stories we walk past. The deadly simple empowering feature of restorative justice here is that it involves listening to the stories of victims and accused offenders, both groups which the criminological literature shows to be disproportionately poor, powerless and young (Hindelang *et al.* 1978; Braithwaite and Biles 1984). The empirical evidence is that women's voices are actually slightly more likely to be heard in restorative justice conferences than men's voices (Braithwaite 2002: ch. 5), a very different reality from the voices that are heard in the corridors of state power and judicial power. Pranis's point is that by the simple fact of listening to their story we give them power. So long as the core listening principle of restorative justice is retained, this kind of empowerment cannot be threatened by state standards.

Dangers in Standards

While it is good that we are now having debates on standards for restorative justice, it is a dangerous debate. Accreditation for mediators that raises the spectre of a Western accreditation agency telling an Aboriginal elder that a centuries-old restorative practice does not comply with the accreditation standards is a profound worry. We must avert accreditation that crushes indigenous empowerment.

We should also worry about standards that are so prescriptive that they inhibit restorative justice innovation. We are still learning how to do restorative justice well. The healing edge programmes today involve real advances over those of the 1990s and the best programmes of the 1990s made important advances over those of the 1980s. We should even worry about regulatory proposals that are highly prescriptive about how we should define what a standard or a principle of restorative justice is, or which matters should be formulated as rights that are guarantees that should never be breached. I am not sure we have learnt enough yet about what happens in restorative processes to be ready for such prescription.

We must be careful in how we regulate restorative justice now so that in another decade we will be able to say again that the healing edge programmes are more profoundly restorative than those of today. Unthinking enforcement of standards is a new threat to innovating with better ways of doing restorative justice. It is a threat because evaluation research on restorative justice is at such a rudimentary stage that our claims about what is good practice and what is bad practice can rarely be evidence-based.

At the same time, there is such a thing as practice masquerading as restorative justice that is outrageously poor—practice that would generate little controversy among criminologists that it was unconscionable, such as the conference discussed in the next section where a child agreed to wear a t-shirt announcing 'I am a thief'. Such practices are an even greater threat to the future of restorative justice. So we have no option but to do something about them through a prudent standards debate. We can craft open-textured restorative justice standards that allow a lot of space for cultural difference and innovation while giving us a language for denouncing uncontroversially bad practice. This contribution to the standards debate will be a modest one that will not seek to be exhaustive in defining the issues standards must address.

The Principle of Non-Domination

From my civic republican perspective (Braithwaite and Pettit 1990; Pettit 1997), a fundamental standard is that restorative processes must seek to avoid domination. We do see a lot of domination in restorative processes, as we do in all spheres of social interaction. But a programme is not restorative if it fails to be active in preventing domination. What does this mean in practice? It means that if a stakeholder wants to attend a conference or circle and have a say, they must not be prevented from attending. If they have a stake in the outcome, they must be helped to attend and speak. This does not preclude special support circles for just victims or just offenders; but it does mandate institutional design that gives every stakeholder a meaningful opportunity to speak and be heard. Any attempt by a participant at a conference to silence or dominate another participant must be countered. This does not mean the conference convenor has to intervene. On the contrary, it is better if other stakeholders are given the space to speak up against dominating speech. But if domination persists and the stakeholders are afraid to confront it, then the convenor must confront it by specifically asking to hear more from the voice that is being subordinated.

Often it is rather late for confronting domination once the restorative process is under way. Power imbalance is a structural phenomenon. It follows that restorative processes must be structured so as to minimize power imbalance. Young offenders must not be led into a situation where they are upbraided by a 'roomful of adults' (Haines 1998). There must be adults who see themselves as having a responsibility to be advocates for the child, adults who will speak up. If this is not accomplished, a conference or circle can always be adjourned and reconvened with effective supporters of the child in the room. Similarly, we cannot tolerate the scenario of a dominating group of family violence offenders and their patriarchal defenders intimidating women and children who are victims into frightened silence. When risks of power imbalance are most acute our standards should expect of us a lot of preparatory work to restore balance both backstage and frontstage during the process. Organized advocacy groups have a particularly important role when power imbalances are most acute. These include women's and children's advocacy groups when family violence is at issue (Strang and Braithwaite 2002), environmental advocacy groups when crimes against the environment by powerful corporations are at issue (Gunningham and Grabosky 1998).

Of course, holding the threat of a punishment beating, of kneecapping, over the head of a person is an intolerable violation of the principle of non-domination. Common ground among all the restorative justice initiatives in Northern Ireland seems to be to transcend this particular form of domination, though there are competing visions of how to accomplish this. While I am in no position to adjudicate these competing visions, I would like to submit the principle of non-domination and the values that flow from it as a values framework for the debate.

Due process is perhaps the major domain where there have been calls for standards. It seems reasonable that offenders put into restorative justice programmes be advised of their right to seek the advice of a lawyer on whether they should participate in the programme. Perhaps this would be an empty international standard in poorer nations where lawyers are not in practical terms affordable or available for most criminal defendants. But wealthier nations like the United Kingdom can afford higher standards on this issue. Arresting police officers who refer cases to restorative justice processes should be required to provide a telephone number of a free legal advice line on whether agreeing to the restorative justice process is prudent.

In no nation does it seem appropriate for defendants to have a right for their lawyer to represent them during a restorative justice process. Part of the point of restorative justice is to transcend adversarial legalism, to empower stakeholders to speak in their own voice rather than through legal mouthpieces who might have an interest in polarizing a conflict. A standard that says defendants or victims have a right to have legal counsel present during a restorative justice process seems sound. But a standard that gives legal counsel a right to speak at the conference or circle seems an unwarranted threat from the dominant legal discourse to the integrity of an empowering restorative justice process. This does not mean banning lawyers from speaking under any circumstances; if all the participants agree they should hear some expert opinion from a lawyer then that opinion should certainly be invited into the circle. Moreover, I have argued that where lawyers have signed a collaborative law agreement and been trained in collaborative law values and methods, there may be special virtue in hearing from them (Braithwaite 2002: 250–1).

The most important way that the criminal justice system must be constrained against being a source of domination over the lives of citizens is that it must be constrained against ever imposing a punishment beyond the maximum allowed by law for that kind of offence. It is therefore critical that restorative justice never be allowed to undermine this constraint. Restorative justice processes must be prohibited from ever imposing punishments that exceed the maximum punishment the courts would impose for that offence. As someone who believes that restorative justice processes should be about reintegrative shaming and should reject stigmatization, it seems important to prohibit any degrading or humiliating form of treatment. We had a conference in Canberra where all the stakeholders agreed it was a good idea for a young offender to wear a t-shirt stating 'I am a thief'. This sort of outcome should be banned.

Another critical, albeit vague, standard is that restorative justice programmes must be concerned with the needs and with the empowerment not only of offenders, but also of victims and affected communities. Programmes where victims are exploited as props for programmes that are oriented only to the rehabilitation of offenders are morally unacceptable (Braithwaite 2002: ch. 5). Deals that are win-win for victims and offenders but where certain other members of the community are serious losers, worse losers whose perspective is not even heard, are morally unacceptable. The key principle here is equal concern for all stakeholders. The most important way to manifest that concern is through respectful listening, which is also the obverse of banning disrespectful or humiliating, degrading ways of reacting or punishing.

The right to appeal must be safeguarded (Brown 1994; Warner 1994). Whenever the criminal law is a basis for imposing sanctions in a restorative justice process, offenders must have a right of appeal against those sanctions to a court of law. That said, not all of the accountability mechanisms of criminal trials seem appropriate to the philosophy of restorative justice. For example, if we are concerned about averting stigmatization and assuring undominated dialogue, we may not want conferences or circles to be normally open to the public. But if that is our policy, it seems especially important for researchers, critics, journalists, political leaders, judges, colleagues from restorative justice programmes in other places, to be able to sit in on conferences or circles (with the permission of the participants) so there can be informed public debate and exposure of inappropriate practices. Most importantly, it is critical that restorative justice processes can be observed by peer reviewers whose job it is to report on compliance with the kinds of standards I will discuss.

International Standards

In general, UN Human Rights instruments give quite good guidance on the foundational values and rights restorative justice processes ought to observe. The first clause of the Preamble of the Universal Declaration that most states have ratified is:

Whereas recognition of the inherent dignity and of the equal and inalienable rights of all members of the human family is the foundation of freedom, justice and peace in the world . . .

BRAITHWAITE

Obviously freedom, justice and peace have a lot of appeal to someone who values republican freedom to frame the pursuit of justice and peacemaking in restorative justice. In its 30 Articles the Universal Declaration defines a considerable number of slightly more specific values and rights that seem to cover many of the things we look to restore and protect in restorative justice processes. These include a right to protection from having one's property arbitrarily taken (Article 17), a right to life, liberty and security of the person (Article 3), a right to health and medical care (Article 25) and a right to democratic participation (Article 21).

From the restorative justice advocate's point of view, the most interesting Article is 5: 'No one shall be subjected to torture or to cruel, inhuman or degrading treatment or punishment.' Of course, all states have interpreted Article 5 in a most permissive and unsatisfactory way from a restorative justice point of view. The challenge for restorative justice advocates is to take the tiny anti-punitive space this Article creates in global human rights discourse and expand its meaning over time so that it increasingly acquires a more restorative interpretation. This is precisely how successful NGO activists have globalized progressive agendas in many other arenas—starting with a platitudinous initial rights framework and injecting progressively less conservative and more specific meanings into that framework agreement over time (Braithwaite and Drahos 2000: 619–20).

We can already move to slightly more specific and transformative aspirations within human rights discourse by moving from the Universal Declaration of 1948 to the less widely ratified International Covenant on Economic, Social and Cultural Rights of 1976 and the International Covenant on Civil and Political Rights of 1966. The former, for example, involves a deeper commitment to 'self-determination' and allows in a commitment to emotional wellbeing under the limited rubric of a right to mental health. The 1989 Second Optional Protocol of the Covenant on Civil and Political Rights includes a commitment of parties to abolish the death penalty, something most restorative justice advocates would regard as an essential specific commitment. Equally most restorative justice advocates would agree with all the values and rights in the United Nations Declaration on the Elimination of Violence Against Women of 1993, the United Nations Standard Minimum Rules for Non-Custodial Measures of 1990 (the Tokyo Rules) and the Declaration of Basic Principles of Justice for Victims of Crime and Abuse of Power adopted by the General Assembly in 1985. The latter includes some relevant values not so well traversed in other human rights instruments such as 'restoration of the environment' (Article 10), 'compassion' (Article 4), 'restitution' (various Articles), 'redress' (Article 5) and includes specific reference to 'restoration of rights' (Article 8) and 'Informal mechanisms for the resolution of disputes, including mediation, arbitration and customary justice or indigenous practices' which 'should be utilized where appropriate to facilitate conciliation and redress for victims'. (Article 7).

A Proposal

So a proposal for a starting framework for a debate on the content of restorative justice standards might take the values discussed above, all of which can be found in the UN human rights instruments I have discussed. From a civic republican perspective we can distinguish constraining standards that specify precise rights and limits and maximizing standards which, while they might justify specific constraints, are also good consequences in themselves which we should want to maximize.

Constraining standards

- Non-domination
- Empowerment
- Honouring legally specific upper limits on sanctions
- Respectful listening
- Equal concern for all stakeholders
- Accountability, appealability
- Respect for the fundamental human rights specified in the Universal Declaration of Human Rights, the International Covenant on Economic, Social and Cultural Rights, the International Covenant on Civil and Political Rights and its Second Optional Protocol, the United Nations Declaration on the Elimination of Violence Against Women and the Declaration of Basic Principles of Justice for Victims of Crime and Abuse of Power.

Maximizing standards

- Restoration of human dignity
- Restoration of property loss
- Restoration of safety/injury/health
- Restoration of damaged human relationships
- Restoration of communities
- Restoration of the environment
- Emotional restoration
- Restoration of freedom
- Restoration of compassion or caring
- Restoration of peace
- Restoration of a sense of duty as a citizen
- Provision of social support to develop human capabilities to the full
- Prevention of future injustice.

Not only are these values that can be justified from the text of UN human rights instruments, as outlined above, they are also consistent with the empirical experience of what victims and offenders say they want out of restorative justice processes (see Strang 2000), at least at our present limited state of knowledge of these matters. The privileging of empowerment on the first list of standards we are constrained to honour means that stakeholders are empowered to tell their own stories in their own way to reveal whatever sense of injustice they wish to see repaired. This can mean at times quite idiosyncratic conceptions of justice that are not reflected in the second starting list of maximizing standards. The idea is that we must honour the standards on the constraining standards list, but that we are not constrained to accomplish always the standards on the maximizing standards list. Constraining standards (list 1) versus maximizing values (list 2) against which we can evaluate the performance of restorative justice in comparison to its alternatives without always being required to honour the standard. With many types of crime, restoration of the environment, for example, will simply not be relevant, as will healing physical injuries not be relevant when a crime is non-violent. With the maximizing standards, the measure is not that they are always secured, but that they are more likely to be increased across a large number of cases that go into a restorative justice programme compared to cases that do not, and more likely to be increased after a restorative justice process than before. So they are certainly the stuff of useful yardsticks for evaluating restorative justice programmes.

Together these values imply parsimony in the use of punishment; together they say there are many positive approaches to regulation that we can consider before we consider our reluctant willingness to resort to punishment. The first 11 standards on the second priority list are different forms of healing that can all be justified in terms of values in the UN human rights instruments above and the empirical experience of what participants often say is the healing they want out of restorative justice processes. Beyond saying that, I will not mount a detailed defence of them. Obviously, there are many dimensions of a value like emotional restoration—some want relief from the emotion of fear, others from hate, others from shame, others vindication of their character.

The twelfth standard—providing social support to develop human capabilities to the full—is essential as a corrective to the concern that restorative justice may be used to restore an unjust status quo. The key design idea here is that regulatory institutions must be designed so as to nurture developmental institutions. Too often regulatory institutions stultify human capabilities, the design of punitive criminal justice systems being a classic example.

For the final standard, preventing future injustice, there are as many modalities of evaluation as forms of injustice. The one being most adequately researched at this time is prevention of future crime, an evaluation criterion that has shown progressively more encouraging results over the past three years (Braithwaite 2002: ch. 3).

Emergent standards

- Remorse over injustice
- Apology
- Censure of the act
- Forgiveness of the person
- Mercy.

As a list of specific restorative values, the maximizing standards list is unsatisfactorily incomplete. The above list of what we will call emergent standards is nowhere to be found as values in these UN documents. The list of emergent standards differs from the earlier list of maximizing standards in a conceptually important way. It is not that the emergent values are less important than the maximizing values. When Desmond Tutu (1999) says 'No Future Without Forgiveness', many restorative justice advocates are inclined to agree. Forgiveness differs from say respectful listening as a value of restorative justice in the following sense. We actively seek to persuade participants that they ought to listen respectfully, but we do not urge them to forgive. It is cruel and wrong to expect a victim of

SETTING STANDARDS

crime to forgive.[1] Apology, forgiveness and mercy are gifts; they only have meaning if they well up from a genuine desire in the person who forgives, apologizes or grants mercy. Apart from it being morally wrong to impose such an expectation, we would destroy the moral power of forgiveness, apology or mercy to invite participants in a restorative justice process to consider proffering it during the process. People take time to discover the emotional resources to give up such emotional gifts. It cannot, must not, be expected. Similarly, remorse that is forced out of offenders has no restorative power. This is not to say that we should not write beautiful books like Tutu's on the grace that can be found through forgiveness. Nor does it preclude us evaluating restorative justice processes according to how much remorse, apology, forgiveness and mercy they elicit. Some might be puzzled as to why reintegrative shaming does not rate on my list of restorative values. It is not a value, not a good in itself; it is an explanatory dynamic that seeks to explain the conditions in which remorse, apology, censure of the act, forgiveness, mercy and many of the other values above occur. There is redundancy in listing remorse, apology and censure of the act because my theoretical position is that remorse and apology are the most powerful forms of censure since they are uttered by the person with the strongest reasons for refusing to vindicate the victim by censuring the injustice. However, when remorse and apology are not elicited it is imperative for other participants to vindicate the victim by censuring the act.

Let us clarify finally the distinctions among these three lists of standards of restorative justice. The constraining list are standards that must be honoured and enforced as constraints; the maximizing list are standards restorative justice advocates should actively encourage in restorative processes; the emergent list are values we should not urge participants to manifest—they are emergent properties of a successful restorative justice process. If we try to make them happen, they will be less likely to happen in a meaningful way.

Many will find these values vague, lacking specificity of guidance on how decent restorative practices should be run. Yet standards must be broad if we are to avert legalistic regulation of restorative justice that is at odds with the philosophy of restorative justice. What we need is deliberative regulation where we are clear about the values we expect restorative justice to realize. Whether a restorative justice programme is up to standard is best settled in a series of regulatory conversations (Black 1997, 1998) with peers and stakeholders rather than by rote application of a rulebook. That said, certain highly specific standards are so fundamental to justice that they must always be guaranteed—such as a right to appeal.

Yet some conventional rights, such as the right to a speedy trial as specified in the Beijing Rules for Juvenile Justice, can be questioned from a restorative perspective. One thing we have learnt from the victims' movement in recent years is that when victims have been badly traumatized by a criminal offence, they often need a lot of time before they are ready to countenance healing. They should be given the right to that time so long as it is not used as an excuse for the arbitrary detention of a defendant who has not been proven guilty.

---

[1] As Martha Minow (1998: 17) puts it: 'Forgiveness is a power held by the victimized, not a right to be claimed. The ability to dispense, but also to withhold, forgiveness is an ennobling capacity, part of the dignity to be reclaimed by those who survive the wrongdoing.'

BRAITHWAITE

This is an illustration of why at this point in history we need an international framework agreement on standards for restorative justice that is mainly a set of values for
framing quality assurance processes and accountability in our pursuit of continuous
improvement in attaining restorative justice values. There is some hope that the
Committee of Experts established in pursuance of the Declaration of Vienna from
the 2000 UN Congress on the Prevention of Crime and the Treatment of Offenders will
accomplish precisely that.

Not Waiting for the United Nations

At the local level what we need to think about is how to make the quality assurance
processes and accountability work well. We don't have to wait for the United Nations for
this. A local restorative justice initiative can take a very broad list of values, such as the
ones I have tentatively advanced here, and use them as the starting point for a debate on
what standards they want to see accomplished in their programme. A few discussion
circles with all the stakeholders in the programme may be enough to reach a sufficient
level of shared sensibility to make quality assurance and accountability work. Not every
contested value or right has to be settled and written down. The unsettled ones can be
earmarked for special observation in the hope that experiential learning will persuade
one side of the debate to change their view or all sides to discover a new synthesis of views.
I will illustrate with the restorative justice standards debate in Northern Ireland.

Northern Ireland actually has a more mature debate on standards and principles of
restorative justice than any society I know. It is certainly a more sophisticated debate than
in my home country of Australia. I suspect this is because Northern Ireland has a more
politicized contest between state and civil society models of restorative justice than can be
found in other places. Such fraught contexts are where there is the greatest risk of justice
system catastrophes. But they also turn out to be the contexts with the richest prospects
for rising to the political challenges with a transformative vision of restorative justice.
During a short visit to Northern Ireland in 2000 I found the restorative justice
programmes in both the Loyalist and Republican communities inspiring. Partly this is
because of the courage and integrity of the community leaders involved and the
reflective professionalism of those in the state who are open to restorative justice. I have
been struck by the way so many ex-prisoners from both sides I met, who agree on very
little politically, share remarkably similar restorative justice values. We saw them discover
these shared values with other community leaders sitting in the same circle in a
conference organized in Belfast by Kieran McEvoy and Harry Mika (2001). There is hope
in this for Northern Ireland.

The drafting of local charters, as commended in the 'Blue Book' (Auld, Mika and
McEvoy 1997) discussed in Harry Mika and Kieran McEvoy's paper (this issue, see also
McEvoy and Mika 2001a, 2001b and Mika and McEvoy 2001), is consistent with the
approach I commend here. So is the approach Greater Shankill Alternatives has
developed through its local 'Principles of Good Practice' (drafted by Debbie Watters and
Billy Mitchell). There are a lot of similarities between these principles (from the Loyalist
community) and those articulated by the Republican community through statements
such as the 'Standards and Values of Restorative Justice Practice' of Community
Restorative Justice Ireland (from the Republican side). The latter has some distinctively

SETTING STANDARDS

interesting standards as well, such as 'flexibility of approach' and 'evaluation' (and both 'confidentiality' and 'transparency'). There is also indigenous distinctiveness in the proposal that key elements of the charters 'are slated to appear as large murals at strategic locations, in spaces that have traditionally been reserved for the political iconography that is well known within and outside Northern Ireland' (McEvoy and Mika, 2001b). For all the local distinctiveness, both the Republican and Loyalist charters have values that sit comfortably beside the values I have derived from the UN human rights instruments and beside those that the Northern Ireland Office has derived from European human rights instruments (for example, in *Restorative Justice and a Partnership Against Crime* 1998).

Recent email correspondence with Kay Pranis revealed the important work she has been doing on bottom-up values clarification in Minnesota. Let me quote at length from her email:

During the training we do a values exercise right away that becomes a touchstone throughout the rest of the training. We give participants a family conflict dilemma, suggest that the siblings come together for a day to try to work it out and then ask them to imagine they are driving home after the day with their siblings. We pose the question: what would you hope was true of your behavior that day working through the problem with your siblings, regardless of the outcome? They make a list individually, then group in pairs to come up with a consensus list for the pair, then group in fours to develop a consensus list and then we go to the large group and put together a consensus list—which is a list of values. There is always general acknowledgement that the list represents who we would like to be but we don't often achieve that—especially in our conflicts. I then talk about circles as a space that tries to maximize the possibility of staying close to those values in our behavior—the circle is designed to help us be our best selves.

In the training with the staff from time to time someone would say 'But these kids don't have these values so the circle won't work with them.' I didn't think it was true (because every group we do the exercise with comes up with essentially the same list) but didn't have a basis to refute that claim until I did the training with the kids. I modified the conflict situation to make it more relevant for the kids but kept it close to the original and used exactly the same process I use with adults. The kids produced a wonderful list—like the adults but even more elaborate. It was so exciting. Who they want to be looks just like who the adults want to be—but what became apparent in the training was that they don't think the world is a safe place to be that kind of person.

Anyway, it was a great experience for me. The kinds of kids who were in the training would have been very intimidating to me as an adolescent. I was very shy and had no idea of the kinds of environments that other kids experienced—so I only saw the defiance or bullying. It was very healing for me to experience them in their humanity and vulnerability.

Systematic empirical work on such initiatives could test Pranis's observation that surprising degrees of consensus over restorative justice values emerge bottom-up from the normally disenfranchised and could document what those values are. Over time compilations of such empirical work from around the world could be bottom-up democratic inputs for revising the hoped-for UN standards. Compilations for one nation can inform the restructuring of national law.

Once there has been a preliminary discussion of the principles, standards and rights a local programme should honour, training is needed for all new restorative justice convenors to deepen the furrows of shared sensibility around them. Training carries a risk of professionalization. This risk can be to some extent countered by making the training participatory, by giving trainees the power to reframe the curriculum. It need not be long. Three days of training followed by a period when convenors work with an experienced mentor and a follow-up day of reflection on the initial period of practice can turn out excellent convenors. Most people do not make good restorative justice facilitators. But I believe that in any large group of people, say in any 7th grade schoolroom, there will be someone with the ability to be an empowering facilitator of a restorative justice circle with only limited training.

It follows from this view that quality assurance is more important than training. I have sat through more restorative justice training sessions than any sane human being would aspire to and taught many others. As well trained as I am, a good quality assurance programme would weed me out as someone whose talents were better suited to other roles. My main deficiencies as a restorative justice conference facilitator are that I am sometimes too intellectually curious about things that are not important to the parties, I am sometimes more emotionally engaged than is best and my personality causes me to have too much dominance in a room; even when I have my mouth shut, my body language is too inured to leadership—communicating encouragement or doubt when all I should be communicating is attentive listening.

Many deficiencies of this kind can be cured by colleagues who sit in on our circles and communicate with us frankly about how we can improve. Other failings may require that we be gently steered into making a contribution somewhere other than in this frontline role. Either way, the crucial remedy is peer review complemented by feedback from participants. The feedback I mean involves the peer reviewer talking to participants after a conference or circle to elicit any concerns they have about the way the facilitator played out their role. It is this process of post-conference regulatory conversations about the conduct of the conference itself that helps clarify how we should give life to the principles, standards and rights that restorative justice must honour. The 'regular inspection by the independent criminal justice inspectorate' recommended by the Criminal Justice Review for Northern Ireland could be crafted to fulfil this role.[2]

Conclusion

The suggestion here is to do something like the following before setting up a new restorative justice programme:

(1) Assemble stakeholders to reflect on a starting set of principles, standards or rights. These starting objectives might be grounded in the values and rights in UN or European human rights instruments.

---

[2] One of the referees pointed out the double standard that this inspectorate was to be 'created exclusively for restorative justice (and not for any independent inspection of conventional justice organizations or practices)'. I do not know enough to have a view on whether this inspectorate as the referee implies is a statist conspiracy to crush community justice. But on the double standard of restorative justice having to face superior accountability mechanisms than state justice, of the courts being a sufficient check on poor prosecutorial practice but not on poor restorative conference practice, of restorative justice being set evaluation research expectations much higher than have ever been set for the efficacy and justice of courts, these double standards are a good thing. This is because the accountability standards of extant criminal justice institutions are intolerably unsatisfactory from the perspective of restorative justice philosophy, certainly from a civic republican one (see Roche 2001).

SETTING STANDARDS

(2) Secure through this local democratic deliberation a set of local commitments to standards that are widely shared. Secure commitment to continuing regulatory conversations around other standards that stakeholders consider important, but where sensibilities are not shared.

(3) Try to resolve the contested standards through reflexive praxis—restorative justice practice that reflects back on its starting assumptions.

(4) Avoid didactic training. Make the training sessions, especially role-plays, part of this locally reflexive praxis that continually rebuilds the ship of restorative justice while it sails the local seas.

(5) Use peer review not only to counsel against practices that threaten the consensually shared standards but also to advance our understanding of the contested standards through regulatory deliberation.

(6) Aggregate these local regulatory conversations into a national regulatory conversation. If the local regulatory conversations converge on the importance of certain rights that should never be infringed, then the state should stand behind those rights, for example by legislating for them or threatening programme funding when they are flouted. But where there is no democratically deliberated consensus, the state should be wary of national standards that threaten local innovation and local cultural difference.

At the end of the day it is better that restorative justice learn from making mistakes than that it make the mistake of refusing to learn. This mistake usually takes the form of believing that standards and rights should be grounded in the rulings of lawyers whose eyes are blinkered to the reflective practice of justice by the people. Recent experience is ground for optimism that if we regulate flexibly, being mindful of all the local ideas for innovation, richer models of restorative justice can blossom. Critics who believe in a univocal justice system as opposed to a legal pluralist one will look askance at the long list of standards I have suggested might emerge from allowing a thousand flowers to bloom bottom-up. But it may be that citizens will find they like a criminal justice system with a lot of bottom-up aspirations for reducing injustice and perhaps a rather smaller number of top-down constraints on what sort of flowers should be allowed to bloom. Designing research that asks citizens with experience of a restorative justice process to evaluate it on 20 or 30 criteria is actually not difficult, just as it is not impossible to collect objective outcome data on multiple criteria of evaluation. If the worry is that justice innovations that seek to accomplish many things will actually do the most important things badly, then this worry can be tested empirically by such research.[3] Of course we already have a criminal law that at some levels aspires to most of the objectives canvassed here. It aspires to enact criminal laws and execute enforcement that *protects the environment*, without manifesting much interest in empirical research on whether its criminalization strategies actually do improve the environment. Defenders of our criminal law claim that it does many of the things it does to *protect the dignity* of citizens without demanding evaluation

---

[3] If they are right, such critics will be able to specify a set of core evaluation criteria. Programmes that perform well on a large number of non-core standards they set out to maximize will produce poor results on the core criteria. Of course, my hypothesis is that this will prove wrong. My reasons are that injustice is variegated and requires creativity to confront in all its forms and that injustice in the periphery (a refugee camp) is a cause of injustice at the core (the World Trade Centre). While it equally sounds plausible that the best way to advance knowledge might be to create knowledge institutions with highly focused objectives, empirically it is non-focused institutions called universities that win most Nobel Prizes, not specialist research institutes or business laboratories.

research on how dignified citizens believe they have been treated by said institutions, and so on. Evidence and innovation from below instead of armchair pontification from above should be what drive the hopes of restorative justice to replace our existing injustice system with one that actually does more to promote justice than to crush it. It would be a less tidy justice system, but tidiness seems decisively not a good candidate for a justice standards framework.

REFERENCES

ABEL, R. (1981), 'Conservative Conflict and the Reproduction of Capitalism: The Role of Informal Justice', *International Journal of the Sociology of Law*, 9: 245–67.

——(1982), 'The Contradictions of Informal Justice', in R. Abel, ed., *The Politics of Informal Justice, I: The American Experience*, 1–13. New York: Academic Press.

AULD, J., GORMALLY, B., McEVOY, K. and RITCHIE, M. (1997), 'Designing a System of Restorative Community Justice: A Discussion Document', *The Blue Book*. Belfast: The Authors.

COMMUNITY RESTORATIVE JUSTICE IRELAND (n.d.), *Standards and Values of Restorative Justice Practice*. Belfast.

BLACK, J. (1997), *Rules and Regulators*. Oxford: Oxford University Press.

——(1998), 'Talking About Regulation', *Public Law*, Spring: 77–105.

BRAITHWAITE, J. (2002), *Restorative Justice and Responsive Regulation*. New York: Oxford University Press.

BRAITHWAITE, J. and BILES, D. (1984), 'Victims and Offenders: The Australian Experience', in *Victimization and Fear of Crime: World Perspectives*, edited by R. Block. Washington, DC: US Department of Justice.

BRAITHWAITE, J. and PETTIT, P. (1990), *Not Just Deserts: A Republican Theory of Criminal Justice*. Oxford: Oxford University Press.

BROWN, J. G. (1994), 'The Use of Mediation to Resolve Criminal Cases: A Procedural Critique', *Emory Law Journal*, 43: 1247–309.

ECKSTEIN, H. (1975), 'Case Study and Theory in Political Science', in N. Greenstein and N. Polsby, eds., *Handbook of Political Science*, Vol. 7: Strategies of Enquiry. Reading, MA: Addison-Wesley.

GUNNINGHAM, N. and GRABOSKY, P. (1998), *Smart Regulation: Designing Environmental Policy*. Oxford: Clarendon Press.

HABERMAS, J. (1996), *Between Facts and Norms: Contributions to a Discourse Theory of Law and Democracy*. London: Polity Press.

HAINES, K. (1998), 'Some Principled Objections to a Restorative Justice Approach to Working with Juvenile Offenders', in *Restorative Justice for Juveniles: Potentialities, Risks and Problems for Research*, in L. Walgrave, ed., selection of papers presented at the International Conference, Leuven, 12–14 May 1997, pp. 93–113. Leuven: Leuven University Press.

HINDELANG, M. J., GOTTFREDSON, M. R. and GAROFALO, J. (1978), *Victims of Personal Crime: An Empirical Foundation for a Theory of Personal Victimization*. Cambridge, MA: Ballinger.

HOWLEY, P. (2002), Breaking Spears and Mending Hearts, Sydney: Federation Press.

JONES, C. (1993), 'Auditing Criminal Justice', *British Journal of Criminology*, 33: 187–202.

McEVOY, K. and MIKA, H. (2001a), 'Punishment, Politics and Praxis: Restorative Justice and Non-Violent Alternatives to Paramilitary Punishments in Northern Ireland', *Policing and Society*, 11: 359.

——eds. (2001), 'International Perspectives on Restorative Justice', conference report. Belfast: Queen's University.

SETTING STANDARDS

MIKA, H., and McEVOY, K. (2001), 'Restorative Justice in Conflict: Paramilitarism, Community and the Construction of Legitimacy in Northern Ireland'. *Contemporary Justice Review*, 3/4: 291–319.

MINOW, M. (1998), *Between Vengeance and Forgiveness: Facing History after Genocide and Mass Violence*. Boston: Beacon Press.

NADER, L., ed. (1980), *No Access to Law: Alternatives to the American Judicial System*. New York: Academic Press.

PETTIT, P. (1997), *Republicanism*. Oxford: Clarendon Press.

POWER, M. (1997), *The Audit Society: Rituals of Verification*. Oxford: Oxford University Press.

PRANIS, K. (2000), 'Democratizing Social Control: Restorative Justice, Social Justice and the Empowerment of Marginalized Populations', in L. Walgrave and G. Bazemore, eds., *Restoring Juvenile Justice: An Exploration of the Restorative Justice Paradigm for Reforming Juvenile Justice*. Monsey, New York: Criminal Justice Press.

ROCHE, D. (2001), *First By Persuasion: Accountabilities of Restorative Justice*, PhD dissertation. Australian National University, Canberra.

STRANG, H. (2000), *Victim Participation in a Restorative Justice Process: The Canberra Reintegrative Shaming Experiments*, PhD dissertation. Australian National Universityj, Canberra.

STRANG, H. and BRAITHWAITE, J., eds. (2002), *Restorative Justice and Family Violence*. Melbourne: Cambridge University Press.

TUTU, D. (1999), *No Future Without Forgiveness*. London: Rider.

VAN NESS, D. and STRONG, K. H. (1997), *Restoring Justice*. Cinncinnati, OH: Anderson Publishing.

WARNER, K. (1994), 'The Rights of the Offender in Family Conferences', in C. Alder and J. Wundersitz, eds., *Family Conferencing and Juvenile Justice: The Way Forward or Misplaced Optimism?* Canberra: Australian Institute of Criminology.

ZEHR, H. (1990), *Changing Lenses: A New Focus for Criminal Justice*. Scottsdale, PA: Herald Press.

[17]

RESPONSIBILITIES, RIGHTS AND RESTORATIVE JUSTICE

Andrew Ashworth*

Restorative justice is much advocated as a new and fruitful response to offending. This article argues for further debate about the proper division of functions between state, victims, offenders and 'communities', and for greater emphasis upon procedural safeguards and substantive limits in the pursuit of the apparently beneficent goals of restorative justice.

Restorative justice is practice-led in most of its manifestations (see Miers 2001). Although the writings of John Braithwaite (e.g. 1989, 1993, 1999), Howard Zehr (1990), Martin Wright (1996) and others may be a source of inspiration for some practitioners and policy makers, there is also a certain reflexivity at work. The theory of restorative justice has to a large extent developed through practice, and will probably continue to do so. One consequence of this is that there is no single notion of RJ, no single type of process, no single theory. Tony Marshall suggests that a commonly accepted definition of restorative justice would be: 'a process whereby parties with a stake in a specific offence collectively resolve how to deal with the aftermath of the offence and its implications for the future' (Marshall 1999: 5). This usefully identifies three central elements in restorative justice: the importance of process, the notion of stakeholders, and the fairly wide-ranging aspirations for outcomes.

In terms of restorative process, the keynotes are empowerment, dialogue, negotiation and agreement. Professionals should not be dominant: the voices of the stakeholders should be the loudest. The stakeholders are assumed to be the victim, the offender and the community. Turning to restorative outcomes, what is to be restored is broadly stated as 'whatever dimensions of restoration matter to the victims, offenders and communities affected by the crime' (Braithwaite 1999: 6). Restoration is often seen as a form of reintegration, of the community and of individuals. Outcomes are measured chiefly by the satisfaction of the stakeholders in each case, and not by comparison with the outcomes of like cases.

One of the aims of the restorative justice movement is to replace forms of state justice for a wide range of offences and offenders. This means changing the focus of the term 'criminal justice' itself, away from the assumption that it is a matter concerning only the state and the defendant/offender, and towards a conception that includes as stakeholders the victim and the community too. However, it will be argued here that such a process of change should not have the effect of depriving defendants/offenders of safeguards and rights that should be assured to them in any processes which impose obligations as the consequence of committing an offence. Important steps have been

* Vinerion Professor of English Law at All Souls College, University of Oxford. An earlier version of this paper was discussed at a colloquium on 'Restorative Justice in Theory and Practice' in Cambridge. October 2000. Some of the arguments were worked into a separate paper on restorative justice and the English youth justice system, published in the 2001 volume of Current Legal Problems. I am grateful to Kathleen Daly, Antony Duff, Roger Hood, Carolyn Hoyle, Paul Roberts, Prince Saprai, Andrew von Hirsch, Richard Young and Lucia Zedner for comments on earlier versions.

and are being taken to ensure that appropriate standards are respected in restorative processes and outcomes, notably in the United Nations draft 'Basic Principles on the Use of Restorative Justice Programmes in Criminal Justice Matters' (United Nations 2000; see further Braithwaite, this issue). However, there are further and deeper issues to be confronted.

The aim of this article is to generate discussion on four of those issues. First, what should be the role of the state and its organs in the administration of criminal justice and in the determination of criminal justice outcomes? Second, if it is argued that the community should have a more central role in criminal justice, what implications does this have? Third, what are the rights and responsibilities of victims in matters of criminal justice? And fourth, if it is accepted that there must be some kind of 'default system' to deal with cases that cannot be handled through restorative justice, what form should it take?

The Responsibilities of the State

It is central to the philosophy of restorative justice that the stakeholders should be able to participate in dialogue about the offence. Undoubtedly the offender is one stakeholder, but who are the others? It may be claimed that the community and the victim also have a stake in the response to the offence, but what about the state? At a time when statist assumptions are crumbling, when 'neo-liberal' and 'advanced liberal' analyses (e.g. Rose 2000; Shearing 2000) point to the changing role of the state and governmentality, what should be the role of the state in matters of criminal justice?

It is common to refer to the 'public interest' in preventing or prosecuting crime: what does this mean? What is the significance of the phrase 'a crime against society'? The idea seems to be that, when it is decided to make certain conduct a crime rather than simply a civil wrong, this implies that it should not be merely a matter for the victim whether some action is taken against the malefactor; and even that there is a public interest in ensuring that people who commit such wrongs are liable to punishment, not merely to civil suit (Cretney *et al.* 1994). Thus Antony Duff argues for a category 'of "public" wrongs that are properly condemned and dealt with as wrongs by the community as a whole' (Duff 2000: 62), and he illustrates this with crimes of 'domestic' violence:

> But whatever else is unclear about the rights and wrongs of a domestic dispute . . . such violence should surely not be seen as a matter for negotiation or compromise. It should be condemned by the whole community as an unqualified wrong; and this is done by defining and prosecuting it as a crime. (Duff 2000: 62)

These are not propositions with which a restorative justice advocate would necessarily disagree. But another element of the argument is more contentious: that it is the responsibility of the state to ensure that there is order and law-abidance in society, and to establish a system for the administration of criminal justice.

In crude terms, the political theory would be that citizens agree to obey laws in return for protection of their vital interests, though keeping their right of self-defence for occasions of emergency when state protection is unavailable. As David Garland puts it, 'over time, the effective control of crime and the routine protection of citizens from criminal depredations had come to form elements of the promise that the state holds out

ASHWORTH

to its citizens' (Garland 2001: 109–10). This serves as the basis of the justification for maintaining a police force, a system of public prosecutions, the courts, and other aspects of the criminal justice system. Thus Duff regards it as obvious 'that the state owes it to its citizens to protect them from crime' through the criminal law and its administration (Duff 2000: 112).

If a community is, through the legal organs of the state, to take seriously the public wrong done to a citizen, it must not only sympathize with the victim but also censure the offender. It owes it to the victim, whose wrong it shares, and to the offender as a member of the normative community, to try to get the offender to recognize the wrong and to make a suitable apology for it. (Duff 2000: 114)

These arguments in favour of the state's responsibility for criminal justice[1] are joined by other consequential justifications for the state taking over the administration of criminal justice from victims and other individuals—partly to avoid placing on victims the additional burden of having to bring offenders to justice (Reeves and Mulley 2000: 130), and partly to avoid the social instability that would result if people had to 'take the law into their own hands' in responding to offences, which might encourage vigilantism (MacCormick and Garland 1998: 22, 27).

None of this is to rule out some delegation of this function by the state (in whole or in part) to others, either by moving it down to the level of the local community (MacCormick and Garland 1998: 27) or by elements of privatization. Recent decades have seen increasing decentralization and 'responsibilization' in criminal justice (Garland 2001), for a variety of political reasons; one aspect of the restorative justice movement, too, is a relocation of authority over responses to crime (Bayley 2001: 212). It is important to question whether these changes are right in principle, but first we must acknowledge two major failures of the statist approach.

First, in many political systems the prevailing statist approach has neglected (some would say, reinforced) social inequalities. Thus Kent Roach writes of disadvantaged groups having to 'rely on the criminal sanction's false promise of security and equality' (1999: 117), and argues that the state's responsibility for protecting citizens should be viewed in the wider context of public health, and therefore tackled as one element in a social programme to improve the conditions of life of groups who are disproportionately victimized and are not in a position to buy private security or healthcare (*ibid.*: 261). This is a timely reminder of the limitations of focusing criminal policy initiatives on the criminal justice system, rather than locating them in the wider social structure.

Second, and more deeply, there are countries in which the legitimacy of the state and its apparatus, including the criminal justice system, has suffered a serious collapse-obvious examples were South Africa (van Zyl Smit 1999; Shearing 2001) and Northern Ireland (McEvoy and Mika 2001). Some of the restorative justice initiatives in the most difficult social conditions are as much about social control as about responses to crime (see McEvoy and Mika 2001 on Northern Ireland). In still other countries it is possible to say that there have been or are legitimacy deficits, particularly in respect of certain groups (Blagg 1997; Tauri 1999), which suggest that reality lies some distance from basic democratic theory. Conditions of this kind may provide fertile soil for initiatives based on restorative justice, with its emphasis on greater participation and community

---

[1] This is an inevitably crude and truncated discussion of political theory. For another approach, see e.g. Raz (1986: ch. 3).

RESPONSIBILITIES, RIGHTS AND RESTORATIVE JUSTICE

involvement, although even restorative justice initiatives intended to tap into the culture of indigenous communities court the risk of increasing the extent of official power over them (Cunneen 1997; Blagg 1997; cf. Braithwaite 1997).

These deficiencies in relation to social disadvantage and governmental legitimacy have led many restorative justice advocates to the view that the state should not have a prominent position in the administration of criminal justice, and should instead have a residual role in providing facilities and in enforcing post-offence agreements reached by conferences, etc. The facilitative state would leave restorative conferences with deliberative space in which to decide on the most appropriate response to an offender's crime, from which it seems to follow that they might select (within ill-defined outer limits) whatever approach the particular conference prefers. Would this confine the state's role too narrowly? Are there duties that the state should retain, no matter that there are elements of 'rolling back' or 'hollowing out' the state's functions which lead to a measure of privatization and responsibilization?

The focus of these questions must be on the process of responding to crime, a process that (even within restorative justice) involves a measure of public censure and the placing of obligations on offenders. Garland identifies:

> an emerging distinction between the *punishment of criminals* which remains the business of the state (and becomes once again a significant symbol of state power) and the *control of crime*, which is increasingly deemed to be 'beyond the state' in significant respects. And as its control capacity comes to be viewed as limited and contingent, the state's power to punish takes on a renewed political salience and priority. (Garland 2001: 120)

What reasons can be given for state control over punishment and official responses to offences? Two arguments are that criminal justice must be administered 'in the public interest', and that it should ensure respect for human rights. Since, as argued above, a defining feature of criminal offences is that they are offences against the state or collectivity, it is right that the state should ensure that the response is based on general principles duly established and applicable throughout the jurisdiction. This connects closely with the second argument about respect for human rights. The state surely owes it to offenders to exercise its power according to settled principles that uphold citizens' rights to equal respect and equality of treatment. Decisions on sentence should be taken by independent and impartial tribunals (see below), operating on principle and transparently, within a legal framework. There is an important distinction between tribunals responding in a principled manner to relevant factual differences between cases, and responding on the basis of their own views or preferences. The latter is contrary to the rule of law, and at odds with the notion of a *Rechtsstaat*. As John Gardner has argued, one of the implications of acting according to the 'rule of law' is 'that questions of how people are to be treated relative to one another always come to the fore at the point of its application'. This is not to rule out mitigation or mercy in sentencing, but to assert that 'what falls to be mitigated is none other than the sentence which is, in the court's [judgment], required by justice' (Gardner 1998: 36–7). In other words, the power exercised by imposing obligations on offenders in response to their offending ought, in principle, to be exercised consistently as between citizens, according to settled standards.

Although the list of failures of state justice is a lengthy one, the state must, as the primary political authority, retain control over criminal justice and its administration. It must do so for pragmatic reasons concerned with security (Bayley 2001: 218), and it must do so in order to ensure respect for the rule of law and human rights standards. This is not to ignore the shortcomings of human rights declarations and their enforcement, or to overlook the malleability of the 'rule of law' principle. Rather it is to argue that these remain fundamental ideals, which should be taken more seriously rather than discarded. The state ought, out of fairness to the people in respect of whom its coercive powers are being exercised, to insist on 'rule of law' principles and so ensure consistency of response to offences. Insofar as restorative justice approaches are adopted, the state's responsibility should be to impose a framework that guarantees these safeguards to offenders— an aim no less worthy in those societies where state legitimacy is contested. The recent draft UN standards amount to a small but welcome step in this direction (United Nations 2000; Braithwaite, this issue). We should also recall that the state has responsibilities towards victims: in the context of restorative justice, this means that it is wrong in principle to place burdens on victims as part of any criminal justice initiative (Reeves and Mulley 2000).

The Empowerment of Communities

It is the hallmark of many restorative justice approaches that they draw into criminal justice both victims and the wider community (although there is no unanimity on this: some regard the involvement of community members as 'at odds with the principles underlying conferencing': Morris and Maxwell 2000: 215). Garland is among those who have argued for the delegation of sentencing powers to communities (to 'authorities intermediate between the state and the individual': MacCormick and Garland 1998: 27). He does this for reasons similar to those of many restorative justice theorists—that the closer the adjudicators and enforcers are to the offender, the more likely they are to be effective in bringing about the desired changes in behaviour (partly, perhaps, because their legitimacy is more likely to impress itself on the offender).

Much depends, of course, on the conception of community on which reliance is being placed. Every citizen may be seen as a member of several cross-cutting communities: each of us has 'a number of community attachments, articulated in terms of factors such as race, ethnicity, class, gender, age, sexuality, occupation' (Lacey 1998: 144). Some restorative justice advocates would probably claim to have an open and inclusive approach to 'community', but in practice most schemes seem to involve the families of victim and offender, and yet to regard the community (where there are 'community representatives') as a geographical entity. If this means that local communities can adopt separate standards, the result is likely to be a form of 'justice by geography' or 'postcode lottery'. Indeed, the empowerment of communities, howsoever defined, might involve a sacrifice of 'rule of law' values such as consistency, which, it was argued, ought to be standards for criminal justice. Is it right for the state, or for bodies exercising authority delegated by the state, to use its coercive powers differently against each of two people, one who commits an offence in one locality and another with exactly similar background who commits a similar offence in a different locality? Surely not; it happens in both 'conventional' and restorative justice systems, but the difference is that in the former it is regarded as a malfunction to be removed whereas in the latter it may be thought beneficial. The conflict can be represented as one between principle and pragmatism, since there are those who regard the use of local knowledge and local ordering as an

RESPONSIBILITIES, RIGHTS AND RESTORATIVE JUSTICE

essential element of successful social control in contemporary societies (e.g. Braithwaite 2000: 232, and Shearing 2001; cf. van Ness 1993). It is certainly true that policing policies are increasingly responsive to local concerns; and, as one looks across European countries or American states, there may be stark differences in criminal justice policy between neighbouring jurisdictions—federal systems differ, for example, in respect of the allocation of responsibility for the administration of criminal justice. The issue cannot be argued to a conclusion here, but the very least that is required by the principle of the consistent use of state power over offenders is that local decision making should be constrained by general standards of procedural and substantive justice.

Turning from restorative processes to restorative outcomes, what is meant by the goal of 'community restoration'? This is regarded by most advocates as one desirable outcome of restorative justice processes, but its practical meaning turns on two issues which remain unsettled. One is the conception of community that is being used. If the broad aim is to restore the 'communities affected by the crime' (Braithwaite 1999: 6), as well as the victim and victim's family, this will usually mean a geographical community; but where an offence targets a victim because of race, religion, sexual orientation etc., that will point to a different community that needs to be restored. This leads to the second issue: what exactly is community 'restoration', and on what criteria are the form and amount of community restoration to be calculated? Reintegration is a term often used in this context, but its practical implications remain unclear. Many restorative justice theorists and others (e.g. Zedner 1994; Walgrave 1995; Duff 2000: 99–106) regard as the paradigm of community restoration some form of community service (now termed 'community punishment orders' in England and Wales). This is largely a symbolic form of restoration, and therefore it must be necessary to devise a scale of 'wrongs to the community' and to match it with a register of degrees of community restoration (cf. Meier 1998). There seems to be little endeavour among restorative justice theorists to deal with this issue, and certainly nothing comparable to the efforts of desert theorists to work out parameters of proportionality (cf. van Ness 1993 with von Hirsch and Jareborg 1991, and von Hirsch 1993: chs 2 and 4).

A further issue of principle concerns impartiality. It is one thing for critics of 'conventional' criminal justice systems to argue that those systems fail to sentence 'objectively', despite their aspirations, because they fail to avoid discrimination on grounds of class, race or gender. It is quite another thing to devise a system that would avoid problems of bias, or of informal hierarchies growing up, or of local power structures tending to dominate (Lacey 1998: ch. 5). Advocates of community justice stress the importance of inclusion rather than exclusion, and the concept of community is often associated with self-regulation, consent and agreement (Pavlich 2001). There may be examples of sentencing circles and restorative justice conferences that appear to avoid these difficulties, but there is always the danger that, as Adam Crawford has warned, 'the normative appeal of community [may be] confused with empirical reality':

the ideal of community should be forced to confront the empirical reality, which reminds us that communities are often marked (and sustained) by social exclusion, forms of coercion, and the differential distribution of power relations. (Crawford 2000: 290–1; cf. McEvoy and Mika 2001)

Among the problems here might be that majorities in some communities might disagree with certain criminal laws, perhaps laws intended to protect the weak against the strong or to eradicate drunk driving (Johnstone 2001: 55–7). Allowing community-based tribunals to determine the response to such laws is fraught with difficulty. Impartiality is a key value in justice processes, and yet in restorative justice theory it stands in tension with other values such as participation, involvement and empowerment (see Johnstone 2001: 153–8). But the tension is not insoluble, since it would be possible to concede the case for greater participation by members of affected communities while insisting that the power of decision making remains in impartial hands.

Rights and Responsibilities of the Victim

It is common for those writing on restorative justice to insist that all parties 'with a stake in the offence' ought to be able to participate in the disposition of the case, through a circle, conference, etc. (e.g. Llewellyn and Howse 1998: 19). The victim certainly has 'a stake', and Christie's (1977) assertion that the 'conflict' in some sense 'belongs' to the victim has become a modern orthodoxy among restorative justice supporters (e.g. Morris and Maxwell 2000: 207, who write of 'returning the offence to those most affected by it and encouraging them to determine appropriate responses to it'). The approach has ancient roots (Braithwaite 1999: 1–2 for a summary and references), although the growing awareness of the existence of secondary victimization (e.g. Morgan and Zedner 1992 on child victims) demonstrates the complexity of the issues arising.

The politico-historical argument is that most modern legal systems exclude the victim so as to bolster their own power. Originally the state wanted to take over criminal proceedings from victims as an assertion of power, and what now passes for 'normal' is simply a usurpation that has no claim to be the natural order. My concern is not to dispute this rather romantic interpretation of criminal justice in early history (Daly 2000 does this splendidly; also Johnstone 2001: ch. 3) but rather to raise three points of principle which have a bearing on the nature and extent of victims' rights: the principle of compensation for wrongs, the principle of proportionality, and the principle of independence and impartiality.

The first point of principle is the most direct of all in its target. What I want to argue is that the victim's legitimate interest is in compensation and/or reparation from the offender, and not in the form or quantum of the offender's punishment. The distinction between punishment and compensation is not widely appreciated: when a court fines an offender £300 for careless driving in a case where death resulted (but where there was no conviction for the more serious offence of causing death by dangerous driving), newspapers will often report comments such as 'my son's life has been valued at just £300'. However, the size of the fine will usually be related to the offender's culpability (and financial resources), and will not be a 'valuation' of the loss. Compensation for loss, from whatever source, is a separate matter. It may not require a separate civil case: English criminal courts are required to consider ordering the offender to pay compensation to the victim or victim's family, so far as the offender's means allow. However, in many cases the offender will not have the funds to pay realistic compensation. It is now recognized as part of the state's responsibility for criminal justice that it should provide a compensation fund for victims of crimes of violence, at least (see Ashworth 1986 and, on the current scheme, Miers 1997). This is not to deny that victims primarily have a right to compensation from the offender: that is clear on legal and moral grounds, if not always practical.

RESPONSIBILITIES, RIGHTS AND RESTORATIVE JUSTICE

The key question is whether the victim's legitimate interest goes beyond reparation or compensation (and the right to victim services and support, and to proper protection from further harm), and extends to the question of punishment. It would be wrong to suggest that the victim has no legitimate interest in the disposition of the offender in his or her case, but the victim's interest is surely no greater than yours or mine. The victim's interest is as a citizen, as one of many citizens who make up the community or state. In democratic theory all citizens have a right to vote at elections and sometimes on other occasions, and to petition their elected representatives about issues affecting them. If I am an ardent advocate of restorative justice or of indeterminate imprisonment for repeat offenders, I can petition my MP about it, or join a pressure group. Just because a person commits an offence against me, however, that does not privilege my voice above that of the court (acting 'in the general public interest') in the matter of the offender's punishment. A justification for this lies in social contract reasoning, along the lines that the state may be said to undertake the duty of administering justice and protecting citizens in return for citizens giving up their right to self-help (except in cases of urgency) in the cause of better social order. This returns to the earlier argument about the state's responsibility, and to the 'rule of law' values of impartiality, independence and consistency in the administration of criminal justice.

This principle is not opposed by all those who advocate a version of restorative justice. Thus Michael Cavadino and James Dignan (1997) draw a strong distinction between the victim's right to reparation and the public interest in responding to the offence. In their view it is right to empower victims to participate in the process which determines what reparation is to be made by the offender, and reparation to the victim should be the major element of the response. In serious cases some additional response (punishment) may be considered necessary, and they then insist on a form of limiting retributivism in which proportionality sets upper and lower boundaries for the burdens placed on offenders (and also serves as a default setting for cases where a conference or circle proves impossible or inappropriate). It is a matter for regret that few restorative justice theorists refer to Cavadino and Dignan's attempt to preserve as many of the values of restorative justice as possible whilst insisting upon principled limits. They rightly see the distinction between compensation and punishment as crucial, even though their proportionality constraints are looser than many desert theorists would require, and they regard victim involvement as a value to be enhanced where possible. 'Victim personal statements' must now be taken into account by English courts before sentencing: Edna Erez claims that 'providing victims with a voice has therapeutic advantages' (1999: 555; cf. Edwards 2001), but findings from the English pilot projects indicated no great psychological benefits to participant victims and some evidence of disillusionment (Sanders *et al.* 2001: 450).

The second point of principle concerns proportionality. Sentencing is *for* an offence, and respect for the offender as a citizen capable of choice suggests that the sentence should bear a relationship to the seriousness of the offence committed. To desert theorists this is axiomatic: punishment should always be proportionate to the offence, taking account of harm and culpability (von Hirsch 1993: ch. 2), unless a highly persuasive argument for creating a class of exceptional cases can be sustained. It is a strong criticism of deterrent sentencing and of risk theory that they accord priority to predictions and not to the seriousness of the offence committed: von Hirsch and Ashworth (1998: chs 2, 3). The proportionality principle is not the sole preserve of desert theorists: on the contrary, versions of it are widely accepted as limiting the quantum of punishment that may be imposed on offenders, whether as a major tenet of the Council of Europe's recommendation on sentencing (1993: para. A4) or as an element in Nicola Lacey's communitarian approach to punishment (Lacey 1988: 194). Other important functions of the proportionality principle are that it should ensure consistency of treatment among offenders, and that it should give protection against discrimination, by attempting to rule out certain factors from sentencing calculations. It is not being suggested that existing sentencing systems always pursue these principles successfully, but it is vital that they be recognized as goals and efforts made to fulfil them.

The principle of proportionality goes against victim involvement in sentencing decisions because the views of victims may vary. Some victims will be forgiving, other will be vindictive; some will be interested in new forms of sentence, others will not; some shops will have one policy in relation to thieves, others may have a different policy. If victim satisfaction is one of the aims of circles and conferences, then proportionate sentencing cannot be assured and may be overtaken in some cases by deterrent or risk-based sentencing. Two replies may be anticipated. First, it may be argued that in fact the involvement of victims assures *greater* proportionality (Erez and Rogers 1999; Erez 1999; cf. Sanders *et al.* 2001: 451): the actual harm to the victim becomes clear, and in general victims do not desire disproportionate sentences. But these are aggregative findings, whereas the point of the principle is to ensure that in no individual case is an offender liable to a disproportionate penalty. A second reply would be to concede that victim involvement should be subject to proportionality limits, so that no agreement reached in a circle or conference should be out of proportion to the seriousness of the offence. The significance of this concession depends on the nature of the proportionality constraint. There is a range of possible proportionality theories: desert theory requires the sentence to be proportionate to the seriousness of the offence, within fairly narrow bands (von Hirsch 1993: chs 2 and 4), whereas various forms of limiting retributivism recognize looser boundaries. Michael Tonry, for example, argues against the 'strong proportionality' of desert theorists and in favour of 'upper limits' set in accordance with a less precise notion of proportionality (Tonry 1994). Among restorative justice theorists, Braithwaite refers to 'guaranteeing offenders against punishment beyond a maximum' (1999: 105), but it is unclear whether his 'guarantee' adopts as much of proportionality theory as Tonry seems prepared to accept, and whether it imposes similar constraints or even less demanding ones. Most restorative justice theorists would insist that one of their objectives is to reduce levels of punitiveness, not to increase them; but some questions will be raised below about the contours of the 'background' penal system which is envisaged for cases where restorative justice processes fail or are rejected.

The third point is that everyone should have the right to a fair hearing 'by an independent and impartial tribunal', as Article 6.1 of the European Convention on Human Rights declares. This right expresses a fundamental principle of justice. Under the European Convention it applies to the sentencing stage as much as to trials. Do conferences and other restorative justice processes respect the right? Insofar as a victim plays a part in determining the disposition of a criminal case, is a conference 'independent and impartial'? The victim cannot be expected to be impartial, nor can the victim be expected to know about the available range of orders and other principles for the disposition of criminal cases. All of this suggests that conferences may fail to meet the basic standards of a fair hearing, insofar as the victim or victim's family plays a part in determining the outcome.

RESPONSIBILITIES, RIGHTS AND RESTORATIVE JUSTICE

Most restorative justice supporters will be unimpressed with this, because the argument simply assumes that what has become conventional in modern criminal justice systems is absolutely right. But the issue of principle must be confronted, since it is supported by the European Convention, the International Covenant on Civil and Political Rights and many other human rights documents. One reply from restorative justice supporters might be that the required 'impartiality' and 'objectivity' produce such an impersonal and detached tribunal as to demonstrate exactly what is wrong with conventional systems, and why they fail. But that reply neglects, or certainly undervalues, the link between independence, impartiality and procedural justice. Might it be possible to sidestep the objection by characterizing conferences and other restorative justice processes as alternatives to sentencing rather than as sentencing processes, and therefore not bound by the same principles? This might be thought apposite where any agreement reached in the conference or circle has to be submitted for approval by a court, and where the offender may withdraw from the conference and go to the court at any time.

This is an appropriate point at which to question the reality of the consent that is said to underlie restorative justice processes and outcomes. The general principle is that 'restorative processes should be used only with the free and voluntary consent of the parties. The parties should be able to withdraw that consent at any time during the process' (UN 2000: para. 7). This suggests that the offender may simply walk out and take his or her chances in the 'conventional' system. However, the result of doing so would usually be to propel the case into a formal criminal justice system that is perceived to be harsher in general, or that the offender may expect to be harsher on someone who has walked away from a restorative justice process. On some occasions, then, as in plea-bargaining (Sanders and Young 2000: ch. 7; Ashworth 1998: ch. 9), the 'consent' may proceed from a small amount of free will and a large slice of (perceived) coercion. Where the 'consent' is that of young people, and it is the police who explain matters to them, the danger of perceived coercion may be acute (Daly 2001). The United Nations draft principles attempt to deal with some of these issues, by providing that failure to reach agreement or failure to implement an agreement 'may not be used as a justification for a more severe sentence in subsequent criminal justice proceedings' (UN 2000: paras. 15, 16). But it is right to remain sceptical of the reality of consent, from the offender's point of view.

Returning to the right to an independent and impartial tribunal, is it breached if the victim makes a statement about sentencing, written or oral, to the court or other body that is to take the sentencing decision? This refers to statements that go beyond a victim impact statement, and are not limited to the issue of compensation. The ruling of the European Commission on Human Rights in *McCourt* v. *United Kingdom* (1993) 15 EHRR CD110 may be taken to suggest that such a statement on sentence could prejudice the impartiality of the tribunal, but this might be thought to go too far, not least because defendants have the right to make a 'plea in mitigation', in which their lawyers usually argue against certain outcomes and (sometimes) for a certain sentence. A stronger argument here is to return to the principles of compensation and of proportionality, discussed above, and to assert that the victim's view as to sentence should not be received because it is not relevant. Consider the case of *Nunn*, where the defendant had been sentenced to four years' imprisonment for causing the death of a close friend by dangerous driving. When Nunn's appeal against the sentence came before the Court of Appeal, the court had before it some lengthy written statements by the victim's mother and sister, recognizing that some punishment had to follow such a terrible offence, but stating that their own grief was being increased by the thought of the victim's close friend being in prison for so long. They added that the victim's father and other sister took a different view. In the Court of Appeal, Lord Justice Judge said this:

> We mean no disrespect to the mother and sister of the deceased, but the opinions of the victim, or the surviving members of the family, about the appropriate level of sentence do not provide any sound basis for reassessing a sentence. If the victim feels utterly merciful towards the criminal, and some do, the crime has still been committed and must be punished as it deserves. If the victim is obsessed with vengeance, which can in reality only be assuaged by a very long sentence, as also happens, the punishment cannot be made longer by the court than would otherwise be appropriate. Otherwise cases with identical features would be dealt with in widely differing ways, leading to improper and unfair disparity, and even in this particular case . . . the views of the members of the family of the deceased are not absolutely identical. (*Nunn* [1996] 2 Cr. App. R. (S) 136, at p. 140; see also *Roche* [1999] 2 Cr. App. R. (S) 105)

This statement captures the principles well.[2] Neither one victim's forgiveness of an offender, nor another's desire for vengeance against an offender, should be relevant when the community's response to an offence (as distinct from compensation) is being considered. The plea in *Nunn* was for leniency in the outcome, as also in the New Zealand case of *Clotworthy* (see Braithwaite 1999: 87–8). There are other cases where victims and their families campaign for severity, some with a very high profile (e.g. the case of Thompson and Venables, convicted at the age of 11 of the murder of James Bulger, whose family campaigned, with considerable support from the mass media, in favour of prolonging the imprisonment of the offenders). In dismissing an application by James Bulger's father for judicial review of the tariff set by the Lord Chief Justice, the Queen's Bench Divisional Court noted with approval that Lord Woolf had invited the Bulger family to make representations about the impact of their son's death on them, 'but had not invited them to give their views on what they thought was an appropriate tariff' (*R v. Secretary of State for the Home Department, ex parte Bulger, The Times*, 16 February 2001).

The above discussion of the three principles of compensation for wrongs, of independent and impartial tribunals, and of proportionality of sentence, suggests that the substantive and procedural rights of victims at the stage of disposal (sentence) ought to be limited. This should apply whether the rights of victims are being considered in the context of restorative justice or of a 'conventional' sentencing system. The rights of victims should chiefly be to receive support, proper services, and (where the offender is unable to pay) state compensation for violent crimes. There are arguments for going further, so as to achieve some measure of victim participation: this would require the provision of better and fuller information to victims, and the objective would be to enable some genuine participation in the process of disposal 'without giving [victims] the power to influence decisions that are not appropriately theirs' (Sanders *et al.* 2001: 458). This would be a fine line to tread, as the debate following the decision of the US Supreme Court to allow victim impact statements in capital cases demonstrates: *Payne v. Tennessee* (1991) 111 S Ct 2597, discussed by Sarat 1997.

---

[2] The *Nunn* case also points to the practical problem arising where two or more victims have different views on the proper response to the crime. A further complication would be where there is a disagreement between the victim and the community representatives over outcome (cf. Law Commission of Canada 1999: 38), although this should be resolved on the basis that the victim's interest lies in reparation and compensation whereas the state's (or community's) interest lies in measures going beyond that.

Exploring the 'Default Setting': When Restorative Justice Runs Out

Although some restorative justice practitioners and writers express themselves as if there are no aspects of criminal justice with which restorative justice could not deal, most are realistic enough to recognize that provision must be made for some cases to be handled outside restorative justice processes. We have noted that Cavadino and Dignan provide for a 'default system' to deal with cases in which a circle or conference does not prove possible, perhaps because the necessary consents are not forthcoming. Certain writers make much stronger claims for the ability of restorative justice to handle a wide range of disputes in criminal justice, schools, industry, and business regulation (e.g. Wachtel and McCold 2001). But even some of those recognize that there must be some form of 'background system' in place (Braithwaite 1999). If one adds together the groups of offenders for whom such a system may be needed—those who refuse to participate in restorative justice, or whose victims refuse to participate,[3] or who have failed to comply with previous restorative justice outcomes—the numbers might be considerable. It has been argued above that some restorative justice processes themselves are incompatible with principles of justice on independence, impartiality, proportionality, and so on. How does the 'default' or 'background' system measure up to these principles?

Braithwaite explains his background system by reference to this enforcement pyramid, developed in relation to regulatory enforcement (1999: 61):

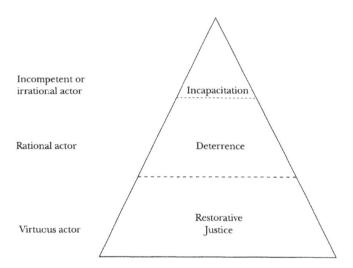

The idea is that one starts with restorative justice at the base of the pyramid. It may be tried more than once. If it clearly fails, then one would move to an 'active deterrence' strategy, which Braithwaite distinguishes carefully from the 'passive deterrence' described in most of the punishment literature (see Ayres and Braithwaite 1992: ch. 2).

---

[3] Some RJ schemes are prepared to proceed with a conference in the absence of the victim, which expands the role of the facilitator or coordinator: see, e.g. Daly (2001) on South Australia.

To have this kind of deterrence in the background helps restorative justice to work, in Braithwaite's view. Nonetheless, he warns that:

> The problem is that if deterrent threats cause defiance and reactance, restorative justice may be compromised by what sits above it in a dynamic pyramidal strategy of deterrence and incapacitation . . . The challenge is to have the Sword of Damocles always threatening in the background but never threatened in the foreground. (Braithwaite 1999: 63-4)

From the point of view of principle, this approach is troubling. It seems that, once we leave the softly, softly world of restorative justice, offenders may be delivered into raging deterrent and incapacitative strategies, with rogue elements like Uncle Harry calling the shots (see the remarkable paragraphs in Braithwaite 1999: 66-7, on Uncle Harry), and with only the vaguest of gestures towards 'guaranteeing offenders against punishment beyond a maximum' (*ibid*.: 105). When Philip Pettit and John Braithwaite state that, in pursuit of the goal of 'community reassurance', sentencers should take account of 'how common that offence has become in the community' and 'how far the offender is capable of re-offending again' (1993, excerpted in von Hirsch and Ashworth 1998: 326), the glass becomes very dark, and the excesses of the 'risk society' seem to beckon.

Braithwaite and Pettit (1990: ch. 7) would answer that current maximum penalties should provide the guarantee in the first instance, and that there should then be a 'decremental strategy' of lowering those maxima progressively so as to reduce levels of punitiveness. But statutory maximum sentences are often very high, and certainly much higher than most proportionality theorists (including Tonry's looser approach to limits) would accept. It is also countered that desert-based critics are not paying attention to the difference between the usual run of consequentialist theories based on ('passive') deterrence and incapacitation, and the meaning of those strategies within a 'republican' framework which respects the dominion of each individual (Braithwaite and Pettit 1990). We should not find these aspects of Braithwaite's restorative justice theory threatening, it is contended, if we looked at the practical meaning of the pyramid of enforcement and took account of the emphasis on penal parsimony in a republican system. But it is not enough to proclaim penal parsimony and yet to give such prominence, even in a 'background system', to deterrent and incapacitative strategies. What types of deterrent strategy are permissible, within what kinds of limits? What forms of incapacitation? To what extent does the background system permit, nay encourage, sentencing on the basis of previous record rather than present offence? The answers to these questions about restorative justice and recalcitrant offenders remain unclear (see von Hirsch and Ashworth 1998: 317-35), but the need for firm safeguards against undue severity does not disappear if a system is labelled 'restorative'. Penal history yields plenty of examples of apparently benign policies resulting in repressive controls.

Conclusions

It has been argued that, despite the decline of statism and the rise of neo-liberal and 'advanced liberal' programmes for the responsibilization of other agencies of security, it should still be acknowledged to be a fundamental role of the state to maintain a system for the administration of justice and to ensure that proper standards of procedural protection are applied. It is recognized that there have been and are failures of state-led criminal justice, just as there have been and are manifest failures of states to deliver security (Garland 2001: ch. 5). The growth of restorative justice schemes is encouraged by both these phenomena. However, it should remain the responsibility of the state towards its citizens to ensure that justice is administered by independent and impartial tribunals, and that there are proportionality limits which should not only constrain the measures agreed at restorative justice conferences etc. but also ensure some similarity in the treatment of equally situated offenders. If the state does delegate certain spheres of criminal justice to some form of community-based conference, the importance of insisting on the protection of basic rights for defendants is not diminished.

Many of the innovations urged by restorative justice advocates ought to be tested and evaluated—the effect on victims and on offenders of face-to-face meetings, the value of apologies, the effect on victims and offenders of reparation agreements, the effect on victims and offenders of victim participation in conferences, and so forth. Too often, however, enthusiasm for such processes leads proponents either to overlook the need for safeguards, or to imply that they are not relevant. The steps being taken to develop standards for restorative justice processes are important in this respect (see UN 2000; Braithwaite, this issue), but they must be accompanied by a re-examination of deeper issues. In order to ensure that there is no deficit of procedural justice or human rights, it was argued above that governments must retain a primary role, that community-based processes and outcomes should be scrutinized closely, and that the proper role of the victim in criminal justice processes should be reappraised. Thus any restorative justice processes for offenders who might otherwise go to court should (a) be led by an independent and impartial person;[4] (b) be required to submit its decisions for court approval; (c) allow the participation of the victim, the offender, and their families or significant others; (d) make provision for access to legal advice before and after any restorative justice processes, at a minimum (Council of Europe 2000, para. 8; cf. UN 2000: para. 12); (e) focus on apology and on the appropriate reparation and/or compensation for the offence; and (f) be required to respect relevant principles, such as not imposing on the offender a financial burden that is not means-related. If, contrary to the argument here, a restorative justice conference is permitted to make proposals for community restoration or other responses going beyond reparation to the individual victim(s), there should be clear and circumscribed proportionality limits for those measures. However, the practical implications of 'restoration of the community' call for closer examination than they have hitherto received.

Criticisms of this kind seem to leave many restorative justice practitioners baffled, however. They may protest that restorative justice processes are not about punishment anyway; that all the safeguards are about offenders, not victims; and that in practice restorative justice encounters no problems about undue severity, etc. On the first point, Kathleen Daly (2000) rightly calls for caution among those restorative justice advocates

---

[4] This raises the question of police-led conferences, used in England in certain types of case (Young 2001). Braithwaite asks 'whether there is something wrong in principle with the police facilitating a conference. Does it make the police investigator, prosecutor, judge and jury?' (1999: 99). He never answers the question of principle, and instead points out the need to have someone assume the role of facilitator, and suggests that police involvement might have beneficial effects on police culture. But the question of principle must surely be answered by stating that this is wrong. It is not appropriate for the police to take on what is a quasi-judicial role, when they are so heavily involved in investigations. More strongly, it is inappropriate for the police to be involved in any 'shaming' of offenders (cf. Cunneen 1997 and Blagg 1997 with Braithwaite 1997). It is insufficient to reply that offenders who have misgivings can withdraw their consent: as stated above, the 'consent' in these situations may take a severely diluted form. This critique is, of course, no less applicable to the ongoing practice of police cautioning of adults.

who claim not to be in the punishment business but to be engaged in constructive and non-punitive responses to wrongdoing. Even if one were to adopt a narrow definition (that only measures intended to be punitive count as punishment), many restorative justice outcomes satisfy that definition inasmuch as they are known to impose obligations or deprivations on offenders: Johnstone 2001: 106–10; cf. Walgrave 2001. The argument that such obligations or deprivations proceed from full consent is, as we have seen, unconvincing. So far as the bias of rights towards offenders is concerned, it must be conceded that most human rights documents do not incorporate victims' rights into their framework—although there are well-known (separate) declarations of victims' rights. This imbalance ought to be rectified, but only after focusing on the arguments presented above. The third point (the absence of severity) may be generally true, since most of those interested in promoting restorative justice seem to oppose penal severity; but attention was drawn above to Braithwaite's 'background system', and even within restorative justice clear limits are important to prevent violations of rights behind a mask of benevolence. Once it is conceded that restorative justice cannot deal with absolutely all criminal cases, the relationship between the formal system and any restorative justice processes must be carefully crafted so as to avoid inequities. This third point is particularly important where enthusiasm for restorative justice leads a government to 'parachute' elements of restorative justice into a system suffused with rather different principles and practices, as has been done with youth justice in England and Wales (Morris and Gelsthorpe 2000; Ball 2000).

References

ASHWORTH, A. (1986), 'Punishment and Compensation: State, Victim and Offender', *Oxford Journal of Legal Studies*, 6: 86–122.

——(1998), *The Criminal Process*, 2nd edn. Oxford: Oxford University Press.

AYRES, I. and BRAITHWAITE, J. (1992), *Responsive Regulation: Transcending the Deregulation Debate*. New York: Oxford University Press.

BALL, C. (2000), 'The Youth Justice and Criminal Evidence Act 1999: A Significant Move towards Restorative Justice, or a Recipe for Unintended Consequences?', *Criminal Law Review*, 211–22.

BAYLEY, D. (2001), 'Security and Justice for All', in H. Strang and J. Braithwaite, eds., *Restorative Justice and Civil Society*, 211–21. Cambridge: Cambridge University Press.

BLAGG, H. (1997), 'A Just Measure of Shame? Aboriginal Youth and Conferencing in Australia', *British Journal of Criminology*, 37/4: 481–501.

BRAITHWAITE, J. (1989), *Crime, Shame and Reintegration*. Cambridge: Cambridge University Press.

——(1993), 'Shame and Modernity', *British Journal of Criminology*, 33/1: 1–18.

——(1997), 'Conferencing and Plurality: Reply to Blagg', *British Journal of Criminology*, 37/4: 502–6.

——(1999), 'Restorative Justice: Assessing Optimistic and Pessimistic Accounts', *Crime and Justice: A Review of Research*, 25: 1–110.

BRAITHWAITE, J. and PETTIT, P. (1990), *Not Just Deserts*. Oxford: Oxford University Press.

CAVADINO, M. and DIGNAN, J. (1997), 'Reparation, Retribution and Rights', *International Review of Victimology*, 4: 233–71.

CHRISTIE, N. (1977), 'Conflicts as Property', *British Journal of Criminology*, 17/1: 1–15.

RESPONSIBILITIES, RIGHTS AND RESTORATIVE JUSTICE

COUNCIL OF EUROPE (1993), *Consistency in Sentencing*, Recommendation R (92) 18. Strasbourg: Council of Europe.

——(2000), *Mediation in Penal Matters*, Recommendation R (99) 19. Strasbourg: Council of Europe.

CRAWFORD, A. (2000), 'Salient Themes towards a Victim Perspective and the Limitations of Restorative Justice', in A. Crawford and J Goodey, eds., *Integrating a Victim Perspective within Criminal Justice*. Aldershot: Ashgate.

CRAWFORD, A. and GOODEY, J., eds. (2000), *Integrating a Victim Perspective within Criminal Justice*. Aldershot: Ashgate.

CRETNEY, A., DAVIS, G., CLARKSON, C. and SHEPHERD, J. (1994), 'Criminalizing Assault: The Failure of the "Offence against Society" Model', *British Journal of Criminology*, 34/1: 15–29.

CUNNEEN, C. (1997), 'Community Conferencing and the Fiction of Indigenous Control', *Australia and New Zealand Journal of Criminology*, 30: 297–320.

DALY, K. (1999), 'Does Punishment Have a Place in Restorative Justice?', unpublished paper presented to the ANZ Criminology conference; www.gu.edu.au/school/ccj/kdaly.html.

——(2000), 'Restorative Justice: The Real Story', unpublished paper presented to Scottish Criminology Conference; www.gu.edu.au/school/ccj/kdaly.html.

——(2001), 'Conferencing in Australia and New Zealand: Variations, Research Findings and Prospects', in A. Morris and G. Maxwell, eds., *Restorative Justice for Juveniles: Conferencing, Mediation and Circles*. Oxford: Hart Publishing.

DUFF, R. A. (2000), *Punishment, Communication and Community*. New York: Oxford Univesity Press.

EDWARDS, I. (2001), 'Victim Participation in Sentencing: The Problems of Incoherence', *Howard Journal of Criminal Justice*, 40: 39–54.

EREZ, E. (1999), 'Who's Afraid of the Big Bad Victim? Victim Impact Statements as Empowerment and Enhancement of Justice', *Criminal Law Review*, 545–56.

EREZ, E. and ROGERS, L. (1999), 'Victim Impact Statements and Sentencing Outcomes and Processes: The Perspectives of Legal Professionals', *British Journal of Criminology*, 39/2: 216–39.

GARDNER, J. (1998), 'Crime: In Proportion and in Perspective', in A. Ashworth and M. Wasik, eds., *Fundamentals of Sentencing Theory*. Oxford: Oxford University Press.

GARLAND, D. (2001), *The Culture of Control: Crime and Social Order in Contemporary Society*. Oxford: Oxford University Press.

JOHNSTONE, G. (2001), *Restorative Justice*. Cullompton: Willan Publishing.

LACEY, N. (1988), *State Punishment*. London: Routledge.

——(1998), *Unspeakable Subjects*. Oxford: Hart Publishing.

LAW COMMISSION OF CANADA (1999), *From Restorative Justice to Transformative Justice*, discussion paper. Ottawa: Law Commission.

LLEWELLYN, J. J. and HOWSE, R. (1998), *Restorative Justice: A Conceptual Framework*. Ottawa: Law Commission of Canada.

MACCORMICK, N. and GARLAND, D. (1998), 'Sovereign States and Vengeful Victims: The Problem of the Right to Punish', in A. Ashworth and M. Wasik, eds., *Fundamentals of Sentencing Theory*. Oxford: Oxford University Press.

McEVOY, K. and MIKA, H. (2001), 'Punishment, Policing and Praxis: Restorative Justice and Non-Violent Alternatives to Paramilitary Punishments in Northern Ireland', *Policing and Society*, 11.

MARSHALL, T. F. (1999), *Restorative Justice: An Overview*. London: Home Office Research, Development and Statistics Directorate.

MEIER, B.-D. (1998), 'Restorative Justice? A New Paradigm in Criminal Law?', *European Journal of Crime, Criminal Law and Criminal Justice*, 6: 125–36.

ASHWORTH

MIERS, D. (1997), *State Compensation for Criminal Injuries.* London: Blackstone.

——(2001), *An International Review of Restorative Justice.* London: Home Office.

MORGAN, J. and ZEDNER, L. (1992), *Child Victims.* Oxford: Oxford University Press.

MORRIS, A. and GELSTHORPE, L. (2000), 'Something Old, Something Borrowed, Something Blue, but Something New?', Comment on the Prospects for Restorative Justice under the Crime and Disorder Act', *Criminal Law Review*, 18–30.

MORRIS, A. and MAXWELL, G. (2000), 'The Practice of Family Group Conferences in New Zealand: Assessing the Place, Potential and Pitfalls of Restorative Justice', in A. Crawford and J Goodey, eds., *Integrating a Victim Perspective within Criminal Justice.* Aldershot: Ashgate.

PAVLICH, G. (2001), 'The Force of Community', in H. Strang and J. Braithwaite, eds., *Restorative Justice and Civil Society*, 56–68. Cambridge: Cambridge University Press.

PETTIT, P. with BRAITHWAITE, J. (1993), 'Not Just Deserts, Even in Sentencing', *Current Issues in Criminal Justice*, 4: 222–32.

REEVES, H. and MULLEY, K. (2000), 'The New Status of Victims in the UK: Opportunities and Threats', in A. Crawford and J Goodey, eds., *Integrating a Victim Perspective within Criminal Justice.* Aldershot: Ashgate.

ROACH, K. (1999), *Due Process and Victims' Rights: The New Law and Politics of Criminal Justice.* Toronto: University of Toronto Press

ROSE, N. (2000), 'Government and Control', *British Journal of Criminology*, 40/2: 321–39.

SANDERS, A., HOYLE, C., MORGAN, R. and CAPE, E. (2001), 'Victim Impact Statements: Can't Work, Won't Work', *Criminal Law Review*, 447–58.

SARAT, A. (1997), 'Vengeance, Victims and the Identities of Law', *Social and Legal Studies*, 6: 163–84.

SHEARING, C. (2000), 'Punishment and the Changing Face of Governance', *Punishment and Society*, 203–20.

——(2001), 'Transforming Security: A South African Experiment', in H. Strang and J. Braithwaite, eds., *Restorative Justice and Civil Society*, 14–34. Cambridge: Cambridge University Press.

TAURI, J. (1999), 'Exploring Recent Innovations in New Zealand's Criminal Justice System: Empowering Maori or Biculturising the State?', *Australia and New Zealand Journal of Criminology*, 32: 153–70.

TONRY, M. (1994), 'Proportionality, Parsimony and Interchangeability of Punishments', in A. Duff, S. Marshall, R. E. Dobash and R. P. Dobash, eds., *Penal Theory and Practice.* Manchester: Manchester University Press.

UNITED NATIONS (2000), *Basic Principles on the Use of Restorative Justice Programmes in Criminal Matters*, www.restorativejustice.org/.ents/UNDecBasicPrinciplesofRJ.htm.

VAN NESS, D. W. (1993), 'New Wine and Old Wineskins: Four Challenges of Restorative Justice', *Criminal Law Forum*, 4: 251–76.

VAN ZYL SMIT, D. (1999), 'Criminological Ideas and the South African Transition', *British Journal of Criminology*, 39/2: 198–215.

VON HIRSCH, A. (1993), *Censure and Sanctions.* Oxford: Oxford University Press.

VON HIRSCH, A. and ASHWORTH, A., eds. (1998), *Principled Sentencing: Readings on Theory and Policy.* Oxford: Hart Publishing.

WACHTEL, T. and MCCOLD, P. (2001), 'Restorative Justice in Everyday Life', in H. Strang and J. Braithwaite, eds., *Restorative Justice and Civil Society*, 114–29. Cambridge: Cambridge University Press.

WALGRAVE, L. (1995), 'Restorative Justice for Juveniles', *Howard Journal of Criminal Justice*, 34: 228–49.

——(2001), 'On Restoration and Punishment', in A. Morris and G. Maxwell, eds., *Restorative Justice for Juveniles*, 17–40. Oxford: Hart.

WRIGHT, M. (1996), *Justice for Victims and Offenders*, 2nd edn. Winchester: Waterside.

YOUNG, R. (2001), 'Just Cops Doing "Shameful" Business: Police-Led Restorative Justice and the Lessons of Research', in A. Morris and G. Maxwell, eds., *Restorative Justice for Juveniles*, 195–226. Oxford: Hart.

ZEDNER, L. (1994), 'Reparation and Retribution: Are They Reconcilable?', *Modern Law Review*, 57: 228.

ZEHR, H. (1990), *Changing Lenses: A New Focus for Criminal Justice*. Scottsdale, PA: Herald Press.

[18]

Feminism, Rape and the Search for Justice[†]

CLARE McGLYNN[*]

Abstract—Justice for rape victims has become synonymous with punitive state punishment. Taking rape seriously is equated with increasing convictions and prison sentences and consequently most feminist activism has been focused on reforming the conventional criminal justice system to secure these aims. While important reforms have been made, justice continues to elude many victims. Many feel re-victimized by a system which marginalizes their interests and denies them a voice. Restorative justice offers the potential to secure justice for rape victims, but feminist resistance has resulted in few programmes tackling such crimes. In *After the Crime*, Susan Miller evidences the positive outcomes of a restorative justice programme tackling serious offences including rape and recommends their development. However, her vision is ultimately limited by her recommendation of only post-conviction restorative processes and the implicit endorsement of the conventional criminal justice system. I argue that feminist strategy and activism must rethink its approach to what constitutes justice for rape victims, going beyond punitive state outcomes to encompass broader notions of justice, including an expansive approach to restorative justice.

Keywords: feminism, justice, rape, sexual violence, restorative justice, punishment

1. Introduction

What constitutes justice for rape victims? Is it seeing the perpetrator convicted and imprisoned for a significant period of time? Is it being believed and treated with respect by prosecuting authorities? Is it receiving compensation, from the offender or the state? Is it having the opportunity to tell one's story in a meaningful way, perhaps directly to the offender? The answer, of course, is that justice for rape victims can take any or all of these forms, as well as many more possibilities. The problem is that it has come to be so closely associated with

[†] A review of Susan Miller, *After the Crime: the Power of Restorative Justice Dialogues Between Victims and Violent Offenders* (New York University Press 2011).

[*] Professor of Law, Durham Law School, Durham University. Email: clare.mcglynn@durham.ac.uk. I would like to thank Vanessa Munro, Erika Rackley and Ian Ward for their helpful comments on an earlier draft of this article.

punitive, carceral punishment that other means of securing justice have been almost completely obscured. As conviction rates for rape and other sexual offences are so low, the end result of such a fundamentally limited approach is that justice eludes most victims of rape and other sexual offences.

In *After the Crime*, Susan Miller offers another possibility, that of restorative justice. After providing rich, in-depth narratives which tell the positive stories of victims and offenders engaging in dialogue, Miller suggests that the potential for the use of restorative justice in cases of 'gendered violence' is 'vast'.[1] Nonetheless, she continues that it is only post-conviction restorative justice programmes which can guard against the 'host of legitimate concerns' over the use of restorative justice in such cases.[2]

Thus, while Miller provides a necessary anti-dote to the long-held feminist resistance to the use of restorative justice for gendered violence, in view of the low conviction rates for such offences, a focus on post-conviction restorative justice offers a constrained vision of justice benefiting only a small number of victims. Furthermore, in her endorsement of post-conviction restorative justice only, Miller enhances the status of the conventional criminal justice system. This is problematic in light of its current punitive and retributive orientation and its systemic marginalization of the interests of victims of gendered violence. In this article, after examining and welcoming Miller's defence of some forms of restorative justice, and focussing on rape and other forms of sexual violence,[3] I will suggest that feminist strategy and activism must rethink its approach to what constitutes justice for rape victims. It must move beyond a predominant focus on punitive state outcomes, with its emphasis on convictions and high prison sentences, to encompass broader notions of justice, including an expansive approach to restorative justice.

2. *Victims' Voices Heard: The Power of Restorative Justice*

After the Crime is a powerful defence of post-conviction restorative justice programmes dealing with serious crimes, including rape and child sexual abuse. The case is made by means of nine vivid narratives which detail the lives and experiences of victims and offenders who engaged in dialogue through the programme 'Victims' Voices Heard' (VVH). VVH is a 'victim-centred' programme in the United States which brings victims into face-to-face contact, post-conviction, with their respective offenders to 'receive information, to tell offenders about the consequences of their violence, and to help them regain control over their lives that was taken from them first by the offender and then

---

[1] Susan Miller, *After the Crime: The Power of Restorative Justice Dialogues Between Victims and Violent Offenders* (New York University Press 2011) 198.

[2] Miller (n 1) 213.

[3] For reasons set out further below, while the literature on restorative justice discusses 'gendered violence' generally, I argue that it is more appropriate to focus on its efficacy for specific forms of such violence. My focus is on rape and other forms of sexual violence.

by the criminal justice system'.[4] It is an intensive programme which has no impact on criminal justice outcomes, such as prison release, and dialogues are preceded by months of preparation. As most restorative projects specifically exclude sexual offences, that VVH includes offences of rape and sexual abuse within its remit marks it out as distinctive.[5] Of the nine cases examined in *After the Crime*, four deal with sexual violence (two stranger rapes and two cases of child sexual abuse by older family members), one involves domestic violence (including marital rape and attempted murder), with the remainder being homicides.

Each of Miller's accounts is based variously on interviews with the offenders, victims, family members and facilitators, together with official and personal documents relating to each case. The stories presented are a skilful blend of easily accessible narratives, with the complex social and political reality of victimhood and offending carefully interwoven. These extremely powerful accounts detail the lives, background, hopes and fears of offenders and victims, offering a multifaceted picture of crime and its effects. In doing so, Miller reaches beyond simplistic accounts of victim 'satisfaction' with restorative programmes, towards a deep understanding of the workings (or failings) of the criminal justice system and the complex, often contradictory, needs and desires of victims.

Having a voice and being heard were key motivations behind victims' decisions to engage with the programme, even for those who had been given the opportunity to participate in their criminal cases.[6] Miller states that participation in VVH gave victims 'the very thing that had eluded them in the criminal justice system: a voice'.[7] Furthermore, victims wanted offenders, 'visibly and publicly', to 'acknowledge the consequences of their actions', as well as wishing to 'give the offenders the emotional baggage they had been carrying all these years'.[8]

Miller reports that the 'restorative success for victims is crystal clear' and the benefits were long-lasting.[9] The whole process, including the many meetings with the facilitator, letter exchanges and the face to face dialogue, was 'transformative, empowering and cathartic and brought [the victims] a sense of peace'.[10] It did not necessarily bring 'closure', but 'facilitated forward movement'.[11] Victims felt 'empowerment' and a restored 'sense of self-control

---

[4] Miller (n 1) 6.
[5] Many such exclusions are the result of feminist resistance to restorative justice. For a discussion of feminism and restorative justice see: James Ptacek (ed), *Restorative Justice and Violence Against Women* (OUP 2010) and John Braithwaite and Heather Strang (eds), *Restorative Justice and Family Violence* (CUP 2002).
[6] Miller (n 1) 163, 175.
[7] ibid 175.
[8] ibid 178–79.
[9] ibid 187–88.
[10] ibid 164.
[11] ibid.

and autonomy'.[12] Furthermore, Miller suggests that the dialogues gave victims back their power: the 'asymmetry of power that was present during the crime and the case processing was reconfigured'.[13] This was particularly important in the cases of gendered violence where victims 'sought empowerment over people and situations over which they had previously had no power'.[14] Nonetheless, where the victims and offenders were strangers prior to the offence, the outcomes 'were more positive'.[15] In these cases, the victims were also most likely to receive unconditional support from families and friends. Offenders who knew their victims did accept responsibility, but 'their contrition rang a little hollow'.[16] The victims still emerged from the programme 'empowered', Miller notes, but these sexual offenders continued to minimize and rationalize their offending.[17]

The overall impact on offenders is more difficult to assess, especially as most remained in prison. Miller reports that offenders felt satisfied that they were able to make some amends for their crimes and express their remorse. Many planned to reform when released from prison and some proposed community action to help others move away from a life of crime. As Miller states, it is only after prison release that we will know whether offenders' resolve to reform will manifest itself, although even a few years after the dialogues, the desire for change remained strong.[18]

To give just one example of the power of the dialogues: Donna survived being raped in her home by an intruder, Jamal. The impact of this offence on Donna was long-lasting, including deep feelings of distrust, self-blame and loathing and a fear of others which effectively made her a prisoner in her own home. Around 10 years after Jamal was imprisoned, Donna started the VVH programme and found it transformative. After the process, she concluded that: 'He no longer controls my life.'[19] Furthermore, she felt able to move on, commenting that: 'I will not let the rape steal my happiness'.[20] Indeed, from having been terrified of her attacker, following the dialogue process Donna reported that she 'wouldn't stop him from getting released'.[21] Jamal expressed his remorse over his offence, apologized, answered Donna's questions and

---

[12] ibid 166.
[13] ibid 178.
[14] ibid 179.
[15] ibid 167.
[16] ibid 171.
[17] ibid. While restorative justice is often criticized for minimizing the harm of an offence, it must be remembered that the traditional criminal justice system is expert at this, via an adversarial process encouraging an offender to refuse to admit guilt and to diminish any harm. As Kathleen Daly and Sarah Curtis-Fawley point out, in the restorative process such behaviors are at least aired and challenged in a way that does not happen in the court room: 'Restorative Justice for Victims of Sexual Assault', in Karin Heimer and Candace Kruttschnitt (eds), *Gender and Crime: Patterns of Victimization and Offending* (New York University Press 2005) 255.
[18] Miller (n 1) 188.
[19] ibid 46.
[20] ibid 55.
[21] ibid 44.

articulated a clear desire to reform and move away from his previous life and behaviours when released.[22]

Overall, therefore, *After the Crime* provides four compelling stories detailing the positive impact of restorative justice dialogues on victims of sexual violence and one relating to domestic abuse. Miller's multifaceted methodology and long-term investment in the research pays dividends and her writing style creates narratives which are moving and inspiring. Furthermore, not only does she convey the experiences and expectations of the victims, but she also manages to open a window into the feelings and perspectives of the offenders, respecting their humanity, but without ever condoning their actions.

3. *Restorative Justice and Sexual Violence: Constraints and Opportunities*

Miller rightly suggests that *After the Crime* will 'shed important light' on debates over the appropriateness of using restorative justice in cases of gendered violence.[23] This highly 'controversial'[24] debate has largely been the domain of feminist communities where discussion of the possibilities of restorative justice has been met with 'deep skepticism'.[25] Critics have characterized it as a 'soft option',[26] warning of the dangers of re-victimization, of risks to women's safety and the concern that a turn to restorative justice will effectively re-privatize sexual violence, thereby reversing the progressive law and policy reforms of recent decades. These are valid concerns though they are sometimes based on myths and generalizations about restorative justice and 'gendered violence'. To be more specific, some feminist resistance appears to be rooted in assumptions about the comparability of restorative justice with forms of civil mediation which feminists have rightly critiqued for their presumption of equality between participants and lack of understanding of the dynamics of domestic abuse.[27] However, restorative justice significantly differs from mediation principally due to the fundamental prerequisite of restorative practices that an offender acknowledges responsibility for the offence.[28] Such an admission clearly establishes the roles of offender and victim: there is no fact-finding. Furthermore, many critiques tend to equate restorative justice with straightforward diversion from the criminal justice system. Over recent

---

[22] ibid 54–55.
[23] ibid 179.
[24] Julie Stubbs, 'Restorative Justice, Gendered Violence and Indigenous Women', in Ptacek (n 5) 105.
[25] James Ptacek, 'Resisting Co-optation – Three Feminist Challenges to Antiviolence Work', in Ptacek (n 5) 19.
[26] As suggested by some victim advocates in Sarah Curtis-Fawley and Kathleen Daly, 'Gendered Violence and Restorative Justice – The Views of Victim Advocates' (2005) 11 Violence Against Women 603–38, 624.
[27] ibid 607.
[28] A commonly cited definition of restorative justice is that given by Tony Marshall: 'a process whereby all parties with a stake in a particular offence come together to resolve collectively how to deal with the aftermath of the offence and its implications for the future': *Restorative Justice: an Overview* (Home Office 1999) 5.

years, however, practice has demonstrated that there is a vast range and variety
of restorative justice programmes which can operate at any stage of the criminal
justice system, having various impacts on outcomes and punishment, or none
at all; or a process can operate outside of the criminal justice system entirely.[29]
It is perhaps revealing that Sarah Curtis-Fawley and Kathleen Daly found in
their interviews with victim advocates that the greatest opposition to restorative
justice was expressed by those who were most unsure of what it was.[30]

Nonetheless, notwithstanding myths and misunderstandings, contention
remains due to the lack of empirical evidence clearly establishing the dangers
or value of restorative justice for sexual offending.[31] There are only a handful
of programmes internationally which use restorative techniques in cases of
sexual violence and even fewer evaluations of such projects. *After the Crime*,
therefore, provides important evidence of the power of restorative justice. It
shows how victims of sexual violence value restorative justice and would
recommend it to others in similar situations.[32] It also responds to concerns
regarding the risks of re-victimization and endangering safety, demonstrating
that restorative justice for sexual violence is viable and can have significant
positive effects. However, while Miller does advocate the use of restorative
justice in cases of serious violence including rape, she only recommends such
schemes post-conviction. This is a considerable limitation on the scope of any
future developments and we need, therefore, to understand in more detail why
she might be making this argument.

Miller distinguishes between what she labels 'therapeutic' restorative justice
and 'diversionary' programmes.[33] Specifically, VVH is 'therapeutic' and
'designed to help victims with their recovery; it is *not* designed to affect the
outcome of criminal cases'.[34] Furthermore, therapeutic programmes 'operate
after offenders have been convicted; their primary goal is to empower and heal
victims'.[35] Miller suggests that it is these specific features which mean that
such schemes can be 'effective in handling crimes of gendered violence'.[36] In
contrast, diversionary programmes are those in which the restorative element
may determine the outcome of the case, are 'offender oriented' and offer an

---

[29] For a discussion, see Mark Umbreit and Marilyn Armour, *Restorative Justice Dialogue – an Essential Guide for Research and Practice* (Springer 2010).
[30] Curtis-Fawley and Daly (n 26) 618. This finding has been confirmed in relation to opinion leaders in New Zealand: Gitana Proietti-Scifoni and Kathleen Daly, 'Gendered Violence and Restorative Justice: the Views of New Zealand Opinion Leaders' (2011) 14 Contemporary Justice Review 269–90.
[31] For an overview of the field, see Mary Koss and Mary Achilles, 'Restorative Justice Responses to Sexual Assault', (2008) VAWnet available at: <http://new.vawnet.org/Assoc_Files_VAWnet/AR_RestorativeJustice.pdf> accessed 19 September 2011.
[32] See also Clare McGlynn, Nicole Westmarland and Nikki Godden, '"I Just Wanted Him to Hear Me": Sexual Violence and the Possibilities of Restorative Justice' (2012) 39 Journal of Law and Society forthcoming.
[33] Miller (n 1) 12.
[34] ibid 6 (original emphasis).
[35] ibid 12.
[36] ibid 13.

'alternative' outcome in lieu of the conventional criminal justice process.[37] According to Miller, there are a 'host of legitimate concerns' with their use for gendered violence including that they 'do little to disrupt' the unequal power relations between offenders and victims and 'risk re-victimizing women and children'.[38] In general, they 'fail many victims'.[39] Diversionary programmes, she concludes, are only appropriate for 'nonviolent property and juvenile cases'.[40]

It can be seen, therefore, that in seeking to defend VVH from the 'great controversy'[41] which courts the use of restorative justice for crimes of gendered violence, Miller emphasizes both the purpose of VVH—recovery and healing— as well as its stage in the criminal justice system, that is post-conviction. Specifically, Miller states that the 'checks and balances' of VVH, plus the fact of incarceration, ensure that victims feel safe, empowered, in control and not vulnerable to re-victimization.[42] It is certainly clear that there is effective screening and risk assessment in the programme and that preparation is taken extremely seriously. However, it is not clear why only post-conviction programmes can deal effectively with these risks. For example, a poorly managed post-conviction programme, without the 'checks and balances' of VVH, could run the real risk of re-victimization and endangering safety. And, on the contrary, a well-managed restorative project operating at different stages of the criminal justice system could effectively manage and monitor risks. This would suggest, therefore, that it is not timing—post-conviction—which per se protects victims, but the exceptional care to risk-assess, prepare and to ensure that any dangers are minimized.

Indeed, it is just such care that is taken in two projects which use restorative conferences to tackle sexual crimes at different stages of the criminal justice system.[43] The Restore programme in the United States, for example, is a diversionary scheme dealing with acquaintance rape and sexual assault.[44] In particular, the programme aims to 'facilitate a victim-centred, community-driven resolution of selected individual sex crimes that creates and carries out a

---

[37] ibid 198.

[38] ibid 213, 13.

[39] ibid 198.

[40] ibid 161. However, many youth justice programmes do net sexual offences. It is the assumption that youth processes do not deal with such serious offences which can lead to their under-examination. For an analysis of this phenomenon in the UK context, see McGlynn and others (n 32).

[41] Miller (n 1) 207.

[42] ibid 198.

[43] There are a wide range of restorative practices, usually involving face to face meetings together with a facilitator, including victim-offender dialogues, circles of support, sentencing circles and conferencing. Restorative conferences bring together the victim, offender, their supporters/family members and potentially other community members or criminal justice personnel. For a discussion of the variety of restorative practices, see Umbreit and Armour (n 29).

[44] See C Quince Hopkins and Mary Koss, 'Incorporating Feminist Theory and Insights into a Restorative Justice Response to Sex Offenses' (2005) 11 Violence Against Women 693–723.

plan for accountability, healing and public safety'.[45] Being specifically designed for sexual offences, the programme understands the power dynamics between victims and offenders and goes to great lengths in its protocols and risk assessments to protect victim safety and to ensure positive outcomes for all parties. Mary Koss, who leads the programme, suggests that its operation demonstrates that 'carefully reasoned, safe, and respectful alternatives can be offered for sexual assault if we collaborate, consult and listen to the needs of our constituencies'.[46] Miller does acknowledge that Restore is 'victim-centred' but states simply that it cannot be compared to the post-conviction approach in VVH, without further explanation.[47]

Another similar programme is Project Restore in New Zealand which focuses on crimes of sexual violence and takes referrals from the court system, as well as community and self-referrals where there has often been no prior contact with the investigatory authorities.[48] The Project is a 'survivor driven organization' and aims to provide a 'sense of justice, support offenders to understand the impacts of their behaviour and facilitate the development of an action plan which might include reparation to the victim and therapeutic programmes for the offender'.[49] A recent evaluation found that the project 'can provide a sense of justice in cases of sexual violence'[50] and Shirley Jülich, one of the project's founders, comments that it offers victims a 'glimmer of hope'.[51]

These projects both show the potential for restorative justice programmes to meet the needs of many victims: such as control over, and participation in, their complaint; an early acknowledgment of responsibility; an opportunity to tell their story and explain the impact of an offence; and the possibility of vindication. Both are examples of community-driven, victim-led restorative innovations which offer victims alternatives to the conventional justice system and, specifically, they tackle only sexual offences. It is this latter feature which is overlooked by Miller in her advocacy of programmes such as VVH for crimes of 'gendered violence' more generally. In common with much of the sceptical feminist literature on restorative justice, Miller's critique largely centres on circumstances of domestic violence.[52] She rightly highlights many of the

---

[45] Mary Koss, 'Restorative Justice for Acquaintance Rape and Misdemeanor Sex Crimes', in Ptacek (n 5) 218–9.

[46] ibid 219.

[47] Miller (n 1) 209.

[48] Shirley Jülich and others, Project Restore: An Exploratory Study of Restorative Justice and Sexual Violence (2010)   <http://aut.academia.edu/documents/0121/2233/The_Project_Restore_Report.pdf>   accessed   19 September 2011.

[49] Jülich (n 48) 1. See also Shirley Jülich, 'Restorative Justice and Gendered Violence in New Zealand – a glimmer of hope', in Ptacek (n 5) 246.

[50] Jülich (n 48) vi.

[51] Jülich, in Ptacek (n 5) 251.

[52] For a discussion of concerns see Julie Stubbs, 'Beyond Apology? Domestic Violence and Critical Questions for Restorative Justice' (2007) 7 Criminology and Criminal Justice 169–87 and Ruth Busch, 'Domestic Violence and Restorative Justice Initiatives: Who Pays if We Get it Wrong?' in Braithwaite and Strang (n 5). On the possibilities of restorative justice for domestic violence, see Carolyn Hoyle, 'Feminism, Victimology and Domestic Violence' in Sandra Walklate (ed), *Handbook of Victims and Victimology* (Willan 2007).

reservations regarding the use of restorative justice for domestic violence, principally due to its integration of psychological and physical abuse, the often lengthy pattern of coercive conduct and the common need for continued contact. However, too often such fears are assumed to be equally applicable to other forms of gendered violence.

While women's experiences of victimization cannot easily be categorized, there are important variations between domestic violence and many forms of sexual violence meaning that they can be treated with some degree of separation.[53] For this reason, the literature is becoming more 'nuanced', with discussion differentiating between different types of gendered violence;[54] an approach which I endorse. My emphasis, therefore, is on considering the applicability of restorative justice for specific types of harm, here sexual violence, whereas Miller stresses the timing of the programme, ie post-conviction. It is perhaps true that if restorative justice only took place post-conviction then some of the worries regarding its use in cases of sexual violence would fall away. However, it is also the case that following such a path means excluding the vast majority of victims from the potential benefits of restorative justice. It is well established that very few victims of sexual violence ever see their attacker convicted of an offence.[55] Therefore, while the development of post-conviction schemes is to be recommended, we must look to a more expansive approach to restorative justice if we are to offer justice to many more victims than is currently the case.

In this light, it is important to examine further Miller's criticisms of diversionary restorative justice. As a general comment, Miller appears to underplay the extensive variety of restorative programmes which is not just limited to Miller's dyad of diversionary and therapeutic schemes. There are many post-conviction restorative schemes which do affect outcomes, such as sentencing or prison release; and there are programmes which operate entirely outside of the conventional criminal justice system. Partly due to this sheer diversity of restorative practices, it is difficult to make definitive claims about efficacy and victim satisfaction. However, the position does not appear to be as clear as Miller perhaps suggests. Although Miller cites extensive research by Umbreit and others as revealing 'positive outcomes of [restorative justice] practices across the board',[56] she concludes that diversionary practices 'fail

---

[53] This is not to suggest that there is no possibility of restorative justice being used in cases of domestic violence. Indeed, there are a range of projects nationally and internationally which deploy restorative techniques and some to apparently good effect: see, for example, Marian Liebmann and Lindy Wootton, *Restorative Justice and Domestic Violence/Abuse* (Home Office Crime Reduction Unit for Wales 2010) and Joan Pennell and Stephanie Francis, 'Safety Conferencing – Toward a Coordinated and Inclusive Response to Safeguarding Women and Children' (2005) 11 Violence Against Women 666–92. What I am suggesting is that there are strong reasons to consider the use of restorative justice separately for domestic violence and sexual violence.

[54] As discussed in Stubbs (n 24) 105.

[55] Kathleen Daly and Brigitte Bouhours, 'Rape and Attrition in the Legal Process: A Comparative Analysis Across Five Countries' (2010) 39 Crime and Justice 565–650.

[56] Miller (n 1) 207.

many victims'.[57] While it is evident that many victims are not satisfied with their experiences, Kathleen Daly's research, to which Miller refers, as well as finding that victims were indeed those least satisfied with the outcome of family conferences, went on to report that victims as well as offenders reported high levels of procedural justice.[58] Daly continued that 'for victims, meeting offenders in the conference setting can have beneficial results' and concluded that the 'evidence is mixed' but that restorative justice is a practice 'worth maintaining and perhaps enlarging'.[59] More recent studies have suggested more widespread victim satisfaction. An evaluation of restorative youth conferencing in Northern Ireland found high levels of victim satisfaction,[60] as has other UK research on a range of restorative interventions, including diversion.[61]

The picture that emerges, therefore, is complex and variable and one which has led Lawrence Sherman and Heather Strang to conclude that the 'evidence on restorative justice is far more extensive, and positive' than is the case for 'many other policies which have been rolled out nationally'.[62] At this juncture, it may be worth recalling that while we need to learn more about restorative processes and their impact, we do in fact already know that the conventional justice system routinely fails victims. The aphorisms 'second-rape' and 'judicial rape' were coined exactly to describe the victim trauma and blame-culture endemic in conventional criminal justice prosecutions of sexual violence.[63]

Indeed, it is such a comparison between the conventional system and restorative processes in relation to sexual offences which Daly examined in later research from South Australia. The study compared the nature and outcomes of youth sexual assault cases processed via formal caution, restorative conference and youth court.[64] It found that although courts can impose more serious penalties, the findings 'challenge those who believe that the court is the place that sends 'strong messages' that serious offending is treated seriously, or that it holds greater potential to vindicate victims than [restorative justice] conferences'.[65] In particular, while offenders readily deny charges and attrition rates are extremely high in the conventional system, the restorative approach ensured a 'greater degree of disclosure of sex offending and victimization which can then be addressed in a constructive manner'.[66]

---

[57] ibid 198.

[58] Kathleen Daly, 'Restorative Justice – the real story' (2002) 4 Punishment and Society 55–79, 69–71, 69.

[59] ibid 71–72.

[60] Catriona Campbell and others, *Evaluation of the Northern Ireland Youth Conference Service* (Northern Ireland Office 2005).

[61] Joanna Shapland and others, *Restorative Justice: The Views of Victims and Offenders* (Ministry of Justice Research Series 3/07 2007).

[62] Lawrence Sherman and Heather Strang, *Restorative Justice: The Evidence* (Smith Institute 2007) 4.

[63] Lee Madigan and Nancy Gamble, *The Second Rape: Society's Continued Betrayal of the Victim* (Macmillan 1991); Sue Lees, 'Judicial Rape' (1993) 16 Women's Studies International Forum 11–36.

[64] Kathleen Daly, 'Restorative Justice and Sexual Assault – An Archival Study of Court and Conference Cases' (2006) 46 British Journal of Criminology 334–356, 339.

[65] ibid 351.

[66] Daly (n 64) 352.

Furthermore, the study showed that the court cases took considerably longer to finalize, possibly adding to the victim's ordeal.[67] In essence, Daly suggests that the results 'underscore the limits of the formal court process in responding to sexual violence' and she suggests that restorative justice critics should take a 'wider view' of the potentially adverse impact of formal court processes on victims.[68] Thus, programmes operating at many stages of the criminal justice system, including diversion, offer some hope and possibility of meeting victim needs, and this to a far wider range of victims.[69]

This leads to a final point about Miller's dichotomizing of diversionary and post-conviction restorative justice, namely the emphasis on the latter being 'therapeutic'. The concern here is twofold. First, the assumption appears to be that it is only the post-conviction programmes similar to VVH that contribute to healing. Yet in all forms of restorative practice, victims express some of the benefits by using terms such as 'closure', or 'moving forward', indicating potential health benefits.[70] Secondly, the emphasis on outcomes being considered only therapeutic, rather than also as a form of justice, limits both the conceptualization and ambition of restorative practices.[71] Therapeutic outcomes and justice are intertwined, with each facilitating the other. Restorative programmes can contribute to healing and thereby offer a sense of justice to some victims of sexual violence, regardless of whether the particular programme operates post-conviction, during the criminal justice system or outside the system entirely. In those post-conviction cases where there is no impact on any conventional outcome, such as prison release, it may be understandable to emphasize victim healing. However, the concern may go deeper. It may be that what is seen to constitute 'justice' is so intimately bound up with the conventional justice system, and its emphasis on convictions and punitive punishment, that the assumption is that 'justice' is done when the offender is incarcerated and then only 'healing' is left. It is such a conceptualization of justice, as being rooted in the conventional criminal justice system, which is considered further below.

---

[67] ibid.

[68] ibid 353.

[69] There are legitimate concerns regarding the rights of offenders in restorative processes, particularly questions of compulsion and the validity of outcomes varying depending on victim preferences. For a debate on these themes, see Chris Cunneen and Carolyn Hoyle, *Debating Restorative Justice* (Hart 2010). However, from a victim-perspective restorative justice is generally viewed as 'offender-friendly' and it is indeed such concerns which have fuelled feminist resistance. In moving forward, we must take appropriate account of offenders' due process rights, as well as ensuring that our notion of justice also meets the interests of victims.

[70] Sherman and Strang (n 62) 8. See also Lawrence Sherman and others, 'Effects of face-to-face restorative justice on victims of crime in four randomized controlled trials' (2005) 1 Journal of Experimental Criminology 367–95 which found positive health benefits in face to face restorative justice processes, which took place at various stages of the criminal justice system including diversion, for victims.

[71] See further the idea of 'therapeutic jurisprudence' as discussed in David Wexler, 'Therapeutic Jurisprudence and its Application to Criminal Justice Research and Development' (2010) 7 Irish Probation Journal 94–107.

4. *Rape Victims and the Search for Justice*

The victims who participated in the VVH programme were 'united in favoring an initial punitive response, conveying their unqualified support for punishment'.[72] Miller emphasizes that the victims would '*not* have favored a diversionary program'.[73] Yet, ultimately, these quests for 'vengeance did not fulfil them'.[74] Although 'punishment for the sake of punishment conveyed that the individual had committed a terrible wrong', it did not 'allay victims' fears'.[75] Miller notes that with the passage of time, the victims' punitive attitudes were tempered; the victims felt 'hollow', as though the 'satisfaction that they were supposed to feel by participating in the formal criminal justice system or knowing their defendants were behind bars was not enough'.[76] Healing, she states, eluded the victims whose desires for 'retribution were eclipsed, but not completely replaced, by the need to find answers and be heard'.[77] In this light, Miller supports schemes such as VVH on the basis that they 'combine elements of both retributive and restorative justice'.[78] The retributive element conforms to the idea that 'most people' would believe that 'punishment for offenders of severe violence should communicate... the abstract societal message that what they did was wrong'.[79] Healing is achieved by the VVH programme itself which works 'in addition to the criminal justice system rather than in lieu of it'.[80]

Miller, and the victims in her study, are not alone in focusing on state-sanctioned retributive justice as the means by which to gain recognition of the serious harm of sexual violence. Feminist activism over the past 30 years has understandably concentrated on securing public acknowledgement that rape is a serious crime, demanding significant punishment, via the criminal justice system. This is because, as Barbara Hudson notes, the formal criminal justice system remains the 'recognized way of demonstrating that society takes something seriously.'[81] The hope has been that in harnessing the power of the state to condemn sexual violence, we could work towards its eradication. This optimism has not, however, borne much fruit. Feminists find ourselves in a situation in which there has been extensive, often feminist-inspired, law reform, yet little evidence of any reduction in the prevalence of sexual violence, few convictions of perpetrators and a system which affords victims little justice.

---

[72] Miller (n 1) 160.
[73] ibid (emphasis in original).
[74] ibid.
[75] ibid.
[76] ibid.
[77] ibid.
[78] ibid.
[79] Miller (n 1) 191.
[80] ibid 169.
[81] Barbara Hudson, 'Restorative Justice and Gendered Violence – Diversion or Effective Justice' (2002) 42 British Journal of Criminology 616–34, 629.

Dianne Martin places the blame for this situation on the dominance of neoliberal punitive attitudes towards crime control over the past two decades. She suggests that it has been those feminist proposals which strengthen the criminal justice process that have been adopted by governments desperate to be seen to be controlling crime and addressing insecurity. In this way, feminist arguments, and credibility, have been used to bolster state power, not in order to empower victims, but as a means of exercising control, particularly over marginalized and vulnerable communities.[82] Kristin Bumiller has vividly described this development as: 'how neoliberalism appropriated the feminist movement against sexual violence'.[83] Bumiller argues that by focussing on the criminal justice system as the key site for recognizing the harm of sexual violence, feminists have played into the neoliberal agenda, in particular its emphasis on individual responsibility and risk-avoidance which reproduces many myths about rape, such as the prevalence of stranger rape.[84] Sexual offenders have been stigmatized and characterized as beyond the law-abiding majority, thereby justifying their punishment but, more significantly, generating the idea that they are different from ordinary men.

Thus, paradoxically, feminism has helped to shape this 'politics of penalization', yet there has been little increase in the conviction and incarceration of sex offenders.[85] In this way, although there have been widespread demands for improvements in victims' rights, reforms remain minimal and piecemeal, with victims' experiences being 'displaced by an outcry focused on controlling the threat of dangerous men'.[86] It has been presumed that punishing offenders is necessarily beneficial for victims. But this is not necessarily so, particularly in the case of sexual offences where a much wider challenge to the culture and attitudes which condone sexual violence is required if victims' rights and sense of justice are to be genuinely improved. The end result is a culture where the 'recognition of harm' is equated with the 'length of a prison term' and 'criminal justice responses which are not punitive are seen to be unresponsive to victims'/women's harms'.[87]

It is this culture which produces victims' expressed wishes for conventional punishment, as it is assumed this is the only way to achieve public condemnation of harm, yet leaves them feeling 'hollow'. An irony, therefore, may be that the therapeutic nature of VVH is required *because of* the failings of the conventional criminal justice system. Victims' needs and desires, their

---

[82] Dianne Martin, 'Retribution Revisited: a Reconsideration of Feminist Criminal Law Reform Strategies' (1998) 36 Osgoode Hall Law Journal 151–88, 153.

[83] Kristin Bumiller, *In an Abusive State: How Neoliberalism Appropriated the Feminist Movement Against Sexual Violence* (Duke University Press 2008).

[84] Bumiller argues, for example, that provisions such as sex offender notification, reinforce myths about stranger rape, rather than contribute to safer communities (n 83) 8. See also Emma Bell, *Criminal Justice and Neoliberalism* (Palgrave 2011).

[85] Bumiller (n 83) 7.

[86] ibid 157–58.

[87] Martin (n 82) 170.

838   *Oxford Journal of Legal Studies*   VOL. 31

varying ideas of justice, have been eclipsed by the seemingly ever-increasing demands for punitive action. It is when we dig further and ask victims about their conceptions of justice that we find a more varied and complex picture which demands a more diverse approach to justice.

In her interviews with victims of domestic and sexual violence, Judith Herman found that punishment, as traditionally conceived and practised by the criminal justice system, was not a key priority for victims.[88] The goal most commonly sought was exposure of the offender as an offender.[89] It was more important to 'deprive the perpetrator of undeserved honour and status than to deprive them of either liberty or fortune'.[90] Furthermore, victims sought validation from the community, by 'denunciation of the crime', which 'transferred the burden of disgrace' to the offender.[91] In this way, while acknowledgement from the offender was important, validation from 'bystanders' was of 'equal or greater importance'.[92] For these reasons, Herman found that victims' needs and wishes are often diametrically opposed to the requirements of formal legal proceedings.[93]

In a similar vein, Jülich found that a common theme arising from survivors of historic child sexual abuse was the desire to tell their story in a way that was meaningful for them and in a safe environment.[94] They were critical of the criminal justice system for 'denying them a voice' and were pessimistic that restorative programmes which might be staffed by the same people responsible for conventional criminal justice provision would engender any significant change.[95]

These findings are echoed in two recent reviews of the experiences of rape victims in England and Wales. Sara Payne concluded that we need a 'redefinition' of what constitutes justice which is 'not just punishing a perpetrator and preventing further crimes'.[96] The subsequent Stern Review concluded that 'support and care for victims should be a higher priority' and that a broader approach to measuring 'success' and outcomes than just a focus on convictions needs to be developed.[97] Furthermore, that while a conviction is

---

[88] Judith Herman, 'Justice from the Victim's Perspective' (2005) 11 Violence Against Women 571–602, 589. This finding is replicated in other studies, for example: Ruth Lewis and others, 'Protection, Prevention, Rehabilitation or Justice? Women's use of the Law to Challenge Domestic Violence' (2000) 7 International Review of Victimology 179; Heather Strang, *Repair or Revenge? Victims and Restorative Justice* (OUP 2002).

[89] Herman (n 88) 593.

[90] ibid.

[91] ibid 585.

[92] ibid.

[93] Herman (n 88) 574.

[94] Shirley Jülich, 'Views of justice among survivors of historical child sexual abuse – implications for restorative justice in New Zealand' (2006) 10 Theoretical Criminology 125–38, 131.

[95] ibid 131, 134–35.

[96] Sara Payne, *Redefining Justice: Addressing the Individual Needs of Victims and Witnesses* (Ministry of Justice 2009) 11.

[97] Baroness Stern, *The Stern Review – An Independent Review into how Rape Complaints are Handled by Public Authorities in England and Wales* (Home Office 2010) 11.

a 'very worthwhile outcome', victims wanted more, such as to be 'treated well' and they 'wanted to know that their experience had been understood and its effects acknowledged'.[98] In essence, Stern concluded, what victims want are processes which 'honour the experience'.[99]

Importantly, honouring the experience does not mean giving up on justice, or punishment, or vindication.[100] For example, this approach echoes the findings of Liz Kelly et al who have stressed the importance for victims of 'procedural justice', even where substantive justice is not forthcoming.[101] Miller also found that victims value procedural justice with many feeling that the preparation process of VVH had been beneficial, with one stating that the dialogue itself was just the 'icing on the cake'.[102] Therefore, even without a conviction and conventional punishment, procedural justice can embed a sense of fairness, of justice. But, in addition, we can find other ways of securing substantive justice, an outcome which is not necessarily tied to the conventional justice system's demand for a conviction and punitive punishment.

Restorative justice is one means by which this can be achieved. It requires the offender to have admitted responsibility, thereby giving some measure of vindication to the victim. It also offers a form of offender accountability by demanding they explain their actions and listen to the harm they have caused. It may be valuable to bear in mind here that restorative justice is an 'alternative punishment' not an 'alternative to punishment'.[103] For these and many other reasons, Barbara Hudson notes that while feminists both for and against restorative justice all agree that offences of sexual violence warrant a significant response, her argument is that restorative justice could carry out the 'traditional functions of criminal justice—retribution, rehabilitation/ reintegration, individual and public protection—better than formal justice does'.[104] In other words, it may offer more *effective* justice.[105] Restorative

---

[98] Stern (n 97) 46. Further, as Wendy Larcombe contends, a focus on conviction rates can work against feminist aims of rape law which include more 'qualitative and victim-centred' outcomes: Wendy Larcombe, 'Falling Rape Conviction Rates: (Some) Feminist Aims and Measures for Rape Law' (2011) 19 Feminist Legal Studies 27–45, 29.

[99] Stern (n 97) 9, 101–02.

[100] Dorothy Vaandering makes the argument that '[j]ustice is honouring the worth of the other': (2011) 14 Contemporary Justice Review 307–28, 324.

[101] L Kelly and others, *A Gap or a Chasm? Attrition in Reported Rape Cases* (Home Office 2005) 87–89.

[102] Miller (n 1) 172.

[103] Anthony Duff, 'Alternatives to Punishment and Alternative Punishments', in W Cragg (ed) *Retributivism and its Critics* (Steiner 1992) 44. See also Bronwyn Naylor who proposes an 'alternative restorative pathway' for cases of adult sexual assault, aspiring to 'symbolic and practical justice' as well as ensuring censure and punishment: 'Effective Justice for Victims of Sexual Assault: Taking up the Debate on Alternative Pathways' (2010) 33 UNSW Law Journal 662–84.

[104] Barbara Hudson 'Restorative Justice and Gendered Violence – Diversion or Effective Justice' (2002) 42 British Journal of Criminology 616–34, 626.

[105] ibid (emphasis in original).

justice, therefore, offers important possibilities and feminists must help to shape its further development.[106]

There are also a myriad of projects which seek to challenge and reduce violence against women by means of various community based activities; determined to resist co-option by the state.[107] These are very clearly 'alternatives' to the criminal justice system, many resolutely refusing any involvement by state bodies or finances.[108] Others similarly recommend a shift of focus from criminal justice, this time towards civil justice, with Ilene Seidman and Susan Vickers advocating greater use of the civil law, especially in meeting the most immediate post-offence needs of victims.[109] Kathleen Daly and Brigitte Bouhours imagine a 'changed societal context' in which ' "sex offenders" are less stigmatized and demonized' and rather than 'negative and punitive legal mechanisms', more 'socially inclusive and integrative approaches' would be deployed.[110] Part of this landscape would be 'mechanisms that encourage admissions by offenders (only those who are factually guilty, of course) at a very early stage', revealing greater levels of sexual offending and according some vindication to victims.[111] The furore surrounding a recent policy proposal in England and Wales, which followed Daly and Bouhours' recommendation to encourage early admissions, demonstrates just how difficult it is going to be to secure such changes.

An increased sentencing discount was to be offered for an early guilty plea.[112] To justify the proposal, the Government offered the example of rape victims as those who may benefit by being saved the trauma of giving evidence at trial. This suggestion was greeted by one front page headline declaring that the Government was 'Soft on Rapists'.[113] Almost the entire debate proceeded

---

[106] Also, greater consideration must be given to the potentially gendered nature of restorative processes more generally, an area which is largely overlooked. For thoughtful interventions on this theme, see Kimberly Cook, 'Doing Difference and Accountability in Restorative Justice Conferences' (2006) 10 Theoretical Criminology 107–24; Fidelma Ashe, 'From Paramilitaries to Peacemakers: the Gender Dynamics of Community-based Restorative Justice in Northern Ireland' (2009) 11 British Journal of Politics and International Relations 298–13; and Gilly Sharpe and Loraine Gelsthorpe, 'Engendering the Agenda: Girls, Young Women and Youth Justice' (2009) 9 Youth Justice: An International Journal 195–208.

[107] For a discussion, see Mimi Kim, 'Alternative Interventions to Intimate Violence: Defining Political and Pragmatic Challenges', in Ptacek (n 5) 193–217.

[108] As considered in Andrea Smith, 'Beyond Restorative Justice: Radical Organizing Against Violence', in Ptacek (n 5) 255–78.

[109] Ilene Seidman and Susan Vickers, 'The Second Wave: An Agenda for the Next Thirty Years of Rape Law Reform' (2005) 18 Suffolk University Law Review 467–91. Similarly, Nikki Godden suggests that greater use could be made of tort law claims based on rape: Nikki Godden, 'Claims in Tort for Rape: A Valuable Remedy or Damaging Strategy?' (2011) 22 Kings Law Journal 157–82.

[110] Daly and Bouhours (n 55) 623. On sexual offenders and the value of restorative justice, see Anne-Marie McAlinden, The Shaming of Sexual Offenders – Risk, Retribution and Reintegration (Hart 2007).

[111] Daly and Bouhours (n 55) 623.

[112] As reported in: Robert Winnett and Christopher Hope, '50pc "discount" in jail term for rapists who enter early guilty plea', The Telegraph, 18 May 2011.

[113] Daily Mail, 19 May 2011.

on the basis that lower prison sentences constituted a travesty of justice.[114] But this was only one approach. The expressed views of many victims, for acknowledgement of the offending, for vindication, for a voice, were drowned out. Indeed, while one victim's objections to the policy were extensively reported in the media, when she later changed her mind on learning more of the actual detail of the policy, her views were conspicuously absent in subsequent reports.[115] In the light of the barrage of public criticism, including from the opposition Labour party and many feminist organizations, the policy was dropped.[116] This is just one further example of feminist rhetoric about the harm of rape being deployed to shore up a punitive approach to punishment and incarceration. Rape was used as a political football and the expressed needs of some victims were lost in a storm of punitive-correctness. What this example also demonstrates is the depth of the challenge to re-orientate and re-imagine our justice system as one which secures justice for rape victims.

5. *Conclusions*

Considerable strategic energy has been directed at the conventional criminal justice system in the hope that it will denounce sexual violence and assist in fulfilling feminist ambitions to eradicate violence against women. We have arrived at a situation, however, in which the investment by feminists has not been repaid. Victims see little justice in the current system which, in its neoliberal manifestation, may in fact have contributed to the culture in which sexual violence is endemic. The idea that increased punitiveness and punishment would secure feminist aims has indeed been the 'ultimate false promise'.[117] In *After the Crime*, Miller is critical of the criminal justice system and recommends many improvements. However, while reform is essential and urgent, by advocating only those restorative justice programmes which operate as an addition to the conventional justice system, she suggests a rather static conceptualization of the criminal justice system. Restorative justice is to be practised only when the formal system has run its course; rather than envisaging restorative justice as being part of a movement to transform the system itself.

It may well be that Miller has taken a strategic decision to advocate post-conviction restorative justice as a first step towards securing greater justice for victims, even if a defence of the conventional system is a by-product of that

[114] With exceptions: see Editorial, 'Ken Clark's Prison Plans are Broadly Right', *The Observer*, 22 May 2011; Clare McGlynn, 'Ken Clarke was Right to Start a Debate on Sentencing in Rape Cases' *The Guardian*, 19 May 2011 <http://www.guardian.co.uk/law/2011/may/19/ken-clarke-debate-sentencing-rape> accessed 19 September 2011.

[115] Ben Chu, 'How the right-wing press lost interest in Gabrielle Brown', *The Independent*, 8 June 2011 <http://blogs.independent.co.uk/2011/06/08/how-the-right-wing-press-lost-interest-in-gabrielle-browne/> accessed 19 September 2011.

[116] Patrick Wintour, 'Kenneth Clarke drops shorter jail terms for rapists after tussle with Cameron' *The Guardian*, 8 June 2011.

[117] Martin (n 82) 184.

strategic judgement. She may also be cautious of any challenge to the due process rights of defendants. However, in focussing her recommendations on only certain restorative practices, and by her implicit endorsement of the current justice system, Miller's vision of justice is constrained. There is also a danger that it largely reinforces, rather than challenges, assumptions about what constitutes justice and what we expect from our criminal justice system. In doing so, it offers little to the vast majority of victims of sexual violence.

We must move forward by listening to the diverse voices of rape victims and recognizing their specific and individual needs. This means ensuring that victim-led justice is no longer synonymous with increasingly punitive attitudes or a predominant focus on convictions and imprisonment. Feminist activism and strategy, therefore, must rethink its approach to what constitutes justice for rape victims, going beyond punitive state outcomes to encompass broader notions of justice, including an expansive approach to restorative justice.

Name Index